BEHAVIORAL APPROACHES TO THERAPY

Spence, Carson, Thibaut

BEHAVIORAL APPROACHES TO THERAPY

Editors and Contributors

Janet T. Spence
University of Texas at Austin

Robert C. Carson
Duke University

John W. Thibaut
University of North Carolina

Albert Bandura
Douglas A. Bernstein
Gerald C. Davison
W. Doyle Gentry
Marvin R. Goldfried
Edward S. Katkin
Leonard Krasner
Donald J. Levis
O. Ivar Lovaas
Richard McFall
Donald Meichenbaum
Richard E. Nisbett
Gordon L. Paul
Martin Seligman
Joyce N. Sprafkin
Thomas G. Stampfl
Stuart Valins

 GENERAL LEARNING PRESS
250 James Street, Morristown, N.J. 07960

Manufactured in the United States of America

Published simultaneously in Canada

Library of Congress Catalog Card Number 75-40855

ISBN 0-382-25080-X

Preface

The chapters in this volume, with the exception of the introductory overview, initially appeared separately, between 1971 and 1975, as modules in the University Programs series in psychology. The modules in this series, written at the invitation of the Editors, are intended for an undergraduate audience at an intermediate or advanced level of training. They contain integrative theoretical and empirical accounts of broad problems in psychology and related disciplines. In designing the series, the Editors attempted to commission clusters of modules on related topics which would provide quite comprehensive coverage of a broad area of psychology and which, when brought together under one cover, could serve as texts for undergraduate or graduate courses.

The unifying theme of this volume is behaviorally-oriented therapies, that is, the therapies that have an intellectual lineage which, although mixed, is dominated by the behavioristic tradition and principles of experimental psychology. While all the essays in this volume are centered on the topic of behavioral therapy or assessment, some of the modules also present basic experimental research and new theoretical approaches.

We would like to thank the American Psychological Association, the many other publishers, and the many authors who have granted permission to reprint extracts, charts and tables. Space does not permit naming them all here, but we have made a conscientious effort to properly cite them at appropriate places in the text.

The three Editors have all been involved to some degree in commissioning the modules reprinted here and bringing them to fruition. The order in which our names are listed reflects the relative degree of responsibility we have taken in the development of this volume.

Janet T. Spence
Robert C. Carson
John W. Thibaut

Contents

Introduction

The attempts by one human being to change the distressing behavior of another go back eons. Approximately half a million years ago Stone Age people apparently believed that aberrant behavior could be eliminated by allowing evil spirits to escape from the brain. As a consequence they practiced trephining, namely chipping away parts of the skull of an afflicted person so that these spirits could escape. These early demonological orientations to abnormal behavior could be found among the ancient Hebrews as well. For example, Jesus is reported to have cured a person with an "unclean spirit" by exorcising the devil and hurling it onto a herd of swine, which were then said to have become possessed and run into the ocean. Similar demonological thinking can be found among the early Chinese, Greeks, and Egyptians; treatments ranged from elaborate prayer rites to extreme measures such as starvation and whipping.

More naturalistic explanations were occasionally advanced, and with them more naturalistic methods of treatment. In the 5th century B.C., the Greek physician Hippocrates, for example, recommended that people suffering from deep depression should seek tranquility and abstain from alcohol and sexual activity. Nonetheless, in the western world, the predominant explanation for peculiar behavior remained demonic possession until after the Middle Ages.

By the beginning of the 19th century, enlightened opinion held that deviant behaviors had physical causes, attributable to disease processes or bad genes. Only in the late 1800's did psychological theories begin to appear and command attention. The most influential of these theories was advanced by Sigmund Freud who, along with his colleague, Joseph Breuer, discovered the cathartic method for treating what they regarded as psychologically rather than physically caused disorders: clients' neurotic difficulties could be relieved if they were encouraged to talk in an emotional fashion about long forgotten events. Their well-known work, *Studies in hysteria* [1955], based largely on the case of Anne O., with whom the method was first used, is viewed by many as initiating the modern discipline of psychotherapy.[1] As psychoanalysis has developed, its basic assumption has been that deviant behavior can best be alleviated by having the client uncover those incidents from the past which underlie current psychological difficulty in order to gain insight into the reasons for present behavior. These reasons for behavior have been interpreted by the therapist from principles set forth in Freud's highly speculative personality theory. It is fair to say that until recently, variants of Freud's psychoanalytic techniques have dominated American psychotherapy.

Theorists like Freud operated almost entirely outside the mainstream of academic experimental psychology. In contrast, during the 1930's and particularly in the 1950's and thereafter, a group of experimentally oriented investigators began to concern themselves with the possibility that principles and procedures derived from experimental psychology might be relevant to the understanding of abnormal behavior and its treatment. Experimentally based techniques, dubbed behavior therapy or behavior modification, did not, of course, arise one morning when a social scientist awoke and said that today was the day behavior therapy was to start. Rather, over a period of years numerous people in the clinical field began to be dissatisfied with the effects of conventional psychotherapies and became convinced that abnormal behavior might be dealt with better by procedures tied to experimental psychology rather than to the more speculative origins that were characteristics of traditional therapy.

In terms of its own historical development, behavior therapy can be viewed as a coming together of several relatively distinct trends. The first is represented by and large by the work done in South Africa in the 1950's (and later in the United States) by Joseph Wolpe, a psychiatrist, and his colleague, Arnold Lazarus, a psychologist. Wolpe and Lazarus tended to emphasize Hullian learning theory as well as Pavlovian (classical) conditioning. Like Freud, they emphasized neurotic anxiety but viewed it as a classically conditioned response. They studied the acquisition and elimination of this learned response in laboratory animals and extrapolated these findings to human beings. For example, Wolpe's doc-

---

1 A recent article by Ellenberger [1972] casts serious doubt on the accuracy of this renowned case report of Anna O.; but its influence remains.

toral thesis concerned the induction of persistent unrealistic fears in laboratory cats and their subsequent successful elimination by "counterconditioning," more specifically, feeding the cats as they were gradually exposed to stimuli that had been present during the original conditioning. This was, in effect, a replication and extension of some pioneering work on counterconditioning done in 1924 by Mary Cover Jones. Wolpe applied this animal experimentation to his therapy with patients: instead of feeding fearful cats, he relaxed fearful humans; and instead of exposing these patients to what they had presumably been conditioned to in the past, he exposed them to graduated doses in imagination of situations which bothered them. This method of systematic desensitization, as he called it, is a prime example of an extension of laboratory research to the clinical situation — certainly a hallmark of behavior therapy.

Related to this Wolpean tradition (as well as to work that was going on at the same time in England in the laboratories of Hans Eysenck and M. B. Shapiro) is the work of Andrew Salter in the United States. In 1949 Salter published an important book entitled *Conditioned Reflex Therapy,* in which he reiterated the theory of the Russian neurophysiologist Ivan Pavlov that human neurotic problems are a result of excessive cortical inhibition. Within this Pavlovian framework, he suggested that most neurotic difficulties could be alleviated by having people become more open emotionally — expressing both their likes and dislikes to others. Although the relationship between Salter's procedures and his theorizing can be questioned, nonetheless his impact on contemporary behavior therapy is unquestionably great.

A second major trend in the development of behavior therapy came from psychologists working with operant conditioning techniques. The initial work can largely be attributed to Ogden Lindsley and B. F. Skinner. Working with severely regressed mental patients in a state hospital in Massachusetts, Lindsley and Skinner [1954] demonstrated that adaptive motor behavior could be taught by systematically reinforcing approximations to a target response, for example, pulling a lever to get a cigarette. In the next dozen years numerous reports were published by other workers demonstrating the utility of regarding much human behavior as operant and therefore amenable to change via various Skinnerian reinforcement procedures. The systematic shaping of new behaviors, along with the extinction of deviant behaviors, became a heavily studied area in behavior therapy, particularly with children and hospital patients.

Behavior therapists were eager to dissociate themselves from earlier "insight" therapies and their highly speculative, largely untestable accounts about what was going on "inside." As a result they originally asserted that the cognitive or thinking capacities of their patients were relatively unimportant in understanding abnormal behavior and helping change it. In fact, those influenced the most heavily by Skinner's antitheoretical, radical behaviorism eschew not only cognitive variables but any internal psychological processes (such as anxiety). In recent years, however, experimental psychologists have developed theories of cognitive behavior in humans to rival the earlier learning theories which concentrated on Pavlovian and operant conditioning in animal subjects. Although the intellectual link is not as direct, the behavior therapy movement has begun to be responsive to this cognitive trend in experimental psychology. An increasing number of behaviorally oriented therapists are becoming concerned with incorporating cognitive factors into their approaches and techniques. In 1954, for example, Julian Rotter made the proposal that clinical psychology align itself with experimental psychology, *particularly* with that portion of the field dealing with the study of expectancy and cognition. The impact of Rotter's book was unfortunately less than it should have been, but gradually a cognitive view took hold in the mid to late 1960's. An important book by Perry London [1964], for example, and a subsequent volume by Goldstein, Heller, and Sechrest [1966] reinforced the suggestion that cognitive variables should play a central role in behavior therapy, a position supported by a case report of Davison [1966]. The most complete statement incorporating cognitive factors into the behavioral tradition, and perhaps also the most influential book in behavior therapy so far, is Albert Bandura's *Principles of Behavior Modification,* published in 1969.

Surely one of the hallmarks of behavioral approaches to therapy is a responsiveness to theoretical and empirical advances in the parent discipline of experimental psychology. No doubt the future will see still more modifications and expansions. This brings us to the present collection of readings.

The selections in this book are noteworthy for several reasons. First, they are written by people who have already made significant contributions to the experimental-clinical literature. Second, each chapter in its own way demonstrates something central about the essence of behavior therapy: the commitment to rigorous thinking, testable hypotheses, careful operationalizing of terms, and to building links between the worlds of the clinic and the laboratory. But perhaps most important of all is that these experts take little for granted. Sacrosanct beliefs have no place in behavior therapy. While the germinal contributions of many workers are rightfully acknowledged, no one's pet idea is off-limits to logical scrutiny and experimental disconfirmation. Science, after all, is supposed to disprove theories and hypotheses whenever possible in order to arrive at better ones. This skeptical stance is absolutely vital for clinical psychology and psychiatry, where all too often the pronouncements of its creative thinkers are accorded an uncritical reverence that I sometimes suspect would be embarrassing to the unusually talented individuals who spawned the ideas.

Nearly all the selections deal with cognitive factors. Whereas, only ten years ago the very mention of concepts like "cognition," "thinking," or "imagery" would have been anathema in behavior therapy circles (and still is among the radical Skinnerians), many researchers and clinicians in behavior therapy have come to believe that systematic attention to human cognitive capacities is both possible and necessary for a more nearly complete scientific understanding of how people acquire maladaptive patterns of behavior and how best to help them change their life styles to something more rewarding.

In the first chapter, behavior therapy's leading theoretician, Albert Bandura, offers a cogent, tightly-reasoned brief on behalf of a behavioral approach that encompasses cognitive and self-regulatory capacities. Without resorting to inferences that are not amenable to experimental test, Bandura leads us through a host of conceptualizations and experimental findings that begin to sketch the outlines of a *social learning theory* that is both complex enough to handle the data and generate nontrivial hypotheses, and simple enough to satisfy the scientist's love of parsimony. While there is still an important place for response-contingent reinforcement in Bandura's scheme, special significance is allotted to the awareness of contingencies and to the role of modelling, particularly in the acquisition of new behavior patterns. The social learning theory proposed by Bandura will be seen by the reader as very much a cognitive theory, with concepts like attention and coding occupying center stage, rather than the overt behavior which has hitherto been the focus of behavior therapy. No doubt this cognitive emphasis will lead to the fruitful integration of social learning theory into the larger framework of experimental cognitive psychology.

Anxiety as a clinical problem continues to be the focus of attention of many behavior therapists. Gordon Paul and Douglas Bernstein provide a theoretical framework for understanding such clinical anxiety in their chapter, which reviews physiological research as well as cognitive and conditioning viewpoints. Like Goldfried and Sprafkin (see below), they advocate a multidimensional approach to the measurement of anxiety, with appropriate cautions about the errors that can creep in with self-report, physiological, and observational indices of any behavior. As we come to expect with any experimental approach to human functioning, there is an emphasis on the specification of the conditions under which a given response occurs; to say that a person is anxious, for example, is not as satisfying to the behaviorist as reporting, as precisely as possible, those conditions under which that person exhibits more or less of a reaction on as many dimensions as can reasonably be assessed. After elaborating a number of learning-based hypotheses as to how anxiety can be acquired and maintained, Paul and Bernstein devote the rest of their chapter to a painstaking analysis of systematic desensitization and other behavioral techniques for reducing anxiety. Paul and Bernstein demonstrate an enviable combination of clinical acumen and attentiveness to experimental niceties. It indeed seems possible to combine clinical sensitivity with scientific rigor.

In the chapter by Thomas Stampfl and Donald Levis, the emphasis continues to be on anxiety. Human psychopathology is conceptualized along the Hullian theoretical lines developed by Mowrer [1939] and Miller [1948]. The view is offered that many neurotic and psychotic behaviors are responses maintained via the reduction of anxiety that has been classically conditioned to intrinsically harmless stimuli. This model is perhaps the most widely accepted in learning-based theories of psychopathology and therapy, even though it has not always been so explicitly stated as here. But Stampfl and Levis go beyond the usual laboratory avoidance situations to point out that, at least with rats, conditioned avoidance responses are nowhere as persistent as the anxiety-based problems of human patients. By comparing the far simpler conditions under which laboratory animals learn avoidance responses with those conditions that seem to characterize the human situation, they generate the idea that human neurotic (and some psychotic) responses are acquired in very complex stimulus situations in which conditioned stimuli are serially ordered, thereby attaching fear to a fantastically large number of cues which, moreover, are hypothesized to go back in time. Moreover, on the basis of laboratory experiments, they demonstrate that highly resistant avoidance responses can be acquired if a series of conditioned stimuli precede shock, rather than the single CS that has typically been employed in such research. If one accepts their view that human fears are acquired in such complex situations, their revised model of the classical conditioning of fear has increased plausibility as an analogue for human fear. In addition, they suggest that the most rapid extinction of fear will take place when the organism is forced to confront those conditioned stimuli that, in the past, were most closely associated with aversive primary reinforcement. For rats, previous noxious learning experiences are easily known. In humans, they are far more difficult to learn, which leads to the formulation of Stampfl's *implosive therapy,* a procedure wherein the therapist encourages increasingly aversive imagery, not permitting the client to escape from the terrifying imaginal situations until a very considerable emotional reaction is elicited and then declines. The assumption is that one has thereby arrived at (or is as close as possible to) the orginal punishing situation, enabling the person to confront the original conditioned stimuli without experiencing pain. Of particular interest (and controversy!) is the therapist's attempt to guide clients, particularly disturbed patients, to psychodynamic themes of the type which Freudian theorists would find understandable. Implosive therapy thus appears to be committed to a psychoanalytically influenced theory of personality development. In introducing psychodynamic themes into therapy, the assumption is that negative emotions have been conditioned to such cues. Stampfl and Levis conclude with a review of the few experiments done thus far with clinical populations, all of them quite favorable to implosion therapy. And as we are accustomed to see in behavior therapy, there is a plea for more research and for continuing assessment of treatment effects via carefully controlled investigations.

Allied to anxiety is the phenomenon of *depression,* the subject of the chapter by Martin Seligman, which illustrates how an experimental psychologist who is clinically oriented can help bridge the gap between the laboratory and the clinical situation. Based on his knowledge of what at least some depressed people are like, as well as the work on learned helplessness in animals, Seligman proposes a model for depression that is more closely derived from experimental work than is most contemporary behavior therapy. He enumerates the similarities in symptomatology, etiology, cure, and prevention, between experimentally induced depression in animals and depression in humans observed clinically. He then demonstrates the fruitfulness of assuming that human depression may be analogous to those situations in which infrahuman organisms learn that nothing they do affects events impinging on them. As we can see in other selections, there is an important role for cognition in this learning-based set of ideas. In many instances, what humans believe about their effects on the environment is more important than what is actually the case. Depressed people can regard themselves and their contributions as worthless even when objective evaluation suggests the contrary and others regard them favorably.

Leonard Krasner provides a comprehensive review of that part of behavior therapy which em-

phasizes the importance of operant conditioning. Speaking on behalf of the majority of the operant group, he contends that quotation marks should always be placed around words such as "abnormal," "sick," and "psychopathological." The use of learning-based procedures like those he reviews is said to rest on the socially relative nature of psychiatric labelling: none of the behavior dealt with clinically is assumed to be different from unremarkable human behavior — except insofar as society's mental health labellers have characterized it. While there continues to be disagreement with the view that behavior therapy — even that portion most aligned with operant conditioning — cannot operate within an illness model of psychopathology, Krasner nonetheless argues his quite radical point of view in a cogent and scholarly manner. One of the major operant techniques is the token economy in which the goal is to promote the acquisition of desirable behavior by prompt delivery (when these behaviors occur) of money-like rewards which can be traded for goods and privileges. One of the more interesting sections of his chapter reviews recent attempts to relate token economies in mental hospitals to the operation of national economies; this illustrates a potentially fruitful expansion of operant research into areas of general importance.

W. Doyle Gentry reviews the relatively new area of behavior therapy of psychosomatic disorders (e.g., low back pain), suggesting that, regardless of the original causes of a particular disorder behavioral approaches can often be useful in reducing the severity of the problem. His chapter manifests an appreciation of disorders that have multiple determinants; some disorders are apparently appropriate to respondent techniques, others to the operant manipulation of consequences. While he views the current evidence as promising, he voices caution in concluding prematurely that any one approach has been shown to be markedly effective.

The chapter by O. Ivar Lovaas emphasizes again the behavior therapist's focus on developing effective procedures for changing behavior in the here and now without being terribly concerned for how it developed. Lovaas's impatience with etiological theories of severe childhood disorders seems to stem from the sterility of current viewpoints in generating useful techniques for change — and anyone who has seen or worked with such children can appreciate the urgency of attempting to improve our ways of helping them. Although one can dispute the contention that psychopathologists should abandon their attempts to uncover the etiologies of severe behavioral disorders, one can be sympathetic with the efforts of serious, inventive therapists like Lovaas to concentrate on change attempts without worrying about etiology. Another feature of the selection is the emphasis on careful measurement and on the use of the operant reversal design with the various children described. Finally, the role of the children's parents illustrates a key feature of behavior therapy, namely, the importance which paraprofessionals can assume in treatment provided they are properly taught the necessary principles of behavior change.

Edward Katkin reviews the research on instrumental learning of autonomic responses and points up some basic issues relevant to behavioral therapy with certain kinds of somatic disorders. The autonomic nervous system emerging from its status as a psychological second-class nervous system, has been the focus of some novel research designed to demonstrate that, under limited and highly controlled circumstances, animals and humans can learn to alter certain parameters of some autonomically mediated behavior such as blood pressure, blood flow, and heart rate [Miller 1948]. The potential practice benefits for those suffering from many different types of disorders is enormous. From his painstakingly careful review of the literature, Katkin concludes that the evidence for instrumental conditioning is weak for galvanic skin responses, stronger for peripheral vasoconstriction, and weak for heart rate. In most of the studies the possibility cannot be ruled out that the human subjects learned to voluntarily alter such functions as muscle and respiration and thereby affect autonomic functions. Of additional importance is the role post-experimental interviews have played in ferreting out cognitive factors that have to be taken into account in much of this human feedback research; once again we see the necessity to include the person's cognitive activity in attempts at complete understanding of behavior.

In a provocative chapter, Richard McFall suggests a response deficit orientation to clinical problems, construing much of behavior therapy in terms of filling performance deficits rather than removing inhibitions. The discrepancy perceived by the client between his current behavior and a preferred behavioral alternative forms the conceptual basis of what he terms "behavioral training", essentially a variety of techniques designed to help clients learn adaptive responses that are lacking. McFall assumes, as do most social learning theorists, that at any given time, a client's behavior is being reinforced to the maximum extent possible; the problem arises when this behavior is negatively evaluated by society or by the individual himself. Thus, while the person may be doing the best he or she can, this best performance may not be good enough. The focus on building new behaviors is aptly summarized by the "dead man's test," attributed by McFall to Ogden Lindsley: the goals of a treatment regimen are inadequately spelled out if a dead man could meet them. These would include, inter alia, not smoking, not being anxious, not being depressed, not hallucinating, and so forth. As McFall persuasively points out, clients typically know what they would like to stop doing — their problems are more often not knowing what *to do*. The performance deficit response-acquisition approach, therefore, focuses much-needed attention on acquiring competence — an emphasis lacking in disease models which stress intrapsychic inhibitions and aberrations. We also see in this chapter a full appreciation of the ethical issues involved in goal-setting and in achieving those goals for which the client contracts. As far as techniques are concerned, McFall proposes the use of a variety of instigation procedures — teaching techniques such as direct instruction and modelling — in contrast to consequation (operant conditioning) procedures, which focus on manipulation of consequences following successive approximations to desired behaviors; the emphasis is on the initiation of new behavior, rather than its maintenance, once it occurs.

The selection by Stuart Valins and Richard Nisbett represents an effort to incorporate a loosely connected set of ideas from social psychology called "attribution theory" into the larger framework of behavior therapy. The basic tenet of attribution theory is that the manner in which humans construe their world — both the external environment and what they notice is happening inside them — plays a key role in how they feel, think, and behave. While the data are far from in, the ideas presented by Valins and Nisbett provide useful directions for research, especially into the always vexing problem of how treatment effects can be maintained once the client exits from the therapy situation.

In the same spirit, Donald Meichenbaum reviews the evidence that important determinants of our emotional behavior are the things we tell ourselves. His review of his own research program lends strong support to the clinical claims of Albert Ellis [1962] that behavior can be changed by altering the manner in which people construe events. As we have already noted in Seligman's chapter, a wide range of hitherto disparate data and theorizing are fruitfully interrelated. Meichenbaum also reviews a variety of behavior therapy techniques which conceptualize covert processes as "little responses," obeying the same laws discovered for observable behavior. He believes that a more nearly complete understanding of the behavior influence enterprise will have to encompass both overt and covert behavioral events — a view independently held also by Goldfried and Sprafkin in the final chapter. Meichenbaum concludes that attention to human cognitive capacities promises to facilitate the kind of extratherapy generalization that is often lacking in behavioral approaches that restrict themselves to overt behavior and external controlling stimuli.

The selection by Marvin Goldfried and Joyce Sprafkin is a concise exposition of the behavioral approach to assessment. The behavior therapist focuses on obtaining information from a client that will be useful for specific interventions. For example, inquiries about anxiety and avoidance are keyed to possible decisions to desensitize, to engage in role-playing, or to employ both techniques. Central to the behavioral viewpoint is the use of behavior as sample rather than as sign of an underlying personality trait. These authors also sound a theme that is common to nearly all the chapters in this book — namely, that contemporary behavior therapy is as mediational as the experimental psychology on which it purports to be based. A thorough behavioral assessment, therefore, will include information on the client's cognitions and feelings as well as his readily observable motoric behavior. Perhaps the most noteworthy feature of the research reviewed is the critical stance assumed by behavioral workers in checking on the reliability — and even honesty — of behavioral observations.

Behavior therapies, as this collection makes clear, are not a finished set of techniques, based on a common underlying rationale. They are constantly evolving, in response to the clinical evidence and to the on-going theoretical and empirical advances in behavioral science as a whole. The works in this book faithfully reflect where behavior therapy is and, more crucially, hint broadly at where it is going.

Gerald C. Davison

BIBLIOGRAPHY

A. Bandura, *Principles of Behavior Modification.* Holt, Rinehart & Winston, 1969.

J. Breuer and S. Freud, *Studien über Hysteria.* (1895). In Standard Edition. London: Hogarth, 1955.

G. C. Davison, "Differential Relaxation and Cognitive Restructuring in Therapy with a 'Paranoid Schizophrenic' or 'Paranoid State.' " Proceedings of the 74th Annual Convention of the American Psychological Association, 1966, 2:177–178.

H. F. Ellenberger, "The Story of 'Anna O.' " A critical review with new data. *Journal of the History of the Behavior Sciences,* 1972, 8:267–279.

A. Ellis, *Reason and Emotion in Psychotherapy.* Lyle Stuart, 1962.

A. P. Goldstein, K. Heller and L. B. Sechrest, *Psychotherapy and the Psychology of Behavior Change,* Wiley, 1966.

O. R. Lindsley and B. F. Skinner, "A Method for the Experimental Analysis of the Behavior of Psychotic Patients." *American Psychologist,* 1954, 9:419–420.

P. London, *The Modes and Morals of Psychotherapy.* Holt, Rinehart & Winston, 1964.

N. E. Miller, "Studies of Fear as an Acquirable Drive. I. Fear as Motivation and Fear-reduction as Reinforcement in the Learning of New Responses." *Journal of Experimental Psychology,* 1948, 38:89–101.

O. H. Mowrer, "A Stimulus-response Analysis of Anxiety and its Role as a Reinforcing Agent." *Psychological Review,* 1939, 46:553–565.

J. B. Rotter, *Social Learning and Clinical Psychology.* Prentice-Hall, 1954.

A. Salter, *Conditioned Reflex Therapy.* Farrar, Straus, 1949.

J. Wolpe and A. A. Lazarus, *Behavior Therapy Techniques: A Guide to the Treatment of Neuroses.* Pergamon, 1966.

1

Social Learning Theory

ALBERT BANDURA

Stanford University

MANY theories have been advanced over the years to explain why people behave as they do. Until recently the most common view, popularized by various personality doctrines, depicted behavior as impelled by inner forces in the form of needs, drives, and impulses, often operating below the level of consciousness. Since the principal causes of behavior resided in forces within the individual, that is where one looked for explanations of man's actions. Although this view enjoyed widespread professional and popular acceptance, it did not go unchallenged.

Theories of this sort were criticized on both conceptual and empirical grounds. The inner determinants were typically inferred from the behavior they supposedly caused, resulting in pseudo explanations. Thus, for example, a hostile impulse was deduced from a person's irascible behavior, which was then attributed to the action of the underlying impulse. Different personality theories proposed diverse lists of motivators, some containing a few all-purpose drives, others embracing a varied assortment of specific drives.

The conceptual structure of psychodynamic theories was further criticized for disregarding the tremendous complexity of human responsiveness. An internal motivator cannot possibly account for the marked variation in the incidence and strength of a given behavior in different situations, toward different persons, at different times, and in different social roles. When diverse social influences produce correspondingly diverse behaviors, the inner cause implicated in the relationship cannot be less complex than its effects.

While the conceptual adequacy of psychodynamic formulations was debatable, their empirical limitations could not be ignored indefinitely. They provided intriguing interpretations of events that had already happened, but they lacked power to predict how people would behave in given situations [Mischel 1968]. Moreover, it was difficult to demonstrate that persons who had undergone psychodynamically oriented treatment benefited more than nontreated cases [Bandura 1969a, Bergin 1966]. Acquiring insight into the underlying impulses through which behavioral changes were supposedly achieved turned out to represent more of a social conversion than a self-discovery process. As Marmor [1962], among others, pointed out, each psychodynamic approach had its own favored set of inner causes and its own preferred brand of insight. The presence of these determinants could be easily confirmed through suggestive probing and selective reinforcement of clients' verbal reports in self-validating interviews. For these reasons, advocates of differing theoretical orientations repeatedly discovered their favorite psychodynamic agents but rarely found evidence for the hypothesized causes emphasized by proponents of competing views. The content of a particular client's insights and emergent "unconscious" could therefore be better predicted from knowledge of the therapist's belief system than from the client's actual social learning history.

It eventually became apparent that if progress in understanding human behavior was to be accelerated, more stringent requirements would have to be applied in evaluating the adequacy of explanatory systems. Theories must demonstrate predictive power, and they must accurately identify causal factors, as shown by the fact that varying the postulated determinants produces related changes in behavior.

The attribution of behavior to inner forces can perhaps be likened to early explanatory schemes in other branches of science. At one time diverse chemical reactions were supposedly caused by movements of a material substance called phlogiston, physical objects were internally propelled by intangible essences, and physiological functioning was ascribed to the action of humors. Developments in learning theory shifted the focus of causal analysis from hypothesized inner determinants to detailed examination of external influences on responsiveness. Human behavior was extensively analyzed in terms of the stimulus events that evoke it and the reinforcing consequences that alter it. Researchers repeatedly demonstrated that response patterns, generally attributed to underlying forces, could be induced, eliminated, and reinstated simply by varying external sources of influence. These impressive findings led many psychologists, especially proponents of radical forms of behaviorism, to the view that the causes of behavior are found not in the organism but in environmental forces.

The idea that man's actions are under external control, though amply documented, was not enthusiastically received for a variety of reasons. To most people it unfortunately implied a one-way influence process that reduced man to a helpless reactor to the vagaries of external rewards and punishments. The view that behavior is environmentally determined also appeared to contradict firm, but ill-founded, beliefs that people possess generalized personality traits leading them to behave in a consistent manner, however variable the social influences.

A more valid criticism of the extreme behavioristic position is that, in a vigorous effort to eschew spurious inner causes, it neglected determinants of man's behavior arising from his cognitive functioning. Man is a thinking organism possessing capabilities that provide him with some power of self-direction. To the extent that traditional behavioral theories could be faulted, it was for providing an incomplete rather than an inaccurate account of human behavior.

In the social learning view, man is neither driven by inner forces nor buffeted helplessly by environmental influences. Rather, psychological functioning is best understood in terms of a continuous reciprocal interaction between behavior and its controlling conditions. The social learning theory outlined in this paper places special emphasis on the important roles played by vicarious, symbolic, and self-regulatory processes, which receive relatively little attention even in most contemporary theories of learning. These differences in governing processes carry certain implications for the way one views the causes of human behavior.

Traditional theories of learning generally depict behavior as the product of directly experienced response consequences. In actuality, virtually all learning phenomena resulting from direct experiences can occur on a vicarious basis through observation of other people's behavior and its consequences for them. Man's capacity to learn by observation enables him to acquire large, integrated units of behavior by example without having to build up the patterns gradually by tedious trial and error. Similarly, emotional responses can be developed observationally by witnessing the affective reactions of others undergoing painful or pleasurable experiences. Fearful and defensive behavior can be extinguished vicariously by observing others engage in the feared activities without any adverse consequences. And behavioral inhibitions can be induced by seeing others punished for their actions.

Man's superior cognitive capacity is another factor that determines, not only how he will be affected by his experiences, but the future direction his actions may take. People can represent external influences symbolically and later use such representations to

2

guide their actions; they can solve problems symbolically without having to enact the various alternatives; and they can foresee the probable consequences of different actions and alter their behavior accordingly. These higher mental processes permit both insightful and foresightful behavior.

A third distinguishing feature of man is that he is capable of creating self-regulative influences. By managing the stimulus determinants of given activities and producing consequences for their own actions, people are able to control their own behavior to some degree. As illustrated later, cognitive and self-regulative influences often serve important functions in causal sequences. The remainder of this paper is devoted to a detailed social learning analysis of how patterns of behavior are acquired and how their expression is continuously regulated by the interplay of self-generated and other sources of influences.

Learning by Direct Experience

In the social learning system, new patterns of behavior can be acquired through direct experience or by observing the behavior of others. The more rudimentary form of learning, rooted in direct experience, is largely governed by the rewarding and punishing consequences that follow any given action. People are repeatedly confronted with situations with which they must deal in one way or another. Some of the responses that they try prove unsuccessful, while others produce more favorable effects. Through this process of differential reinforcement successful modes of behavior are eventually selected from exploratory activities, while ineffectual ones are discarded.

It is commonly believed that responses are automatically and unconsciously strengthened by their immediate consequences. Simple performances can be altered to some degree through reinforcement without awareness of the relationship between one's actions and their outcomes. However, man's cognitive skills enable him to profit more extensively from experience than if he were an unthinking organism. Within the framework of social learning theory, reinforcement primarily serves informative and incentive functions, although it also has response-strengthening capabilities.

Informative Function of Reinforcement

During the course of learning, people not only perform responses, but they also observe the differential consequences accompanying their various actions. On the basis of this informative feedback,

they develop thoughts or hypotheses about the types of behavior most likely to succeed. These hypotheses then serve as guides for future actions [Dulany & O'Connell 1963]. Accurate hypotheses give rise to successful performances, whereas erroneous ones lead to ineffective courses of action. The cognitive events are thus selectively strengthened or disconfirmed by the differential consequences accompanying the more distally occurring overt behavior. In this analysis of learning by experience, reinforcing consequences partly serve as an unarticulated way of informing performers what they must do in order to gain beneficial outcomes or to avoid punishing ones.

Motivational Function of Reinforcement

Because of man's anticipatory capacity, conditions of reinforcement also have strong incentive-motivational effects. Most human behavior is not controlled by immediate external reinforcement. As a result of prior experiences, people come to expect that certain actions will gain them outcomes they value, others will have no appreciable effects, and still others will produce undesired results. Actions are therefore regulated to a large extent by anticipated consequences. Homeowners, for instance, do not wait until they experience the misery of a burning house to buy fire insurance; people who venture outdoors do not ordinarily wait until discomforted by a torrential rain or a biting snowstorm to decide what to wear; nor do motorists usually wait until inconvenienced by a stalled automobile to replenish gasoline.

Through the capacity to represent actual outcomes symbolically, future consequences can be converted into current motivators that influence behavior in much the same way as actual consequences. Man's cognitive skills thus provide him with the capabiity for both insightful and foresightful behavior.

Cognitive Mediation of Reinforcement Effects

A great deal of research has been conducted on whether behavior is learned through the automatic action of consequences or whether the effects of reinforcement are cognitively mediated. Most of these studies have employed verbal conditioning situations in which subjects converse freely or construct sentences and the experimenter rewards certain classes of words but ignores all others. Changes in the incidence of reinforced verbalizations are then examined as a function of whether the participants were aware that their verbal utterances were selectively reinforced and whether they recognized the types of words that produced reinforcement.

Spielberger and De Nike [1966], proponents of an exclusively cognitive view of learning, measured subjects' awareness at periodic intervals throughout the verbal conditioning session. They found that subjects displayed no rise in the number of reinforced responses as long as they remained unaware of the reinforcement contingency, but they suddenly increased their output of appropriate responses upon discovering what types of words were rewarded. Dulany [1962, 1968] similarly found that reinforcing consequences were ineffective in modifying subjects' behavior as long as they were unaware of what they had to do to produce rewarding outcomes. These authors concluded that learning cannot take place without awareness of what is being reinforced. Dulany, who outlined this position in a formal way, contended that the acquired response information gives rise to intentions or self-instructions to produce the required behaviors, the strength of the tendency depending on the incentive value of the consequences. Neither these findings nor the generalizations went uncontested.

Earlier studies by Postman and Sassenrath [1961], who also examined the temporal relation between emergence of awareness and changes in responsiveness, found that reinforcement produced small but significant improvements in performance prior to awareness, but subjects sharply increased appropriate responses after they hit upon the correct solution. Learning, they concluded, can occur without awareness, albeit slowly and quite inefficiently. The resultant increase in correct responses makes it easier to discern what is wanted; once the discovery has been made, the appropriate behavior is readily performed, given adequate incentives. A sudden rise in correct responding with discovery of the reinforcement contingencies is generally regarded as insightful behavior.

The discrepant findings concerning the relationship between awareness and behavior change largely reflected how adequately awareness was measured. Spielberger and De Nike [1966] assessed at infrequent intervals during the learning task (after twenty-five trials) whether subjects figured out the correct responses. Subjects may, therefore, have discerned the reinforcement contingency late in the insight block of trials after a noticeable increase in performance was produced by reinforcement in the absence of awareness. By measuring awareness at shorter intervals, Kennedy [1970, 1971] demonstrated that this is precisely what happens. When data are plotted in twenty-five-trial blocks, awareness seems to precede behavior change, but when these same data are plotted in five- or ten-trial blocks, perform-

ance gains precede awareness for subjects who later recognize the correct types of responses.

Whether emergence of awareness is accompanied by increases, decreases, or no change in performance largely depends on the reward value of the response consequences. People who are aware of appropriate responses in a given situation and who value the outcomes they produce change their behavior in the reinforced direction. On the other hand, those who are equally aware of the reinforcement contingencies but who devalue either the required behavior or the reinforcers not only remain uninfluenced but may even respond in an oppositional manner.

Reinforcing Effects of Response Consequences

Verbal conditioning procedures are adequate for demonstrating that awareness can facilitate changes in behavior, but they are ill-suited for resolving the basic question of whether awareness is a prerequisite for learning or performance change. The limitations are twofold: first, the verbalizations that are modified already exist in the subjects' repertoires so that the task does not involve response learning. Second, since both the responses and their outcomes are observable, experimenters have to rely on subjects' verbal reports of unknown reliability to figure out who is aware of what.

The question of whether learning must be consciously mediated is answered most decisively by studies in which either the reinforced responses or their effects are not attributable to awareness because the action-outcome relationship cannot be observed. Hefferline and his associates [Hefferline & Keenan 1963, Hefferline, Keenan, & Harford 1959] and Sasmor [1966] successfully modified the behavior of adults through reinforcement even though the latter were unable to observe their rewarded responses. In these studies the occurrence of visibly imperceptible muscular responses, detected by the experimenter through electronic amplification, is reinforced either by monetary reward or by termination of unpleasant stimulation. Unseen responses increase substantially during reinforcement and decline abruptly after reinforcement is withdrawn. As might be expected, none of the people could identify the response that produced the reinforcing consequences.

In the preceding investigation, the appropriate responses were unobservable but the reinforcers were. Experiments have been conducted with animals in which the correct responses are noticeable but their reinforcing consequences are not [Chambers 1956, Coppock & Chambers 1954, Coppock, Headlee, &

Hood 1953]. Results of such studies likewise show that responses can be automatically strengthened through selective reinforcement operating below the level of awareness.

Evidence that elementary performances can be increased through reinforcement without the mediating effects of awareness does not mean that people can learn to respond in accordance with relatively complicated principles in this manner as well. For an illustration of how rule-governed behavior is under cognitive control, visualize a task in which subjects are presented with words varying in length, to which they must provide a correct number. Let us select an arbitrary rule wherein the correct number is obtained by subtracting the number of letters in a given word from 97, dividing the remainder by 3, and then multiplying the result by 5. In this situation, appropriate responses are derived from a high-order rule,

$$R = \frac{97 - N \times 5}{3},$$

requiring a three-step transformation of the external stimulus. To achieve errorless performances, one must perform accurately several mental operations in a particular sequence. An unthinking organism is unlikely to show any performance gains, however long its responses may be reinforced.

The overall evidence reveals that response consequences can be informative, motivating, and reinforcing. Therefore, in any given instance, contingent reinforcement may produce changes in behavior through any one or more of the three processes. People can learn some patterns of behavior by experiencing rewarding and punishing consequences, but if they know what they are supposed to do to secure desired outcomes, they profit much more from such experiences. As shown later, while reinforcement is a powerful method for regulating behaviors that have already been learned, it is a relatively inefficient way of creating them.

Learning through Modeling

Although behavior can be shaped into new patterns to some extent by rewarding and punishing consequences, learning would be exceedingly laborious and hazardous if it proceeded solely on this basis. Environments are loaded with potentially lethal consequences that befall those who are unfortunate enough to perform dangerous errors. For this reason it would be ill-advised to rely on differen-

tial reinforcement of trial-and-error performances in teaching children to swim, adolescents to drive automobiles, and adults to develop complex occupational and social competencies. Apart from questions of survival, it is difficult to imagine a socialization process in which the language, mores, vocational activities, familial customs, and the educational, religious, and political practices of a culture are taught to each new member by selective reinforcement of fortuitous behaviors, without benefit of models who exemplify the cultural patterns in their own behavior.

Most of the behaviors that people display are learned, either deliberately or inadvertently, through the influence of example. There are several reasons why modeling influences figure prominently in human learning in everyday life. When mistakes are costly or dangerous, new modes of response can be developed without needless errors by providing competent models who demonstrate how the required activities should be performed. Some complex behaviors, of course, can be produced only through the influence of models. If children had no opportunity to hear speech, for example, it would be virtually impossible to teach them the linguistic skills that constitute a language. It is doubtful that one could ever shape intricate individual words, let alone grammatical speech, by differential reinforcement of random vocalizations. Where novel forms of behavior can be conveyed only by social cues, modeling is an indispensable aspect of learning. Even in instances where it is possible to establish new response patterns through other means, the process of acquisition can be considerably shortened by providing appropriate models. Under most circumstances, a good example is therefore a much better teacher than the consequences of unguided actions.

A number of different theories have been proposed over the years to explain how people learn by observing the behavior of others. Major tenets of these alternative views, and their empirical status, are discussed at length elsewhere [Bandura 1971b]. The social learning analysis of observational learning differs from contemporary learning interpretations principally in the locus of response integration, in the role played by cognitive functions, and in the manner in which reinforcement influences observational learning.

Nonmediated Stimulus-Response Theories

There was no research to speak of on modeling processes until the classic publication *Social Learning and Imitation* by Miller and Dollard [1941]. They advanced the view that in order for imitative learning to occur observers must be motivated to act, they must be provided with an example of the desired behavior, they must perform responses that match the example, and their imitative behavior must be positively reinforced. In experiments conducted to test these assumptions, a model always chose one of two boxes that contained two rewards, and observers received one of the rewards whenever they went to the same box. Observers not only learned to follow the model, but they generalized copying responses to new situations, to new models, and to different motivational states.

These experiments were widely accepted as demonstrations of imitative learning, although they represent only a special form of discrimination place-learning. The model's actions simply informed children where to go but did not teach them any new behavior. Had a light or some other informative cue been used to indicate the correct box, the model's behavior would have been irrelevant and perhaps even a hindrance to efficient performance. Observational response learning, on the other hand, is concerned with how people organize behavioral elements to form new response patterns exemplified by others. Since the theory proposed by Miller and Dollard requires a person to display imitative responses before he can learn them, it accounts more adequately for the performance of previously established matching responses than for their acquisition. It is perhaps for this reason that publication of their research monographs, which contained many provocative ideas, aroused only a passing interest. Despite the prevalence and powerful influence of example in the development and regulation of human behavior, traditional accounts of learning contain little or no mention of modeling processes.

The operant conditioning analysis of modeling [Baer & Sherman 1964, Skinner 1953, Gewirtz & Stingle 1968] relies entirely upon the standard three-component paradigm $S^d \longrightarrow R \longrightarrow S^r$, where S^d denotes the modeled stimulus, R represents an overt matching response, and S^r designates the reinforcing stimulus. Except for deletion of the motivational requirement, Skinner's explanation posits the same necessary conditions (that is, cue, response, reinforcement) for imitation originally proposed by Miller and Dollard. Observational learning, according to the operant view, is presumably achieved through differential reinforcement. When responses corresponding to the model's actions are positively reinforced and divergent responses either nonrewarded or punished, the behavior of others comes to function as cues for matching responses.

The scheme above does not appear to be applicable to observational learning where an observer does not overtly perform the model's responses in the setting in which they are exhibited, reinforcements are not administered either to the model or to the observer, and whatever responses have been thus acquired are not displayed for days, weeks, or even months. Under these conditions, which represent one of the most prevalent forms of social learning, two of the factors ($R \longrightarrow S^r$) in the three-element paradigm are absent during acquisition, and the third factor (S^d, or modeling stimulus) is typically missing from the situation when the observationally learned response is first performed. Like the Miller and Dollard theory, Skinner's analysis clarifies how similar behavior that a person has previously learned can be prompted by the actions of others and the prospect of reward. However, it does not explain how a new matching response is acquired observationally in the first place. As shown later, such learning occurs through symbolic processes during exposure to the modeled activities before any responses have been performed or reinforced.

Social Learning Analysis of Observational Learning

Social learning theory assumes that modeling influences produce learning principally through their informative functions and that observers acquire mainly symbolic representations of modeled activities rather than specific stimulus-response associations [Bandura 1969a, 1971a]. In this formulation, modeling phenomena are governed by four interrelated subprocesses.

Attentional processes. A person cannot learn much by observation if he does not attend to, or recognize, the essential features of the model's behavior. One of the component functions in learning by example is therefore concerned with attentional processes. Simply exposing persons to models does not in itself ensure that they will attend closely to them, that they will necessarily select from the model's numerous characteristics the most relevant ones, or that they will even perceive accurately the aspects they happen to notice.

Among the numerous factors that determine observational experiences, associational preferences are undoubtedly of major importance. The people with whom one regularly associates delimit the types of behavior that one will repeatedly observe and hence learn most thoroughly. Opportunities for learning aggressive behavior obviously differ markedly for members of delinquent gangs and of Quaker groups. Within any social group some members are likely to command greater attention than others. The functional value of the behaviors displayed by different models is highly influential in determining which models will be closely observed and which will be ignored. Attention to models is also channeled by their interpersonal attraction. Models who possess interesting and winsome qualities are sought out, whereas those who lack pleasing characteristics tend to be ignored or rejected, even though they may excel in other ways.

Some forms of modeling are so intrinsically rewarding that they can hold the attention of people of all ages for extended periods. This is nowhere better illustrated than in televised modeling. Indeed, models presented in televised form are so effective in capturing attention that viewers learn the depicted behavior regardless of whether or not they are given extra incentives to do so [Bandura, Grusec, & Menlove 1966].

Retention processes. A person cannot be much influenced by observation of a model's behavior if he has no memory of it. A second major function involved in observational learning concerns long-term retention of activities that have been modeled at one time or another. If one is to reproduce a model's behavior when the latter is no longer present to serve as a guide, the response patterns must be represented in memory in symbolic form. By this means past influences can achieve some degree of permanence.

Observational learning involves two representational systems—an imaginal and a verbal one. During exposure, modeling stimuli produce, through a process of sensory conditioning, relatively enduring, retrievable images of modeled sequences of behavior. Indeed, under conditions where stimulus events are highly correlated, as when a name is consistently associated with a given person, it is virtually impossible to hear the name without experiencing imagery of the person's physical characteristics. Similarly, reference to activities (golfing, skiing), places (San Francisco, Paris), and things (one's automobile, Washington Monument) that one has previously observed immediately elicits vivid imaginal representations of the absent physical stimuli.

The second representational system, which probably accounts for the notable speed of observational learning and long-term retention of modeled contents by humans, involves verbal coding of observed events. Most of the cognitive processes that regulate behavior are primarily verbal rather than visual. The route traversed by a model can be acquired, retained, and later reproduced more accurately by verbal coding of the visual information into a sequence of

right and left turns (for example, RLRRL) than by reliance upon visual imagery of the itinerary. Observational learning and retention are facilitated by such codes because they carry a great deal of information in an easily stored form.

After modeled activities have been transformed into images and readily utilizable verbal symbols, these memory codes serve as guides for subsequent reproduction of matching responses. That symbolic coding can enhance observational learning is shown by studies conducted both with children [Bandura, Grusec, & Menlove 1966, Coates & Hartup 1969] and with adults [Bandura & Jeffery 1971, Gerst 1971]. Observers who code modeled activities into either words, concise labels, or vivid imagery learn and retain the behavior better than those who simply observe or are mentally preoccupied with other matters while watching the performance of others.

In addition to symbolic coding, rehearsal serves as an important memory aid. People who mentally rehearse or actually perform modeled patterns of behavior are less likely to forget them than are those who neither think about nor practice what they have seen. Some of the behaviors that are learned observationally cannot be easily strengthened by overt enactment either because they are socially prohibited or because the necessary appartus is lacking. It is therefore of considerable interest that mental rehearsal of modeled activities can increase their retention [Bandura & Jeffery 1971, Michael & Maccoby 1961].

Some researchers [Gewirtz & Stingle 1968] have been especially concerned about the conditions that produce the first imitative responses on the assumption that they help explain observational learning at later stages of development. There is some reason to question whether initial and later imitations have equivalent determinants. In early years imitative responses are evoked directly and immediately by models' actions. In later periods, imitative responses are usually performed in the absence of the models long after their behavior has been observed. Immediate imitation does not require much in the way of cognitive functioning because the behavioral reproduction is externally guided by the model's actions. By contrast, in delayed imitation, the absent modeled events must be internally represented, and factors such as symbolic transformation and cognitive organization of modeling stimuli and covert rehearsal, which facilitate retention of acquired contents, serve as determinants of observational learning. The difference between physically prompted and delayed imitation is analogous to drawing a picture of one's automobile when it is at hand, and from memory.

In the latter situation, the hand does not automatically sketch the car; rather, one must rely on memory guides, mainly in the form of mental images.

Motoric reproduction processes. The third component of modeling is concerned with processes whereby symbolic representations guide overt actions. To achieve behavioral reproduction, a learner must put together a given set of responses according to the modeled patterns. The amount of observational learning that a person can exhibit behaviorally depends on whether or not he has acquired the component skills. If he possesses the constituent elements, he can easily integrate them to produce new patterns of behavior, but if the response components are lacking, behavioral reproduction will be faulty. Given extensive deficits, the subskills required for complex performances must first be developed by modeling and practice.

Even though symbolic representations of modeled activities are acquired and retained, and the subskills exist, an individual may be unable to coordinate various actions in the required pattern and sequence because of physical limitations. A young child can learn observationally the behavior for driving an automobile and be adept at executing the component responses, but if he is too short to operate the controls he cannot maneuver the vehicle successfully.

There is a third impediment at the behavioral level to skillful reproduction of modeled activities that have been learned observationally. In most coordinated motor skills, such as golf and swimming, performers cannot see the responses that they are making; hence, they must rely on ill-defined proprioceptive cues or verbal reports of onlookers. It is exceedingly difficult to guide actions that are not easily observed or to identify the corrective adjustments needed to achieve a close match of symbolic model and overt performance. In most everyday learning, people usually achieve rough approximations of new patterns of behavior by modeling and refine them through self-corrective adjustments on the basis of informative feedback from performance.

Reinforcement and motivational processes. A person can acquire, retain, and possess the capabilities for skillful execution of modeled behavior, but the learning may rarely be activated into overt performance if it is negatively sanctioned or otherwise unfavorably received. When positive incentives are provided, observational learning, which previously remained unexpressed, is promptly translated into action [Bandura 1965]. Reinforcement influences not only regulate the overt expression of matching behavior, but they can affect the level of observational learning by controlling what people attend to and how actively they code and rehearse what they have seen.

For reasons given above, the provision of models, even prominent ones, will not automatically create similar patterns of behavior in others. If one is interested merely in producing imitative behavior, some of the subprocesses included in the social learning analysis of modeling can be disregarded. A model who repeatedly demonstrates desired responses, instructs others to reproduce them, physically prompts the behavior when it fails to occur, and then administers powerful rewards will eventually elicit matching responses in most people. It may require 1, 10, or 100 demonstration trials, but if one persists, the desired behavior will eventually be evoked. If, on the other hand, one wishes to explain why modeling does or does not occur, a variety of determinants must be considered. In any given instance lack of matching behavior following exposure to modeling influences may result from either failure to observe the relevant activities, inadequate coding of modeled events for memory representation, retention decrements, motoric deficiencies, or inadequate conditions of reinforcement.

Locus of Response Integration in Observational Learning

New patterns of behavior are created by organizing constituent responses into certain patterns and sequences. Theories of modeling differ on whether the response integration occurs mainly at central or at peripheral levels. Operant conditioning formulations [Baer & Sherman 1964, Gewirtz & Stingle 1968] assume that response elements are selected out of overt performances by providing appropriate antecedent stimuli and by rewarding actions that resemble the modeled behavior and ignoring those that do not. The response components presumably thus extracted are sequentially chained by the influence of reinforcement to form more complex units of behavior. Since, in this view, behavior is organized into new patterns in the course of performance, learning requires overt responding and immediate reinforcement.

According to social learning theory, behavior is learned, at least in rough form, before it is performed. By observing a model of the desired behavior, an individual forms an idea of how response components must be combined and temporally sequenced to produce new behavioral configurations.

The representation serves as a guide for behavioral reproduction. Observational learning without performance is abundantly documented in modeling studies using a nonresponse acquisition procedure [Bandura 1969, Flanders 1968]. After watching models perform novel modes of response, observers can later describe the entire pattern of behavior with considerable accuracy, and given the appropriate conditions, they often achieve errorless behavioral reproductions on the first test trial.

It is commonly believed that controversies about the locus of learning cannot be satisfactorily resolved because learning must be inferred from performance. This may very well be the case in experimentation with animals. To determine whether a rat has mastered a maze one must run him through it. With humans, there exists a reasonably accurate index of learning that is independent of motor performance. To measure whether a human has learned a maze by observing the successful performances of a model, one need only ask him to describe the correct pattern of right and left turns. Such an experiment would undoubtedly reveal that people can learn through modeling before they perform.

Role of Reinforcement in Observational Learning

Another issue in contention concerns the role of reinforcement in observational learning. As previously noted, reinforcement-oriented theories [Baer & Sherman 1964, Miller & Dollard 1941, Gewirtz & Stingle 1968] assume that imitative responses must be reinforced in order to be learned. Social learning theory, on the other hand, distinguishes between learning and performance of matching behavior. Observational learning, in this view, can occur through observation of modeled behavior and accompanying cognitive activities without extrinsic reinforcement. This is not to say that mere exposure to modeled activities is, in itself, sufficient to produce observational learning. Not all stimulation that impinges on individuals is necessarily observed by them, and even if attended to, the influence of modeling stimuli alone does not ensure that they will be retained for any length of time.

Anticipation of reinforcement is one of several factors that can influence what is observed and what goes unnoticed. Knowing that a given model's behavior is effective in producing valued rewards or averting negative consequences can enhance observational learning by increasing observers' attentiveness to the model's actions. Moreover, anticipated reinforcement can strengthen retention of what has been learned observationally by motivating people to code and to rehearse modeled responses that have high value. Theories of modeling primarily differ in the manner in which reinforcement influences observational learning rather than in whether reinforcement may play a role in the acquisition process. As shown in the schematization below, the issue in dispute is whether reinforcement acts backward to strengthen preceding imitative responses and their association to stimuli or whether it facilitates learning through its effects on attentional, organizational, and rehearsal processes. It would follow from social learning theory that a higher level of observational learning would be achieved by informing observers in advance about the payoff value for adopting modeled patterns of behavior than by waiting until observers happen to imitate a model and then rewarding them for it.

In social learning theory reinforcement is considered a facilitative rather than a necessary condition because there are factors other than response consequences that can influence what people will attend to. One does not have to be reinforced, for example, to hear compelling sounds or to look at prominent visual displays. Hence, when people's attention to modeled activities can be gained through physical means, the addition of positive incentives does not increase observational learning [Bandura, Grusec, & Menlove 1966]. Children who intently watched modeled actions on a television screen in a room darkened to eliminate distractions later displayed the same amount of imitative learning regardless of whether they were informed in advance that correct imitations would be rewarded or given

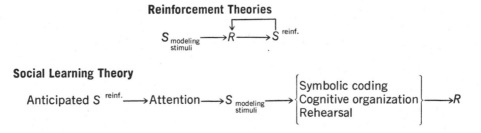

9

no prior incentives to learn the modeled performances. Anticipated reinforcement would be expected to exert greatest influence on observational learning under self-selection conditions where people can choose whom they will attend to and how intensively they observe their behavior.

Both operant conditioning and social learning theories assume that whether or not people choose to perform what they have learned observationally is strongly influenced by the consequences of such actions. In social learning theory, however, behavior is regulated, not only by directly experienced consequences from external sources, but by vicarious reinforcement and self-reinforcement.

The Modeling Process and Transmission of Response Information

A major function of modeling stimuli is to transmit information to observers on how to organize component responses into new patterns of behavior. This response information can be conveyed through physical demonstrations, through pictorial representation, or through verbal description.

Much social learning occurs on the basis of casual or studied observation of exemplary models. As linguistic skills are developed, verbal modeling is gradually substituted for behavioral modeling as the preferred mode of response guidance. By performing sequences of actions as described in instructional manuals, people can learn how to assemble and operate complicated mechanical equipment, how to behave in a variety of unfamiliar social situations, and how to perform vocational and recreational tasks in a skillful manner. Verbal modeling is used extensively because one can convey through words an almost infinite variety of complex behaviors that would be exceedingly difficult and time consuming to portray behaviorally.

Another influential source of social learning is the abundant and varied symbolic modeling provided in television, films, and other pictorial displays. There is a large body of research evidence showing that both children and adults can acquire attitudes, emotional responses, and new patterns of behavior as a result of observing filmed or televised models [Bandura 1969a, Flanders 1968, Lumsdaine 1961]. Considering the large amount of time that people spend watching televised models, mass media may play an influential role in shaping behavior and social attitudes. With further developments in communication technology, it will be possible to have almost any activity portrayed on request at any time on remote television consoles [Parker 1970]. As such forms

of symbolic modeling are increasingly used, parents, teachers, and other traditional role models may assume a less prominent role in social learning.

The basic modeling process is the same regardless of whether the desired behavior is conveyed through words, pictures, or live actions. Different forms of modeling, however, are not always equally effective. It is frequently difficult to convey through words the same amount of information contained in pictorial or live demonstrations. Some forms of modeling may also be more powerful than others in commanding attention. Children, or adults for that matter, rarely have to be compelled to watch television, whereas verbal characterizations of the same activities would fail to hold their attention for long. One might also expect observers who lack conceptual skills to benefit less from verbal modeling than from behavioral demonstrations.

Scope of Modeling Influences

In many instances the behavior displayed by exemplary models must be learned in essentially the same form. For example, driving automobiles or performing surgical operations permit little, if any, departure from established practices. In addition to transmitting fixed repertoires of behavior, modeling influences can, contrary to common belief, create generative and innovative behavior as well.

In studying more complex forms of modeling, persons observe models respond to different stimuli in accordance with a preselected rule or principle. Observers are subsequently tested under conditions where they can behave in a way that is stylistically similar to the model's disposition, but they cannot mimic his specific responses. To take an example, a model constructs from a set of nouns sentences containing the passive voice. Children are later instructed to generate sentences from a different set of nouns with the model absent, and the incidence of passive constructions is recorded. In this higher form of modeling, observers must abstract common features exemplified in diverse modeled responses and formulate a rule for generating similar patterns of behavior. Responses performed by subjects that embody the observationally derived rule are likely to resemble the behavior that the model would be inclined to exhibit under similar circumstances, even though observers had never witnessed the model's behavior in these new situations.

A number of studies have been conducted demonstrating how response-generative rules can be transmitted through modeling. Young children who had no formal grammatical knowledge altered their syntactic style in accord with the rules guiding the modeled verbal constructions [Bandura & Harris 1966, Liebert, Odom, Hill, & Huff 1969, Rosenthal & Whitebook 1970]. In addition, modeling influences have been successful in modifying moral judgmental orientations [Bandura & McDonald 1963, Cowan, Langer, Heavenrich, & Nathanson 1969], delay of gratification patterns [Bandura & Mischel 1965, Stumphauzer 1969], and styles of information seeking [Rosenthal, Zimmerman, & Durning 1970]. Researchers have also begun to study how modeling influences alter cognitive functioning of the type described by Piaget and his followers [Rosenthal & Zimmerman 1970, Sullivan 1967].

The broader effects of modeling are further revealed in studies employing several models who display different patterns of behavior. Observers may select one or more of the models as the primary source of behavior, but they rarely restrict their imitation to a single source, nor do they adopt all of the characteristics of the preferred model. Rather, observers generally exhibit relatively novel responses representing amalgams of elements from different models [Bandura, Ross, & Ross 1963a]. Paradoxical as it may seem, innovative patterns can emerge solely through modeling. Thus, within a given family same-sex siblings may develop distinct personality characteristics as a result of adopting different combinations of parental and sibling attributes. A succession of modeling influences, in which observers later become sources of behavior for new members, would most likely produce a gradual imitative evolution of novel patterns that might bear little resemblance to those exhibited by the original models. In homogeneous cultures, where all models display similar modes of response, imitative behavior may undergo little or no change across successive models. It is diversity in modeling that fosters behavioral innovation.

The discussion thus far has been concerned solely with the process of learning through modeling. A second major function of modeling influences is to strengthen or to weaken inhibitions of responses that observers have previously learned [Bandura 1971b]. The effects that models have on behavioral restraints are largely determined by observation of rewarding and punishing consequences accompanying models' responses. As a result of seeing a model's actions punished, observers tend to inhibit behaving in a similar way. Conversely, observing models engage in threatening or prohibited activities without experiencing any adverse consequences can reduce inhibitions in observers. Such disinhibitory effects are most strikingly revealed in recent therapeutic

applications of modeling principles [Bandura 1971a]. In these studies, people who dread and avoid certain activities are able to perform them in varying degrees after observing others perform the feared behaviors repeatedly without any harmful effects.

The actions of others can also serve as social cues that influence how others will behave at any given time. Response facilitation by modeling can be distinguished from observational learning and disinhibition by the fact that the model's actions neither teach new behaviors nor reduce inhibitions, because the behavior in question, which already exists, is socially sanctioned and therefore is unencumbered by restraints. Inhibitory and disinhibitory effects of modeling are examined later in the context of vicarious reinforcement, while social facilitation effects are given detailed consideration in the discussion of stimulus control of behavior.

Modeling influences can have additional effects, though these may be of lesser importance. The behavior of models directs observers' attention to the particular objects used by the performer. As a result, observers may subsequently use the same objects to a greater extent, though not necessarily in an imitative way. In one experiment, for example, children who had observed a model pummel a large doll with a mallet not only imitated this specific aggressive action but spent more time pounding other things with a mallet than did those who did not see a person handle this particular instrument [Bandura 1962]. Research findings, considered together, disclose that modeling influences can serve as teachers, as inhibitors, as disinhibitors, as response elicitors, as stimulus enhancers, and as emotion arousers.

Regulatory Processes

A comprehensive theory of behavior must explain not only how response patterns are required but how their expression is regulated and maintained. In social learning theory, human functioning relies on three regulatory processes. They include stimulus, cognitive, and reinforcement control. For explanatory purposes, these control functions are discussed separately, although in reality they are closely interrelated.

Stimulus Control

To function effectively a person must be able to anticipate the probable consequences of different events and courses of action and regulate his behavior accordingly. Without a capacity for anticipatory or foresightful behavior, man would be forced to act blindly in ways that might eventually prove to be highly unproductive, if not perilous. Information about probable consequences is conveyed by environmental stimuli, such as traffic signals, verbal communications, pictorial messages, distinctive places, persons, or things, or the actions of others.

In the earliest years of development, environmental stimuli, except those that are inherently painful, exert little or no influence on infants and young children. As a result of paired experiences, either direct or vicarious, formerly neutral stimuli begin to acquire motivating and response-directive properties. Stimulus control over emotions and actions is established in both instances through association, but they differ in what gets associated.

Stimulus Control of Physiological and Emotional Responsiveness

Physiological responses can be most readily brought under the control of environmental stimuli by having two stimulus events occur contiguously. If a formerly neutral stimulus is closely associated with one that is capable of eliciting a given physiological response, the former stimulus alone gradually acquires the power to evoke the physiological response or a fractional component of it. Although some types of automatic responses are more difficult to condition than others, almost every form of somatic reaction that an organism is capable of making, including changes in respiration, heart rate, muscular tension, gastrointestinal secretions, vasomotor reactions, and other indices of emotional responsiveness, has been classically conditioned to innocuous stimuli [Kimble 1961]. Environmental events can likewise acquire the capacity to control cortical activity through association with either external evocative stimuli or direct brain stimulation [John 1967]. Conditioning is by no means confined to events in the external environment. In recent years researchers [Razran 1961, Slucki, Adam, & Porter 1965] have been able to condition physiological reactions as well as defensive behaviors to variations in the intensity of visceral stimulation from internal organs.

The conditioning process described above has important implications for the understanding of, among other things, psychosomatic disorders, defensive behavior, and evaluative reactions having an affective component. In the psychosomatic field Dekker, Pelser, and Groen [1957] established asthmatic attacks in two patients by pairing formerly ineffective stimuli with allergens that evoked respiratory dysfunctions. A careful analysis of the situations in which other patients regularly experienced asthmatic attacks revealed that a varied array of stimuli had acquired controlling value; these included, among other things, radio speeches by influential politicians, children's choirs, the national anthem, elevators, goldfish, caged birds, the smell of perfume, waterfalls, bicycle races, police vans, and horses. Once the conditioned stimuli had been identified in a particular case, Dekker and Groen [1956] were able to induce attacks of asthma by presenting the evocative stimuli in actual or pictorial form.

A great deal of human behavior is under aversive stimulus control. In this form of emotional learning, persons, places, and events become endowed with anxiety-arousing value through association with painful experiences. A prime function of most anticipatory behavior is to provide protection against potential threats. Once established, defensive behavior is exceedingly difficult to eliminate because it derives self-reinforcing power from its capacity to reduce distress. Any protective activities that remove or avoid discomfort aroused by conditioned threats are thereby strengthened even though the fears may no longer be realistically justified. This process is graphically illustrated by the apocryphal case of a compulsive who, when asked by a psychiatrist why he incessantly snapped his fingers, replied that it kept ferocious lions away. When informed that obviously there were no lions in the vicinity, the compulsive client replied, "See, it works." Inhibitions and avoidance responses commonly regarded as neurotic (for example, phobias and obsessive-compulsive rituals) are similarly strengthened by their capacity to lessen subjectively distressing but objectively nonexistent threats. To the extent that formerly aversive situations are successfully avoided, individuals prevent themselves from discovering that current conditions of reinforcement may differ substantially from those in the past, when their anxiety reactions were appropriate.

In an early study Miller [1948] showed how subjective threats can motivate, and fear reduction reinforce, a variety of defensive behaviors in a currently benign environment. Animals were shocked in a white compartment of a shuttle box where they quickly learned to escape the painful stimulation by running through an open door into a black compartment. The formerly neutral white cues thus acquired aversive properties so that the animals continued to run when placed in the white box even after the shocks had been completely discontinued. To examine further acquisition and self-perpetuation of new defensive reactions in the absence of any physical danger, Miller placed the animals in the white compartment with the door closed to prevent escape. The door could be released, however, by rotating a wheel. Wheel turning was rapidly learned and maintained by fear reduction. When environmental conditions were further changed so that wheel turning no longer released the door, but the animal could escape the compartment by pressing a bar, the former response was quickly discarded while the latter became strongly established. An animal psychiatrist observing these winded animals dashing through compartments, turning wheels, and pressing bars to avoid nonexistent shocks would justifiably diagnose them as suffering a serious psychological disorder. Their behavior was clearly out of touch with reality.

Symbolic conditioning. Conditioning principles would have limited explanatory power if emotional responses could be established only through direct physical experiences. It is not uncommon for people to display strong emotional reactions toward certain things or classes of people on the basis of little or no personal contact with them. Such responses are frequently developed on the basis of higher processes in which symbolic stimuli that have acquired positive or negative valence through direct association with primary experiences serve as the basis for further conditioning.

Emotion-arousing words often function as the vehicle for symbolic conditioning. Words that conjure up feelings of revulsion and dread can be effectively used to create new fears and hatreds; conversely, words arousing positive emotions can endow associated events with pleasing qualities. In laboratory investigations of symbolic conditioning neutral syllables have been found to take on negative value through repetitive pairing with adjectives having negative connotations (for example, ugly, dirty), whereas these same items are evaluated as pleasant after they have been associated with positively conditioned words such as beautiful and happy [Insko & Oakes 1966, Staats & Staats 1957]. Preexisting evaluative reactions toward familiar names of persons and nations have also been significantly altered through conditioning methods using emotional words as evocative stimuli [Staats & Staats 1958]. Moreover, Gale and Jacobson [1970] provide some evidence that emotionally charged words can condition autonomic responses as well as evaluative reactions to neutral stimuli. Evaluative responses occur not only toward objects singled out for conditioning, but they also tend to generalize along established associative networks, thus resulting in widespread effects. Das and Nanda [1963], after associating neutral syllables with the names of two aboriginal tribes, conditioned positive and negative reactions to the syllables by pairing them with affective words. The tribes took on positive and negative values in accordance with the evaluative responses developed to the syllables with which they had been associated.

Symbolic conditioning may be achieved to some extent through pictorial stimuli having affective properties. Geer [1968], for example, conditioned autonomic responses to tones with photographs of victims of violent death. The role of conditioning processes is perhaps nowhere more dramatically illustrated than in the marked cross-cultural variations in the physical attributes and adornments that become sexual arousers. What is invested with arousal properties in one society—corpulence or skinniness, upright hemispherical breasts or long pendulous ones, shiny white teeth or black pointed ones, distorted ears, noses, or lips, broad pelvis and wide hips or narrow pelvis and slim hips, light or dark skin color—may be neutral or repulsive to members of another social group. A bold experiment by Rachman [1966] on how fetishes might be acquired throws some light on symbolic conditioning of sexual arousal. After a photograph of women's boots was repeatedly associated with slides of sexually stimulating nude females, males exhibited sexual arousal (as measured by penile volume change) to the boots alone and generalized the conditioned sexual responses to other types of black shoes. Needless to say, these unusual sexual reactions were thoroughly eliminated at the conclusion of the study. Consistent with the latter findings, McGuire, Carlisle, and Young [1965] advance the view that deviant sexuality often develops through masturbatory conditioning in which aberrant sexual fantasies are endowed with strong erotic value through repeated association with pleasurable experiences from masturbation.

Vicarious conditioning. While many emotional responses are learned on the basis of direct experience, much human learning undoubtedly occurs through vicarious conditioning. The emotional responses of another person, as conveyed through vocal, facial, and postural manifestations, can arouse strong emotional reactions in observers. Affective social cues most likely acquire arousal value as a result of correlated experiences between people. That is, individuals who are in high spirits tend to treat others in amiable ways, which arouse in them similar pleasurable affects; conversely, when individuals are dejected, ailing, distressed, or angry, others are also likely to suffer in one way or another. This speculation receives some support in a study by Church [1959], who found that expression of pain by an animal evoked strong emotional arousal in animals that had suffered pain together; it had much less emotional effect on animals that had undergone equally painful experiences but unassociated with suffering of another member of their species, and it left unmoved animals that were never subjected to any distress.

In vicarious conditioning, events take on evocative properties through association with emotions aroused in observers by affective experiences of others. In laboratory studies of this phenomenon, an observer hears a tone and shortly thereafter he sees another person exhibit pain reactions (actually feigned) as though he were severely shocked [Berger 1962]. Observers who repeatedly witness this sequence of events begin to show emotional responses to the tone alone even though no pain is ever inflicted on them. In everyday life, of course, pain may be witnessed from a variety of sources. Observation of failure experiences and the sight of terrified people threatened by menacing animals have, for instance, served as arousers for emotional learning [Bandura, Blanchard, & Ritter 1969, Craig & Weinstein 1965].

Despite the importance of vicarious learning, there has been surprisingly little study of the factors determining how strongly people can be affectively conditioned through the experiences of others. The nature of the relationship between the observer and the sufferer is undoubtedly an influential factor. People are generally less affected emotionally by the adversities of strangers than by the suffering and joy of those close to them and on whom they depend. Observers' sensitivity to expressions of suffering, derived from their past social experiences, may be another contributor. Bandura and Rosenthal [1966], for example, found that the degree to which observers were emotionally aroused affected their level of vicarious conditioning. Those who were under moderate emotional arousal displayed the highest rate and most enduring conditioned autonomic responses, whereas those who were either quite calm or highly aroused showed the weakest vicarious conditioning. Apparently, anguished reactions proved so upsetting to observers who themselves were beset by high arousal that they diverted their attention from the suffering person and sought refuge in distracting thoughts of a calming nature.

It is evident from the preceding discussion that emotional learning is much more complex than is commonly assumed. Emotional responses can be brought under the control of intricate combinations of internal and external stimuli that may be either closely related to, or temporally remote from, physical experiences. The fact that stimulus events can be endowed with emotion-arousing potential on a vicarious basis further adds to the complexity of conditioning processes. Additionally, it will be shown later that formerly neutral stimuli can acquire evocation properties through association with thought-produced arousal. Once conditioned stimuli have acquired eliciting power, this capacity transfers to other sets of stimuli that possess similar physical characteristics, to semantically related cues, and even to highly dissimilar stimuli that happen to be associated in people's experiences.

By associating the term *behaviorism* with odious images of salivating dogs and animals driven by carrots and sticks, critics of behavioral approaches skillfully employ Pavlovian conditioning procedures on their receptive audiences to endow this point of view with degrading properties. The fact that valuation of places, persons, and things is affected by one's emotional experiences, whether they be fearful, humiliating, mournful, or pleasurable, does not mean that such conditioning outcomes reflect a base animal process. To expect people to remain unaffected by paired experiences is to require that they be less than human. Moreover, to be sensitive to the consequences of one's actions indicates intelligence rather than subhuman functioning.

Cognitive Control of Conditioning Phenomena

Both popular accounts and psychological descriptions of conditioning phenomena convey the impression that emotional responsiveness is conditioned automatically through paired stimulation occurring in a certain temporal relationship. This view is typically reinforced by diagrammatic portrayal of the process as a nonmediated one in which conditioned stimuli are directly connected to responses evoked by unconditioned stimuli. Results of several lines of research indicate that, in humans, conditioning phenomena cannot be fully understood without encompassing the influence of cognitive control.

Studies of the relationship between awareness of paired events and degree of learning reveal that conditioning involves more than simply linking stimuli to new responses through contiguous association. Fuhrer and Baer [1965] report an experiment in which one tone was always followed by shock but a different tone was presented alone. People who recognized that one of the tones signified shock responded emotionally whenever it appeared, whereas those who remained unaware of the stimulus contingencies did not. Other researchers have likewise shown that repetitive association of neutral and aversive stimuli does not produce conditioned emotional responses in people who fail to recognize that the two sets of events are related [Dawson & Grings 1968, Dawson & Satterfield 1969].

That awareness is a determinant of conditioning rather than vice versa is convincingly demonstrated by Chatterjee and Eriksen [1962]. People who were informed that shock would follow a particular word in a chain of associations quickly developed conditioned heart-rate responses. In contrast, subjects who were led to believe that the occurrence of shock was not related in any consistent way to their verbalizations evidenced no autonomic conditioning even though they repeatedly experienced the same paired stimulation as their aware counterparts.

The most striking evidence of cognitive control of conditioned responses is provided by studies comparing extinction of emotional reactions to conditioned stimuli in subjects who are informed that the stimuli are no longer followed by painful events and in those who are never told that the threat has ceased to exist. Induced awareness promptly abolishes conditioned autonomic responses [Grings & Lockhart 1963, Notterman, Schoenfeld, & Bersh 1952, Wickens, Allen, & Hill 1963] and avoidance behavior [Lindley & Moyer 1961, Moyer & Lindley 1962], whereas uninformed subjects lose their fear only gradually.

Self-arousal interpretation of conditioning. According to social learning theory, conditioned emotional responses are typically mediated through thought-produced arousal rather than being directly evoked by conditioned stimuli. The power to arouse emotional responses is by no means confined to external events. People can easily make themselves nauseated by imagining revolting experiences. They can become sexually aroused by generating erotic fantasies. They can frighten themselves by fear-provoking thoughts. And they can work themselves up into a state of anger by ruminating about mistreatment from offensive *provocateurs*. Indeed, Barber and Hahn [1964] found that imagined painful stimulation produced subjective discomfort and physiological responses similar to those induced by the actual painful stimulation. The incomparable Satchel Paige, whose extended baseball career provided many opportunities for anxious self-arousal, colorfully described the power that thoughts can exert over visceral functioning when he advised, "If your stomach disputes you lie down and pacify it with cool thoughts."

The findings reported in the preceding section are consistent with the self-arousal interpretation of conditioning. In aware individuals, events that forebode distress activate fear-arousing thoughts that produce emotional responses. On the other hand, those who, for one reason or another, fail to notice that the conditioned stimulus foreshadows pain do not conjure up frightening ideas. As a result, the conditioned stimulus rarely evokes emotional responses even though it is often paired with unpleasant experiences. Sudden disappearance of conditioned emotional responses following awareness that the threat has been removed is also explainable in terms of self-arousal processes. Given such knowledge, conditioned stimuli no longer activate frightening thoughts, and a major source of emotional responses is thus removed.

It follows from self-arousal theory that emotional conditioning can be achieved on a cognitive basis in the absence of physically painful experiences. Grings and others [Bridger & Mandel 1964, Dawson & Grings 1968] provide some evidence on this point. In their experiments, subjects are told that a given stimulus will sometimes be followed by shock, but except for a sample experience, this in fact never occurs. Formerly neutral stimuli acquire arousal capabilities through association with thought-produced emotional responses. That covert self-stimulation plays an influential role in this type of cognitively based conditioning is shown by Dawson [1966]. He reports that the level of emotional conditioning was positively related both to the degree to which subjects believed that they would be shocked and to the severity of pain they anticipated.

Although the development and extinction of conditioned emotional responses are subject to cognitive control, this does not mean that all conditioned responses are necessarily consciously mediated. The degree of cognitive control partly depends on the conditions under which the emotional responses are originally acquired. Bridger and Mandel [1964] found that autonomic conditioning was similar regardless of whether stimuli were associated with threat of shock alone or with threat combined with shock experiences. Emotional responses established on the basis of actual painful experiences, however, were less susceptible to cognitive control. Thought-induced conditioned responses promptly disappeared with the knowledge that shocks would no longer be forthcoming. By contrast, conditioned emotional responses originating in painful experiences persisted for some time despite awareness that the physical threat was completely removed.

These findings may be explained in several ways. It may mean that conditioned responses contain dual components, as Bridger and Mandel suggest. One of the components—created by self-arousal influences—

is readily modifiable by having a person alter his thoughts. The second component may be a non-mediated one that is directly evoked by external stimuli and hence requires disconfirming experiences for its extinction. Snake phobics, for example, will instantaneously respond with fear at the sight of a coiled snake before they have time to cogitate about the potential dangers of reptiles.

An alternative interpretation is that in instances where people either have undergone distressing experiences or there is a remote chance that they might get hurt, external stimuli become such powerful elicitors of fear-provoking thoughts that they are not easily subject to voluntary control. To tell phobics who dread heights that they can gaze down safely from the rooftop of a tall building because of protective railings does not mean that they will be able to turn off thoughts about the horrendous things that could conceivably happen. Here fearfulness is still cognitively mediated but the individual is unable to control his thoughts, however safe the eliciting situations may be.

Nonmediational theories of conditioning assume that associated stimulus events must be registered in the nervous system of the organism. Studies examining the influence of awareness on conditioning should therefore obtain evidence that the input from the stimulus to be conditioned has in fact been received. It is not inconceivable that in experiments where, to reduce awareness, subjects' attention is diverted to irrelevant features of the situation, the conditioned stimuli may not be registered in a sufficiently consistent manner to produce stable conditioned responses. Neural responses to afferent input can be substantially reduced by focusing attention on irrelevant events. In neurophysiological studies by Hernández-Péon, Scherrer, and Jouvet [1956], for instance, auditory neural responses to a loud sound were virtually eliminated in cats when they gazed at mice, attentively sniffed fish odors, or received shocks that disrupted their attentiveness. Horn [1960] noted a similar weakening of neural responses to a light flash during active attention to other sights and sounds.

People who direct their attention to extraneous features may neither experience nor recognize the conditioned stimulus. Absence of conditioning, under such circumstances, may be erroneously attributed to lack of conscious recognition when, in fact, it derives from deficient sensory registration of the stimulus. Proof that awareness is necessary for learning would require evidence that, despite adequate neural registration of the paired environmental events, classical conditioning does not occur unless the relationship between the events is recognized.

Developmental theories of psychological functioning often draw sharp distinctions between associative and cognitive processes as though they represented independent functions. As noted above, cognitive influences can markedly affect performances regarded as associative in nature. Extent of cognitive control can, in turn, be influenced by associative factors. Mandel and Bridger [1967], for instance, demonstrated that awareness hastened fear extinction, but the speed with which aware subjects lost their apprehensions depended on how closely and in what order neutral and aversive stimuli were associated when the fear was first learned. Most changes in behavior undoubtedly result from the interactive effects of associative and cognitive influences.

Disorders Arising from Inappropriate Stimulus Control

The development of stimulus functions has considerable adaptive value, but unfortunately, as alluded to in some of the illustrative material, it can also create needless distress and constricting defensiveness. Dysfunctions of this sort can arise in several different ways. Events that happen to occur in the context of traumatic experiences but are in no way causally related to them sometimes take on aversive properties and produce inappropriate generalization of anxiety reactions. The following letter taken from the advice column of a newspaper illustrates such inappropriate generalization.

Dear Abby:

My friend fixed me up with a blind date and I should have known the minute he showed up in a bow tie that he couldn't be trusted. I fell for him like a rock. He got me to love him on purpose and then lied to me and cheated on me. Every time I go with a man who wears a bow tie, the same thing happens. I think girls should be warned about men who wear them.

Against Bow Ties

In this above example, the letter writer had generalized a whole pattern of social behavior to bow ties, a stimulus one would not expect to be routinely correlated with deceitfulness. To the extent that her anticipatory hostile actions evoke negative counter-reactions in bow-tied men, her defensive behaviors create adverse experiences and are thereby self-perpetuated. Here the inappropriate behavior is maintained by a self-produced reality rather than one that had been in effect in the past but no longer exists under changed conditions of life.

Irrational defensive behaviors often occur on the basis of overgeneralization from events associated with traumatic experiences to others that are similar to them either physically or semantically. In the often quoted study by Watson and Rayner [1920], for example, several pairings of a rat and a loud sound produced in a young boy, not only marked fear of the rat, but the fear generalized widely to other furry objects including rabbits, dogs, fur coats, cotton, wool, and even human hair.

Clinical evidence exists that suggests that relatively innocuous stimuli may be invested with powerful aversive properties through semantic generalization. Walton and Mather [1963] report the case of a woman who suffered from obsessions about being dirty and spent much of her life performing incapacitating hygienic rituals.

> The main feature was compulsive handwashing which appeared to arise from doubts about contamination of herself by dirt. After every daily activity or whenever she believed she may have touched something which had been handled by another person before her, she would wash her hands four or five times (taking fifteen minutes). Door knobs and taps were particularly anxiety-provoking as they were handled most frequently. Going to the toilet would always be followed by handwashing and additional scrubbing of the nails. Taking a bath and washing her hair would occupy several hours due to continual rewashing of herself, the bath, and the washbasin. To avoid contamination, she would ensure that she never brushed against walls or other people's clothing and she always kept her own clothes in a special place untouched by others. Any street or thoroughfare would be examined for patches of dirt. Many such activities, such as turning on taps and opening doors were delegated to her mother. She would in fact never venture outside the house alone lest she were required to handle something and there were no facilities for washing. Sitting on public seats was also difficult for her [p. 169].

The obsessive-compulsive behavior began with her severe guilt and feelings of "dirtiness" because of sexual relations in a love affair with a married man. Eventually, a wide range of stimuli related to urogenital activities and all forms of dirt became disturbing to her.

Maladaptive emotional responses can not only be created by unpleasant paired experiences, but they can be eliminated by therapeutic methods utilizing similar principles [Bandura 1969a, Franks 1969]. This is achieved by repeated exposure to threatening events without the occurrence of any adverse consequences. Several variant procedures have been devised and applied with relatively high success. In the *extinction* method disabling anxieties are removed by gradually exposing clients to progressively more frightening situations or through massive contact with what they fear. Some understandably loathe facing what they dread, thus requiring positive inducements. Therapies based on *counterconditioning* desensitize anxious people by presenting to them the things they fear together with anxiety neutralizers (for example, muscular relaxation, tranquilizing imagery, or the reassurance and security of a supportive person) capable of eliciting highly positive reactions. By reducing the level of anxiety arousal, positive activities allow persons to tolerate threats they might ordinarily avoid without experiencing them as unduly aversive. A third major approach relies upon *modeling* procedures wherein anxiety disorders are eliminated by having anxious clients observe others engaging in threatening activities without experiencing any untoward consequences. After undergoing this form of treatment they lose their fears, they can engage in activities they formerly inhibited, and they develop more favorable attitudes toward the things they abhorred.

Stimulus Control of Action

The same actions can produce markedly different consequences, depending upon the time, the place, and the persons toward whom they are expressed. Driving through a busy intersection on a red signal, for example, will have painfully different effects from crossing on a green light. People therefore come to attend closely to stimuli that predict reinforcement and to ignore those that do not, and they utilize cues that signify probable consequences in regulating their behavior. Stimuli indicating that given actions will be punished or nonrewarded tend to inhibit their performance, whereas those signifying that the actions are permissible or rewardable facilitate their occurrence. The capacity to regulate responsiveness on the basis of information conveyed by antecedent stimuli about likely response consequences provides the mechanism for foresightful behavior.

Stimuli acquire controlling power by being correlated with differential response consequences. Traditional explanations of how stimulus control is developed focus primarily on direct training in which responses are reinforced only in the presence of certain cues but never in a different stimulus context. Stimulus control is undoubtedly established and maintained in many instances through correlation with experienced response consequences. However, man's symbolic capacity enables him to gain such information without having to perform responses and experience them rewarded, ignored, or punished under varied conditions. Much learning of this sort is achieved through verbal explanations that describe situations in which certain actions are regarded as appropriate or out of place. Moreover, as we shall see later, stimulus control can be effectively established by observing how the behavior of others is reinforced in different situations. Although people often guide their actions solely on the basis of what they have observed or been told, maintenance of verbally and vicariously produced stimulus control ordinarily requires periodic confirmation through direct experience.

Interpersonal behavior is partly regulated by characteristics of people that predict the consequences likely to accompany certain courses of action. Children often behave quite differently in the presence of their mothers and their fathers in accordance with their disciplinary practices. The following quotation provides a telling example of an autistic boy who freely expressed destructive behavior with his lenient mother but rarely did so in the presence of his father, who tolerated no aggression.

> Whenever her husband was home, Billy was a model youngster. He knew that his father would punish him quickly and dispassionately for misbehaving. But when his father left the house, Billy would go to the window and watch until the car pulled out. As soon as it did, he was suddenly transformed. . . . "He'd go into my closet and tear up my evening dresses and urinate on my clothes. He'd smash furniture and run around biting the walls until the house was destruction from one end to the other. He knew that I liked to dress him in nice clothes, so he used to rip the buttons off his shirts, and used to go in his pants [Moser 1965, p. 96].

In a formal study of social stimulus control Redd and Birnbrauer [1969] had one adult reward a group of seclusive children for playing cooperatively, while a second adult rewarded them equally regardless of their behavior. Later the mere appearance of the contingently rewarding adult evoked cooperative play, but the noncontingent adult exerted no influence on the children's behavior. When the adults reversed their reinforcement practices their power to elicit play behavior changed accordingly.

People frequently regulate their behavior on the basis of more subtle social cues. To take a common example, parents are quick to issue commands to their children, but they do not always see to it that their requests are heeded. Children are therefore inclined to ignore demands voiced in mild or moderate tones. The parents' mounting anger usually serves as the cue that they will enforce compliance so that only shouts produce results. Indeed, many households are run at a fairly high decibel level.

Of the numerous stimuli that influence how people will behave at any given moment, none is more ubiquitous or effective than the actions of others. People applaud when others clap, they laugh when others laugh, they exit from social functions when they see others leaving, and on countless other occasions their behavior is prompted and channeled by modeling stimuli.

The actions of others acquire controlling properties through selective reinforcement in much the same way as do physical and symbolic stimuli in nonsocial forms. When behaving like others produces rewarding outcomes, modeling cues become powerful determinants of analogous behavior; conversely, when matching actions are treated negatively but dissimilar behavior proves rewarding, models' responses prompt divergent performances in observers. Because people usually display modes of behavior that are appropriate and effective, following good examples is much more reinforcing than tedious trial and error. As a result, modeling cues generally assume high predictive value. Thus, by relying on the actions of knowledgeable models, a novice can behave appropriately in synagogues, in mosques, in saloons, at wedding ceremonies, and in countless other situations, without having to discover the acceptable conduct through shocked or pleased reactions to his unguided performances. The dictum "When in Rome do as the Romans do" underscores the functional value of modeling stimulus control.

People differ in the degree to which their behavior is guided by modeling influences, and not all models are equally effective in eliciting the types of behavior they themselves exemplify. Responsiveness to modeling influences is largely determined by three factors, which derive their power from correlation with conditions of reinforcement. These include the characteristics of the models, the attributes of the observer, and the response consequences associated with matching behavior.

With regard to model characteristics, those who have high status, prestige, and power are much more effective in evoking matching behavior in observers than models of low standing. The force of prestigeful example is well illustrated in a study of behavioral contagion conducted by Lippitt, Polansky, and Rosen [1952]. Children in summer camps rated each other in terms of their power to influence others. Observers then recorded the incidence and sources of behavioral contagion, defined as spontaneous imitation of the actions of another person where he displayed no intent to get others to follow his example. The behavior of a few models who were attributed high power largely determined the conduct of the camp members. The influence of prestigeful modeling is demonstrated even more convincingly by Lefkowitz, Blake, and Mouton [1955]. Pedestrians were more likely to cross a street on a red light when they saw a presumably high-status person in executive attire do it than when the same transgression was performed by the same model dressed in soiled patched trousers, scuffed shoes, and a blue denim shirt.

It is not difficult to explain why model status facilitates matching behavior. The actions of models who have gained some status are more likely to be successful and hence have greater functional value for observers than the behavior of models who possess relatively low vocational, intellectual, and social competencies. In situations where people are uncertain about the wisdom of modeled courses of action, they rely on model characteristics and status-conferring symbols (for example, speech, dress, deportment, possession of material goods), which serve as tangible indicants of past successes. The effects of a model's prestige tend to generalize from one area of behavior to another, as when prominent athletes advise on breakfast cereals as though they were nutrition experts. Unfamiliar persons also gain influence by their similarity to models whose behavior proved successful in the past.

Some efforts have been made to identify the types of people who are most responsive to modeling influences. Observers who achieve better outcomes by following the examples of others than through their own independent behavior are readily susceptible to modeling influences. Therefore, those who have been frequently rewarded for imitative behavior and those who lack self-esteem, who feel incompetent, and who are highly dependent are especially prone to pattern their behavior after successful models [Bandura 1969b, Campbell 1961].

The preceding generalizations must be accepted with reservations because the functional value of modeled behavior overrides the influence of either model or observer characteristics. It is exceedingly unlikely that dull, anxious, and dependent students would gain more from observing skilled ski instructors, brain surgeons, or airline pilots than understudies who are bright, attentive, and self-assured. When modeled activities are highly valued, the more venturesome and talented observers benefit most from exposure to exemplary models. Laboratory studies reporting prosaic correlates of imitativeness typically employ inconsequential modeled behaviors that competent observers would have little incentive to learn.

The attributes of models exert greatest influence when it is unclear what consequences their behavior is likely to have. Observers must therefore rely on status cues that may have been correlated with reinforcement in their past experiences. A prestigeful or attractive model may induce a person to try a given course of action, but if the behavior should prove unsatisfactory, it will be discarded and the model's future influence diminished. For this reason studies in which response consequences are not evident may exaggerate the role played by model characteristics in the long-term control of social behavior.

In everyday life cues that predict the likely consequences of different actions appear as part of a bewildering variety of irrelevant events. To complicate matters further, the rules governing reinforcement often involve particular combinations of several environmental factors. To borrow an example from the study of conceptual behavior, a person is asked to sort a set of pictures that differ in a variety of ways into correct and incorrect piles without being told the relevant feature. Let us arbitrarily designate all pictures containing an adult drinking an alcoholic beverage as positive instances of the concept, and those that do not as negative instances. As the person sorts the pictures on the basis of provisional guesses, he observes which of his placements get rewarded and he eventually abstracts the common feature from the array of irrelevant stimuli. Response consequences are generally determined by the joint presence of several factors. Continuing with the above example, only pictures depicting drinking by an adult at home or in a bar, in the evening, and in the company of others might be considered appropriate, whereas solitary or daytime drinking and imbibing in work settings would not. Here the reinforcement rule combines temporal, social, and situational cues. The important role played by cognitive processes in rule-regulated behavior is discussed later.

Defective stimulus control. Effective social functioning requires highly discriminative responsiveness, often to subtle variations in stimulus events. Some behavior disorders primarily reflect defective stimulus control, due either to faulty reinforcement practices or to a loss of such functions under stressful experiences. Rosenbaum [1953, 1956], for example, found that people were less able to distinguish critical from irrelevant features of the environment under strong than mild threat, and those prone to emotional arousal were most adversely affected in this regard.

Social behavior is extensively regulated by verbal cues. We influence people's actions in innumerable situations by suggestions, requests, commands, and written directives. Because of the importance of symbolic communication in human relationships, deficient or inappropriate responsiveness to verbal stimuli can have serious consequences. As part of a program to develop procedures for modifying psychotic behavior, Ayllon and his associates [Ayllon & Haughton 1962, Ayllon & Michael 1959] provide illustrations of defective verbal control. In one study, a group of schizophrenics with severe chronic eating problems were totally unresponsive to meal announcements or to persuasive appeals. Because of concern for their health, patients were escorted by nurses to the dining room, spoon-fed, tube-fed, and subjected to electroshock "therapy" and other forms of infantilizing and punitive treatments. It appeared that the nurses' coaxing, persuading, and feeding inadvertently reinforced the eating problems. Also, by rewarding nonresponsiveness to verbal requests, they lost their directive function. All social rewards for ignoring the announcement of mealtime and for refusals to eat were therefore withdrawn; following meal call, the dining room remained open for thirty minutes and any patient who failed to appear during that time simply missed his meal. After these consequences were instituted, patients responded in a socially appropriate manner to meal calls and fed themselves.

In his studies of language learning in autistic children, Lovaas [1967] shows how the influence of modeling stimuli can be negated by faulty reinforcement practices. Autistic children who lacked communicative speech imitated the therapist's verbalizations with high accuracy when rewards were made contingent upon correct speech reproductions. By contrast, when children were equally generously rewarded but without regard to the quality of their verbalization, their imitative behavior progressively deteriorated until it bore little resemblance to the verbal responses modeled for them by the therapist.

Reinforcement Control

An organism that responded foresightedly on the basis of informative environmental cues but remained unaffected by the results of its actions would be too obtuse to survive for long. In fact, behavior is extensively controlled by its consequences. Responses that cause unrewarding or punishing effects tend to be discarded, whereas those that produce rewarding outcomes are retained and strengthened. Human behavior therefore cannot be fully understood without examining the powerful influence of reinforcement control.

Traditional theories of reinforcement have been almost entirely concerned with demonstration of how behavior can be regulated by directly experienced conseqeuences arising from external sources. Out of this circumscribed research interest grew the unfortunate impression that behavior theories view man as a manipulable automaton with hardly any self-regulatory capacities. Social learning theory, while acknowledging the important responsive guiding role played by extrinsic feedback, posits a wider range of reinforcement influences. People are not only affected by the experiences created by their actions; they also regulate their behavior to some extent on the basis of observed consequences, as well as those they create for themselves. These three different forms of reinforcement control—direct, vicarious, and self-monitored—are considered next.

External Reinforcement

Some of the most impressive demonstrations of how behavior is controlled by its immediate consequences are found in the treatment of behavior disorders. Such studies usually employ an "intrasubject replication design" in which troublesome behavior is successively eliminated and reinstated by systematic variation of reinforcement contingencies. One case, selected from a large number reported by Harris, Wolf, and Baer [1964], illustrates the four-step procedure.

First, the person who is having difficulties is observed for a time to assess the incidence of the deviant behavior, the contexts in which it tends to occur, and the reactions it elicits from others. In the case under discussion, an extremely withdrawn boy spent about 80 per cent of his time secluded in isolated areas of the nursery school. Observation revealed that the teachers unwittingly reinforced his seclusiveness by paying a great deal of attention to him when he remained by himself, reflecting his feelings of loneliness, consoling him, and urging him to play with others. On the infrequent occasions when he happened to join other children, the teachers took no special notice.

In the second phase of the program a new set of reinforcement practices is instituted. Continuing with the above example, the teachers stopped rewarding solitary play with attention and support. Instead, whenever the boy sought out other children, a teacher joined the group and gave it her full attention. In a short time, the boy's withdrawal declined markedly and he was spending about 60 per cent of his time playing with other children.

After the desired changes have been produced, the

original reinforcement practices are reinstated to determine whether the deviant behavior was in fact maintained by its social consequences. In this third stage, for example, the teachers behaved in their customary way, being inattentive to his sociability but responding with comforting ministrations when he was alone. The effect of this traditional "mental hygiene" approach was to drive the child back into seclusiveness. Clearly, social practices should be evaluated in terms of the effects they have on recipients rather than in terms of the humanitarian intent of the practitioners.

In the final phase, the therapeutic contingencies are reintroduced, the deviant patterns are eliminated, and the adaptive ones are generously rewarded until they then are adequately supported by their natural consequences. In the above case, the teachers gradually reduced their rewarding attentiveness as the boy derived increasing enjoyment from play activities with his peers. In follow-up observations he continued to enjoy his social relationships, which contrasted conspicuously with his previous seclusiveness.

Similar treatments conducted with both children and adults reveal that a wide variety of grossly deviant behaviors—including self-injurious actions, hypochondriacal and delusional preoccupations, infantile and regressive patterns, extreme withdrawal, chronic anorexia, psychogenic seizures, asthmatic attacks, psychotic tendencies, and countless other disorders of long standing—have been successfully eliminated, reinstated, and removed for a second time by altering the amount of social reinforcement they elicit from others.

The regulatory influence of reinforcement has been demonstrated not only with deviant conditions but with all other forms of behavioral functioning as well. Until recently it was widely believed that internal physiological states could be externally aroused but were not subject to reinforcement control. In an ingenious series of studies the eminent psychologist Neal Miller [1969] succeeded in altering visceral responsiveness in animals, including changes in heart rate, blood pressure, blood flow, intestinal contractions, and even rate of urine formation by reinforcing the animals whenever physiological responses of a selected rate or magnitude occurred. The preciseness of reinforcement control is most impressively revealed in a study in which animals were rewarded for relatively greater volume flow of blood to one ear than to the other. The differential reinforcement produced corresponding changes in the amount of blood flow to the two ears.

Preliminary studies indicate that this line of research holds promise for advancing understanding of the development of psychosomatic disorders and their treatment. Voluntary control of one's own physiological functioning is achieved through instantaneous feedback techniques. In this procedure, people are told to maintain a given level of physiological responsiveness during which they are signaled with a tone or light whenever they achieve a desired state of body function. Dworkin and Miller [Miller, Di Cara, Solomon, Weiss, & Dworkin 1970] found that a subject could increase and decrease his diastolic blood pressure to some degree by informative feedback of changes in selected directions. In a fascinating project, Kamiya [1968] succeeded in teaching people to control their alpha brain states (experienced as feelings of serene well-being) by monitoring their brain waves and sounding a tone when they reduced their brain waves to a rhythm between eight to twelve cycles per second. During alpha periods subjects felt relaxed, they exerted no mental effort, and they experienced no visual imagery.

Budzynski Stoyva, and Adler [1970] successfully applied the biofeedback method in treating tension headaches resulting from sustained contraction of scalp and neck muscles. Patients heard a tone with a frequency proportional to the electromyographic (EMG) activity in the monitored forehead muscles. They were instructed to keep the tone low by relaxing their facial muscles. As the patients became more adept at muscular relaxation, the criterion was increased in graded steps requiring progressively more relaxation to achieve low-pitched tones. Through this method patients who had experienced daily headaches over a period of several years quit tensing their facial muscles and eventually eliminated their headaches. The clinical applicability of biofeedback techniques will depend on the degree of voluntary control people can exert on their physiological responses. It would appear from preliminary findings that they possess greater self-regulatory capacities than was previously believed.

Reinforcement control of behavior is further shown by evidence that people behave quite differently depending on the pattern and frequency with which their actions are reinforced. Those who have been rewarded each time they respond are likely to become easily discouraged and to give up quickly when their efforts fail. On the other hand, individuals whose behavior has been reinforced intermittently tend to persist for a considerable time despite setbacks and only occasional success.

Intermittent reinforcement can take a variety of forms. Sometimes behavior is reinforced only after a specified period of time has elapsed (*fixed-interval* schedule), as in pay periods, eating schedules, and recreational cycles. When rewards occur on a fixed temporal basis, the payoff is the same regardless of the person's productivity; hence, behavioral output is relatively low. For this reason people are more often rewarded on the basis of the amount of work they accomplish rather than on the passage of time. In a *fixed-ratio* schedule a person must complete a given amount of work for each reinforcement. Because outcomes depend on one's own behavior, responsiveness remains high.

In everyday life most reinforcements occur not only periodically but in an irregular manner. For instance, superiors rarely check their employees' work at the same time each day, and achievements regarded as adequate on one occasion may be considered insufficient at another. Under *variable-interval* schedules individuals are reinforced at changeable times; in *variable-ratio* schedules the performances required for each reinforcement vary. Since in both instances the rewards occur unpredictably, variable schedules produce higher and more consistent performances than those in which outcomes occur with evident regularity. Even under variable schedules, outcomes occurring on a performance rather than on a time basis produce higher levels of responsiveness. Ferster [Ferster & Skinner 1957] created a striking example of schedule influences by rewarding simultaneously the right-hand responses of a subject on a fixed-ratio and the left-hand responses on a variable-ratio schedule. The subject produced two remarkably different sets of performances, each corresponding to the typical response rates generated by these types of schedules.

As a further way of illustrating schedule control of behavior let us consider how patrons of the gambling devices at Las Vegas might behave under different systems of reinforcement. Given a fixed-interval schedule, where playing a slot machine produces a jackpot each time an hour has elapsed, patrons would deposit a coin and then sit around watching the clock until it was time to insert the next coin for the payoff. Under a fixed-ratio schedule requiring, for example, 25 plays to produce a jackpot, patrons would be seen busily stuffing slot machines at a high, stable rate. If the customary reinforcement was no longer forthcoming after an hour in the first case, and after 25 responses in the second, players would rapidly quit with loud complaints. On a variable-interval schedule—where players receive a jackpot on the average every hour but it can occur unpredictably after 10 minutes, a half hour, or 2 hours—they are likely to wait for a while immediately after gaining a jackpot and then play at a moderate, steady rate. Put on a variable-ratio schedule—where on the average every 25th response produces a payoff but sometimes 5 responses are sufficient, whereas at other times 10, 50, or even as many as 200 responses may

be needed to get a jackpot—players would continue cranking the machine at a rapid pace without a break until their money ran out, fatigue set in, or their spouses intervened. Since the variable-ratio schedule is most powerful in maintaining behavior at minimum costs, owners of gambling casinos understandably favor it. Behavior that has been reinforced on a thin variable-ratio schedule is exceedingly hard to extinguish because one's efforts are sustained by the belief that the actions will eventually prove successful and it takes a long time to realize that the rewards are no longer forthcoming.

In everyday life mixed schedules of reinforcement predominate, with both the number of unreinforced responses and the intervals between reinforcements continually changing. Drivers, for example, are not fined for every traffic violation. Speakers are not equally applauded every time they express their views. And scheduled activities do not always occur on time. Behavior is usually associated with variable outcomes because people are not always around to mediate the reinforcing consequences. Even when they are present, their preferences often differ so that the same actions may be applauded, ignored, or disapproved, depending on with whom one interacts.

The matter of reinforcement control is much more complicated than would appear from the discussion thus far. If people did not have the power of countercontrol, they could be impelled to do almost anything simply by arranging the appropriate consequences. In social interactions, however, participants are dependent upon each other to get what they want and consequently they have some power over each other. When conflicts arise, as they often do, compromise systems are adopted that are acceptable to both parties. As power disparities change, so do reinforcement systems. When employers enjoyed commanding positions, they paid their employees on a piece-rate basis representing various fixed-ratio schedules. As organized labor gained increasing power, it was able to negotiate interval schedules in which prescribed wages were guaranteed on a daily, weekly, monthly, and eventually on an annual basis. In order to ensure high performance, many employers combined ratio and interval schedules by paying fixed wages plus commissions based on individual or group productivity. In many other areas of functioning people understandably strive for power that would enable them to remove bothersome performance requirements for desired outcomes. Further illustrations are provided later of how the potential power of external reinforcement is weakened and counteracted by reciprocal control and by the influence of other reinforcement systems.

The opinion is often expressed that desired activities should be performed for their own sake. It is feared that reinforcing practices may not only interfere with the development of self-determining characteristics but may render people so dependent upon extrinsic supports that they remain unresponsive without payoffs. Some of the more intemperate critics, whose own activities are generously reinforced by salaries, consulting fees, book royalties, and the applause of sympathetic audiences, consider the use of reinforcement to be manipulative and debasing.

The fact that behavior is controlled by its consequences is not a phenomenon created by behavioral scientists, any more than physicists are responsible for the laws of gravity. The process of natural selection has favored organisms adept enough to regulate their behavior on the basis of the effects it produces. Continuing with the above example, a social commentator might express moral indignation over gravitational control of behavior and denounce it as dehumanizing and degrading. A poetic view of man might be more flattering but it would in no way reduce the likelihood that people will continue to fall should they fling themselves off heights. The major purpose of psychological science is not to romanticize human behavior but rather to understand it.

Some of the criticisms that have been levied against reinforcement practices fail to recognize the complexity and the developmental changes in the consequences that influence behavior. At the earliest developmental levels, infants and young children are responsive only to immediate physical events, such as food, painful stimulation, and physical contact. It would be foolhardy for parents to rely on children's self-actualizing tendencies to keep them out of fires, electric outlets, or busy thoroughfares. In the course of development, as physically rewarding experiences are repeatedly associated with expressions of interest and approval, and punishments with disapproval and withdrawal of interest, the social reactions themselves eventually acquire reinforcing properties. At this higher level of psychological functioning behavior is extensively governed by symbolic social reinforcements. It would be a rare, unfeeling person who could remain totally indifferent to the sentiments of others.

Some child-rearing authorities popularized the view that healthy personality development can be achieved only through "unconditioned love." If this principle were, in fact, applied, parents would respond warmly and affectionately regardless of how their children behaved—whether or not they treated others maliciously, stole whatever they wanted, amassed a record of failing grades, showed contempt

for the wishes and rights of others, and demanded immediate gratification of their desires. Unconditioned love, were it possible, would make children directionless, irresponsible, asocial, and quite unlovable. Most readers are probably acquainted with families where parents who attempted to approximate this condition succeeded in producing "self-actualized" tyrants. Guideless interest is clearly not enough. Fortunately, the vast majority of parents are not indiscriminate dispensers of affection. Being human, they tend to be displeased with reprehensible actions. It also comes as no surprise that some of the strongest advocates of unconditional regard are quite selective in their own social responsiveness, approving things they like and disapproving those they do not [Murray 1956, Truax 1966]. And recipients of this differential treatment accommodate to their preferences.

There are a number of symbolic reinforcers, other than social responses, that take on reinforcing functions. Money, having exchange value for countless things that people want, is a dependable and durable generalized reinforcer of behavior. When exemplary achievements are recurrently rewarded, qualitative differences in performance acquire reinforcing value. After signs of progress and merited attainment become a source of personal satisfaction, knowledge that one has done well can function as a reward. However, the reinforcement ensuing from successful results is most likely mediated through self-reinforcement. For this reason, correctness feedback on tasks that are personally devalued or very simple is unlikely to have much reinforcing value. On the other hand, attainments that exceed personal standards of what constitutes a worthy performance activate positive self-evaluations, whereas inadequate accomplishments produce self-dissatisfaction.

Many of the activities that enhance competency are initially tiresome and uninteresting and it is not until one acquires proficiency in them that they assume reinforcing functions. During initial stages of skill development children are often coerced to perform required activities by demands and threats that, more often than not, instill antipathies rather than competencies. This prevalent problem can be largely avoided by rewarding children's efforts, both socially and tangibly, until the behavior is developed to the stage at which it produces more natural reinforcing effects. Thus, for example, children may temporarily require extrinsic encouragement to teach them how to read, but after they become skilled at it they read on their own for the enjoyment it provides. Many other forms of behavior, such as verbal facility and manual skills, which enable people to deal more effectively with their environment, do not require arbitrary rewards to sustain them.

Some performances are also partially maintained by the sensory reinforcement they produce. Infants, for example, repeatedly perform responses for certain sounds and sights and older children and adults spend long hours playing musical instruments that create pleasing sensory feedback. When activities are sustained by the sensory effects they naturally create, the phenomenon is usually designated as intrinsic reinforcement. This process is often distinguished from extrinsic reinforcement, where the outcomes, such as social approval or monetary rewards, represent arbitrary response consequences. The reinforcing value of most forms of sensory feedback is learned rather than inherently furnished. Indeed, many of the things that people enjoy doing for their own sake, whether playing atonal music or writing compositions, were probably experienced originally as somewhat aversive. As a result of repeated exposure, skill acquisition through initial extrinsic reinforcement, and investment of self-esteem rewards in merited performances, however, the activities eventually take on positive value.

The highest level of autonomy is achieved when individuals regulate their own behavior by self-evaluative and other self-produced consequences. The paramount role played by self-reinforcement in controlling human actions is given detailed consideration in a later section of this paper. Behavior is least susceptible to the vagaries of externally occurring reinforcement when effective consequences are either intrinsically related to the behavior or are self-administered. Paradoxically, the types of symbolic and self-regulatory mechanisms that humanistically oriented commentators consider to be antithetical to behavioral approaches are, in fact, most successfully developed by practices derived from principles of social learning.

Vicarious Reinforcement

Human functioning would be exceedingly inefficient, not to mention dangerous, if behavior were controlled only by directly experienced consequences. Fortunately, people can profit greatly from the experiences of others. In everyday situations reinforcement typically occurs within a social context. That is, people repeatedly observe the actions of others and the occasions on which they are rewarded, ignored, or punished. Despite the fact that observed rewards and punishments play an influential role in regulating behavior, vicarious reinforcement has, until re-

cent years, been essentially ignored in traditional theories of learning.

There is a second reason why the study of vicarious reinforcement is critical to the understanding of reinforcement influences. Observed consequences provide reference standards that determine whether a particular reinforcer that is externally administered will serve as a reward or as a punishment. Thus, for example, the same compliment is likely to be discouraging to persons who have seen similar performances by others more highly acclaimed, but rewarding when others have been less generously praised.

Research on the relational character of reinforcing events has shown that the same consequence can have rewarding or punishing effects on behavior depending upon the nature, frequency, or generosity with which one's performances were previously reinforced. However, incentive contrast effects, resulting from discrepancies between observed and directly experienced consequences, have received relatively little attention.

Vicarious Punishment

Vicarious reinforcement is defined as a change in the behavior of observers resulting from seeing the response consequences of others. Vicarious punishment is indicated when observed negative consequences reduce people's tendency to behave in similar or related ways. This phenomenon has been studied most extensively with respect to aggressive behavior. In the typical experiment [Bandura 1965, Bandura, Ross, & Ross 1963b] children are shown a film depicting a model engaging in novel aggressive behaviors that are either rewarded, punished, or unaccompanied by any evident consequences. Witnessing aggression punished usually produces less imitative aggression than seeing it obtain social and material success or go unnoticed.

Because of the variety and complexity of social influences, people are not always consistent in how they respond to aggressive behavior. Rosekrans and Hartup [1967] examined the effects of discrepant observed consequences on imitative aggression. Children who saw assaultive behavior consistently rewarded were most aggressive, those who saw it consistently punished displayed virtually no imitative behavior, while those who saw aggression sometimes rewarded and sometimes punished exhibited a moderate level of aggressiveness.

A second major set of experiments has been concerned with how vicarious punishment affects people's willingness to violate prohibitions. Walters and his associates [Walters, Leat, & Mezei 1963, Walters & Parke 1964, Walters, Parke, & Cane 1965] have shown that witnessing peer models punished for violating prohibitions increases observers' inhibition of transgressive behavior as compared with conditions in which modeled transgressions are either rewarded or simply ignored. Results of a comparative study by Benton [1967] indicate that, under some conditions, observed and directly experienced punishment may be equally effective in reducing deviant behavior. Children who observed peers punished for engaging in prohibited activities later showed the same amount of response inhibition as the punished transgressors.

An interesting experiment by Crooks [1967] reveals that lower species are also highly susceptible to observed punishments. After being tested for the extent to which they handled play objects, monkeys observed distress vocalizations sounded (through a tape recorder) whenever a model monkey touched a particular object; they also witnessed the model's contacts with a control object accompanied by the distress vocalizations played backwards, which did not sound like a pain reaction. In a subsequent test the observing animals played freely with the control item but actively avoided objects that supposedly produced painful experiences for another animal.

In all of the preceding studies the model was punished either verbally or physically by someone else. In many instances persons respond with self-punitive and self-devaluative reactions to their own behavior that may be considered permissible, or even commendable, by others. Numerous experiments, which are discussed later, demonstrate that witnessing punishments self-administered by a model has inhibitory effects on observers with respect to unmerited achievements. Observation of self-punishment by a model has been shown by Porro [1968] to exert similar effects on transgressive behavior. For children who viewed a filmed model exhibit self-approving responses to her transgressions, 80 per cent subsequently handled toys they were forbidden to touch, whereas the transgression rate was only 20 per cent for children who had observed the same model respond self-critically toward her own transgressions.

Vicarious Positive Reinforcement

Behavior can be enhanced as well as reduced by observed outcomes. Vicarious positive reinforcement is evident when observers display an increase in behavior for which they see others rewarded. Results

of numerous experiments generally show that observed rewards produce a greater increase in similar responding than if the exemplified actions have no evident consequences. In the case of behavior that is ordinarily disapproved, however, seeing transgressions go unpunished seems to heighten analogous actions in observers to the same degree as witnessing models rewarded [Bandura 1965, Walters & Parke 1964, Walters, Parke, & Cane 1965]. To the extent that absence of anticipated punishment conveys permissiveness and allays fears, behavioral restraints are thereby reduced and transgressive actions are performed more readily.

Relative Effectiveness of Direct and Vicarious Reinforcement

How do observed consequences compare with directly experienced ones in their power to influence behavior? The answer to this question partly depends upon whether one assesses effects in terms of what is learned or what is performed. By watching the types of consequences produced by different actions in various settings, observers can learn the responses considered appropriate in given situations. Observers generally learn faster than reinforced performers, especially on tasks requiring conceptual behavior [Berger 1961, Hillix & Marx 1960, Rosenbaum & Hewitt 1966]. It is not difficult to find reasons for the relative superiority of vicarious reinforcement. Performers may be impeded in discerning which of their actions lead to success by the need to create, to select, and to enact responses and by the emotional arousal resulting from experienced rewards and punishments. Observers, on the other hand, can give their undivided attention to discovering the correct solutions.

The relative power of vicarious and direct reinforcements is reversed with respect to their motivational effects, as reflected in the capacity to maintain effortful behavior over a long period. One would not recommend to employers, for example, that they maintain the productivity of their employees by having them witness a small group of workers receive pay checks at the end of each month. Seeing others rewarded may temporarily enhance responsiveness but it is unlikely by itself to have much sustaining power. Observation of other people's outcomes, however, can have a continuing influence on the effectiveness of direct reinforcement by providing a standard for judging whether the reinforcements one customarily receives are equitable, beneficent, or unfair. Since both direct and vicarious reinforcements inevitably occur together in everyday life, the interactive effects of these two sources of influence on human behavior are of much greater significance than their independent controlling power. This assumption is borne out by evidence that seeing how others are reinforced can significantly increase or reduce the effectiveness of direct rewards and punishments in changing observers' responsiveness [Condrell 1967, Ditrichs, Simon, & Greene 1967, Marlatt 1968].

Consistent with the preceding findings, explanations of social behavior emphasize relative rather than absolute reinforcement in determining the level of productivity and discontent within a society. Disadvantaged people may be rewarded more generously than in the past but still experience greater discouragement and resentment because the more affluent members of society make more rapid progress, so that the disparity between the groups widens.

Explanation of Vicarious Reinforcement

Vicarious reinforcement is simply a descriptive term that does not explain how observed consequences produce their psychological effects. Social learning theory posits several different mechanisms by which witnessed rewards and punishments alter the actions, feelings, and thoughts of others [Bandura 1971c]. A vicarious reinforcement event may vary in a number of aspects, including the characteristics of the recipient and the reinforcing agents, the type and intensity of consequences, their justifiability, the situation in which reinforcements are administered, and the reactions of the participants. The number and type of mechanisms that are operative in any given instance will therefore depend upon the particular combination of these component factors.

One explanation of vicarious reinforcement is in terms of the *informative function* of observed outcomes. Response consequences accruing to others convey information to observers about the types of actions that are likely to be approved or disapproved. Given knowledge about probable response consequences, people will generally do the things they have seen well received and avoid those that they have seen punished.

The same behavior can produce markedly different consequences depending on the setting in which it is performed. What is permissible in a nightclub may be censurable in a church. Hence, adaptive functioning requires not only response information but knowledge about what actions are appropriate in what setting. In modeling experiments where performers are rewarded for responding in a given context but ignored or punished for exhibiting the same behavior in a different situation, observers *learn to discriminate critical features in their environment.* [McDavid 1964, Wilson 1958]. In this way, vicarious reinforcement increases responding to stimuli correlated with observed rewards and decreases responding to stimuli signifying negative response consequences.

Observed reinforcement is not only informative but can also have *incentive motivational effects.* Seeing others reinforced can function as a motivator by arousing in observers expectations that they will be similarly rewarded for analogous performances. An experiment reported by Bruning [1965] illustrates how variations in the size of observed rewards, while providing equivalent information about the types of responses required for reinforcement, produce different levels of responsiveness through their motivational effects on observers. Children who had observed a performer generously rewarded subsequently responded more rapidly when they received smaller rewards for the same actions, whereas when observed rewards were smaller than the ones observers later received, they worked more slowly. These unexpected findings were attributed by Bruning to the energizing effects of frustration in the undercompensated condition, and to satiation in the beneficent treatment. The frequency with which others were rewarded has also been shown to affect how long observers will persist before they give up when their efforts are never reinforced [Berger & Johansson 1968, Rosenbaum & Bruning 1966]. Variations in the generosity with which other people are reinforced thus determines the speed, the vigor, and the persistence with which others behave.

Models generally exhibit emotional reactions while undergoing rewarding or punishing experiences. Observers are easily aroused by the emotional expressions of others. It was previously shown how vicariously elicited emotions can become conditioned either to the modeled behavior or to environmental stimuli that are regularly associated with performers' distress reactions. As a result of vicarious emotional conditioning, the negatively valenced stimuli or the matching responses are likely to frighten and to inhibit observers. Emotional arousal and behavioral inhibitions can also be extinguished by having fearful observers watch performers engaging in threatening activities without experiencing any adverse consequences. *Vicarious conditioning and extinction of emotional arousal* may therefore partially account for increases and decreases in responsiveness that result from observing affective consequences accruing to models.

In everyday situations people not only see the consequences of another's behavior but how he responds to his treatment. There is some evidence, presented by Ditrichs, Simon, and Greene [1967], that the performer's responsiveness to reinforcement significantly affects how observers later react when they themselves are rewarded for displaying similar behavior. Children who observed models give progressively more hostile responses for social approval later increased their own output of hostile responses under positive reinforcement, whereas when models gave progressively fewer rewarded hostile responses or reacted in random fashion, observers did not increase their expression of hostility even though they were positively reinforced whenever they did so. *Susceptibility to direct reinforcement influences* is thus increased by observed positive responsiveness and reduced by observed resistance.

In addition to the aforementioned effects of vicarious reinforcement, social status can be conferred on performers by the manner in which their behavior is reinforced. Punishment tends to devalue the model and his behavior, whereas the same model assumes emulative qualities when his actions are praised and otherwise rewarded [Bandura, Ross, & Ross 1963b, Hastorf 1965]. *Modification of model status,* in turn, influences the degree to which observers pattern their own actions after behavior exemplified by different models. There are conditions, of course, where observed punitive treatment enhances rather than lowers the recipient's social status. People who risk punishment for upholding their basic rights and beliefs gain the admiration not only of their peers but of others as well, especially when the protest is directed at social practices that violate the professed values of society. It is for this reason that authoritative agencies are usually careful not to discipline deviators in ways that might martyr them.

Observed reinforcements can alter the *valuation of reinforcing agents* as well as recipients. When societal agents misuse their power to reward and punish, they undermine the legitimacy of their authority and generate strong resentment. Under these conditions seeing inequitable punishment, rather than prompting compliance, may free incensed observers from self-censure of their own actions and thus increase transgressive behavior. This is most likely to occur when retaliative counterreactions are self-justified as rectifying past grievances or preventing further maltreatment. Otherwise considerate people can thus be readily provoked by observed injustice to behave cruelly without remorse.

None of the foregoing explanations assumes that vicarious reinforcement produces its effects by strengthening connections between stimuli and responses. Such a mechanism of operation would require observers, not only to perform covert matching responses concurrently with the model, but to experience indirectly the reinforcements. A reinforcement process of this type is not implausible, though it seems highly improbable.

Although the preceding discussion is concerned with possible mechanisms through which vicarious reinforcement affects observers, the alternative explanations apply equally to interpretation of how direct reinforcement influences performers. Reinforcements convey information to performers about the types of responses that are appropriate; selective reinforcement directs performers' attention to correlated environmental stimuli that signify probable response consequences; previous reinforcements create expectations that motivate actions designed to secure desired rewards and to avoid injurious outcomes; punishing experiences can endow persons, places, and things with fear-arousing properties that inhibit responsiveness; a given history of positive or negative reinforcement can alter people's self-evaluations in ways that affect their willingness to exhibit behaviors that are discrepant with their self-attitudes and the determination with which they perform them; and finally, the treatment one receives alters liking and respect for the reinforcing agent.

Self-Reinforcement

The discussion thus far has illustrated how people regulate their behavior on the basis of response consequences that they either observe or experience firsthand. If actions were determined solely by external rewards and punishments, people would behave like weathervanes, constantly shifting in radically different directions to conform to the whims of others. They would act like segregationists with a racial bigot, like John Birchers with a zealous Bircher, like Communists with a devoted Communist, like Republicans with a staunch conservative, and like scoundrels with a villainous character. Close scrutiny of social interactions would most likely reveal, barring powerful coercive pressures, steadfast adherence to ideological positions rather than compliant behavior reversals. Anyone who attempted to change a Bircher into a Communist, or a Catholic into an atheist, would quickly come to appreciate the existence of potent internal sources of behavior control.

The notion that behavior is controlled by its consequences is unfortunately interpreted by most people to mean that actions are at the mercy of situational influences. In fact, behavior can, and is, extensively self-regulated by self-produced consequences for one's own actions. In writing a term paper or preparing a manuscript for publication, for example, authors do not require someone sitting at their sides differentially reinforcing each written statement until a satisfactory version is produced. Rather, authors possess a standard of what constitutes an acceptable work and they engage in repeated self-corrective editing of their own writing performances until they are satisfied with what they have written. The self-editing often exceeds external requirements of what would be satisfactory to others. Indeed, some people are such severe self-editors that they essentially paralyze their own writing efforts. In most other areas of functioning people similarly set themselves certain performance standards and respond to their own behavior in self-satisfied or self-critical ways in accordance with their self-imposed demands. Because of their greater representational and self-reactive capacities, humans are less dependent upon immediate external supports for their behavior. The inclusion of self-reinforcement phenomena in learning theory thus greatly increases the explanatory power of reinforcement principles as applied to human functioning.

After a self-monitoring reinforcement system has been developed, a given action typically produces two sets of consequences—a self-evaluative reaction and an external outcome. These two sources of reinforcement can occur in several different patterns. Sometimes people are rewarded socially or materially for behavior that they devalue. Anticipation of self-reproach for personally repudiated actions provides an important motivating influence to keep behavior in line with adopted standards in the face of opposing influences. There is no more devastating punishment than self-contempt. Under conditions where self-devaluative consequences outweigh the force of rewards for accommodating behavior, external influences prove relatively ineffective. On the other hand, when external inducements, whether rewarding or coercive, prevail over self-reinforcing influences, individuals exhibit cheerless compliance. Humans, of course, are equipped with facile cognitive capacities for reconciling distressing discrepancies. Disliked actions can be, and often are, justified so that losses in self-respect are minimized as long as the self-deception remains convincing.

An opposite type of conflict between external and self-produced consequences arises when people are punished for engaging in activities they value highly. Here, the relative strength of self-approval and external censure determine whether the behavior will be discarded or maintained. Another common situation

is one where external reinforcement for certain activities is minimal or lacking and individuals sustain their efforts largely through self-encouragement. External reinforcement exerts greatest influence when it is harmonious with, rather than contravenes, self-produced consequences. People strive actively to achieve and to maintain such conditions. They do this by selectively associating with persons who share similar behavioral standards, thus ensuring social support for their own system of self-evaluation.

There are three major aspects of self-reinforcement that warrant detailed comment. These issues are concerned with questions of how self-monitoring reinforcement systems are established; how effective they are in regulating behavior; and what maintains them.

Establishment of Self-Reinforcing Functions

Self-reinforcement functions can be acquired in several different ways. One of these is through the process of selective reinforcement. People learn to evaluate their behavior partly on the basis of how others have reacted to it. Parents and other socialization agents subscribe to certain norms of what constitute worthy performances. They are generally delighted and respond approvingly when children achieve or exceed desired standards and displeased when their performances fall short of the valued level. As a result of such differential treatment children eventually come to respond to their own behavior in self-approving and self-critical ways, depending on how it departs from evaluative standards set by others. Some indirect support for the effects of direct training on self-reinforcement practices is provided by Kanfer and Marston [1963]. They found that adults who had received indulgent treatment subsequently rewarded their performances more generously than did those who had been stringently trained, even though the actual achievements of both groups were comparable.

People not only prescribe self-evaluative standards for others, they also exemplify them in response to their own behavior. It is amply documented in psychological research that modeling is another influential means of transmitting systems of self-reinforcement. In the procedure typically used to study this process, children or adults observe a model performing a task in which he adopts either a high or a low performance standard for self-reinforcement. On trials in which the model achieves or exceeds his self-imposed demand, he rewards himself tangibly and voices self-praise; but when his attainments fall short of self-prescribed requirements, he denies himself freely available rewards and reacts in a self-derogatory manner. Observers later perform the task alone, receiving a predetermined set of scores. The performances for which they reward and punish themselves are recorded.

Results of such experiments show that people tend to adopt standards of self-reinforcement displayed by exemplary models, they evaluate their own performances relative to that standard, and then they serve as their own reinforcing agents. In a study by Bandura and Kupers [1964] children who observed a model set a high standard of self-reinforcement later rewarded themselves sparingly and only when they achieved superior performances, whereas children exposed to models who considered low achievements deserving of self-reward tended to reinforce themselves for mediocre performances. A control group of children, who had no exposure to models, did not reward themselves selectively for differential levels of achievement. Subjects in the experimental conditions not only adopted the modeled standards of self-reinforcement but matched variations in the generosity with which the models rewarded their own performances.

Social groups contain members of widely differing abilities, so that a given individual must select the modeled standards against which to evaluate his own accomplishments. His level of self-satisfaction and of self-disappointment will be determined to a large extent by the models with whom he compares himself. A study by Bandura and Whalen [1966] found that children readily adopted self-reinforcement patterns displayed by either low-achieving models who were satisfied with mediocre performances or moderately competent models subscribing to self-reward standards within their reach. According to social comparison theory, people tend to choose reference models similar in ability and to disregard those who are too divergent from themselves. Consistent with this view, children rejected lofty standards of superior models and adopted lower self-reward requirements within the range of their achievements.

Although there is an understandable reluctance to emulate exacting norms of distinguished models, it is nevertheless not uncommon for people to adopt stringent standards of self-reinforcement. Indeed, universities are heavily populated with students who are self-satisfied only with superior performances in whatever academic work they undertake. We conducted an experiment in our laboratory to explore some of the social conditions that might lead people to emulate austere standards of self-reinforcement even though adherence to such demands results in

frequent self-dissatisfaction [Bandura, Grusec, & Menlove 1967].

Children observed a highly capable adult who rewarded himself only when he obtained superior scores that children rarely achieved when they later performed the same task. Prior to this experience, the adult model treated half the children in a warm, rewarding manner and the others in a neutral, businesslike fashion. The quality of the social relationship was varied on the assumption that the reward-ingness of a model, which tends to increase interpersonal attraction, would facilitate emulation of the model's exacting norms.

Adherence to high performance standards is generally publicly acclaimed. Without societal valuation most people would forego lofty aspirations if only because their attainment requires arduous work and much self-denial of readily available gratifications. To measure the effects of observed social rewards, with half the children in the experiment the adult model was praised for adhering to stringent standards of self-reinforcement, but with the remaining children the model received no social recognition for his high-standard-setting behavior.

Ordinarily, individuals are exposed to a variety of modeling influences, many of which operate in opposing directions. Speculations about the influence of multiple modeling on social learning generally assign importance to conflicting identification with adult and peer models. To study how children resolve the problem of simultaneous exposure to antagonistic modeling influences, half the children in each subgroup observed both the stringent adult and a peer model who displayed a low standard of self-reward. When faced with a conflict between adult and peer standards, children would be predisposed toward peer modeling. Not only would a peer be viewed as a more appropriate comparison model but emulation of high aspirations results in frequent self-criticism of one's performances, which discourages adoption of such standards. It was assumed, however, that the tendency for peer modeling to reduce the impact of adult modeling might be counteracted by opposing influences arising from positive ties to the adult model and from social recognition of high-standard-setting behavior.

Children exposed to conflicting modeling influences were more inclined to reward themselves for low achievements than children who had observed only the adult model consistently adhering to a high standard of self-reinforcement. Children were also more likely to impose severe criteria of self-reward on themselves when the adult model received social recognition for his high-standard-setting behavior than when the model's stringent achievement demands went unrecognized. However, contrary to expectation, children who had experienced a highly nurturant interaction with the adult model were more likely to accept the low performance standard set by the peer than if the adult was less beneficent. A nurturant relationship was apparently interpreted by the children as permissiveness for lenient self-demands.

Comparison of subgroups receiving various combinations of treatments revealed that the influence of the peer's liberal self-reward was effectively negated by praising the adult's high-standard-setting behavior. The most austere pattern of self-reinforcement was displayed by children who experienced a relatively nonnurturant relationship with the adult model, who had no exposure to conflicting peer norms, and who witnessed the adult receive social recognition for holding to high standards. These children, who rarely considered performances that fell below the adult's criterion worthy of self-reward, displayed unyielding self-denial. The adoption and continued adherence to unrealistically high self-evaluative standards is especially striking considering that the self-imposition of rigorous performance demands occurred under conditions where the children were at liberty to reward themselves whenever they wished without anyone around to judge their actions. Moreover, since children rarely attained the modeled standard, adopting it as an index of personal merit resulted in repeated self-devaluation and self-forbiddance of freely available rewards.

In everyday life it is not uncommon for people to differ in what they practice and in what they preach. Some parents, for example, lead a frugal self-denying life but are lenient in what they demand of their children; others are self-indulgent while expecting their children to subscribe to high standards of achievement entailing long hours of work and sacrifice of many day-to-day pleasures. A number of researchers have investigated the effects of such discrepancies on the development of self-reinforcement patterns [McMains & Liebert 1968, Mischel & Liebert 1966, Rosenhan, Frederick, & Burrowes 1968]. The findings generally show that children reward themselves most sparingly when stringent standards have been consistently modeled and imposed, whereas social learning conditions in which adults both model and impose lenient performance demands produce children who reward themselves generously for mediocre attainments. Discrepant practices, on the other hand, in which models prescribe stringent standards for others but impose lenient ones upon themselves, or impose austere demands on themselves and lenient ones on others, reduce the likelihood that high standards of self-reward will be adopted.

The manner in which self-reward patterns may be passed on through a succession of models has been demonstrated by Mischel and Liebert [1966]. Children who had adopted high standards of self-reinforcement displayed by adults later modeled and applied the same standards in relation to peers. Marston [1965a] has likewise shown in an experiment with adults that seeing models reinforce their performances either generously or sparingly not only affected how liberally observers rewarded their own behavior but influenced the frequency with which they later reinforced another person performing the same task.

The laboratory findings corroborate field studies demonstrating that in cultures where austerity is consistently modeled and taught as the dominant social norm people not only reward themselves sparingly, but because of the emphasis on personal responsibility for high standards of conduct, self-denying, self-punitive, and depressive reactions are prevalent [Eaton & Weil 1955]. By contrast, in societies where liberal self-gratification patterns predominate, people usually reward themselves generously for minimal performances [Hughes, Tremblay, Rapoport, & Leighton 1960].

Self-Reinforcement and Self-Concept

Accounts of personality theories frequently draw sharp distinctions between phenomenological approaches in which the self-concept is a central feature and behavioral orientations that supposedly dismiss self-evaluative phenomena. Behavior theories differ among themselves, of course, in what they choose to study and in what they regard as the nature and locus of the causes of human behavior. It is evident from the preceding discussion that self-evaluative and self-reinforcing functions assume a prominent role in social learning theory. It will be recalled that individuals who had been exposed to models favoring lenient standards of self-reinforcement were highly self-rewarding and self-approving for comparatively mediocre performances; conversely, persons who observed models adhering to stringent performance demands displayed self-denial and self-dissatisfaction for objectively identical accomplishments. These contrasting self-reactions to one's own behavior illustrate how self-esteem, self-concept, and related self-evaluative processes can be conceptualized within a social learning framework. From this perspective, self-esteem is the result of discrepancies between a person's behavior and the standards that he has selected as indices of personal merit. When behavior falls short of one's evaluative standards, the person judges himself negatively or holds himself in low self-esteem. On the other hand, when performances coincide with, or exceed, a person's standards he evaluates himself favorably, which is considered indicative of high self-esteem.

The self-concept also reflects the phenomenon of self-reinforcement. Self-concept usually signifies a person's tendency to regard different aspects of his behavior positively or negatively. In measuring this personality characteristic individuals are presented with a set of evaluative statements in the form of adjective check lists, Q-sorts, or inventories and are asked to rate which statements apply to them. The individual responses are then summed to provide a global index of self-evaluation, which represents his self-concept. Within a social learning approach, a negative self-concept is defined in terms of frequent negative self-reinforcement of one's behavior; conversely, a favorable self-concept is reflected in a disposition to engage in high positive self-reinforcement. Marston [1965b] has conceptualized the phenomena subsumed under the term self-concept in much the same way.

Personality theories often attribute variations in behavior to differences in values. Behavioral approaches treat values largely in terms of incentive preferences. As we have already observed, the kinds of responses a person makes are affected by the positive and negative outcomes they are likely to produce. Traditional value theory, however, is more concerned with valuation of behavior than of external outcomes. Established personality theories tend to regard values as global personal entities that influence behavior but they fail to explain exactly how values control specific actions. Within the social learning framework, self-reinforcement is the control mechanism. The behavioral standards represent the values and the anticipatory self-satisfaction and self-criticism for actions that correspond to or deviate from the adopted standards serve as the controlling influences.

Dysfunctions in self-reinforcement systems often assume major importance in psychopathology through their capacity to create excessive self-punishment and aversive conditions that can maintain deleterious forms of deviant behavior. Many of the people who seek psychotherapy are behaviorally competent and free of debilitating anxiety, but they experience a great deal of personal distress stemming from excessively high standards of self-evaluation often supported by unfavorable comparisons with models noted for their extraordinary achievements. As an unidentified pundit once remarked, "If you compare yourself with others, you may become vain or bitter; for always there will be greater and lesser persons than oneself." Yet social comparisons are inevitable, especially in societies that place a high premium on competitiveness and individual achievement. Ironically, talented individuals who have high aspirations that are possible but difficult to realize are especially vulnerable to self-dissatisfaction despite their notable achievements. As Boyd [1969] graphically describes this phenomenon, "Each violinist in any second chair started out as a prodigy in velvet knickers who expected one day to solo exquisitely amid flowers flung by dazzled devotees. The 45-year-old violinist with spectacles on his nose and a bald spot in the middle of his hair is the most disappointed man on earth." Linus, the security-blanketed member of the Peanuts clan, also alluded to this phenomenon when he wisely observed, "There is no heavier burden than a great potential."

In its more extreme forms, a harsh system of self-reinforcement gives rise to depressive reactions, chronic discouragement, feelings of worthlessness, and lack of purposefulness. Excessive self-disparagement, in fact, is one of the defining characteristics of psychotic depression. As Loeb, Beck, Diggory, and Tuthill [1967] have shown, depressed adults evaluate their performances as significantly poorer than do nondepressed subjects, even though their actual achievements are the same. People also suffer from considerable self-devaluation when they experience a loss in ability due to age or physical injury but continue to adhere to their original standards of achievement. In the latter instances, most of their performances are negatively self-reinforced to the point where they eventually become apathetic and abandon activities that previously brought them a great deal of personal satisfaction.

When a person's behavior produces self-punishing consequences, any activities that avert or reduce these disturbing effects are thereby strengthened and maintained. A variety of deviant behaviors can serve as means of escaping or avoiding self-generated distress. Some people whose accomplishments bring them a sense of failure resort to alcoholic self-anesthetization; others escape into grandiose ideation where they achieve in fantasy what they failed in reality; others protect themselves against self-condemnation for their lack of advancement by developing delusions of persecution; still others are tragically driven by relentless self-disparagement to suicide; and many renounce pursuits that have self-evaluative implications and gravitate to social groups that embrace an antiachievement norm.

The preceding discussion portrays the personal misery that can result from stringent self-reinforcement. Social problems also arise from deficient or deviant self-reinforcement systems. Individuals who have failed to develop well-defined standards necessary for adequate self-regulating reinforcement and those who make self-reward contingent upon skillful performance of antisocial behavior readily engage in transgressive activities unless deterred by externally imposed controls. Similarly, individuals who set low behavioral standards for themselves are inclined to upset others by their indifference to achievement requirements.

Behavior-Regulating Function of Self-Produced Consequences

Psychologists have examined not only how people learn to respond to their own actions in self-rewarding and self-punishing ways but the degree to which they can control their own behavior by self-produced consequences. Bandura and Perloff [1967] compared the relative effectiveness of self-monitored and externally applied systems of reinforcement in an experiment that proceeded as follows: children worked at a manual task in which they could achieve progressively higher scores by performing increasingly more effortful responses. Eight complete rotations of a wheel were required to advance 5 points, so that, for example, a total of 16 cranking responses was required to achieve a score of 10, 24 responses to attain a score of 15, and a total of 32 cranking responses to reach the maximum score of 20. Children in the self-reinforcement condition selected which of these achievement levels they would strive for and rewarded themselves whenever they attained their self-prescribed standard of performance. Children who performed under externally administered reinforcement were individually matched with members in the self-reward group so that the same achievement standard was externally set for them and the rewards were automatically delivered whenever they reached the predetermined level. To determine whether subjects' behavioral productivity was due to response reinforcement or to gratitude for the rewards that were made available, children in an incentive control group performed the task after they had received the rewards without any strings attached. A fourth group

worked without any rewards at all to estimate the number of responses children would perform solely through interest in the task itself. Because the capacity to maintain effortful behavior is one of the most important features of a reinforcement operation, the dependent measure was the number of cranking responses the children performed until they no longer wished to continue the activity.

Children whose behavior was positively reinforced either by themselves or by others performed substantially more responses than children who received the rewards in advance or were never rewarded. Girls were equally productive under externally and self-administered reinforcement. Although boys also worked hard when they rewarded their own performances, they were even more responsive under conditions where reinforcement was externally regulated.

Of special interest is the prevalence with which children in the self-monitored condition willingly imposed upon themselves highly unfavorable schedules of reinforcement. Not a single child chose the lowest score, which required the least effort, while approximately half of them selected the highest achievement level as the minimal performance meriting self-reward. Moreover, a third of the children later raised their initial standard to a higher level, without a commensurate increase in amount of self-reward, thereby requiring of themselves more work for the same recompense.

Why did children work themselves so hard when no one required them to do so? Since the experiment was not designed to provide evidence on this point, we can only speculate. It can be reasonably assumed that most older children have adopted standards of achievement through modeling and the evaluative reactions of others. Moreover, they are likely to have been criticized on many occasions for being self-satisfied with performances judged to be unworthy. Hence, under conditions where persons are provided with opportunities to optimize their material outcomes by resorting to behavior that has low self-regard value, conflicting tendencies are aroused. On the one hand, they are tempted to maximize rewards at minimum effort costs to themselves; they can achieve this by simply lowering their performance standards. On the other hand, reward for low-quality performances evokes self-reproof, which, if sufficiently strong, may inhibit undeserving self-compensation. Apparently, children were willing to deny themselves rewards over which they had full control rather than risk self-disapproval for unmerited self-reward. Many of the children, in fact, set themselves performance requirements that incurred high effort costs at minimum material recompense. These findings are at variance with what one might expect on the basis of reward-cost theories, unless such formulations include the self-esteem costs of rewarding devalued behavior.

In recent years psychologists have been developing self-reinforcement procedures that would enable people to control their own behavior more effectively. These methods are applied most extensively to the modification of behaviors that are personally disturbing or that create chronic difficulties for others. Given clearly defined objectives and some practice on how valued rewards can be self-administered contingently, children are able to manage their aggressive and scholastic behavior as well as or better than their teachers through self-reinforcement practices [Goodlet & Goodlet 1969, Glynn 1970, Lovitt & Curtis 1969]. Self-administered aversive consequences have been used with some degree of success to reduce stuttering, obsessional ruminations, craving for addictive drugs, and deviant sexual behavior [Bandura 1969a].

Recent investigations of techniques of self-control also assign a principal role to self-managed reinforcement [Ferster, Nurnberger, & Levitt 1962, Harris 1969, Stuart 1967]. In such treatment programs changes in highly refractory behavior are induced by having people regulate the stimuli that ordinarily control undesired and competing response patterns. However, unless positive consequences for self-controlling behavior are also arranged, the well-intentioned practices are usually short-lived.

Self-controlling behavior is difficult to maintain because it tends to be associated, at least initially, with relatively unfavorable conditions of reinforcement. Prepotent activities such as heavy drinking by alcoholics and excessive eating by obese people are immediately rewarding, whereas their detrimental consequences are not experienced for some time. Conversely, self-control measures usually produce immediate unpleasant effects while the personal benefits are considerably delayed. Self-reinforcement practices are, therefore, employed to provide immediate support for self-controlling behavior until the benefits that eventually accrue take over the reinforcing function. This is achieved by having individuals select a variety of activities that they find rewarding and make them contingent upon the performance of desired behavior.

The preceding studies primarily involve self-administration of tangible reinforcers. Of considerable interest is evidence that imagined consequences can serve a reinforcing function in regulating overt behavior. Weiner [1965] reports an experiment in which inappropriate motor responses by adults were either punished by withdrawal of monetary points or by having the subjects imagine the same loss of monetary points, or their performances had no consequences. He found that imagined aversive consequences and the actual occurrence of the same negative outcomes both reduced responding compared to the condition involving no feedback. Covert self-punishment, however, produced somewhat weaker reductive effects.

Although experimental demonstrations are lacking, there is every reason to expect that people can increase desired behavior by covert self-reward. The operation of covert self-reinforcement complicates interpretation of behavior changes accompanying external reinforcements. It may not be the lights, the scores, and the evaluative statements used as rewards in psychological experiments that are reinforcing; rather, such extrinsic events serve as cues that elicit covert self-satisfaction or self-criticism in subjects. It would follow from this line of reasoning that correctness feedback on tasks that are personally devalued or regarded as trifling is unlikely to activate self-reward and hence will not operate as a positive reinforcement. On the other hand, behavioral improvements are possible in the absence of extrinsic rewards because people can easily supply them to themselves. Preliminary findings of studies of self-reinforcement processes suggest that learning approaches hold considerable promise for increasing people's capacity to regulate their own feelings, thoughts, and actions.

Conditions Supporting
Self-Reinforcement Systems

Since self-reinforcement systems are developed through social influence, there is no reason to assume that, once established, they become autonomous regulators completely impervious to subsequent social influences. An interesting, but inadequately explored, question is what supports self-reinforcing actions. No elaborate theory is needed to explain why people reward themselves. The challenging question requiring explanation is why people deny themselves available rewards over which they have full control, why they adhere to exacting standards that require difficult performances, and why they punish themselves. Several different interpretations have been proposed.

Conditioned relief. In the view advanced by Aronfreed [1964], people punish themselves because such responses have become endowed with anxiety relief value through prior conditioning experiences. This classical conditioning interpretation assumes that when parents discipline their children they often voice their criticism as they cease punishing them. If verbal criticism is repeatedly associated with the termination of punishment, criticism eventually becomes a relief signal indicating that punishment will soon end, thus allaying anxiety. Thereafter, when transgressive behavior arouses anticipatory fear, people criticize themselves for its conditioned tranquilizing effects. Self-critical responses persist, according to Aronfreed, because they are automatically reinforced by anxiety reduction.

To test this theory, Aronfreed conducted an experiment in which children performed an ambiguous task; on periodic occasions a buzzer sounded indicating that they had erred, at which point they were reprimanded for behaving the "blue" way and deprived of some candy. For one group the critical label "blue" was uttered as the buzzer and punishment were terminated; for a second group the label coincided with the onset of the buzzer and punishment; while with control children the blue label was verbalized as the buzzer was turned off without any accompanying punishment. On subsequent trials, during which the buzzer signaled a transgression, children who experienced labeling at the termination of punishment were more inclined to verbalize the critical label than either the controls or children receiving labeling at onset of punishment, who did not differ from each other.

These findings are consistent with a conditioned reinforcement view, but other aspects of the data cast doubt on this interpretation. After transgressing, the children rarely uttered the critical label on their own and did so only after the punisher prompted it from them through a series of questions concerning their actions. Given anxiety arousal, one would expect an anxiety reducer to be performed quickly and spontaneously. Why endure discomfort if one can promptly relieve it by a soothing self-critical word? The children's initial reluctance but later differential use of the critical label can be more adequately explained in terms of its assumed functional value rather than its conditioned tranquilizing properties. Children for whom the critical label brought on punishment would have little reason to use it. On the other hand, those who had earlier observed that the critical verbalization terminated punishment would be inclined to try it as a defensive maneuver in the face of the punisher's probing. Once having seen that uttering the critical word apparently eliminated at least the punisher's verbal reprimand, children would tend to repeat it for its presumed instrumental value. Moreover, when children did use the blue label on signaled errors, it remains unclear whether they were simply reporting that they performed the "blue" way or whether they were in fact voicing self-criticism. An adequate test of the conditioning view of self-criticism, therefore, requires a situation in which children are provided with opportunities to actually criticize their actions in the absence of the punisher, thereby removing any possible external gains for such behavior. It might be noted in passing that the conditioning theory would also require several complicated assumptions to explain how people adopt self-punishing responses by observing punishments self-administered by a model for devalued behavior without observers receiving any direct painful treatment.

Reduction of self-generated distress. When a person performs inadequately or violates his own standards of conduct, he is likely to experience self-deprecatory and other types of distressing thoughts. During the course of socialization the sequence of transgression—internal distress—punishment—relief is repeatedly experienced. In this process performance of punishable behavior creates anticipatory fears that often persist in varying degrees until the person is reprimanded. Punishment not only terminates worries over discovery of the transgression and possible social condemnation, but it also tends to restore the favor of others. Thus, punishment can provide relief from thought-produced anguish that is enduring and often more painful than the actual reprimand itself. This phenomenon is most vividly illustrated in extreme cases where people torment themselves for years over relatively minor transgressions and do not achieve equanimity until after making reparations of some type. Self-punishment may serve a similar distress-relief function. Having criticized or punished themselves for undesirable actions, individuals are likely to discontinue further upsetting ruminations about their behavior.

The way in which self-punishment can be maintained by averting anticipated threats is strikingly demonstrated by Sandler and Quagliano [1964]. After monkeys learned to press a lever to avoid being shocked, a second contingency involving self-administered punishment was introduced. A lever press prevented the occurrence of the original shock, but it also produced an electric shock of lesser magnitude. As the experiment progressed, the self-administered shock was gradually increased in intensity until it equaled the one being avoided. However, the animals showed no reduction in self-punishment even though this behavior no longer served as a "lesser of two evils." Even more interesting, after the avoided shock was permanently discontinued but lever-pressing responses (which had now become objectively functionless) still produced painful consequences, the animals continued to punish themselves needlessly with shock intensities that they had previously worked hard to avoid. This experiment reveals how self-punishment can become autonomous of contemporaneous conditions of reinforcement and be maintained through its capacity to forestall imagined threats that no longer exist.

In psychotic disorders, self-punishment is often powerfully maintained by delusional contingencies that have little relationship to reality. In a case to be cited later, a man who judged trivial acts as heinous sins could relieve his fright of hellish torment and feelings of self-contempt only by performing exceedingly self-punitive behaviors for long hours.

The preceding analysis of self-punishment can be applied as well to self-disappointing performances as to moral conduct. Like transgressive behavior, inferior performances can be a source of disconcerting thoughts and social disapproval that individuals will strive to reduce by criticizing or punishing themselves.

External reinforcement. Although self-punishment can be reinforced by its capacity to end or at least to reduce thought-produced distress, self-reinforcing responses are partly sustained by periodic external reinforcement. Adherence to high standards of self-reinforcement is actively supported through a vast societal system of rewards involving praise, social recognition, and a variety of awards and honors, whereas few accolades are bestowed on people for rewarding themselves on the basis of mediocre performances. To the extent that people choose a reference group whose members share similar behavioral norms for self-reinforcement, a given individual's self-evaluations are undoubtedly influenced by the actual or anticipated reactions of members whose judgments he values. When a person's immediate reference group is small and select, his self-evaluations are not much influenced by the views of others, and he sometimes appears to be an "inner-directed" person [Riesman 1950], although, in fact, he is highly responsive to a few individuals whose good opinion he prizes. The man is rare who regards his behavior so highly that the reactions of his fellows have no effect on his self-evaluation.

In everyday life high evaluative standards are not only favored, but negative sanctions are frequently applied to discourage inappropriate positive self-reinforcement. Rewarding oneself for inadequate or undeserving performances is more likely than not to evoke critical reactions from others. Similarly, lowering one's performance standards is rarely considered praiseworthy.

Self-punishment often serves as an effective means of lessening negative reactions from others. When misdeeds are almost certain to evoke disciplinary actions, self-punishment may be the lesser of two evils. Stone and Hokanson [1969] show how self-punitive behavior can be effectively maintained by its self-protective and emotion-reducing function. When adults could avoid painful shocks by administering to themselves shocks of lesser intensity, self-punitive responses not only increased but were accompanied by reduction in autonomic arousal.

Finally, verbal self-punishment can be a good way of extracting commendations from others as well. By criticizing and belittling themselves, people can predictably get others to enumerate their noteworthy accomplishments and abilities, and to issue reassuring predictions that continued effort will produce future triumphs. In summary, self-reinforcing behavior is intermittently reinforced by both subjectively created contingencies and various external sources.

Cognitive Control

If human behavior could be fully explained in terms of external stimulus conditions and response consequences, there would be no need to postulate any additional regulatory mechanisms. Actions are not always predictable from these external sources of influence, however, because cognitive factors partly determine what one observes, feels, and does at any given moment. In the present discussion, cognitive events refer to imagery, to representations of activities in verbal and other symbols, and to thought processes. There are several ways in which cognitive functioning enters into the regulation of human behavior. These are discussed next.

Cognitive Representation of Reinforcement Contingencies

It was previously shown that repeated paired stimulation generally fails to produce conditioned responses as long as the connection between stimulus events goes unnoticed. Response consequences similarly have little or no effect on behavior when the relationship between one's actions and outcomes is not recognized. On the other hand, cognitive representation of conditions of reinforcement typically results in abrupt improvements in performance, indicative of insightful functioning.

Another interesting way of analyzing the process of cognitive control is to pit the power of belief against experienced reinforcement in the regulation of behavior. Several researchers have systematically explored the degree to which cognitive influences attenuate, distort, or nullify the effects of response consequences. Kaufman, Baron, and Kopp [1966] conducted a study in which motor responses of adults were rewarded each minute on the average (variable-interval schedule). One group was correctly informed about how often their performances would be rewarded, whereas other groups were misled into believing that their behavior would be reinforced either every minute (fixed-interval schedule) or after they had performed 150 responses on the average (variable-ratio schedule). Beliefs about the prevailing conditions of reinforcement outweighed the influence of experience consequences. Although all subjects actually received the same pattern of reinforcement, those who thought they were being rewarded once every minute produced very low rates of response (mean = 6); those who thought they were reinforced on a variable-ratio schedule maintained an exceedingly high output (mean = 259); while those who were correctly informed that their behavior would be rewarded on the average every minute displayed an intermediate level of responsiveness (mean = 65).

Human behavior is regulated to a large extent by anticipated consequences of prospective actions. Individuals may accurately assess the customary effects of given activities but fail to act in accordance with existing conditions of reinforcement because of false hope that their actions may eventually produce favorable outcomes. In one study some children persisted in imitating nonfunctional responses of a model that were never reinforced in the erroneous belief that their continued imitativeness might change his reinforcement practices [Bandura & Barab 1971]. People also lead themselves astray by inaccurate expectations when they wrongly assume that certain changes in their behavior will alter future response consequences.

The oft-repeated dictum that behavior is controlled by its immediate consequences holds up better under close scrutiny for anticipated consequences than for those that actually impinge on the organism. In most instances customary outcomes are reasonably good predictors of behavior because the consequences that

people anticipate for their actions are accurately derived from, and therefore correspond closely to, prevailing conditions of reinforcement. Belief and actuality, however, do not always coincide, because anticipated consequences are also partly inferred from observed response consequences of others, from what one reads or is told, and from a variety of other cues that, on the basis of past experiences, are considered reliable forecasters of likely outcomes. When actions are guided by anticipated consequences derived from predictors that do not accurately reflect existing contingencies of reinforcement, behavior is weakly controlled by its actual consequences until cumulative experiences produce more realistic expectations.

In some of the more severe behavior disorders, psychotic actions are so powerfully controlled by bizarre subjective contingencies that the behavior remains unaffected by its external consequences. This process is vividly illustrated in the passages quoted below [Bateson 1961], taken from a patient's account of his psychotic experiences in an insane asylum during the early 1800's. The narrator had received a scrupulously moralistic upbringing, according to which actions ordinarily viewed as fully acceptable were judged by him to be deviant, sinful, and likely to provoke the wrath of God; consequently, many innocuous acts elicited dreadful apprehensions, which in turn motivated and maintained exceedingly painful atonement rituals designed to forestall the imagined disastrous consequences.

> In the night I awoke under the most dreadful impressions; I heard a voice addressing me, and I was made to imagine that my disobedience to the faith, in taking the medicine overnight, had not only offended the Lord, but had rendered the work of my salvation extremely difficult, by its effect upon my spirits and humours. I heard that I could only be saved now by being changed into a spiritual body. . . . A spirit came upon me and prepared to guide me in my actions. I was lying on my back, and the spirit seemed to light on my pillow by my right ear, and to command my body. I was placed in a fatiguing attitude, resting on my feet, my knees drawn up and on my head, and made to swing my body from side to side without ceasing. In the meantime, I heard voices without and within me, and sounds as of the clanking of iron, and the breathing of great forge bellows, and the force of flames. . . . I was told, however, that my salvation depended on my maintaining that position as well as I could until the morning; and oh! great was my joy when I perceived the first brightness of the dawn, which I could scarcely believe had arrived so early [pp. 28–29].

In the experiences described above, the anxiety instigators and the influential response consequences are both internally created. Acceptance of medicine, an act later considered a rebellion against, and mistrust of, the Almighty, aroused dreadful hallucinations of Hadean torture, which could be banished only by performance of arduous bizarre behavior. The nonoccurrence of subjectively feared, but objectively nonexistent, threats undoubtedly serves as an important source of reinforcement, maintaining many other types of psychotic behavior. Given fictional contingencies with a powerful internal reinforcing system, a person's behavior is likely to remain under very poor environmental control even in the face of severe external punishments and blatant disconfirming experiences.

> When I opened the door, I found a stout man servant on the landing, who told me that he was placed there to forbid my going out, by the orders of Dr. P. and my friend; on my remonstrating, he followed me into my room and stood before the door. I insisted on going out; he, on preventing me. I warned him of the danger he incurred in opposing the will of the Holy Spirit, I prayed him to let me pass, or otherwise an evil would befal him, for that I was a prophet of the Lord. He was not a whit shaken by my address, so, after again and again adjuring him, by the desire of the Spirit whose word I heard, I seized one of his arms, desiring it to wither; my words were idle, no effect followed, and I was ashamed and astonished.
> Then, thought I, I have been made a fool of! But I did not on that account mistrust the doctrines by which I had been exposed to this error. The doctrines, thought I, are true; but I am mocked at by the Almighty for my disobedience to them, and at the same time, I have the guilt and the grief, of bringing discredit upon the truth, by my obedience to a spirit of mockery, or, by my disobedience to the Holy Spirit; for there were not wanting voices to suggest to me, that the reason why the miracle had failed, was, that I had not waited for the Spirit to guide my action when the word was spoken, and that I had seized the man's arm with the wrong hand [p. 33].

> The voices informed me, that my conduct was owing to a spirit of mockery and blasphemy having possession of me . . . that I must, in the power of the Holy Spirit, *redeem myself,* and rid myself of the spirits of blasphemy and mockery that had taken possession of me.
> The way in which I was tempted to do this was by throwing myself on the top of my head backwards, and so resting on the top of my head and on my feet alone, to turn from one side to the other until I had broken my neck. I suppose by this time I was already in a state of feverish delirium, but my good sense and prudence still refused to undertake this strange action. I was then accused for faithlessness and cowardice, of fearing man more than God.

> I attempted the command, the servant prevented me. I lay down contented to have proved myself willing to obey in spite of his presence, but now I was accused of not daring to wrestle with him unto blows. I again attempted what I was enjoined. The man seized me, I tore myself from him, telling him it was necessary for my salvation; he left me and went down stairs. I then tried to perform what I had begun; but now I found, either that I could not so jerk myself round on my head, or that my fear of breaking my neck was really too strong for my faith. In that case I then certainly mocked, for my efforts were not sincere.

> Failing in my attempts, I was directed to expectorate violently, in order to get rid of my two formidable enemies; and then again I was told to drink water, and that the Almighty was satisfied; but that if I was not satisfied (neither could I be sincerely, for I knew I had not fulfilled his commands), I was to take up my position again; I did so; my attendant came up with an assistant and they forced me into a straight waistcoat. Even then I again tried to resume the position to which I was again challenged. They then tied my legs to the bed-posts, and so secured me [pp. 34–35].

Grotesque homicidal actions provide other striking illustrations of how behavior can come under bizarre symbolic control. A study of presidential assassins [Weisz & Taylor 1970], for instance, shows that, with one exception, the murderous assaults were partly under delusional control. The assassins were driven to acts of violence by divine inner voices commanding them to do so, by delusional beliefs that the victim was conspiring to harm them, and by grandiose convictions that it was their heroic responsibility to eliminate maleficent leaders in positions of power. The assassins, being unusually seclusive in their behavior, shielded the delusional beliefs from corrective social influences.

Representational Guidance of Behavior

Symbolic processes play a prominent role in the acquisition and retention of response patterns as well as in their expression. The memory trace of momentary influences is short-lived, but such experiences often have lasting behavioral effects. This condition is made possible by the fact that transitory external events are coded and stored in symbolic form for memory representation. Patterns of behavior that have been observed and other experiences long past can thus be reinstated by visualizing them or by representing them verbally. These internal models of the outside world can serve as guides to overt action on later occasions. It will be recalled from the earlier discussion of learning processes that internal representations of patterned behavior are constructed from observed examples and from informative feedback to one's trial-and-error performances.

Representational mediators are especially influential in early phases of response acquisition. After action patterns have become routinized through over-learning, they are usually performed smoothly and automatically without requiring intermediary imaginal or verbal guidance. Skilled performance can, in fact, be disrupted by visualizing or thinking about what one must do next while carrying out the activity.

Thought Control of Action through Covert Problem Solving

Man's efforts to understand and to manage his environment would be exceedingly wearisome, and perilous as well, if optimal solutions to problems could be arrived at only by performing alternative actions and suffering the consequences. Fortunately. most problem solving occurs in thought rather than in action. Man's higher mental capacities, for example, enable him to design sturdy dwellings and bridges without having to build them until he hits upon a structure that does not collapse. Alternative courses of action are generally tested in symbolic exploration and either discarded or retained on the basis of calculated consequences. The best symbolic solution is then executed in action.

Symbols that represent external events, operations, and relationships are the vehicle of thought. Most thinking occurs in terms of language symbols. By manipulating words that convey relevant information, one can gain an understanding into causal processes, arrive at solutions, and deduce consequences. Thinking also occurs in numerical and other symbols. The functional value of thought depends upon close correspondence between the symbolic system and external events so that the latter can be substituted for the former. Thus, subtracting the number 2 from 10 yields the same outcome as physically performing the operation of removing two objects from a group of ten. Symbols can be manipulated much more easily than their physical counterparts, which greatly increases the scope and power of symbolic problem solving. Since symbols are the instruments of thought, the level of symbolization development partly determines reasoning capacities.

The process by which people learn to attain solutions covertly has received comparatively little attention, despite its focal role in human functioning. Being a private activity, of course, it is not readily accessible to empirical investigation. Such cognitive skills are usually developed by performing operations initially on actual objects and then gradually translating the external processes to covert symbolic ones of increasing complexity and abstraction. In the teaching of arithmetic principles, for instance, children first learn the formal operations of addition and subtraction by combining and withdrawing real ob-jects. Pictorial representations are also used in early phases as aids to acquiring arithmetic skills. After children have learned to solve arithmetic problems through physical manipulation of things, the objects are symbolized by numbers. Correct solutions are now achieved by manipulation of numerical symbols on paper, where each step can be checked and corrected. The process at this stage is still partially overt but the solutions are symbolic. Eventually the symbolic solutions are achieved covertly by having children think out the problem within their heads. Overt and covert operations do not differ in any fundamental way, although covert problem solving generally makes heavy demands on memory processes. For this reason various diagrammatical and mechanical aids are used when solutions to problems require complex chains of symbolic activities.

Interaction of Controlling Influences

The three major systems by which behavior is regulated do not operate independently. Most actions are simultaneously controlled by two or more of the component influences. Moreover, the various systems are closely interdependent in acquiring and retaining their power to determine behavior. In order to establish and to maintain effective stimulus control, for example, the same actions must produce different consequences, depending on the cues that are present. If walking through intersections on red or green signals left one equally vulnerable to being knocked down by automobiles, pedestrians would quickly disregard traffic lights and rely on other informative cues to guide them safely through busy thoroughfares. Earlier we noted how the effectiveness of verbal and other social influences is negated by faulty reinforcement practices and reinstated by ensuring that predictable consequences will ensue for responding in a particular way to certain stimulus situations.

The preceding comments illustrate how stimulus determinants of behavior can be markedly affected by how they are correlated with reinforcing consequences. Stimulus and cognitive influences, in turn, can alter the impact of prevailing conditions of reinforcement. Conditioned aversive stimuli can acquire such powerful control over defensive behavior that people avoid renewed encounters with feared persons or things. In instances where the original threats no longer exist, their self-protective behavior is insulated from realistic reinforcement control.

Even when the things one dislikes or fears are not completely avoided, stimuli having strong emotion-arousing potential provoke defensive behaviors that predictably create adverse reinforcement contingencies where they may not ordinarily exist. We might draw again on the advice column of a newspaper counselor to illustrate this process.

Dear Abby:

I have trouble with blondes. Every time I go for a girl and she is a blonde she turns out to be a gold-digger. I notice on TV whenever they have a gold-digger she is blonde. The last blonde I went with asked me to buy a record every time I took her out. She kept me busted buying her records. Should I pass up all blondes from now on?

Blonde Trouble

Dear Blonde Trouble:

Plenty of golden heads have golden hearts.

Abby

To the extent that the correspondent's distrust of blondes leads him to behave in ways that provoke unfriendly counteractions from them, the negative valence of blonde hair is repeatedly strengthened, and it in turn prompts actions that produce reciprocal negative reinforcement. Both processes thus support each other.

The way in which beliefs and conscious recognition of environmental contingencies can enhance, distort, or even negate the influence of reinforcing consequences has already been amply documented and needs no further illustration. Cognitive events, however, do not function as autonomous causes of behavior. Their nature, their valence, and their occurrence are under stimulus and reinforcement control. Analysis of cognitive control of behavior is therefore incomplete without specifying what controls the influential cognitions.

Cognitively based conditioning, for example, cannot occur unless the thoughts that serve as sources of emotional responses have been endowed with arousal potenial. The research of Miller [1951] and Grose [1952] demonstrates that thoughts can acquire emotion-provoking properties through generalization from reinforcing experiences associated with overt responses. In these studies it was found that thoughts corresponding to verbalizations that had been punished generated physiological arousal, whereas thoughts representing nonpunished verbalizations elicited no emotional reactions. If the painful experiences are sufficiently intense, however, they can condition such potent aversive properties that the disturbing thoughts themselves are completely inhibited [Eriksen & Kuethe 1956, Marks & Gelder 1967]. In personality theories, thought inhibition is usually designated as repression.

Thoughts remain partly under external stimulus control. Thus, the thoughts elicited in a hospital are markedly different from those aroused in a discotheque. A simple cue from a past experience can reinstate reveries of bygone events. And perturbing trains of thought can be turned off by directing one's attention to absorbing matters that elicit superseding cognitive activities. This form of self-control, in which thought-produced arousal is diminished by engrossment in absorbing literary material, televised programs, vocational and avocational pursuits, and other engaging projects, is widely used to restore a sense of well-being.

The rules and principles that people use to guide their actions do not arise in a mental vacuum. When rules defining appropriate behavior in given situations are not explicitly designated, they are arrived at largely through information conveyed by observed or experienced response consequences. Provisional hypotheses that produce responses resulting in reinforcement are retained, partially correct hypotheses are successively refined on the basis of differential response feedback until the right one is hit upon, and hypotheses that give rise to faulty performances are promptly discarded. While it is true that implicit rules govern behavior, the rules themselves are partly fashioned out of reinforcement experiences.

Considering the intricate interdependence of stimulus, reinforcement, and cognitive control systems, the sharp distinctions frequently drawn between reinforcement and cognitive theories are of questionable value. It has been customary in psychological theorizing to construct entire explanatory schemes around a single form of behavioral control, to the relative neglect of other obviously influential determinants and processes. Some theories have tended to concentrate upon stimulus control effected principally through association of experiences; others have primarily focused upon external reinforcement control; and advocates favoring cognitive interpretations confine their interest largely to symbolic mediators. These resolute allegiances to part processes may encourage intensive investigation of subsystems, but considered alone, they do not provide a complete understanding of human behavior.

Social Learning as a Reciprocal Influence Process

In the social learning view, psychological functioning involves a continuous reciprocal interaction between behavior and its controlling conditions. Early attempts to incorporate both individual and environmental determinants in personality theory simply depicted behavior as caused by these two sets of influences. In the widely cited equation $B = f(P, E)$, actions were presumably best understood by considering the joint effects of personal attributes and environmental pressures. The major weakness of this type of formulation is that it treats response dispositions and the environment as independent entities. Contrary to this assumption, the environment is only a potentiality, not a fixed property that inevitably impinges upon individuals and to which their behavior eventually adapts. Behavior partly creates the environment and the resultant environment, in turn, influences the behavior. In this two-way causal process the environment is just as influenceable as the behavior it controls.

Illustrations of how behavioral disposition and the environment affect each other can be found even in simple experiments with animals. To study defensive reactions to threats, Sidman [1966] devised a situation in which animals could postpone the occurrence of painful shocks for a given period by depressing a lever. Shocks, for example, may be scheduled to occur every minute, but each bar press forestalls it for thirty seconds so that animals have an effective means for controlling the punitiveness of their environment. Under these conditions animals that quickly learn the adaptive behavior create for themselves an environment that is essentially free of punishment. Others who, for one reason or another, are slow in acquiring the requisite coping responses experience a highly unpleasant milieu. Though the *potential environment* is identical for all animals, the *actual environment* varies in accordance with their behavior. Is the animal controlling the environment or is the environment controlling the animal? What we have here is a two-way control system, and it is arbitrary which aspect of it we choose to record. When changes in the animals' behavior are selected for analysis, the environmental contingencies appear to be the controllers of behavior. If, instead, one examines the amount of punishment created by each subject, it is the environment that is controlled and modified by the animals' actions, and it can therefore vary considerably for different subjects and at different times for the same subject. In examining how behavior determines the environment, one might, for instance, administer alcohol to one group and water to another within the same programmed milieu and then compare the types of aversive environments subjects create for themselves under intoxicated and under sober conditions.

The rewarding aspect of an environment is also only a potentiality until actualized through appropriate actions. A researcher once studied the behavior of schizophrenic and normal children in a room containing an extraordinary variety of reinforcing devices including, among other things, a pinball machine, a color wheel, a television set, a phonograph, an electric train, a picture viewer, an electric organ, and candy- and trinket-vending machines. To actuate these various playthings, children had simply to deposit available coins, but only when a light was turned on; coins deposited when the light was off extended the period that the device would remain inoperative. Normal children rapidly learned the requisite behavior and created an unusally beneficent environment for themselves. On the other hand, the schizophrenic children, who failed to master this simple skill, experienced the same potentially rewarding environment as a depriving and emotionally disturbing place.

In the preceding examples, the features of the potential environment were highly restricted. Social environments, on the other hand, provide a much greater latitude for creating contingencies that can in turn affect one's own behavior. People can converse on a multiplicity of topics, they can do a variety of things, and in other ways their potential range of responsiveness is exceedingly broad. In a given social interaction the behaviors of the participants largely determine which aspects of their respective repertoires are actualized and which remain unexpressed. Some people bring out the best in others, while other individuals have a talent for bringing out the worst in those with whom they interact.

In examining sequential interchanges between children, Rausch [1965] found that the immediately preceding act of one person was the major determinant of the other person's response. In approximately 75 per cent of the instances, hostile behavior elicited unfriendly responses, whereas cordial antecedent acts seldom did. Aggressive children thus created through their actions a hostile environment, whereas children who displayed friendly interpersonal modes of response generated an amicable social milieu. With little effort we could readily identify problem-prone individuals with aversive styles of behavior that predictably produce negative social climates wherever they go. Far from being ruled by an imposed environment, people play an active role in constructing their own reinforcement contingencies through their characteristic modes of response.

It might be argued that if each person partly creates his own environment there is no one remaining to be influenced. This apparent paradox overlooks the fact that reciprocity is rarely perfect because one's behavior is not the sole determinant of subsequent events. Situational factors, the roles that people occupy, and other considerations partly determine what one can or cannot do in response to the actions of others. Furthermore, controlling and counteracting influences usually occur in an alternating pattern, rather than concurrently, until each participant gets what he wants.

The operation of reciprocal reinforcement processes in the unwitting production of troublesome child behavior illustrates the point. On most occasions children's mild requests go unheeded because the parent is disinterested or preoccupied with other activities. If further bids also go unrewarded, the child will generally display progressively more intense behavior that becomes increasingly aversive to the parent. At this stage in the interaction sequence the child is exercising aversive control over the parent. Eventually the parent is forced to terminate the troublesome behavior by attending to the child, thereby reinforcing obstreperous responsiveness. Since the child gains parental attention and the parent gains temporary peace, the behavior of both participants is rewarded, although the long-term effects benefit neither. As shown in this example, detrimental reciprocal systems are often unknowingly created and mutually sustained when particular social practices evoke deviant behavior, which, due to its aversive properties, creates the very conditions likely to perpetuate it.

Interpersonal difficulties are most likely to arise when a person has developed a narrow range of effective behaviors and must thereby rely on coercive methods to force desired actions from others. Nagging complaints, aggressiveness, thinly veiled threats, helplessness, sick-role behavior, and emotional expressions of rejection, suffering, and distress are compelling means of controlling others, especially if the relationship involves some mutual dependence. The manner in which one treats conditions of this sort differs substantially, depending on whether such behaviors are viewed as by-products of intrapsychic disturbances or in terms of their functional value in influencing the responsiveness of others. Deleterious reciprocal interactions are most effectively modified by withdrawing the reinforcement supporting coercive behavior and by developing more constructive means of securing desired reactions from others.

Because social control involves a two-way process, it is exceedingly doubtful that the *Brave New Worlds* and the *1984*s will ever be attainable, even as knowledge about the conditions governing human behavior increases. Wherever you have controllers you have countercontrollers as well. Both parties usually experience some feeling of powerlessness in achieving the outcomes they desire. Parents voice discouragement because they cannot get their children to follow their wishes, whereas children feel constrained by their parents from doing what they want. At universities the administrators, faculty, students, and alumni all feel that the other constituencies are unduly influential but that they themselves have insufficient power to alter the institutional practices. In government functioning Congress feels that the executive branch has excessive power, and conversely the executive branch feels thwarted in achieving its programs by congressional countercontrol. Whatever the levels of interaction might be, no one party is able to manipulate the other at will. Indeed, reciprocal influence systems are protected by legal and social codes designed to prevent easy use of imperious control with impunity.

BIBLIOGRAPHY

Justin Aronfreed, "The Origin of Self-Criticism." *Psychological Review*, 1964, 71:193–218.

Teodoro Ayllon and E. Haughton, "Control of the Behavior of Schizophrenic Patients by Food." *Journal of the Experimental Analysis of Behavior*, 1962, 5:343–352.

Teodoro Ayllon and Jack Michael, "The Psychiatric Nurse as a Behavioral Engineer." *Journal of the Experimental Analysis of Behavior*, 1959, 2:323–334.

Donald M. Baer and James A. Sherman, "Reinforcement Control of Generalized Imitation in Young Children." *Journal of Experimental Child Psychology*, 1964, 1:37–49.

Albert Bandura, "Social Learning through Imitation." In Marshall R. Jones, ed., *Nebraska Symposium on Motivation: 1962*. University of Nebraska Press, 1962.

Albert Bandura, "Influence of Models' Reinforcement Contingencies on the Acquisition of Imitative Responses." *Journal of Personality and Social Psychology*, 1965, 1:589–595.

Albert Bandura, *Principles of Behavior Modification*. Holt, Rinehart & Winston, 1969a.

Albert Bandura, "Social-Learning Theory of Identificatory Processes." In David A. Goslin, ed., *Handbook of Socialization Theory and Research*. Rand McNally, 1969b.

Albert Bandura, "Psychotherapy Based upon Modeling Principles." In Allen E. Bergin and Sol L. Garfield, eds., *Handbook of Psychotherapy and Behavior Change*. Wiley, 1971a.

Albert Bandura, ed., *Psychological Modeling: Conflicting Theories*. Aldine Atherton, 1971b.

Albert Bandura, "Vicarious and Self-Reinforcement Processes." In Robert Glaser, ed., *The Nature of Reinforcement*. Merrill, 1971c.

Albert Bandura and Peter G. Barab, "Conditions Governing Nonreinforced Imitation." *Developmental Psychology*, 1971, in press.

Albert Bandura, Edward B. Blanchard, and Brunhilde Ritter, "The Relative Efficacy of Desensitization and Modeling Approaches for Inducing Behavioral, Affective, and Attitudinal Changes." *Journal of Personality and Social Psychology*, 1969, 13:173–199.

Albert Bandura, Joan E. Grusec, and Frances L. Menlove, "Observational Learning as a Function of Symbolization and Incentive Set." *Child Development*, 1966, 37:499–506.

Albert Bandura, Joan E. Grusec, and Frances L. Menlove, "Some Social Determinants of Self-Monitoring Reinforcement Systems." *Journal of Personality and Social Psychology*, 1967, 5:449–455.

Albert Bandura and Mary B. Harris, "Modification of Syntactic Style." *Journal of Experimental Child Psychology*, 1966, 4:341–352.

Albert Bandura and Robert Jeffery, *"Role of Symbolic Coding and Rehearsal Processes in Observational Learning."* Unpublished manuscript, Stanford University, 1971.

Albert Bandura and Carol J. Kupers, "The Transmission of Patterns of Self-Reinforcement through Modeling." *Journal of Abnormal and Social Psychology*, 1964, 69:1–9.

Albert Bandura and Frederick J. McDonald, "The Influence of Social Reinforcement and the Behavior of Models in Shaping Children's Moral Judgments." *Journal of Abnormal and Social Psychology*, 1963, 67:274–281.

Albert Bandura and Walter Mischel, "Modification of Self-Imposed Delay of Reward through Exposure to Live and Symbolic Models." *Journal of Personality and Social Psychology*, 1965, 2:698–705.

Albert Bandura and Bernard Perloff, "Relative Efficacy of Self-Monitored and Externally-Imposed Reinforcement Systems." *Journal of Personality and Social Psychology*, 1967, 7:111–116.

Albert Bandura and Ted L. Rosenthal, "Vicarious Classical Conditioning as a Function of Arousal Level." *Journal of Personality and Social Psychology*, 1966, 3:54–62.

Albert Bandura, Dorothea Ross, and Sheila A. Ross, "Imitation of Film-Mediated Aggressive Models." *Journal of Abnormal and Social Pyschology*, 1963a, 66:3–11.

Albert Bandura, Dorothea Ross, and Sheila A. Ross, "A Comparative Test of the Status Envy, Social Power, and Secondary Reinforcement Theories of Identificatory Learning." *Journal of Abnormal and Social Psychology*, 1963b, 67:527–534.

Albert Bandura and Carol K. Whalen, "The Influence of Antecedent Reinforcement and Divergent Modeling Cues on Patterns of Self-Reward." *Journal of Personality and Social Psychology*, 1966, 3:373–382.

Theodore X. Barber and Karl W. Hahn, Jr., "Experimental Studies in 'Hypnotic' Behavior: Physiological and Subjective Effects of Imagined Pain." *Journal of Nervous and Mental Disease*, 1964, 139:416–425.

Gregory Bateson, ed., *Perceval's Narrative: A Patient's Account of His Psychosis, 1830–1832*. Stanford University Press, 1961.

Alan A. Benton, "Effects of the Timing of Negative Response Consequences on the Observational Learning of Resistance to Temptation in Children." *Dissertation Abstracts*, 1967, 27:2153–2154.

Seymour M. Berger, "Incidental Learning Through Vicarious Reinforcement." *Psychological Reports*, 1961, 9:477–491.

Seymour M. Berger, "Conditioning through Vicarious Instigation." *Psychological Review*, 1962, 69:450–466.

Seymour M. Berger and Sandra L. Johansson, "Effect of a Model's Expressed Emotions on an Observer's Resistance to Extinction." *Journal of Personality and Social Psychology*, 1968, 10:53–58.

Allen E. Bergin, "Some Implications of Psychotherapy Research for Therapeutic Practice." *Journal of Abnormal Psychology*, 1966, 71:235–246.

L. M. Boyd, "Most Disappointed Men in the World." *San Francisco Chronicle*, March 15, 1969.

Wagner H. Bridger and Irwin J. Mandel, "A Comparison of GSR Fear Responses Produced by Threat and Electric Shock." *Journal of Psychiatric Research*, 1964, 2:31–40.

James L. Bruning, "Direct and Vicarious Effects of a Shift in Magnitude of Reward on Performance." *Journal of Personality and Social Psychology*, 1965, 2:278–282.

T. Budzynski, J. Stoyva, and C. Adler, "Feedback-Induced Muscle Relaxation: Application to Tension Headache." *Journal of Behavior Therapy and Experimental Psychiatry*, 1970, 1:205–211.

Donald T. Campbell, "Conformity in Psychology's Theories of Acquired Behavioral Dispositions." In Irwin A. Berg and Bernard M. Bass, eds., *Conformity and Deviation*. Harper, 1961.

Randall M. Chambers, "Effects of Intravenous Glucose Injections on Learning, General Activity, and Hunger Drive." *Journal of Comparative and Physiological Psychology*, 1956, 49:558–564.

Bishwa B. Chatterjee and Charles W. Eriksen, "Cognitive Factors in Heart Rate Conditioning." *Journal of Experimental Psychology*, 1962, 64:272–279.

Russell M. Church, "Emotional Reactions of Rats to the Pain of Others." *Journal of Comparative and Physiological Psychology*, 1959, 52:132–134.

Brian Coates and Willard W. Hartup, "Age and Verbalization in Observational Learning." *Developmental Psychology*, 1969, 1:556–562.

K. N. Condrell, "Vicarious Learning of a Discrimination Learning Problem as a Function of Reinforcement and Set." *Dissertation Abstracts*, 1967, 28:1221.

Harold W. Coppock and Randall M. Chambers, "Reinforcement of Position Preference by Automatic Intravenous Injections of Glucose." *Journal of Comparative and Physiological Psychology*, 1954, 47:355–357.

Harold W. Coppock, C. P. Headlee, and W. R. Hood, "Negative Reinforcing Effects of Insulin Injections." *American Psychologist*, 1953, 8:337.

Philip A. Cowan, Jonas Langer, Judith Heavenrich, and Marjorie Nathanson, "Social Learning and Piaget's Cognitive Theory of Moral Development." *Journal of Personality and Social Psychology*, 1969, 11:261–274.

Kenneth D. Craig and Malcolm S. Weinstein, "Conditioning Vicarious Affective Arousal." *Psychological Reports*, 1965, 17:955–963.

Judith L. Crooks, "Observational Learning of Fear in Monkeys." Unpublished manuscript, University of Pennsylvania, 1967.

J. P. Das and P. C. Nanda, "Mediated Transfer of Attitudes." *Journal of Abnormal and Social Psychology*, 1963, 66:12–16.

Michael E. Dawson, "Comparison of Classical Conditioning and Relational Learning." Unpublished MA thesis, University of Southern California, 1966.

Michael E. Dawson and William W. Grings, "Comparison of Classical Conditioning and Relational Learning." *Journal of Experimental Psychology*, 1968, 76:227–231.

Michael E. Dawson and James H. Satterfield, "Can Human GSR Conditioning Occur without Relational Learning?" *Proceedings of the American Psychological Association*, 1969, 69–70.

E. Dekker and J. Groen, "Reproducible Psychogenic Attacks of Asthma: a Laboratory Study." *Journal of Psychosomatic Research*, 1956, 1:58–67.

E. Dekker, H. E. Pelser, and J. Groen, "Conditioning as a Cause of Asthmatic Attacks." *Journal of Psychosomatic Research*, 1957, 2:97–108.

Raymond Ditrichs, Seymore Simon, and Barry Greene, "Effect of Vicarious Scheduling on the Verbal Conditioning of Hostility in Children." *Journal of Personality and Social Psychology*, 1967, 6:71–78.

Donelson E. Dulany, "The Place of Hypotheses and Intentions: an Analysis of Verbal Control in Verbal Conditioning." In Charles W. Eriksen, ed., *Behavior and Awareness—A Symposium of Research and Interpretation*. Duke University Press, 1962.

Donelson E. Dulany, "Awareness, Rules, and Propositional Control: a Confrontation with S-R Behavior Theory." In Theodore R. Dixon and David L. Horton, eds., *Verbal Behavior and General Behavior Theory*. Prentice-Hall, 1968.

Donelson E. Dulany and Daniel C. O'Connell, "Does Partial Reinforcement Dissociate Verbal Rules and the Behavior They Might be Presumed to Control?" *Journal of Verbal Learning and Verbal Behavior*, 1963, 2:361–372.

Joseph W. Eaton and Robert J. Weil, *Culture and Mental Disorders*. Free Press, 1955.

Charles W. Eriksen and James L. Kuethe, "Avoidance Conditioning of Verbal Behavior Without Awareness: a Paradigm of Repression." *Journal of Abnormal and Social Psychology*, 1956, 53:203–209.

Charles B. Ferster, John I. Nurnberger, and Eugene B. Levitt, The Control of Eating." *Journal of Mathetics*, 1962, 1:87–109.

Charles B. Ferster and B. F. Skinner, *Schedules of Reinforcement*. Appleton, 1957.

James P. Flanders, "A Review of Research on Imitative Behavior." *Psychological Bulletin*, 1968, 69:316–337.

Cyril M. Franks. *Behavior Therapy*. McGraw-Hill, 1969.

Marcus J. Fuhrer and Paul E. Baer, "Differential Classical Conditioning: Verbalization of Stimulus Contingencies." *Science*, 1965, 150:1479–1481.

Elliot N. Gale and Marsha B. Jacobson, "The Relationship between Social Comments as Unconditioned Stimuli and Fear Responding." *Behaviour Research and Therapy*, 1970, 8:301–307.

James H. Geer, "A Test of the Classical Conditioning Model of Emotion: the Use of Nonpainful Aversive Stimuli as Unconditioned Stimuli in a Conditioning Procedure." *Journal of Personality and Social Psychology*, 1968, 10:148–156.

Marvin S. Gerst, "Symbolic Coding Processes in Observational Learning." *Journal of Personality and Social Psychology*, 1971, 19:7–17.

Jacob L. Gewirtz and Karen G. Stingle, "Learning of Generalized Imitation as the Basis for Identification." *Psychological Review*, 1968, 75:374–397.

E. L. Glynn, "Classroom Applications of Self-Determined Reinforcement." *Journal of Applied Behavior Analysis*, 1970, 123–132.

G. R. Goodlet and M. M. Goodlet, "Efficiency of Self-Monitored and Externally Imposed Schedules of Reinforcement in Controlling Disruptive Behavior." Unpublished manuscript, University of Guelph, 1969.

William W. Grings and Russell A. Lockhart, "Effects of 'Anxiety-Lessening' Instructions and Differential Set Development on the Extinction of GSR." *Journal of Experimental Psychology,* 1963, 66:292–299.

Robert F. Grose, "A Comparison of Vocal and Subvocal Conditioning of the Galvanic Skin Response." Unpublished doctoral dissertation, Yale University, 1952.

Florence R. Harris, Montrose M. Wolf, and Donald M. Baer, "Effects of Adult Social Reinforcement on Child Behavior." *Young Children,* 1964, 20:8–17.

Mary B. Harris, "A Self-Directed Program for Weight Control: a Pilot Study." *Journal of Abnormal Psychology,* 1969, 74:263–270.

Albert H. Hastorf, "The 'Reinforcement' of Individual Actions in a Group Situation." In Leonard Krasner and Leonard P. Ullmann, eds., *Research in Behavior Modification.* Holt, Rinehart & Winston, 1965.

Ralph F. Hefferline and Brian Keenan, "Amplitude-Induction Gradient of a Small-Scale (Covert) Operant." *Journal of the Experimental Analysis of Behavior,* 1963, 6:307–315.

Ralph F. Hefferline, Brian Keenan, and Richard A. Harford, "Escape and Avoidance Conditioning in Human Subjects without Their Observation of the Response." *Science,* 1959, 130:1338–1339.

Raúl Hernández-Péon, Harold Scherrer, and Michel Jouvet, "Modification of Electric Activity in Cochlear Nucleus during 'Attention' in Unanesthetized Cats." *Science,* 1956, 23:331–332.

W. A. Hillix and Melvin H. Marx, "Response Strengthening by Information and Effect on Human Learning." *Journal of Experimental Psychology,* 1960, 60:97–102.

G. Horn, "Electrical Activity of the Cerebral Cortex of the Unanesthetized Cat during Attentive Behavior." *Brain,* 1960, 83:57–76.

Charles C. Hughes, Marc-Abelard Tremblay, Robert N. Rapoport, and Alexander H. Leighton, *People of Cove and Woodlot: Communities from the Viewpoint of Social Psychiatry.* Basic Books, 1960.

Chester A. Insko and William F. Oakes, "Awareness and the 'Conditioning' of Attitudes." *Journal of Personality and Social Psychology,* 1966, 4:487–496.

E. Roy John, *Mechanisms of Memory.* Academic, 1967.

Joe Kamiya, "Conscious Control of Brain Waves." *Psychology Today,* 1968, 1(11):57–61.

Frederick H. Kanfer and Albert R. Marston, "Determinants of Self-Reinforcement in Human Learning." *Journal of Experimental Psychology,* 1963, 66:245–254.

Arnold Kaufman, Alan Baron, and Rosemarie E. Kopp, "Some Effects of Instructions on Human Operant Behavior." *Psychonomic Monograph Supplements,* 1966, 1:243–250.

Thomas D. Kennedy, "Verbal Conditioning Without Awareness: the Use of Programmed Reinforcement and Recurring Assessment of Awareness." *Journal of Experimental Psychology,* 1970, 84:484–494.

Thomas D. Kennedy, "Reinforcement Frequency, Task Characteristics, and Interval of Awareness Assessment as Factors in Verbal Conditioning Without Awareness." *Journal of Experimental Psychology,* 1971, 88:103–112.

Gregory A. Kimble, *Hilgard and Marquis' Conditioning and Learning.* Appleton-Century-Crofts, 1961.

Monroe Lefkowitz, Robert Rogers Blake, and Jane S. Mouton, "Status Factors in Pedestrian Violation of Traffic Signals." *Journal of Abnormal and Social Psychology,* 1955, 51:704–705.

Robert M. Liebert, Richard D. Odom, Jae H. Hill, and R. L. Huff, "Effects of Age and Rule Familiarity on the Production of Modeled Language Constructions." *Developmental Psychology,* 1969, 1:108–112.

Richard H. Lindley and Kenneth E. Moyer, "Effects of Instructions on the Extinction of a Conditioned Finger-Withdrawal Response." *Journal of Experimental Psychology,* 1961, 61:82–88.

Ronald R. Lippitt, Norman Polansky, and Sidney Rosen, "The Dynamics of Power." *Human Relations,* 1952, 5:37–64.

Armin Loeb, Aaron T. Beck, James C. Diggory, and Robert Tuthill, "Expectancy, Level of Aspiration, Performance, and Self-Evaluation in Depression." *Proceedings of the 75th Annual Convention of the American Psychological Association,* 1967, 2:193–194.

O. Ivar Lovaas, "A Behavior Therapy Approach to the Treatment of Childhood Schizophrenia." In J. P. Hill, ed., *Minnesota Symposia on Child Psychology,* vol. 1. University of Minnesota Press, 1967.

Thomas C. Lovitt and Karen A. Curtis, "Academic Response Rate as a Function of Teacher- and Self-Imposed Contingencies." *Journal of Applied Behavior Analysis,* 1969, 2:49–53.

Arthur A. Lumsdaine, ed., *Student Response in Programmed Instruction.* National Academy of Sciences–National Research Council, 1961.

John W. McDavid, "Effects of Ambiguity of Imitative Cues upon Learning by Observation." *Journal of Social Psychology,* 1964, 62:165–174.

R. J. McGuire, J. M. Carlisle, and B. G. Young, "Sexual Deviations as Conditioned Behavior: a Hypothesis." *Behavior Research and Therapy,* 1965, 2:185–190.

Michael J. McMains and Robert M. Liebert, "Influence of Discrepancies between Successively Modeled Self-Reward Criteria on the Adoption of a Self-Imposed Standard." *Journal of Personality and Social Psychology,* 1968, 8:166–171.

Irwin J. Mandel and Wagner H. Bridger, "Interaction between Instructions and ISI in Conditioning and Extinction of the GSR." *Journal of Experimental Psychology,* 1967, 74:36–43.

Isaac M. Marks and Michael G. Gelder, "Transvestism and Fetishism: Clinical and Psychological Changes during Faradic Aversion." *British Journal of Psychiatry,* 1967, 113:711–729.

Gordon A. Marlatt, "Vicarious and Direct Reinforcement Control of Verbal Behavior in an Interview Setting." Unpublished doctoral dissertation, Indiana University, 1968.

J. Marmor, "Psychoanalytic Therapy as an Educational Process: Common Denominators in the Therapeutic Approaches of Different Psychoanalytic 'Schools'." In Jules H. Masserman, ed., *Science and Psychoanalysis.* vol. 5, *Psychoanalytic Education.* Grune & Stratton, 1962.

Albert R. Marston, "Imitation, Self-Reinforcement, and Reinforcement of Another Person." *Journal of Personality and Social Psychology*, 1965a, 2:255–261.

Albert R. Marston, "Self Reinforcement: the Relevance of a Concept in Analogue Research in Psychotherapy." *Psychotherapy: Theory, Research and Practice*, 1965b, 2:1–5.

Donald N. Michael and Nathan Maccoby, "Factors Influencing the Effects of Student Participation on Verbal Learning from Films: Motivating versus Practice Effects, 'Feedback,' and Overt versus Covert Responding." In Arthur A. Lumsdaine, ed., *Student Response in Programmed Instruction*. National Academy of Sciences–National Research Council, 1961.

Neal E. Miller, "Studies of Fear as an Acquirable Drive: I. Fear as Motivation and Fear-Reduction as Reinforcement in the Learning of New Responses." *Journal of Experimental Psychology*, 1948, 38:89–101.

Neal E. Miller, "Learnable Drives and Rewards." In S. S. Stevens, ed., *Handbook of Experimental Psychology*. Wiley, 1951.

Neal E. Miller, "Learning of Visceral and Glandular Responses." *Science*, 1969, 163:434–445.

Neal E. Miller, Leo V. Di Cara, Henry Solomon, Jay M. Weiss, and Barry Dworkin, "Learned Modifications of Autonomic Functions: a Review and Some New Data." *Circulation Research*, Supplement I, 26 & 27, 1970; 3–11.

Neal E. Miller and John Dollard, *Social Learning and Imitation*. Yale University Press, 1941.

Walter Mischel, *Personality and Assessment*. Wiley, 1968.

Walter Mischel and Robert M. Liebert, "Effects of Discrepancies between Observed and Imposed Reward Criteria on Their Acquisition and Transmission." *Journal of Personality and Social Psychology*, 1966, 3:45–53.

Don Moser, "Screams, Slaps, and Love." *Life*, May 7, 1965, 90A–101.

Kenneth E. Moyer and Richard H. Lindley, "Supplementary Report: Effects of Instructions on Extinction and Recovery of a Conditioned Avoidance Response." *Journal of Experimental Psychology*, 1962, 64: 95–96.

Edward James Murray, "A Content-Analysis Method for Studying Psychotherapy." *Psychological Monographs*, 1956, 70(13), whole no. 420.

Joseph M. Notterman, William N. Schoenfeld, and Philip J. Bersh, "A Comparison of Three Extinction Procedures Following Heart Rate Conditioning." *Journal of Abnormal and Social Psychology*, 1952, 47:674–677.

Edwin P. Parker, "Information Utilities and Mass Communication." In Harold Sackman and Norman Nie, eds., *Information Utility and Social Choice*. AFIPS Press, 1970.

Catherine R. Porro, "Effects of the Observation of a Model's Affective Responses to Her Own Transgression on Resistance to Temptation in Children." *Dissertation Abstracts*, 1968, 28:3064.

Leo Postman and Julius Sassenrath, "The Automatic Action of Verbal Rewards and Punishments." *Journal of General Psychology*, 1961, 65:109–136.

Stanley Rachman, "Sexual Fetishism: an Experimental Analogue." *Psychological Record*, 1966, 16:293–296.

Harold L. Rausch, "Interaction Sequences." *Journal of Personality and Social Psychology*, 1965, 2:487–499.

Gregory Razran, "The Observable Unconscious and the Inferable Conscious in Current Soviet Psychophysiology." *Psychological Review*, 1961, 68:81–147.

William J. Redd and Jay S. Birnbrauer, "Adults as Discriminative Stimuli for Different Reinforcement Contingencies with Retarded Children." *Journal of Experimental Child Psychology*, 1969, 7:440–447.

David Riesman, *The Lonely Crowd*. Yale University Press, 1950.

Mary A. Rosekrans and Willard W. Hartup, "Imitative Influences of Consistent and Inconsistent Response Consequences to a Model on Aggressive Behavior in Children." *Journal of Personality and Social Psychology*, 1967, 7:429–434.

Gerald Rosenbaum, "Stimulus Generalization as a Function of Level of Experimentally Induced Anxiety." *Journal of Experimental Psychology*, 1953, 45:35–43.

Gerald Rosenbaum, "Stimulus Generalization as a Function of Clinical Anxiety," *Journal of Abnormal and Social Psychology*, 1956, 53:281–285.

Milton E. Rosenbaum, "The Effect of Stimulus and Background Factors on the Volunteering Response." *Journal of Abnormal and Social Psychology*, 1956, 53:118–121.

Milton E. Rosenbaum and James L. Bruning, "Direct and Vicarious effects of Variations in Percentage of Reinforcement on Performance." *Child Development*, 1966, 37:959–966.

Milton E. Rosenbaum and Oliver J. Hewitt, "The Effect of Electric Shock on Learning by Performers and Observers." *Psychonomic Science*, 1966 5:81–82.

David Rosenhan, F. Frederick, and Anne Burrowes "Preaching and Practicing: Effects of Channel Discrepancy on Norm Internalization." *Child Development*, 1968, 39:291–301.

Ted L. Rosenthal and Joan S. Whitebook, "Incentives versus Instructions in Transmitting Grammatical Parameters with Experimenter as Model." *Behaviour Research and Therapy*, 1970, 8:189–196.

Ted L. Rosenthal and Barry J. Zimmerman, "Modeling by Exemplification and Instruction in Training Conservation." Unpublished manuscript, University of Arizona, 1970.

Ted L. Rosenthal, Barry J. Zimmerman, and Kathleen Durning, "Observationally-Induced Changes in Children's Interrogative Classes." *Journal of Personality and Social Psychology*, 1970, 16:681–688.

Jack Sandler and John Quagliano, "Punishment is a Signal Avoidance Situation." Paper read at Southeastern Psychological Association meeting, Gatlinburg, Tenn., 1964.

Robert M. Sasmor, "Operant Conditioning of a Small-Scale Muscle Response." *Journal of the Experimental Analysis of Behavior*, 1966, 9:69–85.

M. Sidman, "Avoidance Behavior." In Werner K. Honig, ed., *Operant Behavior*. Appleton-Century-Crofts, 1966.

B. F. Skinner, *Science and Human Behavior*. Macmillan, 1953.

Henry Slucki, Gyorgi Adam, and Robert W. Porter, "Operant Discrimination of an Interoceptive Stimulus in Rhesus Monkeys." *Journal of the Experimental Analysis of Behavior*, 1965, 8:405–414.

Charles D. Spielberger and L. Douglas De Nike, "Descriptive Behaviorism versus Cognitive Theory in Verbal Operant Conditioning." *Psychological Review,* 1966, 73:306–326.

Arthur W. Staats and Carolyn K. Staats, "Attitudes Established by Classical Conditioning." *Journal of Abnormal and Social Psychology,* 1958, 57:37–40.

Carolyn K. Staats and Arthur W. Staats, "Meaning Established by Classical Conditioning." *Journal of Experimental Psychology,* 1957, 54:74–80.

Lewis J. Stone and Jack E. Hokanson, "Arousal Reduction via Self-Punitive Behavior." *Journal of Personality and Social Psychology,* 1969, 12:72–79.

Richard B. Stuart, "Behavioral Control of Overeating." *Behaviour Research and Therapy,* 1967, 5:357–365.

J. S. Stumphauzer, "Increased Delay of Gratification in Young Prison Inmates through Imitation of High-Delay Peer-Models." Unpublished doctoral dissertation, Florida State University, 1969.

Edmund V. Sullivan. "The Acquisition of Conservation of Substance through Film-Mediated Models." In D. W. Brison and Edmund V. Sullivan, eds., *Recent Research on the Acquisition of Conservation of Substance, Education Monograph.* Toronto: Ontario Institute for Studies in Education, 1967.

Charles B. Truax, "Reinforcement and Nonreinforcement in Rogerian Psychotherapy." *Journal of Abnormal Psychology,* 1966, 71:1–9.

Richard H. Walters, Marion Leat, and Louis Mezei, "Inhibition and Disinhibition of Responses through Empathetic Learning." *Canadian Journal of Psychology,* 1963, 17:235–243.

Richard H. Walters and Ross D. Parke, "Influence of Response Consequences to a Social Model on Resistance to Deviation." *Journal of Experimental Child Psychology,* 1964, 1:269–280.

Richard H. Walters, Ross D. Parke, and Valerie A. Cane, "Timing of Punishment and the Observation of Consequences to Others as Determinants of Response Inhibition." *Journal of Experimental Child Psychology,* 1965, 2:10–30.

D. Walton and M. D. Mather, "The Application of Learning Principles to the Treatment of Obsessive-Compulsive States in the Acute and Chronic Phases of Illness." *Behaviour Research and Therapy,* 1963, 1:163–174.

John B. Watson and Rosalie Rayner, "Conditioned Emotional Reactions." *Journal of Experimental Psychology,* 1920, 3:1–14.

Harold Weiner, "Real and Imagined Cost Effects upon Human Fixed-Interval Responding." *Psychological Reports,* 1965, 17:659–662.

Alfred E. Weisz and Robert L. Taylor, "American Presidential Assassinations." In David N. Daniels, Marshall F. Gilula, and Frank M. Ochberg, eds., *Violence and the Struggle for Existence.* Little, Brown, 1970.

Delos D. Wickens, Charles K. Allen, and Frances A. Hill, "Effects of Instruction and UCS Strength on Extinction of the Conditioned GSR." *Journal of Experimental Psychology,* 1963, 66:235–240.

William C. Wilson, "Imitation and Learning of Incidental Cues by Preschool Children." *Child Development,* 1958, 29:393–397.

2

Anxiety and Clinical Problems: Systematic Desensitization and Related Techniques

GORDON L. PAUL
University of Illinois at Urbana-Champaign
DOUGLAS A. BERNSTEIN
University of Illinois at Urbana-Champaign

Systematic desensitization refers to a package of therapeutic procedures developed to treat problems in which maladaptive conditioned anxiety is central. "Anxiety" and related escape or avoidance behaviors ("defense mechanisms") have traditionally been considered the major component of problems exhibited by people suffering from "psychoneurotic" or "acute psychotic" reactions. The empirical and theoretical contributions leading to our present understanding of anxiety, and related diagnostic and therapeutic procedures, however, have largely culminated in the past twenty years.

Before presenting the conceptual background for systematic desensitization and related techniques, several features of terminology used in this paper should be made clear: First of all, the term "behavior" simply refers to the organism's activity. Thus "behavior" encompasses physiological and emotional activity and cognitive and ideational activity as well as motoric activity. Second, most of the terms describing human behavior, and terms such as "principles of learning or performance," "stimulus," and "response," refer to functional relationships among phenomena rather than to static properties of objects or activities. Finally, "explanatory" concepts regarding fully developed human behavior are necessarily hypotheses rather than facts. While we attempt to stay at an empirical–descriptive level as much as possible, we have explicitly invoked a *utility criterion* in our alternative explanatory constructs and principles. That is, our conceptualizations are based on constructs and principles that we have found provide maximum utility by most adequately accounting for known facts of human and animal behavior, while simultaneously suggesting principles and procedures for the clinical task of changing human behavior. Such an approach results in the belief that a combination of functional learning principles, physiological responses, and genetic factors can "explain" behavior, normal and abnormal, as well as or better than any other available conceptual system, and to date provides greater clinical utility [Paul 1969d].

We wish to apologize at the outset for the rather "heavy" nature of much of the material to be covered. Human beings are complex organisms who can get fouled up in many ways. Any approximation to understanding how we can get disarranged in relationship to anxiety, and consequently how we may get "straightened out" again, necessarily deals with complex factors and interrelationships. A glossary summarizing basic terminology and principles of functional learning and performance is included in an appendix to aid the reader in wading through the more technical aspects. We believe the material we are presenting will assist you in understanding many aspects of human behavior and show the exciting developments in clinical treatment that have occurred in recent years.

A Conceptual Model for Anxiety and Associated Clinical Problems

Nearly everyone has at some time experienced an emotion he calls anxiety. Precise agreement about what we really mean by the term, however, is not easy. The difficulty of definition stems from the fact that "anxiety" is not a single, unitary "thing" that a person either "has" or does not "have." It is also necessary to distinguish among those conditions or events that produce anxiety (the eliciting stimuli), the resulting physiological and cognitive reactions of the individual (the anxiety response), and cognitive or motor behaviors invoked to reduce or prevent anxiety reactions (escape and avoidance behavior). Finally, because of frequent confusion in both technical and everyday language, we must distinguish between anxiety as a state and anxiety as a personality trait. Our coverage here is sufficient only to give an orientation to the nature of problems we discuss later. Charles D. Spielberger's 1966 anthology *Anxiety and Behavior* (especially the chapters by Spielberger, Malmo, Wolpe, Schacter, Mandler and Watson, Spence and Spence, and Eriksen) provides a more detailed coverage of the vast literature on anxiety and references to original sources.

Physiological Arousal and the Ascending Reticular Activating System (ARAS)

We shall consider "anxiety," as have others, a shorthand term for a very complex pattern of *response*, characterized by subjective feelings of apprehension and tension associated with physiological arousal involving the sympathetic branch of the autonomic nervous system. In 1951 Lindsley reported a series of electrophysiological studies of the central nervous system related to physiological arousal. (Note that *physiological arousal* in reference to anxiety should not be confused with sexual arousal, which Masters and Johnson found involves predominantly the parasympathetic branch of the autonomic nervous system in early stages before orgasm, and the sympathetic branch only later.) Lindsley's investigations were directed toward the brain stem reticular formation, a diffuse multineuronal pathway receiving collaterals from both ascending and descending nerve tracts and projecting through subcortical structures directly to the cortex. He found that brain stem stimulation produced shifts in behavior from drowsiness to vigilance and alertness, while progressive destruction produced shifts toward drowsiness and inertia to the point where massive stimulation had no effect in rousing the organism. Coinciding with these changes in motor behavior, recordings of "brain waves" on the electroencephalogram (EEG) revealed parallel changes in the cerebral cortex, with shifts from a relaxed cortex to an activated cortex accompanying stimulation of the reticular formation, and shifts in the opposite direction accompanying progressive destruction. Lindsley called the reticular–cortical matrix the Ascending Reticular Activating System (ARAS), since the intensity of cortical arousal appeared to be correlated with the output from the ARAS. He further proposed a dimension of physiological arousal in which behavioral intensity paralleled EEG activation, ranging from coma or deep sleep through relaxed states to alert attentiveness, finally culminating in agitation, excitement, or panic with a flooding cortical stimulation.

Further research by Malmo and many other physiological psychologists found that levels of cortical activation are related to a variety of physiological activity mediated by the autonomic nervous system: heart rate, blood volume, skin temperature, sweat gland activity, respiration, pupillary changes, hormonal changes, gastrointestinal activity, muscle tremors, muscle tension, and the like. Lindsley and Malmo observed that return circuits from cortical and subcortical areas of the brain also provided a basis for activation and inhibition of the ARAS. Thus physiological arousal need not depend only on sensory impulses from external stimuli, but could result from higher level symbolization and thinking in humans—from ideas, images, and the perceptual discriminations of the present or from those of the past stored as memories. As an example of this, it is not uncommon to hear someone say,

"I get scared all over again just thinking about it." Similarly, people with strong anxiety reactions to specific objects are often upset by the mere thought of that object, even if it is not nearby.

Arousal and Behavioral Efficiency

The significance of the arousal dimension was readily appreciated by psychologists once its anatomical and behavioral correlates had been outlined. Two applications were particularly important because they unified a mass of theoretical and empirical data that had obvious relevance for understanding human behavior. In particular, this nonspecific energizing system (the ARAS) provided a physiological basis for the learning concept of drive [Hebb 1955] and what we call affective behavior or emotion [Schacter 1964]. From the drive aspect, the efficiency of cognitive and motoric learning and performance has been found to be a function of the existing level of drive or physiological arousal. For any given task, the quality of an individual's performance seems to bear an "inverted-U" relationship to the level of arousal (see curve A, figure 1).

Over a broad plateau of medium-range arousal, behavioral efficiency is optimized with sufficient energization to maintain effort, attention, instrumental acts, necessary discriminations, and so on, for either acquiring new knowledge and behaviors or performing previously learned skills and habits. An arousal level less than, or more than, the optimum level for a given task impairs performance. Thus at the low end of the arousal curve, the individual is simply too lethargic, drowsy, or turned off to put forth sufficient effort or to attend to the cues necessary to guide his action efficiently. As arousal increases above the optimum level, responses irrelevant to the task also become energized and compete with appropriate goal-oriented behavior, while at the same time generalization gradients are raised, leading to a breakdown of necessary discriminations for efficient regulation. Given sufficient increases in physiological arousal, overenergization of skeletal muscles results in paralysis or "freezing," while cortical flooding results in disorganization and the breakdown of necessary discriminations, eventually leading to unconsciousness or fainting, all obviously incompatible with efficient performance.

Although the inverted-U relationship between arousal and behavioral efficiency presumably holds for nearly all cognitive or motoric tasks, with the exception of the extremes of the arousal dimension, the shape of the inverted-U (peak, breadth, slope) is determined by the difficulty of the task for the individual. Thus the optimal level of arousal, and the degree to which increases or decreases in arousal facilitate or impair performance, depends on the complexity of the task requirements and the stage of practice, skill, or ability of the individual. For what might loosely be called "easy" tasks, that is for very well-learned habits, skills, or associations (a cab driver applying brakes at a red light, a professional ball player hitting a baseball, an Afro-American responding "beautiful" on hearing "black") or for noncomplex tasks (normal adults turning a knob on request, reading numbers from 1 to 10, acquiring a simple, classically conditioned response) the point of optimum arousal is quite high, with less slope and greater breadth along the arousal dimension lower than the optimum, and very steep slope over a narrow range of arousal above the optimum (see curve B, fig. 1). In the latter instances, behavioral output and performance efficiency appear to improve along with increases in drive or physiological arousal until very near the point of cortical flooding, panic, and breakdown of all discriminations. Other tasks, in contrast, can be considered "difficult" for a given individual either because he is in the learning stages that involve many response components or because of competing responses (a high school sophomore applying brakes at a red light the first time he is at the wheel, a neophyte Little Leaguer hitting a baseball the first time at bat, the KKK bigot learning to respond "beautiful" on hearing "black") or because the tasks require many fine discriminations (normal adults reproducing a circle by coordinated knob turning on a child's Etch-A-Sketch, counting backward from 999 by

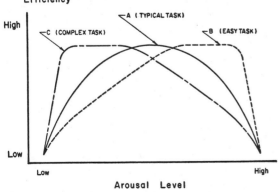

Figure 1. The inverted-U relationship between physiological arousal and behavioral efficiency.

7's, learning to solve second-order differential equations). With complex, difficult tasks, the point of optimum arousal is lowered to a relaxed–attentive level, with less slope and greater breadth along the arousal dimension above the optimum, and steeper slope over a narrower range of arousal below the optimum. With such difficult task demands, behavioral efficiency falls off rapidly with drowsiness or lack of vigilance, but it is also impaired with slight increases in arousal that are considerably lower on an absolute level than those that continue to facilitate performance of easy tasks (see curve C, fig. 1).

Physiological Arousal and Emotion

So far we have been discussing the effects of physiological arousal levels on the quality of performance *during* given degrees of energization from the aspect of drive. In addition, from both drive and emotional aspects, physiological arousal is motivationally related to the nature and directionality of other responses. Under the usual circumstances of living, with sufficient stimulus input from the environment to require some attention but without stressful stimuli, most organisms adapt so as to maintain a moderate level of arousal. Small variations around the adaptation level are experienced as pleasurable and are actively sought out by the organism [Hebb 1955, McClelland 1951]. Those stimulus conditions that produce small changes in physiological arousal from the usual adaptation level may serve as positive reinforcers, motivating instrumental acts to increase contact with those stimuli resulting in either mild increases or decreases in arousal until the organism adapts to the new stimulus conditions. On the other hand, intense levels of physiological arousal are typically experienced as negative emotions, and the stimuli producing such high arousal levels are experienced as aversive. Thus the stimulus conditions that produce extremely high levels of physiological arousal may serve as negative reinforcers, motivating instrumental acts to remove or avoid contact with them.

The effects above of physiological arousal, both in influencing performance and in directing behavior through reinforcing functions, appear to hold for lower mammals as well as for humans. The past social learning history and higher processes of cognition and symbolization of humans, however, play an important role in determining the affective aspects of physiological arousal and the consequent reinforcing properties guiding other behaviors. It has long been known that excitation of the sympathetic branch of the autonomic nervous system, like that occurring in physiological arousal, is characteristic of emotional states. Duffy in 1962 and Schachter in 1964 reviewed much experimental evidence supporting the hypothesis that an emotional state or response consists of a state of physiological arousal and a cognition related to that state of arousal. Given a particular degree of arousal, the person labels and identifies the state on the basis of the precipitating stimulus conditions as interpreted by past experience. Thus, while the degree of arousal present at any given time should bear the same relationship to the quality of performance (inverted–U dependent on task difficulty) no matter what the accompanying emotion, the affective component and resultant reinforcing or guiding functions of eliciting stimuli are quite dependent on associative learning and attribution of the "cause" of physiological arousal.

Extremely high levels of arousal appear to be regularly experienced as aversive or negative emotions and to motivate instrumental or operant behaviors to remove contact with the stimulus conditions eliciting such reactions. The accompanying emotion, however, may be labeled "fear or anxiety," "guilt," "agitated depression," or "anger," depending on the individual's interpretation of the eliciting stimulus conditions, as determined by the cues present in the immediate situation and by prior associative learning. Thus in states involving extreme arousal leading to negative or aversive affects, labeling the state may serve to guide instrumental behaviors in terms of how the individual attempts to remove the eliciting stimuli—escape, avoid, attack, attempt to recover, and the like.

With somewhat lower degrees of physiological arousal, the cognitive interpretation and labeling may result not only in discriminations among negative affects, but perhaps in the arousal state's being labeled positive rather than negative. Thus, depending on prior associative learning and cues in the current situation, the same increase in physiological arousal may be interpreted as pleasant and labeled as "euphoria," "excitement," or "joy," or as an unpleasant emotion such as those associated with extremely high levels of arousal. In this case, the cognitive interpretations leading to "pleasant" or "unpleasant" labels determine the positive or negative reinforcing properties of the eliciting stimuli, and resultant direction of intrumental behaviors—that is, behaviors geared (at least temporarily) either to increase contact with the eliciting stimulus conditions (for positively experienced affects) or decrease contact (for negatively experienced affects). In a similar vein, decreases in arousal below usual adaptation levels are experienced as pleasant ("relaxed," "calm," "relieved") or unpleasant ("depressed," "blue," "down") partially as a result of the cognitive interpretation of the stimulus conditions producing the decrease in arousal and the prior associative learning regarding these states.

In addition to cognitive interpretation and past learning, prior setting events also appear to influence the affective experience of increases or decreases in physiological arousal, very likely as a function of the homeostatic regulation of the body. Thus with continued stimulation leading to relatively high levels of arousal, even when the state is initially experienced as positive, fatigue eventually occurs and decreases in arousal are likely to be experienced as a pleasant emotion. Similarly, low levels of arousal initially experienced as a pleasant state eventually result in boredom, and small increases in arousal are likely to result in positive affective experiences.

"It's a GAS"

Most emotional reactions that become of sufficient concern to result in psychological treatment involve overarousal in some way. Later we discuss specific classes of stimuli that elicit high degrees of arousal. For the moment we note that stress constitutes a broad class of stimulus conditions that produce increases in physiological arousal, typically experienced as negative affect. Any time a person is in a situation that poses a threat to desired goals or homeostatic organismic conditions, thus placing strong demands for adjustment on him, we can say that he is being stressed. Examples of stressful situations for humans are easy to find: an important academic examination, an argument with one's spouse, a major operation, a job interview, prolonged exposure to cold or heat, and so on.

So far our discussion has focused primarily on the nature and effects of physiological arousal at a specific point in time or over relatively brief time periods. Our understanding of physiological arousal, negative emotions, and related clinical problems, however, has been considerably enhanced by studies of the biochemical and physiological reactions to long-term stress, especially by the work of Selye [1969]. Working with animals and humans in the late 1940's and early 1950's, Selye found a nonspecific pattern of hormonal reaction with both fast and slow components resulting from *continuous* exposure to *any* noxious agent or event, in addition to specific reactions resulting from the particular stressor.

Selye called the nonspecific pattern of long-term response the *General Adaptation Syndrome* (GAS), which evolves through three stages: the alarm reac-

tion, the stage of adaptation or resistance, and the stage of exhaustion. On exposure to a specific stressor the fast component of the GAS (the alarm reaction) occurs primarily as a function of the discharge of adrenalin into the blood stream. The alarm reaction thus appears to correspond to the immediate elicitation of high levels of physiological arousal and negative affect. During the alarm reaction, the organism's susceptibility to the increased intensity of the particular stressor and to the occurrence of any other extraneous stressors is reduced. If the stress is severe enough, and unavoidable (even by fainting), death occurs within hours or days of initiation of the alarm reaction. With less intense, nonfatal stressors, however, prolonged exposure brings the slow components of the GAS into play through pituitary–adrenal hormones so that the alarm reaction gives way to the stage of resistance. The level of physiological arousal remains high but decreases somewhat through adaptation, while the parasympathetic branch of the autonomic nervous system partially counteracts the sympathetic discharge. Through increased effort, the organism is able to endure the particular stressor and resist further debilitating effects.

While resistance to extraneous stressors also increases temporarily, even during the stage of resistance the organism coping with a specific stressor becomes more vulnerable to extraneous sources of stress. The emotional experience remains negative and unpleasant, with a lower threshold for eliciting the alarm reaction should other aversive stimulus conditions be confronted. If the stress is severe enough and applied long enough, the hormonal reserve becomes depleted, resulting in fatigue, and eventually the organism enters the stage of exhaustion with decreased ability to resist either the original or extraneous stressors. The affective experience is likely to be "depression." In fact, the organism will experience a temporary period of fatigue and decreased physiological arousal with an affective experience of depression, if stressors are removed after a period of time during an extended alarm reaction or during the stage of resistance; presumably the period of decreased arousal allows the restoration of the biochemical balance of the body.

Some Clarification of Terms

We now return to our definition of anxiety for further clarification. We indicated earlier that "anxiety" may be regarded as a shorthand term for a very complex pattern of response, characterized by subjective feelings of apprehension and tension associated with physiological arousal involving the sympathetic branch of the autonomic nervous system. Although anxiety level may be synonymous with physiological arousal level in relation to the learning or performing of other behaviors (for the affective experience appears irrelevant in these relationships), "anxiety state," "anxiety reaction," or "anxiety response" by definition refer to physiological arousal that is affectively uncomfortable or aversive.

We should make clear that our use of "anxiety level" or simply "anxiety" typically refers to the degree of physiological arousal and cognitive distress existing at a particular moment in time—the extent to which an anxiety state has been elicited. "Anxiety reaction" or "anxiety response" refers to the *increase* in physiological arousal and cognitive distress that occurs on perception of specific eliciting stimulus conditions—the immediate reaction of the individual to stimulus events by the evocation of anxiety states. Thus anxiety reactions or high levels of anxiety are seen as transitory states of response depending on the presence of specific eliciting stimulus conditions or stressors.

The latter use of "anxiety" to describe a response *state* occurring at a particular moment should be distinguished from a common use of "anxious" to describe a relatively enduring personality *trait*—"he is an anxious person." Such "trait anxiety" refers to the degree to which an individual is *predisposed* to respond with anxiety reactions to a wide range of stimuli. An individual with high trait anxiety, however, would not appear anxious at any given moment in time unless there was an effective eliciting stimulus for an anxiety response. Similarly, "general anxiety" typically refers to the chronic level of physiological arousal and cognitive distress because of the presence of a wide variety of eliciting stimuli in an individual's life situation, without distinguishing the specific nature of the eliciting stimuli. As we see later, treating anxiety and related clinical problems requires specification of the precise eliciting stimulus conditions for each individual and, thus, while trait anxiety and general anxiety may provide a description of some aspects of a client's behavior, as well as a global means of evaluation, neither is sufficiently specific with regard to eliciting stimulus conditions to provide a basis for treatment programming. Rather, the specific stimulus dimensions maintaining general anxiety must be identified for efficient treatment.

Problems in Assessing Anxiety

Anxiety is a useful construct because of the consistent relationships among this pattern of response, environmental conditions, and other behavior of the individual. Specific components of the anxiety response, however, may vary widely over different individuals or in the same individual over different times. Furthermore, each specific component of the anxiety response may be influenced or modified by other contingencies unrelated to anxiety, making assessment of the "degree of anxiety" for either research or clinical purposes a very complex undertaking. Since the anxiety response involves both physiological and cognitive components, direct assessment covers three channels of measurement: self report, physiological, and observable or motoric. For severe anxiety responses all three channels regularly coincide and little difficulty is encountered. Each of them, however, is subject to increasing problems as the anxiety response becomes less severe or continues over time.

Verbal assessment of the degree of anxiety through self reports on questionnaires, on paper and pencil scales, or in interviews is subject to all the problems posed by this mode of measuring any behavior. The most serious concern is that the individual's response may not be a valid report of experience or of other behaviors. Being a response system under direct voluntary control, verbal reports may function instrumentally to achieve other anticipated consequences for the individual, leading to ratings or statements that are simply untrue and that depend on the individual's perception of the assessment situation. Lower degrees of anxiety than actually experienced may be reported if some positive consequence or avoiding a negative consequence is anticipated for doing so (a client who has undergone some treatment procedure may not wish to continue or "upset" his therapist by reporting anxiety reactions; a young man may assume he will lose face and appear unmasculine if he admits to being distressed). Similarly, higher degrees of anxiety than actually experienced may be reported for similar reasons (a client may enjoy the attention of a therapist so much that he reports greater distress to maintain contact; a student may report anxiety to a teacher to explain a poor examination performance because the immediate consequences appear more positive than if he admitted that he had not studied).

Even if an individual is motivated to provide valid self reports, verbal assessment of anxiety is still subject to problems. In interviews, the bias or expectancies of the interviewer may subtly influence verbal reports by selective focusing of questions or by reinforcing statements of greater or lesser distress through differential attention. In all modes of verbal assessment the habitual response styles of the individual (a tendency to use or not use extremes on scales or descriptive adjectives, to exaggerate or deny experiences, or to agree or disagree) may influence the validity of the degree of apprehension and tension reported. When questions relate to previous experiences or responses, simply forgetting or actively suppressing painful experiences may play a role. The individual may not be able to report precise data concerning a prior experience because of his failure to attend or discriminate his own responses at the time of stress. Similarly, if the questions themselves elicit anxiety in the assessment situation, discriminations may break down or evasive tactics may be invoked to reduce anxiety. Contrast effects in relation to the general anxiety level or previous extremes of anxiety may also influence self report differentially over individuals.

Because of the cognitive interpretation of physiological arousal involved in the anxiety response, the lack of recent exposure to the stimulus conditions that in the past elicited anxiety can influence verbal reports. Thus treatment conditions or other life experiences may have brought about changes such that no increase in physiological arousal is elicited if the individual is exposed again to those stimulus conditions, but in the absence of such exposure his verbal report may be based on expectations of distress as previously experienced. Similarly, experiences may lead the individual to believe that no distress will now occur, and to consequent verbal reports based on such positive expectations when, in fact, actual exposure to the stimulus conditions would lead to increased physiological arousal, unpleasant affect, and consequent relabeling. Failure to relate response assessment appropriately to stimulus conditions also occurs if the assessors attempt to measure anxiety states with instruments designed to measure general anxiety or traits. Finally, verbal assessment may suffer from a failure to specify the exact information sought, allowing the individual to introduce idiosyncratic meaning or interpretations or confuse reports of stimulus and secondary behaviors with reports of the anxiety state sought.

In spite of the multitude of potential problems with self report as a mode of assessment of anxiety, it remains an efficient means of data collection, and the only way to obtain direct information regarding cognitive experience. A great deal of technical knowledge and skill, however, is required to insure the validity and utility of verbal reports as data for either programming, clinical treatment or evaluative research.

Because of the central role of physiological arousal in defining anxiety, assessing physiological activity at first glance appears to provide an easy channel of measurement. Unfortunately, this is not the case. The activity of the autonomic and central nervous systems is reflected in electrical and chemical discharges and in changes in the activity of the organs and viscera. To understand the complexity of an energy system like the human body requires much technical knowledge and skill, knowledge not only of the specific anatomical or physiological components to be measured, but also of the characteristics of the assessment apparatus for each particular measure and of the statistical properties of the data obtained by such devices. Direct internal measurement (that is, inside the skin) is expensive, time consuming, and frequently painful, so that practicality requires that most physiological assessment of humans be peripheral (that is, outside the skin via analysis of body fluids, recording of electrical activity, sound, volume changes, and so on). Unfortunately, peripheral measures are especially vulnerable to artifacts that may reduce the validity of the data. In addition, each physiological system is influenced not only by emotional stimuli leading to diffuse physiological arousal, but by physical activity, drugs, temperature, diet, size, and other factors as well. Thus a person's heart rate could be increased by having him jump up and down as well as by "scaring" him (presenting an anxiety-eliciting stimulus); the sweat gland activity in the palm of his hand could be increased by raising the temperature as well as by increasing stress, and so on. Obviously, knowing the stimulus conditions under which physiological measurements are obtained is crucial to rule out other sources of influence. Since anxiety is defined as a response to eliciting stimuli, physiological arousal must be further assessed in the presence of the potential eliciting stimuli. The latter requirement can be met regularly in research assessments, but it severely limits the practicality of many physiological measures in day-to-day clinical work. The symbolic presentation of potential eliciting stimuli through pictures or visual imagery widens those limits.

Although direct physiological measurements are much less subject to purposeful distortion than self-report measures, the individual motivated to outfox the assessor can influence the outcome of some of them. Those response systems under direct voluntary control as well as under autonomic regulation may be invalidated as accurate measures of anxiety states in the same fashion as verbal reports: within limits, the individual may increase or decrease respiratory rate and regularity below or above what would "naturally" occur by autonomic regulation; he may voluntarily increase muscle tension as measured on an electromyograph (EMG) to show greater tension than autonomic regulation would show (although tonic muscle tension apparently cannot be lowered directly by voluntary effort without specific training). Some degree of indirect control can be exerted on other physiological measures by voluntarily performing a behavior that itself elicits effects opposite to those produced by the physiological arousal resulting from the stimuli presented (looking at a light to produce pupillary constriction, remembering the last time you ate a dill pickle to increase saliva flow, imagining your hand in ice water to lower skin temperature, recalling an upsetting event to produce arousal when presented with neutral stimuli, or closing your eyes and visualizing a relaxing scene to reduce arousal when presented with anxiety-eliciting stimuli). These indirect control procedures are typically effective only with mild degrees of stress. In severe anxiety reactions, the sympathetic arousal appears strong enough so that in the absence of special training, most people are unable to alter specific responses indirectly, without escaping from the eliciting stimuli.

In general, under high degrees of stress all sympathetically innervated physiological systems show the effects of increased arousal. Thus, with extreme reactions, nearly any of the measures (increases in heart rate, palmar sweat, blood sugar, tonic muscle tension, respiratory rate; decreases in blood volume, saliva flow, respiratory regularity, visceral blood supply) provide an adequate index of anxiety elicitation compared with neutral stimulus conditions. Under less extreme degrees of arousal, however, fewer systems are likely to be involved, and each system may come into play in different order for different people. These discrepancies appear to be valid. Either because of prior learning, or the genetically endowed nervous system, or prior system pathology, each individual shows a "relative response stereotypy" in the pattern of physiological responses over a broad range of eliciting stimuli. One person may readily respond to mild stress with changes in heart rate, muscle tension, and gastrointestinal motility; another with changes in respiratory rate and palmar sweat; a third with changes only in heart rate. With small increases in physiological arousal only the most responsive physiological system or systems show changes for each individual. Greater increases in arousal lead to more intensive reactions in the most responsive systems and bring more systems into play.

Clinically, knowledge of relative response stereotypy helps us understand some "psychophysiological disorders," but response stereotypy has also caused difficulty in measuring arousal, since the correlations among different autonomic measures of response to the degree of stress that can ethically be introduced in experiments are necessarily low. Further discrepancies in physiological measures occur over time with continued stress, as the individual enters later stages of the GAS, differentially adapting in various measures, and as the parasympathetic system becomes relatively activated. Multiple measurement of physiological responses is therefore necessary to insure measuring the most responsive systems for all individuals; the responsive measures then need to be reduced to a single composite index to assess physiological arousal. The necessity for multiple measurement, in addition to assessment in the presence of potential eliciting stimuli, further restricts the practicality of physiological assessment in clinical service work. Study of physiological arousal, however, is important enough to require multiple measurement in evaluative research dealing with the treatment of anxiety and related problems.

The third channel of measuring anxiety involves the use of external observers to record manifestations of anxiety in the individual's motor behavior or performance. This source of data (without actual recording), along with the individual's verbalizations, provides the major basis for inferences of degree of anxiety for both the man on the street and the practicing clinician. Without specifying and standardizing the behaviors to be observed and the assessment context, however, such "naturalistic" observation is subject to all the potential problems of self report, except that the source of possible invalidation is the observer. That is, conflicting motivation, biased expectancies, habitual response styles, selective attention and discrimination, experiential contrast effects, idiosyncratic interpretations, confusion of stimuli and secondary responses with anxiety states, and the like may all operate to invalidate observer judgment in the same way they invalidate the individual's own report. As with self report and physiological assessment, a great deal of technical knowledge and skill is required to insure the validity and utility of observational assessments. But with standardization and specification of the behaviors to be observed and of the assessment context, extremely high reliabilities are possible, using trained observers whose bias has been removed, and in "blind" circumstances where the observers are unaware of treatment conditions or the use to be made of their observations.

Two classes of observational assessment of anxiety are typically used, each subject to different problems. The first class is the *direct* assessment of either (1) the observable effects of physiological arousal and the signs of affective distress on physical and motor functioning (hand tremors, moistening lips, heavy breathing, excessive perspiration, facial grimaces, gross body movement) or (2) of the direct interference of arousal on performance (speech blocks, stammers, impaired motor dexterity, inability to recall). As in physiological measures, direct observational assessment is meaningful only in relationship to the presence of potential eliciting stimuli. Because most observable manifestations of anxiety result from the overenergization of physiological arousal, the problems of physiological response stereotypy also occur in direct observational assessment. Thus, with less than maximum degrees of arousal, only the effects of the most responsive systems are observed, and these differ with individuals. Additionally, since most observable effects are in motor behavior or skeletal muscles, within limits the individual may increase or decrease the frequency or intensity of specific behaviors beyond the direct effects that would "naturally" occur as a result of autonomic discharge alone. The differential complexity of task requirements interacting with the stage of practice for each individual may also influence the degree of interference with specific performance, so that any single behavior or performance in isolation may not represent the degree of anxiety. As in specific physiological measurements, observable behaviors and performances may be influenced by other conditions as well as by the degree of physiological arousal. It is the relatively greater intensity and/or frequency of such behaviors or performance decrements in the presence of eliciting stimulus conditions that allows the interpretation of anxiety.

The second class of observational assessment of anxiety is the *indirect* assessment of physiological arousal and negative affect by observing the secondary approach–avoidance behaviors that may be partially controlled by the degree of anxiety elicited by specific stimuli. These assessments may take the form of measuring the relative intensity or frequency of behaviors learned or maintained to reduce anxiety, as a secondary response to potential anxiety eliciting stimuli. The latter behaviors may be motoric (compulsive handwashing, overeating) or cognitive and ideational (tangential thought progressions, misperception of stimuli, idiosyncratic word associations). In either case, the assumption is that increased anxiety results in increases in those behaviors that in the past have reduced the anxiety reaction, either by being incompatible with the anxiety response or by avoiding or escaping the eliciting stimuli or their cognitive representations. Another form of indirect observational assessment is "free operant" measurement, in which the individual's relative frequency of approach toward, or avoidance of potential eliciting stimulus conditions is observed in natural or standardized environments. The assumption here is that the more severe the anxiety associated with a given class of stimuli, the more those stimuli will be avoided.

A related form of indirect observational assessment is the Behavioral Avoidance (or Approach) Test (BAT), in which a potential anxiety eliciting stimulus is located in a standardized environment and the individual is instructed to approach the stimulus object or event and engage in progressively more intimate contact or interaction. The degree of physical approach and/or intimacy of contact accomplished before the individual refuses to go further is observed, the assumption being that the more severe the anxiety elicited by the stimulus, the earlier in the sequence the individual will terminate approach, or institute escape or avoidance.

The major problem with all indirect observational assessment procedures is that the specific focus of assessment consists of operant behaviors of the person which are under direct voluntary control. While many escape or avoidance responses may become so overlearned as to be habitual, occurring without specific attentional focus, even habitual responses may be modified when the individual's attention is redirected. As with other assessment modes, it is easy to identify severe anxiety reactions through secondary behavioral effects; no manner of encouragement or external demand could prevent escape or avoidance for long, and if it did, panic or fainting would readily be observed. As the degree of anxiety becomes less severe, however, other sources of influence become progressively more potent in motivating approach or avoidance of given stimulus conditions, to the point at which anxiety may play no role at all and other factors may totally control approach behaviors. In fact, all the problems of the potential lack of validity of self–report measures as a response system under direct voluntary control also apply to the observational assessment of secondary behaviors. Thus, in mild or moderate degrees of anxiety, the situational context of assessment, the level of demand for approach behavior, and the perceived positive or negative consequences for a given degree of approach may be more potent motivating factors in determining secondary motoric behaviors than the degree of anxiety experienced. These motoric behaviors may further interact with other individual characteristics (tolerance for distress, knowledge and experience in interacting with the stimuli involved, prior cultural experience) relatively independently of anxiety level.

Such individual characteristics can contribute significantly to the lack of communality of measurement among avoidance tests and other modes of assessment. For example, if two individuals experienced the same degree of anxiety in relation to a specific eliciting stimulus, but one was offered a hundred dollars to approach the stimulus and the other offered nothing, interpreting the avoidance index for anxiety in isolation would inappropriately indicate the paid participant to be less anxious, while the other three modes of assessment would find him to be more anxious (since he was in closer proximity to the eliciting stimulus than his unpaid colleague). Thus to interpret approach–avoidance behaviors as an index of anxiety, it seems necessary to institute high demand conditions for approach behavior and to assess further the degree of anxiety at the same point on the approach gradient over two or more time periods by the modes we described earlier.

In summary, assessing anxiety for either research or clinical purposes is a highly complex and technical undertaking. Each of the three channels of measurement is subject to particular problems. By taking a multimethod approach, in which all three channels are used to assess the degree of response in relation to specific eliciting stimulus conditions, however, the nature of the eliciting stimuli, the intensity and extensity of the anxiety reaction, and the effects of anxiety on other behaviors can be meaningfully determined. For research purposes, all three channels of assessment should be regularly employed. Unfortunately, assessments in external life environments by trained observers or physiological measures are frequently impractical for day-to-day clinical work. In this situation, the clinician attempts to standardize his own observations of client behavior and assessments of client self reports and to train the client to become a valid observer of his own physiological, affective, and motoric behavior in relation to specific stimuli in the life environment.

Development and Maintenance of Anxiety

Since anxiety is a response to eliciting stimuli, understanding the nature of potential eliciting stimuli is essential in order to comprehend the clinical problems related to anxiety and the treatment procedures designed to alter them. As we said earlier, any condition that places strong demands for adjustment on an organism by threatening desired goals or homeostatic organismic conditions constitutes stress and may elicit an immediate anxiety response, followed by the slower GAS pattern if the stress continues over a long time. Developmentally, such responses are quite adaptive, since the organism is energized to take action to remove dangerous, possibly life–threatening conditions. Although genetic factors may provide nervous and endocrine systems more or less responsive to stress for each individual, a number of environmental condi-

tions or events appear to function as stressors, or anxiety-eliciting stimuli, across individuals and species without benefit of prior learning (that is "unconditioned" stimuli). Such unconditioned stimuli are generally noxious or painful and thus threaten the homeostatic balance of the body. Thus wounds, physical trauma, impeded respiration, and so on all serve to elicit anxiety without prior experience. Rapid changes in physical orientation or support (falling, whirling, being thrown through the air) typically function as unconditioned stressors, although the introduction of learning contingencies may later result in relabeling the emotional experience as positive under certain conditions (An example, riding a roller coaster). In general, almost any physical stimulus—noise, heat, cold, light, pressure, shock—in high enough intensity may serve as an unconditioned, eliciting stimulus for anxiety or stress responses.

As the organism matures and interacts with the environment it acquires a learning history, through which objects, events, and interactions take on a variety of stimulus functions, including positive and negative reinforcing functions and discriminative stimulus functions. Further, at least in humans, such experience becomes cognitively organized through higher symbolic processes, so that new experiences are interpreted on the basis of past experience stored as memories, and behavior is then based on hypotheses or expectancies regarding the value of reinforcing consequences and their probable occurrence, given different courses of action [Dulany 1968].

From an early point in psychological development, once a minimal learning history has been acquired, certain other stimulus conditions will elicit anxiety, more on the basis of posing a threat to desired goals than as an immediate threat to homeostatic regulation. These stimulus conditions may still be considered "unconditioned," since anxiety may occur without earlier experience with the specific conditions involved. Some of these stimulus conditions and the resulting anxiety reactions are often seen in infants and young children, before the learning history has broadened experience and introduced more complex cognitive organization. One such set of stimulus conditions is the introduction of novel stimuli that cannot readily be assimilated with prior experience, as may be seen in the baby who cries uncontrollably when a stranger (even kindly rich old Uncle George) picks him up for the first time. Similarly, disconfirmation of positive expectancies, or the loss of customary or anticipated positive reinforcers, may be stressful in the absence of prior experience, such as frequently happens when a young child goes off for his first two-week summer camp stay.

Of all such stimulus conditions, the most important, because of their pervasiveness and regular occurrence, are *conflict situations*. Conflict conditions exist when a course of action results in contradictory or opposing consequences, or when discriminative stimuli, which provide guidance regarding the probable occurrence of positive or negative reinforcers, are unclear, confused, or simultaneously indicate equal probability of opposing consequences. Thus conflict conditions are those that typify the "damned-if-you-do-damned-if-you-don't" situation we are all familiar with. Frequently occurring classes of conflict conditions are referred to in terms of the directionality of the instrumental acts placed in opposition. "Approach–avoidance conflict" refers to a situation in which alternative courses of action may result either in the occurrence of both positive and negative reinforcers or alternatively in the loss of a positive reinforcer simultaneously with the escape or avoidance of a negative consequence. "Approach–approach conflict" refers to a situation in which alternative courses of action would each result in the occurrence of a positive reinforcer and simultaneously the avoidance or loss of another positive reinforcer. "Avoidance–avoidance conflict" refers to a situation in which alternative courses of action would each result in the escape or avoidance of a negative consequence but simultaneously result in the occurrence of another negative consequence.

These conflict conditions may be elaborated and become more stressful: [a] with the occurrence of two or more discriminative stimuli, [b] when additional courses of action, each with simultaneous contradictory consequences, become available, or [c] when the opposing stimulus functions differ over time (positive now, negative tomorrow). The major point to remember is that conflict conditions may serve as stressors, whether or not prior experience has been obtained with the specific conflict situation confronting the individual.

As our discussion has indicated, previously neutral or even positive stimuli can acquire anxiety-eliciting functions through association with stimulus conditions that already evoke anxiety, following the classical conditioning paradigm. Acquiring a conditioned anxiety response is illustrated in a simple way by the famous case of "Little Albert" [Watson & Raynor 1920], who was taught to fear white rats under controlled conditions. The child was frightened with a loud noise (anxiety was elicited by the presentation of an unconditioned eliciting stimulus) while he was playing with a gentle white rat (contiguous with the occurrence of an initially neutral or positive stimulus). After five such

pairings of the rat and the noise, the sight of the rat, unaccompanied by the noise, elicited fear reactions in the child; and the rat had become a conditioned stimulus for anxiety.

Theoretically, any feature or characteristic of objects, events, or interactional settings to which an organism is attending at the time an anxiety response is elicited can acquire anxiety-eliciting stimulus properties. If the original anxiety reaction is severe, or if the organism is confined and able to attend to only one stimulus complex, a single occurrence may be sufficient to establish a conditioned anxiety response, as when a person who has been involved in a serious car accident becomes quite anxious riding in a car and may even refuse to enter one. Conditioned anxiety (or, more accurately, the acquisition of conditioned eliciting stimulus functions) may also develop through repeated exposure to mildly stressful conditions in which common stimulus characteristics are regularly contiguous in time or space with the mild anxiety reaction. An example of the latter is a teacher's becoming a conditioned stimulus for anxiety in a child if several other children in the class regularly stressed the child by placing him in conflict situations. Since the source of the mild stress would not be consistent, any feature of the environment that was consistent, such as the teacher, the room, or the school building, might acquire eliciting stimulus properties.

Humans and higher mammals can acquire conditioned anxiety responses through vicarious learning and higher–order conditioning or associative learning, without necessarily being exposed to unconditioned stressors except at the earliest stages of development [Bandura 1969]. Higher–order conditioning simply means that the anxiety-eliciting stimuli that provide the basis for the acquisition of new conditioned stimulus functions were themselves acquired, not unconditioned. Similarly, the observation of stimulus conditions that result in physical trauma or strong anxiety reactions for others and the verbal description of potentially dangerous stimulus conditions can under certain circumstances provide a background leading to anxiety if the individual is himself confronted with those stimulus conditions in the future. Such processes serve a very adaptive function, since our survival as a species would be endangered if each of us had to be shot or hit by a truck to learn to respond with anxiety, and consequent escape or avoidance behaviors, at a gun shoved in our faces or a truck bearing down on us.

Other stimulus conditions may take on anxiety-eliciting functions without direct exposure to previous anxiety-eliciting stimuli through generalization. Thus stimuli whose physical attributes, appearance, or functions are similar to conditioned anxiety-eliciting stimuli may also elicit anxiety, depending on the degree of similarity. Such stimulus generalization also serves an adaptive purpose, since, for example, we do not need to experience anxiety and learn to avoid being burned by first touching every object that could have this effect. Rather, after once being burned by touching a hot stove, a child appropriately generalizes this experience to other objects or events with similar physical attributes (fire), appearance (other stoves), or functions (heat-producing furnaces or electric heaters). Generalization may also occur in relation to other stimuli contiguous in time or space with a conditioned anxiety-eliciting stimulus. The closer an individual approaches the occasion for the occurrence of a stressful event, or the place where a dangerous event has occurred, the greater the anxiety elicited. Temporal or spatial generalization also serves an adaptive purpose, since we may learn to anticipate the occurrence of strong eliciting stimuli, take evasive action to escape the mild anxiety resulting from approximation to the dangerous event, and thereby avoid the dangerous event altogether. The "time–binding" ability of humans to use thoughts, ideas, and images not only to recall past experiences but to anticipate and interpret future courses of action and events allows us to be particularly adaptive in avoiding physical trauma and objective dangers with minimal experience of anxiety or exposure to threatening conditions.

So far we have seen how learning may be appropriately related to anxiety to serve adaptive functions for the individual. Unfortunately, learning may not always result in appropriate and adaptive behaviors — that is, behavior in the individual's best interest to maximize positive and minimize negative consequences. Inappropriate or maladaptive learning provides the basis for many clinical problems.

Anxiety may be related to maladaptive learning in three primary ways. In the first, anxiety is actually an appropriate reaction to the stimulus conditions the individual finds himself in, but his inappropriate learning of other behaviors either produces the eliciting stimulus conditions or prevents their modification. There are several different sorts of inappropriate learning that lead to ineffective dealing with the physical or social environment. Behavioral or learning deficits, for example, may exist when the individual has not acquired the skills necessary to perform adequately in certain situations. Consider a young man who has not had the opportunity to learn the social skills necessary to keep a conversation going with young women. The ensuing rejection will undoubtedly elicit anxiety, which might be an appropriate conditioned response but is a secondary result of his own inappropriate social behavior. Similarly, a college professor may not have learned to say "no" to requests for future services, with the result that he is in an approach–avoidance conflict situation because of conflicting time demands that are a consequence of his own inappropriate verbal behaviors.

Other inappropriate behaviors may have been positively acquired under deviant environmental conditions: the behavior may have been positively reinforced under one set of circumstances but in a different environment, or after a change in the existing environment it is no longer adaptive. A young woman may have developed a repertoire of social behavior in a large city high school in which, for "survival," she was assertive and demanding, like her close friends. On a small college campus, however, this behavior might be considered obnoxious, and result in aversive, punishing responses from others and consequent anxiety reactions on her part — which are appropriate to such eliciting stimuli. Similarly, a highly trained aeronautical engineer may find his job skills no longer adequate to earn a living when government contracts are not renewed, with resultant anxiety appropriately elicited by such conditions.

Other maladaptive behaviors resulting in anxiety reactions may be a function of inappropriately learning reinforcement schedules and modes of conflict resolution. For example, a college student may find "socializing" more pleasant than studying and inappropriately engage in the immediately more rewarding activity of not opening his textbooks until the night before exams. Then, realizing that he cannot cover the course material or that he does not know enough for performing successfully in the exam an anxiety reaction appropriate to such conditions is likely to occur.

In all the examples above of the first way anxiety may be related to maladaptive learning, the anxiety is a reaction resulting from other behaviors that are a function of inappropriate learning. Such anxiety is called *reactive anxiety* and is treated clinically by modifying the other behaviors that result in the anxiety reaction (for example, teaching new skills) rather than focusing directly on the anxiety response.

The second way anxiety may be related to maladaptive learning is when it is an inappropriate reaction itself, occurring in response to stimulus conditions that, objectively, provide no threat or danger. Just as anxiety may be appropriately conditioned to previously neutral stimuli, the stimulus characteristics that take on anxiety-eliciting properties may be irrelevant to actual danger or threat and thus inappropriately elicit anxiety. Such maladaptive acquisition of conditioned anxiety reactions is most obvious in the case of "traumatic neuroses," where intense anxiety reactions are elicited as a result of a major catastrophe, such as a bomb exploding nearby, being caught in a building destroyed by an earthquake, or being in a severe automobile accident. Because of the intensity of the unconditioned anxiety response, and the consequent breakdown of discriminations, any feature of the external or internal environment that happens to make an impact on the individual at the original catastrophe might become conditioned stimuli for anxiety, later eliciting an anxiety reaction when there is no danger. Further, through stimulus generalization, objects, events, or interactions only somewhat similar to those associated with the original trauma may inappropriately elicit anxiety as a conditioned response—a factory whistle (rather than the sound of a falling bomb), sitting close to a wall (rather than a wall falling in), or riding in a bus (rather than in an automobile).

Of course, few of us are confronted with such extreme physical dangers. Most instigating conditions for the development of inappropriate conditioned anxiety in humans appear to result, not from catastrophes but from repeated exposure to mildly stressful conditions, especially conflict situations, in which common stimulus features are present. Behaviors leading to reactive anxiety carried on over a period of time may lead to acquiring conditioned anxiety to features of the environment regularly associated in time or space with the occurrence of reactive anxiety. Deviant models (in person, print, or television) may provide inappropriate warnings, threats, or examples that vicariously sensitize the observer to respond with conditioned anxiety to objectively nonthreatening stimuli. A young woman constantly warned of the danger of being raped by "evil men" may over time develop an anxiety response to all men, without being hurt, abused, or raped by anyone.

Any circumstance that elicits intense anxiety responses may, theoretically, provide the basis for the development of inappropriate conditioned anxiety. Therefore, an individual already under stress for some time (second stage of the GAS) is more likely to acquire inappropriate conditioned anxiety responses because of his lower tolerance for stress. Similarly, in approach-avoidance or avoidance-avoidance conflict situations, the avoidance tendency may be based on conditioned anxiety, thereby allowing for the compounding of anxiety in the presence of the same stimuli. Because of the cognitive aspects of anxiety, components of the anxiety response may function as "response-produced cues," which lead to intensification of the response. Mild anxiety may be elicited from some external or internal stimulus, the individual labels the sensations accompanying that mild response (trembling, or "butterflies in the stomach") as fear or anxiety, and then responds to the label with even more anxiety. Being aware of an increase in anxiety can itself act as a stressor, and the "feedback loop" of response–label–response may lead to progressive intensifications.

The higher symbolic processes of humans appear to make us uniquely capable of such spiral progressions of anxiety—bootstrapping" (recall the ARAS) through the things we tell ourselves, increasing the probability of overgeneralization and higher-order conditioning. Semantic generalization on the basis of similarity of meaning can produce very inappropriate anxiety responses. Let us consider a young girl who grows up in an extremely rigid, puritanical environment, where sexual activity is characterized as dirty, sinful, and punishable. By the time she reaches adolescence, the girl is likely to consider even minor approximations to sex, like hand holding, as threatening behaviors. Through generalization even the word "sex" may act as a stressor and produce an anxiety response. This strong set of vicariously conditioned anxiety responses may interfere massively with her enjoyment of, or even participation in sex as an adult and would probably result in the label of "frigidity" in a clinical setting.

One may ask why a person who has at one time acquired an association between anxiety and a previously neutral stimulus continues to respond with anxiety to that stimulus even after it is inappropriate to do so. That is, why would not a frigid woman thaw out as a result of repeated experiences with sexual behavior? Why do people afraid of elevators, either as a result of direct or vicarious conditioning, not get over their fear once they have taken a few elevator rides and realize that there really is no danger?

These questions lead us directly into the third way anxiety can be related to inappropriate learning: the development or maintenance of behavior problems through reinforcement of escape or avoidance behavior. We might assume that if a person who has learned a maladaptive or irrational anxiety response exposes himself to the feared stimuli, the anxiety will disappear over time (through a process known as *extinction*). While this is a theoretically correct assumption, much maladaptive conditioned anxiety is not so relieved. Rather, when the person attempts to enter a stressful situation, he experiences anxiety and at some early point leaves (escapes) that situation before fully experiencing its harmless nature (seeing that no noxious unconditioned stimulus occurs). Because it is followed immediately by reduced anxiety, the behavior that is strengthened, and thus made more likely to occur the next time, is the escape response. As escape behaviors become stronger, they begin to occur earlier and earlier on approach to the anxiety–provoking situation, until the individual does not enter the situation at all and thus *avoids* rather than escapes it. Since avoidance of anxiety altogether is even more comfortable than escaping after it has begun, avoidance behaviors are strengthened over time and the conditioned anxiety response is maintained intact.

Even if a person does not avoid or escape an anxiety-eliciting situation, complete reduction in conditioned anxiety is not always the result. This is especially true if the anxiety is not incapacitating. Many college students are tense and anxious before and during academic examinations. The anxiety may be as mild as a slightly queasy stomach or as severe as an anxiety "attack," complete with loss of appetite, heart palpitations, vomiting, and dizziness. If in spite of these effects, the student takes the exam and passes, the extremely rewarding reduction in anxiety following the test reinforces the entire chain of behaviors preceding it. This chain usually includes overstudying if successful exam performance results. As long as "test anxiety" does not become severe enough to cause flunking, it may be maintained at a fairly constant level, but considered part of the person's test–taking style rather than a behavior problem.

Operant or instrumental escape and avoidance behaviors, whether ideational or motoric, may thus contribute to maintaining conditioned anxiety responses by preventing the occurrence of extinction. In fact, to the extent that the individual is successful in avoiding anxiety-eliciting stimuli, he may not appear anxious to outside observers nor experience anxiety himself. Such avoidance behavior may therefore be quite adaptive for the individual. Instrumental avoidance behaviors, however, may be developed that are themselves maladaptive, either in preventing the individual from engaging in behavior with ultimately positive consequences, or in developing bizarre avoidance responses that ultimately have negative consequences. Such maladaptive avoidance behaviors are likely when the conditioned anxiety providing the basis for reinforcement is itself inappropriate, or when the conditioned anxiety is of high intensity, such that the immediate reduction of anxiety is a more powerful reinforcer of escape or avoidance behaviors than a delayed negative consequence; that is, the gradient of reinforcement favors an ultimately maladaptive behavior. Consider an individual who has developed an inappropriate conditioned anxiety reaction to au-

thority figures. Such a person might possess vocational skills that qualify him for important advances, high salary, and other benefits. Because the anxiety elicited by the administrators who make promotions, however, he avoids working where they might observe him and thereby loses the opportunity for the ultimate positive consequences of advancement. The gradient of reinforcement is often seen to operate where a particular source of escape or avoidance becomes habitual, often through providing positive effects in addition to reducing anxiety, as do drugs, alcohol, or sex. Any source of anxiety, appropriate or inappropriate, may provide a basis for maladaptive habitual behavior. An individual may develop the use of alcohol as a habitual mode of escape or avoidance, since the immediate effects (mild positive disinhibition, physical relaxation antagonistic to anxiety, "blotting out" and thereby escaping or avoiding perception of anxiety-eliciting stimulus conditions) are quite positive, while the aversive effects (loss of job, social criticism, consequences of poor decisions, and so on are delayed in time.

The Problems Brought to the Clinician

Throughout our discussion of anxiety and physiological arousal and their interrelationship with behavioral efficiency and learning, we have alternatively mentioned "the organism" or "the individual" rather than referring to "clients" or "patients." This use of terms has been purposeful, since we view the phenomena involved as natural events and processes that operate similarly not only for people labeled as suffering from psychological problems, but for "normals" and lower level mammals as well. In 1963 Wilson surveyed the literature on clinical studies of human behavior pathology and integrated the major features of neurotic behavior with findings from laboratory studies of humans and animals on experimental neuroses, conflict, frustration, and traumatic avoidance learning. Wilson concluded,

> research raises the possibility that the same principles control behavior pathology in more than one species. The unique features of human pathology seem to be traceable to the complex cognitive processes through which the problem is expressed, rather than a fundamental difference in how the pathology originates. We would tentatively conclude that the indispensable feature of pathology is a strong anxiety reaction keyed to significant aspects of the individual's experience. [p. 145].

Since Wilson's review, many surveys and writers have offered convincing data that sociocultural factors, learning deficits, modeling, external reinforcement contingencies, and other events are in many clinical cases more important determinants of maladaptive behavior than anxiety. Further, whether or not an individual or his behavior is considered pathological or abnormal, and therefore changeworthy through entry into psychological treatment, is seen as a social action in itself. In 1969 Ullmann and Krasner described this process in the following way:

> an individual may do something . . . under a set of circumstances . . . which upsets, annoys, angers, or strongly disturbs somebody (e.g., employer, teacher, parent, or the individual himself) sufficiently that some action results. . . that it, the individual may enter treatment [p. 21].

From this framework, we make two observations. [1] Beyond very severe or grossly deviant emotional reactions or maladaptive behaviors, the problems that result in an individual's becoming a "client" in psychological treatment may not differ at all from those that do not lead him to enter treatment, since the action of entering treatment is partially a function of the tolerance for distress of the individual and those around him, and of the circumstances in which the maladaptive behavior occurs. Even in severe or grossly deviant reactions, the principles of development and maintenance of the problem behavior are considered to be the same as less intense reactions. [2] Because of the negative affect associated with anxiety, the disruption of behavioral efficiency, and the bizarre nature of some avoidance responses, stress and anxiety are likely to be involved in the initiation, development, and maintenance of a wide variety of behaviors that are sufficiently upsetting to the individual or those in his environment to result in his seeking out psychological treatment.

Appropriate "Targets" for Systematic Desensitization

Obviously, many people seen by behavior–change agents (therapists) complain about anxiety and tension as at least part of their problem. Many others suffer from the effects of stress, even though they do not specifically label the problem as such.

Systematic desensitization, the major topic of the presentation to which we now turn, was designed as a therapeutic technique to alleviate some of these problems. Difficulties stem from many sources and, depending upon the nature and history of the problem, may or may not be appropriate for the application of systematic desensitization and related techniques.

As a general rule, systematic desensitization is useful only where *conditioned, inappropriate* anxiety plays a central role. The range of problems *not* appropriate for systematic desensitization and the range of treatment techniques designed to deal with them are very wide [Bandura 1969, Franks 1969, Ullmann and Krasner 1969, Paul 1969d].

The clinician who finds no evidence of anxiety, behavioral disruption, or escape or avoidance behaviors encounters little difficulty. He does not entertain systematic desensitization or related clinical procedures as possible components of treatment. But when any of these features are present, the clinician is faced with important diagnostic decisions, because the client's problems may look as if they fit into the "conditioned, inappropriate" anxiety category when in fact they do not. Since unwise and inappropriate application of any treatment procedure cannot result in a successful outcome, it is vital in all cases that both the source of the client's anxiety and its effects on his environment be carefully analyzed.

The major discrimination to be made before systematic desensitization and related techniques are decided on as appropriate is to distinguish instances of unconditioned anxiety and reactive anxiety from instances of inappropriate conditioned anxiety. Furthermore, verbal reports of anxiety that serve as operants to achieve other goals, rather than as valid reports of experience, must be discriminated. Finally, "depression" resulting from overwork, fatigue, or loss or absence of reinforcers, not involving conditioned anxiety, should be distinguished from depression resulting from continued stress (third phase of the GAS), termination of stress, or absence of reinforcers as a function of inappropriate conditioned anxiety, since the former does not involve systematic desensitization as part of a treatment program. These differential diagnostic decisions typically require several sessions in which the clinician determines the covariance of the three channels of assessment of anxiety, and the temporal relationships to specific stimulus conditions and to other behaviors. Frequently, historical information provides hypotheses regarding differential diagnostic decisions, which the clinician and client must test in the current life environment. The latter sequence of assessment is typical for day-to-day clinical service work, in which clients present problems and clinicians fit a program of treatment to those problems and the client's life situation. (In research evaluating the efficacy of therapy, the assessment criteria may be previously established, and clients selected to "fit" the questions being asked in the research.) Whenever the behavior problem does *not* centrally involve an anxiety response that is inappropriate to the circumstances in which it is occurring or is a reactive rather than conditioned response, systematic desensitization and related techniques are not appropriate means of handling it.

Based on our previous analysis, the problems in which inappropriate conditioned anxiety is centrally important, for which systematic desensitization and related techniques are considered appropriate, are of five major kinds, each of which may overlap in a given individual:

1] *Conditioned anxiety of sufficient duration or intensity to cause extreme subjective distress is elicited in the absence of objective danger or threat.* This is the relatively "pure" anxiety response, which occurs in continued or intermittent exposure to eliciting stimulus conditions without means of escaping or avoiding. Typically, the clients' complaints are obviously related to anxiety. The stimuli may be either simple (in the sense of a single, clear-cut class of stimulus events or objects) or complex (involving multiple classes of stimuli, conflict with one or more branches involving inappropriate conditioned stimuli, and/or vague, broadly generalized stimuli difficult to identify). Extreme episodes of intense anxiety ("nervous breakdowns," "acute psychotic episodes") may be involved, or lower intensity, chronic states may be typical.

2] *The response pattern of anxiety becomes sufficiently specific to produce tissue change of the sort seen in so-called psychophysiological or psychosomatic disorders.* Because of physiological response stereotypy, either continuous or intermittent anxiety over long periods of time can result in tissue change or damage in the most responsive physiological systems. Similarly, specific physiological systems become overworked in later stages of the GAS, and the interaction of intermittent periods of anxiety with biological cycles puts added stress on specific systems. Many physical problems (migraine headache, peptic ulcer, ulcerative colitis, dermatoses, high blood pressure, asthma, chronic fatigue) may have anxiety as a basis. When the anxiety is elicited by inappropriate stimuli, systematic desensitization may be the treatment of choice. When tissue damage has occurred, however, medical treatment to repair the damage is essential, and systematic desensitization may prevent reoccurrences.

3] *The current or prior intensity of conditioned anxiety results in the breakdown of efficient performance of complex behavior.* Several classes of clinical problems may be involved when inappropri-

ate conditioned anxiety is the basis of a breakdown in performance. Nearly any cognitive or motor performance can suffer as a result of the inverted-U relationship between arousal and behavioral efficiency. A client's specific problem would therefore be a function of the task demands placed on him by his job, family, friends, or other life circumstances. "Inability to talk at a party," "can't think straight," "can't study," "stutter," "no longer hit the basket" might be complained of or observed to occur in clients for whom task demands for complex performance coincide with the occurrence of inappropriate eliciting stimuli in which physiological arousal is elicited above the optimal level. At the other end of the dimension, nearly any cognitive or motor performance could suffer as a result of the inverted-U relationship when underarousal (below the optimal level) results as a reaction to prior intense levels of anxiety (reactive depression). Here, the breakdown in performance is likely to be nonspecific, involving tasks required during the period of fatigue or depression. Finally, sexual problems in which sympathetic enervation interferes with parasympathetic control of behavior (such as impotence, premature ejaculation, and frigidity) may result from inappropriate conditioned anxiety. In cases involving reactive underarousal, rest and absence of stress are instituted to restore normal physical functioning before systematic desensitization is undertaken. Where breakdown of performance of complex behavior is the predominant feature, anxiety may or may not be presented as an initial referral problem or complaint.

4] *Adaptive behavior in the client's repertoire is inhibited to avoid inappropriate conditioned anxiety reactions.* Clinical problems of this sort involve escape and avoidance behavior, and the individual either stops doing things he can do or actively goes out of his way to avoid specific stimulus situations. The classical phobia, in which a specific stimulus object or a specific set of stimulus conditions is actively avoided, is the most obvious problem of this kind. Someone with a phobic reaction to airplanes may take a week to drive across the country rather than ride a few hours in a plane. A mailman "with a cat phobia" may stop delivering mail to a house with a pet cat on the porch. A "claustrophobic" may not apply for a job because the only way to get to the office is in an elevator. Since the inhibition of behavior is not openly bizarre, and infrequently occurring phobic objects can be avoided without much difficulty, individuals suffering from phobias are seldom referred for services, and they may not even be detected by observers. If the phobic object cannot be avoided, however, the resulting anxiety reaction (as in 1 above) may suffice to lead the individual to seek treatment. Also, if anxiety-eliciting stimuli are many or frequent, the inhibition of adaptive behavior may actually interfere with other aspects of the individual's life. In some cases inhibition may become so widespread that nearly all sources of external reinforcement are shut off, leading to depressive reactions. As in 2 above, the individual referred to treatment for "failing to do things" may or may not present anxiety as an initial referral problem or complaint. But behavior of this kind very often provides one branch of a conflict situation that may be quite dominant on initial referral.

5] *Maladaptive behaviors are learned and maintained to alleviate or avoid inappropriate conditioned anxiety reactions.* These problems also involve escape and avoidance behaviors, but of a nature that is itself maladaptive, either because of their bizarre nature, which is sufficiently beyond the experience of most people who react negatively, or because they violate laws, cultural standards, or work requirements so that the ultimate consequences at a given time and place are uniformly negative. In this class of anxiety-related problems are many traditional psychotic and neurotic "symptoms", such as amnesias, compulsions, delusions, tangential thought, and the like, in which a bizarre behavior may be adopted either as an immediate escape from the perception of anxiety-eliciting stimuli and maintained by avoidance of that perception, or as an activity that removes the individual from exposure to situations where anxiety-eliciting stimuli are more probable. Many sexual problems involving objects or acts that are deviant in a particular culture, such as fetishes or homosexual behavior, may involve inappropriate conditioned anxiety to the more usual and accepted stimulus objects or activities. Any habitual source of relief from anxiety may become excessive and maladaptive, particularly when multiple reinforcement is obtained. Frequent clinical problems of the latter sort occur through the use of drugs, alcohol, food (obesity), and sex (compulsive masturbation, nymphomania, satyriasis). The range of unusual stimuli to which the human organism may become conditioned, and the range of unusual behaviors that we may adopt by chance to escape or avoid resulting anxiety reactions, is nearly without limit. As with 4 above, behavior of this kind frequently provides one

branch of a conflict situation that may be dominant on initial referral. More often, the maladaptive avoidance behavior itself is the predominant complaint, and anxiety may or may not be presented as an initial problem.

Systematic Desensitization Therapy

The principles on which systematic desensitization is based have been used unsystematically for centuries to overcome traumatic anxiety reactions—probably without the users knowing the underlying principles. "A little hair of the dog that bit you" summarizes a common sense practice followed by many parents. If a small child has been frightened by a dog, a wise parent is likely to comfort the child by holding him, and perhaps giving him candy to chew while simultaneously petting a dog at arms length, then closer, then having the child first touch and then pet the dog himself. Unfortunately, unsystematic common sense approaches in therapy rely greatly on trial and error, so that each problem must be faced anew, with possible unnecessary distress for the client.

The period from 1920 to 1950 saw massive experimental laboratory research on methods of producing and eliminating classically conditioned responses in both animals and humans, which provided a systematic basis for the effectiveness of procedures like those we described above for the child afraid of dogs. On the basis of this laboratory research and related theory, Wolpe formulated a counterconditioning hypothesis to guide the treatment of maladaptive anxiety, which he termed the *reciprocal inhibition principle.* According to this principle, the ability of given stimuli to evoke anxiety is permanently weakened if "a response antagonistic to anxiety can be made to occur in the presence of anxiety-evoking stimuli so that it is accompanied by a complete or partial suppression of the anxiety responses" [1958, p. 71]. In his search for procedures that might produce responses incompatible with anxiety, Wolpe was struck by the promise of a technique called "progressive relaxation training," which Jacobson had reported in 1938. Jacobson's training procedures appeared to produce both a reduction in physiological arousal and a pleasant affective tone —a response state, by definition, that would be incompatible with anxiety.

Progressive relaxation training required some period of time to develop the relaxed state. Therefore, the incompatible response of relaxation could not be immediately elicited on the appearance of an anxiety-eliciting stimulus. It would also be impractical for a therapist to pile his office full of potential anxiety-eliciting stimuli in order to gain control over the timing of stimulus presentation. Besides, most anxiety-eliciting stimuli of clinical concern involve people, social events, and past or future situations, and these could not easily be controlled or brought into an office. Since the eliciting stimulus conditions for anxiety involve the perception of "threatening" stimuli, Wolpe began experimenting with phobic clients who were asked to confront anxiety-eliciting stimuli only by visualizing (a "cue-producing response") their presence. He concluded that the imaginal representation of stimulus conditions was as effective in eliciting anxiety as the actual occurrence (although clients sometimes needed additional training in appropriate visualization), thereby providing much flexibility and control.

Problems still existed, however, since anxiety reactions severe enough to cause clinical difficulty also appeared too strong to be suppressed by the rather fragile relaxed state resulting from progressive relaxation training, at least in a few weeks of training. Wolpe resolved this problem by drawing on "gradual approach" procedures, used by several earlier therapists, which had formed the basis for medical desensitization treatment of allergies. By selecting stimuli far enough out on the stimulus generalization gradient from the anxiety-eliciting target stimulus, an anxiety response could be elicited that was weak enough to be suppressed by prior relaxation training. By constructing a hierarchy of specific stimuli, running from items far out on the stimulus generalization gradient (eliciting weak anxiety responses) through items closer to the target stimulus (eliciting stronger anxiety responses), the therapist could apparently suppress anxiety by first training the client in relaxation and then repeatedly presenting stimuli low on the hierarchy. As weaker items lost their power to elicit anxiety by presentation in the presence of a relaxed state, some generalization apparently occurred to the next higher items, for the next stimulus in the hierarchy could now be presented and the relaxed state would be sufficient to suppress the anxiety response. By proceeding up the hierarchy of stimuli, the target (most anxiety-eliciting) stimulus could finally be presented and relaxation would be sufficient to inhibit the anxiety normally occurring in the absence of the relaxed state. After repeated presentations of the target stimulus, visualization in the absence of relaxation would fail to elicit anxiety, this new absence of response apparently transferred, "invariably," to the real-life confrontation of the previously anxiety-eliciting stimulus conditions.

The Technical "Package"

Systematic desensitization thus refers to a package of treatment procedures that systematically includes: [a] training in deep relaxation to provide a state incompatible with anxiety; [b] constructing hierarchies of anxiety-eliciting stimuli to provide specific, controllable items for the client to visualize; [c] desensitization proper—suppressing anxiety through graduated presentation of the anxiety-eliciting stimuli from weakest to strongest while the client is in the relaxed state. The procedures themselves appear deceptively simple; because of many subtle nuances of timing and other parameters, however, even experienced therapists typically require several months of supervised training to learn to apply skillfully all aspects of systematic desensitization, as it has been used in well-controlled evaluative studies and in most skilled clinical work. Most reports of systematic desensitization have based details of procedure on one of four identifiable approaches, those of Wolpe, Arnold A. Lazarus, Lang, or Paul, each of which follows the complete package but with minor variations in the timing or sequence of various aspects of treatment [Paul 1969c, pp. 150–154]. In general, the features of these major approaches appear sufficiently similar to allow the generalization of findings from one to the other.

Relaxation training is typically a much abbreviated version of the Jacobson technique. The major goal of relaxation training is to reduce physiological arousal and produce at least neutral, preferably positive affect. Since the autonomic and cortical activity to be reduced is not under direct voluntary control, relaxation training usually focuses on the skeletal muscles and respiration, which are partially under direct voluntary control. The client is usually asked to recline on a couch or recliner chair that provides complete physical support. The therapist instructs the client systematically to tense and hold small muscle groups, a hand and a forearm, for example, and then release them; some degree of relaxation or reduction of tonic muscle tension is naturally produced during the release. (You may get some idea of the sensation by resting your arm on a desk or chair, making a tight fist, holding it tense for seven seconds, and *abruptly* releasing your fist. The sensations of warmth and relaxation you notice during the first ten to twenty seconds after release are a mild form of the sensations that relaxation training produces in the entire body.) By repeating this tension-release cycle several times systematically with all muscle groups in the body, and holding a deep breath concurrent with tension and releasing it for normal breathing at the same time he releases muscle tension, the client can usually produce a state of reduced physiological arousal with no detectable tension at all in one to six training sessions. Further, if the client focuses his attention on the sensations during release phases, he can passively learn to produce relaxation by simply recalling the sensations previously experienced during release phases.

The specific order in which muscle groups are taken varies among the major approaches, as does the timing of tension-release cycles. No differences in effectiveness have been reported as long as the sequence in which muscle groups are taken is systematic, tension is maintained for at least five to seven seconds, and the release phase for each group is at least twenty to thirty seconds, with progress from one group to another contingent on an absence of detectable tension in the first group. The complexity of relaxation–training technique is evident in a book written to serve as a therapist training manual [Bernstein & Borkovec in press]. Initially, about half of each therapy session is devoted to relaxation training, and the client is asked to practice the procedures at home. Over time the number of muscle groups is systematically reduced by combining smaller groups. Eventually the client is able to produce deep relaxation in any or all parts of his body in less than four minutes without first having to tense his muscles at all, but simply by recalling previous relaxation. This ability allows the client to relax without reclining.

Relaxation may sometimes be induced by direct suggestion or hypnotic procedures, relying on prior associations to reduce physiological arousal. Direct suggestion has been effective, but requires longer to produce deep relaxation and produces less extensive effects than abbreviated relaxation training [Paul 1969e]. No matter how it is achieved, a deep and consistent state of relaxation is necessary to inhibit anxiety.

Anxiety hierarchies are constructed by the therapist in collaboration with the client, based on the client's reports on the specific nature and relative strength of the stimuli that elicit maladaptive anxiety. The hierarchy is simply a list of the entire range of these anxiety-eliciting stimulus conditions systematically ordered along an equal-interval scale from the weakest to the strongest. These specific conditions thus fall along a primary or secondary stimulus generalization gradient from the most severe stimulus.

The items in an anxiety hierarchy should be highly specific and concrete. Thus an item in a test anxiety hierarchy might be "sitting at your desk in your room, on the night before the final exam, reading your [some specified] text," rather than "studying for an exam." Note that the former version gives the client more cues than the latter to help him visualize the item.

In addition to constructing the anxiety hierarchy during the early treatment sessions, the therapist also collects information about important factors that might change the intensity of the items within the hierarchy. The information is very helpful during desensitization proper since it allows the therapist to reduce the potency of specific items if they appear to be too strong for their serial position or to insert items that had not been planned for originally (all hierarchies are considered tentative and subject to constant revision). With social anxiety, for example, it is important to know that the number of people in a group influences the degree of anxiety elicited. Thus, if during desensitization proper, the client has trouble visualizing without anxiety, "you're at Jim's dinner party, sitting down at the table with Jim and eight of his friends," the therapist can change the item to ". . . six of his friends." When the new item has been mastered, the more troublesome one is likely to be easier to tolerate.

Since more than one anxiety hierarchy may be employed with a client, several items from each hierarchy may be presented in one session. Several hierarchies may also be completed sequentially over sessions. The number of items making up a hierarchy differs widely depending on the difficulty and complexity of the problem. Relatively simple problems (for example, a circumscribed phobia) may require hierarchies of only ten to fifteen items, while more complex problems (for example, major social-evaluative anxiety) in which many environmental factors qualify the strength of a given stimulus item may require fifty, sixty, or even one hundred items.

There are two basic types of anxiety stimulus hierarchies: spatial–temporal and thematic. Spatial-temporal hierarchies contain items that gradually and systematically approach a single object or event along a space or time dimension, for example, waking up on the morning of the exam, eating breakfast on the morning of the exam, walking toward the exam room, fifteen minutes before the exam. Note that the hierarchy approaches a single event in space and time; which could be a dog, a speech, a job interview, a party, or whatever.

A thematic hierarchy, on the other hand, does not usually involve the space-time dimension. Rather, its items are listed along some dimension of thematic similarity such as physical attributes, functions, or meaning. Thus a thematic hierarchy includes items that are progressively more anxiety producing but not necessarily part of the same event or object, for example, waiting for the English exam to begin, waiting for the French exam to begin, waiting for the math exam to begin. The thematic dimension employed here is the type of exam, which (for the hypothetical client) varied from the easiest to the most difficult. Thematic hierarchies may be focused on relatively simple targets such as types of exams, or types of dogs, or they may (and often do) deal with more complex themes involving mediated generalization such as rejection, criticism, and death.

In clinical practice it is rare that only a simple spatial-temporal or thematic hierarchy is used; more often, a combination is found. In combined hierarchies there is usually a major thematic dimension composed of spatial-temporal subdimensions. Thus, in our test anxiety example, a combined hierarchy might include items like waking up on the morning of the English exam, eating breakfast on the day of the English exam, walking toward the English exam room, fifteen minutes before the exam . . . waking up on the morning of the French exam; eating breakfast on the morning of the French exam. . . . The more complicated either the thematic or spatial-temporal dimensions become, the more elaborate the combined hierarchy is.

Whether the anxiety hierarchy employed in systematic desensitization is spatial-temporal, thematic, or a combination of both, its adequate construction is central to the success of the technique. To the extent that interitem steps are inappropriately large or items do not accurately represent the client's particular anxiety dimension(s), the degree of effectiveness of anxiety reduction in the *real* fear-stimulus situation is reduced. At the current state of development the identification of central stimulus dimensions and the construction of appropriate hierarchies depend more on the therapist's knowledge and clinical acumen than on his skills in either relaxation training or desensitization proper, both of which can be taught relatively quickly.

Desensitization proper can begin after hierarchies have been constructed, the client can reliably achieve a deep state of relaxation, and imagery has been tested (or trained) to assure that the client visualizes clearly, can start and stop images on request, and that visualization of anxiety-eliciting stimuli in the absence of relaxation does in fact increase anxiety. An easy and rapid communication system is established for the client to indicate when images are clear and when any anxiety, tension, or discomfort is experienced. Such indications are usually made by signaling with the left or right index finger, but may be verbal. Deep relaxation is induced, and the client reminded of the need to indicate even the slightest disruption of relaxation. He is then asked to visualize the lowest item on the anxiety hierarchy. After an appropriate exposure time with clear imagery, he is instructed to stop visualizing and focus his attention on feelings of deep relaxation. In the absence of any indication of anxiety (a "perfect" hierarchy with strong relaxation), each item is repeated until the entire hierarchy is completed. Of course, the therapist makes certain that each item has been imagined without disturbance before moving on to the next one.

If an anxiety response occurs during an item presentation, that presentation is immediately terminated and all further activity halted until the client again achieves deep relaxation, often aided by imagining a previously agreed upon neutral or pleasant scene. A diluted version of the anxiety-provoking item is then presented (dilution can be achieved by shortening the presentation or by adding a factor known to reduce the item's intensity), or in some cases a lower item is introduced. Ultimately, any item causing an anxiety response is repeated until it can be tolerated in its strongest form for a longer period than was initially required. The specific parameters of timing item duration and criteria for moving on vary some among the major approaches. Their effectiveness, however, does not appear to differ so long as a minimum criterion of two ten-second visualizations without anxiety (one twenty-second visualization for an item that previously disrupted relaxation) is maintained before moving to higher items.

Each desensitization session concludes with a successfully completed item, which is the first one presented at the next session. The number of items presented per session usually depends on how well the hierarchy was constructed and thus how much anxiety it generates. An ideal hierarchy spaces items so that an anxiety response never occurs. The number of items completed per session then depends solely on the time available. More often, however, some anxiety occurs, necessitating backtracking and item revision. The usual range is from about three to ten items per session, or until about forty-five minutes have elapsed. Overlong sessions may tire some clients; desensitization proper, however, has occasionally been conducted for as long as three hours in emergencies (producing therapist fatigue).

Obviously, progress in the visualized hierarchy should be paralleled by progress in the real-life anxiety situation. If it is not, the therapist must begin to look for defects in procedure or lapses in client cooperation, so that relevant remedial steps can be taken.

Sometimes continuous assessment of progress is possible. With acrophobia (fear of height), for example, the client can be asked to expose himself to the real-life situations covered during each desensitization session (without attempting items not yet visualized). While this is an ideal assessment situation, the target problem may not allow continuous monitoring of progress. If, for example, the hierarchy being desensitized involves arranging for and going out on a date, the therapist cannot assess progress in lower segments of the hierarchy without "trapping" the client into the rest of the chain, perhaps before he is ready to handle it.

An Illustrative Case

Let us present an actual clinical case example to bring together our earlier discussion of the development of anxiety-based clinical problems and the foregoing account of the modification of such problems through systematic desensitization. In the interest of clarity, the following material focuses mainly on those aspects of a case that relate directly to systematic desensitization. The reader should be aware that other facets of the client's problems and other treatment techniques, which we mention only in passing, were also taken into account and dealt with intensively.

Mr. M., an unmarried professional man in his early thirties, referred himself to a psychological clinic because he felt he was homosexual. His problem was longstanding and had previously been dealt with in individual and group therapy on an outpatient basis as well as during a short period of hospitalization. The client reported that while he had never actually engaged in any overt homosexual activity, he frequently found himself paying more attention to the physical attractiveness of males than of females and that he enjoyed the company of males more than females. Mr. M was often very tense and uncomfortable with people (especially new acquaintances) partly because he was worried that he would do something stupid and partly because of guilt over his attraction to males. His discomfort caused him to withdraw from or avoid social situations and to become very depressed. Thus he had few friends, although, somewhat surprisingly, he was occasionally having sexual intercourse with a girl he had known for a long time. Mr. M did not see this heterosexual activity as evidence against his being homosexual; rather, he felt that it was too "mechanical" and noted that it was often accompanied by fantasies of homosexual relations.

As a child, Mr. M. had been a somewhat overweight, nonathletic bookworm, a marked contrast to his outgoing, athletic brother. His family and peers considered him a sissy, and in high school he was labeled "effeminate" by classmates. After attending Catholic primary and secondary schools, he entered a seminary, where he formed several close relationships with other young men and with one individual in particular. At one point a teacher labeled this friendship "potentially homosexual." This evaluation upset Mr. M greatly and marked the beginning of his concerns over being homosexual and of his attempts to seek help for the "problem."

This case is a good example of a presenting problem that is not obviously based on a conditioned anxiety response and might not at first seem an appropriate target for systematic desensitization. While it is easy, however, to think of homosexual behavior in terms of a person's attraction to same-sex partners, many people are labeled (by themselves and others) "homosexual" because they are *repelled* by members of the opposite sex. In many such cases the problem is not mainly one of breaking the same–sex attraction but of eliminating a conditioned anxiety response (along with its operant escape and avoidance components) to opposite-sex partners and then allowing for (or teaching) appropriate heterosexual behaviors.

It became fairly clear after about three diagnostic sessions that Mr. M's main problem was that as a result of early experience and some unfortunate labeling, he had never developed the social skills necessary for satisfying heterosexual relationships. He was a "loser," socially speaking. In addition because of how people (especially females) responded to him, he learned to [a] associate social situations with anxiety (respondent conditioning), and [b] avoid or escape such situations to gain relief from the anxiety (operant conditioning). Thus Mr. M's concerns about homosexuality were brought about initially by the label others placed on his behavior, which he then adopted. While his feelings toward males supported this label, they did not justify it. Since his only strong relationships had been with males (mainly because of the circumstances of his education and his social-skills deficits), it is not surprising that in adult life he was more strongly attracted to people with whom he associated some comfort (that is, males) than to those from whom he had received only rejection.

Mr. M was caught in the middle of the kind of double approach-avoidance conflict we discussed earlier. He was attracted to males but repelled by the guilt and cultural taboos associated with such feelings. On the other hand, he knew he should be attracted to females (and he wanted to be "normal"), but was repelled by them. The byproducts of this conflict were the depression, tension, and guilt reported to the therapist.

The treatment consisted of eliminating the approach-avoidance conflict by social–skill training, altering attitudes about positive feelings toward males, and so forth. Our concern, however, is only with the elimination of Mr. M's conditioned anxiety response to social situations, especially those involving females. The client was introduced to progressive relaxation training at the second session because of the high degree of tension he experienced on a day-to-day basis and because it would allow for early use of systematic desensitization. By the fourth session he was well on his way to developing relaxation skill, and at that point the therapist began working with him at outlining desensitization hierarchies relating to social situations.

As it turned out, two hierarchies were used. The first was thematic, dealing with a wide variety of social stimuli. It consisted of twenty-three items, ranging from easy situations like "you are reading at a library table" through intermediate settings like "saying 'hello' to your secretary when you arrive at the office" and "talking to your parents on the telephone" to very difficult items like "asking [girl's name] to go to a movie with you" and "sitting in [name of authority figure's] office while he reads and evaluates a paper you wrote." The items jump around from situation to situation, but though their situational context differs they are all systematically related to one another since they represent increasing degrees of difficulty for the client along a "social evaluative" dimension or theme.

A second hierarchy was constructed to deal in a more specialized way with one of the more difficult situations represented on the original, thematic hierarchy—arranging for and going on a date with a new girl. It was a spatial-temporal hierarchy because its twenty items described the actual sequence of events (along space and time rather than thematic dimensions) preceding and during a date, beginning with items like "looking up [girl's name] phone number" and "dialing [girl's name] phone number" and progressing through increasingly stressful visualizations like "sitting together in the movie theater waiting for the picture to begin," "leaving the theater and [girl's name] says, 'What shall we do now?'," and "sitting in the car in front of [girl's name] house."

Once the hierarchies had been constructed (which took part of two sessions) and Mr. M had indicated that the items were correctly spaced in difficulty, desensitization proper began. Both hierarchies were successfully visualized without anxiety in eleven sessions, each of which was devoted partly to desensitization and partly to discussing and planning ways to elimi-

nate some of Mr. M's other problems.

The client was seen for nineteen sessions over five months. At the end of his contact with the therapist, many changes had taken place in Mr. M's attitudes and behavior. Among the most important was that he no longer felt uncomfortable and anxious in the social-evaluative situations that had previously been so difficult for him to handle. He found that as he relaxed more in such settings (and applied some of the social skills he had been taught) other people responded positively, thus maintaining (reinforcing) his social behavior and reducing the probability of escape or avoidance. Mr. M began to feel better about himself; he was no longer depressed and spent less and less time worrying about being homosexual. He did not stop thinking about it; rather the problem simply became irrelevant. He just did not think about it because he had learned not to feel guilty about appreciating good-looking males and because he was far too busy being a socially active heterosexual. Shortly after the termination of therapy, Mr. M became engaged and was married. He reported feeling extremely well and experiencing none of the depression that had been so characteristic of him.

While it is always nice when case reports like this one have a "happy ending," we must resist the temptation to make too much of such success. Even though it is clear that Mr. M changed a great deal, especially in his response to previously stressful situations, the changes cannot be related in a cause–effect fashion to the operation of systematic desensitization alone. Many other specific and nonspecific factors could have had (and probably did have) a role in his behavioral changes. Thus such positive case examples, encouraging as they are, must ultimately be replaced by confirming data from research employing higher-level-of-product factorial designs before cause–effect statements about the effectiveness of systematic desensitization can be justified. Some data of this kind are available on the effectiveness of systematic desensitization. A foundation in the principles and problems of evaluative research in behavior modification, however, must be provided before evidence for claims of specific degrees of effectiveness and efficiency can be presented.

A Note on Designs in Evaluative Research

All scientific research is nothing more than a special way of answering questions so that the information gained, as well as the procedure used, are public, reproducible, and communicable to others. The purpose of scientific research on clinical procedures (behavior-modification techniques) is to discover cause–effect relationships between the things a therapist does and the changes observed in client behavior. These relationships are discovered by carefully and systematically manipulating one aspect of the treatment situation, while holding all other aspects constant and observing the effects that the manipulation has on client behavior.

We may, for example, be interested in how the length of therapy sessions is related to therapy success. Research might take the form of asking five therapists to conduct one-hour sessions with their clients, while five other therapists hold two-hour meetings. Assessment of the change in client behavior from before to after treatment would lead the researcher to conclude that either more or less benefit occurred for long-session versus short-session clients. While this hypothetical research design is an example of how scientific method might be applied to questions about length of therapy sessions, it contains many flaws. Factors in addition to differences in session length (for example, differences in therapist techniques and in severity of client problems) could also affect success of therapy; thus the original question cannot be answered by the design employed. The principles and methods of evaluative research on anxiety-reduction techniques are basically the same as those of research in any other area, except possibly for the greater complexity of variables. Hence the clinical researcher must be even more vigilant than other scientists about errors in his research designs.

To provide valid information about specific questions, research must be designed so that the data obtained can be interpreted unambiguously. If the design employed does not allow unambiguous interpretation of results, it is a mistake to act as if it did. Unfortunately many researchers make errors inevitable because they ask the wrong question in the first place. Questions like "Does behavior therapy work with neurotics?" or "Does electric shock help schizophrenics?" are just about impossible to answer with any research design because the variables are too complex. What do you mean by behavior therapy? What is a neurotic or a schizophrenic? What kind and how many shocks? When both the independent and dependent variables in a design are inadequately specified because the original questions were poorly phrased, it becomes not just unlikely but impossible that anything of value can be learned from the research.

One methodologist [Paul 1969a] has suggested that progress in behavior–modification research lies in asking specific experimental questions within the framework of the ultimate question: *What* treatment, by *whom*, is most effective for *this* individual with *that*

specific problem, under *which* set of circumstances, and *how* does it come about? Of course, no one study can ever completely answer this rather long question. But it is possible for knowledge about it to accumulate through many studies, in which the particular aspect of the question is identified and all relevant classes of variables are adequately described, measured, and/or controlled. Researchers need to ask specific questions about the *classes* of clients, therapists, techniques, and problems and separate the effects of each. Ideally, then, an anxiety-reduction study should tell us unambiguously that the procedure works well when conducted by this *type* of therapist with that *type* of problem for that *type* of client.

Research Design and Possible Level of Product

As we have stated, each type of research design has limits on the quality of data it can generate. In behavior-modification research, designs range in complexity and sophistication from simple reports of case studies like Mr. M's to elaborate group designs in which several independent variables are simultaneously studied in combination with each other and special control groups are included. Obviously, the level of product from each of these designs differs, with more information about the specific nature of cause-effect relationships generally coming from higher-level designs. It is important, however, to realize that something can be learned from almost every design. The trick is to recognize what that something is in a given instance. The following outline (adapted from Paul 1967, 1969a) of level of product possible in designs that have been employed in research on systematic desensitization and related techniques (summarized in table 1) provides an idea of what can be expected from a given study and the basis of our conclusions on treatment effectiveness.

Individual case study without measurement. This type of study simply reports what a therapist did with a single client and the changes that took place in that client's behavior, as in Mr. M's case. While it was the typical approach of behavior–modification research before 1920, in its simplest form (that is, uncontrolled observation by the therapist with no formal, specified measures of either the problem or the degree of improvement) it has essentially no scientific value. The anecdotal case report can really only raise questions not answer them, although it can serve to interest others in new therapy techniques and thus generate researchable hypotheses.

The problems with this design should be obvious. The basis for all scientific evidence is that at least one comparison is made somewhere in the experi-

Table 1. Summary of Level of Product Possible from Various Research Designs.

Design	Level of Product
Case study (without measurement)	Crude hypotheses
Case study (with measurement)	Correlational conclusions; stronger hypotheses
Nonfactorial group design (without no-treatment control group)	Correlational conclusions; stronger hypotheses
Nonfactorial group design (with no-treatment control group)	Some general cause-effect relationship established
Factorial group design (with No treatment control group and attention–placebo control group	Specific cause–effect relationship established
Laboratory analogues	Specific cause–effect relationship established for analogue version of targets, treatments, subjects, and therapists (see text)

SOURCE: Adapted from G. L. Paul, 1967.

ment. In the anecdotal case study the only comparison is between what happened and what is assumed would have happened without treatment. Unfortunately any change in client behavior could have been the result of factors like the mere passage of time or the client's faith in the therapist or his particular treatment (the placebo effect). In fact, because of their presence in nearly any therapeutic interaction, nonspecific placebo effects are particularly in need of control for evaluation of anxiety-reduction procedures. Thus the level of product from such case reports is only that of an aid in the development of crude hypotheses about treatment effectiveness.

Individual case study with measurement. Improvement of the case study can be made by using standardized multiple measurement procedures. For example, a person who is afraid of cats is exposed to and asked to handle one on several occasions over many months before treatment, immediately after treatment, and at regular follow-up points. If it is discovered that reduction in the anxiety elicited occurred and was maintained only after the experimental treatment, then the hypotheses formed about the effects of treatment can be stronger. This design can provide a level of product that suggests correlational relationships, one that shows that as one effect varies, so do the others. But it is still not at the level of cause–effect evidence because the effects of suggestion, expectation of help, nonspecific characteristics of the therapist and the treatment, nontherapy related events, and many other

factors can still be partly, or even completely responsible for the behavior change observed.

For many problem behaviors, a multiple-baseline design can strengthen the level of product. For example, in a case of operant overeating an experimenter could alternate periods of treatment (designed to reduce weight) with no-treatment periods. If he found that weight loss occurred during a treatment period, stopped during no treatment, began again during treatment, and so on, he would have improved the single-subject design to its highest level of product. Here the hypothesis of a cause–effect relationship between treatment and change is strong indeed and is limited only by the fact that variables such as therapist and/or subject characteristics, repeated testing, and repeated treatments may have had an effect of their own. Even if the latter factors were active, however, they would most strongly affect (that is, limit) the generalizability of the results not the validity of the cause-effect relationship found. Thus we would know that the treatment was effective, but we could not be sure why or to what extent it could be applied to other clients, therapists, and the like. Unfortunately, multiple-baseline designs are seldom appropriate for treating problems in which inappropriate conditioned anxiety is central. Once a therapeutic reduction in anxiety has been obtained and the client has appropriately interacted with previously anxiety-eliciting stimulus conditions, anxiety reduction is likely to be not only maintained but furthered. A variant of this design is possible when several unrelated anxiety-eliciting stimuli are present in a client and each is treated separately and sequentially. To the extent that changes regularly occur only in those conditions being treated at the time and not in others, this design approximates the level of product of the multiple-baseline design.

Nonfactorial single–group design. This design may be thought of as basically a combination of case studies. Thus, instead of reporting the results of one case, an experimenter may report the results of several cases at the same time. While more impressive than its single-subject counterpart, in its simplest form the single-group design shares all the problems of the anecdotal case study. If standardized multiple prepost assessments are added to this design, the level of product is increased, since a relationship between treatment and behavior change, if found, applies to more than one subject. Obviously, multiple assessment procedures or the use of alternate treatment and no-treatment periods, multiple baselines, and so on would make the design even stronger. For problems involving conditioned anxiety, however, the impracticality of using powerful single-subject designs restricts the single-group design to strengthening hypotheses and correlational conclusions.

Nonfactorial group design with untreated controls. This is the classic experiment: one group gets treatment while another, the control group, does not. Often this design is elaborated so that two or more treatments are compared with each other and with a no-treatment control group. For example, a researcher may be interested in whether systematic desensitization is effective with claustrophobia (fear of closed places) and, in addition, whether its effectiveness surpasses that of the procedures already in use. He might design an experiment in which one group of claustrophobic clients is treated with systematic desensitization by one therapist, while another group is administered "standard" procedures by a different therapist. A third group would be given no treatment at all (in many studies people in the no-treatment group are put on a waiting list).

While this is a strong design because the treatments can be directly compared with each other and also with no-treatment conditions in terms of producing changes in clients with comparable problems, it does have its weaknesses. It can establish some cause-effect relationships (if the treated groups show significantly more anxiety reduction than the untreated group, it can be concluded that treatment was responsible), but it cannot tell which treatment worked better. Any difference in effectiveness among the treatments could have been the result of the characteristics of the particular therapist who conducted the treatments (perhaps one was just more competent and sensitive than the other), placebo effects in treatment (perhaps one therapist or treatment procedure inspired more confidence than the other), or interactions between these and other variables like client characteristics (perhaps one of the therapists is generally more effective with the type of client used in the study).

Many researchers interested in studying anxiety-reduction techniques like systematic desensitization feel that if they have employed a control group (usually a no-treatment group), they have designed a completely adequate experiment. The inclusion of a no-treatment control group in an anxiety-reduction experiment, however, does not guarantee that all the research questions can be answered unambiguously. The most probable reason for this situation is that experimenters often forget to ask themselves exactly what they want to control. If you want to control for the effects of the passage of time or spontaneous improvement, a no-treatment control is the ticket. If, on the other hand, you need to control for the effects of the client's faith in the therapist or other nonspecific

ingredients, a special control condition must be developed in which client faith and therapist attention are the only factors that could have produced a reduction in anxiety. Obviously the choice of control groups in anxiety-reduction research must be preceded by consideration of the question "Control for what?"

Factorial group design with untreated and nonspecific-treatment controls. This rather long description refers to the best of the behavior-modification designs as regards level of product. Quite simply, all relevant *combinations* of treatments, therapists, and problems are represented in the design, along with some control subjects who receive no treatment and others who receive partial treatment to control for nonspecific effects about which specific questions are *not* being asked. This type of study in which several variables are studied in combination is called a *factorial design.* For example, two kinds of treatments for claustrophobia, A and B, are conducted by two therapists, X and Y, with each therapist responsible for treating half of the individuals in the A and B groups. This factorial design results in four groups, which differ in the therapist–treatment combination. (X–A, X–B, Y–A, Y–B).

There is no single factorial design for studying techniques of anxiety reduction. The designs are as different and as complex as the number and nature of the questions require. The basic model of the factorial design is the group design with untreated controls and measurement before and after treatment. Factors, levels of factors, and groups are added to the design as necessitated by the questions asked in such a way that each independent variable occurs in combination with every other independent variable. For example, in the hypothetical study of claustrophobia we mentioned above, the fact that the same therapists conduct systematic desensitization and a standard treatment could allow separation of specific treatment effects. Factorial and partial factorial designs are complex and expensive to conduct. Because they control relevant sources of both nontreatment and nonspecific treatment variance, however, they are the most effective way to provide evidence of specific cause-effect relationships between specific treatment techniques and change in client behavior.

Laboratory analogues. All of the designs we have mentioned may be conducted in a laboratory rather than in a clinical setting. Often a controlled laboratory setting is the best place for research on behavior modification, especially to find out *how* rather than *whether* a particular treatment technique operates. To find out how, an analogy is made between variables in the clinic and in the laboratory so that clients become subjects and treatments become experimental conditions. To the degree that the laboratory study differs in important ways from the problems and procedures in the clinical treatment setting, however, the results of the laboratory analogue are not useful in contributing to knowledge of clinical treatment. Thus, in reading a laboratory analogue study about treatments for anxiety reduction, we must ask, "How is this experiment analogous to a clinical situation and how does it clearly differ?" The number and importance of the differences must then be assessed to determine how relevant the findings are to problems and procedures in actual clinical settings.

This determination is not always easy because there are many ways to set up a laboratory analogue of anxiety-reduction therapy, and each contains advantages and disadvantages. It is important to understand that the experimenter's choice is dictated not by which is the perfect analogy (there probably is no such thing), but by which analogy best suits his purposes. A laboratory analogue study can be like or unlike a clinical situation in at least four major areas: subjects, target problems, treatments, and therapists. A desensitization analogue study that is most like a clinical situation, then, employs as subjects only persons who seek help with a clinically disturbing problem and as therapists practicing, professional ones who administer treatments identical to those provided in a clinic.

Faithful analogy in all four areas is not always necessary or possible, however, and at this point the experimenter's goals become relevant. Let us suppose, for example, that an experimenter is interested in discovering the best way to teach systematic-desensitization techniques to therapists unacquainted with it. The need for subjects and problems identical to those found in the clinic is less important than the need to employ as students persons who are in fact practicing therapists who do not know much about systematic desensitization.

On the other hand, if you are working on the problem of programming computers to conduct systematic desensitization, the need for accurate analogy in the therapist area disappears; but it is important that the computer-administered version of systematic desensitization be identical to that used by human therapists. Early in such a research program the need for subjects and problems precisely like those found in clinical practice is minor because the emphasis is on simply determining whether or not the computer can desensitize *any* conditioned anxiety response. Later, however, the experimenter would need to apply the computer-based treatment to real subjects with real problems to provide evidence for the machine's usefulness in clinical settings.

The main thing to remember in dealing with analogue research concerning techniques for reducing anxiety is that the accuracy of analogy in each area we mentioned above becomes important only if the experimenter plans to generalize about it beyond the contrived laboratory setting. If you want to make statements about the effectiveness of systematic desensitization on phobias, for example, you should make certain that [a] the subjects employed are really phobic (that is, avoid the eliciting stimulus conditions and demonstrate anxiety in the presence of the eliciting stimulus), [b] the systematic desensitization procedure used is an accurate version of its clinical counterpart (unless you want only to make statements about the effectiveness of an artificial treatment not in use clinically), and [c] the treatment is conducted by people competent to do so (if the therapists administer procedures incorrectly, you cannot draw conclusions about the effectiveness of systematic desensitization).

While clinical field studies frequently suffer from the use of low-level designs, unusual procedures, confounding of variables, or other design errors [Paul 1969b, 1969c], laboratory analogue studies less frequently reflect pure experimental–design errors. Unfortunately, too many laboratory analogue studies mistakenly assume direct generalization to clinical problems or settings, while failing to meet some or all of the requirements for doing so [Bernstein & Paul, 1971]. For example, in many analogue studies on systematic desensitization, subjects (usually undergraduate psychology students required to take part in several hours of experimentation) are selected as phobics on the basis of a single verbal report, often supplemented by a test of their willingness to touch a supposedly phobic object such as a rat or snake. These same measures are readministered after treatment. The problem here is that in the first test the subjects know that fear of snakes is being assessed, and thus the social situation demands that they not touch the animal (or do so only reluctantly). In the posttreatment test the demand is reversed, so that touching the snake is now appropriate and socially desirable. Since it has been shown that such subjects may be extremely compliant [Orne 1962] and may act like phobics or "normals" depending on how the fear test is set up [Bernstein 1970a], doubt is immediately cast upon whether the persons used in most such analogue research are really phobic in the clinical sense. As our discussion of problems in assessing anxiety indicated, this is a particular problem when using such operant assessment modes. While it may be true that real phobics are hard to find in a college population [Lang 1968], there is no excuse for using nonphobics to evaluate a treatment for phobia. In fact, no study purporting to investigate treatment procedures designed to reduce anxiety has meaning or relevance unless the existence of an anxiety response in the presence of eliciting stimuli is well documented before treatment.

Similar problems of comparability exist for treatment techniques used in analogue research. Important aspects of treatment techniques like systematic desensitization are often altered in the laboratory for convenience or to save time. Even though the changes made may strain the analogy badly, the laboratory version is referred to in the published report as "systematic desensitization." While it is true that if data are available to justify major procedural changes (that is, if we discover through separate controlled research that the change does not seriously alter the effectiveness of treatment), those changes need not result in reduction of the strength of the analogue. In most cases, however, such data are not available or presented. Thus the reader of behavior-modification literature must be aware that an experimenter's referring to his treatment technique as "systematic desensitization," or "client–centered therapy," or so on does not always guarantee that an accurate version of the treatment is actually being assessed.

A closely related problem is that of the competence of therapists in analogue studies to conduct the treatments involved. A therapist who is either unskilled in a particular treatment (even if that treatment is an accurate version of clinical procedures) or, more generally clinically deficient (for example, insensitive or offensive) is likely to bias results in such a way that a fair test of the treatment technique is not made. Of course, if the question is whether the treatment can be used by clinically unskilled or inexperienced persons (for example, nonprofessional therapists), then this criticism does not apply. Unfortunately, many studies designed to answer questions relating to treatment procedures use as therapists individuals whose general clinical experience is minimal and whose familiarity with the specific treatment procedures is brief or nonexistent. Ideally, the therapists involved in such analogue studies should be persons who are actually, or come as close as possible to real therapists in skill and experience.

When conducted appropriately, laboratory analogue research is a useful tool, which can be employed by the clinical researcher interested in systematic desensitization or in any other behavior-modification technique. It cannot, however, provide all the answers to

all the questions that must be asked about a treatment technique. Procedures and conclusions based on laboratory research must ultimately be tested in applied settings to determine their validity in clinical practice. Such acid tests may have disappointing or ambiguous results, which send the experimenter/clinician back to his laboratory. But ideally research on any behavior-modification technique should progress in a clear-cut, if not orderly fashion from case studies to laboratory analogue work designed to establish and refine the procedures, back to case-study tests with "real clients," and then on to more sophisticated control-group and factorial designs aimed at experimentally determining both the effectiveness of the treatment and how it works. Once a body of empirical knowledge has been accumulated on a specific set of treatment procedures, even lower level designs may accumulate to provide a combined level of product that is higher than any individual study.

Research on Effectiveness of Systematic Desensitization

Of all clinical treatment packages in current use for treating specific classes of problems, systematic desensitization comes closer than any other to approximating the ideal sequence for developing and evaluating treatment procedures. Extrapolating from principles established in the experimental laboratory with animals and humans, Wolpe experimented at the clinical-case-study level with several procedures for overcoming conditioned anxiety responses. His first report of the treatment technique and clinical outcome of a series of individual cases appeared in the *South African Medical Journal* in 1952. During the 1950's a few reports of additional series of individual cases appeared in American and British journals by Wolpe and his students, such as Arnold A. Lazarus and Stanley Rachman; it was not until the publication of Wolpe's book *Psychotherapy by Reciprocal Inhibition* [1958], however, that much attention was paid to the new technology.

During the early 1960's several series of case studies by different therapists were reported, systematic desensitization was brought into the laboratory for further formalization and modification, and controlled evaluation studies of both nonfactorial and factorial designs began to appear. Since 1966 controlled investigations of systematic desensitization have outnumbered uncontrolled reports; the interplay between controlled clinical studies, laboratory investigations, and clinical case trials, however, continues in a concurrent, if not orderly way. Some indication of the degree of activity surrounding systematic desensitization may be seen by noting that only thirteen reports appeared on the technique during the ten years following Wolpe's 1952 paper. In contrast, the next five years saw sixty-two reports, and the next five over one hundred and twenty. These reports range from single and multiple case reports all the way to highly sophisticated factorial experiments employing multiple-assessment techniques and a variety of relevant controls. Detailed descriptions and critiques of systematic desensitization evaluative research on a study-by-study basis are available in separate review papers [Paul 1969b, 1969c, Borkovec 1970]. These reviews encompass over one hundred and fifty separate reports on the work of hundreds of therapists with thousands of clients. Most of them were based on experimental designs whose level of product was less than optimal. In addition, however, there have been several well-controlled studies whose designs allow for evaluation of specific cause-effect relationships between systematic desensitization therapy and change in the client's behavior.

The results of these experiments have been overwhelmingly positive in establishing the specific effectiveness of systematic desensitization. Moreover, some of this research clearly demonstrates the superiority of desensitization over other more traditional treatment approaches in handling anxiety-related behavior problems. Most of the lower level designs provide data consistent with the results of cause-effect experiments. While these lower level designs cannot themselves establish the effectiveness of treatment, they can and do supplement and support the cause-effect conclusions found in higher product-level studies. Once the effectiveness of a treatment package has been established through higher level experimentation, the results of lower level designs are more believable. In systematic desensitization, these lower level studies not only support positive conclusions of overall effectiveness but provide important information about the range of clients, target problems, therapists, treatment settings, and procedural variations over which systematic desensitization may be successfully employed.

Systematic desensitization has been reported effective in cases representing the full range of distressing behaviors where conditioned anxiety is a fundamental component, including social-evaluative anxiety, some types of depression, impotence, frigidity, stuttering, "pervasive anxiety," some psychophysiological disorders as well as problems involving concrete phobic objects. Research at all levels of sophistication has reported the technique effective with both males and females, most ranging in age from fifteen to fifty, living in various socioeconomic circumstances in North America, Europe, and South Africa. Clients as young as five and as old as seventy have been reported in the literature; no well-controlled studies, however, have yet appeared at these extremes of age (modifications of procedures have usually been required with young children).

The few reports that failed to find systematic desensitization an effective treatment for anxiety appear to be largely a result of inappropriate assessment, in which either reactive anxiety or problems unrelated to anxiety were treated. Client personality characteristics have not been found to interact with the success of the treatment so long as motivation is present; few studies, however, have yet focused directly on this issue. Psychotic behavior by a client obviously requires some change in nonspecific interaction and focus. Conflicting reports have appeared on the effectiveness of systematic desensitization with this group, some therapists (including the authors) reporting success and others not. No well-controlled studies with a psychotic population have yet appeared. The severity or duration of elicited anxiety per se is apparently related to the length of time required for treatment but not to effectiveness.

The range of therapists and therapy settings in the successful use of systematic desensitization has also been reported to be very broad by many lower product-level studies. Positive results have been reported in public and private hospitals and clinics, day-care centers, university clinics and counseling centers, clients' homes, private therapists' offices, and so forth. There is, then, no reason to believe that the effectiveness of systematic desensitization interacts in any significant way with the physical setting in which it is conducted. Therapists of both sexes and of various theoretical persuasions have been reported to be effective (in both controlled and uncontrolled research) in administering systematic desensitization, but inexperienced therapists tend to do far less well than those with both general clinical skill and specific training and supervised experience with the treatment package. The major negative influence of therapists is in the assessment area, where inexperienced therapists are more likely to fail in identifying appropriate targets and hierarchies. Otherwise, therapist characteristics appear to make little contribution to the effectiveness of systematic desensitization per se.

Therapists inexperienced with the specific treatment procedures may inadvertently introduce unusual technique variations. Even within the restrictions of the standard desensitization treatment package (relaxation training, hierarchy construction, and item presentation) great variability in the details of administration is possible, and it is important to know how much such variation affects treatment results. In relaxation training, for example, the number and nature of specific muscle groups, the duration of tension and release, the number of tension-release cycles per muscle groups, the use of direct versus indirect suggestion (or even hypnosis), and many other factors vary across the four standard versions we described earlier. There is, however, no evidence that the ultimate effects of the four major procedures are significantly different. Other more drastic procedural variations in relaxation training (for example, the use of drugs, tape-recorded instructions, and alpha-wave feedback conditioning) may result in important and meaningful differences in the relaxation state produced and may thus alter the effectiveness of desensitization [Paul & Trimble 1970]. Much more research on such factors is badly needed since no comparative data are currently available.

Hierarchy-construction procedures are still more art than science and, thus variation is almost boundless. The major variations have been in hierarchies that are individualized versus standardized (that is, where for convenience in research or other settings each of several clients is desensitized to the same set of items) and spatial-temporal versus thematic. Few firm conclusions can be drawn from the research literature except that [a] spatial-temporal hierarchies appear easier to construct and may be completed faster than thematic ones, and [b] standardized hierarchies may be used successfully if the items represent the anxiety dimension of the most distressed client (with this method less anxious clients are overtreated, but no one is given less desensitization than is required).

Procedural variations are perhaps most obvious in desensitization proper. Some of them are so extreme that they make it impossible, or at least unreasonable to call them systematic desensitization at all. On the other hand, some variations that look extreme at first glance are not really so different from standard procedures. For example, it has been found that desensitization can be effectively administered to groups of clients experiencing similar or related problems. The major variations here are in modified rules for relaxation training and hierarchy construction, in which treatment must be paced, as we noted above, for the most anxious client at any point in time. In addition, there is a great deal of solid evidence now available indicating that specially designed computers can administer systematic desensitization with excellent success.

These variations really involve the mode of presentation of fairly standard procedures, but many other reports include changes in the procedures themselves. While the four major versions of systematic desensitization we mentioned earlier differ in this area (that is, in the number of items presented per session, the number of presentations of each item, the duration of item presentation, the criteria for successful completion of an item, and other factors), they are sufficiently similar to produce essentially comparable results. Minor changes in procedural parameters do not necessarily have negative effects on treatment outcome, but all the variations we have discussed so far remained within the limits of the principles of systematic desensitization. Further research on this type of procedural variation is necessary to determine the combination of parameters that is most effective and efficient in producing the behavior change desired.

Unfortunately, many so-called variations of desensitization procedures actually violate the basic principles of systematic desensitization. Examples include presentation of hierarchy items for standard durations (regardless of the client's response to them), or while the client *tenses* his or her muscles, or for only one brief exposure; relaxation training that is ineffective because it is extremely brief or allows no feedback from the client; tape-recorded desensitization proper, which allows for no consequences of an anxiety signal from the client. Such techniques may be extremely interesting and potentially useful (after being subjected to careful research scrutiny), but they cannot be considered versions of systematic desensitization. Thus data (positive or negative) on the effectiveness of procedures that are superficially similar but fundamentally unrelated to systematic desensitization are not relevant for the overall evaluation of that technique or its legitimate variants.

Research on "Mechanisms" in Systematic Desensitization

Variations in procedure naturally lead to concern about the underlying mechanisms of operation of systematic desensitization. Once an effective treatment package has been established the how and why of effectiveness are extremely important. The more we understand the basis for effectiveness, the more we may be able to avoid variations in procedure that are likely to reduce effectiveness, and, conversely, the more precise we may become in detailing specific parameters for maximizing effectiveness.

As we stated earlier, any attempt to determine specific cause-effect relationships for specific treatment techniques requires control for nonspecific factors in treatment. Research on mechanisms of change must also take these factors into account. Paul has discussed possible nonspecific factors that may be operative in any treatment contact to reduce anxiety and thus add "noise" to the evaluation of specific parameters [1966, pp. 85–89]. The client's simply being accepted for treatment, in addition to being given an internally consistent rationale for the development of problems and a clear plan for alleviating them, may limit the response-label-response feedback spiral and restrict alternative, possibly irrational conceptualizations, which increase anxiety for clients with major life problems. Similarly, some anxiety reduction is likely to occur as a function of the therapist's providing a model of relaxed confidence and serving as a warm, interested, social-reinforcing agent (that is, a stimulus eliciting comfort and relief). Some extinction or counterconditioning of anxiety may occur as the client simply talks about anxiety-eliciting events (that is, symbolically confronts eliciting stimuli) in the context of a comfortable therapeutic relationship. Overgeneralizations may be halted by discrimination learning as the client sorts out the relationship between his responses and various aspects of his environment. This result is especially likely during hierarchy construction for systematic desensitization if the sources of anxiety are complex or social.

Three major approaches have been taken in research directed at discovering the underlying mechanisms of effectiveness for systematic desensitization per se. The first approach is a comparison of the effectiveness of the complete treatment package with the effectiveness of other treatment procedures that leave out specific components of the total package. Thus, for example, all procedures might be conducted intact for one group, while another would receive all procedures except relaxation training. Several well-controlled studies have been conducted using such a subtraction method, generally finding that the complete systematic desensitization package is more effective than nonspecific factors and than the package without all of its components. Similarly, the complete package has operated effectively without many of the nonspecific factors (for example, rationale, warm, attentive therapist) being present. Merely constructing an anxiety hierarchy has not been found to contribute to effectiveness either positively or negatively; this aspect, however, has not yet been investigated in a controlled study with complex stimuli (see Bandura 1969, Lang 1969 for detailed, study-by-study review of subtraction studies).

The second major approach to discovering mechanisms of effectiveness is a comparison of the effectiveness of the total package with other treatment procedures that modify specific components on the basis of parallel or contradictory principles. For example, the standard package might be compared with another treatment that is identical except that progress through the hierarchy continues even if the client responds with anxiety, or except that the client might be instructed to maintain tension rather than relaxation during item presentation. Although this approach is theoretically quite sound, only a few well-controlled studies have contributed knowledge through such designs, again supporting the procedures of the standard package [Lang 1969]. Unfortunately, many studies conducted with this approach contribute little or nothing to our understanding of systematic desensitization because of innumerable analogue research errors [Bernstein & Paul 1971].

The third major approach to discovering mechanisms of effectiveness is to isolate experimentally specific components of the treatment package. Then the detailed response to them during the administration process is investigated to determine if they operate as the underlying principles predict. For example, relaxation training procedures might be studied in detail to determine if the reduction in physiological arousal assumed by the reciprocal inhibition principle actually occurs; or hierarchy items might be mixed up and presented to subjects to determine if physiological response still maintains the original hierarchical ordering. Surprisingly few studies have been undertaken within this framework; those that have been reported, however, generally support the original package and underlying principles (for example, imaginal presentation of items produces arousal, relaxation inhibits stress responses, response–contingent relaxation is more effective than direct suggestion) [Lang 1969, Mathews 1971, Paul & Trimble 1970].

Many studies have focused on questions of counterconditioning versus extinction as the primary principle operating in systematic desensitization [Lang 1969]. This question appears to us to be relatively unimportant. The procedures of systematic desensitization do not in fact attempt to *replace* anxiety responses with relaxation responses as a full-scale counterconditioning program would; rather, relaxation is used to suppress anxiety responses—thus modified counterconditioning. Whether or not this inhibition of anxiety allows extinction or adaptation to take place, or whether a response of not responding becomes positively associated to the previously anxiety-eliciting stimuli, does not appear to have much theoretical or practical value beyond the academic. (Although a related question of the relative effectiveness of extinction procedures involving the elicitation of anxiety is quite important). The major question, rather, is whether relaxation inhibits anxiety, and whether systematic desensitization with relaxation is more effective than the same procedures without relaxation. Current research evidence suggests that it is.

In summary, while other factors operate in systematic desensitization, as in all other treatments, the current research on mechanisms of change does not provide any solid evidence to challenge either anxiety response suppression as the primary basis of effectiveness or the full procedural package as the method of choice. On the other hand considerable positive support exists in the research literature to favor these conclusions. As the severity of anxiety experienced by clients or subjected to investigation decreases, however, other factors and modes of operation are likely to take on increasing significance.

Related Procedures for Reducing Conditioned Anxiety

Many therapeutic techniques have been developed in accordance with the same conceptual model of anxiety and related clinical problems on which systematic desensitization is based. In addition, several clinical procedures initially introduced by therapists of other theoretical persuasions have been re-examined and incorporated into this social-learning approach in a more consistent and systematic way. Few of the other procedures have as yet been subjected to the extensive investigation that characterizes systematic desensitization, nor is their effectiveness as well documented (with one exception). All, however, are based on the same guiding principles and appear promising at least at the case-study-with-measurement level of product, which is as strong as the evidence for any other treatment for conditioned anxiety with the exception of systematic desensitization. We give only a brief overview of related procedures here. The reader interested in details of application may consult recent books and journals in which many of these techniques are illustrated [Bandura 1969, Kanfer & Phillips 1970, Ullmann & Krasner 1965, 1969, Wolpe 1969, Wolpe & Lazarus 1966, *Behavior Research and Therapy, Behavior Therapy, Behavior Therapy and Experimental Psychiatry, Journal of Abnormal Psychology, Journal of Applied Behavior Analysis, Journal of Consulting and Clinical Psychology*].

As we stated earlier, several treatments have been called systematic desensitization that vary procedures enough to make generalization of findings from the total systematic desensitization package unwarranted.

Nevertheless, the same guiding principles are involved, and some positive case reports have appeared. Some variations have been reported in which relaxation is induced, but the symbolic presentation of hierarchy items has been through a verbal narrative by the client, or through colored slides or graded movies. Other investigators working with mild anxiety responses have done away with the hierarchy altogether and merely repeated the strongest anxiety-eliciting stimulus. Still others have maintained images when anxiety occurs and imposed additional stimuli for relaxation in the presence of the anxiety-eliciting image. A variant called cognitive desensitization does away with relaxation training and relies only on repeated presentation of the hierarchy images to extinguish anxiety responses. Theoretically, most of these variations in procedure may be useful when anxiety responses are very weak, or in some cases when unique difficulties with imagery or relaxation prevent the standard systematic desensitization procedures from being employed. For most cases involving strong anxiety reactions, however, the standard procedure would appear to be the treatment of choice.

In vivo desensitization is a related set of procedures found to be effective when anxiety-eliciting stimuli consist of concrete physical objects or situations. This form of desensitization uses the same basic principles and procedures as the standard version except that live rather than visualized stimuli make up the anxiety hierarchy. Thus the client is gradually exposed to increasingly potent real-life stimuli, with the therapist always insuring that anxiety is no longer elicited by the weaker stimuli before proceeding to the stronger. Sometimes *in vivo* desensitization is conducted while the client is deeply relaxed in the therapist's office, with the therapist presenting the physical stimuli; but more often *in vivo* procedures are employed outside of the office.

An example of the former procedure was the treatment of a young woman whose intense fear of flashbulbs led her to take extreme and often embarrassing measures to avoid being photographed. The client was trained in deep relaxation and a flashbulb hierarchy was constructed, which began with very easy items like "taking someone else's picture with a nonflash camera" all the way up to "having your picture taken with a flash camera at close range." The items between these extremes were graded carefully so that none of them represented a major increase in difficulty. At each treatment session the client was first relaxed and then, while still comfortably seated in the reclining chair, exposed to several hierarchy items. As with imaginal desensitization, progress to a higher item was always preceded by repeated mastery (no evidence of anxiety) of the item just below it. If the client reported becoming uncomfortable, she was instructed to close her eyes and relax until she was ready to continue. This procedure was very successful, and the client was awarded several attractive photographs of herself at the conclusion of the program.

More typically, *in vivo* desensitization exposes the client to specific stimulus contexts outside the therapist's office, since it is impractical for a therapist to collect the range of potentially threatening stimuli that a client might present. Frequently, such *in vivo* procedures start only after the client is well trained in relaxation, so that he may approach an anxiety-eliciting stimulus until a mild increase in anxiety is detected, stop at that point and relax, continue until another mild increase in anxiety is detected, stop and relax, and so on until the most extreme anxiety-eliciting stimulus is mastered. With relatively mild anxiety responses, relaxation training often may not be included at all. Rather, the client may simply be instructed to approach the real-life stimuli gradually, in a hierarchical order, stopping at each point that anxiety is detected until the response extinguishes. For example, a young man who feared entering a hospital was instructed to drive toward the hospital until mild anxiety was experienced, and at that point to park and engage in any mildly pleasant activity (he chose reading a book). As soon as no anxiety was detectable, he was to proceed, stopping again when a detectable increase in anxiety occurred. After once reaching the hospital parking lot, he was to continue stopping and reading on benches along the walk until he could sit in the emergency room for fifteen minutes without anxiety. In this instance of mild anxiety he was able to progress to the parking lot from his home (about four miles) in about two hours on the first evening, on to the entrance in a similar period of time on the second evening, and to meet the waiting-room criterion within a week.

With somewhat more severe anxiety, specific anxiety-reducing stimuli or actions, frequently the reassuring presence and encouragement of the therapist, may be programmed along with *in vivo* desensitization. Especially in cases in which skill deficits and conditioned anxiety are both present, modeling procedures may be combined with therapist-accompanied *in vivo* desensitization. In this approach the client observes another person, often the therapist (either live or on film or videotape), fearlessly engage in the behaviors the client finds aversive. The client is then asked to engage in the feared behavior at each step along the hierarchy, immediately following the model.

Thus the client observes a model who behaves calmly and appropriately while demonstrating that, in fact, no harm or discomfort need occur in the situation. These functions of modeling may inhibit anxiety in the feared situation long enough to allow other more adaptive behaviors to be reinforced, much as relaxation and graded hierarchy presentations do in standard desensitization. The client may then attempt the confrontation of each successive stimulus situation himself, with the support of the therapist, allowing for *in vivo* extinction to occur.

Beyond the requirements of systematically graded exposures to anxiety-eliciting stimuli and inhibition of strong anxiety, there are few firm rules for the use of *in vivo* desensitization, and each therapist usually devises his own programs. The technique can be used by itself as a main therapeutic tool or along with systematic desensitization, both as a booster treatment and as a means of assessing transfer to live situations. Thus a therapist can ask his client to practice items *in vivo* that have already been desensitized in imagination. *In vivo* techniques also appear helpful with persons who are unable to [a] learn deep relaxation, [b] produce clear visual images, or [c] experience emotional arousal in response to visualized fear stimuli. When anxiety-eliciting stimuli are limited, concrete, and physical, the combined modeling *in vivo* desensitization procedure has been found to be extremely effective and is the treatment of choice, especially with children.

Since it is clear that relaxation is a state or condition incompatible with anxiety, it is often extremely desirable to provide anxious clients with a means to produce and experience feelings of deep relaxation under unanticipated anxiety-producing circumstances. Such self-produced relaxation skills may also substantially increase the effectiveness of *in vivo* desensitization programs. *Differential relaxation training* is a procedure often used as an adjunct to other techniques. After the client has obtained some facility with progressive relaxation, he is taught to analyze the specific muscle groups required to perform any given task and to differentially relax all other parts of his body. In driving a car, for example, some slight tension in the hands and forearms (to steer) and in the right calf and foot (to operate the accelerator) is all that is required beyond the normal muscle tonus necessary to stay awake without falling over. An analysis of tension produced, however, may reveal that the client is squeezing the steering wheel with both hands, pressing on the floor boards with his left leg, sitting forward with his back and neck tense, and so on. The extra tension is probably a result of an unnecessarily high arousal level for the task requirements. By selectively focusing on progressive relaxation of those muscles that are not required for the task, the client may lessen the tension-produced fatigue as well as partially reduce the anxiety level *in vivo*.

Conditioned relaxation to a self-produced cue is a promising technique because of its potential utility in a wide range of circumstances. This procedure consists of first training the client in progressive relaxation and then associating other responses, which are under the client's direct voluntary control, with the relaxed state. After the client is totally relaxed, he is instructed to focus all of his attention on his breathing and then to subvocalize a cue word such as "calm" or "relax" each time he exhales. The therapist repeats the word in synchrony with exhalation several times, and the client then continues for many more pairings. After repeating this procedure for four or five weeks, with the client giving additional pairings on his own each night following relaxation practice, the ability of the self-produced responses (cue word and exhalation) to bring about relaxation is tested in the office. The client is presented with a threatening stimulus until some degree of anxiety is experienced and then instructed to take a deep breath and subvocalize the cue word on exhalation. If a relaxation response is achieved, the client may be instructed to use this cue any time he begins to feel a slight increase in anxiety in any real-life situation.

Another means of investing self-produced words such as "calm," "control," or "relax" with the power to produce relaxation (especially in clients who have difficulty in learning progressive relaxation skills) is by associating them with the *relief* of strong tension or anxiety. *Anxiety-relief conditioning* begins by subjecting the client to a continuous and uncomfortable electric shock. He is instructed to tolerate the shock as long as possible and then to say aloud a cue word such as "calm" or "relax." As soon as he says the cue word the shock is terminated, resulting in a marked sensation of relief. Several weeks of continuous pairing of the cue word with shock termination may associate strong feelings of relief and relaxation responses with that word. Later, when the client is in disturbing situations, this association may allow him to subvocalize the cue to reduce anxiety.

Self-produced relaxation has been employed in several ways. It may be incorporated into a standard systematic desensitization procedure as a quick means of restoring relaxation following an anxiety response to a hierarchy item; it may be used as an anxiety inhibitor in therapist-conducted *in vivo* desensitization; or it may be used as the basis for a client–conducted *in vivo*

program. As an example of the last possibility, a claustrophobic client could be trained in progressive relaxation and then given instructions to practice pairing the word "relax" with exhalation in the relaxed state (or with shock termination if anxiety-relief is being used). After an office test of the cue's ability to bring about anxiety reduction, the claustrophobic client could be instructed to try out the effects of the cue in progressively more difficult real-life situations. He might first enter a large empty room, which was poorly ventilated, and then, if successful (that is, if no anxiety is experienced or if reduction of anxiety occurs on use of the cue word), move on to smaller, more crowded situations until all the previously anxiety-producing settings are no longer a problem. If self-produced relaxation to such a cue producing response is carefully used at the moment of very mild anxiety, it could theoretically be self-reinforcing and self-perpetuating. Empirically, however, the strength of the association between the relaxation response and the cue word and exhalation as eliciting stimuli is so fragile that one or two attempts to use it in the presence of extreme anxiety may extinguish the conditioned relaxation, thus undoing several weeks' work.

Many other therapeutic procedures are based on incompatible or competing responses other than relaxation. Theoretically, any action or event that elicits cognitive and physiological responses other than anxiety can serve as a stimulus with some ability to reduce anxiety. Thus training in some dominant motor response, instruction in methods of distraction, eating, reading, or many other activities may be used to provide anxiety-competing responses for *in vivo* desensitization programs, either as self-control approaches by the client or as therapist controlled treatments in the office. Many of these procedures were developed empirically by therapists of other theoretical persuasions and incorporated more systematically into a social-learning framework.

Assertion training is one approach that has been incorporated and widely used with clients who experience conditioned anxiety in social situations. If a client can be taught to state or assert his feelings (positive or negative) to others in an anxiety-eliciting context instead of merely attending to his own arousal, anxiety is likely to be reduced as a function of distraction and of the competing motor responses. (Additionally, reactive anxiety is likely to be reduced since other people respond more favorably to appropriate assertion than to inappropriate social avoidance or submissiveness. In the case of aversive behavior by others, they are likely to change their behavior or "leave the field" in response to client assertion, thus reducing aversive stimulation.) Assertion training typically involves therapist modeling and client rehearsal of the new assertive behavior in therapy sessions (providing some *in vivo* desensitization), followed by prescribed actions in specific contexts in the real-life anxiety-eliciting social situation. Behavioral prescriptions for assertion also use gradual approach from easy situations in which success is assured through more difficult ones, thus allowing *in vivo* desensitization of anxiety to occur.

Similarly, clients may be taught to say things to themselves (produce incompatible cognitions) in the presence of anxiety-eliciting stimuli that will compete with the elaboration, through labeling, of conditioned anxiety responses, or that will prompt them to perform other incompatible behaviors, thus allowing *in vivo* desensitization to occur. Ellis has elaborated an entire approach of psychotherapy, called *rational-emotive therapy*, in which the instigation of incompatible cognitions, assertions, and a variant of *in vivo* desensitization are the primary procedures used to treat conditioned anxiety [1962]. Reliance on the ability of thoughts and images to elicit emotional responses incompatible with anxiety, without prior training, is also part of a procedure called *emotive imagery*. This technique is typically used with children who may be too young for relaxation training. The therapist therefore relies on establishing a positive affective state by engaging the child in play and fantasy activities that are especially engrossing and gradually introducing the anxiety-eliciting stimuli into the fantasy.

Sexual functioning is perhaps the most frequent area of behavior in adults in which conditioned anxiety causes a breakdown in performance. Systematic desensitization and *in vivo* desensitization based on relaxation are very effective treatment procedures for such problems as impotence (failure of a male to obtain or maintain an erection), frigidity (failure of a female to obtain or maintain vaginal lubrication or orgasm), premature ejaculation (ejaculation with a flaccid penis, or with an erect penis before or immediately after insertion), and so forth. If anxiety is not severe enough to totally inhibit sexual feelings or functioning, however, the parasympathetic enervation involved in early stages of sexual arousal or the relaxation typically following orgasm may with proper timing provide physiological responses that are incompatible with anxiety. Thus a man or woman who becomes sufficiently anxious to prevent sexual functioning in the presence of a potential sex partner may not become anxious when alone. Therefore a systematic and graded program of masturbation may be used as

a basis for desensitization in which the client systematically visualizes a hierarchy of sexual stimuli and activities while masturbating in the privacy of the home. By keeping sexual arousal stronger than the anxiety-evoking images, both desensitization of anxiety and increased sexual arousal in response to the imagined stimulus may occur.

When a cooperative sex partner for the client is available, the therapist can apply the principles of *in vivo* desensitization based on sexual arousal directly within the interpersonal context of sexual activity. After cooperation of both sexual partners is assured, they are instructed to engage in only that degree of sexual foreplay that is comfortable for the distressed individual. It is also made explicit that the cooperating partner must never urge or force the other to go beyond that point, and that no expectation of complete intercourse or critical evaluation of performance is involved early in the program. Many additional factors, such as education and skill training, are particularly important in dealing with sexual problems; systematic desensitization and related techniques involving behavioral prescriptions, with session-by-session monitoring of progress, however, form the core of treatment when conditioned anxiety is involved.

So far we have been discussing treatment techniques based on gradual approach and incompatible response principles. All have gradually exposed the client to increasingly potent versions of the anxiety-eliciting stimuli while preventing the occurrence of anxiety, thus assuring the emission and reinforcement of new, more adaptive responses in previously aversive situations. Even when the underlying principle guiding specific techniques involved extinction rather than active response suppression, the procedures we have discussed so far have relied on gradual approaches in which the therapist attempts to manage timing so that the client experiences little or no anxiety during treatment. Several therapists have employed a parallel set of procedures based on the principle of extinction, in which they attempt to expose the client to the most severe anxiety-evoking stimuli under conditions in which escape is impossible. Theoretically, the most severe conditioned anxiety is elicited but gradually extinguishes, because no unconditioned source of anxiety is present to reinforce the conditioned response.

Such forced extinction procedures may use either *in vivo* or imagined presentation of anxiety-eliciting stimuli. As an example of *in vivo* procedures, a claustrophobic client might be required to enter a small, crowded, poorly ventilated room, without gradual approaches through less difficult stimulus contexts.

The room would elicit severe anxiety in the client, who would not be allowed to leave until a marked reduction in anxiety occurred. Since some degree of spontaneous recovery of conditioned anxiety is expected, these sessions would be repeated until anxiety was not elicited on the initial entry. If the anxiety-eliciting stimulus was a response-produced cue based on some action of the individual, the client might be instructed to produce that action actively and repeatedly in a similar way ("negative practice"). Imaginal presentation of eliciting stimuli has also been used with forced-extinction procedures. One of the most popular techniques is called "flooding," in which anxiety-eliciting stimuli equivalent to the top items on a desensitization hierarchy are presented for the client's continued visualization, without training competing responses and without gradual approximations of stimuli lower on the stimulus generalization gradient. The client is literally flooded with those stimuli that elicit maximum anxiety until a reduction in anxiety occurs. As with *in vivo* forced-extinction procedures, sessions are typically repeated until no anxiety at all is elicited.

A related procedure, used with traumatic neurosis for years, is *abreaction*—the re-experiencing or reliving through imagery and concurrent vocalizations of an original traumatic incident that may have established conditioned anxiety. The underlying principles are parallel to flooding techniques (that is, extinction because of the unreinforced evocation of the conditioned anxiety response in the safe context of the therapist's office). Abreaction occasionally occurs without preplanning by the therapist. For example, during history taking, hierarchy construction, or desensitization proper, some specific stimulus may elicit a chain of associations that redintegrates a traumatic experience in its entirety. When a specific traumatic stimulus context is known to exist as a probable cause of severe conditioned anxiety, abreaction may be used programmatically, sometimes in conjunction with hypnotic techniques or hypnotic drugs to aid in reducing competing associations and in narrowing the client's focus to the relevant stimulus context. The transfer of learning or extinction from drug to nondrug states, however, is somewhat questionable [Paul, Tobias & Holly, in press]. Although abreaction is quite dramatic when it occurs (and therefore provides material for many movies and television programs), the number of clients for whom a single traumatic incident forms the basis for maladaptive conditioned anxiety is so small that planned or unplanned abreaction is a relatively rare event in actual treatment.

In both *in vivo* forced extinction and imaginal procedures, the stimuli the client confronts are those conditioned ones that he may realistically expect to encounter in real life. Stampfl [1967] introduced a forced extinction approach involving imagined presentation of anxiety-eliciting stimuli that differs from flooding and abreaction in that stimuli are not restricted to inappropriate conditioned stimuli or realistic past experiences. Stampfl called the procedure *implosive therapy* [Stampfl & Levis, in press]. Rather than restricting stimulus presentation to realistic conditions, implosive therapy relies on the therapist's ingenuity in describing conditions for the client to imagine that will maximize anxiety, no matter how realistic, unrealistic, or fantastic they may be. For example, "A snake is gnawing its way up through your throat and out your eyeball," "You're running a power lawnmower back and forth across your husband—see the blood spurting, hear him cry out, see his face fly past you." According to reports of therapists who use this technique, a point is reached at which the anxiety level starts to decline (extinguish) no matter what horrible or gory events are imagined. At this point the anxiety-eliciting stimuli from the real-life context are woven into the descriptions and presumably become extinguished.

Forced extinction procedures are obviously less pleasant than other alternatives for both client and therapist. Additionally, reports of the success of flooding and implosive procedures have been contradictory, so the most reasonable conclusion on their effectiveness in treating conditioned anxiety may be one of openminded skepticism, pending much further research.

Many other specific techniques for dealing with problems centering on maladaptive conditioned anxiety have been reported by individual therapists from time to time. The procedures above, however, cover most approaches used by a significant number of therapists and the approaches with the strongest empirical and research support. In current clinical practice, depending on the severity of the client's anxiety responses and the nature of eliciting stimulus conditions, any or all of them may be used in combination and applied in a systematic way. Frequently, unless anxiety is severe, other procedures may be attempted before a systematic desensitization program is undertaken, since they are typically less time consuming for the therapist. Forced extinction techniques are the most questionable of all those we have described because of the possibility of increasing the client's maladaptive anxiety under some conditions and the absence of stronger research support. In general, however, all of the procedures are beginning to receive attention in the experimental literature.

Current Status of Systematic Desensitization and Related Techniques

The current research status of systematic desensitization as a specific therapeutic package for the treatment of problems involving inappropriate conditioned anxiety is overwhelmingly positive. Some well-controlled studies have established cause-effect evidence with specific classes of eliciting stimuli and several broad classes of both anxiety and secondary responses. Lower level designs and case studies with objective measurement generally support the extension of findings from controlled studies to other classes of eliciting stimuli, secondary responses, and both clients and therapists with different personal characteristics. When anxiety is strong and involves eliciting stimulus conditions that are complex, social, or include mediated generalization, systematic desensitization would be the treatment of choice. Research on underlying mechanisms in general supports response suppression and successive-approximation or gradual-approach principles as the primary active ingredients operative in systematic desensitization. Of related techniques, only *in vivo* desensitization combined with modeling procedures has received as strong research support as systematic desensitization, although nearly all of the gradual-approach incompatible-response techniques have been found effective in a few controlled studies. When eliciting stimulus conditions are concrete and physical, *in vivo* desensitization with modeling is the preferred treatment, especially with children. Well-controlled factorial designs have not yet been conducted to evaluate the effectiveness of any technique with sexual problems involving conditioned anxiety. But the near perfect hit rate of systematic desensitization and *in vivo* desensitization obtained from reports of sexual partners—especially when compared with poor reports from traditional approaches—suggests that these procedures are the best bet at present. Forced extinction procedures currently rest on less firm research support than any of the other techniques. Our preference, because of the unpleasantness of the procedures and their potential for inadvertently increasing anxiety, is to hold back forced extinction techniques as a last-resort approach until more solid research data have accumulated to establish effectiveness and to guide the focus and timing of application.

Well-controlled factorial studies comparing the effectiveness of various procedures are beginning to appear, and should become much more frequent in the future. Research that "tests the limits" of the range of clients, problems, therapists, and procedural variations of systematic and *in vivo* desensitization will be extremely important now that basic effectiveness has been established, as will further research on underlying mechanisms. Related techniques have just begun to receive adequate attention, but we hope the next ten years will show extensive research on them. Probably cognitive variables, their modification and interaction with other aspects of behavior will be the focus of increasing clinical research activity within a social-learning framework. Ten years hence many changes in systematic desensitization and related techniques and many totally different procedures, equally or more effective, may have resulted from the research we have anticipated. However, the strength of the research existing to date assures us that the procedures we've described are sound enough that they will never be found to deserve a place along side some of the now forgotten therapy "breakthroughs" of the past, such as bloodletting and powdered "unicorn" horn.

Before concluding, we remind the reader that we have been concerned only with a conceptual model for conditioned anxiety, related clinical problems, and the most promising therapeutic techniques for dealing with them. Because we are focusing on a specific area in this way, it is all too easy for readers unfamiliar with clinical work to gain the impression that anxiety may account for all clinical problems, or that the therapeutic techniques we have described may be applied in isolation as a completely adequate approach. We wish to point out explicitly that nothing could be farther from the truth. Rather, the clinical status of systematic desensitization and related techniques is no more or less than a portion of the technology used in helping clients overcome problems of a specific nature. Many other problems having nothing to do with maladaptive conditioned anxiety are brought to the clinic and require other therapeutic procedures. Even when maladaptive conditioned anxiety is adequately removed or reduced as a problem by the techniques we have described, the client may simply become "teachable" and still need to acquire new behaviors to increase satisfactions, experience pleasure, and prevent future problems or anxiety reactions from being developed. Thus the techniques we have described would systematically be applied in combination with each other and with still other therapeutic techniques as only part of an integrated treatment program designed to alleviate the problems unique to a specific client and his specific environmental circumstances.

It should also be clear that all therapeutic techniques derived from social-learning principles are typically applied in the context of a human relationship. While our goal, indeed, is to bring psychological-treatment technology closer and closer to an applied science, in which specific classes of human problems may be changed in specified ways by known treatment procedures, we do not mean that treatment techniques can be applied to clients as you would apply a wrench to a piece of broken machinery. Rather, when the context of treatment involves human relationships, the characteristics of that relationship and the nonspecific aspects of the therapist's behavior in forming and sustaining relationships cannot be ignored.

We mention this point here because the introduction and clinical status of new treatment procedures may get off the track in several ways. This deviance is especially likely when procedures are based on a different way of conceptualizing human problems than has been traditional, as is the case with systematic desensitization and related techniques (for example, problems as a natural consequence of individual history rather than mental illness, specific distressing behaviors as primary or secondary learned responses rather than symptoms of an underlying problem in the active unconscious). One reason the clinical status of these therapeutic techniques has indeed gotten off the track is the way clinicians have adapted procedures into practice. On the one hand is a number of older, experienced clinicians who have been introduced to the new procedures and principles by reading a few accounts and hearing a paper presentation or two, and who were sufficiently impressed to attempt to incorporate them into their work. Unfortunately, many older clinicians have practiced in such an impressionistic fashion that new procedures are applied without a complete understanding of the principles and without the necessary rigor. On the other hand is a number of people who may have a good understanding of the underlying principles and the need for rigor in application, but who are new to clinical work. These inexperienced clinicians may not attend to the nonspecific aspects of the clinical interaction such as establishing rapport, showing interest and respect for the complexity of the client's problems, being sensitive to the perceptions, desires, and emotional state of the client, or just maintaining motivation and open communication. Errors in either direction are likely to lower the effective clinical status of any treatment approach or technique from that which current research evidence indicates is possible. Although most practitioners are not likely to use procedures without adequate training in both specific and nonspecific

skills, in psychological services, as in medicine, law, or any other service, "let the buyer beware" is still a wise maxim. We hope the information we have presented will not only acquaint the reader with the exciting and promising developments currently taking place, but will also provide the potential consumer with a guide for evaluating the marketplace.

APPENDIX A

Summary of Basic Principles and Concepts of Learning and Performance

In essence almost all principles of learning and performance have their basis in two fundamental descriptive laws. [1] The law of effect, which, loosely stated, says that to the extent possible an organism tends to do things that pay off or are pleasant and tends not to do things that do not pay off or are unpleasant. [2] The law of contiguity, which says that events occurring together in time tend to be associated and take on the same functional properties (meaning). From these ancient observations masses of experimental research have empirically established many other principles. Although several different explanatory theories have been proposed to account for the empirical findings, most of the findings are well established. Our preference has been to take an eclectic, functional learning approach, rather than to accept any single theory. The glossary that follows should assist the reader who is unfamiliar with the area in understanding the principles and terminology used. Most of the following definitions have been abstracted from basic texts, and the reader is referred to the original sources for elaboration [Bandura & Walters 1963, Bijou & Baer 1961, Dollard & Miller 1950].

I. Concepts and Principles of Instrumental Learning (Operant "Conditioning")
   A. Basic Concepts
      1. Operant behavior: responses functionally related to consequences of responding (that is, under control of stimuli following them)
         a. Operant strength: rate or frequency of occurrence; sometimes magnitude or latency
         b. Operant level: strength of an operant before it is affected by reinforcement
         c. Discriminated operant: operant behav-

ior also under control of a preceding discriminative stimulus

2. Reinforcement: operant-stimulus contingencies that strengthen an operant
3. Stimulus functions:
   a. Neutral stimuli: stimulus events whose occurrence following an operant has no effect on operant strength
   b. Discriminative stimuli: stimulus events that mark the time or place of reinforcement (precede operants, but do not elicit responses—"cues")
   c. Reinforcing stimuli:
      [1] Positive reinforcer: stimulus event whose occurrence following an operant strengthens the operant
      [2] Negative reinforcer: stimulus event whose removal, termination, or avoidance following an operant serves to strengthen the operant
      [3] Primary reinforcer: stimulus effective as positive or negative reinforcer from the beginning of psychological development (for example, food, temperature)
      [4] Acquired reinforcer: stimulus that achieves positive or negative reinforcing power through prior service as discriminative stimulus
4. Setting event: stimulus-response interaction the occurrence of which affects stimulus-response relationships that follow (for example, satiation of a reinforcer reduces its effectiveness; deprivation of a reinforcer increases its effectiveness)

B. Operations and Principles
   1. Conflict: simultaneous application of opposing stimulus functions (for example, operants produce contradictory reinforcers)
   2. Extinction: weakening of a response to operant level following neutral stimulus consequences
   3. Punishment: weakening of an operant by:
      a. production or application of a negative reinforcer (that is, hurt or aversion)
      b. removal or avoidance of a positive reinforcer (that is, loss)
   4. Reward: strengthening of an operant by:
      a. production or application of a positive reinforcer
      b. removal or avoidance of a negative reinforcer (that is, relief)

5. Reinforcement schedules: patterns of contingencies between operants and reinforcers
   a. Continuous reinforcement: operant is reinforced every time it occurs, resulting in rapid acquisition and rapid extinction on termination of reinforcement
   b. Intermittent reinforcement: operant is not reinforced every time it occurs, resulting in slower acquisition and slow extinction on termination of reinforcement
6. Reinforcement extensity and intensity: the greater the past frequency (extent) and strength (intensity) of reinforcement, the greater the operant strength
7. Temporal gradient of reinforcement: the more immediately a response is reinforced, the more effectively is its strength changed
8. Response chaining: series, pattern, or set of responses gradually developed by reinforcing only the set
9. Shaping (successive approximation): selective reinforcement of responses approximating final performance with concurrent extinction of others
10. Response generalization: strengthening one response by direct reinforcement results in indirect strengthening of other responses to the extent that they are similar to the reinforced response
11. Stimulus generalization: other stimuli take on functional stimulus properties (for example, discriminative or reinforcing) to the extent that they are similar to an original stimulus with those properties

II. Concepts and Principles of Classical (Respondent) Conditioning
A. Basic Concepts
   1. Respondent behavior: responses functionally related to antecedent events (that is, elicited by stimuli preceding them)
      a. Respondent strength: magnitude and frequency of occurrence; sometimes latency
      b. Unconditioned response: respondent elicited by an unconditioned stimulus
      c. Conditioned response: respondent elicited by a conditioned stimulus
   2. Respondent conditioning: a stimulus ini-

tially having no power to elicit a respondent may come to have such power if it is consistently associated with a stimulus that has the power to elicit the respondent

3. Eliciting stimuli: stimulus events that have the power to bring about (elicit) respondents

 a. Unconditioned stimuli: stimulus conditions effective as eliciting stimuli from the beginning of psychological development

 b. Conditioned stimuli: stimulus conditions that acquire eliciting-stimulus properties through association with unconditioned stimuli

 c. Higher order conditioned stimuli: conditioned stimuli that acquire eliciting-stimulus properties through association with other conditioned stimuli

B. Operations and Principles

 1. Conflict: simultaneous application of stimuli that elicit contradictory respondents

 2. Extinction: weakening of a conditioned response by repeatedly presenting the conditioned stimulus without an unconditioned stimulus

 3. Counterconditioning: weakening or replacing a conditioned response by pairing the conditioned stimulus with stimuli that elicit stronger, incompatible respondents

 4. Deconditioning: weakening or removing a conditioned response by pairing the conditioned stimulus with conditions that prevent the occurrence of the conditioned response

 5. Respondent reinforcement: strengthening the response to a conditioned stimulus by pairing with an unconditioned stimulus

 6. Principles of reinforcement (schedules, extensity, intensity, temporal gradient) and principles of stimulus and response generalization of instrumental learning also apply to respondent reinforcement, respondents, and eliciting stimuli

III. Concepts and Principles of Mediational Theorists

A. Basic Concepts

 1. Stimulus functions:

 a. Drive stimuli: strong stimulus events that impel action by internal activation (quantitative aspect of stimulus intensity)

 [1] Primary drives: stimuli possessing drive properties from the beginning of psychological development

 [2] Secondary drives: stimuli possessing drive properties because of prior association with primary drives

 b. Cues: qualitative properties of stimuli determining the where, when, and what of a response (essentially, discriminative stimulus functions)

 c. Cue–producing responses: overt or covert responses that function as part of the stimulus pattern leading to another response (originally thought of as only a part of the cue or discriminative stimulus function, but may also provide eliciting stimulus functions)

 d. Expectancy: implicit response-produced cue functioning as a probabalistic discriminative stimulus

 2. Mediational processes: implicit cue-producing responses (thoughts, ideas, images, language) hypothesized to follow all other principles of learning and performance

 3. Model: source of behavioral patterns

 a. Symbolic model: source of behavioral patterns communicated by cue-producing responses

 4. Habit: a consistently recurring, learned stimulus-response association (theoretically, a construct referring to modifications in the nervous system

 5. Response hierarchy: relative order of different responses by their tendency to be evoked in a given stimulus situation

 6. Stimulus hierarchy: relative order of different stimuli by their tendency to evoke a given response

B. Operations and Principles

 1. Reactive inhibition: weakening of a response resulting from the effort of responding

 2. Conditioned inhibition: positively acquired negative response of not responding

 3. Spontaneous recovery: return of an extinguished response following a period of rest (presumably resulting from dissipation of reactive inhibition)

 4. Observational learning: acquisition of covert cue-producing responses via contiguity

a. Imitation: matching of observed performance of a model following observational learning

b. Latent learning (latent performance): acquisition of cue-producing responses that do not lead to performance change until later presentation of discriminative and reinforcing stimuli

c. Vicarious reinforcement: observer's performance modified after observed consequences to a model

5. Principles of performance in conflict

a. An approach gradient exists such that the tendency to approach a positive reinforcer becomes stronger with decreasing distance in time or space

b. An avoidance gradient exists such that the tendency to escape or avoid a negative reinforcer becomes stronger with decreasing distance in time or space

c. The avoidance gradient is steeper than the approach gradient

d. The effect of increasing drive associated with a gradient is to raise the entire gradient (increasing strength of responses and increasing generalization)

e. The stronger of two competing responses at any given time is the one that will occur

BIBLIOGRAPHY

Albert Bandura, *Principles of Behavior Modification.* Holt, Rinehart and Winston, 1969.

Albert Bandura and Richard H. Walters, *Social Learning and Personality Development.* Holt, Rinehart, and Winston, 1963.

Douglas A. Bernstein, "Problems in Behavioral Fear Assessment." Paper presented at Western Psychological Association, Los Angeles, 1970.

Douglas A. Bernstein and Thomas D. Borkovec, *Progressive Relaxation Training: A Manual for Therapists.* Research Press, in press.

Douglas A. Bernstein and Gordon L. Paul, "Some Comments on Therapy Analogue Research with Small Animal 'Phobias.'" *Behavior Therapy and Experimental Psychiatry,* 1971, 2, 225–237.

Sidney W. Bijou and Donald Baer, *Child Development I.* Appleton-Century-Crofts, 1961.

Thomas D. Borkovec, *The Comparative Effectiveness of Systematic Desensitization and Implosive Therapy and the Effect of Expectancy Manipulation on the Elimination of Fear.* Unpublished doctoral dissertation, University of Illinois, 1970.

John Dollard and Neil E. Miller, *Personality and Psychotherapy.* McGraw-Hill, 1950.

Elizabeth Duffy, *Activation and Behavior.* Wiley, 1962.

Don E. Dulany Jr., "Awareness, Rules, and Propositional Control: A Confrontation with S-R Behavior Theory." In T. R. Dixon and D. L. Horton, ed., *Verbal Behavior and General Behavior Theory,* Prentice-Hall, 1968.

Albert Ellis, *Reason and Emotion in Psychotherapy.* Lyle Stuart, 1962.

Cyril M. Franks, ed., *Behavior Therapy: Appraisal and Status.* McGraw-Hill, 1969.

Donald O. Hebb, "Drives and the C.N.S. (Conceptual Nervous System)." *Psychological Review,* 1955, 62:243–254.

Edmund Jacobson, *Progressive Relaxation.* University of Chicago Press, 1938.

Frederick Kanfer and Jeanne S. Phillips, *Learning Foundations of Behavior Therapy.* Wiley, 1970.

Peter J. Lang, "Fear Reduction and Fear Behavior: Problems in Treating a Construct." In J. M. Schlein, ed., *Research in Psychotherapy, Vol. III.* American Psychological Association, 1968.

Peter J. Lang, "The Mechanics of Desensitization and the Laboratory Study of Human Fear." In Cyril M. Franks, ed., *Behavior Therapy: Appraisal and Status.* McGraw-Hill, 1969.

Donald B. Lindsley, "Emotion." In S. S. Stevens, ed., *Handbook of Experimental Psychology.* Wiley, 1951.

Donald B. Lindsley, "Psychophysiology and Motivation." In M. R. Jones, ed., *Nebraska Symposium on Motivation,* University of Nebraska Press, 1957.

William H. Masters and Virginia E. Johnson, *Human Sexual Response.* Little, Brown, 1966.

Andrew M. Mathews, "Psychophysiological Approaches to the Investigation of Desensitization and Related Procedures." *Psychological Bulletin,* 1971, 76: 73–91.

David C. McClelland, *Personality.* Sloane, 1951.

Martin Orne, "On the Social Psychology of the Psychological Experiment: With Particular Reference to Demand Characteristics and Their Implications." *American Psychologist,* 1962, 17:776–783.

Gordon L. Paul, *Insight vs. Desensitization in Psychotherapy: An Experiment in Anxiety Reduction.* Stanford University Press, 1966.

Gordon L. Paul, "The Strategy of Outcome Research in Psychotherapy." *Journal of Consulting Psychology,* 1967, 31:109–118.

Gordon L. Paul, "Behavior Modification Research: Design and Tactics." In Cyril M. Franks, ed., *Behavior Therapy: Appraisal and Status.* McGraw-Hill, 1969a.

Gordon L. Paul, "Outcome of Systematic Desensitization I: Background, Procedures, and Uncontrolled Reports of Individual Treatment." In Cyril M. Franks, ed., *Behavior Therapy: Appraisal and Status.* McGraw-Hill, 1969b.

Gordon L. Paul, "Outcome of Systematic Desensitization II: Controlled Investigations of Individual Treatment, Technique Variations, and Current Status." In Cyril M. Franks, ed., *Behavior Therapy: Appraisal and Status.* McGraw-Hill, 1969c.

Gordon L. Paul, "There Is No Substitute for Knowledge." *International Journal of Psychiatry,* 1969d, 8:907–910.

Gordon L. Paul, "Physiological Effects of Relaxation Training and Hypnotic Suggestion." *Journal of Abnormal Psychology*, 1969e, 74:425–437.

Gordon L. Paul and Ralph W. Trimble, "Recorded vs 'Live' Relaxation Training and Hypnotic Suggestion: Comparative Effectiveness in Reducing Physiological Arousal and Inhibiting Stress Response." *Behavior Therapy*, 1970, 1:285–302.

Gordon L. Paul, Lester L. Tobias, and Beverly L. Holly, "Maintenance Psychotropic Drugs in the Presence of Active Treatment Programs: A 'Triple-Blind' Withdrawal Study with Long-term Mental Patients." *Archives of General Psychiatry*, in press.

Stanley Schachter, "The Interaction of Cognitive and Physiological Determinants of Emotional State." In L. Berkowitz, ed., *Advances in Experimental Social Psychology I.* Academic Press, 1964.

Hans Selye, "Stress: It's a G.A.S." *Psychology Today*, 1969, September: 25–56.

Charles D. Spielberger, ed., *Anxiety and Behavior*. Academic Press, 1966.

Thomas G. Stampfl and Donald J. Levis, "Implosive Therapy." In R. M. Jurjevich, ed., *Handbook of Direct and Behavior Psychotherapies*. North Carolina Press, in press.

Leonard P. Ullmann and Leonard Krasner, *Case Studies in Behavior Modification*. Holt, Rinehart and Winston, 1965.

Leonard P. Ullmann and Leonard Krasner, *A Psychological Approach to Abnormal Behavior*. Prentice-Hall, 1969.

John B. Watson and R. Raynor, "Conditioned Emotional Reactions." *Journal of Experimental Psychology*, 1920, 3:1–14.

Ronald S. Wilson, "On Behavior Pathology." *Psychological Bulletin*, 1963, 60:130–146.

Joseph Wolpe, "Objective Psychotherapy of the Neuroses." *South African Medical Journal*, 1952, 26:825–829.

Joseph Wolpe, *Psychotherapy by Reciprocal Inhibition*. Stanford University Press, 1958.

Joseph Wolpe, *The Practice of Behavior Therapy*. Pergamon, 1969.

Joseph Wolpe, and Arnold A. Lazarus, *Behavior Therapy Techniques*. Pergamon, 1966.

[Preparation of this manuscript was supported in part by Grants MH-17376 and MH-15553 from the National Institutes of Mental Health, United States Public Health Service.]

3

Implosive Therapy: Theory and Technique

THOMAS G. STAMPFL

University of Wisconsin at Milwaukee

DONALD J. LEVIS

State University of New York at Binghamton

THE phenomena that are the province of abnormal psychology represent a diversity of mystifying behaviors that have challenged man's scholarly and scientific efforts for centuries. Many individuals have devoted their entire lifetimes to attempts to understand the bewildering ramifications of behavior that characterize neurotic, psychotic, and other types of persons who are categorized as abnormal.

An enormous amount of time, effort, and money has been committed to the goal of developing effective methods of treatment and prevention. In general, the search for the causes of abnormal behavior and the conditions that tend to maintain such behavior are thought to constitute the first steps in any rational approach to the problems of treatment and prevention. At first glance, these initial steps appear insoluble because of the diversity of the unusual and puzzling behavior emitted by persons who are labeled as neurotic or psychotic. The following examples of such behavior should help to illustrate the complexity of the task at hand.

Neurotic Behavior

To an observer it seems incomprehensible that a woman could be so terrified of water that she wears a life preserver when she takes a bath. Or that a college professor is so fearful of locomotives that the sound of a locomotive whistle located one-half mile away evokes such terror that he runs around in a circle while screaming at the top of his voice [Leonard 1927]. What seems so surprising is that such neurotic individuals frequently appear normal in other ways. For example, they usually understand perfectly that such situations are quite harmless and realize that there is no reason for them to react in the extreme manner that they do. Though well aware of the irrationality of their behavior, they seem helpless to change it.

Another example of neurotic behavior is seen in a woman, a psychiatric patient, who is so obsessed with thoughts of fire that she spends most of her day checking and rechecking electrical appliances to be certain they are turned off. However many times she makes certain that a particular electrical appliance is "off" the nagging doubt somehow remains that maybe it is still "on." Consider that this woman actually has checked a particular appliance ten times in a one-hour period and even has pulled the plug out. Consider also that she is in good contact with reality and on an intellectual level is certain that the appliance is no longer "on." Nevertheless, she feels impelled to check it again and yet again. Furthermore, she thinks she smells smoke and regularly searches for the source. She may sit helplessly for hours carefully watching a fire-pot used by a construction crew convinced that at any moment some part of the fire, perhaps a piece of paper, will blow towards her house and ignite it. It is interesting to note that this patient was so distraught concerning her obsessive and compulsive behavior that *she was seriously considering setting her house on fire deliberately in order to "get it over with."* This thought evoked even more anxiety and led to further compulsions to prevent such a possibility from occurring.

A male patient responded in a similarly compulsive manner to thoughts of dirt and contamination. He regularly engaged in cleaning rituals (dusting and washing various objects) including repetitious handwashing. He turned light switches on and off with his elbows, and would frequently wear gloves when touching common objects such as money or door knobs. The sight of anything that actually contained· "dirt" such as a wastepaper basket would prompt him to wash his hands. After toileting, he would wash and rewash his hands many times.

The range of neurotic behaviors may be extended almost indefinitely. Thus another patient is inhibited sexually to an extreme degree and takes numerous precautions to avoid men. She also is tormented by thoughts of eternal damnation in hell and feels that she will sell her soul to the devil. It is estimated that tens of thousands, perhaps a total of several million individuals in the United States suffer from one or another of the different types of neurotic reactions. Any current abnormal psychology text may be consulted to review the variety of deviant and maladaptive behaviors characteristic of the neurotic.

Why don't people just make up their "minds" to stop their neurotic behavior when they "know" that their fears are groundless? Unfortunately, any attempt by the neurotic individual to "fight" his symptomatic behavior regularly results in an unbearable anxiety reaction that frequently progresses to a panic-like intensity. The symptomatic behavior temporarily alleviates this anxiety and usually prevents further increases in it from occurring. An example of this is seen in a man who refused to engage in his compulsive dressing ritual one morning. Seized with unbearable anxiety as he drove to work, he was forced to return home in order to carry out his compulsive behavior, which consisted of a particular sequence of putting on his garments while dressing and a specific order of buttoning them.

In effect, these individuals are punished by an increase in anxiety for trying to "fight" their symptoms. As every attempt to stop their maladaptive behavior fails, a "Why try?" reaction develops. This state appears to be quite similar to Seligman's concept of "learned helplessness" and many, even those who seek psychological help, truly feel that there is nothing they can do about their·problems. They give up trying and attempt to live their lives as best they can with their handicaps [Seligman 1969].

Psychotic Behavior

Abnormal behavior which is labeled as psychotic seems even more baffling. The neurotic at least seems to be aware of the irrationality of his actions and is in "good contact with reality." The psychotic ordinarily does not appear to be aware of the irrationality of his behavior and displays "poor contact with reality." Thus, one psychotic patient insists with absolute conviction that he receives secret messages from TV sent by his enemies announcing his imminent annihilation. He imports a similar sinister meaning to the marking on packaged goods found in supermarkets. Another psychotic patient insists in a similar way that "cowboys and Indians" are after him. Others appear to be completely convinced that they are Jesus Christ, Queen Mary, J. Edgar Hoover or God Himself, that they possess ten billion dollars, or are giving birth to kittens. Still others report that their food contains captive people and worms, while still others hear voices telling them that they are dirty and evil, that they spread disease, and that they are doomed. Some psychotic patients lie huddled in a fetal position, speak rarely or not at all, and may spread their feces around and then eat them.

These descriptions again represent only a small fraction of the variety of delusions, hallucinations, and other types of deviant behavior that occur in psychotic individuals. Patients such as these constitute the bulk of the mental hospital population.

Although many kinds of psychotherapy have been developed for treatment of these disorders, the newest and perhaps most promising have been based on learning principles established in the experimental laboratory. Operant Conditioning Therapy, Systematic

Desensitization, and Implosive Therapy are examples of these new approaches and have been referred to collectively as Behavior Therapies [Levis 1970]. The purpose of this module is to describe one of these new approaches, Implosive Therapy (IT). A discussion from an IT point of view on how fear is learned, how it is maintained over time, and how it can be unlearned will be given. This will be followed by a description of the IT procedure, examples of its applications, and a review of the supporting literature.

Fear Acquisition

Although the complexity and diversity of deviant behaviors appear to defy a common etiology, few investigators would object to the statement that learning plays an important role in the development of both normal and psychopathological behavior. Even the analytically trained Franz Alexander [1965] concluded that the therapeutic process is best understood in learning terms. The controversy, however, is whether it is feasible to apply existing learning or conditioning laws to complex human behavior. Since the available evidence is insufficient, any strong pro or con statements to the above proposition would be premature. Kimble [1961, p. 436] perhaps stated the issue best:

It may, some day, be known whether the laws of conditioning do or do not explain (say) psychopathological behavior. But that day is still far in the future. For the time being all that is possible is to attempt the explanation of complex phenomena in simpler terms. It is to be expected that the resulting explanations will be incomplete and imperfect. Complex behavior, if it is explainable at all in these terms, certainly involves the simultaneous operation of many principles of conditioning. Unfortunately, these principles are not exactly known, and we know even less about the way in which they combine and function together.

Despite the imcompleteness of the learning model, data do exist that suggest that some principles developed under laboratory conditions are operating, at least partially, in more complex, less well-defined situations. As Eysenck has reasoned [1960, p. 5]:

If the laws which have been formulated are, not necessarily true, but at least partially correct, then it must follow that we can make deductions from them to cover the type of behavior represented by neurotic patients, construct a model which will duplicate the important and relevant features of the patient and suggest new and possibly helpful methods of treatment along lines laid down by learning theory.

Conditioning Paradigm

One such analysis of human psychopathology suggests that patients have learned through a conditioning sequence to become afraid when exposed to certain stimuli that may comprise either some external event like a tall building or a snake and/or an internal event such as an image or thought that they are going to lose control or become crazy. The fear conditioned to the stimulus situation in question provides an unpleasant motivating source that the patient attempts to avoid. This avoidance response, if successful in removing some or all of the aversive stimulus, is reinforced by a reduction in fear. Clinicians frequently label the resulting avoidance behavior as the patient's symptoms.

Before attempting to give a more detailed presentation of the learning relationships, which are assumed to exist in the model outlined above, it may prove helpful to review the basic conditioning procedure of the laboratory where the principle under discussion was developed originally. In the interest of clarity, an attempt will be made also to draw analogies between the laboratory situation and the hypothesized conditioning of human psychopathology.

The avoidance conditioning paradigm provides a basic procedure for investigating those variables responsible for developing conditioned fear. Infrahuman subjects, such as the white rat, are conditioned frequently in a two-compartment rectangular box. Although dimensions vary, one can describe the apparatus as an elongated narrow box, about three feet in length, five inches wide, and ten inches high. Frequently, a barrier about three inches in height is extended from the surface of the floor in order to divide the box into two equal compartments. The walls of both compartments are typically painted black, and the floor of both compartments consists of grid bars through which an electric shock can be administered by the experimenter.

Following the typical procedure, a laboratory rat is placed into the apparatus for a fifteen-minute exploratory period. This period prior to the onset of conditioning provides the subject with sufficient time to satisfy its "curiosity" about the new environment. At the end of the exploratory period, the experimenter presents a "neutral" stimulus, e.g., a tone for a predetermined duration such as six seconds. Following the sixth second, shock is presented. This six-second period of tone and the period of shock presentation is defined as the CS-UCS interval. To *escape* the shock, the rat must jump over the hurdle into the next compartment. Such a response terminates both the shock and the tone. A 60-second waiting period referred to as the intertrial interval is usually allowed to elapse before the next trial is begun. The tone is presented again for a six-second period and again followed by shock. To escape the shock the subject must jump back into the compartment from which he previously came. With continued trials this shuttling behavior becomes well established.

Thus, the basic fear conditioning paradigm of the laboratory involves simply the pairing of a "neutral" stimulus with an aversive stimulus. With sufficient pairings of tone and shock, the tone, especially the segment just preceding shock onset, will tend, upon presentation, to elicit fear. The tone now becomes a *conditioned stimulus* (CS) capable of eliciting fear (anxiety) in the absence of the *unconditioned stimulus* (UCS) of shock. Shock is labeled a UCS or unlearned stimulus because the inherent properties of this stimulus upon presentation regularly produces aversiveness. If the animal jumps into the opposite compartment within the first six seconds after CS onset, the response immediately terminates the tone and prevents the onset of shock. Such responses successfully remove the rat from the aversive situation of the CS and UCS and are referred to as *conditioned avoidance responses* (CARs).

According to Mowrer's [1947] two-factor theory of avoidance learning, the animal in the above situation is learning two different responses. First of all, it is learning to become afraid of the tone CS, which can be conceived as a cue signaling the danger of being exposed to shock. The sequence of events by which fear is learned to the CS simply results from the pairing of the CS with the UCS. This type of learning is commonly referred to as *classical conditioning*. With repeated trials of the CS-UCS pairing, fear to the CS becomes strengthened. The second behavior that the animal learns is how to protect itself from these aversive events. This type of learning is referred to as *instrumental learning*. Besides the aversive characteristics of conditioned fear, stimuli generated by the fear response is viewed as having motivational or drive properties that can heighten the subject's activity. This acquired drive will eventually result in the animal moving from one compartment of the shuttlebox to the other. If this skeletal response is made contingent with CS offset, as is the case when an avoidance procedure is used, the response will be reinforced by a reduction in the aversive stimulation. In other words, the animal learns to escape the aversive conditioned stimuli by making an active instrumental response, which results in its termination. Thus fear onset serves as a drive to activate the avoidance response, while fear reduction provides the condition necessary for reinforcement of the instrumental response.

The above model is believed to be applicable to the understanding of human psychopathology. Psychopathology is assumed to arise as a result of past specific experiences of punishment and pain, which confer strong emotional reactions to initially non-punishing (neutral) stimuli. The conditioning events in the human are usually far more complex than in the typical laboratory experiment. The acquisition of "danger signals" in the human may have resulted from aversive events in the early socialization period of the child, for example, parental punishment (spanking, slapping, deprivation of food) for transgressive (forbidden) behavior. Other significant conditioning factors may be events related to aversive peer group experiences (being bullied, teased, beaten) or from aversive natural events (injuries resulting from falling, being burned, being cut, and so forth). Current aversive events (trouble with the in-laws, losing one's job, ill health, etc.) also can contribute to affective arousal. As a consequence of such CS-UCS pairings, neutral stimuli acquire aversive properties that are then capable of secondarily motivating behavior (drive properties). Defensive maneuvers and symptoms of the patient are believed to result from attempts on his part to avoid or terminate these conditioned stimuli that function as danger signals.

One might view the model suggested for human psychopathology as an oversimplification since its present form was developed at the infrahuman level. However, it is frequently forgotten that the essence of this theory was first offered not to explain rats' behavior but the behavior of human psychiatric patients. As Freud wrote, "Since we have reduced the development of anxiety to a response to situations of danger, we shall prefer to say that the symptoms are created in order to remove or rescue the ego from the situation of danger. If symptom formation is prevented, then the danger actually makes its appearance. . . ." [1936, p. 85].

Let us now return to our laboratory example of avoidance conditioning. The hypothesis is being offered that human methods of dealing with anxiety-provoking situations follow essentially the same strategy of the rat, i.e., to escape as quickly as possible the presence of the feared CS and avoid the possibility of UCS onset. However, differences do exist between the animal laboratory and the human conditioning situation. The topography of the human avoidance response may take a different form from the avoidance response of the rat discussed in our experiment because human responses not only involve physical removal from anxiety producing cues, but also, as mentioned earlier, take the shape of defense mechanisms and symptoms. The CSs also may be qualitatively different from those used in the laboratory in that the CS complex to which the human patient has been previously conditioned usually involves not only external cues (e.g., sight of an elevator, smell of a particular food, or the sound of a train), but also internal cues like thoughts and images. As Dollard and Miller [1950] have reasoned, the child frequently is punished for acts that have been carried out in the past, so that punishment (the UCS) becomes associated with the thought of the act and not the act itself. Generalization of fear from the act or overt behavior which previously led to punishment may well occur to the mere thought or symbolic representation of this act. These thoughts now become elicitors of anxiety and, in turn, are frequently avoided by the patient through the response of "not-thinking" about them, which is similar to the Freudian concept of repression. Nevertheless, the mechanism for conditioning of fear is believed to be the same in both the laboratory and real-life situation (the pairing of a "neutral" stimulus with a UCS), as well as the mechanism for strengthening the avoidance response (a reduction in fear-eliciting cues).

Unfortunately, the laboratory experiment as previously presented falls far short in producing results comparable to that obtained from the clinical literature. First of all, learning is very slow in the shuttlebox situation. In fact, it is our experience [Levis 1970a; Levis & Stampfl 1972] following the above outlined shuttlebox procedure, that a fourth of the rats do not reach a learning criterion of ten consecutive avoidance responses after 150 training trials. Once shock is discontinued, those subjects that do learn rarely make more than 50 consecutive avoidance responses before they stop responding. Although in some situations reports of relatively efficient and persistent avoidance responding with dogs have been noted [Brush 1957; Solomon & Wynne 1953], the infrequency of this finding with rats is of considerable concern. In fact, reports of nearly complete failures to obtain successful avoidance conditioning with rats and of short-lived conditioning are strikingly in evidence in the literature [Anderson & Nakamura 1964; Feldman & Bremner 1963; Fitzgerald & Brown 1965; Meyer, Cho, & Wesemann 1960; Mowrer 1940]. This type of finding presents a paradox for those investigators interested in extrapolating from the animal literature since human conditioned avoidance responses that take the form of neurotic and psychotic symptoms apparently resist extinction for years in the absence of any physical danger (the UCS).

Can the disparity between the patient and infrahuman findings be reconciled? Perhaps a closer analysis of an actual human conditioning situation observed by the first author will provide us with the answer [Stampfl & Levis 1969]. Twin boys were "drawing" various figures with stones on the side of their father's new automobile, which was parked in the driveway next to their house. Their father appeared in the door of the house, uttered a roar, and rushed toward his sons picking up a shovel on the way. In an extremely menacing manner he approached the boys with the

shovel upraised; he then swung the shovel several times but missed hitting them. He finally put down the shovel, took a firm grasp of their shoulders and dragged them into the house. For an hour or so the boys were punished intermittently; the sounds clearly were audible, the father alternating between using a belt and using his hands. The cries and screams were of considerable intensity, and the crying did not subside completely until several hours later.

One of the critical differences between a traumatic event of this kind and that of the animal laboratory consists in the complex sequential stimulation that usually precedes and accompanies punishment in the human situation.

What is the conditioned stimulus in this description? Is it the complex proprioceptive, visual, and tactual stimulation associated with the boys picking up the stones, the complex stimulation correlated with their "drawing" on the side of the car, seeing their father in the doorway, the auditory stimulation associated with his roar, the complex stimuli related to seeing him picking up the shovel, rushing down the steps, swinging the shovel, or being dragged into the house? Would the conditioned stimulus include the sight of the belt or hand of the father as it landed on various parts of the body, the preparatory responses made with the muscular tension accompanying them before being hit, the autonomic feedback from the emotional reactions, proprioceptive feedback from the postures adopted, feedback from the motor responses in struggling to escape, the auditory stimulation emanating from the father commenting on their worthlessness, or the auditory stimulation related to their cries and screams? Do context stimuli acquire aversive properties also? Are the sight of the clouds in the sky, the tunes they were humming, the thoughts they were having, the unique arrangement of the furniture in the rooms, the style of the automobile, etc., also elements of the conditioned stimulus?

Fear Maintenance

The Role of CS Complexity

It should be clear from the above example that the events preceding the onset of physical pain involved a *complex* of stimuli and not just one isolated cue, which is the usual manipulation made in the animal conditioning laboratory. Furthermore, the pattern of cues that are potentially conditionable are ordered sequentially or serially in the above example (picking up the stones, "drawing" on the side of the car, seeing their father in doorway, etc.) An important point to note is that a stimulus element, such as the clouds in the sky, may have no anxiety-eliciting potential in itself, but could add to the total anxiety-eliciting potential of the stimulus pattern when it functions in context. Another point is that stimuli closely associated with pain are still considered to be conditioned aversive stimuli, not unconditioned stimuli. That is to say, the sight of the belt descending through the air and the sight of it on the body is an essentially "neutral" stimulus that in and of itself does not elicit pain but only acquires its aversive properties through its close association with the resulting pain. Furthermore, a cue relating to the traumatic event may activate or redintegrate (i.e., reestablish) other internal cues such as thoughts and images stored in memory, and a stimulus pattern associated with a single traumatic event may have an associative linkage with the patterns representing other previously conditioned traumatic events.

Unfortunately, most of the conditioning laws developed in the laboratory stemmed from a paradigm in which only one external cue was manipulated. The variable of CS complexity surprisingly has remained a relatively unexplored parameter in the American infrahuman avoidance conditioning literature [Razran 1965; Baker 1968]. According to Wickens [1965], knowledge of the laws of stimulus-response connections will be of very limited value for prediction of behavior if, when in the context of complex environments, the functional stimulus for the response cannot be identified by the predictor.

It is clear from our work with patients that the CS patterns that are being avoided involve rather complex and varied stimulus elements. Returning to our analysis of the shuttlebox avoidance situation, one problem which becomes immediately apparent, if you view conditioning as occurring to a stimulus complex, is that the situation preceding shock (CS-UCS interval) is not very distinctive from the situation following shock (intertrial interval), a point recognized also by other investigators [Denny, Koons, & Mason 1959; McAllister & McAllister 1962]. Conditioning occurs not just to the tone that precedes shock but also to the apparatus cues associated with the conditioning chamber (e.g., color, floor surface, size of the box). In the typical shuttlebox situation the same background cues are present during both the situation that precedes shock and the situation that follows shock. In theory, this occurrence has a two-fold effect. First, it reduces the amount of reinforcement since the subject escapes fewer conditioned aversive stimuli; and second, it facilitates extinction of the avoidance response since the background cues are present during the intertrial interval in which shock is absent. Exposure of the

CS complex, or part of it, in the absence of the UCS is a condition that leads to extinction.

If our assumptions about the importance of the apparatus cues is correct, then we need to alter the environments between where the rat is shocked and where the intertrial interval (the safe, nonshock period following a response) is spent. This task can be easily accomplished by presenting the CS-UCS interval in, for example, a black box with grid floors and permitting the animal to run or jump into a white box with a solid floor. Since the apparatus cues of the two compartments are highly distinctive, the rat should be able to discriminate between these two situations quite easily. However, we are now faced with the additional problem of transferring the animal from the "safe" side of the apparatus to the shock side in order to start a new trial. This task can be achieved by transferring the animal, by hand, by a specially designed transport box [Levis 1970b] or through an automatic arrangement [Baum 1965]. Another feature of this experimental situation is that the subject makes a response in only one direction, rather than shuttling back and forth from one compartment to the other as described in our shuttlebox experiment. Thus, this type of paradigm has been labeled a *one-way* or one-directional avoidance situation. The difference in apparatus cues, the addition of transport cues, and the fact that the animal always responds in the same direction rather than jumping back in a compartment that was previously associated with shock should enhance the learning of the avoidance response and persistence of this response once shock is discontinued. This expectation is clearly supported; rats typically learn the avoidance response after an average of only three shock trials, and once shock is discontinued, they tend to respond for a 100 trials or so before extinguishing [Levis 1966a; Levis et al. 1970; Theios & Dunway 1964].

Making it easier for the rat to discriminate between situations safe and noxious by embedding the tone CS in a complex stimulus situation produced by differential apparatus cues is a step in the right direction. But, 100 or even 200 trials of consecutive avoidance responding before an animal extinguishes does not yet approach the persistence of responding noted for patients. However, one of the key elements of our human fear conditioning example with the twin boys was the observation that components of the CS complex were ordered serially (S1 followed by S2 followed by S3, etc.). This observation would suggest that instead of presenting the rat with a tone for 18 seconds before shock is introduced, a better procedure would be to divide the CS-UCS interval into three distinctive CS segments. Thus, the rats could be presented a sequence in which tone (S1) is presented for the first six seconds, followed by flashing lights (S2) for six seconds, followed by a buzzer (S3) for six seconds, and then followed by shock. Before we describe what happens when such a procedure is introduced in our one-way avoidance situation, let us briefly discuss the theoretical importance of serial CS presentation.

The Role of Serial CS Presentation

We have argued that human psychopathology resists extinction because the patient's symptoms (avoidance responses) terminate the conditioned fear cues before sufficient exposure to these cues can occur to produce a substantial extinction effect. It has also been argued that the cues the patient is avoiding are multiple and ordered sequentially. Returning to our analogue model developed for the rat, we are suggesting that greater resistance to extinction can be achieved by dividing the CS interval into two or more distinctive segments ordered serially (e.g., tone followed by lights followed by a buzzer). After conditioning, a response by an animal to the first component of the serial (tone) is expected to result in greater conservation or maintenance of fear to the next component when the second component is a different stimulus from the first (lights) than when it is the same type of stimulus (another tone) [Levis & Stampfl 1972; Solomon & Wynne 1954].

An additional hypothesis generated by this model is that by maintaining the strength of the CS segments closer in temporal proximity to the UCS, these segments (S2 and S3) upon exposure can function as effective secondary conditioners. That is to say, when the strength of anxiety to the short CS segment becomes extinguished through repeated exposures to this segment, an increase in response latency produces exposure to a longer, more anxiety-loaded segment of the CS. If sufficient anxiety is conserved to the longer CS exposure, it will, upon presentation, secondarily condition anxiety to the previous parts of the chain. Thus, by incrementing the anxiety level of the previous extinguished segment, this shorter CS segment will now reacquire the capacity to establish the CAR to this portion of the CS without the aid of primary reinforcement. At the same time, because of the CS exposure in the absence of the UCS, the anxiety associated with the longer CS exposure undergoes a decrement. As long as there is sufficient anxiety to some segment of the CS-UCS interval, this reinstating process should repeat itself. Therefore, if a situation could be constructed where the long CS exposure occurs rarely (intermittently) and, upon occurring, reconditions the short CS exposure to elicit the avoid-

ance response, extinction to the total chain should be retarded. A similar process of avoided serial cues is believed to be a major factor in sustaining the fear response in humans where a number of sequential stimulus patterns are assumed to be learned.

Perhaps the above concepts will be more easily understood in the context of a laboratory experiment [Levis 1966b]. The apparatus was divided equally into two distinctive compartments. One compartment was black with a grid floor, the other was white with a solid wood floor. A drop-gate completely separated the two compartments when it was lowered. An 18-second CS-UCS interval was presented in the black compartment only. An escape response immediately lowered the gate and terminated both the CS and UCS, while an avoidance response immediately lowered the gate and terminated the CS preventing UCS presentation. Subjects remained in the white compartment for a 60-second intertrial interval. At the end of the intertrial interval the subject was taken from the white (safe) compartment and placed into the black (shock) compartment immediately initiating the next trial. The designated 18-second CS-UCS interval consisted of the background and handling cues, plus the presence of three distinct stimulus segments of six-second duration ordered serially. The first six-second segment consisted of the gate being raised (permitting a response) followed by a period of silence. From the sixth to the twelfth second flashing lights were presented, and from the twelfth to the eighteenth second a buzzer was presented. The offset of the buzzer on the eighteenth second was followed by shock.

Only one to three shock trials were required for subjects to reach the acquisition criterion of ten consecutive avoidance responses. The shock was then turned off initiating the extinction phase of the experiment. The first three or four avoidance responses occurred to the buzzer and/or to the lights. However, by the fifth trial subjects were responding to the first six-second CS segment. Apparently, some of the aversiveness associated with the shock transferred back to the onset of the CS-UCS intervals. In fact, for approximately the first 100 trials most subjects responded within one or two seconds after the onset of the CS-UCS interval. These short latency responses helped conserve the anxiety associated with the remaining segments of the chain since short latency responses prevent exposure to the remaining segments. As the number of avoidance responses increased, overt signs of fear (e.g., defecation, urination) diminished. It appeared that as the skeletal avoidance response became overlearned, only a minimal amount of anxiety was needed to produce the response. After a number of short CS exposures, longer latency responses started to occur, although most subjects responded to the first six-second segment for two to three hundred trials. Finally, the subject remained in the situation long enough to be exposed to the second segment of flashing lights. Since in the subject's conditioning history there was little exposure to the lights without subsequent shock, this segment still generated a high level of anxiety. Upon its exposure, a reoccurrence of overt signs of fear were noticeably followed by a quick avoidance of the stimulus. On the next few trials, a short latency response usually would be made to the first six-second segment. Apparently the second segment in the series "recharged" or secondarily reinforced the subject's anxiety to the first segment. Most rats responded to the first segment for another 50 or 100 consecutive trials. Exposure to the second segment again recharged the first segment. However, with more and more exposure to the lights, extinction to the lights increased. The subject now responded mainly to the second segment. After approximately 500 or 600 trials, enough extinction occurred to the lights for subjects to remain in the situation long enough to be exposed to the buzzer, the third stimulus segment in the series. The buzzer, which probably had the highest anxiety attachment since it was the closest segment to shock onset, recharged the lights which, in turn, reinforced the silent period, again resulting in short latency responses. Thus, by this process of intermittent secondary reinforcement, a sort of "seesaw effect" occurred that resulted in extreme resistance to extinction.

Subjects were run 100 extinction trials a day until they extinguished by making one response of 120-second latency or more. Because most subjects continued to respond for some time, the experimenter extinguished before they did and terminated the experiment after 1000 trials. Most subjects apparently would have resisted extinction well past this mark. One subject tested emitted 921 responses to the first segment, 75 to the second and had only 4 short exposures to the buzzer, the third CS segment. Subjects which were tested under the same background conditions, but were presented with only one CS (buzzer) during the eighteen-second CS-UCS interval, extinguished on the average around 150 trials. We are in the process of carrying out more systematic work on this model [Levis 1966a, 1970b; Levis & Stampfl 1972; Levis et al. 1970].

To extend our analogue further, one could then view this extreme resistance to extinction in the absence of any physical danger as "irrational" behavior. However, from the rat's point of view, if one may anthropomorphize, the behavior is anything but irrational. As far as the rat is concerned, the avoidance response (the symptom) is adaptive since it serves to reduce the learned anxiety experienced in the feared situation. In order to really test the situation to determine whether shock has been turned off, the animal has to expose itself to the total stimulus complex that it has previously learned to avoid. Since the testing of this hypothesis by the conditioned subject would result in a substantial increase in anxiety, the law of least resistance usually wins out.

Fear Extinction

Following the reasoning associated with the human treatment procedure, in order to administer therapy to the rat (i.e., produce fast extinction), one only has to prevent the subject's avoidance response and directly force it to experience the total CS complex in the absence of primary reinforcement. Neal Miller [1951] advocated essentially the same strategy when he stated that, "Experimental extinction is more effective when the animal is in the original punished situation that evokes the most intense fear." Since the procedures employed in implosive therapy depend very heavily on this principle of direct experimental extinction, it is interesting to observe that Solomon, Kamin, and Wynne [1953] have based their conservation of anxiety hypothesis on exactly the same principle:

> . . . the best way to produce extinction of the emotional response would be to arrange the situation in such a way that an extremely intense emotional reaction takes place in the presence of the CS. This would be tantamount to a reinstatement of the original acquisition situation, and since the UCS is not presented a big decremental effect should occur [p. 299].

A number of experimental studies have corroborated this interpretation. Studies by Baum [1970], Black [1958], Denny, Koons, and Mason [1959], Hunt, Jernberg, and Brady [1952], Knapp [1965], Weinberger [1965], and others indicated that extinction of a learned emotional response proceeds with greatest rapidity when the organism is exposed to stimulus conditions most closely approaching those which were originally associated with painful stimulation. To achieve this state of affairs in the laboratory, one needs only to block the avoidance response to the CS during extinction by inserting a barrier between the shock and safe compartments. This procedure is commonly referred to as a response prevention technique of extinction.

Our own work and others [Shipley, Mock, & Levis 1971] indicates that both fear and avoidance responding extinguishes quite rapidly (usually within a few trials) using a response prevention procedure. To illustrate the point that rapid extinction of the avoidance response occurs after the elicitation of a strong emotional response to the previous conditioned stimulus complex, the following example from the second author's laboratory will be given [Levis, 1966b]. The conditioning situation was identical to the one-way avoidance example previously outlined. However, after ten consecutive avoidance responses were made to a three-component serial CS, the safe side of the apparatus was altered to look identical to the shock side. The white walls were changed to black, and the solid floor was removed exposing a grid floor. Shock was turned off. Because of methodological reasons beyond the scope of this paper, the response was not blocked by a barrier. The rat was permitted to continue its avoidance responding, which were now occurring to the first stimulus in the sequence with most response latencies being a second or under in duration. On the first test trial, the rat appeared to the experimenter to be quite surprised when it first jumped into the safe box that now resembled the shock side. Immediately after the response, the CS sequence was represented during the safe period (intertrial interval). The animal remained immobile during the presentation of S1, urinated during the presentation of S2, and when S3 occurred (the stimulus that was previously closest to shock onset), the rat jumped straight up into the air and grasped with its teeth a small light bulb mounted near the ceiling of the apparatus that served as a constant source of illumination for the chamber. The experimenter was so surprised, he checked the equipment because it appeared as if the animal received a very strong shock through the grid bars of the floor. Upon inspection this turned out not to be the case since the grid bars were not connected by wire. The animal stayed suspended by his teeth in midair for some time until gravity forced it to lose its grip. Upon hitting the grid floor, the rat again bolted up into the air and grasped the lamp. This time it fell faster, and finally it stopped jumping. By the tenth extinction trail, the animal refused to jump into the safe side, and by the twentieth trial, the rat was actively exploring the shock box, and the flashing lights and buzzer appeared to have little behavioral effect since it finally fell asleep in their presence. The repeated exposure to the feared situation in the absence of any physical pain led to a strong emotional response, which was followed by an unlearning of fear to the conditioned stimulus complex.

Six Steps of Treatment by Implosive Therapy

The principles of extinction developed by experimental psychologists in laboratory research were used to provide the foundation and guide lines for the procedures employed in IT.

The steps followed in treating patients with IT may be summarized as follows:

1. Diagnostic Interviews

The first task of the therapist is to identify as accurately as possible those conditioned aversive stimuli that are presumed to mediate the emotional responses (e.g., anxiety, anger, depression), which are determinants of the symptoms and problems of the patient.

In order to accomplish this goal, the therapist conducts two standard diagnostic interview sessions with the patient. At this time, the therapist lists both internal stimuli (images, thoughts, impulses) and external stimuli (stimuli associated with public events, e.g., phobic objects, social situations, parental arguments, etc.).

2. Training in "Neutral" Imagery

At the end of the second diagnostic interview, the therapist instructs the patient to close his eyes. The patient is asked to visualize in detail various "neutral" scenes such as watching TV, eating a meal, driving a car, and so forth. Events involving home, school, games, play, and others may be described. From time to time the therapist requires the patient to focus closely on the details of these scenes. For example, the patient is asked to observe very closely the facial expression of a person to whom he is speaking, or to pay attention to the reflectance of the chrome of an automobile toward which the patient is walking. The characteristic muscular "feel" experienced in a scene where the patient is hitting a ball with a tennis racquet (baseball bat, etc.) also is observed closely.

The scenes chosen by the therapist are those which do not evoke emotionality in the patient. If the patient appears to experience any emotion to the scenes that are described, the scene is quickly changed in the direction of emotional neutrality. Part of this procedure includes having the patient pay attention to any sensations in the various anatomical parts of his body (e.g., head, neck, shoulders, stomach).

The procedure followed in the "neutral" imagery phase allows the therapist to establish a crude baseline for the ability of the patient to imagine various stimuli. Also, the therapist establishes himself as the essential director of the scenes. The patient also learns (the therapist explicitly emphasizes this point) that one can imagine things and events that may actually have never happened or may even be impossible.

3. Implosive Extinction Sessions

At the beginning of the third session, the therapist usually has the patient "replay" the "neutral" imagery practiced in the previous session. Then the therapist directs scenes in which stimuli are included that generate emotional responses (fear, anger, guilt, etc.). The emotional reactions elicited are thought to provide the basic motivation for the patient's symptoms and problems. The therapist may take a few minutes to "set the stage" for the scene but then attempts to maximize emotional arousal by presenting the aversive stimuli as vividly and realistically as possible. Repetition of the key aversive stimuli is followed by progressive expansion to other sets of aversive cues thought to be critical to the patient's symptoms. Any attempt on the part of the patient to avoid the imagined aversive stimuli is prevented by the therapist. The essence of the procedure is to force repeated exposures to the aversive stimuli that underlie the patient's difficulties.

4. Hypothesized Approximations

Since it is frequently difficult to identify *precisely* some types of aversive stimuli (e.g., unreported past conditioning events), the therapist may make "guesses" that represent hypothesized stimulus approximations of the unidentified aversive stimuli. To the extent that there is some similarity between the hypothesized approximation, which reflects the "guess" of the therapist, and the actual aversive stimuli controlling the patients' deviant or maladaptive behavior, then, some extinction should be conferred on the critical aversive stimuli through a generalization of extinction effect.

5. Homework Assignments

At the end of the first therapy session, the patient is asked to practice in imagery the aversive scenes used during the session as a homework assignment. Many more extinction trials for the critical aversive stimuli are obtained through the use of this procedure. Homework assignments also are given at the end of subsequent sessions. As the patient acquires more skill and understanding for the basic principles of learning used in IT, he may apply the principles to almost any new problem of adjustment in his daily living with little or no help from the therapist.

6. Duration of treatment

In each session that follows, aversive stimuli used in previous sessions are repeated and a progressive expansion of additional aversive stimuli are introduced. New homework assignments are given. The sessions are continued and the conditioned aversive stimuli are repeated until little or no emotional arousal to them is observed in the patient. Typically the patient reports that the symptomatic behavior is eliminated or is so markedly reduced that it no longer interferes with his daily life adjustment. At this time treatment is terminated. However, additional follow-up sessions spaced at increasingly greater intervals may be arranged in order to allow an assessment of the long range stability of the improvements that have been achieved.

Through this procedure the Implosive therapist systematically uses the principle of extinction, which includes the use of overlapping generalization of extinction gradients in the treatment of deviant behavior. The symptoms and problem behavior of the patient are hypothesized to be motivated by mediating emotional reactions under the control of internal and external conditioned stimuli. The main emotional mediating responses consist of conditioned fear (anxiety) and/or conditioned anger reactions that were acquired as a consequence of past experiences involving punishment, frustration, and pain.

The Case Of The Bottomless Bathtub

It should be evident that in the case of the woman so terrified by water that she wore a life preserver when she took a bath that the principle of extinction could be applied by having the patient vividly imagine again and again that she was taking a bath *without a life preserver.* Such a procedure would represent a symptom contingent cue.

However, in applying the principle of extinction to individual patients, the IT therapist capitalizes on the fact that frequently a train of associatively linked thoughts or images is related to the symptom. Thoughts, images, or even impulses to behave in various ways may also function as part of the total number of conditioned stimuli that evoke emotional reactions related to the patient's problem. For example, diagnostic interviews had revealed that the feeling or thought that the bathtub was bottomless was related to her phobia. The patient was well aware of the irrationality of this belief, but nothing she could do dispelled her conviction that the bathtub might be bottomless. It now becomes more understandable why she felt she had to wear a life preserver. If one cannot swim (and she could not) it makes sense to wear a life preserver in a bottomless bathtub. The report of the patient of her feeling that the tub might be bottomless illustrates a second class of cues susceptible to extinction. Thus the IT therapist might have the patient imagine that she was taking a bath without a life preserver *in a bottomless bathtub.* The inclusion of the bottomless nature of the bathtub is classified as a "reportable cue."

It seems clear that the taking of a bath in a bottomless bathtub without a life preserver when one cannot swim is a dangerous situation. Such a situation may lead to drowning. Therefore, the therapist instructs her to imagine that while taking the bath without her life preserver she sinks under the water and drowns. But imagined drowning is not real drowning. Imagined drowning functions as a conditioned stimulus and is susceptible to extinction. It is true that she experienced much anxiety while going through the first repetitions of drowning. However, after a number of repetitions less and less anxiety is experienced. A "ho-hum" reaction of, "Well, I'm drowning again" is finally elicited. This is true even when the therapist emphasizes her struggling and helplessness while drowning. As predicted by the principle of experimental extinction, *repetition is the key to success of the procedure.* The inference of the therapist that "drowning" is part of the aversive conditioned stimulus complex is classified as an "hypothesized cue." Subsequently, variations on the basic theme of drowning were introduced. Following five implosive extinction sessions, the patient reported that she no longer wore a life preserver while taking a bath and experienced very little anxiety when taking it. It must be remembered that the patient also practiced the imagery as a homework assignment and that two diagnostic interview sessions preceded the implosive extinction sessions.

Original Conditioning Events

Some of the variations introduced by the therapist to the bottomless bathtub sequence were related to original events reported by the patient during the diagnostic interviews. Also, a number of additional memories were recalled by the patient following the implosive extinction sessions. These two sources of information revealed that the patient had lived on a farm during her early childhood. Once she had a very frightening experience when she fell into a ditch filled with water. Her mother had scolded and punished her for playing so close to the water. Furthermore, her mother had constantly warned her of the dangers of going near an old well on the farm and had described to her repeatedly how children could fall and drown in such deep water. In general, most patients do not readily recollect such incidents and are very surprised when memories of this nature emerge during or following the implosive extinction sessions.

A learning interpretation of psychopathological behavior assumes that the observed symptomatic behavior is a product of earlier conditioning events in the life history of the patient. Therefore, some of the variations in imagery introduced by the therapist included a number of these original conditioning events. For example, the bathtub was changed into a ditch and also into a deep well. The scolding and punishing mother was included in the "replay" of such scenes. Such reproductions contain auditory as well as visual stimuli (the therapist will speak for the mother on occasion). Cues of this type are classified in the category of "original conditioning events."

Hypothesized Psychodynamic Cues

The final class of cues used in Implosive Therapy are those directly related to traditional psychodynamic theory. It should be noted that these cues are reinter-preted in terms of a learning or conditioning model of behavior. This class of cues appears to be most useful for patients whose symptoms seem to be unusually resistant to change. This seems to be true for patients in which the symptoms have lasted for many years and/or a history of failure to obtain change by other methods of treatment have occurred. The psychodynamic cues also appear to be especially useful in cases where more profound behavioral disturbance seems to exist. For example, hospitalized psychotic patients appear to benefit appreciably from the inclusion of such cues.

In the case of the patient who was terrified of water there were other problems that she reported. Implosive therapists usually find phobic behavior a reasonably easy type of behavior to reverse; thus they encourage the patient to report other types of problems. Frequently, some of these problems are more difficult to solve and require more effort and experience on the part of the therapist. For example, this patient reported that she was prone to severe feelings of depression and experienced much difficulty in interpersonal relationships, especially those involving other women. She bitterly resented her mother-in-law but was totally unable to express herself and her point of view in this relationship. Based on information secured from the diagnostic interviews and from much additional material obtained during and following the five implosive extinction sessions of her water phobia, the following picture of her relationship with her parents emerged.

In early childhood she had been a favorite of her father and did not get along well with her mother. Her mother had punished her frequently and she remembered how bitterly resentful she had felt toward her mother. Her mother had ruled her with a stern hand and any expression of resistance or rebellion to her mother's peremptory commands were quickly and completely squelched. From the point of view of psychodynamic theory it is interesting that she finally recalled that on several occasions she wished that her mother were dead. In fact, she reported that vague fantasies of actually killing her mother had occurred to her. The presence of such "death wish impulses" is a fairly frequent interpretation of traditional psychoanalytic theory. Implosive theory assumes that anger, aggression, and "death wish impulses" are conditioned responses that function as anxiety evoking conditioned stimuli. One might infer that part of the difficulty in her relationship to her mother-in-law is a displacement (response generalization) of the anger response originally conditioned to her mother. In learning terms the mother-in-law is a generalized CS and the anger is a generalized response. Her inability to express herself assertively is a result of the anxiety conditioned to the assertive responses that are a consequence of the punishments given by her mother when as a child she had attempted to be assertive in relation to her mother.

One interpretation of psychodynamic theory is that depression may result, at least in part, from anger or hostility that cannot be directed externally. Anger and hostility are "internalized," that is, directed toward the self. When this state of affairs exists feelings of depression may result. The learning model employed in Implosive Therapy interprets the "internalized anger" as a result of a set of avoidance responses. These avoidance responses are motivated by the anxiety reactions acquired to the external expression of anger (the external expression of anger is conceived as a CS). However, the anger or hostility itself is a conditioned emotional response to stimuli associated with primary frustration and punishment. This network of conditioned stimuli is a result of her conditioning history and is represented in her nervous system.

Therefore, the IT therapist, following the first five implosive sessions, branches off into a set of scenes related to past incidents of frustration and punishment that involved her mother. In reproducing these scenes, she is directed to express strong feelings of anger and resentment toward the mother. In this procedure verbal, physical, and primary process types of aggression are included as expressions of the anger reactions. During and following such a procedure, it is common for the patient to "remember" many more specific incidents that occurred in the past. These incidents are "replayed" with the aggression component included. Current figures (e.g., mother-in-law) are also used in some of the aggression scenes.

According to the learning model of IT, two processes are occurring. First, the anxiety conditioned to the aggression CS should be reduced through extinction since the expression of aggression is not followed by real punishment (primary reinforcement). By reducing the anxiety component, one would expect the patient to become more assertive, more able to stand up for her own rights. Second, since the emotional response of anger is itself a conditioned response, *the repetition of the anger or hostility reaction in the absence of primary frustration and pain will lead to a decrement in the total anger component.*

The patient received seven implosive extinction sessions along these lines. Fourteen sessions after beginning treatment, which included two nonimplosive diagnostic interviews, this patient had not only lost her fear of water but was no longer suffering from any pronounced depressive episodes. Furthermore, she reported that she no longer experienced much difficulty with older women, was able to express herself

far more assertively without anxiety and, in fact, had a much better relationship with her mother-in-law. These gains had been maintained for several years.

Thus five broad classes of cues are employed for reproduction in imagery: symptom contingent cues; reportable cues; cues relating to original conditioning events; hypothesized cues related to the symptom contingent, and reportable cues; and hypothesized cues related to the original conditioning events. The fifth class of cues is that related to psychoanalytic interpretations. The most commonly reproduced stimuli associated with these five classes of cues are those involving punishment, aggression, oral, anal, and sexual material, rejection, bodily injury, loss of impulse control, acceptance of conscience, and feedback stimuli from autonomic and central nervous system activity. Of course, more than one type of class and set of stimuli may be combined in the reproduction of a single scene.

It should be clear to the reader now how the persons described earlier would be treated with the IT method. In the case of the woman obsessed with the thought that fire might break out, and who spent most of her day checking ashtrays and electrical appliances while thinking she could smell smoke, the procedure is an obvious one. Such a patient is instructed to imagine in vivid and detailed scenes that she fails to check the ashtrays or appliances and that, as a result of her negligence, a terrible fire breaks out.

To be sure, some strong anxiety reactions result from the reproduction of such imagery. Imagined fires (conditioned stimuli) are not real fires (unconditioned stimuli), however, and the fear of imagined anticipated fires decreases. After a sufficient number of fire repetitions (she is given homework assignments to practice the fire theme), she behaves far more rationally at home. She now checks ash trays and appliances once or twice and then forgets about them. Furthermore, the patient reports how foolish it seems to her now that she once had such fears.

In the case of the male patient who was a compulsive hand washer, it seemed clear that he was responding to thoughts of dirt and contamination. This patient was repeatedly instructed to imagine scenes that involved exposure to dirt and contamination. In these scenes, he uses his fingers to turn the light switches on and off and then fails to wash his hands. Much exposure to dirt and contamination results. For example, he discovers that the light switch is crawling with bacteria; nevertheless, he is instructed to touch it again and then rub it on his body and then lick his finger. But again, imagined contamination is not real contamination and his anticipation of dirt loses its panic-inducing qualities. After a few sessions the patient reports that his hand washing has decreased markedly and that he never bothers to turn off light switches with his elbows. In cases similar to these, a number of additional variations may be included that touch on original conditioning events and other classes of cues and responses such as sex, guilt, and aggression. Many compulsive symptoms can be reasonably traced back to conditioning events involving early toilet and cleanliness training. These events are "replayed" and in severe cases psychoanalytic cues are introduced. For example, not only is the original training approximated, but in addition the patient falls through the seat of an outhouse (an outhouse is used to emphasize the dirt and possibilities of contamination) and hits with a splat in the soft, brown, mushy, moist, smelly mass of material beneath. After much interaction with this foul fecal material, the patient is transferred (in imagery) to a septic tank. In his "new" septic tank home, which is now his permanent abode, he cooks, eats, bathes, sleeps, and even throws cocktail parties. Each and every activity affords ample opportunity for exposure to fecal material, dirt, and contamination. Occasionally, psychoanalytic retentive and expulsive themes are reproduced in imagery. Such themes are usually reserved for extremely severe neurotic patients or for psychotic patients.

Frequently the IT therapist combines two or more classes of cues in a single scene. For example, in the case of the female patient who was sexually inhibited (fear of sexual stimuli) and who also was tormented by thoughts of eternal damnation in hell (partly as anticipated punishment for sexual thoughts and impulses), the theme was developed (fifth implosive session) of a blatant love affair with the devil in hell. Eternal damnation and punishment follow such sexual activity. Imagined sexual intercourse with the devil in hell is a complex conditioned aversive stimulus, as is the imagined punishment (eternal damnation). The repetition of this theme leads to a progressive reduction in the irrational elements of her fear of sex and hell.

The clinical success of IT with severe neurotic patients led to an attempt to treat the hospitalized psychotic mental patient with similar methods. It seemed reasonable to make this transition since severe neurotic patients frequently display much "psychotic-like" mental processes on occasion. Following treatment the "psychotic-like" signs appear to be reduced as well as the neurotic ones.

A major feature of psychotic disorders (such as schizophrenia) is described as poor reality contact. Delusions, hallucinations, and disturbance in the thought processes are characteristic of such patients. Surprisingly, the hospitalized psychotic patient could

be analyzed in almost the same way as the neurotic one. That is, the two-factor model of avoidance learning could be employed to interpret the sources of motivation for the occurrence of delusions, hallucinations, disturbance in the thought processes, and apparent loss of reality contact in the psychotic patient. Although this analysis is somewhat more complex than the neurotic one, it is still a reasonably simple one. For example, the patient who has the delusion that he is Jesus Christ, or possesses billions of dollars, may be interpreted as engaging in avoidance responses that serve to protect him from exposure to conditioned stimuli which, when activated, induce negative emotional reactions in him. These conditioned stimuli include a network of associated thoughts, images and impulses as in the neurotic patient. The loss of reality contact itself seems to represent one grand set of avoidance responses that serve to protect him from exposure to "reality" stimuli, which would redintegrate the thoughts, images, or impulses that function as conditioned aversive stimuli. Like the neurotic patient, these stimuli seem to have acquired their properties as a result of the previous conditioning history. [For additional information concerning the technique and theory see Stampfl 1966, 1970; Stampfl & Levis 1967, 1968, 1969].

Experimental Support

A number of investigators interested in validating the theory and techniques of behavior therapies used to treat anxieties, such as Implosive Therapy or Wolpe's [1958] Systematic Desensitization technique, have engaged in research dealing with the "fears" (usually of rats or snakes) of nonpatient populations. These studies, which are usually carried out in a laboratory setting with college students as subjects, have been labeled "analogue therapy" studies. A few comments about this research strategy are in order since the credibility of the analogue approach has recently been challenged by Cooper, Furst, and Bridger [1969]. These authors concluded that "studying the treatment of snake fears may be irrelevant to the understanding of treating clinical neuroses."

In defense of analogue research, Levis [1970c] has argued that such laboratory studies are of value when they are used as vehicles to obtain information about various treatment manipulations, to develop ideas or hypotheses, to clarify theoretical issues, or to check the validity of previous findings. The laboratory setting using nonpatient populations is attractive because it permits the selection of homogeneous target behaviors, the equation of avoidance tendencies, the operational definition of independent and· dependent measures, and the selection of appropriate control conditions. Unfortunately, such experimental precision is exceedingly difficult to obtain when using patient populations. Anyone who has involved himself with therapy-outcome research is aware of the numerous problems confronting the researcher in execution of their study. Typical difficulties encountered involve problems associated with drug control and effects, administrator interference, ethical considerations, patient selection and participation, establishment of control groups, and the equating of therapists on such dimensions as experience, skill, and commitments. It is precisely because of this lack of experimental control that outcome patient research has not covered the range of questions raised at the analogue level of analysis.

Nevertheless, critics of analogue research are quite correct in questioning the conclusions of investigators who over-generalize from data collected on nonpatient populations and suggest that the results of their studies directly support the therapeutic effectiveness of the treatment technique they are investigating. The naïveté of some behavior therapists on this issue is disconcerting. Furthermore, an argument can also be made that too much effort is being placed in the analogue area and that some of this effort is at the expense of carrying out badly needed patient work. For example, despite the fact that Wolpe's systematic desensitization technique has been known to the scientific community for over fifteen years, the majority of the work on this behavioral technique (which is considerable) has involved analogue research. The authors could only find six published experimental reports of this procedure with patient populations.

Implosive Therapy has also been the topic of analysis by analogue researchers, and work in this area is on the increase. Unfortunately, the first published report of the theory and technique of Implosive Therapy to receive any widespread circulation appeared in December, 1967. Sufficient time has not yet elapsed to permit extended experimental work. Nevertheless, evidence is available that suggests Implosive Therapy is effective in treating nonpatient subjects' isolated fears of rats or snakes [Barrett 1969; Borkovec 1972; Hogan & Kirchner 1967, 1968; Kirchner & Hogan 1966; Prochaska 1971].

The above analogue work will not be reviewed in detail here since the authors strongly believe that this type of data should not be used in direct support of a therapeutic technique designed to treat patient populations. Thus, the review in this section will only concentrate on experimental studies using Implosive Therapy with patient populations. To date, four such studies have appeared in the literature and they will be presented in chronological order of their appearance.

Hogan Study

The first research report dealing with the effectiveness of Implosive Therapy on a patient population was carried out by Robert Hogan [1966]. In this investigation, fifty patients from the intensive treatment ward of a state hospital were evaluated. These patients were assigned to Implosive-trained therapists and non-Implosive oriented therapists by the ward physician. The non-Implosive therapists were traditional in orientation and basically administered what is referred to as conventional treatment. The assignments were made on the basis of time available in each therapist's schedule and without knowledge that the study was in progress. As a result, twenty-six patients were assigned to Implosive Therapy and twenty-four to a non-Implosive treatment procedure that served as the control group.

Statistical tests revealed that the two groups of patients did not reliably differ from each other on such variables as sex, age, education, intellectual ability, and length of prior treatment.

After assignment to a ward, the patient was administered the Minnesota Multiphasic Personality Inventory (MMPI). The pre-therapy MMPI scores were used to establish the similarity of the Implosive and non-Implosive groups with regard to the character and degree of initial disturbance. Statistical tests revealed there were no significant differences between groups. Each patient in the study lived within a semicontrolled environment in that the patient came into daily contact with the same fellow patients and the same members of the hospital staff. In addition to each patient's individual therapy treatment program, patients participated in group therapy, occupational therapy, recreational work, and educational programs routinely outlined for all patients in this hospital setting. Full ground privileges were also given to each patient in this study.

The post-treatment MMPI's were administered at the time a patient was released from the hospital or transferred from the ward. This option was ultimately determined by the physician, after consultation with the members of the intensive treatment staff. The interim between pre- and post-testing established the period of time of treatment. The Implosive group averaged 4.9 months in treatment and the controls averaged 8.2 months. The individual therapists for both treatment procedures were psychologists. They had similar academic and therapy experience prior to the investigation, and all therapists were aware that the study was in progress.

Before we discuss the results of this study, it may prove helpful to outline briefly what the MMPI is supposed to measure. The MMPI is considered to be one of the most carefully constructed objective personality questionnaires so far developed. It consists of more than 500 questions that are answered by the person as being either true or false. The test is designed to assess many different phases of personality especially useful in detecting mental disorder. Among other things it appraises is the degree to which a person is anxious or depressed, whether his thinking is disturbed, whether he ruminates excessively, has paranoid thoughts, is concerned with problems of sexual identification, or has symptoms involving hypochondriasis, hysteria, phobias, and other "nervous" manifestations. An advantageous feature of this test is that more than ten percent of the MMPI questions are subtly designed to evaluate the degree to which a person is deliberately making himself look worse or better. By comparing these validity scales with predetermined standards, the tester is able to estimate the truthfulness of the person examined. Another advantage of this test is that the scales of the test are empirically determined, which takes into account the fact that patients have varying degrees of self-understanding and that they may interpret many items on the exam differently. That is to say, the relation between what is said on the test and what the subject actually does is not always expected to be a literal one. People who tend to respond affirmatively or negatively to certain questions or a group of questions have empirically been shown to manifest certain behaviors like depression. The basic test is constructed to yield scores for ten clinical scales and four validity scales.

Although the problem of adequately determining the effectiveness of a given therapeutic procedure is complex and little agreement in the field exists as to what is the best or best set of measures to employ, the use of the MMPI does provide certain advantages as noted in the preceding paragraph. It is an objective measure that is well constructed, empirically derived, and extensively validated [Dahlstrom & Welsh 1960]. Furthermore, it has been used frequently in the evaluation of treatment [Barron & Leary 1955; Gallagher 1953; Kaufman 1950; Mogar & Savage 1964; Schofield 1950, 1953] and shows promise in forecasting the adjustment of people following therapeutic intervention [Johnston & McNeal 1965].

Returning to Hogan's study, comparison of the pre- and post-MMPI's of the Implosive and non-Implosive treatment groups revealed that the Implosive group shifted significantly away from pathology on five MMPI scales, while no significant changes were noted in the control group from pre- to post-therapy testing. Since testers have traditionally considered MMPI T-scores of seventy and above as a sign of pathology, Hogan analyzed shifts in these extreme scores. The results revealed a statistically significant shift away from pathology for the Implosive group when compared to the non-Implosive treatment group. Similar results were obtained when all T-scores eighty and above were considered. The Implosive group shifted an average of -11.47 T-scores in the seventy and above analysis and -8.12 when scores eighty and above were considered. The control, non-Implosive treated group showed a mean shift of $-.59$ when scores seventy and above were evaluated and an average shift of $+.88$ for scores eighty and above.

Hogan introduced a second yardstick for improvement. Each patient was followed for one year after treatment. At the end of this time, cases released or discharged from the hospital were considered successful, while patients who were transferred to other units, and/or rehospitalized were classified as failures. Eighteen of the twenty-six implosive patients were classified as successful as opposed to eight out of twenty-four control patients. This difference between groups was found to be statistically reliable.

Levis and Carrera Study

The results of the Hogan study were encouraging and prompted Levis and Carrera [1967] to investigate the effectiveness of Implosive Therapy with non-hospitalized outpatients. Their study was designed as an exploratory study to determine the feasibility and value of more extensive evaluations. Aware of the fact that "new" therapies appear to be more effective initially, Levis and Carrera attempted to provide a stringent test of the Implosive Therapy technique. To accomplish this objective, only patients who displayed relatively severe signs of psychopathology were treated with Implosive Therapy, and the number of treatment sessions given them were limited to ten. As an additional handicap, only one of the two Implosive therapists treating the patients had previous experience using the technique.

The MMPI was selected as the measure of evaluation to facilitate comparison with the Hogan study. The prediction was made that the clinical scales signifying pathology (T-score above seventy) for the Implosive Therapy-treated group would decrease more than those of the control groups.

Forty psychotherapy patients were divided into one experimental (IT) and three control groups (CT1, CT2, and WT) with ten subjects per group.

The experimental group, Group IT, received one or two one-hour standard diagnostic interviews followed by ten hours of Implosive Therapy. One Implosive therapist treated seven patients and the other, three. An attempt was made to remove all possible bias in preselection factors for Group IT. The subjects were accepted for Implosive treatment simply upon meeting certain predetermined MMPI criteria that will be described below. The subjects who did not meet the necessary test requirements were excluded from this study and treated by another method. No subject in this group terminated Implosive treatment prematurely. The subjects were not requested to pay for treatment.

The control groups consisted of two treatment groups and one nontreatment group. Group CT1 received a conventional type of treatment (a combination of insight and supportive therapy) for essentially the same number of hours as Group IT. Group CT1 was employed as a control for both the number of therapy sessions and duration of treatment.

Patients were kept in treatment after evaluations for the present study were made. Three of the four therapists who treated the subjects in Group CT1 were third-year psychiatric residents, while the fourth therapist was an experienced clinical psychologist (Ph.D.). The subjects were preassigned to the therapists by a supervisor who believed patients were good candidates for psychotherapy. Four subjects in Group CT1 terminated treatment prior to ten hours of therapy. These subjects were replaced. Seven of the ten patients in this group were charged a fee which averaged three dollars a session.

Group CT2, the second treatment control group, received conventional treatment for an average of thirty-seven hours. This group was treated by one of the Implosive therapists before he had any knowledge about Implosive Therapy. Group CT2 was employed as a control for possible skills and personal qualities of the therapist that might be operating independently of the treatment technique and because it was thought desirable to compare Group IT with a group in which treatment was terminated. Patients were accepted for treatment upon request. No subject included in this group received less than ten sessions. The subjects were not requested to pay for treatment.

The final control group, Group WT, consisted of nontreated patients who previously had been placed on a waiting therapy list. This group was employed as a control for the possible therapeutic effects resulting from the commitment to and expectation of professional treatment, rather than from formal treatment.

All subjects in Group WT received one intake interview by a psychiatrist before being placed on a waiting list. The forty persons whose names had been most recently listed were sent a form letter requesting their cooperation in a research study. It was pointed out that only individuals who had not begun therapy were desired, and participation would in no way affect being called for treatment. Twenty patients cooperated, and only ten of these met the necessary requirements.

Pre- and post-treatment MMPIs were administered to each subject. For the treatment subjects tests were administered by the patient's therapist. Tests were administered within a week prior to and after completion of treatment. Post-tests for Group WT were taken approximately three months after completion of the pretest, and all tests were administered by mail. Each therapy subject was required to have low scores on the several validity scales of the MMPI so that it could be assumed that their responses to the ten clinical scales were valid [Dahlstrom & Welsh 1960]. An additional criterion of three or more T-scores about seventy on any of the clinical scales was required for all subjects so as to obtain a relatively severe degree of test pathology. Because of the practical difficulty in meeting the latter criterion, one of the ten subjects in each of the four groups was included with only two T-scores above seventy.

Specific subclassification and differentiation among psychotic, personality, and psychoneurotic disorders were not made because of difficulty in objectively determining a diagnosis. However, in order to give some indication of the types of profiles encountered, the Meehl-Dahlstrom PNI rules [Dahlstrom & Welsh 1960, p. 469; Meehl & Dahlstrom 1960] were applied to all pretest MMPIs. For Group IT seven patients were classified as psychotic-curve types (P), one as a neurotic-curve type (N), and two as indeterminate (I). For the control groups the breakdown was as follows: Group CT1 (four Ps, four Ns, and two Is); Group CT2 (five Ps, two Ns, and three Is); and Group WT (six Ps, one N, and three Is). All of the therapists participating in the study reported that each of the patients they treated was capable of functioning in society without the need of hospitalization.

Although the main interest of the investigators was in the scale scores representing pathology (defined as T-scores above seventy), a look at the mean difference score between pre- and post-MMPIs for all subjects proved of value. These scores showed a greater decrease for Group IT on each of the ten standard scales except the Hypomania scale. The mean difference score across all standard scales for Group IT (M $=-53.1$) was significantly different from the mean of the control groups (M$= -8.0$). This later finding is of interest since Johnston and McNeal [1965] found some justification from follow-up data for considering patients improved if a reduction of the sum of the T-scores on the clinical scales for each patient was twenty points or greater.

For Group IT, seventeen of the forty-eight pretest scores above seventy dropped into the normal range after treatment, while five of the forty-two T-scores dropped for Group CT1, four of forty-six for CT2, and three of forty-one for Group WT. If T-scores above eighty are considered, fifteen of the twenty-six pretest T-scores for Group IT dropped below eighty on the post-test while no change in total number of T-scores above eighty occurred for the combined control groups. The reason for analyzing scores above eighty separately was to determine whether the extreme scores were more likely to show changes in the positive direction (regression toward the mean phenomenon). This clearly was not the case for the control conditions. Furthermore, the mean T-score decrease for all scores above seventy was far greater after treatment for Group IT (-8.3) than for Groups CT1 (-1.0), CT2 ($-.3$), or WT (-1.9). This latter finding is quite consistent with the data of Hogan [1966] who reported that his Implosive group shifted an average of -11.5 T-score points in the seventy and above analysis while the non-Implosive-treatment group showed a mean shift of $-.6$.

A statistical analysis of the differences between Group IT and the combined control groups for T-scores above seventy on the ten standard scales was made. A single score was obtained for each subject by computing the difference for each of the patient's pretest scale scores above seventy from the respective post-test score and calculating a mean of these difference scores. These scores were ranked, and the median was obtained. According to the Fisher exact probability test, Group IT and the control groups differed significantly in the proportion of scores assigned above and below the median. Group IT had the greater proportion of patients showing a decrease in the direction away from pathology.

A final comparison was made between subjects treated by the newly trained Implosive therapist and Group CT2, which also was treated by the same therapist. The Implosive Therapy subjects (N=7) had a mean difference score across all the standard clinical scales of -50.9, while Group CT2 (N=10) had a mean shift of -8.7. For scores above seventy, Implosive Therapy subjects dropped on the average of -8.1 score points, while Group CT2's mean decrease was only $-.3$.

The consistent trend of Group IT to shift away from psychopathology on the MMPI also was in agreement with clinical observations and verbal reports of subjects. (For example, patients reported a marked decrease in feelings of anxiety, depression, obsessional thoughts, compulsive behavior, and phobic reactions.) These latter data, however, were not systematically recorded or compared with responses from control groups.

Since the control groups failed to show any marked improvement on the test measures, the authors concluded that some evidence is present that the effects of Group IT were not due to the number of therapy sessions, the skills and personal qualities of the therapists independent of the treatment technique, the termination of treatment, or the effects resulting from the commitment to and expectation of professional treatment. Unfortunately, long-term follow-up data were not obtained, in part due to job relocation of the investigators.

Boulougouris, Marks, and Marset Study

The third study to be reviewed was carried out by Boulougouris, Marks, and Marset [1971]. They treated sixteen psychiatric patients with phobic disorders. Nine of the phobic disorders were classified as agoraphobics (fear of open spaces) and seven specific phobics, the phobias all being more than one year in duration with the mean duration of symptoms being twelve years. The mean age of patients (seven men and nine women) was thirty-three years. The experimental design consisted of a crossover technique in which half the subjects received Wolpe's [1958] Systematic Desensitization procedure for the first six therapy sessions followed by six therapy sessions involving Implosive Therapy. For the remaining half of the subjects the order of therapy presentation was reversed. Treatment was given two or three times weekly with the average treatment time taking five weeks. Five of the patients were treated as inpatients and eleven as outpatients. Most of the patients were taken off drugs and their main reason for seeking treatment centered on problems presented by their phobic disorder. The mean delay in crossing over from one treatment technique to the other was six days.

The patients were treated by ten therapists, all novices to both Systematic Desensitization and Implosive Therapy. Each patient had all twelve treatment sessions from the same therapist. The content of the Implosive sessions mainly dealt with symptom-contingent cues. Clinical assessment made by each patient, each therapist, and an independent medical assessor on scales described by Gelder and Marks [1966] as well as physiological assessments were made before the start of treatment and two days after the end of the sixth and twelfth sessions. The clinical ratings were continued at intervals to a year's follow-up.

Since the therapist and assessor's rating correlated

0.78 and 0.89 with one another for the treated phobia and total phobic condition respectively, the investigators combined them for one "doctors' rating score" for purposes of analysis. Analyses of these data revealed that the Implosive condition produced significant improvement in the ratings of the treated phobia and total phobic condition when compared with Systematic Desensitization therapy. However, both treatment procedures showed a reliable improvement in the ratings. The physiological assessment indices showed the same basic results. Implosive Therapy patients displayed a significantly greater decrease in heart rate and in skin conductance indices during the presentation of phobic test scenes when compared to Desensitization subjects. On no measure were the Systematic Desensitization data found to be reliably superior to the Implosive Therapy data.

The one-year follow-up data suggested that the patients continued to improve although some had no further treatment. The respective contributions of Systematic Desensitization or Implosive Therapy could not be isolated since all subjects received both treatment procedures.

After considerable discussion of methological issues, the authors concluded that the Implosive Therapy technique was the more effective form of treatment. These data support their preliminary finding with four phobic patients [Boulougouris & Marks 1969].

Boudewyns and Wilson Study

The final study to be reviewed was carried out by Boudewyns and Wilson [1972]. This study provides the most extensive analysis of the Implosive Therapy technique to date. The present study investigated the effects of Implosive Therapy (IT); Desensitization therapy (DT) using free association, a technique developed by Wilson and Smith [1968]; and Milieu therapy (MT) on psychiatric inpatients at a Veterans Administration Hospital. Patients under the age of fifty, whose highest significantly elevated clinical scale (T-score seventy or above) on the MMPI was either the depression or the psychasthenia scale were accepted for the study. These two clinical scales were used as criterion measures since they are most commonly elevated for VA patients [Gilberstadt & Duker 1965]. Of the thirty-seven patients asked to participate in the study, only one declined. The mean age of the volunteer patients was 39.8 years.

The two authors and two advanced clinical psychology trainees served as therapists. The first author of this study, trained in Implosive Therapy by Thomas Stampfl, the originator of that therapy, trained the other three therapists in this technique. The sec-

ond author, originator of the particular version of the desensitization therapy technique that was employed, trained the others in desensitization therapy. At the beginning of the study, both trainee-therapists expressed negative attitudes toward some aspects of Implosive Therapy, while one was negative and the other neutral toward the desensitization approach.

Twelve patients were assigned to each of the three groups. In the two individual therapy treatment conditions, Groups IT and DT, subjects were seen for not more than twelve one-hour sessions (mean number of therapy sessions per patient equaled 11.4 hours). Within this limit, the number of spacing of therapy sessions were left to the discretion of the individual therapist. The mean number of days to complete all therapy contacts was 34.3 days. All patients were released from the hospital within thirty days after completion of therapy.

Each therapist was randomly assigned six patients, three each from Groups IT and DT. All subjects were given a similar ward milieu. To evaluate the effectiveness of the ward milieu, the third group (Group MT) was formed. The milieu therapy involved an intensive ward program involving occupational therapy, industrial therapy, physical therapy, group therapy, and individual counseling by residents, medical students, nurses, and nursing students. Group MT subjects were told that the milieu program had been planned specifically for them by the ward team and that psychological tests would be used to help determine the effectiveness of these activities.

None of the patients in the study were allowed to take anti-psychotic tranquilizers (e.g., chlorpromazine) during therapy.

Boudewyns and Wilson employed multiple criterion measures in assessing the treatment effectiveness of the various groups. The MMPI and the Mooney Problem Checklist were administered to all patients prior to therapy, immediately following therapy, and six months after therapy. Prior to therapy, each subject was also asked to identify the personal goals he hoped to attain as a result of his therapy. Patients were then requested to rate their present psychological distance from that goal on a seven-point scale, where one was identified as "no evidence of movement toward the goal" and seven was "attainment of the goal." Furthermore, patients were encouraged to name at least one "significant other" (e.g., wife, mother, father) who would be willing to specify and rate the goals they felt the patients should work for. Finally, two behavioral measures were used following discharge from the hospital after a one-year period: [1] the total number of subjects in each group who had been readmitted at least once to a hospital for psychiatric purposes during that year and [2] the total number of months spent in gainful employment during that year.

Boudewyns and Wilson also evaluated process measures during the course of the treatment for subjects in Group IT and DT. A set of rating scales based on Buss' [1962] two-factor view of anxiety were developed to allow subjects to report their perceived physiological arousal (PPA) during therapy. Following each therapy session, nine items (heart racing, heavy breathing, blushing, tightness in muscles, etc.) were self-rated. A five-point rating scale was used for each response. A single PPA score was calculated for each individually treated therapy subject by averaging ratings of all items across all therapy sessions.

In analyzing the MMPI results, the authors sought to obtain a single score that best represented a patient's change. They chose the criterion scale used to select subjects for their study (depression or psychasthenia) which represented the scale showing the greatest amount of pathology. For this criterion scale, Group IT subjects' scores dropped (away from pathology) on post test a total of −18.9 T-score points. Group DT subjects dropped a total of −8.9 points, and Group MT subjects showed a drop of −4.6 points. Statistical comparisons were made on this measure between Groups IT and MT, DT and MT, and IT and DT. The comparison between Groups IT and MT produced borderline significance, while the other comparisons did not produce a statistically reliable result. At the six-month follow-up period the following MMPI changes were reported: Group IT dropped −19.5; Group DT, −6.3; and Group MT, −0.4). At this point, the difference between Groups IT and MT was found statistically significant but the other comparison still was not.

Of the ten standard MMPI clinical scales, the group means of four were elevated above seventy T-scores across all three groups on initial testing. The means of three of these scales in Group IT fell within normal limits (below seventy T-scores) at post-therapy, while only one reached normal limits for Group DT, and none fell below seven T-scores for Group MT. At the six-month follow-up testing period, two of the three means that had dropped below seventy T-scores for Group IT remained in normal limits, while all four means either rose or stayed above seventy T-scores for Groups DT and MT.

Of the total number of the MMPI clinical scales that suggested pathology before therapy, 45 percent in Group IT, 35 percent in Group DT, and 15 percent in Group MT fell within normal limits immediately following therapy. At the six-month follow-up the percentages were 43 percent for Group IT, 31 percent for Group DT, and 19 percent for Group MT. Of those scales that fell within normal limits immediately follow-

ing therapy, 83 percent in Group IT, 36 percent in Group DT, and 25 percent in Group MT stayed within normal limits at the six-month follow-up testing period.

The Mooney Problem Checklist data were consistent with the MMPI data. Only Group IT's mean gain score reached significance when compared to Group MT at both post-testing and at the six-month follow-up period. None of the other group comparisons were significant. At the six-month follow-up period, both Groups DT and MT's means suggested that problems increased for subjects in these groups, which was not the case for subjects in Group IT.

The patients' ratings of their progress toward each predefined goal of therapy at post-testing revealed that subjects in both Groups IT and DT displayed significantly greater gain scores than subjects in Group MT. For goals defined by "significant others," only the mean gain score for Group IT was reliably greater than that obtained for the other two groups.

The one-year follow-up data did not reveal any reliable differences among groups for patients readmitted to a psychiatric ward during the year subsequent to discharge, or for time spent in gainful employment during the one year after discharge. One patient was readmitted in Group IT, two in Group DT, and four in Group MT.

The process data collected during therapy revealed that the mean PPA score for subjects in Group IT was .significantly greater than the mean for the subjects in Group DT, indicating the expected finding that IT subjects felt more physiological arousal during therapy sessions. The PPA scores were not found statistically to be related to therapy outcome. No variations in therapist effectiveness were found. Interestingly, the attitude of the two trainee-therapists toward Implosive Therapy was considerably more positive after completion of the study. Both strongly believed that Implosive Therapy had been the most effective procedure and both currently are using it in their own clinical practice.

The authors concluded that Implosive Therapy was more effective than milieu therapy alone. The effects of desensitization therapy were seen as equivocal, since encouraging trends reflected in psychological test scores at post-therapy, for the most part, did not sustain themselves at the six-month follow-up period.

It is interesting to note that the four published experimental reports to date with patient populations support our clinical observations about the effectiveness of Implosive Therapy. The question of validation, however, cannot be resolved by a few studies and may well take at least another twenty years of systematic work. It is also encouraging to note that in each of the studies reviewed, the authors were quite frank in discussing the methodological limitations of their work, and all remained cautious in their interpretations. It is imperative that the issue of Implosive Therapy's effectiveness (and for that matter any other therapy system) be answered by "hard" experimental data with multiple outcome evaluations and long-term follow-up data rather than by wishful thinking.

Historical Note

The basic procedures of Implosive Therapy and the utilization of the basic two-process theoretical model as it applies to the actual treatment of patients were originated by Thomas G. Stampfl, who treated the first patients with IT procedures in 1957. A year later Stampfl trained George Golias and Robert Hogan who were the first therapists to acquire proficiency with Implosive techniques. Over a period of three years, these three therapists worked together to extend the therapeutic technique for the treatment of a variety of symptoms such as depressive reaction, sexual deviation, and psychotic behavior. The next person to become actively interested in the technique was Donald J. Levis, who first became acquainted with the technique in 1959. In collaboration with Stampfl, and over a period of eight years, a further critical analysis of the learning principles underlying the major features of the theoretical model was made. Levis was extremely active in the experimental laboratory as it was recognized early that experimental tests of some of the extensions made to the two-process model were needed. Ten years later after its original conception Stampfl concluded that sufficient data had been collected in both the clinical and laboratory setting to warrant the publication of the IT model and technique.

Numerous other individuals such as Richard Carrera, were also instrumental in actively acquiring proficiency with the technique. Others by their interest and support encouraged continued work with the therapy. Among them, the authors wish to express their debt of gratitude to O. H. Mowrer, Perry London, J. McV. Hunt, Frank Kobler, E. Joseph Shoben, Cooper Clements, John Scanlon, and Gerald Rosenbaum.

BIBLIOGRAPHY

F. Alexander, "The dynamics of psychotherapy in the light of learning theory." *International Journal of Psychiatry*, 1965, 1:189–197.

N. H. Anderson and C. Y. Nakamura, "Avoidance decrement in avoidance conditioning." *Journal of Comparative and Physiological Psychology*, 1964, 57:196–204.

T. W. Baker, "Properties of compound conditioned stimuli and their components." *Psychological Bulletin*, 1968, 70:611–625.

C. L. Barrett, "Systematic desensitization versus implosive therapy." *Journal of Abnormal Psychology*, 1969, 74:587–592.

F. Barron and T. Leary, "Changes in psychoneurotic patients with and without psychotherapy." *Journal of Consulting Psychology*, 1955, 19:237–245.

M. Baum, "An automatic apparatus for the avoidance training of rats." *Psychological Report*, 1965, 16:1205–1211.

M. Baum, "Extinction of avoidance responding through response prevention (flooding)." *Psychological Bulletin*, 1970, 74:276–284.

A. H. Black, "The extinction of avoidance responses under curare." *Journal of Comparative and Physiological Psychology*, 1958, 51:519–525.

T. D. Borkovec, "Effects of expectancy on the outcome of systematic desensitization and implosive treatment for analogue anxiety." *Behavior Therapy*, 1972, 3:29–40.

P. A. Boudewyns and A. E. Wilson, "Implosive therapy and desensitization therapy using free association in treatment of inpatients." *Journal of Abnormal Psychology*, 1972, 79:259–268.

J. C. Boulougouris and I. M. Marks, "Implosive (flooding) a new treatment for phobias." *British Medical Journal*. 1969, 2:721–723.

J. C. Boulougouris, I. M. Marks, and P. Marset, "Superiority of flooding (implosion) to desensitization for reducing pathological fear." *Behaviour Research & Therapy*, 1971, 9:7–16.

E. Brush, "Traumatic avoidance learning: the effects of conditioned stimulus length in a free-responding situation." *Journal of Comparative and Physiological Psychology*, 1957, 50:541–546.

A. Cooper, J. B. Furst, and W. H. Bridger, "A brief commentary on the usefulness of studying fears of snakes." *Journal of Abnormal Psychology*, 1969, 74:413–414.

W. G. Dahlstrom and G. S. Welsh, *An MMPI handbook*. University of Minnesota Press, 1960.

M. R. Denny, P. B. Koons, and J. E. Mason, "Extinction of avoidance as a function of the escape situation." *Journal of Comparative and Physiological Psychology*, 1959, 52:212–214.

J. Dollard and N. E. Miller, *Personality and Psychotherapy*. McGraw-Hill, 1950.

H. J. Eysenck, ed., *Behaviour Therapy and the Neuroses*. Pergamon, 1960.

R. S. Feldman and F. J. Bremner, "A method for rapid conditioning of stable avoidance bar pressing behavior." *Journal of Experimental Analysis of Behavior*, 1963, 6:393–394.

R. D. Fitzgerald and J. S. Brown, "Variables affecting avoidance conditioning in free-responding and discrete-trial situations." *Psychological Report*, 1965, 17:835–843.

S. Freud, *The problem of anxiety*. Norton, 1936.

J. J. Gallagher, "MMPI changes concomitant with client-centered therapy." *Journal of Consulting Psychology*, 1953, 17:443–446.

H. Gilberstadt and J. Duker, *A handbook for clinical and actuarial MMPI interpretation*. Saunders, 1965.

R. A. Hogan, "Implosive therapy in the short term treatment of psychotics." *Psychotherapy: Theory, Research and Practice*, 1966, 3:25–31.

R. A. Hogan and J. H. Kirchner, A preliminary report of the extinction of learned fears via short term implosive therapy. *Journal of Abnormal Psychology*, 1967, 72:106–109.

R. A. Hogan and J. H. Kirchner, "Implosive, eclectic verbal, and biblio-therapy in the treatment of fears of snakes." *Behavior Research and Therapy*, 1968, 6:167–171.

H. F. Hunt, P. Jernberg, and J. V. Brady, "The effect of electroconvulsive shock (E.C.S.) on a conditioned emotional response: the effects of post-E.C.S. extinction on the reappearance of the response." *Journal of Comparative and Physiological Psychology*, 1952, 45:589–599.

R. Johnston and B. F. McNeal, "Residual psychopathology in released psychiatric patients and its relation to readmission." *Journal of Abnormal Psychology*, 1965, 70:337–342.

P. Kaufmann, "Changes in the MMPI as a function of psychiatric therapy." *Journal of Consulting Psychology*, 1950, 14:458–464.

G. A. Kimble, *Hilgard & Marquis' Conditioning and Learning*. Appleton, 1961.

J. H. Kirchner and R. A. Hogan, "The therapist variable in the implosion of phobias." *Psychotherapy: Theory, Research, and Practice*, 1966, 3:102–104.

R. K. Knapp, "Acquisition and extinction of avoidance with similar and different shock and escape situations." *Journal of Comparative and Physiological Psychology*, 1965, 60:272–273.

W. E. Leonard, *The locomotive-god*. Appleton, 1927.

D. J. Levis, "Effects of serial CS presentation and other characteristics of the CS on the conditioned avoidance response." *Psychological Reports*, 1966a, 18:755–766.

D. J. Levis, "Implosive therapy, part II: the subhuman analogue, the strategy, and the technique. In S. E. Armitage, ed., *Behavioral modification techniques in the treatment of emotional disorders*. Battle Creek, Michigan: V.A. Publication, 1966b, 22–37.

D. J. Levis, ed., *Learning approaches to therapeutic behavior change*. Aldine, 1970.

D. J. Levis, "Serial CS presentation and shuttlebox avoidance conditioning: a further look at the tendency to delay responding." *Psychonomic Science*, 1970a, 20:145–147.

D. J. Levis, "Between-trial transporting of animals: a methodological consideration." *Behavior Research Methods & Instrumentation*, 1970b, 2:157–160.

D. J. Levis, "The case for performing research on nonpatient populations with fears of small animals: a reply to Cooper, Furst, and Bridger." *Journal of Abnormal Psychology*, 1970c, 76:36–38.

D. J. Levis and R. N. Carrera, "Effects of 10 hours of implosive therapy in the treatment of outpatients: a preliminary report." *Journal of Abnormal Psychology*, 1967, 72:504–508.

D. J. Levis and T. G. Stampfl, "Effects of serial CS presentation on shuttlebox avoidance responding." *Learning and Motivation*, 1972, 3:73–90.

D. J. Levis, S. Bouska, J. Eron, and M. McIlhon, "Serial CS presentation and one-way avoidance conditioning: a noticeable lack of delayed responding." *Psychonomic Science*, 1970, 20:147–149.

W. R. McAllister and D. E. McAllister, "Role of CS and of apparatus cues in the measurement of acquired fear." *Psychological Reports*, 1962, 11:749–756.

P. E. Meehl and W. G. Dahlstrom, "Objective configured rules for discriminating psychotic from neurotic MMPI profiles." *Journal of Consulting Psychology*, 1960, 24:375–378.

D. R. Meyer, C. Cho, and A. F. Wesemann, "On problems of conditioning discriminated lever-press avoidance responses." *Psychological Review*, 1960, 67:224–228.

N. E. Miller, "Learnable drives and rewards." In S. S. Stevens, ed., *Handbook of Experimental Psychology*. Wiley, 1951.

R. E. Mogar and C. Savage, "Personality change associated with psychedelic (LSD) therapy: a preliminary report." *Psychotherapy: Theory, Research & Practice*, 1964, 1:154–162.

O. H. Mowrer, "Anxiety-reduction and learning." *Journal of Experimental Psychology*, 1940, 27:497–516.

O. H. Mowrer, "On the dual nature of learning—a reinterpretation of 'conditioning' and 'problem-solving.'" *Harvard Educational Review*, 1947, 17:102–148.

J. O. Prochaska, "Symptom and dynamic cues in the implosive treatment of test anxiety." *Journal of Abnormal Psychology*, 1971, 77:133–142.

G. Razran, "Empirical codification and specific theoretical implications of compound-stimulus conditioning: Perception." In Prokasy, W. F. ed., *Classical Conditioning: A Symposium*. Appleton, 1965.

W. Schofield, "Changes in Response to the MMPI Following Certain Therapies." *Psychological Monographs*, 1950, 64: (5 Whole No. 311).

W. A. Schofield, "A further study of the effects of therapies of MMPI responses." *Journal of Abnormal and Social Psychology*, 1953, 48:67–77.

M. E. P. Seligman, "For helplessness: can we immunize the weak?" *Psychology Today*, 1969, June: 42–44.

R. H. Shipley, Lou Ann Mock, and D. J. Levis, "Effects of several response prevention procedures on activity, avoidance responding, and conditioned fear in rats." *Journal of Comparative and Physiological Psychology*, 1971, 77:256–270.

R. L. Solomon and L. C. Wynne, "Traumatic Avoidance Learning: Acquisition in Normal Dogs." *Psychological Monographs*, 1953, 67: No. 354, pp. 19.

R. L. Solomon and L. C. Wynne, "Traumatic avoidance learning: the principle of anxiety conservation and partial irreversibility." *Psychological Review*, 1954, 61:353–385.

R. L. Solomon, L. J. Kamin, and L. C. Wynne, "Traumatic avoidance learning: the outcomes of several extinction procedures with dogs." *Journal of Abnormal and Social Psychology*, 1953, 48:291–302.

T. G. Stampfl, "Implosive therapy, part I: the theory. In S. G. Armitage, ed., *Behavioral modification techniques in the treatment of emotional disorders*. Battle Creek, Michigan: V. A. Publication, 1966, 12–21.

T. G. Stampfl, "Implosive therapy: an emphasis on covert stimulation." In D. J. Levis, ed., *Learning approaches to therapeutic behavior change*. Aldine, 1970.

T. G. Stampfl and D. J. Levis, "The essentials of implosive therapy: a learning-theory based psychodynamic behavioral therapy." *Journal of Abnormal Psychology*, 1967, 72:496–503.

T. G. Stampfl and D. J. Levis, "Implosive therapy—a behavioral therapy?" *Behavior Research and Therapy*, 1968, 6:31–36.

T. G. Stampfl and D. J. Levis, "Learning theory: an aid to dynamic therapeutic practice." In L. D. Eron & R. Callahan, eds., *Relationship of theory to practice in psychotherapy*. Aldine, 1969.

J. Theois and J. E. Dunaway, "One-way versus shuttle avoidance conditioning." *Psychonomic Science*, 1964, 1:251–252.

N. M. Weinberger, "Effects of detainment on extinction of avoidance responses." *Journal of Comparative and Physiological Psychology*, 1965, 60:135–138.

O. Weininger, W. J. McClelland, and R. Arima, "Gentling and weight gain in the albino rat." *Canadian Journal of Psychology*, 1954, 8:147–151.

D. D. Wickens, "Compound conditioning in humans and cats." In W. F. Prokasy, ed., *Classical Conditioning*. Appleton, 1965.

A. Wilson and F. J. Smith, "Counterconditioning therapy using free association: a pilot study." *Journal of Abnormal Psychology*, 1968, 73:474–478.

J. Wolpe, *Psychotherapy by reciprocal inhibition*. Stanford University Press, 1958.

4

Learned Helplessness and Depression in Animals and Men

MARTIN E. P. SELIGMAN
University of Pennsylvania

It is easy to overlook one of the most important psychological components of our world: control. You walk into a dark room, throw a switch, and the room is flooded with light. You have an attack of sharp pains in your right side, and afraid of appendicitis, you rush to the nearest doctor. Your infant brother screams in hunger and his cries bring your mother, bottle in hand. In all three examples, and in virtually everything we do, there is an element of control. Some responses that we make alter our environment, and it is a truism that we strive to control our world.

Experimental psychologists interested in learning have traditionally studied the behavior of animals and men faced with rewards and punishments that they could affect with voluntary responses. So, for example, in a typical instrumental learning experiment the subject can make some response or refrain from making it and thereby bring reward or ward off punishment. Nature, however, is not always so benign in its arrangement of the contingencies. Most of the time we face events that we can control by our actions, but we also face many events about which we can do nothing at all. These uncontrollable events can significantly debilitate men and animals. They can produce passivity in the face of trauma, inability to learn that responding is effective, and emotional stress and depression. In short, exposure to uncontrollable events produces a reaction that can be characterized as *helplessness*.

Since it is the lack of control that produces helplessness, we must first define *control* and *uncontrollability*. The definitions must be made within the context of instrumental learning. Learning theorists have usually described the relations between instrumental responding and outcomes by a line depicting the conditional probability of a reinforcement following a response, that is, $p(RFT/R)$. This line varies from 0 to 1. At 1, every response produces a reinforcement (continuous reinforcement); at 0, a response never produces reinforcement (extinction). Intermediate points on the line represent various degrees of partial reinforcement — for example, at .50 the response is followed by the reinforcement half of the time. A simple line, however, does not exhaust the relations between response and outcomes to which organisms are sensitive; rewards or punishments sometimes occur when no specific response has been made. It would be a woefully maladaptive subject, S, that could not learn about such a contingency. Rather than representing instrumental learning as occurring along a single dimension, we can better describe it using the two-dimensional space shown in the following figure. The horizontal axis $[p(RFT/R)]$ represents the traditional dimension, probability of reinforcement following a response.

At right angles to the probability of reinforcement given a response is the probability of reinforcement given the absence of *that* response. This dimension is represented along the vertical-axis. Animals and men, it will be contended here, learn about variations along *both* dimensions. The subject may therefore learn the extent to which reward or escape from punishment occurs when it does not make a specific response at the same time as it learns the extent to

which these events occur when it does make a specific response.

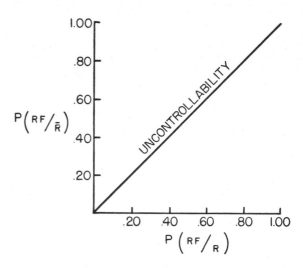

The concept of control is defined within this instrumental training space. Whenever there is something the organism can do or not do that changes what it gets, it has control. Specifically, a response *controls* a reinforcer *if and only if*:

$$p(RFT/R) \neq p(RFT/\bar{R})$$

That is, the probability of reinforcement given a response is different from the probability of reinforcement in the absence of that response. Furthermore, when a response will not change what happens, the response and reinforcement are independent. Specifically, when a response is independent of a reinforcer, $p(RFT/R) = p(RFT/\bar{R})$. When this is true of all responses, the reinforcer is *uncontrollable* and nothing the organism does matters.

In the last decade, laboratory psychologists have turned to the investigation of uncontrollable events. When organisms are faced with important events that no voluntary responses they make can alter, the result is *learned helplessness*. In this module, I will survey the symptoms, the cause, the cure, and the prevention of learned helplessness; finally, I will examine the possibility that learned helplessness bears a close relationship to the disorder known in man as depression.

Symptoms of Learned Helplessness

Passivity

The most prominent symptom of learned helplessness is *passivity*. Organisms that have experienced uncontrollable traumatic events have trouble initiating coping responses when they later face new traumas — even traumas they otherwise could easily escape. Here is what happens in a typical dog helplessness experiment [Overmier & Seligman 1967]:

An experimentally naive dog is placed in a shuttlebox. At the onset of the first painful, but not damaging, electric shock, the dog runs frantically about. After about 30 seconds it accidentally scrambles over the barrier and escapes the shock. On the next trial, the dog crosses the barrier more quickly. This pattern continues until the dog learns to avoid shock altogether. Interestingly, any given dog either learns to escape normally or consistently fails to escape on almost every trial. An intermediate outcome is rare. Among experimentally naive dogs, only about 6 percent fail to escape the shock.

But consider what happens when a dog has first been strapped into a hammock and given electric shocks that he cannot affect by his responding. Such helpless dogs show a strikingly different pattern of behavior. When later put into the shuttlebox, their initial reactions are much the same as those of a naive dog. The helpless dog, however, soon stops running and sits or lies down, quietly whining, until the shock ends. The dog does not cross the barrier and escape; rather, it seems to give up and passively accept the shock. On succeeding trials, the dog continues to fail to escape and takes as much shock as the experimenter chooses to give.

My associates and I have studied the shuttlebox behavior of over 150 dogs pretreated with inescapable shocks. *Two-thirds* of these dogs did not learn to escape the shock by jumping the hurdle. This failure is highly maladaptive since it means that the dog takes 50 seconds of strong, pulsating shock on each trial in the shuttlebox.

A typical experimental procedure that produces failure to escape shock is as follows: On the first day, the subject is strapped into a hammock and given 64 unsignaled, inescapable electric shocks, each 5.0 seconds long and of 6.0 ma intensity. The shocks occur randomly in time. Twenty-four hours later, the dog is given 10 trials of escape-avoidance training in the shuttlebox. A tone begins each trial, and the tone remains on until the trial ends. The tone-shock interval is 10 seconds. If the dog jumps the barrier (set at shoulder height) during this interval, the tone stops and there is no shock. Failure to jump during the tone-shock interval leads to a 4.5 ma shock that continues until the dog jumps the barrier. If the dog fails to jump within 60 seconds after the onset of the tone, the trial automatically terminates. The performance that typically results is that the dogs pretreated with inescapable shocks respond much more slowly than those not so pretreated, if they escape the shock at all.

Passivity produced by experience with responding that has no effect is not unique to the dog. Mice that have received inescapable shock have trouble learning to swim out of a cold water maze. Cats that have received inescapable shock do not flee shock later on. Young monkeys that have been placed in pits, a particularly dramatic instance of an environment in which responding is useless, are later deficient in social play and exploration. Even the lowly goldfish and cockroach are poor at coping with shock after experiencing an inescapable shock [see Seligman 1975, for a review].

The white rat and the beginning psychology student are the most widely used subjects of psychological experiments. The preference for the rat is more due to the convenient fact that so much else is known about its behavior and physiology than to any conceptual reason, but still some experimenters will not believe a phenomenon is real until it has been demonstrated in the white rat. Until recently, the rat proved a difficult creature to produce learned helplessness in. Although a substantial number of experiments were done involving inescapable shock, by and large they showed rather small, if any, effects on later response initiation [Anderson, Cole, & McVaugh 1968; De Toledo & Black 1967; Dinsmoor & Campbell 1956a; b; Looney & Cohen 1972; Mullin & Mogenson 1963; Weiss, Krieckhaus, & Conte 1968]. Unlike dogs, rats given prior inescapable shock were typically only a bit slower to escape shock on the first few trials or slower to acquire avoidance — they did not sit and passively take shock.

After intensive experimentation, however, several investigators have now independently produced substantial helplessness in rats [Maier, Albin, & Testa 1973; Maier & Testa 1975; Seligman & Beagley 1975; Seligman, Rosellini, & Kozak 1975]. In doing so, one crucial factor emerged: The response tested for must be difficult and not something the rat does very readily. So, for example, if rats are first exposed to inescapable shock and then tested on a simple escape response like pressing a bar once or fleeing to the other side of a shuttlebox, no deficits are found. If, however, the response requirement is increased so that the bar must be pressed three times for shock to end or the rat has to run from one compartment of a shuttlebox to another and back again, then the rat that has experienced inescapable shock escapes very poorly. In contrast, rats that had prior escapable shock or no shock perform even the more difficult responses without giving up. So to the extent that a response is natural to the point of being all but automatic in the rat, experience with uncontrollable shock will not interfere with later shock escape. If the response is somewhat unnatural and is therefore performed "deliberately," the rat shows helplessness following uncontrollability.

Men respond to inescapability very much as rats and dogs do. In one experiment, Hiroto [1974] presented college students with loud noise. One group was helpless, that is, no response they made turned off the noise; a second group could escape the noise by pressing a button; a third group received no noise. The students were then taken to a finger shuttlebox (moving their hands back and forth across the shuttlebox turned off the noise). Those who previously escaped noise by button pushing readily learned to "jump" in order to control noise in the shuttlebox, as did the no-experience group. The helpless group tended merely to sit with their hands in the shuttlebox and passively take the noise.

Hiroto also related learned helplessness to a personality variable — external versus internal locus of control [Rotter 1966]. *Externals*, people who believe that reinforcement comes from the outside and is due to luck, were more susceptible to learned helplessness than *internals*, people who believe that their own actions control reinforcement. Hiroto also found that if the subjects were told that the shuttlebox task was a chance rather than a skill task, they were more helpless. He concluded that the objective conditions

of uncontrollability, the personality characteristic of externality, and the perceptual set of chance all act in the same way to produce helplessness. They result in the subject believing that his responding is independent of reinforcement and therefore useless.

Glass and Singer [1972] have performed an extensive series of studies of the effects of uncontrollable stress on men. In an attempt to mimic the urban environment, their subjects listened to a 108 db concatenation of the sounds of two people speaking Spanish, one person speaking Armenian, a mimeograph machine, a calculator, and a typewriter. Subjects who could terminate the noise at will were much more persistent at problem solving, found the noise less irritating, and did better at proofreading than subjects who could not control the noise. Merely believing they could control the noise by pressing a panic button, even if they never actually exert control, was sufficient to prevent helplessness.

Passivity produced by helplessness is not only general across species; it also occurs across tasks — in escape and avoidance of electric shock, cold water, and loud noise. Passivity is evident in that the subject's exploration and play are reduced and social status in dominance hierarchies goes down. Response initiation is impaired even when there is a history of uncontrollable outcomes that are not traumatic. Hiroto and Seligman [1975] tried to produce helplessness by using insolvable "discrimination problems" rather than inescapable noise. In a typical discrimination learning problem, a person or animal confronts two stimulus cards, one white and one black. On some trials, black is on the left, white on the right; on other trials this is reversed. Behind one of these cards, say the black one, reward is consistently found: some bran mash for a rat, candy for a child, a dime or "correct" for an adult. The problem is solvable since picking the black card will consistently produce reward and picking the white card will consistently produce no reward. Reward is therefore controllable. Children, adults, rats, and even earthworms learn to solve such problems. Just as a solvable discrimination problem is controllable in the same sense that an escapable shock is controllable, an unsolvable discrimination problem is controllable in the same sense that an inescapable shock is uncontrollable.

Consider what happens when there is no solution to a discrimination problem. Procedurally, this means baiting the white cards and the black cards randomly so that on half the trials chosen at random, black is rewarded, and on the other half white is correct. This also means that on half the trials the left side is correct and on the other half, the right side. Such an experiment becomes a helplessness experiment, for the probability of getting a reward when the subject chooses left is 0.5; when the subject chooses black, it is also 0.5. Reward is independent of the subject's response, and thus by definition it is uncontrollable.

With the formal similarity of unsolvability and inescapability in mind, Hiroto and I gave college students four sets of solvable, unsolvable, or no discrimination problems. Then all groups were given the finger shuttlebox with loud noise to be escaped. Individuals who had solvable discrimination problems or no prior problems escaped noise with alacrity. The unsolvable group now sat and took the noise. These results led us to believe that response initiation to control noxious events may be impaired by prior experience with uncontrollable *reward,* not merely punishment.

Animals may also be helpless with respect to obtaining food. In an experiment with pigeons, Engberg, Hansen, Welker, and Thomas [1972] claimed they had produced *learned laziness,* a first cousin of learned helplessness. One group of hungry pigeons first learned to press a treadle for grain (the mastery group). Members of the second group received the same grain, but regardless of what they did, food and responding were independent (the helpless group). The third group (control) received no grain. All the pigeons were then given an autoshaping task in which the pigeons had to learn to peck a lighted key paired with grain. The mastery group learned to peck the key fastest; the control group was second; but the helpless group learned only very slowly. Finally, all three groups were shifted to a schedule in which they had to learn to *refrain* from pecking to get grain. Again, the mastery pigeons learned fastest; the group with no initial experience was second; and the helpless pigeons were slowest. It is clear that inescapable positive reinforcers also make animals less able to initiate responses for future reinforcers.

Associative Retardation

The second central symptom of learned helplessness is *associative retardation* [Seligman, Maier, &

Solomon 1971]. Dogs that have first learned that responding and relief from punishment are independent show a cognitive as well as a motivational deficit. Even when they do make a response that turns off shock, they have trouble *learning* that the response works. Whenever a naive dog makes even one response that turns off shock in a shuttlebox, he immediately catches on and begins to jump back and forth across the barrier. A dog that has previously received inescapable shock, however, occasionally jumps the barrier and escapes shock but then reverts to passively taking the punishment. He fails to profit from exposure to the barrier-jumping–relief contingency.

Miller and Seligman [1975] found that learned helplessness in man also results in this kind of cognitive deficit. Three groups of students were first exposed to loud noise that was escapable or inescapable, or to no noise at all. Then they confronted two new tasks, one of skill and one of chance. In the skill task they received ten trials, on each of which they were to sort cards into categories based on shape within a 15-second period. Unknown to the subjects, the experimenter arranged to have them succeed or fail on any given trial by saying "time is up" either after they had finished sorting all the cards or before. So they went through a prearranged run of successes and failures. At the end of each trial, the subject rated (on a zero to 10 scale) what he thought his chances of succeeding on the next trial would be. Subjects who were previously helpless in escaping loud noise showed very little change in their expectancy for success after each new success and failure. They perceived that their responses would not affect the results. Control subjects and those who had escaped noise showed great expectancy changes following each success and failure, thus demonstrating their belief that outcomes were dependent on their actions. The three groups did not differ in expectancy changes following success and failure in a "chance" task that they perceived as a guessing game. Thus learned helplessness produces a cognitive set in which people believe that success and failure are independent of their own skill; this suggests that they would therefore have difficulty learning that responses work when they actually do.

Hiroto and Seligman [1975] also reported cognitive deficits in human subjects in another form. After exposure to escapable, inescapable, or no noise, three groups were given a series of twenty anagrams to solve. There was a pattern to the anagrams: Each was arranged with its letters in 34251 order — e.g., ISOEN, DERRO, OURPG, and so on. Two kinds of cognitive deficits emerged. First, students subjected to inescapable noise were less able to solve each of the anagrams. Second, students who had received inescapable noise also had difficulty catching on to the pattern. Prior exposure to unsolvable discrimination problems, incidentally, produced the same disruption in anagram solution as did inescapable noise.

Lack of Aggression and Competitiveness

Maier, Anderson, and Lieberman [1972] examined shock-elicited aggression as a function of helplessness in rats. When a male rat is given strong electric shock, he will fiercely attack any other male rat that happens to be present. Maier and his colleagues found that rats that had first received inescapable shock were not very aggressive when later shocked in the presence of other rats. In contrast, rats that had learned to control shock were hyperaggressive. Similarly, my associates and I have found that helpless rats consistently lose out to rats that had first escaped shock when both are placed on an electrified floor with an unshocked pedestal large enough only for one. We have also found that dogs that received inescapable shock as puppies lose in competition for food to dogs that had experience with controllable shock.

Time Course

Learned helplessness, at least in the dog, dissipates in time. Overmier and Seligman [1967] found that after one session of inescapable shock, dogs were helpless in the shuttlebox one day later. Dogs tested two days or a week later, however, did not exhibit this helplessness. The time course (dissipation of learned helplessness) can be eliminated, however, if the dog first receives multiple sessions of inescapable shock. If the dog is reared from birth in the laboratory with only a limited past history of controlling reinforcers, the time course also seems to be eliminated. Further, Overmeir and I have found that after one session of inescapable shock, a markedly higher percentage of laboratory-reared dogs become helpless than nonlaboratory-reared dogs. This discrepancy suggests that dogs reared in a natural environment have been immunized by past history. (This phenomenon will be discussed further below.)

Physical Symptoms

Neal Miller, Jay Weiss, and their colleagues at Rockefeller University [Miller & Weiss 1969; Weiss 1968; Weiss, Glazer, & Pohorecky 1974; Weiss, Stone, & Harrell 1970] have discovered several other correlated symptoms of inescapable shock in rats. They find that rats receiving inescapable shock lose weight and eat less than rats receiving escapable shock or no shock. In addition, the brains of rats that receive inescapable shock are depleted of norepinephrine, an important transmitter substance in the central nervous system. Rats who escape shock show elevated norepinephrine levels.

Stress and Mood

Weiss [1971] reported that rats receiving uncontrollable shock were more prone to develop ulcers than rats receiving no shock or controllable shock. His well-done series of studies contradicts a previous set of studies of "executive" monkeys by Brady [1958] in which it was found that monkeys able to turn off shock during lengthy sessions were more ulcer-prone than "nonexecutive" monkeys who passively endured the same shock. Thus it seems that helpless animals are more rather than less anxious than executive animals. Moreover, human subjects in the experiment by Glass and Singer [1972] discussed earlier report that uncontrollable noise is more stressful than controllable noise. A complementary inference is also possible: Organisms that control their environment may be happier than those that passively receive the same reinforcers. For example, Carder and Berkowitz [1970] demonstrated that rats prefer food that they have to work for to free food. Similarly, Watson [1970] placed a spinning mobile over the cribs of two groups of infants. Whenever those in one group pressed their pillows, the mobiles spun. The other group was helpless: The mobile spun just as much, but independently of their responses. Watson found that the mastery groups smiled more than the helpless group, so it seems possible that controlling reinforcers produces pleasure and not controlling them produces boredom and even, perhaps, depression.

In summary, experience with uncontrollable trauma has been demonstrated to produce six effects. There are two *basic* effects: (1) Animals become passive in the face of trauma; i.e., they are slower to initiate responses that would alleviate trauma, and they may not respond at all. (2) Animals are retarded at learning that their responses control trauma: if the animal makes a response that produces relief, he may have trouble "catching on" to the response-relief contingency. This maladaptive behavior appears in a variety of species, including man, and over a range of tasks that require voluntary responding. Additional effects are that aggressiveness and competitive behaviors are reduced; the passivity dissipates in time; anorexia, weight loss, ulcers, and norepinephrine depletion result from uncontrollability of trauma in the rat; and more stress results from uncontrollable than controllable aversive events. Similar passivity and cognitive deficit are observed in organisms that have received inescapable reward. In subsequent tasks they too are less efficient in learning to obtain positive reinforcement.

The Causes of Learned Helplessness

It is not trauma per se that produces interference with later adaptive responding, but not having control over trauma. The passivity of animals in the face of trauma and their difficulty in benefiting from response-relief contingencies seems to result from their having learned that responding and trauma are independent — that trauma is uncontrollable. This is the heart of the learned helplessness hypothesis.

My colleagues and I have tested and confirmed this hypothesis in several ways. We began by ruling out alternative hypotheses. For one, it is unlikely that dogs have become adapted by pretreatment with shock, since we have found that making the shock in the shuttlebox very intense or very mild does not attenuate the phenomenon. Another possibility is that the dogs subjected to inescapable shock have learned some motor response pattern that is accidentally paired a few times with reinforcement and that later competes with barrier jumping in the shuttlebox. This hypothesis also seems unlikely because interference occurs even if the dogs are

paralyzed by curare and can make no overt motor response during shock.

Seligman and Maier [1967] performed a direct test of the hypothesis that learning that shock was uncontrollable, and not shock per se, causes helplessness. One group of animals was placed in a hammock and trained to press a panel with their noses or heads in order to turn off shock. Paired with each escape subject was a yoked control animal, also in a hammock, that received exactly the same shocks but could do nothing about them. Thus the yoked group differed from the escape group only with respect to the degree of instrumental control it had over shock. A naive control group received no shock in the hammock. When tested in the shuttlebox, only the yoked group was helpless. Both the naive control group and the escape group responded normally. We thus demonstrated that it was not the shock itself, but not controlling shock, that produced later failure to escape.

Maier [1970] provided more dramatic confirmation of the hypothesis. In response to the criticism that what gets learned during uncontrollable trauma is not a cognition set, as we have proposed, but some motor response reinforced by shock termination that is incompatible with jumping, Maier reinforced the most antagonistic response he could find. One group of dogs (passive-escape) was tied down in the hammock. Only by *not* moving, by remaining passive and still, could these dogs terminate shock. Another group of ten (yoked) received the same shock in the hammock, but could do nothing to escape it. A third group received no shock. The hypothesis that what responses get learned during the initial session produce later helplessness predicts that when dogs are later tested in the shuttlebox, the passive-escape group should be the most helpless, since its members had been explicitly reinforced for *not* moving during shock. Our cognitive-set hypothesis makes a different prediction: Dogs in the escape condition could *control* shock, even though it took a passive response to do it, whereas those in the nonescape condition could not. Some response, even one that competes with barrier jumping, produced relief for the escape animals. It is the possibility of *control*, not a specific response-reinforcement responser that is the crucial bit of learning. As we predicted, the dogs in the yoked group were predominantly helpless in the shuttlebox escape, and the naive controls escaped normally. The passive-escape group at first looked for "still" ways of minimizing shock in the shuttlebox. Failing to find them, they all became active and began to escape and avoid. Thus, it is not trauma per se, nor interfering motor habits, that produces failure to escape, but having learned that no response at all can control trauma.

Maier and Testa [1975] have provided further evidence to demonstrate that the expectancy of independence between responding and shock termination, and not motor interference or norepinephrine depletion, is crucial in producing learned helplessness. The reader will recall that rats that received inescapable shock are not helpless when they later have to cross a shuttlebox once to escape, but that they become helpless if they have to go across and then back. In order to test whether the deficit depended on difficulty in seeing the relationship between responding and shock termination or on the difficulty of *performing* the double crossing, Maier and Testa did a clever thing. They had the rats learn a single crossing to escape, but with a slight delay in shock termination. That is, when the rat ran across, the shock stopped, but not until one second later. In this experiment the response effort is identical to the easy single crossing; what differs is that the contingency is hard for the rat to see. From a motor-deficit point of view, no helplessness should occur; but to the extent that helplessness produces a cognitive difficulty in seeing response-outcome contingencies, the single crossing with a delay should interfere with acquisition of the escape response.

Any view of helplessness that merely postulates difficulty in responding would not predict a deficit in this situation [Anisman & Waller 1973; Bracewell & Black 1974; Weiss, Glazer, & Pohorecky 1974]. As Maier and Testa expected, rats that had received inescapable shock failed to learn to cross with the one-second delay, whereas rats that had received no shock learned well. Similar results occurred when the contingency was obscured by partial reinforcement (50 percent shock termination) of the crossing. Finally, Maier and Testa tried to make the double-crossing contingency clearer for rats receiving inescapable shock, while holding response effort constant. After the rat crossed the shuttlebox once, shock was very briefly turned off but immediately went back on, only to terminate when the second response was made. Here the contingency was clearer, but the response requirement was difficult. As the researchers expected, rats that had received inescapable shock were *not* helpless. Interference with responding is therefore not sufficient to explain the cause of rat helplessness; it is necessary to postulate cognitive deficit — difficulty in seeing that responding works.

Cure of Learned Helplessness

We have so far found only one treatment for helplessness in dogs and rats. According to the hypothesis, the animal fails to escape because of the expectation that no instrumental response will stop the shock. By forcibly exposing the animal to the fact that responding produces reinforcement, we thought we should be able to change this expectation. We found that forcibly dragging the dogs with long leashes from side to side in the shuttlebox, so that they experienced that changing compartments was accompanied by termination of the shock, produced recovery from helplessness that was complete and lasting [Seligman, Maier, & Geer 1968]. This procedure was successful with every animal, but it took many, many draggings. A directly analogous procedure has the same therapeutic effect on helpless rats [Seligman, Rosellini, & Kozak 1975].

The behavior of the dogs during the training was noteworthy. At the beginning of the procedure, a good deal of force had to be exerted to pull the animal across the center of the shuttlebox, but as training progressed, less and less force was needed. A stage was usually reached in which a slight nudge of the leash would send the dog into action. By the end, each dog initiated its own response, and thereafter failure to escape was very rare. The initial problem seemed to be one of "getting going."

We had first tried other procedures, but with little success. Removing the barrier, calling to the dog from the safe side, dropping food into the safe side, kicking the dangerous side of the box, tempting the dog by dropping Hebrew National salami on the safe side — all failed. Until the animals were physically forced to make the correct response repeatedly, the response did not occur, and the dog was not effectively exposed to the response-relief contingency.

In an experiment to find other ways of overcoming helplessness, Dorworth [1971] gave electroconvulsive shock to six chronically helpless dogs and found that three were cured. But so little is known at this point about the physiology and psychopharmacology of learned helplessness that we can say with confidence only that *directive therapy* — forcing the animal to see that its responding succeeds — works reliably.

Prevention of Learned Helplessness

Dramatic successes in medicine have come more frequently from prevention than from treatment, and inoculation and immunization have probably saved many more lives than cures have. Surprisingly, therefore, psychotherapy is almost exclusively limited to curative procedures; preventive procedures only rarely play an *explicit* role. In studies of dogs and rats we have found behavioral immunition to be an easy and effective means of preventing learned helplessness. Dogs that first become experienced at mastering shock do not become helpless after subsequent inescapable shock. Moreover, dogs that begin by learning to escape shock in the shuttlebox press the panels four times as often in the hammock during the inescapable shocks as do naive dogs, even though pressing panels has no effect on shock [Seligman & Maier 1967; Seligman, Rosellini, & Kozak 1975].

Other findings from our laboratory support the idea that early experience in controlling trauma may protect organisms from the helplessness caused by inescapable trauma. It will be recalled that approximately two-thirds of dogs of unknown history that are given inescapable shock become helpless, but that one-third respond normally. Why do some of these dogs become helpless and others not? Could it be possible that those dogs who do not become helpless even after inescapable shock have had a pre-laboratory history of controllable trauma? Seligman and Groves [1970] tested this hypothesis by raising dogs singly in cages in the laboratory. In comparison with dogs of unknown history, these cage-reared dogs had very limited experience in controlling anything. They proved on testing to be more susceptible to helplessness: It took four sessions of inescapable shock to produce helplessness one week later in dogs of unknown history, but only two sessions were needed to cause helplessness in the cage-reared dogs. Lessac and Solomon [1969] also reported that dogs reared in isolation seem prone to failure to escape. Dogs that are deprived of natural opportunities to master reinforcers in their developmental history, it seems, are more vulnerable to helplessness than naturally immunized dogs.

Richter [1957] discovered that when wild rats were squeezed in his hand until they stopped struggling, they drowned suddenly when placed in a water tank from which there was no escape. Unlike unsqueezed rats who swam for 60 hours before drowning, these rats died within 30 minutes. Richter reported that he could prevent sudden death by a technique that resembles our immunization procedure: If he held the rat then let it go, held it again then let it go, sudden death did not occur. Further, if after holding it, he put the rat in the water, took it out, put it in again and rescued it again, sudden death was prevented. These procedures, like our own, may provide the rat with a sense of control over trauma and thereby immunize against sudden death caused by inescapable trauma.

What, then, do we know about learned helplessness in the face of trauma?

Table 1 summarizes what we have learned to date. As for symptoms, we see passivity, difficulty in learning that response produces relief, deficits in aggression and competition, dissipation in time, disturbance of appetite, norepinephrine depletion, and increased stress. Learned helplessness is caused by learning that responding and trauma are independent, not by trauma per se. It can be cured by forcibly

Table 1. *Learned helplessness.*

Symptoms	Passivity
	Difficulty learning that responses produce relief (associative retardation)
	Lack of aggression
	Dissipates in time
	Weight loss, anorexia
	Norepinephrine depletion
	Ulcers and stress
Cause	Learning that responding and trauma are independent
Cure	Directive therapy: forced exposure to responding producing relief
	Electroconvulsive shock
	Time
Prevention	Immunization with mastery over trauma

exposing the animals to the fact that responding produces relief, and perhaps by electroconvulsive shock. It can be prevented if the animal first has experiences in which his responses control reinforcement, and then he is confronted with uncontrollability.

Depression in Man

One major form of psychopathology in man bears such striking resemblance to learning helplessness that learned helplessness can be considered a laboratory model of it. That disorder is depression. The following case history presents a typical depressive pattern.

Recently Mel, a 42-year-old business executive who was temporarily unemployed, came to see me for some "vocational advice." Actually, it was his wife who first contacted me. She had read a popular article of mine on helplessness and asked if I would talk with her husband, because he looked helpless to her. For the last twenty years, Mel had been a rising executive. Up until a year ago, he had been in charge of production for a multimillion-dollar space-related concern. With the winding down of the space program, he had lost his job and been forced to take a new executive position in a company he described as "backbiting." After six miserable and lonely months he had quit, and for the last month he had been sitting listlessly around the house, making almost no effort to find work. The slightest annoyance drove him up a wall; he was unsocial and withdrawn. Finally, his wife prevailed on him to take a set of vocational guidance tests to help him find a more satisfying job.

When the results of the tests came back, the vocational guidance company recommended that he become a worker in an assembly line. The tests revealed that he had a low tolerance for frustration, that he was incapable of taking on responsibility, that he was unsociable, and that routine, prescribed work fit his personality best. The advice came as a shock, since Mel had twenty years of high executive achievement behind him, was usually outgoing and persuasive, and was considerably brighter than the average assembly line worker. But the tests actually reflected his present state of mind: He believed himself incompetent; he saw his career as a failure; he

found every small obstacle to be an insurmountable barrier; he was not interested in other people; and he could barely force himself to get dressed, much less to make important career decisions. This profile did not give a true picture of Mel's long-term history; rather, it reflected the disorder of depression — a process, probably transient, that had been going on since Mel lost his job.

The prevalence of depression in America today is staggering. Over and above the mild depressions we all occasionally suffer, the National Institute of Mental Health estimates that "four to eight million Americans may be in need of professional care for the depressive illness" [Williams, Friedman, & Secunda 1970]. Unlike most other forms of psychopathology, depression can be lethal. "One out of every two hundred persons affected by a depressive illness will die a suicidal death." This estimate is probably on the low side. In addition to the immeasurable cost in individual misery, the economic cost is great. Loss of time at work and treatment costs alone amount to "between 1.3 and 4.0 billion dollars per annum."

The most useful and best-confirmed typology of depression is the "endogenous-reactive" dichotomy [Carney, Roth, & Garside 1965; Kiloh & Garside 1963; Mendels 1968; Schuyler 1975]. Reactive depressions are precipitated by some external event, whereas endogenous depressions are a response to some internal physical or endogenous process. These depressions are not triggered by any external event; they just sweep over the sufferer.

Reactive depressions, the kind familiar to us all, are by far the most common. They account for roughly 75 percent of all depressions and are initiated by some external event such as the death of a member of the family. A reactive depression is not cyclical, is not usually responsive to physical therapies like drugs and electroconvulsive shock (ECS), does not have genetic predisposition, and is usually somewhat milder in all its symptoms than endogenous depression.

In contrast, endogenous depressions are usually cyclical and can be either bipolar or unipolar. Bipolar depression is called *manic depression* — the individual cycles from despair to a neutral mood to the hyperactive and superficially euphoric state of mania back to neutrality down to despair and so on. Early in this century, *all* depressions were mistakenly called manic-depressive illnesses, but it is now known that depression usually occurs without mania, and mania can occur without depression. Unipolar depression consists of a regular cycle from neutrality to despair to neutrality to despair. Endogenous depressions often respond to drug treatment and ECS and may be hormonal in origin. They may have genetic components and are often more severe in their symptoms than reactive depressions. Reactive depressions are the focus of the learned helplessness model of depression although endogenous depressions have much in common psychologically with reactive depressions.

Symptoms of Depression

Each of the symptoms that we have seen in learned helplessness has parallels in depression.

Lowered Voluntary Response Initiation

Depressed men and women do not do much. The word *depression* itself probably has its etymological roots in the reduced activity of the patient. I recently suggested to a depressed woman patient who had let her appearance go to seed that she go out and buy herself a new dress. Her response was typical: "Oh, Doctor, that's just too hard for me." Systematic studies of the symptoms of depression capture this behavioral manifestation in a number of ways [Grinker, Miller, Sabshin, Nunn & Nunnally 1961]:

> Isolated and withdrawn, prefers to remain by himself, stays in bed much of the time.
>
> Gait and general behavior slow and retarded. Volume of voice decreased, sits alone very quietly.
>
> Feels unable to act, feels unable to make decisions.
>
> Gives the appearance of an "empty"person who has "given up."

Paralysis of the will is a striking feature of severe depression:

> In severe cases, there often is complete paralysis of the will. The patient has no desire to do anything, even those things which are essential to life. Con-

sequently, he may be relatively immobile unless prodded or pushed into activity by others. It is sometimes necessary to pull the patient out of bed, wash, dress and feed him. In extreme cases, even communication may be blocked by the patient's inertia [Beck 1967, p. 28].

Social deficits in depression reflect lowered response initiation. Ekman and Friesen [1974] have done a fascinating series of filmed studies of the hand motions that depressives make in the course of chatting with an interviewer. Two categories of hand motions accompany conversation. *Illustrators*, are sweeping gestures that go along with the words to emphasize and illustrate what is being said. These are voluntary and conscious, for if you interrupt and ask the speaker what he just did, he can tell you accurately. On the other hand, *adaptors* are small, tic-like motions such as nose picking or hair pulling. These are involuntary and are not conscious; if interrupted, the speaker cannot usually report them. When depressives arrive at the hospital, they make many adaptors but few illustrators. As they get better, they make more illustrators and fewer adaptors, indicating a recovery of voluntary response initiation.

Other social responses are also diminished in depressives. When someone says "good morning" to a depressed person, and timing how long it takes him to respond, the depressed person will be slow to answer [Lewinsohn 1974]. Moreover, it will take him even longer to reply with a social amenity, such as "and how are *you?*" The reader can check this out in any phone conversation with a friend he knows to be depressed.

The lowered voluntary response initiation that defines learned helplessness, then, is pervasive in depression. It produces passivity and social unresponsiveness; in extreme depression, it can produce stupor.

Negative Cognitive Set

Suppose that I had been able to convince the depressed patient who had let her appearance go to seed that it was not too hard for her to go out and buy a dress. Her next line of defense would probably be along these lines: "But I'd probably take the wrong bus, and even if I found the right store, I'd pick out something that didn't fit and was the wrong style.

Anyway, I'm so unattractive that a new dress wouldn't help.'' Depressed people believe their responses to be even more ineffective than they are. Small obstacles to success are regarded as impassable barriers. Difficulty in dealing with a problem is seen as complete failure, and even outright success is often misconstrued as failure. Beck [1967] views this ''negative cognitive set'' as the universal hallmark of depression.

This discrepancy between the objective performance (even though, as we have seen, it is not all that good to begin with) and the depressive's subjective view of performance is striking. Friedman [1964] found that depressed patients performed more poorly than normals in reaction to a light signal and took longer to recognize common objects, but even more striking was their subjective estimate of how poorly they thought they would do:

> When the examiner would bring the patient into the testing room, the patient would immediately protest that he or she could not possibly take the tests, was unable to do anything, or felt too bad or too tired, was incapable, hopeless, etc. . . . While performing adequately the patient would occasionally and less frequently reiterate the original protest, saying ''I can't do it,'' '' I don't know how,'' etc.

This is also our experience in testing depressed patients in the laboratory. If we ask a depressive after an intellectual speed test how slow they were, they will tell us that they were even slower than they had actually been.

An important test of the learned helplessness model is to determine if inescapable noise and unsolvable problems result in the same symptoms as in naturally occurring depression. Miller and Seligman [in press] found that inescapable noise produced a negative cognitive set in nondepressed students. Subjects showed small changes in their expectancies for success and failure in a skill task; they treated their successes and failures in the skill task just as if it had been a task of chance in which their responses did not matter. In contrast, subjects who received escapable noise or no noise showed great expectancy changes when they failed or succeeded in skill, but small changes in chance. These subjects were not depressed, so we then asked ourselves whether depression itself, with no pretreatment with noise, would produce the same negative set as that produced by exposure to inescapable noise in nondepressed subjects.

In our learned helplessness model depression is not a generalized pessimism, but *pessimism specific to the effects on one's own skilled actions*. We therefore placed groups of depressed and nondepressed subjects in tests of skill and of chance, and in both tasks the subject experienced the same experimentally manipulated pattern of success and failure. We found that depressed and nondepressed students did not differ in their *initial* expectancies of success. Then after each success and each failure, we asked the subjects how well they thought they would do on the next trial, as we had in our earlier experiment with the subjects who had been given prior experience with inescapable noise. The results were very different for depressed and nondepressed people once the two groups had experienced success and failure. The nondepressed subjects, believing that their responses mattered in the skill task, showed much greater expectancy changes than they did in the chance task. The depressed groups, however, did not change their expectancies any more in skill than they did in chance. Further, the more depressed an individual was, the less his expectancies changed in skill. Such subjects apparently believed that their responses mattered no more in skill than they did in chance. So both experimentally induced helplessness and naturally occurring depression produce pessimism about skilled action.

Miller and Seligman [1975] provided more evidence for the symmetry of depression and learned helplessness by looking at the anagram solution test. As was discussed earlier, prior inescapable noise impairs ability to solve anagrams like ''OSIEN.'' Time to solve, the number of failures before solving, and the number of trials to catch on to a pattern in the anagrams were increased by uncontrollability. These subjects were not depressed, however. Does depression produce the same negative cognitive set as measured by impairment of anagram solution as laboratory-induced helplessness? To test this, we gave three groups of students escapable noise, inescapable noise, or no noise. Half of each group was depressed, as measured by the Beck Depression Inventory (BDI), a mood scale. The other half was not depressed as defined by their Inventory responses. As predicted, depressed subjects who had no noise, just like nondepressed subjects who had inescapable noise, did very poorly on anagrams: They solved fewer anagrams, took longer on the ones they did solve, and had more trouble catching on to the pattern. In addition, the more depressed an individual was, the worse he did on anagrams. So again, depression produces the same deficits as laboratory-induced helplessness.

Lack of Aggression

Depressed people are usually less aggressive and less competitive than nondepressed people. Not only is the behavior of depressed patients depleted of hostility, but even their dreams are less hostile. This symptom forms the basis for the Freudian view of depression. Freud [1917] claimed that the hostility of depressed people was directed inward toward themselves rather than outward. Be this as it may, the *symptom* corresponds to the depleted aggression and competitiveness of helpless dogs and rats.

Time Course

Depression, like learned helplessness in dogs, often dissipates in time. When a man's wife dies, sometimes he is depressed for only a few hours; sometimes for weeks, months, or even years. But time usually heals. One of the most tragic aspects of suicide is that if the person could have suspended action for a few weeks, the depression might well have lifted. When catastrophe strikes, time courses of depression parallel dog helplessness.

Loss of "Libido"

In this common symptom of depression, food does not taste as good, sex is less exciting, interest in friends and loved ones drops off. Also, just as in helpless rats *weight loss* is observed in moderate and severe depression. In addition to the parallels to Weiss' [1968] work on anorexia and weight loss in helpless rats, norepinephrine (NE) may also be depleted in depression, as it is in helpless rats. Schildkraut [1965] proposed the *catecholamine hypothesis* which postulates the cause of depression as a deficiency of NE at receptor sites in the brain. The evidence for it is indirect: Two kinds of antidepressant drugs, MAO inhibitors and tricyclics, have the common property of keeping NE available in the brain [Cole 1964; Davis 1965; Klerman & Cole 1965]. The drug reserpine, originally given to lower the blood pressure of heart patients, occasionally causes depression and also depletes NE, among

many other effects. AMPT, a specific NE depletor, produces social withdrawal and other depressive behavior in monkeys [Redmond, Maas, Kling, & De-Kirmenjian 1971] and failure to escape shock in rats [Abramson & Seligman unpublished]. These findings may correspond to the NE deficits seen by Weiss in helpless rats.

Etiology of Depression

Our research suggests that the cause of depressive reaction, like learned helplessness, may be the belief that responding is useless in bringing relief or succor. What kind of events set off reactive depressions? Some are failure in work or school; death, loss, rejection, or separation from loved ones; physical disease; financial setback; and growing old. There are others, but these capture the flavor of events that often precipitate depression. In addition, they all have something in common: The depressed patient has learned or believes that he cannot control those parts of his life that relieve suffering or bring him gratification. In short, he believes that he is helpless. Consider a few of the common precipitating events. What is the meaning of job failure or incompetence at school? Frequently it means that all a person's efforts have been in vain: He cannot find responses that control reinforcement. When an individual is rejected by someone he loves, he can no longer control this significant source of gratification and support. When a parent or lover dies, the bereaved is powerless to produce or influence love from the dead person. Physical disease and growing old are helplessness situations par excellence. In these conditions, the person finds his own responses ineffective and his life dependent on others.

Cure of Depression

Not terribly much is known, as opposed to what is claimed, about the cure of depression. So far, there is no cure-all. From the helplessness point of view, the central issue should be getting the patient to believe that his responding does produce the reinforcers he values. Some methods by which the patient is shown that his responding *is* effective have been claimed to be therapeutic. One example is assertive training, in which the patient rehearses making assertive responses, is induced to tell off an abusive attendant; and then sees the attendant mend his ways [Taulbee & Wright 1971]. Graded task assignments in which patients perform harder and harder work and are thereby exposed to graduated success seem to be effective antidepressant therapy [Burgess 1968]. As in learned helplessness, electroconvulsive shock treatment is reported therapeutic in depression, and time is, as mentioned, usually effective in mitigating it.

Individuals often adopt their own strategies for dealing with their own minor depressions. Asking for help and getting it, as well as helping someone else (or even caring for a pet), are two strategies that may help alleviate minor depressions and build up control. My own strategy is to force myself to work — to sit down and write a paper, read a difficult text or an article from a technical journal, or do a math problem. What better way for an intellectual to see that his efforts can still be effective and to bring gratification than to plunge into writing, heavy reading, or problem solving? The problem is getting started. If I begin to solve the math problem and give up halfway through, the depression gets worse.

Many psychotherapies claim to be able to cure depression. There exist, however, few well-controlled studies of the effectiveness of any form of psychotherapy for depression. The evidence I presented is selective: Only those treatments that seem compatible with helplessness were discussed. It is possible that when other therapies work, it is because they also reinstate the patient's *sense of efficacy*. What is needed now is experimental evidence to isolate the effective variable in the psychological treatment of depression. It is also essential that untreated control groups be run, since depression dissipates in time of its own accord.

Prevention of Depression

If little is known about the cure of depression, even less is known about its prevention. We can speculate, however, that the life histories of individuals who are particularly resistant (or resilient) to depression may have been filled with mastery. People who have had extensive experience controlling and manipulating the sources of reinforcement in their lives may perceive their future optimistically. Those who are particularly susceptible to depression may have had lives relatively devoid of mastery; their lives may have been filled with situations in which they were helpless to influence sources of suffering and gratification.

A summary of the findings of depression that have been discussed is shown in table 2. A comparison of this table with table 1 shows the many parallels between depression and learned helplessness. These parallels suggest similarity of cause, cure, and prevention and thus may point the way to effective treatment of human depression.

Table 2. *Depression.*

Symptoms	Passivity
	Negative cognitive set
	Introjected hostility
	Time course
	Loss of libido
	Norepinephrine depletion
	Ulcers (?) and stress
	Feelings of helplessness
Cause	Belief that responding is useless
Cure	Recovery of belief that responding produces reinforcement
	Electroconvulsive shock
	Time
Prevention	Inoculation (?)

BIBLIOGRAPHY

Lyn Abramson and M. E. P. Seligman, "The Effects of AMPT and Imipramine on Learned Helplessness in the Rat." Unpublished.

H. S. Akiskal and W. T. McKinney, "Depressive Disorders: Toward a Unified Hypothesis." *Science*, 1973, 182:20–28.

D. C. Anderson, J. Cole, and W. McVaugh, "Variations in Unsignaled Inescapable Preshock as Determinants of Responses to Punishment." *Journal of Comparative and Physiological Psychology*, 1968, 65: monograph supplement 1–17.

H. Anisman and T. G. Waller, "Effects of Inescapable Shock on Subsequent Avoidance Performance: Role Response Repertoire Changes." *Behavioral Biology*, 1973, 9:331–355.

A.T. Beck, *Depression*. Hoeber, 1967.

R. J. Bracewell and A. H. Black, "The Effects of Restraint and Noncontingent Pre-shock on Subsequent Escape Learning in the Rat." *Learning and Motivation*, 1974, 5:-53–69.

J. V. Brady, "Ulcers in 'Executive' Monkeys." *Scientific American*, 1958, 199:95–100.

E. Burgess, "The Modification of Depressive Behavior." In R. Rubin and C. Franks, Eds., *Advances in Behavior Therapy*. Academic Press, 1968.

B. Carder and K. Berkowitz, "Rats' Preference for Earned in Comparison with Free Food." *Science*, 1970, 167:1273–1274.

M. W. P. Carney, M. Roth, and R. F. Garside, "The Diagnosis of Depressive Syndromes and the Prediction of E. C. T. Response." *British Journal of Psychiatry*, 1965, 111:659–674.

J. O. Cole, "Therapeutic Efficacy of Antidepressant Drugs." *Journal of the American Medical Association*, 1964, 190:448–455.

J. Davis, "Efficacy of Tranquilizing and Antidepressant Drugs." *Archives of General Psychiatry*, 1965, 13:522–572.

L. De Toledo and A. H. Black, "Effects of Preshock on Subsequent Avoidance Conditioning." *Journal of Comparative and Physiological Psychology*, 1967, 63:493–499.

J. A. Dinsmoor and S. L. Campbell, "Escape-from-shock Training Following Exposure to Inescapable Shock." *Psychological Reports*, 1956a, 2:43–49.

J. A. Dinsmoor and S. L. Campbell, "Level of Current and Time Between Sessions as Factors in Adaptation to Shock." *Psychological Reports*, 1956b, 2:441–444.

T. R. Dorworth, "The Effect of Electroconvulsive Shock on 'Helplessness' in Dogs." Unpublished doctoral dissertation, University of Minnesota, 1971.

P. Ekman and W. V. Friesen, "Non-verbal Behavior in Psychopathology." In R. J. Friedman and M. M. Katz, eds., *The Psychology of Depression: Contemporary Theory and Research*. Halstead, 1974.

L. A. Engberg, G. Hansen, R. L. Welker, and D. Thomas, "Acquisition of Key-Pecking Via Autoshaping as a Function of Prior Experience: 'Learned Laziness'?" *Science*, 1972, 178:1002–1004.

Sigmund Freud, "Mourning and Melancholia." In *Collected Works*. London, Hogarth, 1917, pp. 243–258.

A. S. Friedman, "Minimal Effects of Severe Depression on Cognitive Functioning." *Journal of Abnormal Social Psychology*, 1964, 69:237–243.

D. C. Glass and J. E. Singer, *Urban Stress: Experiments on Noise and Social Stressors*. Academic Press, 1972.

R. Grinker, J. Miller, M. Sabshin, R. Nunn, and J. Nunnally, *The Phenomena of Depression*. Hoeber, 1961.

D. S. Hiroto, "Locus of Control and Learned Helplessness." *Journal of Experimental Psychology*, 1974, 102:187–193.

D. S. Hiroto and M. E. P. Seligman, "Generality of Learned Helplessness in Man." *Journal of Personality and Social Psychology*, 1975, 31:311–327.

L. G. Kiloh and R. F. Garside, "The Independence of Neurotic Depression and Endogenous Depression." *British Journal of Psychiatry*, 1963, 109:451–463.

G. L. Klerman and J. O. Cole, "Clinical Pharmacology of Imipramine and Related Antidepressant Compounds." *Pharmacological Review*, 1965, 17:101–141.

M. Lessac and R. L. Solomon, "Effects of Early Isolation on the Later Adaptive Behavior of Beagles: A Methodological Demonstration." *Developmental Psychology*, 1969, 1:14–25.

P. Lewinsohn, "A Behavioral Approach to Depression." In R. J. Friedman and M. M. Katz, eds., *The Psychology of Depression: Contemporary Theory and Research*. Halstead, 1974.

T. A. Looney and P. S. Cohen, "Retardation of Jump-up Escape Responding in Rats Pretreated with Different Frequencies of Noncontingent Electric Shock." *Journal of Comparative and Physiological Psychology*, 1972, 78:317–322.

S. F. Maier, "Failure to Escape Traumatic Shock: Incompatible Skeletal Motor Responses or Learned Helplessness?" *Learning and Motivation*, 1970, 1:157–170.

S. F. Maier, R. W. Albin, and T. J. Testa, "Failure to Learn to Escape in Rats Previously Exposed to Inescapable Shock Depends on the Nature of the Escape Response." *Journal of Comparative and Physiological Psychology*, 1973, 85:581–592.

S. F. Maier, C. Anderson, and D. A. Lieberman, "Influence of Control of Shock on Subsequent Shock-elicited Aggression." *Journal of Comparative and Physiological Psychology*, 1972, 81:94–100.

S. F. Maier and T. J. Testa, "Failure to Learn to Escape by Rats Previously Exposed to Inescapable Shock is Partly Produced by Associative Interference." *Journal of Comparative and Physiological Psychology*, 1975, 88:554–564.

J. Mendels, "Depression: The Distinction Between Symptom and Syndrome." *British Journal of Psychiatry*, 1968, 114:1549–1554.

W. R. Miller and M. E. P. Seligman, "Depression and Learned Helplessness in Man." *Journal of Abnormal Psychology*, 1975, 84:228–238.

W. R. Miller and M. E. P. Seligman, "Depression, Learned Helplessness, and the Perception of Reinforcement." *Behavior Research Therapy*, in press.

N. Miller and J. M. Weiss, "Effects of Somatic or Visceral Responses to Punishment." In B. A. Campbell and R. M. Church, eds., *Punishment and Aversive Behavior*. Appleton-Century-Crofts, 1969, pp. 343–372.

A. D. Mullin and G. J. Mogenson, "Effects of Fear Conditioning on Avoidance Learning." *Psychological Reports,* 1963, 13:707–710.

J. B. Overmier and M. E. P. Seligman, "Effects of Inescapable Shock Upon Subsequent Escape and Avoidance Learning." *Journal of Comparative and Physiological Psychology,* 1967, 63:23–33.

D. E. Redmond, J. W. Maas, D. Kling, and H. DeKirmenjian. "Changes in Primate Social Behavior after Treatment with Alpha-methyl Para-tyrosine." *Psychosomatic Medicine,* 1971, 33:97–113.

C. Richter, "On the Phenomenon of Sudden Death in Animals and Man." *Psychosomatic Medicine,* 1957, 19:191–198.

J. Rotter, "Generalized Expectancies for Internal vs. External Control of Reinforcement." *Psychological Monographs,* 1966, 80:whole no. 609.

J. J. Schildkraut, "The Catecholamine Hypothesis of Affective Disorders: A Review of Supporting Evidence." *American Journal of Psychiatry,* 1965, 122:509–522.

D. Schuyler, *Depression.* Aronson, 1975.

M. E. P. Seligman, "Depression and Learned Helplessness." In R. J. Friedman and M. M. Katz, eds., *The Psychology of Depression: Contemporary Theory and Research.* Halsted, 1974.

M. E. P. Seligman, *Helplessness: On Depression, Development and Death.* Freeman, 1975.

M. E. P. Seligman and G. Beagley, "Learned Helplessness in the Rat." *Journal of Comparative and Physiological Psychology,* 1975, 88:534–541.

M. E. P. Seligman and D. Groves, "Non-transient Learned Helplessness." *Psychonomic Science,* 1970, 19:191–192.

M. E. P. Seligman, D. Klein, and W. R. Miller, "Depression." In H. Leitenberg, ed., *Handbook of Behavior Therapy.* Appleton-Century-Crofts, in press.

M. E. P. Seligman and S. F. Maier, "Failure to Escape Traumatic Shock." *Journal of Experimental Psychology,* 1967, 74:1–9.

M. E. P. Seligman, S. F. Maier, and J. Geer, "The Alleviation of Learned Helplessness in the Dog." *Journal of Abnormal and Social Psychology,* 1968, 73:256–262.

M. E. P. Seligman, S. F. Maier, and R. L. Solomon, "Unpredictable and Uncontrollable Aversive Events." In F. R. Brush, ed., *Aversive Conditioning and Learning.* Academic Press, 1971, pp. 347–400.

M. E. P. Seligman, R. A. Rosellini, and M. J. Kozak, "Learned Helplessness in the Rat: Time Course, Immunization, and Reversibility." *Journal of Comparative and Physiological Psychology,* 1975, 88:542–547.

E. S. Taulbee and H. W. Wright, "A Psycho-Social-Behavioral Model for Therapeutic Intervention." In C. D. Spielberger, ed., *Current Topics in Clinical and Community Psychology, III.* Academic Press, 1971, pp. 92–125.

J. S. Watson, "Smiling, ·Cooing, and 'the Game.' " Paper read at American Psychological Association Meeting, Miami, 1970.

J. M. Weiss, "Effects of Coping Response on Stress." *Journal of Comparative and Physiological Psychology,* 1968, 65:251–260.

J. M. Weiss, "Effects of Coping Behavior in Different Warning Signal Combinations on Stress Pathology in Rats." *Journal of Comparative and Physiological Psychology,* 1971, 77:1–13.

J. M. Weiss, H. Glazer, and L. Pohorecky, "Coping Behavior and Neurochemical Changes in Rats." Paper presented at the Kittay Scientific Foundation Conference, New York, March 1974.

J. M. Weiss, E. E. Krieckhaus, and R. Conte, "Effects of Fear Conditioning on Subsequent Avoidance Behavior and Movement." *Journal of Comparative and Physiological Psychology,* 1968, 65:413–421.

J. M. Weiss, E. A. Stone, and N. Harrell, "Coping Behavior and Brain Norepinephrine in Rats." *Journal of Comparative and Physiological Psychology,* 1970, 72:153–160.

T. A. Williams, R. J. Friedman, and S. K. Secunda, *Special Report: The Depressive Illnesses.* National Institute of Mental Health, November 1970.

5

The Operant Approach in Behavior Modification

Leonard Krasner

State University of New York, Stony Brook

In the period after World War II, a new approach to observing and changing human behavior began to develop. During the succeeding decades this approach, which is known as "behavior modification" or "operant conditioning," has achieved growing acceptance and usage by individuals professionally engaged in assisting human beings with a variety of behavioral problems.

We will discuss the operant approach in its historical context, offer illustrations that emphasize its application to adult behavior, and examine its social and ethical implications. Although we will detail concepts, theories, and a technology, actually we will describe the behavior of individuals variously labeled as therapists, researchers, paraprofessionals, psychologists, psychiatrists, nurses, or attendants, working with other people in environmental settings such as laboratories, clinics, hospitals, homes, and schools. In emphasizing the operant conditioning approach, selective studies involving research and its application will be reviewed. There will be no attempt to be exhaustive since we are dealing with a field that has grown in recent years to the point where there are a multitude of published reports of operant applications to "clinical" problems and these are continuously being supplemented by additional reports.

Any model purporting to explain how human behavior develops and is changed should be clearly differentiated from other existing models. In this instance, behavior modification has arisen as an alternative to an intrapsychic model of psychopathology that utilizes psychotherapy as its major mode of changing behavior.

Psychotherapy, as an interpersonal healing process, can be traced back to the eighteenth-century hypnotic technology of Franz Anton Mesmer. However, it is to Sigmund Freud, with his emphasis on verbally interacting with an unhappy individual in a one-to-one relationship, that the modern-day origin of psychotherapy is credited. The major features of psychotherapeutic interaction include a verbal exchange, interpretation of the clients' verbalizations, expectancy of some alleviation of problems on the clients' parts, the therapist's belief in his ability to assist the patient, the use of the relationship in the therapeutic process, and the belief that change in feelings and/or verbal behavior in the therapy situation will carry over to the patient's real life on the outside. Psychotherapy made sense within a model of man that viewed his overt behavior as a result of the interplay of dynamic forces within an autonomous being or a "personality."

In contrast, the behavior modification approach developed from a model of human behavior that places major, but not exclusive, emphasis on the impact of environmental events on behavior. This module will focus upon one stream of development within the overall behavior modification (using that term as the generic one) approach, namely the stream that utilizes operant methodology.

Historical Context

The development of behavior modification has been traced through fifteen streams of development in the history of psychology and psychiatry [Krasner 1971]. Of these, the stream influenced by the research and theories of B. F. Skinner [1938, 1956, 1972] has been the major influence on the operant approach to be described in this module.

Behavior modification represents an uneasy alliance of investigators who have more in common in terms of theory, rationale, and technique of application than differences between them. In fact, behavior modification has enough communality and differentiation from other approaches that it may be said to represent a paradigmatic break with previous models [Kuhn 1970]. Behavior modification generally focuses on changing behavior *directly* (rather than indirectly through psychic manifestations), emphasizes "learning" theories, uses procedures derived from the experimental and social psychology laboratories, offers an educational or social model of deviancy rather than a medical or disease model of psychopathology, and insists on research objectivity and the generation of data [Krasner & Ullmann 1973].

It is difficult to differentiate the various techniques used by the practitioners of behavior modification into discrete categories. At one point in time, it was relatively simple to describe behavior modification research in terms of a few general procedures such as operant conditioning, systematic desensitization, modeling, and extinction. Early reviews of the techniques and research involved were organized around these procedures. Bandura [1961] reviewed behavior therapy using the topics of extinction, discrimination learning, reward, punishment, and social imitation. Grossberg [1964] organized around the topics of aversion, negative practice, positive conditioning, reinforcement withdrawal, and desensitization. Kalish [1965] reduced the techniques to those of extinction and of conditioning.

Within this broad theoretical context, the operant approach more specifically emphasizes the concept that behavior is determined by its consequences. The organism operates upon its environment and the nature of the feedback it receives from that environment determines subsequent response. The operant approach emphasizes the impact of positive environmental response (a reward or *reinforcement*) on increasing the likelihood of a behavior reoccurring. In so doing, the operant approach deals with *probability* of response. A behavior followed by positive consequences is more *likely* to be repeated than if it is not. Finally, the operant approach emphasizes the role of the individual's social environment. If behavior is determined by social consequences, then effort must be expended in rearranging these consequences (by design of physical environments, planning social institutions, training key environmental figures such as parents or teachers) so as to develop and maintain desirable behavior.

If a bit of behavior is to be modified by the consequences of that behavior, then a systematic manipulation of rewards and punishments is involved. An organism performs an act that is followed by an environmental event. If the individual repeats the act, then we may label the environmental event as a *reinforcing stimulus*. Behaviors are more likely to be repeated if they are followed by environmental consequences, which can be called *reinforcements*. Experimental examples of such reinforcement are abundant. They include: the bar-pressing by the rat, which is followed by a food pellet [Skinner 1938]; verbalization of an emotional word, followed by an experimenter saying, "Good" [Krasner 1958]; a man's shaving himself followed by a token [Atthowe & Krasner 1968]; the report of having looked up information on a particular vocation in the library followed by a counselor's nod of approval [Krumboltz 1966]; fluent speech for thirty seconds in a stutterer followed by a ticking of a clock indicating that he has earned 10¢ [Goldiamond 1965].

Reviews

There are now available a considerable number of reviews of the general field of operant methodology, approach and theory [Catania 1968; Ferster & Skinner 1957; Honig 1966; Keller & Schoenfeld 1950; Rachlin 1970; Reese 1966; Reynolds 1968; Skinner 1938, 1953, 1957, 1961; Staats 1964; Ulrich 1967; Verhave 1966]. This approach has developed a highly technical set of terms and concepts, which we will not try to define here except as they may occur in the descriptions of applied operant work.

Another series of books have specifically reviewed the application of operant approaches to changing deviant or undesirable human behavior [e.g., Bandura 1969; Ferster & Perrot 1968; Franks 1969; Kanfer & Phillips 1970; Liberman 1972; Rickard 1971; Ulrich, Stachnik, & Mabry 1966, 1970]. Else-

where the writer [Krasner 1962, 1971; Krasner & Ullmann 1965, 1973; Ullmann & Krasner 1965, 1969] offered a series of concepts that are basic to and useful in conceptualizing and utilizing operant conditioning to influence human behavior.

Broad Concepts

Reynolds offers an excellent introduction to the operant approach:

> Operant conditioning is an experimental science of behavior. Strictly speaking, the term operant conditioning refers to a process in which the frequency of occurrence of a bit of behavior is modified by the consequences of the behavior. Over the years, however, operant conditioning has come to refer to an entire approach to psychological science. This approach is characterized in general by a deterministic and experimental analysis of behavior. It is also characterized by a concentration on the study of operant or instrumental behavior, although not to the exclusion of the study of instinctive and reflexive behavior.
>
> As an approach to the study of behavior, operant conditioning consists of a series of assumptions about behavior and its environment; a set of definitions which can be used in the objective, scientific description of behavior and its environment, a group of techniques for the experimental study of behavior in the laboratory; and a large body of facts and principles which have been demonstrated by experiment.
>
> Operant conditioning is concerned with the relationship between the behavior of organisms and their environment. Research in operant conditioning gathers knowledge about behavior from the experimental study of the effects on behavior of systematic changes in the surrounding environment. Operant conditioning attempts to understand behavior by gaining knowledge of the factors that modify as an objective science; it is restricted to the study of factors that can be observed, measured, and reproduced. The psychologists who use this approach differ greatly in their degree of commitment to the principles of operant conditioning. At one extreme of commitment are those who accept only the experimental techniques because they are convenient methods for studying behavior. At the other extreme are those who accept, at present partly on faith, the beliefs and findings of operant conditioning as being truly descriptive of behavior and as guides to the conduct of their personal lives [1968, pp. 1–2].

This statement summarizes the main features of operant methodology: the intensive study of individual subjects, the control of the experimental environment, the control of individual behavior, the emphasis on objective observation and recording of behavior, the importance of consequences of behavior, the empirical nature of the approach, and the intense involvement of most of its proponents.

Only a relatively few years ago a module surveying research on operant procedures as applied in the context of behavior modification would have been simple. There were only a few studies, such as those of Skinner and Lindsley [1956], which unequivocally belonged in this category. These important studies involved the application of operant procedures, which had been developed with animals as subjects in the psychology laboratory, to "psychotic" human beings living in a mental hospital. In a crude sense, it could be said that early results of operant work with adults demonstrated that when a "psychotic" patient was put in a large Skinner box, his performance was as lawful as that of a pigeon or a rat.

Currently, in the 1970s, the number of reports of operant work has expanded enormously. Further, it is impossible to limit the boundaries of operant applications to behavior problems in the laboratory or even in the mental hospital. Research has been extended to the clinic, the schoolroom, the home, the community, and beyond!

The studies to be described in this module will involve two types of characteristics. First, they will be studies that concern the manipulation of consequences of behavior or reinforcement so as to influence subsequent behavior of adult human beings. Second, the behavior to be influenced is such that it has been labeled *undesirable* or *maladaptive* by a person who is in a power position vis-à-vis the individual. This includes studies done in a laboratory context since even in this situation, artificial as it may be, the decision has been made by the experimenter, that a certain behavior should be changed with the focus on the process of change itself.

It is important to emphasize that operant procedures should be approached within a framework that conceptualizes the behavior to be changed as deviant not as psychopathological. The implications of the latter view (the medical model) is that deviant behaviors are symptoms which, if removed, will be replaced by other undesirable behavior (symptom substitution) unless underlying causes are extirpated. The implication of the view expressed in the quotation below (social labeling) is that deviant behavior is a learned social phenomenon; hence changed behavior will represent "real" changes in the individual because every change will have social consequences influencing the individual's environment specifically by eliciting new responses from others.

> Behavior which is called abnormal must be studied as the interaction of three variables: the behavior itself, its social context, and an observer who is in a position of power. Rather, an individual may do something (e.g., verbalize hallucinations, hit a person, collect rolls of toilet paper, refuse to eat, stutter, stare into space, or dress sloppily) under a set of circumstances (e.g., during a school class, while working at his desk, during a church service) which upsets, annoys, angers, or strongly disturbs somebody (e.g., employer, teacher, parent, or the individual himself) sufficiently that some action results (e.g., a policeman is called, seeing a psychiatrist is recommended, commitment proceedings are started) so that the society's professional labelers (e.g., physicians, psychiatrists, psychologists, judges, social workers) come into contact with the individual and determine which of the current sets of labels (e.g., schizophrenic reaction, sociopathic personality, anxiety reaction) is most appropriate. Finally, there follow attempts to change the emission of the offending behavior (e.g., institutionalization, psychotherapy, medication). The label applied is the result of the training of the labeler and reflects the society which he represents. The labeling itself leads others to react to the individual in terms of the stereotypes of that label (e.g., "Be careful, he's a dangerous schizophrenic;" "Poor girl, she's hysterical.") [Ullmann & Krasner 1969, p.21].

Early Clinical Applications

Most of the applications of operant conditioning to modifying deviant or unusual behavior has been within the behavioral model of deviancy as outlined above. It is the model that influences the behavior of the behavior modifier in its conceptualization of what is the nature of the individual patient's problems. This major point will be illustrated more clearly in later sections that describe research on the application of operant procedures to such problem behaviors as depression, excessive alcoholic drinking, or "schizophrenic" behavior.

Fuller [1949] was probably the first investigator to report on the deliberate application of operant procedures in a clinical setting. He worked with an eighteen-year-old "vegetative idiot" and was able to "shape" the movement of the boy's right arm by successive approximations, using a warm sugar-milk solution as a reward. Fuller's study included many of the characteristics of later operant reports, including the fact that the physicians in the institution thought it would be impossible for the boy to learn anything. However, Fuller demonstrated that an appreciable addition had been added to the "idiot's" repertoire in four sessions.

A major step forward in the application of operant procedures to human behavior was taken by Ogden Lindsley and B. F. Skinner in their research program with psychotic patients at Metropolitan State Hospital in the early 1950s in which the lever-pulling responses of patients to a "vending machine" was investigated under different conditions of reward. In fact, in one of the first reports of their work [Lindsley, Skinner, & Solomon 1953] they used the term "behavior therapy" in the title. This was the first such use of this term in the modern literature [Wolpe 1968]. Subsequent users of operant procedures generally preferred to use the term "behavior modification" to describe their work [Krasner & Ullmann 1965; Ullmann & Krasner 1965], although it has been adopted by behaviorally oriented therapists who used nonoperant techniques, such as systematic desensitization.

The early reports of the performance of "disturbed" individuals foreshadowed much of the later operant work. In one of the first formal reports of the early studies at Metropolitan State Hospital, Lindsley [1956] presented four general assumptions that are useful in analyzing the behavior of psychotic patients. These were: (1) the need to increase the precision of the measurement of behavior itself determining the conditions under which behavior occurs; (2) the seeking of physical events in the patient's environment controlling his behavior; (3) the application of the experimental method in its most rigorous and objective manner; (4) the use of behavioristic descriptions of the patient.

Based on these assumptions, Lindsley proceeds to suggest five methodological advantages of the operant method: (1) high experimental control; (2) automatic recording and scheduling to eliminate experimental bias; (3) high generality involving many situations, subjects, and species; (4) the free operant nature of the method, which eliminates variability and increases sensitivity to individual behavior; (5) the lack of instructions permitting the study of nonverbal behavior and studying individuals who do not communicate. These descriptions of the operant methodology are still applicable to later studies and are offered repeatedly as among the major advantages of this approach.

It is of interest to note that even in these early studies, operant procedures were used in combination with other behavior influencing methods such as modeling. For example, Lindsley describes what happens when the subject did not respond to a vending machine dispensing candy in front of which he had been placed. If the patient did not make a response within 15 minutes, the experimenter entered the room, pulled the knob himself and ingested a reinforcement with obvious relish. He then left, saying nothing. If no response was made for 15 minutes after this demonstration, the experimenter again entered, placed the patient's hand on the knob, and helped him pull it. Then the patient was given a reinforcement.

Lindsley [1960] reported additional data on individual performance on tasks similar to those reported in the earlier paper. The emphasis again was on the *observation of the behavior* of the patients.

> To a behaviorist a psychotic is a person in a mental hospital. If psychosis is what makes, or has made this person psychotic, then psychosis is the behavioral deviation that caused this person to be hospitalized or that is keeping him hospitalized. Looked at from this point of view, very few psychotics are at this moment behaving psychotically. Neither is there any assurance that they will behave psychotically when we wish to evaluate or to sample their behavior in a brief test conducted at irregular intervals. In fact psychosis defined in terms of the behavior that hospitalizes a person is most often highly infrequent. Most patients are hospitalized because the time of occurrence of their infrequent psychotic episodes cannot be predicted [p. 66].

This quotation captures the way in which operant investigators approach their work.

The importance of the early Lindsley and Skinner

studies was primarily to demonstrate the feasibility of operant conditioning procedures with psychotic patients. The early studies of Peters and Jenkins [1954] and King, Armitage, and Tilton [1960] are worthy of mention as preludes to later operant conditioning studies although they were not specifically performed within the operant framework. However, their procedures were similar, in general principles, to the Lindsley and Skinner studies. In one instance Peters and Jenkins introduced the notion of exposing the patients to deliberate deprivation (of sugar) to enhance the likelihood of responsivity to the reinforcement used (fudge candy).

The Research Design in Operant Studies

There are several reasons for beginning our review of specific operant conditioning studies with some comments on research design. Applications of the operant paradigm developed from early studies that were avowedly "experimental" in nature. At the great risk of oversimplification, it might be argued that the studies that we shall later describe involving behavior modification procedures in hospitals, schools, homes, and the community developed from early experiments in a psychological laboratory with a single rat pressing a lever in the classical Skinner box. Throughout the development of operant conditioning there has been a close link between "basic research" (often, but not exclusively, with animals) and application.

Further, by the very nature of its theoretical structure, operant conditioning has emphasized the necessity for training in the observation of behavior and the collection of data on the interaction between an individual organism and its environment. This research orientation has been considered the real strength of the operant orientation (and its basic weakness according to some critics).

The investigators in operant conditioning have emphasized own-control experimentation. In this section we shall illustrate this kind of design in the context of attempting to discern the basic variables involved in the operant approach.

We will start with a dogmatic assertion with which many investigators with different theoretical frameworks may disagree: The variables involved in operant research are the same as those in any other types of behavior modification or behavior influence research [Krasner & Ullmann 1973]. Sometimes this point is overlooked because of the belief that operant conditioning investigations impose a different set of standards. The variables involved may be categorized into those of influencer, influencee, situation, and the interaction among the three.

The therapist (or behavior modifier, or operant conditioner) may be viewed as a social reinforcer to, or educator of, other people [Krasner 1962]. Thus anything that enhances the influencing impact of the therapist's role is of importance. These would include "personality characteristics" and refer to the therapist's behavioral characteristics that can be specified, rather than to amorphous personality labels such as "warmth" or "empathy." Clear specifiable variables that may affect the therapist behavior include years of experience, prestige among peers, socio-economic background, degree of self-confidence, value system, theoretical orientation, "expectancy" of success, and techniques used. Similar sets of variables influence the behavior of the subjects, clients, or influencees. Situational variables include the influence of the environment in which the operant interaction is taking place (e.g., "laboratory," classroom, hospital, ward, etc.). Some of the verbal conditioning studies described below illustrate the systematic investigation of the interaction between the variables of influencer, influencee, and situation.

In the research studies, it is undesirable to conceptually separate the specific "reinforcement" (e.g., head nod, "mm hmm," candy, token) which is so integral a part of the operant technique from the reinforcer. This means that it is necessary to include the characteristics of the dispenser of reinforcement within the design of an operant study control. The "power" of reinforcement with human beings lies not in a token or food or a "very good" per se, but in these items *plus* the "giver" of the "good things." The operant studies have generally not given sufficient cognizance to this important element in the behavior influence process.

Since reinforcers are so crucial in the operant approach, then what comprises a reinforcer and how does the investigator determine what stimulus may serve as a reinforcer? In some instances there is an attempt to determine the likelihood of an object serving as a reinforcer before the study. Staats and his associates [1962] had their children preselect toys that were then to be used as reinforcers. Barrett [1962] asked his patient in advance what music he liked. Hutchinson and Azrin [1961] ascertained that their subjects were heavy smokers before using cigarettes as reinforcers. Cautela [1967] has developed a check list of reinforcers which his subjects fill out before starting to work with him. Ayllon and Azrin [1968a] report on a technique of reinforcer-sampling that can be used in situations in which reinforcers are available, but rarely used, by individuals who have previously demonstrated an interest in these reinforcers. There clearly is a very pragmatic approach to reinforcers; they can be anything that works to affect output of behavior. However, what will serve as a reinforcer for any given individual must be determined by observation and assessment of the individual's behavior in a natural setting.

Research in the general area of psychotherapy has alternated in fadistic style between emphasis on outcome and on process. Outcome studies generally have been so difficult to do and the results so discouraging that they were almost wholly abandoned in the 1950s for the easier to do, less meaningful, and more autistic type of process studies. The situation has been summarized by Paul as follows,

> Historically, behavior modification research has been dichotomized into "process" and "outcome" investigations, depending upon whether questions were asked about the "ultimate" change in clients' behavior after treatment termination (outcome) or about the way in which intratreatment phenomena transpired (process). On the one hand, the process-outcome dichotomy must be seen as a false one to be set aside, since the establishment of solid cause-effect relationships for outcome necessitates the specification of independent variables often considered under "process." On the other hand, "process" may refer to studies designed to answer questions related to determining **mechanisms** of change or testing competing explanatory hypotheses of **how** changes come about. While experimental operations and designs may focus on both sets of questions concurrently, it is possible and often desirable for behavior modification research to focus on outcome questions without including the necessary operations for identifying mechanisms of change [1969, p.36].

It seems clear that if we had to dichotomize the operant studies described in this module as process

or outcome, they are clearly outcome studies. Yet, as Paul makes clear, this is no longer a meaningful distinction. The process is subsumed within the investigation of the outcome. This can be illustrated by the usual design of an operant study, frequently labeled as ABA (or ABAB), in which the frequency (operant level) or baseline of a target behavior is measured (A), and then a new procedure is introduced (B) and withdrawn (A) as the behavior continues to be measured.

As an example of this design, Agras, Leitenberg, and Barlow [1968] report an investigation in which the effect of therapists' verbal behavior (social praise) on agoraphobic behavior could be determined. They worked with three subjects who had been severely phobic for one, fifteen, and sixteen years, respectively. The authors isolated the behavior with which they wished to work. They described it as the individual's difficulty in leaving a dependent situation. They designated *time* spent away from the clinic and *distance* walked from the clinic as the *target behavior* under measurement and treatment. A baseline period (the A of the ABA design) was set up in which the patient was asked to walk by himself as far as he could along a measured distance from the clinic. During the baseline period the therapist maintained a pleasant relationship with the patient but made no comment on the distance walked or time spent away. Reports of improvement made by the patient were also ignored. In the *reinforcement* phase (the B period) the first trial of every day, and all trials that met a slowly increasingly more difficult criterion of time spent away, were reinforced by verbal phrases such as "good," "you're doing well," and "excellent" spoken with appropriate enthusiasm. During the reinforcement phase remarks made by the patient to the nursing staff about progress were also praised. The *nonreinforcement* period (the second A of the design) consisted of a return to baseline conditions, stopping selective praise but taking care to maintain a generally pleasant supportive attitude towards the patient. In this way a distinction between general support and selective social reinforcement could be made. A fourth phase would then constitute a return to the reinforcement period (B) to determine if the target behavior then returns to its previous strength.

There are variations of this design. (1) The testing of an interaction between two variables (baseline, one experimental procedure introduced and effects measured, then a second procedure introduced and the effects measured. This gives the effects of procedure A *plus* procedure B. Then procedure A can be withdrawn, procedure B withdrawn, and both can then be reintroduced); (2) a comparison of different procedures with the same subject (baseline, procedure A introduced, procedure A withdrawn, procedure B introduced, then withdrawn, etc.).

There are further variations of this design possible, depending upon the ingenuity of the experimenter. In fact it would seem that it is this design, the *own-control* design, which is a unique contribution of the operant investigators. (The own-control is not the only design used since the usual kinds of control groups are also used in some studies, but it is by far the predominant design.) The interesting point here is that despite the animal origins of the early operant work, despite the rigid experimental genesis of operant conditioning, it has come full cycle to the basic tenets of the clinical approach, that of assessing change relative to the individual's own behavior. Changes in individual client's behavior is the basic yardstick against which success in treatment procedures must be measured.

Verbal Conditioning

The verbal conditioning studies represent a major aspect of the operant approach for a variety of reasons. They represent the first systematic set of studies with human beings that demonstrated the feasibility of applying this approach. They demonstrate that human verbal behavior, perhaps the most important (at least with the most consequences) of human behaviors was modifiable through operant procedures. These studies also represented a link with psychotherapeutical treatment approaches that place emphasis on the importance of "talk." Furthermore, they offered technique for assessing an individual's amenity to operant conditioning. And, they offered a useful experimental means of investigating and systematically exploring the effects of the many variables involved in the one-to-one relationship.

In effect, the verbal conditioning studies involve one individual using his behavior in a systematic and contingent manner to influence the likelihood of the other emitting certain specified bits of verbal behavior.

For example, in Greenspoon's early study [1954], his subjects were asked to, "Say all the words that you can think of." The specific response class selected to be reinforced was that of *plural nouns*. Thus, whenever the subject verbalized a plural noun, the experimenter responded with an "mm-hum." This response indicates that the other person ("experimenter") is paying attention and thus serves as a *generalized reinforcer*. The verbal conditioning studies have been extensively reviewed since their origin in the early 1950s [Greenspoon 1962; Holz & Azrin 1966; Kanfer 1968; Krasner 1958, 1962, 1965; Salzinger 1959; Williams 1966].

In his comprehensive review of this field, Kanfer [1968] observes that research on verbal conditioning has undergone four stages of development: (1) demonstration; (2) reevaluation; (3) application; (4) expansion. This is a useful way of conceptualizing the growth of these studies particularly as they are related to behavior therapy research.

The studies in the first stage *demonstrated* that verbal behavior could be brought under the control of environmental stimuli; hence verbal behavior followed the same principles as did the motor behavior of humans and of animals. In that sense the early verbal conditioning studies were similar to other early operant conditioning studies; they demonstrated that reinforcement, *under certain conditions*, can systematically influence verbal behavior.

The second stage, that of *reevaluation*, demonstrated that influencing verbal behavior was a far more complex phenomenon than the first simple operant explanations made it seem to be. Responsiveness to verbal conditioning was affected by variables such as social setting, previous experience with the examiner, the expectations of both participants, variations in the meaning of reinforcing stimuli, and other variables. It became increasingly clear that verbal conditioning involved the full gamut of the social influence process variables.

In the third stage, *application,* verbal conditioning studies were used to change specific verbal behavior with therapeutic intent [e.g., Isaacs, Thomas, & Goldiamond 1960]. A study by Williams and Blanton [1968] was one of the first in which the verbal conditioning techniques were used as therapy. The subjects in the treatment groups were told that they had been referred for "psychotherapy." Eighteen nonpsychotic patients were assigned to three treatment groups. Two groups received conditioning by verbal reinforcement, one for emitting statements expressing *feeling,* the other for emitting statements without discriminable feeling content. The third group received psychotherapy as usually administered. After an initial operant-level session, treatment was administered for nine half-hour sessions, the same therapist conducting all sessions. Recordings of the sessions were scored for number of statements expressing feelings over sessions for all groups. The percentage of feeling statements increased for the group receiving reinforcement for that category, and for the group receiving ordinary psychotherapy. For the group receiving reinforcement for statements without feeling content, the percentage of feeling statements decreased slightly, but the percentage of nonfeeling statements did not increase. The subjects did not express awareness of the reinforcement contingency. Thus, in this study, the verbal conditioning was at least as effective a procedure as traditional psychotherapy, perhaps a dubious distinction.

Ince [1968] offers a variation of the Williams and Blanton "verbal conditioning as psychotherapy" factorial design. It involves a return to the more "traditional" ABA single study design. An experimental setting was designed to replicate a psychotherapist's office, and subjects were seen daily. Variable interval reinforcement was employed to modify the rate of emission of positive self-reference statements. The results demonstrated that the verbal reinforcement exerted a definite, marked effect on the verbal behavior of the subjects. All subjects were conditioned to the schedules. Ince concludes that serious consideration should be given to the use of verbal conditioning in "actual psychotherapy." He even reports the anecdotal evidence of subjects reporting that they felt "much better" after the sessions because of the help they got in talking things over. It should be clear from this study that results in verbal conditioning studies emphasize the importance of the most minute therapist behavioral cues in controlling the "patients' " behaviors.

The fourth stage of development of these studies, which Kanfer labels the *expansion* stage, involves those studies investigating theoretical issues related to the capability of human beings for self-regulation.

These include processes such as vicarious learning, [Kanfer 1965a], the role of awareness in learning, [Krasner 1966], self-reinforcement and self-control [Kanfer & Marston 1963], and the associative relationship of words.

In perspective, it is clear that verbal conditioning studies are a research technique that developed as a combination of operant conditioning and clinical interests in verbal behavior. Many of the early investigators were interested in the process of psychotherapy, which during the early 1950s was primarily of the evocative model. Here, at last, it seemed as if operant conditioning offered a technique for setting up an analog of psychotherapy in a rigorously objective manner. It is clearer now that verbal conditioning and psychotherapy are not the *same* process, nor is one an analog of the other. However, some verbal conditioning does take place in evocative psychotherapy, and some of the relationship variables of the latter cannot, and should not, be eliminated from the former.

In an earlier paper [Krasner 1958], it was possible to cover the approximately thirty-five verbal conditioning studies then in the literature. Since then the number of verbal conditioning studies has increased to well over one thousand, and almost every conceivable variable in the situation has been investigated, often with contradictory findings. As these studies multiplied, it became obvious that the variables involved were very complex, and were not always adequately controlled. The major uncontrolled variable in these studies has been the examiner—his expectancies, biases, and the interactions of his "characteristics" with other variables of the situation. Studies investigating several variables at the same time have demonstrated complex interactional effects [Sarason & Minard 1963]. It has been this very sensitivity of verbal conditioning to the many variables of human interaction that has emphasized its usefulness as a research device.

These interactions can be illustrated by two studies, both relevant to psychotherapy. Sapolsky [1960] used the Schutz FIRO-B scale of interpersonal "needs" to determine the relative "compatibility" of two given individuals. He hypothesized that the influence process in verbal conditioning would be most effective when subjects (S's) and experimenters (E's) "needs" were "compatible" with each other. In one study, he assigned students as Ss and as Es on a basis of compatibility of personality "needs" for one group, and incompatibility of "needs" for another. During the acquisition period the compatible group was conditioned, but incompatible Ss-Es were not. During the extinction period (E out of room), compatible Ss did not extinguish in their use of reinforced pronouns, whereas incompatible Ss increased their use of the pronouns to the level obtained by the compatible Ss. A second similarly designed study used an experimental "set" of high personal "attraction" on the part of the Ss instead of compatibility. The resulting curves were almost identical with those in the first study. The implications of these studies are (1) the influencing process is most effective when the personality of the S and the E are "compatible"; (2) the influencing process is most effective when the S expects or has the "set" that he will like the E; (3) the influencing process, even with an incompatible E, is effective when he is physically removed, and (4) the relationship between S and E can be experimentally manipulated.

Taylor [1968] replicated part of these findings by investigating the relationship between *interpersonal orientation* as measured by the FIRO-B. The more "interpersonally" (positive) oriented the individual subject is, the more susceptible he is to verbal conditioning. Unfortunately this later study did not directly study interaction as such but only the orientation of the subject. The effects of the converse of a "positive" subject "attitude" has been also demonstrated; "hostile" examiners inhibit conditioning [Bryan & Lichtenstein 1966; Weiss, Krasner, & Ullmann 1960].

As we have emphasized, research in verbal conditioning, as with other operant approaches to human behavior, has offered an opportunity to explore the effects of manipulating and controlling relevant behavior influence variables (e.g., is verbal reinforcement more effective in producing change when administered by a, let's say, "warm," prestigeful examiner to an "extroverted" subject?). The source of hypotheses of what may be relevant variables for these studies have come from current "personality" theories, which has been a source of difficulty as evidenced by the fact that the findings of most studies using these traditional variables usually do not replicate.

It is necessary to approach human behavior by focusing on observing with "operant eyes" just how people perform in interpersonal situations. This kind of approach can be illustrated by the work of Goldiamond and Dyrud [1968]. They have explicitly extended the operant investigation of verbal behavior into the area of behavioral analysis of psychotherapy. They point out that "although words can now control machine behavior and computer processes, the major function served by verbal behavior, that is, its major consequence, is the control of the behavior of other people and ourselves" [p. 54]. They make the same kind of connection that many of the verbal conditioner experimenters have, namely, that there is a similarity between the operant conditioning strategy in research and that of the practitioner of psychotherapy.

Goldiamond and Dyrud argue that "If the transactions of psychotherapy can be translated into the observational and procedural terms of the experimental analysis of behavior, a corollary task is to utilize that representational system to describe the functional relations between dependent and independent variables in an ongoing therapy session and establish them where advisable" [p. 64]. The use of such language ties in with a literature of laboratory-derived procedures for the establishment, maintenance, and alteration of behavior. Goldiamond and Dryud then go on to explain that they

> . . . . decided to observe therapy sessions further, to ascertain the relevant transactive units and procedures employed in the change . . . . An example of such analysis is provided by a discussion after a session, when the observer asked the therapist if he was trying to provide certain possibilities for the patient. The therapist agreed that the analysis was correct. "Well," asked the observer, "why not state these openly." "Because I want the patient to find out for herself," was the answer. Rather than argue this point, both observer and therapist then decided to observe what therapist procedures defined "having the patient find out for herself." It turned out that the procedures employed were almost identical with operant abstraction training, in which stimuli are used which are intentionally multidimensional, rather than clearly occasioning the appropriate response [p. 64]. Much of the verbal conditioning research with nods and "uh-huhs" may be beside the point when it assumes that such reinforcers change behavior therapeutically. They may merely keep the patient talking and maintain the behaviors of going through the im-

plicit program. The brunt of the therapy may be borne by the content of the transactions. We have discovered in our research that our "uh-huhs" and nods, and many questions and statements, as well, merely serve to maintain behavior. When reinforcements are given which shape behavior these are quite often noticeable and quite rare [p. 83].

The patient has the undivided attention of the therapist, and the nods and "uh-huhs" may be merely conditioned reinforcers or discriminative stimuli accompanying such attention. The therapy session, with its questions, restatements and approval, may provide the patient with an opportunity to behave verbally; and Premack's investigations (1959), as well as extension by others, indicate the reinforcing power of the opportunity to behave. Goldiamond and Dyrud go on to argue that,

One of the questions we have addressed ourselves to is what behaviors this reinforcer, namely, the opportunity to talk at length, is contingent upon. One behavioral requirement involves using the language of the therapist. When the patient is speaking in one language, for example, is describing an experience in terms of his own feelings, a therapist with a different language, say, a behavioral one, may continually interrupt him and ask for a clarification which amounts to a redefinition in behavioral terms. The patient will soon come to talk in the behavioral language of the therapist [pp. 73–74].

These investigators report on their study of traditional psychotherapy as carried on by a psychoanalytically oriented psychotherapist. The assessment and observation of the "traditional" psychotherapeutic interaction via operant eyes represents a major extension of the approach described in this module [Ferster 1972].

On Generalization

One of the major questions that keeps arising with operant research, as with all behavior modification research, is that of "generalization." It is relatively easy to change behavior in an institutional setting or in a clinic office. But the evidence is equivocal that such changes carry over to meaningful situations in the real world. Investigators utilizing operant approaches have restructured the question of generalization so that it can be handled within its model. The question is not phrased as, "Does this behavior carry over to another situation?" but rather, "What behavior is desirable in this new situation?"

Although laboratory studies and individual case studies using operant procedures have to some extent attempted to approach problems of generalization (e.g., changing classroom behavior and measuring changes in behavior out of the classroom), most of the so-called token economy programs conducted in institutional settings have not attempted such measures. The token programs, in which desired behaviors are systematically rewarded by tokens which can be exchanged for tangible rewards or privileges, approach outside behavior change in a somewhat different manner. The goal of institutional change usually is to bring about such behavior that the individual will be able to function adequately in a situation outside the institution. In order to do that, the new extra-institutional situation must be analyzed to determine what behaviors are necessary in order that the individual may maximize social reinforcement for himself. What are the kinds of things a person can do so that he may present himself to others as a social stimulus that elicits positive reinforcement from them?

Rather than a generalized attempt to change behavior within the institution with the *hope* of subsequent change on the outside, it must first be determined what behaviors will "pay off" for the individual in a foster home, in his own home, or living with other patients in a community setting. For example, if the patient is to move into a home, living with other ex-patients, then the important behaviors to develop include cooking, housecleaning, shopping, management of money, gardening, and general maintenance of the appearance of the home. This latter is extremely important since it will elicit favorable response from neighbors who will perceive the ex-patient's efforts as enhancing property values rather than as a potential danger to the community.

At this point we will offer illustrations of operant procedures in various settings starting with the process of assessment, the first step in the actual application of modification techniques.

Assessment Procedures in the Operant Approach

Assessment may be considered as part of the operant procedure in a number of ways. One group of investigators argues that the operant approach opens the way to use behavioral principles in the assessment and classification of deviant behaviors [Ferster 1965; Kanfer & Saslow 1965; Sidman 1962]. A second linkage of operant approach with assessment procedures is to utilize the responsiveness to social reinforcement, as in a verbal conditioning study, as a means of predicting responsiveness to some other kind of behavior influence procedure [Krasner 1965; Patterson 1965]. Another variation is to view responsiveness to social reinforcement as an indicator or short-trial period of responsiveness to operant treatment procedures. Still another way of looking at this is to argue that there is a close interrelationship between assessment and the modification of behavior. Whatever assessment procedures are developed must be related to the actual operations in the treatment procedure [Mischel 1968].

Standard assessment procedures (such as the Rorshach) have limited usefulness in relation to operant techniques. An illustration of the development of new techniques would be Cautela's [1967] report of a Reinforcement Survey Schedule, which offers an opportunity for the client to assess the environmental events that he finds reinforcing.

Operant Approaches to Changing Disease Entities

An important element in the operant approach is the implicit, and often explicit, reconceptualization of what constitutes disease. From our point of view, this is an integral and necessary part of the operant approach, but not all investigators would agree.

Since we have discussed the more general aspects of the alternative implications of the disease versus social psychological models, we can now present illustrations of how this approach involved the literal breakdown of "disease entities" into component behaviors and the changing of these behaviors by manipulating their consequences. Implicit in Lindsley and Skinner's early operant studies is a view of schizophrenia as a collection of undesirable behaviors in terms of their social consequences for the individual. For example, Ullmann and Krasner [1969] point out that the key behavioral indicants for the label of schizophrenia are: disorganized thinking,

apathy, social withdrawal, and verbalizations that are bizarre or aversive to listeners. Within this framework they cite a series of operant studies designed to change specific behaviors of schizophrenia patients in each of these categories. In effect, this is an approach to treating schizophrenia by *changing its component behaviors*.

Disorganized Thinking

If we start with "disorganized thinking," subsumed under it would be tasks involving *abstract thinking*. An illustrative study is one by Meichenbaum [1966a] in which he reinforced the abstract interpretation of proverbs. He used four groups of schizophrenic patients. The first group, a "contingent positive" one, was given social reinforcement for appropriate and abstract interpretation of proverbs. A second group received noncontingent positive reinforcement; they received social reinforcement regardless of the quality of their response. The third group received contingent negative reinforcement whenever a vague, false, or absurd response was given (examples of negative reinforcement were "uh, uh"; "no"; and "poor"). The contingent positive group significantly increased the verbalization of abstract meanings as compared with the other three groups. In the control group, the experimenter remained neutral throughout. Further performance on a test of abstract thinking, the similarities test, significantly improved only in the contingent positive group. Thus, one important element subsumed under the rubric of disorganized thinking, that involving abstractions, could be modified.

Other studies using the verbal operant conditioning paradigm have directly manipulated other measures of disorganized thinking in experimental situations. Ullmann, Krasner, and Edinger [1964], working with schizophrenic patients whose total hospitalization averaged 15 years, obtained significant changes in a word association test by verbal conditioning common word associations. Panek [1967] also significantly influenced emission of common word associations by using tokens in a response contingent manner. In both of these studies, the investigators placed the behavior change in ability to give common word associations within the context of being indicative of a change in the ability to do abstract thinking.

Wagner [1968] also worked within the same conceptual framework. He examined the effects of training schizophrenics to *attend to* stimuli and to *respond* correctly to abstract discriminative stimuli under conditions of contingent and noncontingent reinforcement. An elaborate training procedure using contingent reinforcement was devised to reinforce "abstract responses." By these contingent reinforcement procedures he was able to significantly improve the abstractibility of the schizophrenic patients. Wagner concluded that his study demonstrated the modifiability of the schizophrenic's abstracting ability and "carr[ied] the implication that the extent to which corrective modification occurs is dependent upon the degree to which the training situation provides reinforcement for making abstracting responses" [p. 88].

Apathy

A second category of schizophrenic behavior that has been manipulated by operant conditioning procedures is *apathy*. Most observers would agree that schizophrenics are "apathetic" in appearance and behavior, but that is too molar a concept with which to work. How can the concept of apathy be differentiated into measurable and modifiable behaviors? One aspect of apathy involves verbal behavior. We could assume that the inability to verbalize emotionally toned statements is a form of apathy. In a series of verbal operant conditioning studies [Ullmann, Krasner, & Sherman 1963; Weiss, Krasner, & Ullmann 1963] the number of *emotional* words used by schizophrenic patients was significantly increased by contingent social reinforcement. Salzinger and his coworkers [Salzinger & Pisoni 1958; Salzinger, Portnoy, & Feldman 1964] reported similar results with conditioning positive self-reference statements.

A second aspect of apathy deals with motor behavior. Schaefer and Martin [1966] analyzed the apathy of schizophrenic patients as a *lack* of the kind of behavior that will elicit reinforcement from others. They worked with forty schizophrenic patients whose medical records indicated apathy in the pre-observation period. Based on observations of the patients' behavior on the ward, they concluded that the best measure of apathy was the *absence* of "concomitant" behavior—talking, singing, playing music, painting, reading, listening to others, listening to the radio, watching TV, engaging in group activity. The investigators decided that the target behavior for these patients should be the enhancement of these concomitant behaviors. If these behaviors could be changed, then it could be concluded that "apathy" was modifiable. The forty patients were divided into two groups of twenty each, experimental and control groups. Using token reinforcement with the experimental group, the target concomitant behaviors were significantly increased. Here again the operant conditioning significantly changed a series of "schizophrenic" behaviors.

Social Withdrawal

A third set of such behaviors can be labeled "social withdrawal." One of the first studies applying operant procedures to schizophrenic behaviors (after the initial Lindsley-Skinner series) was that of King, Armitage, and Tilton [1960] who performed a by-now classic, study of modifying the schizophrenic behavior of social withdrawal. Their approach involved the "shaping" of patient behavior starting with that behavior that was available and attempting to move it in the direction of what was deemed more socially desirable behavior. These investigators worked with schizophrenic patients assigned to four experimental groups of twelve each. The procedures included a recreation therapy group, an operant interpersonal group, a verbal therapy group, and a no-treatment control group. This last group was the experimental group representing the application of operant conditioning procedures. This study also was the first investigation using control groups as bases of comparison for operant procedures in a mental hospital. Further, most of the elements involved in the later development of the operant approach were present in this study. In fact, the very use of the term "interpersonal" in the descriptive label for the experimental group indicated a greater sensitivity to what is involved than many later studies.

There were three phases in the operant-interpersonal approach. In the first, the therapist demonstrated the use of a machine and its lever, which had to be pulled to obtain a reinforcement. The therapist modeled the procedure and then guided the participation of the patient to the point of putting a candy reinforcer in the patient's mouth, if necessary. In the second phase, the possible movements of the lever became more complex (for example, could be moved right and left, as well as toward and away). In the third phase, the therapist slowly introduced verbal behavior into the situation by giving directions toward the formulation of the problem. The therapist and patient began to work together as a team, first one doing something, then the other. Task-oriented verbal interactions were encouraged, such as "Who does what next?" Patients would also begin to work with each other. The therapist might even deliberately make a mistake so that the patient could point out the error. In effect, in the task-oriented situation, speech was highly relevant and reinforced. A basically simple situation became a complex, cooperative one. The investigators collected a series of measures of adjustment before and after therapy. All of the measures pointed to the operant-interpersonal technique as being more effective.

Bizarre Verbalization

A fourth area of deviant schizophrenic behavior is that of bizarre verbalization. Peculiar speech usually annoys other people who do not understand it and are often frightened by it. A major variant of bizarre speech is no speech at all, which is perhaps even more annoying and frightening to others. Thus the task of the therapist is either to modify the bizarreness of the speech or to help develop a verbal repertoire.

Wilson and Walters [1966] used three groups of four subjects each who had a very low rate of speech. The task for all subjects was to tell what was happening on slides that depicted everyday scenes. During the first session, all subjects were treated alike. The experimenter remained silent save for standard prompts. During sessions two through seven, two groups of subjects were exposed to a verbalizing *model,* an experimenter who talked rapidly and continuously about each slide. One of these two groups was reinforced with pennies for the production of words while the other was exposed to the model treatment only and did not receive the penny reinforcement. A third group received neither model nor response contingent reinforcement, but both this group and the model-only group received money at the end of each session so that take-home pay was held constant. The eighth session was a nonrein-

forcement session similar to the first. During sessions nine through fourteen all groups received modeling plus reinforcement, and the final two sessions, number fifteen and sixteen, were again nonreinforcement. The gain by the model-plus-reinforcement group produced a significant linear trend (upwards) and that of the model-only group approached statistical significance. The rate of speech in both the model-plus-reinforcement and the model-only groups decreased when the situation was returned to that of the first session. In trials nine through fourteen, there was a significant improvement for the model-plus-reinforcement group and the former control group, but, interestingly for future treatment strategies, not in the model-only group. The gains were maintained in session fifteen but all groups decreased in session sixteen. In summary, the production of words in the model-plus-reinforcement group quadrupled. Thus, to the extent that apathy involves a reduced output of words, this aspect of schizophrenia may be directly modified.

Another approach to the speech of the hospitalized schizophrenic patient deals with response contingent reinforcement aimed towards developing a type of speech likely to lead to societal approval. Ullmann and his colleagues [1965] performed the following experiment: Each of five experimenters saw twelve patients, four each in three conditions. The situation was a 20-minute, semistructured clinical interview. After a baseline period during which the interviewer made no response except to ask questions, the experimental conditions were instituted.

In one group, whenever the subject emitted "healthy talk" the examiner would smile, nod his head, and show approval. In the second group, the experimenter did the same thing whenever the patient emitted "sick talk." Healthy talk, in contrast to sick talk, was defined in terms of the verbalization of comfort rather than discomfort, liking or approach behavior as distinct from disliking and avoidance behavior, good physical and mental health as distinct from poor physical and mental health, personal assets rather than personal liabilities, presence rather than absence of motivation, realistic, nonpathological statements as distinct from bizarre ideation, and optimism, well-being, self-esteem, contentment, enthusiasm, and favorable perceptions of others rather than negative self-references, discontent, upset, and anxiety. A third group served as a control. In order to approximate the number of experimenter-emitted reinforcing stimuli without biasing the patient in either a sick talk or healthy talk direction, the experimenter emitted his approving behaviors whenever the patient used a plural noun. The results were that the group reinforced for healthy talk decreased in the percentage (sick talk divided by sick talk plus healthy talk) of sick talk, while the group reinforced for sick talk and the control group reinforced for plural nouns showed a tendency approaching statistical significance to increase the relative frequency with which they emitted sick talk. The differences among the groups were significant.

Two personality scales had been administered before the induction of experimental conditions. One of these was significantly correlated with the percentage of sick talk emitted during the baseline period, while one was not. There was a significant change when the tests were readministered after the interview period in the scale that had been correlated with the percentage of sick talk, while there was no significant postexperimental difference among the groups in the scale that had not been correlated with the target verbal class. In short, the relative rate of emission of aversive (grouch, gripe, and grotesque) talk could be directly manipulated and an effect was obtained on an independent test measure.

Further work, with a more restricted definition of "sick talk" in the direction of bizarre verbalization and with interviews on ten successive days, has been completed by Meichenbaum [1966b]. This work provided an elaborate series of checks on the transfer of improved verbal behavior under direct selective reinforcement to other tasks and people.

This review of a series of operant conditioning studies illustrates an approach to a medical classification such as schizophrenia via a breakdown of the label into component behaviors. This is not to imply that individuals with the label are "cured," but rather that these studies represent an illustration of an approach to modifying deviant behavior, which in turn offers an opportunity to break out of the disease model straightjacket.

Operant Approaches to Specific Disorders

By the early 1970's, there were very few, if any, specific types of behavioral disorders for which there were not at least several reports by investigators influenced by the operant approach. We have concentrated thus far on the major categories of deviant or maladaptive behavior such as schizophrenia, which was an early target of the operant approach. More recently the behaviors usually categorized under the diagnostic categories of "neuroses" or even the usual problem behaviors of living have been approached. Many of these earlier had been the targets of behavior therapists influenced by Wolpe [1958] and the respondent conditioning of Pavlov.

Examples of the later operant work are anxiety reduction [Anthony & Duerfeldt 1970], phobias [Leitenberg, Agras, & Thomson 1968], obesity [Moore & Crum 1969; Bernard 1968; Horan & Johnson 1971], improved study behavior [Jackson & Van Zoost 1972], addiction [O'Brien, Raynes, & Patch 1971], and depression [Lewinsohn, Weinstein, & Shaw 1969].

Case Reports

A number of reports based on the operant approach are essentially case studies, although they frequently involve some own-control procedures. These reports are significant because they suggest areas of investigation to which more carefully controlled research studies may be applied, and are of major use to practitioners who may utilize the specific technique.

An example is a study by Burgess [1969] on the application of contingency management to depressive behaviors. Burgess, following the implication of Ferster's [1966, 1973] view of depression as resulting from decreased reinforcement, argues that a broad class of active, task-oriented responses can be labeled as a performing behavior class. "Retarded motor-response rate, sad face and body appearances, and mournful verbalizations can be labeled a depressive behavior class. As the frequency of performing behaviors begins to diminish, the very absence of those behaviors becomes the occasion for reinforcement. Concurrent with the extinction of performing behaviors may be the conditioned acquisition of depressive behaviors" [p. 193]. It would follow from this analysis that the treatment procedures should involve the reversal of all contingencies. Reinforcement should be made contingent upon performing behaviors, and depressive behaviors that are not being responded to should extinguish.

Following this paradigm, Burgess reports on the treatment of six clients seen in a university counseling center. The treatment methods ran as follows: If the history of the individual indicated the loss of a specific reinforcer that was available, efforts to reinstate it were made. If reinforcement losses were more generalized or nonspecific, the client was required from the first to emit a few performing behaviors that required minimal effort for completion. The client's attention was brought to bear on the importance of successful completion rather than on the nature or value of the task. Task requirements gradually were increased so that behaviors accelerated in frequency, duration,and quality, and sucessively approximated former behaviors from the client's repertoire. If available, a mate was taught to augment treatment by providing reinforcement specified according to prescribed contingencies. Clients were seen daily for the first week to maximize therapist-reinforcing power and then seen with decreasing frequency as natural reinforcers began to become effective. Therapist attention and approval were used as reinforcers during the interviews as the clients reported either orally or in writing about their activities. No attention was paid to depressive behaviors after the first interview. It should be noted that techniques changed as a function of individual reinforcement histories, contingencies, and environmental components. Burgess concluded that,

> . . . contingency management, which promotes reinforcement for the completion of performing behaviors and extinction of depressive behaviors seems to be effective for the treatment of depression when reinstatement of a reinforcer cannot be accomplished. All clients were able to perform in their life situation with at least passable facility within three weeks of treatment inaguaration. Case reports, however, are not adequate to establish the efficacy of any treatment method. The need for controlled research is obvious [1968, p.199].

A variation of the case report is represented by more systematically own-control designed studies which also derive from the earlier operant investigations. They combine a research approach with clinical applications (a genuine "real life" problem). They use a baseline period that measures the target behavior before any attempt at modification is made

so as to provide a comparison point from which to measure the effectiveness of the procedure. These studies stress quantification and measurement of behavior, often with the individual involved trained to quantify his own behavior. The ABA, off-on-off design is usually used. Social influence procedures are usually used in such a way as to maximize the likelihood of the operant procedures working. In addition, there is usually a follow-up over a period of some time, and there is some attempt to determine if there have been changes in other behaviors that may be related to the target behaviors; they may move directly into the home of the subject to set the conditions for change.

A prototype of these studies, and one of the most interesting and ingenious of them, is Stuart's report [1969]. The design was an own-control one with a baseline period, a treatment period, and then a follow-up report. The general framework was that of treatment of marital problems. Stuart presents certain assumptions about the character of marital interaction upon which his treatment procedure rests. These assumptions are important because they lay the basis for the extension of the operant approach into the everyday activities of individuals seeking help in an outpatient setting. Stuart assumes that the exact pattern of interaction which takes place between a husband and his wife at any point in time is the most rewarding of all the currently available alternatives. While the specifics may vary for each couple, most married adults expect to enjoy reciprocal relations with their partners. In order to modify an unsuccessful marital interaction, it is essential to develop the power of each partner to mediate rewards for the other. Based upon this formulation, the "operant interpersonal approach" (a term which Stuart uses in a manner similar to that of King, Armitage, and Tilton [1960]), seeks to construct a situation in which the frequency and intensity of mutual positive reinforcement is increased. The treatment procedure follows from this assumption in a logical manner.

The first step is to train the couple in the logic of the approach. The next step is to ask each of the two partners to list the three behaviors that each would like to accelerate in the other. Even this phase comprises elements of training, that of training people in the ways of observing and conceptualizing a behavioral sequence. The third step is to train each individual to transfer the observed data onto a graph on which each person is to keep a record of the other's positive behavior. Step four consists of working out a series of exchanges of desired behaviors. "The typical couple complain of a 'lack of communication' which is a euphemism for a failure to reinforce each other" [p. 628]. At this point Stuart introduced a token system into the home situation. Stuart reports on the use of such a system with four couples who had sought treatment in a last effort to avoid a divorce. One behavior much desired by the wives was to have their husbands converse with them more fully. The wives were instructed to purchase a timer and to give the husband a token after each hour in which the husband talked with his wife for a sufficient time to meet her criterion. However, an important part of the procedure was that within the first 30 minutes the wife had to provide her husband with cues as to his performance if it was unsatisfactory. If she failed to do this he had to be given a token at the end of the hour, even if he did not perform adequately. With the four couples, tokens were redeemable at the husband's request "from a menu stressing physical affection." [p. 678]. A different "menu" was constructed for each couple that took into account the baseline level of sexual activity, the desired level of activity, and the number of hours available for non-sexual (conversational) interchange. On this basis, husbands were charged three tokens for kissing, and/or "lightly petting" with their wives, five tokens for "heavy petting," and fifteen tokens for intercourse. The results indicated that, as compared with baseline measures, the "rates of conversation and sex increased sharply after the start of treatment and continued through 24 and 48 week followups" [p. 680]. The participants were asked to fill out inventories about their own satisfaction and their perception of their spouse's satisfaction in marriage. These reports indicated a great increase in self-satisfaction and satisfaction with the spouse as the behaviors changed. The actual number of sessions which were held with the therapist (by each individual couple) were only seven.

This study emphasizes most of the major points about the operant approach. In effect, the individual is trained so that he is able to provide new stimuli to the key people in his life so as to elicit different behaviors from them. "Each spouse was directed in specific modifications of his own behavior in an effort to modify the behavioral environment in which his partner's behavior occurred" [p. 680]. Actually the therapist did not introduce anything really new in terms of behavior. Stuart points out that he merely suggested behaviors, which had doubtless been requested, cajoled, and demanded by each party many times in the past. In that sense they were not of a different order than the many items of behavior that pay off for a hospitalized patient in a token economy (in the one instance conversing more, in the other self-grooming). But in this instance the therapist clarified and spelled out the contingencies involved. He introduced the clear expectation of change in the partners and, most important of all, took the situation out of a coercive context. In the home situation when a request is put in the form of a demand, which is what had been occuring in these families, then adherence to the request involves the reinforcing of "demands," something usually held to be undesirable by most people. The importance of the gamelike qualities that the therapist gave to the treatment should not be ignored. In fact, the game was termed "prostitution" because Stuart felt that all games must have names and prostitution appealed to the fantasies of all concerned.

An Operant Approach to Depression

Although depression has been one of the more recent target behaviors for the operant approach, once the concept was reconceptualized in behavioral terms, most of the standard operant approaches have been utilized in influencing depressive behavior. The decrease of positive reinforcement in the origin and maintenance of depression has previously been reported [Lazarus 1968; Lewinsohn, Weinstein, & Shaw 1969]. Ferster [1973] offered a cogent behavioral analysis of depression that linked the onset of depression with other behaviors resulting from a deficit or loss of reinforcement.

An illustration of how the operant investigator approaches depression is that of Hersen and his colleagues [1973], who utilized a "token economy" to influence "neurotic depression." During an earlier study, these workers had used token reinforcement procedures on an experimental psychiatric ward consisting of patients who were young veterans. They found a two-fold increase in the sheer output of behavior when compared with productivity in baseline periods. During the course of that study, the clinical staff observed that patients bearing diagnoses of "depression" appeared markedly less depressed during contingency management phases. Moreover, depressed patients reported to staff that when they were involved in token-economy activities, they tended to "obsess" less about themselves, and felt that there was an improvement in their condition.

By increasing the patient's activity level (e.g., hospital job tasks, occupational therapy, etc.) via contingent reinforcement, an increased range of social contact was provided. Increased social stimulation probably permitted both the elicitation and reinforcement of target responses of talking, smiling, and activity level. By contrast, in baseline conditions, patients decreased their involvement in social situations, thus restricting the availability of reinforcement.

Examples of Operant Applications

An example of the extension of the operant approach to more general problems of living (as against the more serious disorders with which the operant group initially coped) is that of inefficient "study habits." The interest in study habits arose because there appeared to be good evidence of a close relationship between study habits and academic performance.

Jackson and Van Zoost [1972] reported a study in which forty-seven university freshmen were randomly assigned to two reinforcement conditions, self-administered reinforcement and external reinforcement, and to two control groups, no reinforcement and no treatment. All treatment subjects viewed identical videotaped presentations on study skills that included exercises, but the experimental groups varied in the way in which they could earn back a $10 deposit. For both reinforcement conditions, a significant gain in study habits was found that was maintained over a four-month follow-up. The study was repeated with thirty-five students including upperclassmen, assigned to the three treatment groups. All subjects showed significant increases in study habits. However, no condition produced a gain in academic performance beyond chance. The authors then conclude that the lack of significant differences in grades for people whose study habits improve would lead to the "obvious conclusion that there is

more to academic output than knowledge about study skills" [p. 195].

The importance of this illustration is that operant-reinforcement techniques are generally effective in changing a specific behavior. However, generally assumed relationships between two sets of behavior may be oversimplification and not hold up in terms of assumed one-to-one relationships. A priori, it certainly seemed that study habits and grades should be related. But, as in most sets of human behaviors, the relationship is quite complex and the belief that if you change one, and only one, then the other would automatically change has to be sharply questioned.

It should be noted that there are studies that do demonstrate a change in study habit performance can influence change in grades. For example, Benecki and Harris [1972] utilized a self-control, self-reinforcement, and self-punishment procedure to improve study habits. Subjects receiving the lessons showed a significant gain in grade-point average for the three semesters following the study when compared with those not receiving the lessons.

The field of physical rehabilitation offers an excellent opportunity for the operant approach because of the types of motor behavior involved. Further, much of the behavior modification must be done "in the field," in the hospital, or in the home where the handicapped individual lives. The term "rehabilitation," of course, has a wide range of meaning, covering as it does both the physically and socially handicapped. Several studies illustrate the range of operant applicants in this field of problem behavior.

Ince [1968] reported the application of the standard operant conditioning procedures to modify the behavior of two disabled individuals without the use of laboratory facilities or sophisticated equipment." In both instances the specific disabling behaviors were measured for baseline, a reinforcement procedure was introduced, and change in performance was measured. In one instance the target behavior was "ambulation" (walking from 5 to 20 feet, and making various turns) in a patient suffering from Parkinson's disease. The second behavior was "typing" by a young girl suffering from a disease involving loss of control of muscles and limbs. In both instances the reinforcement was a verbal statement such as "very good." The performance of the target behavior in both cases significantly improved, and increased self-confidence was manifested by other positive behavioral changes. Ince concludes cautiously,

> There were probably variables other than the specific reinforcements at work in both cases which it was not possible to control for. Perhaps social reinforcement from family and friends played a role. Perhaps practice can account, at least in part, for the effects obtained. Further work obviously needs to be done along these lines. I would like to make one more point, namely that despite disabilities which at first appear beyond modification, either because of their apparent severity or because of the nature of the setting, there is much that can be done for the disabled person using behavior modification techniques [p. 10].

Zimmerman and his associates [1969] also reported the application of operant approaches to a community sheltered workshop setting and to the problem of increasing productivity in multiply handicapped clients. Sixteen clients who were participating in a special prevocational training program for hard-core handicapped people served as the subjects of the investigation. Clients admitted to the prevocational training program had either been previously denied entrance into a workshop program because of poor prognosis for productive employment or had been exposed to previous workshop experiences and had failed to make satisfactory progress. Twelve of the sixteen clients were exposed to a set of preliminary procedures designed to give them experience receiving and exchanging tokens (point cards) for tangible goods and services. These clients together with four additional clients were subsequently exposed as a group to a series of successive control and experimental conditions designed to assess the effects of token reinforcement on productivity. While the sixteen clients were treated as a group with respect to the introduction and removal of experimental conditions, each client served as his own control in the sense that he received token reinforcement that was programmed on the basis of his own recent work history. Throughout the investigation, the clients worked five days a week for six hours a day. The twelve clients exposed to the preliminary procedures, and later all sixteen clients, worked daily in a 500-square-foot area of the Industrial Services (subcontract) Department. This area, immediately adjacent to the offices of two of the work supervisors, contained six work tables, and two to four clients worked at a given table. A materials handler provided the work materials and monitored the number of work units completed throughout each day. Each client worked on a given job throughout the investigation. All but one of the clients performed each day on a Western Electric terminal board assembly task, while the remaining client folded Goodwill bags.

Fifteen clients were assigned to two weeks of token training procedures. Then they were put on a work contingent program that related work performance to receipt of tokens. There was a period of alternation between contingent and noncontingent reinforcement and a return to baseline. The authors concluded that work contingent token reinforcement can significantly increase productivity, that the removal of token reinforcement can lead to a significant decrease in productivity, and that factors other than token reinforcement contingencies can also significantly increase productivity. The first two results systematically replicated results previously obtained by other investigators with other groups of handicapped people and in other settings. The third result suggested that factors other than token reinforcement contingencies can significantly contribute to results obtained in token reinforcement studies and, thus, investigators using such an approach should consider employing additional control conditions besides those which involve the removal of token reinforcement or token contingencies.

Henderson and his group at Spruce House [Henderson & Scoles 1970; Henderson 1969] report a token economy program which, while having many of the features of the Zimmerman program, had certain other features. The program was designed to differ from a state hospital in three ways: it was operated in a non-stigmatizing "house" rather than in a mental hospital; it undertook to strengthen social and vocational coping behaviors which were often punished within the typical state hospital setting. The emphasis at Spruce House was on the modification of overt behavior through a system of rewards. Adaptive vocational and social behavior and counter-symptomatic behavior were reinforced, and maladaptive behavior was ignored. The social responses of staff members and other patients were made contingent on adaptive or desirable social behaviors by the patient. Behavior revealing delusions or hallucinations was ignored, and social approach responses were socially reinforced.

For regressed patients, primary reinforcers such as candy and cigarettes were used. For example, a patient was given candy when he was working and not when he was standing about. A patient on a reading program was given a piece of candy for every so many words that he read successfully, with this rate of "payment" specified to him in advance. Another part of the system was based on secondary reinforcing tokens, called "grickles," which were earned by patients for appropriate vocational or social behavior and were then exchanged for meal extras, candy, passes, phone calls, and special privileges.

A work-habituation program was constructed hierarchically. Work projects were conducted six mornings and three afternoons a week. Jobs that required the least initiative or interpersonal competence yielded the smallest token payments. With successive promotions, jobs required greater responsibility, independence, and interaction with others, and the pay was correspondingly higher. Promotion was ordinarily accomplished by earning the maximum available number of grickles for the job previously held. Consistent performance within a job was brought about by the awarding of bonuses at the end of each work period, at the end of each work day, and at the end of each work week. Social program activities were conducted three afternoons and six evenings a week. They included dances, athletics, field trips, role playing, discussion groups, crafts and games. Within the experimental facility, some activities involved only residents and staff, others involved volunteers from the community. Still other activities were held within the community itself. Token reinforcements were awarded for participation in an activity and for social responses at four different levels. The least token reinforcement attached to nonsocial participation in an activity. Superficial conversation with other persons, interpersonal transactions indicative of "social involvement," and the occurrences of initiative or role modeling resulted in successively higher token payments. Residents who engaged in interesting conversations with community persons were paid bonuses in order to foster the transition of the resident into the community.

The results of these studies are similar to those of other operant studies. Based on the first thirteen months of its operation Henderson concludes that the general hospitals return subjects to the community more rapidly than Spruce House does, but that a larger proportion of Spruce House subjects are employed once they return to the community than those returned from other facilities.

Token Economy Programs

Token economy programs are the most recent illustration and culmination of the operant conditioning approach. They are a good example of the point made throughout this module that the operant techniques cannot be separated from a more general social influence approach. The critique and evaluation of these studies will differ if they are considered solely as operant conditioning, or if they are put in a social influence context.

Basic Elements of Token Economy Programs

Token economy may be defined in terms of the operation involved in planning for it, setting it up, and carrying it out. First, there is systematic *observation* of the *behavior* of the people for whom the program is intended and the *consequences* of this behavior in the specific situation in which it is occurring. This may be in the classroom, on a hospital ward, in the home, or in the community. The unit of observation goes beyond the specific act of an individual to include the response elicited from the environment by the behavior. Thus it is insufficient to observe that a child "left his seat." The full observational unit is that the child left his seat, the teacher said, "Go back to your seat," three children laughed, and another child started to leave his seat.

Second, there is the *designation* of certain specific behaviors as *desirable,* hence reinforceable. On a hospital ward, this may include such behaviors as dressing oneself or making a bed; or in a classroom, staying in one's seat or raising a hand. These behaviors are usually those that someone (the teacher, ward nurse, or the individual) determines are socially useful and of initial low frequency. Later we shall stress the value decisions implicit in deciding that a certain behavior (e.g., staying in one's seat) is desirable.

The third element is the determination of what environmental events may serve as *reinforcers* for the individual. What are the good things in life for these individuals? What are they willing to work for? For the hospitalized adult, it may include a bed, a pass, or a chance to sit in a favorite chair. For the child in the classroom, it may include candy, toys, or a chance to go on an interesting trip.

The fourth element is the *medium of exchange,* the token, which connects elements two and three. The token *stands for* the backup reinforcer. It can act as a discriminative or reinforcing stimulus, or both. The token may be a tangible object such as a plastic card or a green stamp that one can handle, or it may be a mark on a piece of paper, or a point scored, which the individual knows is there but to which he has no direct access. Despite the label of *token* economy, the tokens themselves are merely a gimmick, a training device to help teachers and others included in the classroom (or hospital ward) to learn how to observe behavior and its consequences, how to use their own behavior in a reinforcing manner, how to respond contingently, and how to arrange the environment to maximize the possibility of the individual child (or patient) receiving reinforcing stimuli at the appropriate time.

The fifth element is the *exchange rules.* The planning of a token economy must specify the economic relationship between the amount of tokens an individual may earn and the cost of the good things in life. If a person can earn only (at most) ten tokens a day and the cheapest item he can purchase costs one hundred tokens, the system will not work. Conversely, if he can earn one hundred tokens and he can take care of all his desires for only ten tokens, this system will not work either. We must take into consideration the economic constraints that determine the values and effects of specific reinforcers.

The goals of a token program are to develop behaviors that will lead to social reinforcement from others, enhance the skills necessary for the individual to take a responsible social role in the institution and eventually to live successfully outside the hospital. Basically the individual learns that he can control his own environment in such a way that he will elicit positive reinforcement from others.

Staats [1965] was one of the first to use *tokens* to replace primary reinforcers in an experiment designed to help in training reading discrimination in children. In his study, the children's responses were reinforced with marbles, which were exchangeable for various backup reinforcers. Staats reported that there were scheduling effects that depended upon the way in which tokens and backup reinforcers were related in addition to the schedules involving the manner in which tokens were made contingent upon the behavior of the individual.

Ayllon and his colleagues [Ayllon 1963; Ayllon & Haughton 1962, 1964; Ayllon & Michael 1959] reported a series of applications of operant principles to a mental hospital setting. These represented dramatic illustrations of the ABA design and opened the way for introduction of the more encompassing token economy program.

Ayllon and Azrin [1965] reported on the results of the first application of a token economy to a psychiatric hospital ward. The behaviors selected for reinforcement included such things as serving meals, cleaning floors, sorting laundry, washing dishes, and self-grooming. Reinforcement consisted of the opportunity to engage in activities that had a high level of occurrence when freely allowed. The reinforcers selected were part of the naturalistic environmental context.

Ayllon and Azrin made no a priori decisions about what might be an effective reinforcer for schizophrenic patients. Instead, their approach involved the observation of patients' behavior to discover what patients *actually did*. They applied the general principle expressed by Premack [1959] that any behavior with a high frequency of occurrence can be used as a reinforcer. Thus, the reinforcers included such things as having a room available for rent; selecting people with whom to dine; passes; a chance to speak to the ward physician, chaplain, or psychologist; opportunity to view TV; or obtaining candy, cigarettes, and other amenities of life. Tokens served as *acquired* reinforcers that bridge the delay between behavior and an ultimate reinforcement. The investigators placed particular emphasis on the objective definition and quantification of the responses and reinforcers, and upon programming and recording procedures.

Ayllon and Azrin reported a series of six experiments. In each they demonstrated that target behavior *systematically* changed as a function of the token reinforcement. One experiment is typical of the procedures developed by these investigators. The response in which they were interested consisted of off-ward work assignments. A patient would select from a list of available jobs and receive tokens for the one which he preferred. After ten days he was told that he could continue working on his job, but there would be *no* tokens for the work. Of the eight patients involved, seven immediately selected another job that had previously been nonpreferred. The eighth patient switched a few days later. In the third phase of the experiment, the contingencies were reversed and the preferred jobs led to tokens. All eight patients immediately switched back to their original jobs.

The results of the six experiments demonstrated that the reinforcement procedure was effective in maintaining desired performance. In each experiment the performance fell to a near zero level when the established response-reinforcement relation was discontinued. On the other hand reintroduction of the reinforcement procedure restored performance almost immediately and maintained it at a high level.

The Ayllon and Azrin token economy functioned on a ward in a midwestern state hospital with a population of long-term female patients. Another token economy program [Atthowe & Krasner 1968; Krasner 1968] was set up in a Veteran's Administration Hospital in California with male patients averaging fifty-eight years of age and a median length of hospitalization of twenty-four years. Most of these patients had been labeled chronic schizophrenics and the remaining had an organic label. As a group, their behavior was apathetic and indifferent, manifested by inactivity, dependency, and social isolation. The procedures used were similar to those developed by Ayllon and Azrin. However, one of the major differences was in the amount of total control exerted by the experimenters. The Atthowe and Krasner program was designed to be an *open* ward on which patients could come and go, *if,* of course, they had the right number of tokens for the gatekeeper. The token economy had to compete with the extra-ward economy that used dollars and cents as their tokens. Many kinds of economic problems had to be faced. To cope with these problems, special procedures had to be developed, such as a banking system to foster savings, a monthly discount rate to cut down hoarding, and names on tokens to prevent stealing.

Prior to the introduction of tokens, most patients refused to go to any of the activities available to them

and showed little interest in their environment. The patients sat or slept on the ward during the day. In effect, their behavior represented the end point of years of shaping of compliant and apathetic institutional behavior. The investigating team decided that there were better things in life for these people to do than to sit and waste away their lives. Among the valued things were: enacting the role of responsible people who are adept at self-grooming, keeping living facilities clean, dressing neatly, holding a job, and interacting with other people. Responsibility also involved their being responsive to normal social reinforcement. Thus each time tokens were given they were accompanied by social reinforcement, such as the phrases, "Good," "I'm pleased," "Fine job," and an explicit statement as to the contingencies involved, e.g., "You received three tokens because you got a good rating from your job supervisor."

This token economy program was a significant success as measured by changes in specified behavior, observer's ratings, and reactions of hospital staff. The changes in behaviors, such as attendance at group activity, were a function of the number of tokens (value) given for the activity. Group attendance increased as more tokens were given for them and then decreased as the "pay off" returned to its previous value.

The greatest changes were in the appearance and atmosphere of the ward and in the staff expectations of what the patients were capable of doing. The token program had an enormous effect on the attitudes of staff throughout the hospital. The staff found that they could have a therapeutic effect on patient behavior by the kinds of acts they performed. Staff morale increased and it became a matter of prestige to work on the token ward. Finally, in the hospital where the Atthowe and Krasner program was underway, two additional wards adopted similar token economies as a way of life because of its apparent usefulness in changing patient behavior.

Winkler [1970] reported on the results of a token economy program that had many of the same features as that of the earlier programs with some additional novel features. Winkler's program was established in a closed female ward in Gladesville Hospital, New South Wales, Australia, with patients averaging forty-nine years of age and twelve years of hospitalization. The patients' behavior was characterized by an excessive amount of violence and screaming, as well as apathy and general lack of response to the ward environment. Winkler gave particular emphasis to economic factors. For example, prices and wages were initially arranged so that the patients' average daily income tended to exceed their average daily expenditure. This basic economic fact of life, that income must equal or exceed outgo, is probably necessary for a viable economy. However, the economic aspects of token economy may be in dispute, just as a Keyesian approach in our broader society may differ from a more standard conservative approach.

Winkler reported a significant improvement in staff morale as indicated by a drop in absenteeism. Absenteeism in the four months after the program began was 24 percent below the absenteeism for the four months before the program, while in a comparable ward, absenteeism over the same periods dropped only 3 percent. This emphasizes, as is clear in every study, that staff morale as mediated by the training program is a necessary ingredient in an operant program. It usually occurs when the staff gets feedback as to the effectiveness of its procedures.

Without exception, Winkler reported improvement in every type of behavior that was reinforced. In addition, behaviors that were not specifically in the program, such as violence and loud noise, decreased. Winkler also carried out a number of studies designed to determine whether the patients' behavior were really under control of the tokens. In one experiment tokens for shoe cleaning were stopped for three weeks and then reintroduced. There was an immediate decrease of this behavior with a discontinuation of tokens and an immediate increase when they were reintroduced. Similar results occurred with other behaviors.

Winkler [1968b] reported on the third phase of his program, which was concerned with the effect on behavior and the relationships between the number of tokens in the patients' possession, the system's economic balance, and amount of reinforcement (wages). At any one time, a token system can be regarded as having a certain economic balance. This balance may be regarded as the discrepancy between total patient income (i.e., the total number of tokens given to the patients) and total patient expenditure (i.e., the total number of tokens spent). Under normal circumstances in a token system, the economic balance determines the speed with which patients accumulate tokens, and hence is involved in determining the number of tokens in the patients' possession at any one time. This variable was called savings. If income consistently exceeds expenditure over a period of time, savings will automatically increase, and if expenditure exceeds income, savings will decrease.

Both economic balance and savings are affected by many different factors in a token system, but they are perhaps most strongly affected by changes in wages and changes in prices.

Studies were designed to separate savings from economic balance in order to examine whether savings did affect token earning behavior. Savings and economic balance were manipulated independently. Savings were manipulated by abruptly changing the currency used in the system. For three weeks a new token was made the only legitimate currency, and the old tokens were useless until the three weeks ended. In effect, savings were abruptly reduced to zero for all patients. Simultaneously all prices were dropped to one token, wages remaining unchanged. Expenditure was therefore lowered and economic disequilibrium, with income exceeding expenditure, occurred. Under the usual token system such a disequilibrium would not occur without high savings. But with the new tokens the disequilibrium coincided initially with low savings. Hence if savings and not economic balance were affecting performance, token-earning behavior would improve rather than deteriorate. Thus, it was hoped that the disequilibrium created by reduced prices would be held as constant as possible during the three-week experimental period. This would automatically insure savings, would increase rapidly and steadily while the economic balance was constant, and so provide a further test of the relationship between savings and token earning behavior.

In six of the seven token-earning behaviors, mean daily performance in the first week of the experiment was higher than the baseline performance. The percentage improvements ranged from 2 to 52 percent, indicating that despite the disequilibrium favoring income, the drop in savings coincided with improved performance. Tidy appearance was the only behavior that did not improve. In six of the seven token-earning behaviors, mean daily performance in the first week of the experimental period was superior to mean daily performance in the third week of the experiment when savings were high. In the third week, six of the seven behaviors had deteriorated from 16 to 44 percent below the initial baseline. Getting up was the only behavior not to deteriorate increasingly. If savings were controlling behavior, then the behavioral deterioration to a level below the baseline would indicate that savings in the third week of the experimental period exceeded savings prior to that period.

This first experiment then indicated a close relationship between savings and token-earning behavior. Behavior under low savings was better than behavior under high savings and reduction in savings improved behavior. The improvement in behavior when the economic balance was altered in favor of income and the change in behavior during the three weeks of disequilibrium suggest that the economic balance does not affect behavior directly, but through the way it affects savings. Changes in economic balance may operate on behavior in other ways but the present study suggests that one important way in which changes in balance affect behavior is the way they affect savings.

Winkler concluded that these two analyses suggest that the process by which savings control behavior involves more than a simple fluctuation in primary deprivation level. The failure of savings to be affected by prices suggests that savings may operate to some extent independently of what they can buy, and the absence of a drop in purchasing with low savings suggests that the patients were working harder to avoid the loss of rewards rather than being motivated by an actual deprivation. Further analysis of the relationship between token deprivation and primary deprivation should clarify these issues.

Another variation of experimental design in token programs was reported by Lloyd and Garlington [1968]. Seven types of behavior of thirteen chronic schizophrenic female patients were rated during four experimental phases. During conditions 1 and 3, the patients were giving a token allowance in the morning on a noncontingent basis. During conditions 2 and 4, tokens were paid on a contingent basis, that is, the patients received tokens commensurate with the ratings of their behavior (e.g., neatness, bedmaking, eating habits). These ratings were higher during conditions 2 and 4 than during conditions 1

and 3. The authors concluded that *contingent* tokens were controlling the behavior of the patients.

This kind of design is more sophisticated than the simpler off-on-off (ABA) in that the B part is not the usual reversal of procedures that would be involved if the alternative to tokens were simply no tokens. Rather, the tokens received remained constant, but the variable being tested most relevantly is that of contingency. Thus the B part of the design becomes *noncontingent* tokens rather than no tokens.

Other successful token economy programs with adult psychiatric patients have been reported by Steffy and his colleagues [1969], Gericke [1965], and others cited in this section. Token economy programs have been extended to other groups of individuals including mental retardates, delinquents, adolescents, and classroom behavior problems. Krasner and Atthowe [1968] offer a bibliography of over fifty reports of token programs in various parts of the world.

However, the effects of the token economy must be evaluated critically in a research context, just as other operant procedures must be. The problems in doing token economy research are as complex as in any other area of investigation involving human behavior change, and perhaps more so. Institutional research is particularly difficult because of the problems involved in controlling relevant variables. Most evidence from research in mental hospitals would point to the fact that some change in the behavior of patients can be brought about by almost any program involving some kind of "total push." The enthusiasm, positive expectation, increased and more focused attention and interest of the staff brought about by participation in a prestigeful research program all provide additional and massive amounts of social reinforcement that is likely to bring about and maintain new and desirable patient behavior. The goal of the research investigator using a token economy is to demonstrate first, significant behavioral change, and, second, that the change is a function of the specific techniques involved in the token program.

The token economy program, insofar as research techniques are concerned, may be divided into four categories.

1. Those programs that are primarily demonstrational projects, and in which no attempt is made to control variables. Although change may be observed, it is difficult to attribute it to the tokens, per se. Many of the programs reported belong in this category.

2. Those programs using base rate and own controls, essentially the ABA design. Measurement is taken of the operant rate of patient behaviors for a specific period of time. The token program is introduced and the same behaviors continue to be measured. The token contingencies may be removed and again the behavior continues to be measured. Then the token contingencies are reintroduced. The Ayllon and Azrin program is an illustration of this. Atthowe and Krasner changed the value (number of tokens given) of various activities and measured change in rate of performance. For example, this is illustrated by the change in rate of patient attendance in group activities as the rate of tokens increased from one to two and back again to one.

3. The effectiveness of the token economy procedure is tested by the use of control groups that receive either no specific treatment or a different treatment. A study by Marks, Sonoda, and Schalock [1968] illustrates this approach. They worked with twenty-two chronic schizophrenic males who were divided into eleven matched pairs based on rated hospital adjustment. One member of each pair was assigned to Group A, called "reinforcement therapy," and the other patient of the pair was assigned to Group B, called "relationship therapy." In Group A each patient received poker chips as tokens for individual specified behaviors. The cost of meals was ten tokens per meal. Initially the reinforced behaviors were selected by the staff. Later the goals were frequently set by the patients themselves. Selected behaviors were tailored to the individual and his progress. One man might be rewarded for simply receiving and paying tokens, another for improving his appearance, another for discussing discharge plans with a social worker, another for expressing feelings. The relationship therapy (Group B) was designed to enlarge and deepen the patient's self-understanding and self-acceptance by daily psychotherapy meetings. The nine therapists involved avoided giving social reinforcement at the appearance of specific behaviors. Each subject received both forms of treatment for approximately ten weeks

each. To assess these therapies, eighteen pre- and post-measures were taken. Most of these measures included work, social, and conceptual performance. The authors concluded that both therapies were effective in improving the behavior of chronic hospitalized patients. However, reinforcement therapy was more *economical* of staff time. They concluded also that "reinforcement can be used in a 'psychodynamic' way. It can be used to shape self-assertive, critical, and dominating behaviors as well as the more conforming ones. Under both therapies there are more evidences of changes in behavioral efficiency than of changes in self-regard or personality structure" [p. 401].

4. Performance in the token economy program is related to performance in another learning task. Panek [1967] worked with thirty-two chronic schizophrenics from the Atthowe-Krasner ward. He conditioned common word associations from the Kent-Rosanoff and Russell-Jenkins lists with positive and negative contingencies of verbal and token reinforcement. The study then compared success in learning of word associations with total number of total ward token transactions. This latter figure was taken as a measure of the responsivity to reinforcement, that is, the patient who *earned* the most tokens and *spent* the most tokens was considered most *responsive* to the token program. The results showed significant increase of common word associations under either positive (saying "right" and giving a fractional ward token) or negative (saying "wrong" and taking away a fractional ward token) reinforcement, but there were no significant differences under the two contingencies. Most important, learning-rate rankings were significantly correlated with rankings of total token usage. This is one of the few studies that have demonstrated that the individual who is responsive in one conditioning task, such as a token economy, is also responsive in an individual verbal conditioning task. This suggests the possibility of utilizing the conditioning task as a predictor for response to token-type reinforcement programs. It also relates to a previous series of studies [Krasner, Ullmann, & Fisher 1964; Krasner, Knowles, & Ullmann 1965] which demonstrated that verbal conditioning of "attitudes" in one task was significantly correlated to performance in another task requiring motor performance.

Impact on Ward Staff

A good description of the impact of a token economy on the behavior of ward staff has been provided by McReynolds and Coleman [1972]:

> Favorable changes in both on ward and off ward staff attitudes toward patients as a result of a year's involvement in the token program is an encouraging, if not especially surprising, finding. Also impressive to the present observers, though difficult to measure systematically, are the qualitative changes in patient-staff interactions evident in the increased frequency of mutual smiles and other verbal and non-verbal communications of concern. Such changes in staff attitudes and behavior appear to relate to a number of aspects of their involvement in the token economy. First, training seminars and lectures were carefully focused to influence staff thinking about the treatment and treatability of patients. As such the training procedures themselves represent an attitude change procedure. More importantly, however, the effects of the reinforcement procedures were readily and repeatedly observed by staff. The limited but meaningful nature of initial target behavior made it easy for ward staff to judge the effects of the token reinforcement procedures. That is, the proof of the treatability of the patients and the efficacy of the token reinforcement was obvious to each staff member. Also important in this "see-for-yourself" aspect of token economy is the focus on appropriate patient behavior as part of the reinforcement procedures as opposed to the usual crisis-only policy of attending only to those patients who are disturbing other patients, staff or ward tranquility. Thus, token reinforcement procedures produced a significant change in the input of information on typical patient behavior received by staff, information capable of reversing the latters' opinion and attitudes about patient capabilities. Lastly, the reinforcement in the form of praise and attention given to the token ward from both inside and outside the hospital served to further identification with the token program and engender feeling of pride in both their role as *treatment* personnel and their patients as legitimate, worthwhile therapy candidates [p. 33].

The Growth of Token Economies

There has been a sharp increase in the range and scope of token economy programs in recent years. Most have followed the pattern of the earlier programs, but there have been some unique features developed. Kazdin [1971] reported on a token rein-forcement system in a sheltered workshop for adult retardates. In this program, the peers administer the token reinforcers. This is an important development in that it involves the training of peers, hence influencing their behavior as an integral part of the program.

A study by Birky, Chambliss, and Wasder [1971] compared female psychiatric residents discharged from a token economy and from two traditional psychiatric programs on a number of variables. There were no significant differences in the number of patients discharged from the token economy program and the two others, but, length of continuous hospitalization was significantly greater for the residents discharged from the token economy, who had been hospitalized markedly longer (mean of 15.81 years), when compared to those residents discharged from either of the comparison programs (means of 2.11 and 0.66 years). The efficacy of the token program was attributed to its focus on eliminating nonfunctional behaviors while developing adaptive behaviors (e.g., dieting, food preparation, grooming, housekeeping, laundry, and shopping skills).

In a similar program, Gripp and Magaro [1971] worked with schizophrenic patients who were selected because of chronic illness or disruptive behavior and transferred to a token economy ward. In this program there was an attempt to maximize the likelihood of success by staff training and promoting morale. Members of the staff were chosen for their "optimism," for example. Not only was there patient improvement in cognitive and affective concomitants of psychoses, but fewer gains were noted for controls. The staff also changed positively as shown by a "Ward Atmosphere Test." The investigators noted about patient behavior, however, that although significant changes resulted, it was not clear that token reinforcement (as opposed to staff expectancies) accounted for all of the results.

As a typical usage of token economy, we have the program of Maley, Feldman, and Ruskin [1973] which emphasized careful evaluation of the effectiveness of their program. The results were described as indicating that "the token economy subjects were better oriented, had more skill in making business purchases and discriminations, and were better able to follow commands. Token economy subjects were rated as being more cooperative and communicative, more socially desirable, more appropriate in mood, and as exhibiting less psychotic behavior'' [p. 141].

Other token economy programs with adult hospitalized patients have been reported by Lloyd and Abel [1970], Shean and Zeidberg [1971], Suchotliff and his associates [1970], Upper and Newton [1971], and Fernandez, Fischer, and Ryan [1973], and are comprehensively evaluated by Kazdin and Bootzin [1972].

Token Economy in the Classroom

O'Leary and Becker [1967] introduced the use of a token reinforcement program in a large public school class of seventeen black children with behavior problems. Observations were focused on the eight most disruptive children. Two observers recorded behaviors labeled deviant (for example, pushing, talking, making a noise, and chewing gum) every 30 seconds for an hour and a half on three days a week. Behaviors manifested during the observation periods were classified as either disruptive or non-disruptive.

On the first day of training, the experimenter put the following words on the blackboard: "In Seat, Face Front, Raise Hand, Working, Pay Attention, Desk Clear." The experimenter then explained that tokens would be given for these behaviors and that the tokens could be exchanged for backup reinforcers of candy, comics, perfume, and so on. The teacher, during several brief class interludes, rated the extent to which each child had met the criteria.

For the first three days, tokens were exchanged at the end of each period; tokens were then accumulated before being cashed in, first for two days, then for three and finally, four days. The process was designed gradually to fade out the backup reinforcer, so that the more traditional acquired reinforcers of teacher's praise would take over. In addition, group points (exchanged for ice cream) were awarded for quietness of the group during the rating period. Further techniques of verbal praise, ignoring (extinction), and time-out-from-reinforcement were used as appropriate. During the baseline observation period, the disruptive-deviant behavior ranged from 66 to 91 percent of the observations. The daily mean of observed deviant-disruptive behavior dropped to a range of from 4 to 32 percent during the period of token training. The authors concluded that "With the introduction of the token reinforcement system, a dramatic, abrupt reduction in deviant behavior occurred.... The program was equally successful for all children observed, and repeated anecdotal evidence suggested that the children's appropriate behavior generalized to other situations" [O'Leary & Becker 1967, p. 637].

This program contained most of the elements that were to characterize future token programs in the classroom and which had appeared in the earlier mental hospital and retardation applications, namely: systematic observation; explicit selection of the desired behaviors, with the assistance of the teacher, as alternatives to undesirable behavior; the exchange system; the training of the teacher in a new role; the use of additional behavior influence techniques such as social reinforcement; and the careful charting of behavior by trained observers.

O'Leary and his associates [1969] replicated the earlier study in a more systematic manner to determine the separate effects of the variables utilized in the previous study. They worked with seven children in a second grade class of twenty-one children. After a period of baseline observations, they successively introduced Classroom Rules (e.g., on the blackboard, the rule, "We sit in our seats"), Educational Structure (e.g., the teacher structured her program into four sessions of 30 minutes each), and Praising Appropriate Behavior while ignoring Disruptive Behavior. None of these procedures consistently reduced disruptive behavior in six of the seven target children; the three procedures were successful with one of the children. When a token reinforcement program was introduced, the frequency of disruptive behavior declined in five of the remaining six children.

Withdrawal of the token programs then resulted in increased disruptive behavior in these five children. The reinstatement of the token program reduced disruptive behavior in four of the five children. Follow-up data indicated that the teacher was able to transfer control from the token and backup reinforcers to more common educational reinforcers such as stars and occasional pieces of candy. Improvements in academic achievement during the year may have been related to the token program, and attendance records appeared to be enhanced during the token phases. The token program was used only in the afternoon and the data did not indicate any generalization of appropriate behavior from the afternoon to the morning.

This particular study is cited because it illustrates many important points about token economy programs in the classroom that become more focused by the observations of the same investigators replicating their earlier work. Clearly there are many complex and subtle variables involved in this kind of program that become more obvious from the authors' comparison of the results of the two studies:

> Although a token reinforcement program was a significant variable in reducing disruptive behavior in the present study, the results are less dramatic than those obtained by O'Leary and Becker (1967). A number of factors probably contributed to the difference in effectiveness of the programs. The average of disruptive behavior during the base period in the 1967 was 76%; in the present study it was 53%. The gradual introduction of the various phases of the program was probably less effective than a simultaneous introduction of all the procedures, as in the previous study. In the earlier study, the children received more frequent ratings.... In the 1967 study, the class could earn points for popsicles by being quiet while the teacher placed ratings in the children's booklets; in the present study, group points were not incorporated into the general reinforcement program. In the 1967 study, the teacher attended a weekly psychology seminar where teachers discussed various applications of learning principles to classroom management. An *esprit de corps* was generated from that seminar that probably increased the teacher's commitment to change the children's behavior.... A number of children in the present study had an abundance of toys at home and it was difficult to obtain inexpensive prizes which would serve as reinforcers; in the earlier study, selection of reinforcers was not a difficult problem since the children were from disadvantaged homes [O'Leary et al. 1969, pg. 11–12].

Thus additional considerations that must be added to any evaluation of token programs include baseline levels of the target behaviors; the phasing of the program; the frequency of certain teacher behaviors; the use of group reinforcers; the consequences of a teacher training program (and available reinforcers for the teacher); and the availability of reinforcers for the children in their total environment. There are still more complexities, as we shall see after describing some other programs.

In the elaborate token programs of Hewett, Taylor, and Artuso [1969], fifty-four children with learning and behavior problems, most of whom had been labeled "emotionally disturbed," were assigned to six different classrooms with nine students each. The age of the children ranged from eight to eleven. Hewett and his group describe their program as involving an "engineered classroom" rather than a token economy. However, the principles of both are the same. The experimental condition of the project involved rigid adherence to the engineered classroom design and systematic reliance on the giving of *checkmarks*. The control condition of the project consisted of any approach the teacher chose to follow, including aspects of the engineered design, except the use of tangible or token rewards. Conventional grading, verbal phrase, complimentary written comments on completed assignments, and awarding privileges for good work were all acceptable. The independent variable was adherence to the engineered design. The dependent variable was the student "task attention" and academic functioning level in reading and arithmetic. Specific criteria for a student's task attention, as measured by observers, was established.

The student's task was significantly facilitated by the experimental condition. Reading achievement was not significantly affected by either the experimental or control condition but gains in arithmetic fundamentals were significantly correlated with the presence of the experimental condition.

The study by Hewett and his colleagues was a forerunner and prototype of applying token programs to "disturbed" children. This program was more complex in its involvement of more teachers, the use of comparative control groups rather than own-control baselines, the focus on academic target behaviors, and the testing of the removal and reinstatement of the token programs.

Wolf, Giles, and Hall [1968] reported a token economy designed to develop and maintain the academic behavior of children with low scholastic achievement in a community setting. This report described the results of the first year of after-school remedial education for such children from the fifth and sixth grade in a poor, urban area. The remedial program incorporated standard instructional material, the mastery of which was supported by token reinforcements.

The reinforcement procedure resembled a trading-stamp plan. Each child was given a folder containing groups of four differently colored pages divided into squares. The different colors signified different sorts of rewards. After a child had completed an assignment correctly, he was given points by the teacher who marked the appropriately colored squares. At first, points were given after each problem that was worked correctly. As the student acquired a more accurate output, the amount, difficulty, or both, of work needed to obtain points was gradually increased.

The number of points to be given to a child for particular work was decided by the teacher. This decision was sometimes determined partially through negotiation with the child—a unique feature of this program. Filled pages of points were redeemable, according to their color, for a variety of goods and events including weekly trips to outdoor events or to the movies, food, money, articles that were available in the store, and long-range goals such as clothes, inexpensive watches and secondhand bicycles. The children could earn tokens in each of three areas: regular classroom work; work completed in the remedial classroom; and six-week report card grades.

With this basic paradigm, Wolf, Giles, and Hall performed several experimental analyses of the token procedures. In the overall program, they compared the academic achievement of their experimental students during the year with that of a matched control group (fifteen in each group). The results indicated that the remedial group gained 1.5 years on the Stanford Achievement Test as compared to 0.8 of a year for the control group; these differences were significant at the 0.01 level. There was a similar significant difference in report card grades. The authors conclude:

> . . . The remedial program's effectiveness in maintaining the children's participation was indicated by the high attendance record, and the fact that whenever the opportunity was given them, the children chose to attend class on regular school holidays . . . The cost of the program, which was substantial, must be contrasted with the longterm cost to society in terms of human as well as economic resources lost by not educating these children adequately. The cost could be reduced significantly by utilizing the potential reinforcers which already exist in almost every educational setting. Properly used, such events as recess, movies, and athletic and social activities could be arranged as consequences for strengthening academic behavior [1968, pp. 63–64].

Thus we see in this study the introduction of application of token economy to "the disadvantaged" of our population, changes in price structure to "shape" the quality and quantity of classroom work, the child entering the decision-making process, the introduction of long-range goals, and the utilization of reinforcing events beyond the classroom, as well as a greater utilization of the "natural" reinforcers of the classroom.

Other token programs have involved money receipts with institutionalized female adolescent offenders [Meichenbaum, Bowers, & Ross 1968]; tokens for good performance on a "news" test [Tyler & Brown 1968]; plastic washer tokens as tickets for special events [Bushell, Wrobel, & Michaelis 1968]; tokens given to school dropouts in a Neighborhood Youth Corps who were "hired" to complete remedial workbook assignments [Clark, Lachowicz, & Wolf 1968]; contingent tokens in a remedial reading program [Haring & Hauck 1969]; points, used as tokens, along with "time out" procedures and parental involvement in working with disruptive fourth- to six-graders [Walker, Mattson, & Buckley 1969]; poker chips to increase "instruction following behavior" in retardates [Zimmerman et al. 1969]; tokens dispensed by peers in an individualized reading program [Winett et al. 1971]; and tokens to extinguish tantrum behavior [Martin et al. 1968].

The Token Economy as a "Real" Economy

A modified use of a token economy program which extends the possiblity of utilization of these programs in the classroom has been reported by Krasner and Krasner (1973). This is a unique token program which took place in a fifth-grade classroom. Previous token programs have emphasized remedial goals. In this classroom, the token economy was a program in which the development of the economy served as a learning experience itself. Gerald Martin of the Three Village Central School District, Setauket, New York, initiated a token program in the form of a *simulated society* in a fifth-grade class. Martin started the program in the role of a king with divine rights, and with an initial royal treasury of a dozen bottle caps as the token capital. Gradually, the token economy developed and soon took on a life of its own. The behavior of the children was determined by the shifting directions of the economy as it progressed from a system of slavery to capitalism and then to socialism. The initial goal of this program, as determined by the teacher, was for the children to learn about and to be more appreciative of historical and economic processes by reproducing them, to some extent, via the concept of a token economy. The children learned the connection between their behavior and the functional relationship between prices and wages. The children then were able to control the program by introducing a new and increasingly more complex relationship between "prices" and "wages" in much the same manner as in the world outside the classroom. This was evidenced by the spontaneous development of a welfare program to take care of those who did not earn enough tokens to function in the economy. A considerable sophistication in economic functioning and human behavior developed on the part of the children.

Behavior Theory and Economic Theory

Winkler [1970] reported the first investigations of the relationship between economic variables such as prices, wages, and savings in a token economy program in a psychiatric hospital. Linking the social learning principles of token programs with economic theory, it has been pointed out that "Token economy procedures need a combination of social and economic planning. When an economist (for example, Galbraith 1967) relates a 'general theory of motivation' to the economic structure of society, he is presenting hypotheses that can be tested in small social units such as hospital wards, by means of a token economy" [Krasner 1968, p. 172]. Such linkages are also possible and necessary in the classroom.

The concepts of token economy and of economics interact in three ways: (1) Economic principles (e.g., the law of supply and demand) can be used to understand why existing traditional token economies work or do not work; (2) economic and behavioral principles can be used in the design of innovative economies; (3) token economies can also be used to test economic theory. Winkler and Krasner [1971] reported on research using token economies with chronic psychiatric patients to clarify these interactions. The implications of this type of economic research go beyond the treatment of psychiatric patients to any token economy that operates with similar rules, be it in a classroom, correctional institution, or a delinquent rehabilitation unit.

Various simple principles that have been well established in operant laboratories such as reinforcement can be found to operate in token economies. It should also be possible to demonstrate in token economies the operation of at least simple economic principles. The phenomena found in token economies fit into the economic principles developed in the analysis of national economies.

In addition to augmenting the theoretical base for understanding token economies, the investigation of economies can provide ideas for the design of new, perhaps more effective, token economies. Research on the interface between economic theory and token economies would, therefore, seem to be essential to a complete understanding of token economies and valuable in the design of innovative token programs, particularly in the classroom.

Operant Conditioning of Autonomic Function

There is one group of operant studies that must be mentioned because of their implications for future research. They are of recent origin and have just begun to be extended to include specific treatment procedures. These are the studies of instrumental conditioning of autonomic function [Miller, 1969]. Among the autonomic functions that have been operantly conditioned in humans are brain waves, galvanic skin response, heart rate, and electrodermal fluctuations.

An early illustrative study by Lang, Stroufe, and Hastings [1967] demonstrated the remarkable control that an individual can attain over his heart rate when heart beat is viewed as an operant response. They presented their subjects equipment that measured heart rate. The task of the subject was to maintain his own heart rate within certain limits on the dial of the measure. Lang and his associates found that when subjects received visual feedback on each trial as to how successful they were, they literally were able to maintain their heart response so that it was within the prescribed limits (in contrast to a control group that did not receive feedback). Subjects were also able to control their heart rate on instruction. It was not clear to the investigators what mechanism was used to control heart rate except that it was clear that respiration, an obvious choice, was not the mechanism used. Similar results were reported by Shearn [1962] where delay of shock was made contingent on accelerated heart rate.

Ascough and Sipprelle [1968] also demonstrated that spontaneous increase and decrease in heart rate can be brought under control of operant verbal conditioning. Their results showed significant conditioning effects with increasing differences from the original baseline over a group of sessions even when possible mediating responses were taken into account. As with the Lang study, the possibility of respiratory changes being responsible for changes in heart rate was ruled out. Reports of operant conditioning of spontaneous electrodermal fluctuations have been reported by Crider, Shapiro, and Tursky [1966] and Kimmel and Kimmel [1963].

These studies open many possibilities of application of operant procedures to problems involved in the area of psychosomatic disorders. The relationship between autonomic functioning and overt behavior is a major field of operant investigation.

Training in Operant Procedures

Because of the nature of the procedures, the operant approach lends itself very readily to the "training"of others. As we have indicated previously, there are several ways in which one can conceive of the operant approach. One can view it as a mechanical process by which one systematically plans a contingent relationship between a behavior and its consequent reinforcer. To this a careful schedule of reinforcement is applied, which gives the whole process an aura of scientific exactitude. On the other hand, the operant approach can be more loosely conceived as a process in which one individual is trained to observe behavior and its consequences (his own and that of others) in such a way that his or her behavior can be used to influence the likelihood of the other person acting in a way that would affect his environment in order to increase positive consequences. This latter concept is coming to predominate the approach of the operant conditioner as a trainer of human beings.

One of the most important developments of the operant paradigm is the reconceptualization of treatment into training. Ludwig, Marx, and Hill [1971] reported on their use of a "double conditioning" operant treatment paradigm designed to modify the behavior of chronic schizophrenics. It involved the training of these patients through operant conditioning procedures to act in turn as behavioral therapists for fellow chronic schizophrenics.

An experimental program was initiated on a special treatment unit at a state hospital. Before the start of the program, the nursing and aide staff trained in the basic principles of learning theory and operant conditioning via movies, video tapes, reading references, seminars, and practice sessions. The investigators also attempted to determine the likes and dislikes of all patients in terms of food and extra "goodies" in order to find the most powerful primary reinforcers.

Twenty-seven patients who had been diagnosed as chronic schizophrenics, and were regarded as treatment failures of traditional psychiatric therapies, were divided into nine trios. Two members of each trio were assigned to serve as "guardian therapists" for the third who was the more regressed "charged" patient.

> . . . the training of these patients through operant conditioning procedures to act in turn as behavioral therapists for fellow chronic schizophrenics . . . . A standardized hierarchy of response levels, ranging from simple eye contact to complex forms of social behavior, was constructed for all charge patients. Daily 45-minute behavior therapy (BT) sessions were held in which the guardians together with two staff systematically administered both social (e.g., praise) and primary reinforcements (e.g., ice cream, soda, cigarettes, chocolate, etc.) to the charge patients to induce him to progress to advanced levels in the response hierarchy. An arbitrary figure of 80 per cent correct responses constituted the criterion used to gauge when it was appropriate to thin out the differential reinforcement rate, as well as when to proceed to the next higher level in the hierarchy. Each of the BT sessions was divided into 3-minute time blocks with guardians altering turns in conditioning their charge. As guardian patients worked, they were given considerable praise, encouragement and instruction from assigned staff. At the end of each time block, they would be given one coupon for effort and one for performance if they earned it. These coupons (secondary reinforcers) were negotiable for assorted 'goodies' and 'treats' [Ludwig, Marx & Hill 1971, p. 683].

Loeber's "Engineering the Behavioral Engineer" [1971] asks the question, "In what ways are experimenters who apply conditioning principles to their subjects, themselves susceptible to those principles? What sort of reinforcements and schedules are most influential for their performance as conditioners?" [p.321].

Twenty-eight nursing staff members treated, by operant methods, a simulated head-banging patient. They were randomly assigned to four experimental conditions, involving improvement versus nonimprovement of the "patient" and promise of reward versus no promise of reward. It had been expected that both the promise of reward and improvement of the "patient" would increase the accuracy of the subjects in applying the "therapy." This expectation was borne out in the case of promise of reward, but not for the improvement condition.

The clear-cut effect of a promise of monetary reward has obvious implications for behavior modification programs regarding training and maintenance of an adequate performance level by nursing staff members who administer them. Provision of monetary reinforcers may often be difficult in practical settings, but there are other potentially useful reinforcers that could be applied, such as upgrading, social reinforcers, and selection of preferred days off. It would certainly seem justified to search for and make use of reinforcements for nursing staff members, in a planned and contingent manner.

Operant Approaches in the Community

One of the most recent developments in the application of behavior modification has been in community mental health centers. This is illustrated by the works of Goodson [1972], Rinn [1972], and Turner [1971] in the Huntsville, Madison County (Alabama) Mental Health Center.

Behavior modification techniques as such are now used in many settings, but there is a difference between the use of an isolated technique within the context of a setting that has a dynamic or eclectic orientation, and the organization of an entire community mental health structure around the behavior modification approach described throughout this module, as is being done at the Huntsville Center.

The characteristics of this mental health center in both their in-patient and out-patient centers are as follows: accountability to the public; the setting of behavioral goals for each individual client; the systematic progress to the goals with careful measurement; training clients to collect data on their own progress; the concept of teaching clients rather than healing clients; community-centered programs designed to keep clients out of the state hospitals; and individual treatment programs built around response contingent approaches. This center has become a prototype of what can be done in the community, influenced by the operant point of view.

Operant Conditioning and Behavior Control

Any material on operant conditioning procedures and behavior modification must touch upon the social implications of behavior control, and issues of the desirability and inevitability of behavior control have been extensively discussed elsewhere [Rogers & Skinner 1956; Krasner 1962, 1969; Kanfer 1965; Goldiamond 1965]. We will discuss only one aspect of this problem, that of the possible misuse of these procedures. These misuses arise primarily because of the apparent simplicity of the operant techniques. Bachrach and Quigley summarized this in their reference to operant procedures by saying, "It is, therefore, a field in danger of being ruined by amateurs" [1966, p. 510].

An illustration of the relationship among the behavior modification programs, social planning, and ethical issues has occurred in several recent incidents in a midwestern state hospital and in a Vietnamese mental hospital. The principles involved in both incidents are similar. In the first incident a token program was introduced on a female ward and, to make the tokens more effective, traditional hospital *physical* restraints were reintroduced. Patients who could exhibit control of their behavior were given tokens with which they could eventually buy their way out of restraints. Not surprisingly this set of procedures came to the attention of people outside the hospital, such as relatives and newspaper people. An uproar resulted in a hospital investigation stopping the program, serious damage to all future behavior programs, and the resignation of several staff members who were involved.

The societal concern about the consequences of what the behavior planner is doing is certainly justified. The use of restraints to develop a situation from which one can use tokens to escape indicates a lack of awareness of the real purpose of token programs as outlined here, i.e., the training of staff to respect the individual and to treat him as a responsible person who is learning to cope with and control his environment.

The other incident is reported in the *American Journal of Psychiatry* by L. H. Cotter [1967], an American psychiatrist who tells of his having read about some of the studies previously described, and draws the conclusion that shock was the essential ingredient in operant conditioning. Cotter brought this form of American enlightenment with him on a visit to a Vietnamese mental hospital. He was in a hurry since he had only two months so he gave the 130 male patients a choice between electroconvulsive therapy (ECT) three times a week and working for their living in the hospital. The rationale was that ECT "served as a negative reinforcement for the response of work for those patients who chose to work rather than to continue receiving ECT." The treatment worked well with the male patients, most of them quickly volunteering for work. He then tried it with a ward of 130 women patients with much less success since at the end of treatment only 15 women were working. Cotter then introduced another American procedure—work or no food, which apparently was more effective. Cotter pointed out that these were not cruel methods but rather was like giving an injection to a sick person. It may hurt a little but it is for his own benefit. Besides, he observed, the Vietnamese are smaller people than the Americans and thus never had bone fractures, a not uncommon concomitant to ECT in this country. To cap off his magnificent achievements with operant conditioning, and as a contribution in our war effort in Vietnam, he worked out an arrangement with a team of American special forces, the Green Berets. He learned that the Green Berets were unsuccessful in utilizing Viet Cong prisoners to tend the crops in the headquarters area. Apparently using the same techniques, Cotter was able to supply the Green Berets with his mental patients to tend the crops. This helped the war effort and increased the self-esteem of the patients who were now a part of the team. Admittedly these ex-patients were now placed under fire of the Viet Cong but, as Cotter concludes, a little stress such as a war situation (for example, the people in London bore up well under fire) is psychiatrically healthy. Thus we have another successful application of operant conditioning!

It is easy to mock this effort but it points up what must be considered to be a basic misunderstanding of behavior therapy. The aim of the program is to arrange the environment in such a way that there is an increased likelihood of the individual learning new behaviors more likely to elicit positive reinforcement from others in the environment. The major technique in all forms of behavior therapy in institutional settings involves training people such as nurses aids, psychologists, and psychiatrists so that they can react to the individual not as a sick patient but as a responsible individual who is acquiring new skills in learning to behave adequately in his environment. To introduce a procedure such as electric shock or physical restraints is to communicate denigration of the individual and thus to defeat the purpose of the training program. You cannot shape responsible behavior in an individual while at the same time treating him inhumanely. You cannot build a new social environment with any chance of enhancing human dignity based on procedures inducing indignity because the means will distort and destroy the ends. Further, it is not completely certain that all therapists would consider the behavior of tilling soil to produce food for soldiers to kill Viet Cong as a necessarily desirable social goal, but that clearly is a value decision.

Cotter's program was not an operant conditioning one since it did not involve any of the principles of contingent reinforcement, nor was it any form of behavior therapy since it demonstrated no respect for the integrity of the individual. It was a clear program of coercion and demonstrates the dangers inherent in the misunderstanding and potential misuse of operant conditioning procedures.

Environmental Design

It is increasingly obvious that the application of operant conditioning is moving in the direction of *environmental design*. If behavior is determined by environmental consequences, then it is reasonable to assist the individual in planning to increase the availability of reinforcers in his environment. The concept of the "environment" would include, among many things, architecture of living space, climate control, and planning for occupational and recreational time. The token economy programs have already moved in this direction [Cohen et al. 1968].

Skinner foresaw the consequences of extending operant conditioning research into a utopian society in his science-fiction novel, *Walden Two* [1948]. As a society, Walden Two is based upon operant conditioning principles just as in a token economy. The extension of research in this direction poses important theoretical and ethical issues [Krasner 1969]. Actually, many social and economic problems could be translated into terms that permitted systematic investigation by operant procedures. For example, what is the effect of a guaranteed annual wage upon human behavior? An important economic problem of this type can be translated into a comparison of programs involving contingent versus noncontingent reinforcement.

Future of Operant Research

As in other areas of research, current studies and theories foreshadow at least the more immediate directions that operant research will take. The trouble with writing a section predicting things to come is that most likely such "things" are here already. For example, it is a safe prediction that operant research will not remain "pure" since it is questionable whether it ever has been "pure."

One social influence procedure, which will be combined with operant techniques such as token economies, will be to change the theoretical model within which the token program operates. Until recently, a mental hospital has been a hospital with all of the consequences thereunto, and residence in a hospital has been ipso facto an indication of sickness. As has been indicated, a major offensive is underway against the "medical model" of psychopathological labeling. It is manifested by daring changes in hospital settings such as those [Jones, Kahn, & Wolcott 1964] in which hospital personnel wear street clothes and patients are referred to as personnel. Rothaus and his associates [1963] reported on a study utilizing role playing which demonstrated that patients make a better impression on perspective employees when they play a role stressing problem behavior rather than recovery-from-illness behavior. Future studies should demonstrate that token programs are successful to the extent that they are set up in an atmosphere in which the patients are reacted to as *responsible individuals* and not as sick patients.

One of the major controversies involving operant conditioning procedures involves the relationship between behavior and the so-called cognitive functions. The controversy appears in different forms. For example, in the verbal conditioning area it is phrased in terms of the relationship between behavior change or conditioning and awareness [Krasner 1967]. In other operant conditioning studies this issue may be expressed in terms of relation between behavior change and the amount and kind of information given to the subject. For example, if a patient is told by a nurse the reason for his receiving a token, does this mean that we have departed from the operant conditioning paradigm?

There are a number of points that should be made about this issue. As we have tried to make clear throughout the module, operant techniques with their focus on manipulating consequences of behavior have to be considered within a broader framework of behavior influence. Crucial research studies eventually will demonstrate that the operant technique significantly adds to the maximimization of this behavior. In any given situation, be it labeled "research" or "psychotherapy," the behavior required of the subject or the patient is communicated implicitly or explicitly. This, of course, is a paraphrasing of the concept of the effect of the demand characteristics of the situation [Orne 1962]. In effect, given a situation in which the experimenter or therapist maximizes the behavior influence variables as expressed by demand characteristics, subject and experimenter biases and expectancies, and experimenter prestige, then operant techniques such as the contingent giving of a token or verbalizing "good" significantly add to the modification aspects of the situation.

The analogue at this point is the study by Paul [1966] using a desensitization technique. As a control group, Paul devised a situation that included the procedures likely to enhance placebo effects. This included offhand statements by the receptionist that the subject was lucky to see an "excellent therapist," the spelling out in explicit terms to the subject of the rationale of the treatment, and communication of expectancies of being helped. Of the two experimental groups, one received systematic desensitization and the second received traditional psychotherapy. The results indicated that the placebo-control group was about as effective as the traditional psychotherapy procedure in bringing about change in the target behavior (anxiety in interpersonal situations). The very specific desensitization procedures *added* to the behavior influence procedures of the other two techniques *significantly* augmenting their effectiveness in changing the target behavior. Thus far there has been no analogous study with the use of operant techniques. Investigators using operant techniques should concentrate on demonstrating that these procedures add to the behavior influence variables rather than, as some have suggested, the elimination of these aspects of the influence process.

This has been increasingly recognized in operant conditioning studies. For example, early verbal conditioning studies invariably used control groups that received no reinforcement. It eventually became obvious that this was inadequate control. When a subject is in a situation in which another individual never responds to him, then that situation becomes aversive and certainly not an adequate control. Even a random reinforcement group presents problems. Harmatz and Lapuc [1968] argue that the ideal control subject would receive the same number of reinforcements, spaced exactly the same way as his experimental counterpart, but delivered noncontingently. A yoked control paradigm would result in this ideal control since the experimental subject and his yoked control receive exactly the same reinforcement, except that for the control subject they are administered noncontingently. Thus once again a growth and sophistication of design has to take into consideration the effects of the situation upon the human being. The progression of operant studies has been steadily in the direction of recognizing and incorporating the basic variables that influence human behavior.

Conclusions

It is obvious from current operant studies that the movement is in the direction away from one-to-one treatment to milieu or environmental manipulation. Yet, the focus in these approaches still remains upon bringing about changes in the individual, through the mechanism of the behavior of other people. The difference between the current operant-based approaches and previous dynamic-based ones is not a real change from one-to-one relationship, but in the nature, role, and function of the "one" at the thera-

peutic end. It has shifted from an individual in the social role of a healer—therapist, physician, psychiatrist, or psychologist—to that of a natural member of the environment—a nurse, aide, teacher, parent, peer, or research experimenter. The latter individual is now behaving "therapeutically" (with intent to change behavior in a socially desirable direction) towards the target individual. This behavior, programmed by the training procedures received, is taking place in a "natural" setting (e.g., hospital, school, home) rather than in an artificial setting (e.g., the therapist's office).

Further, the view that the behavior dealt with by operant procedures is too molecular or atomistic, hence inconsequential, simply does not hold up. As a change in behavior is brought about, even a small change, it is the "whole" individual to whom others react, not a part of a person.

Summary

This module has presented an overview of research in operant approaches to modifying human deviant behavior. The research investigations in this area are characterized by

1. working within a *social learning* framework of deviancy;
2. the extension of experimental *laboratory* studies of humans and animals to real life problem behaviors;
3. a close linkage of experimental *attitudes* with clinical problems;
4. the development of new *assessment* procedures based on observation of behavior;
5. the necessity of conceptualizing operant research within a broader behavior influence framework;
6. the apparent effectiveness of operant approaches in modifying a wide category of behaviors;
7. the complexity of the three sets of variables involved in operant research—influencer, influencee, and situational;
8. the extension of training of key environmental figures into the community;

9. the clinical usefulness of operant research designed as own-control;

10. the broad social and ethical implications which are inherent in the extension of operant research to social planning; and

11. the final comment, which no self-respecting research investigator can neglect, the need for more carefully controlled and ingenious variations of current operant research that will move the field more clearly into recognition of its place within a psychology of behavior influence.

BIBLIOGRAPHY

S. Agras, H. Leitenberg, and D. H. Barlow, "Social Reinforcement in the Modification of Agoraphobia." *Archives of General Psychology,* 1968, 19:423–427.

R. M. Anthony, and P. H. Duerfeldt, "The Effect of Tension Level and Contingent Reinforcement on Fear Reduction." *Behavior Therapy,* 1970, 1:445–464.

J. C. Ascough, and C. H. Sipprelle, "Operant Verbal Conditioning of Autonomic Responses." *Behaviour Research and Therapy,* 1968, 6:363–370.

J. M. Atthowe, Jr., and L. Krasner, "A Preliminary Report on the Application of Contingent Reinforcement Procedures (Token Economy) on a 'Chronic' Psychiatric Ward." *Journal of Abnormal and Social Psychology,* 1968, 73:37–43.

T. Ayllon, "Intensive Treatment of Psychotic Behaviour by Stimulus Satiation and Food Reinforcement." *Behaviour Research and Therapy,* 1963, 1:53–61.

T. Ayllon, and N. H. Azrin, "The Measurement and Reinforcement of Behavior of Psychotics." *Journal of Experimental Analysis of Behavior,* 1965, 8:357–383.

T. Ayllon, and N. H. Azrin, "Reinforcer Sampling: A Technique for Increasing the Behaviour of Mental Patients." *Journal of Applied Behavior Analysis,* 1968a, 1:13–20.

T. Ayllon, and N. H. Azrin, *The Token Economy: A Motivational System for Therapy and Rehabilitation.* Appleton-Century-Crofts, 1968b.

T. Ayllon, and E. Haughton, "Control of the Behavior of Schizophrenic Patients by Food." *Journal of Experimental Analysis of Behavior,* 1962, 5:343–352.

T. Ayllon, and E. Haughton, "Modification of Symptomatic Verbal Behavior of Mental Patients." *Behaviour Research and Therapy,* 1964, 2:87–97.

T. Ayllon, and J. Michael, "The Psychiatric Nurse as a Behavioral Engineer." *Journal of the Experimental Analysis of Behavior,* 1959, 2:323–334.

A. J. Bachrach, and W. A. Quigley, "Direct Methods of Treatment." In I. A. Berg and L. A Pennington, eds., *Introduction to Clinical Psychology,* 3rd ed. Ronald Press, 1966.

A. Bandura, "Psychotherapy as a Learning Process." *Psychological Bulletin,* 1961, 58:143–159.

A. Bandura, *Principles of Behavior Modification.* Holt, Rinehart & Winston, 1969.

B. H. Barrett, "Reduction in Rate of Multiple Ties by Free Operant Conditioning Methods." *Journal of Nervous and Mental Disease,* 1962, 135:187–195.

W. M. Benecke, and M. B. Harris, "Teaching Self-Control of Study Behavior." *Behaviour Research and Therapy,* 1972, 10:35–41.

J. L. Bernard, "Rapid Treatment of Gross Obesity by Operant Techniques." *Psychological Reports,* 1968, 23:663–666.

H. J. Birky, J. E. Chambliss, and R. Wasden, "A Comparison of Residents Discharged from a Token Economy and Two Traditional Psychiatric Programs." *Behavior Therapy,* 1971, 2:46–51.

J. H. Bryan, and E. Lichtenstein, "Effects of Subject and Experimenter Attitudes in Verbal Conditioning." *Journal of Personality and Social Psychology,* 1966, 3:182–189.

E. P. Burgess, "The Modification of Depressive Behaviors." In R. D. Rubin and C. M. Franks, eds., *Advances in Behavior Therapy, 1968,* Academic, 1969.

D. Bushell, Jr., P. A. Wrobel, and M. L. Michaelis, "Applying 'Group' Contingencies to the Classroom Study Behavior of Preschool Children." *Journal of Applied Behavior Analysis,* 1968,1:55–61.

A. Catania, ed., *Contemporary Research in Operant Behavior.* Scott, Foresman, 1968.

J. R. Cautela, "Covert Sensitization." *Psychological Record,* 1967, 20:459–468.

M. Clark, J. Lachowicz, and M. Wolf, "A Pilot Basic Education Program for School Dropouts Incorporating a Token Reinforcement System." *Behaviour Research and Therapy,* 1968, 6:183–188.

H. L. Cohen, I. Goldiamond, J. Filipczak, and R. Pooley, "Training Professionals in Procedures for the Establishment of Educational Environments.'' Educational Facility Press, IBR, Maryland, 1968.

L. H. Cotter, ''Operant Conditioning in a Vietnamese Mental Hospital.'' *American Journal of Psychiatry*, 1967, 124:23–28.

A. Crider, D. Shapiro, and B. Tursky, ''Reinforcement of Spontaneous Electrodermal Activity.'' *Journal of Comparative and Physiological Psychology*, 1966, 61:20–27.

J. Fernandez, I. Fischer, and E. Ryan, ''The Token Economy: A Living-Learning Environment.'' *The British Journal of Psychiatry*, 1973, 122:453–455.

C. B. Ferster, ''Classification of Behavioral Pathology.'' In L. Krasner and L. P. Ullmann, eds., *Research in Behavior Modification*. Holt, Rinehart & Winston, 1965.

C. B. Ferster, ''Animal Behavior and Mental Illness.'' *Psychological Record*, 1966, 16:345–356.

C. B. Ferster, ''Clinical Reinforcement.'' *Seminars in Psychiatry*, 1972, 4:101–115.

C. B. Ferster, ''A Functional Analysis of Depression.'' *American Psychologist*, 1973, 28:857–869.

C. B. Ferster, and M. C. Perrot, *Behavior Principles*. Appleton-Century-Crofts, 1968.

C. B. Ferster, and B. F. Skinner, *Schedules of Reinforcement*. Appleton-Century-Crofts, 1957.

C. M. Franks, ed., *Behavior Therapy: Appraisal and Status*. McGraw-Hill, 1969.

P. R. Fuller, ''Operant Conditioning of a Vegetative Human Organism.'' *American Journal of Psychology*, 1949, 62:587–590.

J. K. Galbraith, *''The New Industrial State.''* Houghton, Mifflin, 1967.

O. L. Gericke, ''Practical Use of Operant Conditioning Studies in a Mental Hospital.'' *Psychiatric Studies and Projects*, 1965, 3:1–10.

I. Goldiamond, ''Self-Control Procedures in Personal Behavior Problems.'' *Psychological Reports*, 1965, 17:851–868.

I. Goldiamond, and J. E. Dyrud, ''Some Applications and Implications of Behavior Analysis for Psychotherapy.'' In J. M. Shlien et al., eds., *Research in Psychotherapy, Vol III*. American Psychological Association, 1968. pp. 54–89.

W. H. Goodson, Jr., ''In and Out—A Behaviorally Oriented Inpatient Service.'' Huntsville-Madison County (Alabama) Mental Health Center, 1972.

J. Greenspoon, ''The Effect of Two Nonverbal Stimuli on the Frequency of Members of Two Verbal Response Classes.'' *American Psychologist*, 1954, 9:384.

J. Greenspoon, ''Verbal Conditioning.'' In A. J. Bachrach, ed., *Experimental Foundations of Clinical Psychology*. Basic Books, 1962.

R. F. Gripp, and P. A. Magaro, ''A Token Economy Program Evaluation with Untreated Control Ward Comparisons.'' *Behaviour Research and Therapy*, 1971, 9:137–149.

J. M. Grossberg, ''Behavior Therapy: a Review.'' *Psychological Bulletin*, 1964, 62:73–88.

N. G. Haring, and M. A. Hauck, ''Improving Learning Conditions in the Establishment of Reading Skills with Disturbed Readers.'' *Exceptional Children*, 1969, 35: 341–351.

M. G. Harmatz, and P. S. Lapuc, ''A Technique for Employing a Yoked Control in Free Operant Verbal Conditioning Experiments.'' *Behaviour Research and Therapy*, 1968, 6:483.

J. D. Henderson, ''The Use of Dual Reinforcement in an Intensive Treatment System.'' In R. D. Rubin, and C. M. Franks, eds., *Advances in Behavior Therapy*, Academic Press, 1969.

J. D. Henderson, and P. E. Scoles, ''Conditioning Techniques in a Community-Based Operant Environment for Psychotic Men.'' *Behavior Therapy*, 1970, 1:245–251.

M. Hersen, R. M. Eisler, G. S. Alford, and W. S. Agras, ''Effects of Token Economy on Neurotic Depression: An Experimental Analysis.'' *Behavior Therapy*, 1973, 4:392–397.

F. M. Hewett, F. D. Taylor, and A. A. Artuso, ''The Santa Monica Project: Evaluation of an Engineered Classroom Design with Emotionally Disturbed Children.'' *Exceptional Children*, 1969, 35:523–529.

W. C. Holz, and N. H. Azrin, ''Conditioning Human Verbal Behavior.'' In W. K. Honig ed., *Operant Behavior: Areas of Research and Application*. Appleton-Century-Crofts, 1966.

W. K. Honig, ed., *Operant Behavior: Areas of Research and Application*. Appleton-Century-Crofts, 1966.

J. J. Horan, and R. G. Johnson, ''Coverant Conditioning through a Self-Management Application of the Premack Principle: Its Effect on Weight Reduction.'' *Journal of Behavior Therapy and Experimental Psychiatry*, 1971, 2:243–249.

R. R. Hutchinson, and N. H. Azrin, ''Conditioning of Mental-Hospital Patients to Fixed-Ratio Schedules of Reinforcement.'' *Journal of the Experimental Analysis of Behavior*, 1961, 4:87–95.

L. P. Ince, ''Behavior Modification in a Rehabilitation Service.'' Paper Presented at Annual Convention

American Psychological Association, San Francisco, Calif., 1968.

W. Isaacs, J. Thomas, and I. Goldiamond. "Application of Operant Conditioning to Reinstate Verbal Behavior in Psychotics." *Journal of Speech and Hearing Disorders,* 1960, 25:8–12.

B. Jackson, and B. Von Zoost, "Changing Study Behaviors through Reinforcement Contingencies." *Journal of Counseling Psychology,* 1972, 19:192–195.

N. Jones, M. Kahn, and O. Wolcott, "Wearing of Street Clothing by Mental Hospital Personnel." *International Journal of Social Psychiatry,* 1964, 10:216–222.

H. I. Kalish, "Behavior Therapy." In B. B. Wolman, ed., *Handbook of Clinical Psychology.* McGraw-Hill, 1965.

F. H. Kanfer, "Vicarious Human Reinforcement: A Glimpse into the Black Box." In L. Krasner and L. P. Ullmann, eds., *Research in Behavior Modification.* Holt, Rinehart, & Winston, 1965(a), pp. 244–267.

F. H. Kanfer, "Issues and Ethics in Behavior Manipulation." *Psychological Reports,* 1965(b), 16:187–196.

F. H. Kanfer, "Verbal Conditioning: A Review of its Current Status." In T. R. Dixon and D. L. Horton, eds., *Verbal Behavior and General Behavior Theory.* Prentice-Hall, 1968.

F. H. Kanfer, and A. R. Marston, "Determinants of Self-Reinforcement in Human Learning." *Journal of Experimental Psychology,* 1963, 66:245–254.

F. H. Kanfer, and J. S. Phillips, *Learning Foundations of Behavior Therapy.* Wiley, 1970.

F. H. Kanfer, and G. Saslow, "Behavioral Analysis." *Archives of General Psychiatry,* 1965, 12:529–538.

A. E. Kazdin, "The Effect of Response Cost in Suppressing Behavior in a Prepsychotic Retardate." *Journal of Behavior Therapy and Experimental Psychiatry,* 1971, 2:137–140.

A. E. Kazdin, and R. R. Bootzin, "The Token Economy: An Evaluative Review." *Journal of Applied Behavior Analysis,* 1972, 5:343–372.

F. S. Keller, and W. N. Schoenfeld, *Principles of Psychology.* Appleton-Century-Crofts, 1950.

E. Kimmel, and H. D. Kimmel, "A Replication of Operant Conditioning of the GSR." *Journal of Experimental Psychology,* 1963, 65:212–213.

G. F. King, S. G. Armitage, and J. R. Tilton, "A Therapeutic Approach to Schizophrenics of Extreme Pathology: An Operant-Interpersonal Method." *Journal of Abnormal and Social Psychology,* 1960, 61:276–286.

L. Krasner, "Studies of the Conditioning of Verbal Behavior." *Psychological Bulletin,* 1958, 55:148–170.

L. Krasner, "The Therapist as a Social Reinforcement Machine." In H. H. Strupp and L. Luborsky, eds., *Research in Psychotherapy,* Vol 2., American Psychological Association, 1962.

L. Krasner, "Verbal Conditioning and Psychotherapy." In L. Krasner and L. P. Ullmann, eds., *Research in Behavior Modification.* Holt, Rinehart & Winston, 1965, pp. 211–228.

L. Krasner, "Behavior Modification Research and the Role of the Therapist." In L. A. Gottschalk and A. H. Auerbach, eds., *Methods of Research in Psychotherapy.* Appleton-Century-Crofts, 1966.

L. Krasner, "Verbal Operant Conditioning and Awareness." In K. Salzinger and S. Salzinger, eds., *Research in Verbal Behavior and Some Neurophysiological Implications.* Academic Press, 1967, pp. 57–77.

L. Krasner, "Assessment of Token Economy Programmes in Psychiatric Hospitals. In R. Porter, ed., *The Role of Learning in Psychotherapy.* London: Churchill, 1968.

L. Krasner, "Behaviour Therapy: Ethics and Training." In C. M. Franks, ed., *Behavior Therapy: Appraisal and Status.* McGraw-Hill, 1969.

L. Krasner, "Behavior Therapy." In P. Mussen, ed., *Annual Review of Psychology,* Vol. 22. Annual Reviews, 1971.

L. Krasner, and J. M. Atthowe, Jr., "Token Economy Bibliography." State University of New York, Stony Brook, 1968.

L. Krasner, J. B. Knowles, and L. P. Ullmann, "Effect of Verbal Conditioning of Attitudes on Subsequent Motor Performance." *Journal of Personality and Social Psychology,* 1965, 1:407–412.

L. Krasner, and M. Krasner, "Token Economies and Other Planned Environments." In *The Seventy-Second Yearbook of the National Society for the Study of Education.* National Society for the Study of Education, 1973.

L. Krasner, and L. P. Ullmann, eds., *Research in Behavior Modification.* Holt, Rinehart & Winston, 1965.

L. Krasner, and L. P. Ullmann, *Behavior Influence and Personality: The Social Matrix of Human Action.* Holt, Rinehart & Winston, 1973.

L. Krasner, L. P. Ullmann, and D. Fisher, "Changes in Performance, as Related to Verbal Conditioning of Attitudes Toward the Examiner." *Perceptual Motor Skills,* 1964, 19:811–816.

J. D. Krumboltz, ed., *Revolution in Counseling.* Houghton, Mifflin, 1966.

T. S. Kuhn, *The Structure of Scientific Revolutions,* 2nd

ed. University of Chicago Press, 1970.

P. J. Lang, L. A. Stroufe, and J. E. Hastings, "Effects of Feedback and Instructional Set on the Control of Cardiac-Rate Variability." *Journal of Experimental Psychology*, 1967, 75:425–431.

A. A. Lazarus, "Learning Theory and the Treatment of Depression." *Behaviour Research and Therapy*, 1968, 6:83–89.

H. Leitenberg, W. S. Agras, and L. E. Thomson, "A Sequential Analysis of the Effect of Selective Positive Reinforcement in Modifying Anorexia Nervosa. *Behaviour Research and Therapy*, 1968, 6:211–218.

P. M. Lewinsohn, M. S. Weinstein, and D. A. Shaw, "Depression: A Clinical Research Approach." In R. D. Rubin and C. M. Franks, eds., *Advances in Behavior Therapy, 1968*. Academic Press, 1969, pp. 231–240.

R. P. Liberman, *A Guide to Behavioral Analysis and Therapy*. Pergamon Press, 1972.

O. R. Lindsley, "Operant Conditioning Methods Applied to Research in Chronic Schizophrenia." *Psychiatric Research Reports*, 1956, 5:118–153.

O. R. Lindsley, "Characteristics of the Behavior of Chronic Psychotics as Revealed by Free-Operant Conditioning Methods." *Diseases of the Nervous System*, 1960, 21:(monograph supplement) 66–78.

O. R. Lindsley, B. F. Skinner, and H. C. Solomon, *Studies in Behavior Therapy: Status Report I.* Waltham, Mass.: Metropolitan State Hospital, 1953.

K. E. Lloyd, and L. Abel, "Performance on a Token Economy Psychiatric Ward." *Behaviour Research and Therapy*, 1968, 6:407–410.

K. E. Lloyd, and W. K. Garlington, "Weekly Variations in Performance on a Token Economy Psychiatric Ward." *Behaviour Research and Therapy*, 1968, 6:407–410.

R. Loeber, "Engineering the Behavioral Engineer." *Journal of Applied Behavior Analysis*, 1971, 4:321–326.

A. M. Ludwig, A. J. Marx, and P. A. Hill, "Chronic Schizophrenics as Behavioral Engineers." *Journal of Nervous and Mental Disease*, 1971, 152:31–44.

R. F. Maley, G. L. Feldman, and R. S. Ruskin, "Evaluation of Patient Improvement in a Token Economy Treatment Program." *Journal of Abnormal Psychology*, 1973, 82:141–144.

J. Marks, B. Sonoda, and R. Schalock, "Reinforcement Versus Relationship Therapy for Schizophrenics." *Journal of Abnormal Psychology*, 1968, 73:397–402.

M. Martin, R. Burkholder, T. L. Rosenthal, R. G. Tharp, and G. L. Thorne, "Programming Behavior Change and Reintegration into School Milieux of Extreme Adolescent Deviates." *Behaviour Research and Therapy*, 1968, 6:371–384.

W. T. McReynolds, and J. Coleman, "Token Economy: Patient and Staff Changes." *Behaviour Research and Therapy*, 1972, 10:29–34.

D. H. Meichenbaum, "Effects of Social Reinforcement on the Level of Abstraction in Schizophrenics." *Journal of Abnormal and Social Psychology*, 1966b, 71:354–362.

D. H. Meichenbaum, "Sequential Strategies in Two Cases of Hysteria." *Behaviour Research and Therapy*, 1966a, 4:89–94.

D. H. Meichenbaum, K. S. Bowers, and R. R. Ross, "Modification of Classroom Behavior of Institutionalized Female Adolescent Offenders." *Behaviour Research and Therapy*, 1968, 6:343–353.

N. E. Miller, "Learning of Visceral and Glandular Responses." *Science*, 1969, 163:434–445.

W. Mischel, *Personality and Assessment*. Wiley, 1968.

C. H. Moore, and B. C. Crum, "Weight Reduction in a Chronic Schizophrenic by Means of Operant Conditioning Procedures: A Case Study." *Behaviour Research and Therapy*, 1969, 7:129–131.

J. S. O'Brien, A. E. Raynes, and V. D. Patch, "An Operant Reinforcement System to Improve Ward Behavior in In-Patient Drug Addicts." *Journal of Behavior Therapy and Experimental Psychiatry*, 1971, 2:239–242.

K. D. O'Leary, and W. C. Becker, "Behavior Modification of an Adjustment Class: A Token Reinforcement Program." *Exceptional Children*, 1967, 33:637–642.

K. D. O'Leary, W. C. Becker, M. B. Evans, and R. A. Saudargas, "A Token Reinforcement Program in a Public School: A Replication and Systematic Analysis." *Journal of Applied Behavior Analysis*, 1969, 2:3–13.

M. T. Orne, "On the Social Psychology of the Psychological Experiment: With Particular Reference to Demand Characteristics and Their Implication." *American Psychologist*, 1962, 17:776–783.

D. M. Panek, "Word Association Learning by Chronic Schizophrenics under Conditions of Reward and Punishment." Paper read at Western Psychological Association Annual Convention, 1967.

G. R. Patterson, "Responsiveness to Social Stimuli." In L. Krasner and L. P. Ullmann, eds., *Research in Be-*

havior Modification. Holt, Rinehart & Winston, 1965, pp. 157–178.

G. L. Paul, *Insight Versus Desensitization in Psychotherapy*. Stanford University Press, 1966.

G. L. Paul, "Behavior Modification Research: Design and Tactics." In C. M. Franks, ed., *Behavior Therapy: Appraisal and Status*. McGraw-Hill, 1969.

H. N. Peters, and R. L. Jenkins, "Improvement of Chronic Schizophrenic Patients with Guided Problem Solving, Motivated by Hunger." *Psychiatric Quarterly Supplement*, 1954, 28:84–101.

D. Premack, "Toward Empirical Behavior Laws. I. Positive Reinforcement." *Psychological Review*, 1959, 66:219–233.

H. Rachlin, *Introduction to Modern Behaviorism*. Freeman, 1970.

E. P. Reese, *The Analysis of Human Operant Behavior*. William C. Brown, 1966.

G. S. Reynolds, *A Primer of Operant Conditioning*. Scott, Foresman, 1968.

H. C. Rickard, ed., *Behavioral Intervention in Human Problems*. Pergamon Press, 1971.

R. Rinn, "The Use of Behavior Modification with Outpatients in a Comprehensive Community Mental Health Center." Paper presented at the annual meeting of the Southeastern Psychological Association, Atlanta, Georgia, 1972.

C. R. Rogers, and B. F. Skinner, "Some Issues Concerning the Control of Human Behavior: A Symposium." *Science*, 1956, 124:1057–1066.

P. Rothaus, P. G. Hanson, S. E. Cleveland, and D. L. Johnson, "Describing Psychiatric Hospitalizations: A Dilemma." *American Psychologist*, 1963, 18:85–89.

K. Salzinger, "Experimental Manipulation of Verbal Behavior: A Review." *Journal of Genetic Psychology*, 1959, 61:65–94.

K. Salzinger, and S. Pisoni, "Reinforcement of Affect Responses of Schizophrenics during the Clinical Interview." *Journal of Abnormal and Social Psychology*, 1958, 57:84–90.

K. Salzinger, S. Portnoy, and R. S. Feldman, "Experimental Manipulation of Continuous Speech in Schizophrenic Patients." *Journal of Abnormal and Social Psychology*, 1964, 68:508–516.

A. Sapolsky, "Effect of Interpersonal Relationships upon Verbal Conditioning." *Journal of Abnormal and Social Psychology* 1960, 60:241–246.

I. G. Sarason, and J. Minard, "Interrelationships among Subject, Experimenter, and Situational Variables." *Journal of Abnormal and Social Psychology*, 1963, 67:87–91.

H. H. Schaefer, and P. L. Martin, "Behavioral Therapy for 'Apathy' of Hospitalized Schizophrenics." *Psychological Reports*, 1966, 19:1147–1158.

G. D. Shean, and A. Zeidberg, "Token Reinforcement Therapy: A Comparison of Matched Groups." *Journal of Behaviour Therapy and Experimental Psychiatry*, 1971, 2:95–105.

D. W. Shearn, "Operant Conditioning of Heart Rate." *Science*, 1962, 137:530–531.

M. Sidman, "Operant Techniques." In A. J. Bachrach, ed., *Experimental Foundations of Clinical Psychology*. Basic Books, 1962, pp. 170–210.

B. F. Skinner, *The Behavior of Organisms*. Appleton-Century-Crofts, 1938.

B. F. Skinner, *Walden Two*. Macmillan, 1948.

B. F. Skinner, *Science and Human Behavior*. Macmillan, 1953.

B. F. Skinner, "A Case History in Scientific Method. *American Psychologist*, 1956, 11:221–233.

B. F. Skinner, *Verbal Behavior*. Appleton-Century-Crofts, 1957.

B. F. Skinner, *Cumulative Record*. Rev. ed., Appleton-Century-Crofts, 1961.

B. F. Skinner, *Cumulative Record: A Selection of Papers*, 3rd ed. Appleton-Century-Crofts, 1972.

A. W. Staats, *Human Learning*. Holt, Rinehart & Winston, 1962.

A. W. Staats, "A Case in and a Strategy for the Extension of Learning Principles to Problems of Human Behavior." In L. Krasner and L. P. Ullmann, eds., *Research in Behavior Modification*. Holt, Rinehart & Winston, 1965, pp. 27–55.

A. W. Staats, C. K. Staats, R. E. Schutz, and M. M. Wolf, "The Conditioning of Textual Responses Using "Extrinsic" Reinforcers." *Journal of Experimental Analysis of Behavior*, 1962, 5:33–40.

R. A. Steffy, et al., "Operant Behaviour Modification Techniques Applied to a Ward of Severely Regressed and Aggressive Patients." *Canadian Psychiatric Association Journal*, 1969, 14:59–67.

R. B. Stuart, "Operant-Interpersonal Treatment for Marital Discord." *Journal of Counseling and Clinical Psychology*, 1969, 33:675–682.

L. Suchotliff, S. Greaves, H. Stecker, and R. Berke, "Critical Variables in the Token Economy." *Proceedings of the annual convention of the American Psychological Association*, 1970, 5:517–518.

E. W. Taylor, "Interpersonal Orientation and Verbal Conditioning Effects." *Proceedings of the 76th Annual Convention, American Psychological Association,* 1968, 3:541–542.

A. Turner, *Huntsville-Madison County Mental Health Center Programs and Evaluations.* 1971.

V. O. Tyler, and G. D. Brown, "Token Reinforcement of Academic Performance with Institutionalized Delinquent Boys." *Journal of Educational Psychology,* 1968, 59:164–168.

L. P. Ullmann, R. G. Forsman, J. W. Kenny, T. L. McInnes, Jr., I. P. Unikel, and T. R. Zeisset, "Selective Reinforcement of Schizophrenics' Interview Responses." *Behaviour Research and Therapy,* 1965, 2:205–212.

L. P. Ullmann, and L. Krasner, *Case Studies in Behavior Modification.* Holt, Rinehart, & Winston, 1965.

L. P. Ullmann, and L. Krasner, *A Psychological Approach to Abnormal Behavior.* Prentice-Hall, 1969.

L. P. Ullmann, L. Krasner, and R. L. Edinger, "Verbal Conditioning of Common Associations in Long-Term Schizophrenic Patients." *Behaviour Research and Therapy,* 1964, 2:15–18.

L. P. Ullmann, L. Krasner, and M. Sherman, "MMPI Items Associated with Pleasantness of Emotional Words Used in Thematic Story-Telling." Veterans' Administration, Palo Alto, Calif., *Research Reports.* 1963, p. 25.

R. Ulrich, "Behavior Control and Public Concern." *Psychological Record,* 1967, 17:229–234.

R. Ulrich, T. Stachnik, and J. Mabry, *Control of Human Behavior.* Scott, Foresman, 1966.

R. Ulrich, T. Stachnik, and J. Mabry, *Control of Human Behavior.* Vol. 2, Scott, Foresman, 1970.

D. Upper, and J. G. Newton, "A Weight-Reduction Program for Schizophrenic Patients on a Token Economy Unit: Two Case Studies." *Journal of Behavior Therapy and Experimental Psychiatry,* 1971, 2:113–115.

T. Verhave, ed., *The Experimental Analysis of Behavior.* Appleton-Century-Crofts, 1966.

B. R. Wagner, "The Training of Attending and Abstracting Responses of Chronic Schizophrenics." *Journal of Experimental Research in Personality,* 1968, 3:77–88.

H. M. Walker, R. H. Mattson, and N. K. Buckley, "Special Class Placement as a Treatment Alternative for Deviant Behavior in Children." In Monograph 1, Department of Special Education, University of Oregon, Eugene, Oregon, 1969.

R. L. Weiss, L. Krasner, and L. P. Ullmann, "Responsivity to Verbal Conditioning as a Function of Emotional Atmosphere and Pattern of Reinforcement." *Psychological Reports,* 1960, 6:415–426.

R. L. Weiss, L. Krasner, and L. P. Ullmann, "Responsivity of Psychiatric Patients to Verbal Conditioning: 'Success' and 'Failure' Conditions and Pattern of Reinforced Trials." *Psychological Reports,* 1963, 12:423–426.

J. H. Williams, "Conditioning of Verbalization: A Review." *Psychological Bulletin,* 1966, 62:383–393.

J. H. Williams, and R. L. Blanton, "Verbal Conditioning in a Psychotherapeutic Situation." *Behaviour Research and Therapy,* 1968, 6:97–103.

F. S. Wilson, and R. H. Walters, "Modification of Speech Output of Near-Mute Schizophrenics through Social-Learning Procedures." *Behaviour Research and Therapy,* 1966, 4:59–67.

R. A. Winett, C. S. Richards, L. Krasner, and M. Krasner, "Child Monitored Token Reading Program." *Psychology in the Schools,* 1971, 8:259–262.

R. Winkler, "Management of Chronic Psychiatric Patients by a Token Reinforcement System." Paper presented at the annual meeting of the Australian Psychological Society, Brisbane, Australia, August 1968 (a).

R. Winkler, "Healthy and Unhealthy Economies." Paper presented at the annual meeting of the Australian Psychological Society, Brisbane, Australia, August 1968(b).

R. Winkler, "Management of Chronic Psychiatric Patients by a Token Reinforcement System." *Journal of Applied Behavior Analysis,* 1970, 3:47–55.

T. Winkler, and L. Krasner, "The Contribution of Economics to Token Economies." Paper presented at the annual meeting of the Eastern Psychological Association, New York City, April 1971.

M. M. Wolf, D. K. Giles, and R. V. Hall, "Experiments with Token Reinforcement in a Remedial Classroom. *Behaviour Research and Therapy,* 1968, 6:51–64.

J. Wolpe, *Psychotherapy by Reciprocal Inhibition.* Stanford University Press, 1958.

J. Wolpe, "Outgoing Presidential Report." *Association for Advancement of Behavioral Therapy,* 1968, 3:1–2.

J. Zimmerman, et al., "Effects of Token Reinforcement on Productivity in Multiply Handicapped Clients in a Sheltered Workshop." *Rehabilitation Literature,* 1969, 30:34–41.

6

Behavioral Treatment of Somatic Disorders

W. DOYLE GENTRY
Duke University Medical Center

The use of behavioral techniques in treating *mental* disorders has been well documented in the fields of clinical psychology and psychiatry [Agras 1972; American Psychiatric Association 1973; Bandura 1969; Franks 1969; Krasner 1971; Lazarus 1971; Meyer & Chesser 1970]. A host of behavioral techniques collectively termed behavior modification, behavior therapy, conditioning therapy, reinforcement therapy, operant conditioning, behavioral engineering, and contingency management have been applied to child and adult patients manifesting numerous types of problems: depression, anxiety, phobic behavior, obsessions and compulsions, mental retardation, sexual and marital problems, and behaviors associated with schizophrenia (delusions, hallucinations), among others. Reference to two earlier modules in this series [Lovaas 1972; Paul & Bernstein 1973] provide an appreciation of the history and development of behavioral techniques in treating autistic children and patients with problems of anxiety.

In this module we will explore the recent application of behavioral techniques to physical, or *somatic*, disorders, focusing on the use of these techniques to treat problems of bodily dysfunction. Such disorders as irregular heart rate, high blood pressure, chronic pain, and diarrhea have already been identified as medical disabilities to be treated by a physician. They are viewed by health care professionals and laymen alike as being beyond direct voluntary control or the influence of external, environmental forces. More recently it has been proposed that behavioral principles are useful in treating physical as well as mental difficulties, applicable wherever illness, disease, or maladaptive behavior are present.

Treatment Models

Medical Model

The traditional and most widely accepted approach to understanding and treating most somatic disorders is the *medical*, or *disease*, model. According to this model, all overt, maladaptive somatic behavior—e. g., coughing, grimacing, or reporting that one "has a headache"— can be symptoms of an underlying, pathological disease. The actual disease or underlying cause of the visible symptoms (or behavior) usually is inferred whether or not it can be identified. In addition, the cause is viewed as being organic, or physiological, for example, germs, lesions, or viral infections. Treatment is focused internally, with the physician attempting to correct the patient's disease chemically and/or surgically. Only secondary attention is given to the external, visible, somatic behavior, what is frequently referred to as "symptom relief" or "symptom management."

Psychosomatic Model

A model similar to the medical one for diagnosing and treating somatic disorders is the *psychosomatic* model. This approach views some types of physical illness as being, in some instances, a response to an underlying, unconscious, emotional conflict. As Kimball [1970] describes it in his review of conceptual developments in psychosomatic medicine during the last thirty years, the underlying conflict may be an expression of a patient's specific personality pattern, it may be tied to the onset of a specific conflict, or it may be a manifestation of a patient's specific attitudes toward a situation, situations, or in his life. The psychosomatic model differs from the medical model in that it focuses on psychic, rather than organic, causes of illness, but it is similar to the medical model in that (a) it views overt somatic behavior as the symptom of an underlying process, (b) it views illness behavior as a response to an earlier event or condition (conflict), and (c) it focuses the treatment inward in attempting to correct the mental or emotional condition of the patient by resolving the specific conflict. The treatment chosen is long-term analytic psychotherapy.

The use of the psychosomatic model in treating somatic disorders has been illustrated by Alexander [1939, p.175] who stated in a classic paper on hypertension: ". . . patients suffering from hypertension have a characteristic psychodynamic structure. This consists in a very pronounced conflict between passive, dependent, feminine, receptive tendencies and over-compensatory, competitive, aggressive hostile impulses which lead to fear and increase a flight from competition towards the passive dependent attitude." He suggested that this state of "emotional paralysis," involving a chronic inhibition of hostile, aggressive tendencies, resulted in a chronic elevation of blood pressure. He also felt that "one cannot hope that through psychotherapy the blood pressure can be brought back to a normal level" (p. 178). According to Alexander psychotherapy seems to offer greater promise in *preventing* hypertension. This view of the therapeutic inadequacy of the psychosomatic model has remained about the same since that time.

Behavioral Model—Respondent

Another approach to understanding and treating physical disorders is what might be called, in behavioral, psychological terms, a *respondent* model. This approach is similar in many respects to the medical and psychosomatic models already described. For instance it looks for the cause, roots, or stimulus of a somatic disorder in an antecedent event or condition, for example, an underlying state of tension or anxiety characterized by subjective and physiological properties. In some cases the stimulus-response relationship between physical tension and the disorder is clearly identified. Budzynski, Stoyva, and Adler [1970] observed a close relation between electromyographic (EMG) activity in scalp and neck muscles and reported intensity of headaches in patients suffering from tension headaches. In other cases the stimulus-response relationship is simply inferred. In either case the focus of treatment is internal (as was true of the other two models); it is intended to reduce or eliminate the patient's anxiety or tension. The therapeutic techniques used include systematic desensitization, relaxation training, and corrective biofeedback. These techniques and the theoretical principles underlying them are discussed in detail in the module by Paul and Bernstein [1973].

Behavioral Model—Operant

The other behavioral approach to somatic disorders is the *operant* model. In this model the emphasis is on the relationship between overt somatic behavior and its consequences in the external environment. Maladaptive somatic behavior is defined as the *operant,* and the derived consequences, positive or negative, are the *reinforcement.* The motivating force that initially produces and/or maintains the disorder is believed to come from the patient's exterior world rather than his interior one; the force is social, or interpersonal. Treatment includes various experimental methods for delivering or withholding positive and negative reinforcement, collectively called operant conditioning or behavior modification.

Review of the Literature

The application of behavioral techniques for treating somatic disorders has evolved progressively from animal experimentation to experimentation with normal human subjects and finally to actual patient-care studies. In the following discussion the major disorders that have been treated with such techniques will be described.

Cardiac Disorders

The area of the behavioral treatment of somatic disorders perhaps most often studied is that of cardiac disorders.

Miller and DiCara [1967; Miller 1969; DiCara 1970] have shown in a series of animal experiments that rats can learn to alter their heart rates under conditions of positive reinforcement and punishment. In seeking to obtain pleasurable electrical stimulation or to avoid (or escape) a painful electrical shock, the rats demonstrated significant increases or decreases respectively in their heart rates. In addition they learned to change their heart rates independently of changes in other bodily systems, for example, blood pressure and intestinal contractions, and they retained this ability over a period of time.

Similar studies have shown effective learning of heart rate change in normal humans who are free of disease. Shearn [1962] found that adult men could learn to accelerate their heart rate temporarily in order to delay painful electric shock, compared to control subjects who received an equivalent number of shocks on a noncontingent basis (that is, changes in heart rate did not delay shock). Ascough and Sipprelle [1968] have noted that verbal praise from an experimenter ("that's good"), when systematically applied, can produce a rise or fall in the heart rate of women college students, again compared to subjects who received the same feedback noncontingently. Engel and his coworkers [Engel & Chism 1967; Engel & Hansen 1966; Levene, Engel, & Pearson 1968] have shown that monetary reward can affect heart rate slowing, speeding, and alternate speeding and slowing in college students paid one-half cent per second for the amount of time they spent responding appropriately in each of the three studies. Heart rate speeding appeared easier to learn than heart rate slowing. While all of those tested learned to accelerate their rate under the reward condition, only half learned to slow their heart rate under similar conditions.

The same approach used in animal and human experimentation studies was applied to patients suffering from a malfunctioning heart. In one study Weiss and Engel [1971] attempted to train eight patients who had been hospitalized for premature ventricular contractions (PVCs) to control their heart rate. Each patient was taught to increase or decrease his rate according to visual cues: a green light signaled heart rate speeding and a red light, heart rate slowing. If the patient responded correctly, a yellow light (reward) indicated a successful performance. Patients were thus able to monitor their heart rate continuously. Five of the patients in the study learned to slow or speed their heart rate systematically and eventually showed a significant decrease in PVCs associated with the training experience. Four of these patients showed a continuation of lessened PVC activity for up to twenty-one months after being discharged from the hospital. Of the remaining three patients who failed to learn to control their heart rate and thus reduce the frequency of PVCs, two subsequently died of cardiac dysfunction. One of these "failure" patients had an unusually diseased heart which was perhaps incapable of beating regularly despite the patient's attempts to learn heart rate control. The other two appeared to be under the influence of competing reinforcement contingencies such as excessive alcohol consumption or disability compensation. Other studies by Engel and Melmon [1968] and Bleecker and Engel [1973] have observed a reduction in other types of irregular heart rate such as cardiac arrhythmias and chronic atrial fibrillation as a result of similar training in heart rate control. In all three studies on actual patients the primary reinforcement influencing behavior change appears to have been the rewarding aspects of survival, which seem to have been more or less a direct consequence of successful performance in the training phase of the experiments.

Hypertension

Another considerable area of study is that of the behavioral change of blood pressure. This includes animal studies, experiments with normotensive humans, and patient-care studies of essential hypertension.

As was true of heart rate, Miller and DiCara [1967] found that rats could learn to increase or decrease their blood pressure in order to avoid or escape the punishment of painful electric shock. Recording systolic blood pressure from a catheter inserted in the abdominal aorta of the animals, these investigators noted that animals rewarded for increasing blood pressure showed an overall rise of 22.3 percent above baseline pressure; those rewarded for decreasing pressure showed an average drop of 19.2 percent. Yoked-control rates (those receiving the same number of shocks regardless of changes in blood pressure) showed no noticeable change in pressure. Also, the blood pressure changes were not accompanied by corresponding changes in the animals' heart rates or body temperatures during training. Plumlee [1969] found similar conditioned elevations in diastolic blood pressure in primates which learned to avoid painful shock by producing such responses.

Shapiro and coworkers have concentrated on demonstrating the conditioning of blood pressure in normal human subjects. In the first of a series of studies [Shapiro, Tursky, Gershon, & Stern 1969] twenty male college students with normal resting blood pressures were rewarded for increases or decreases in systolic blood pressure (SBP). Reward consisted of visual and auditory feedback as to how successful the subject was on each of twenty-five trials in addition to the opportunity to view a slide of a nude from *Playboy* magazine projected on a screen. The subjects rewarded for decreases in SBP showed a significant drop in pressure, compared to those who were rewarded for increases in SBP. The latter, however, failed to show a significant increase in SBP despite their being systematically reinforced for this increase. In a second study in this series Shapiro, Schwartz, and Tursky [1972] reported similar findings for subjects rewarded for changes in diastolic blood pressure (DBP). In this study the subject's reinforcement consisted of visual and auditory (light, tone) feedback for successful performance in each training trial, which, in turn, led to an opportunity to view slides of nudes and attractive landscape scenes and to receive monetary bonuses. Other studies in this series [Shapiro, Tursky, & Schwartz 1970a, 1970b; Schwartz 1972] revealed that heart rate and blood pressure conditioning can occur in the same subjects, both in an integrated fashion (both systems jointly) and a differentiated fashion (one system without the other). Elder, Leftwich, and Wilkerson [1974] have also demonstrated successful modification of both SBP and DBP in volunteer college students, although the results were of lesser magnitude.

Three studies illustrate the use of behavioral techniques in treating patients with essential hypertension. Benson, Shapiro, Tursky, and Schwartz [1971] attempted to modify arterial SBP in seven patients diagnosed as having moderate to severe hypertension. All of these patients were receiving outpatient treatment for their abnormal blood pressure condition, and six of the seven were on antihypertensive medication at the time of the study. Benson and others trained the patients to control their blood pressure, using the same procedures they had used in the previous experiments on normotensive human subjects (visual and auditory feedback indicating a successful lowering of SBP in each trial, projected slides of scenic landscapes, and monetary rewards). Patients were conditioned until they no longer showed further decline in pressure. This goal took from eight to thirty-four conditioning sessions, depending on the patient. A comparison of SBP levels before and after training indicated that six of the seven patients profited from the conditioning. In addition, the effect appeared to be specific to blood pressure; no consistent changes in heart rate were observed for any of the patients. In a later study Elder, Ruiz, Deabler, and Dillenkoffer [1973] found that visual feedback and/or feedback paired with verbal praise from the experiment ("good," "very good")lowered the DBP of eighteen male hypertensives as much as 25 percent below baseline during conditioning and that the therapeutic effect tended to persist for at least a week after training.

Finally, Brady, Luborsky, and Kron [1974], using a *respondent* behavioral technique, found that three of four labile hypertensive patients exposed to metronome-conditioned relaxation training showed a significant decrease in DBP below their own baseline levels, which in some cases persisted over an extended period of time. Here, rather than receiving immediate feedback for altering their blood pressure, patients were simply told to lie down, close their eyes, and listen to a tape recording of instructions to "relax" and "let go," paced with the rhythmic beats of an auditory metronome set at sixty beats per minute [Brady 1973].

Asthma

Behavioral techniques, both operant and respondent, have been used successfully in treating asthmatic behavior in children and adults.

Using the operant approach, Neisworth and Moore [1972] and Gardner [1968] noted that a combination of an extinction procedure for coughing behavior and positive reinforcement for incompatible noncoughing behavior led to a dramatic reduction in asthmatic behavior in very young children. Extinction involved the stopping of parental attention and medication following actual or threatened asthmatic attacks. Positive reinforcement, on the other hand, involved giving the children money or tokens (which could be exchanged for toys) either for "settling down and relaxing" or for coughing less over a period of time. In both investigations the patients were tested several months later (six months in one case and eleven in the other), and the beneficial effects of the conditioning procedure were found to persist.

In another operant study Creer [1970] noted that the use of time out from positive reinforcement was effective in decreasing the number of hospitalizations as well as the duration of hospitalization for asthmatic children admitted for severe coughing behavior. He found that when the normally positive consequences of hospitalization (socializing with other children, watching television, and receiving "tender loving care" from the nurses) were eliminated, asthmatic children were less apt to spend time in the hospital and that they exhibited less asthmatic behavior which might necessitate such entry. In one child's words, "The hospital is no fun no more" (p. 120).

Similarly, Alexander, Chai, Creer, Miklich, Renne, and Cardoso [1973] demonstrated the effectiveness of aversive consequences. They successfully altered the coughing pattern of a hospitalized, severely asthmatic, fifteen-year-old boy by teaching him to "suppress" coughing (increase the latency of response) to specific stimuli known to elicit such behavior, in order to avoid painful electric shock which was applied to the boy's forearm. After seventy-five conditioning trials over a period of three days, the boy reported "no urge to cough" upon inhaling shampoo, a stimulus that had previously triggered violent bouts of coughing. In subsequent training sessions he was able to suppress coughing to the odor of beef grease after about fifty conditioning trials, to bath soap after fifteen trials, and hair spray after being exposed to it only once.

Members of this same group of investigators have also used the respondent approach in treating asthmatic behavior. Alexander, Miklich, and Hershkoff [1972] found that relaxation training was effective in reducing subjective feelings of tension and in increasing the peak expiratory flow rate in asthmatic children compared to a control group of youngsters who did not receive this type of treatment. Davis, Saunders, Creer, and Chai [1973] observed that relaxation training alone and relaxation training plus biofeedback (the subject is able to "hear" his level of muscle tension via headphones) were successful in reducing asthma symptoms (peak expiratory flow rate) with children experiencing nonsevere asthma. The same techniques, however, were not successful, compared to a control condition, with children suffering from severe asthmatic behavior. In addition, the combination of relaxation training and biofeedback appeared to be more effective than relaxation training alone in improving the respiratory behavior of the subjects.

Moore [1965] reported that while relaxation training, suggestion, and systematic desensitization were all effective in altering the *subjective* reports of patients about the number of asthma attacks they had each week, only the desensitization technique produced *objective* improvement in respiratory function.

Finally, Cooper [1964] has demonstrated the use of relaxation in alleviating anxiety and reducing asthmatic behavior in a young woman whose asthma had not responded to drug therapy. He also noted a continued improvement in the patient for at least sixteen months after being discharged from

treatment, during which time she had only four attacks.

Chronic Pain

Fordyce and coworkers [Fordyce, Fowler, & DeLateur 1968;Fordyce, Fowler, Lehmann, & DeLateur 1968] have reported success in treating patients with chronic orthopedic pain, using behavioral (operant) techniques. In a typical case, Fordyce, Fowler, and DeLateur [1968] systematically manipulated medication, attention, and rest as positive reinforcers for nonpain behavior in a thirty-seven-year-old woman who manifested an eighteen-year history of debilitating back pain. At the beginning of treatment she complained of continuous pain, habitually took analgesic medication throughout the day, and was virtually unable to engage in any type of activity for more than twenty minutes without resting. The behavioral program consisted of (a) providing medication on a time-contingent rather than pain-contingent basis (i.e., at specific time intervals, not when the patient experienced and/or complained of pain); (b) providing social reinforcement (staff attention and praise) for nonpain behavior, for example, increased ward activity and nonreinforcing (extinction) pain behavior such as moaning, grimacing, and inactivity; (c) providing social reinforcement for increased walking; and (d) providing programed rest periods as a reward for more involvement in occupational therapy. After eight weeks of inpatient treatment and twenty-three weeks of outpatient treatment, the woman had improved dramatically in all areas of behavior. She could be active for as long as two hours at a time without complaining of pain or needing rest; she could walk farther and faster than before, and "she was taking driving lessons so as to be independently mobile in the community" (p.106). In addition, she had learned to function without the use of pain medication.

Headaches

In only one study published to date have operant procedures been applied to a patient suffering from headaches [Yen & McIntire 1971]. Yen and

McIntire reported the case of a fourteen-year-old girl who initially complained of having two to seven headaches a day and who subsequently experienced a rapid reduction in the frequency of such complaints as a result of a response-cost procedure. In this procedure the girl was asked to record each headache—its time of occurrence, probable cause, and what she did about it—before she was allowed to complain verbally or receive any medication. The aim of the procedure was to disrupt the usual relationship between reporting the disorder verbally and immediate positive social reinforcement (attention), rest, and medication. At the onset of treatment the frequency of headache complaints was reduced to only one a day, and by the end of five weeks there were almost no complaints.

Several studies have used respondent techniques in treating migraine and tension headaches. Lutker [1971], for example, found that teaching a patient to relax whenever she felt a "pressure build-up" helped eliminate migraine headaches. The patient had suffered from severe attacks six to eight times weekly for about eight years. Mitchell and Mitchell [1971] found that a combination of of systematic desensitization and training in making assertive responses was effective in reducing both the frequency and the duration of migraine headaches when compared to relaxation training alone or no treatment.

Using corrective biofeedback, Budzynski and colleagues [Budzynski, Stoyva, & Adler 1970] were successful in treating patients with tension or muscle-contraction headaches. Patients were trained in deep muscle-relaxation by listening to and then altering the level of muscle tension in their scalp and neck muscles. They were able to "hear" (get feedback) their own muscle activity by means of earphones which translated electromyographic activity (EMG) into an audible tone. Their task was to "keep the tone low in pitch"; the lower the tone, the more relaxed the muscles. External manipulation of the auditory feedback made it increasingly difficult for the patient to lower the tone, i.e., the required progressive lessening of EMG activity; therefore the patient gradually learned to become more relaxed. After four to eight weeks of biofeedback experience, all of the patients reported significantly less intense headaches, which corresponded with their lessened EMG activity. A three-month follow-up indicated continued improvement. The patients generally reported an increased awareness of the times when they were becoming tense, an increased ability to reduce the tension, and a decreased tendency to overreact to stress (eg., "things don't seem to bother me as much as they used to").

In a subsequent study Budzynski, Stoyva, Adler, and Mullaney [1973] duplicated their findings and concluded that after three to six twenty-minute feedback sessions, chronic tension-headache patients improved considerably.

A similar procedure for treating tension and migraine headaches, called "autogenic feedback training," has been described by Sargent, Green, and Walters [1973]. Patients were trained to increase the flow of blood in their hands, which is associated with an increase in hand temperature, by visualizing autogenic phrases such as "I feel quite relaxed," "my arms and hands are heavy and warm," "warmth is flowing into my hands," "they are warm," while at the same time receiving visual feedback from a "temperature trainer," a device that indicates the differential temperature between the midforehead and right index finger. Sargent and his colleagues used this procedure with sufferers of migraine and tension headaches. The technique proved more effective with migraine headaches (where 63 percent of the patients undergoing treatment improved) than with tension headaches (where improvement in only 33 percent was noted).

Related to this finding is the report by Wickramaskera [1973] that two migraine patients responded postively to autogenic feedback training related to changes in hand temperature after failing to respond to EMG feedback training.

Spasms

Sachs and Mayhall [1971] reported successful treatment of spastic behavior in a twenty-year-old cerebral palsied man, using an operant punishment technique. The patient received a painful electric shock in his hand immediately following each gross head movement or spasm (irrelevant movement of arms, legs, or body) during thirty-minute treatment sessions. Spastic behavior decreased from an average of fifty-four and eighty-two responses per session before treatment to only three responses per session after eight treatment sessions. The punishment procedure produced an immediate decrease in gross head movements and a more gradual decline in spasms.

Neurodermatitis

Three cases have been reported involving the use of behavioral techniques in alleviating severe scratching behavior associated with chronic skin disorders. In all three cases patients' long-standing dermatological problems, which were of sufficient intensity to produce bleeding, had not responded to traditional medical treatment, including ointments, lotions, and X-ray therapy.

Allen and Harris [1966] used a combination of extinction for scratching behavior and positive reinforcement for nonscratching behavior in treating a five-year-old girl whose excessive scratching had resulted in bleeding as well as large sores and scabs over the upper part of her body. The child was ignored whenever she scratched herself, no matter how bloody the results. At the same time, she was rewarded with parental approval and attention whenever she engaged in constructive play activities and did not scratch. The child was also given gold stars and primary reinforcement (cookies, candy, beverages) for nonscratching behavior. At the end of six weeks of such treatment she was free of the destructive scratching, and her scratches had begun to heal. At a four-month follow-up check, the successful outcome had been maintained.

Similarly, Walton [1960] used an extinction technique successfully to eliminate a skin disorder of two years' duration in a twenty-year-old woman. He had the girl's family and fiance withdraw their attention to her scratching.

Finally, Ratliff and Stein [1968] used a combination operant and respondent approach to treat severe scratching behavior in a young man. Initially a program of aversive conditioning was established in which the patient was shocked when he scratched any part of his body. The conditioning, however, upset him and thus did not produce a complete reduction of the disorder. Another approach was used in which the patient was trained to relax anytime he felt the "urge to scratch" (p. 398). This approach led to a complete cessation of such behavior, and at a six-month follow-up the man reported no return of the scratching.

Spasmodic Torticollis

Several case studies have been reported using behavioral techniques in treating spasmodic torticollis, or "wry neck," that is, gross distortions in head placement and general head immobility.

In one report [Brierley 1967] two patients, each with a two-year history of disabling torticollis, received painful electric shock to their wrists whenever their heads deviated from a normal position in a specially made headset. Both patients improved in a fairly short time (ten to twelve sessions), quickly resumed normal functioning in areas such as driving and working, and were still free of the disorder in follow-up several months later.

Agras and Marshall [1965] have used negative practice to treat torticollis in two patients, with success in one case but not in the other. Negative practice involved having the patient duplicate the tic behavior several hundred times in each treatment session as well as in practice sessions at home. Success was determined by both the clinical absence of the torticollis behavior and a reduction in excessive muscle activity evident in electromyography.

Bernhardt, Hersen, and Barlow [1972] found that simple instructions to the patient to keep his head in a normal position were ineffective in alleviating wry neck. However, negative feedback, which consisted of a white light that was flashed each time the patient failed to maintain the desired head position, effectively relieved the wry neck. Instructions and feedback combined were also effective in decreasing torticollis but not to the same extent as with feedback alone.

Vocal Nodules

Gray, England, and Mohoney [1965] have used systematic desensitization in treating benign vocal nodules in a twenty-nine-year-old woman. Before behavioral treatment was begun the patient had experienced hoarseness for six months, which had led to the total loss of her voice. She was trained in deep muscle-relaxation and learned to relax in three types of situations that had previously elicited anxiety reactions: (a) the disciplining of her children, (b) her relationship with her husband, and (c) her relationship with another man with whom she was emotionally involved. After fifteen treatment sessions over a period of three weeks, she was symptom-free. In fact, "a laryngeal examination by the laryngologist revealed that the vocal folds had cleared, with only slight vestiges of former swelling" (p.192).

Seizures

Gardner [1967] used behavioral techniques to treat seizure behavior of a nonorganic origin in a ten-year-old girl. The child's seizure activity appeared to be the result of inadvertent modeling of somatic dysfunction by the child's mother who had recently been hospitalized for an intense headache and of parental shaping of deviant somatic behavior. That is, the parents had progressively given in to the child's tantrum behavior and somatic complaints, which increasingly became indistinguishable from one another. Treatment consisted of having the parents act "deaf and dumb" (extinction) when the child manifested seizures and instead giving the child attention (positive reinforcement) for engaging in constructive nonseizure behavior such as playing with other children and helping her mother. Within two weeks of starting treatment the child had dropped from six to eight seizures per week to none. In addition, her tantrum behavior had completely disappeared. At the end of twenty-six weeks of follow-up the parents were told to begin paying attention again to the child's tantrum and seizure behavior. The result was that

> within 24 hours of the deliberate reinstatement of parental attention for S's somatic complaints, this class of behavior showed a sharp increase to about one per hour. Then S manifested a seizure. As instructed, the parents then returned to the

initial treatment plan of reinforcing appropriate behavior while ignoring deviant behavior. Subsequent to the parents' reinstatement of these contingencies, S manifested no more seizure behavior . . . (p. 211).

Two reports by Sterman and coworkers [Sterman & Friar 1972; Sterman, MacDonald, & Stone, in press] illustrate the use of behavioral treatment with organic, epileptic seizures. In both cases patients received corrective biofeedback training to reduce sensorimotor electroencephalographic (brain wave) activity associated with the occurence of seizures. Patients were provided with visual (slides of nature scenes) and auditory (chime) feedback to show EEG activity of a certain desired frequency. They were also told to relax and think positive thoughts in order to produce an internal state that might activate the feedback apparatus. All of the patients responded positively to the training experience, as shown by clinical seizure records kept by the patient and by EEG records. For one of the patients the treatment was so effective that over the eighteen-month training period she reported only seven seizures compared to the twenty-one or more per year she had previously had.

Vomiting

Lang and Malamed [1969] have reported a dramatic case in which aversive conditioning (punishment) was used to eliminate persistent, ruminative vomiting in a nine-month-old infant. The infant received painful electric shocks in his leg at the beginning and throughout each episode of vomiting. All such behavior was eliminated after six treatment sessions. In addition, the infant gained weight, became more active, and was generally more responsive to other humans. A six-month follow-up showed no recurrence of the disorder.

Wolf, Birnbrauer, Williams, and Lander [1965] extinguished vomiting in a young, retarded girl in a classroom setting. Ordinarily the girl was excused from class when she vomited (positive rein-forcement), but with the extinction procedure, she was not permitted to leave; she had to remain in class which continued. Furthermore, she was rewarded with teacher attention and praise as well as candy, for classroom behavior that did not include vomiting. Initially her rate of vomiting increased, but soon (after thirty class days) dropped to zero where it remained. Removal of the operant procedure led to an immediate return to the maladaptive behavior and its reintroduction to a final cessation of the vomiting behavior.

Chronic Diarrhea

Hedberg [1973] has demonstrated the effectiveness of systematic desensitization in treating a patient with chronic diarrhea of twenty-two years' duration. When treatment began the patient had an average of ten bowel movements a day and an average of three "accidents" a week. She was able to maintain bowel control only up to thirty seconds. As a result, she had stopped all of her community activities (shopping, going to church, and so on, as well as many personal relationships.

Treatment involved twelve sessions of systematic desensitization dealing with situations of interpersonal anxiety over a six-week period. Bowel control was achieved by the eighth session with a simultaneous increase in social and physical activities. After two years she was defecating only once a day and was able to control her bowels for hours if necessary.

Incontinence

While there are many reports available that describe successful treatment of fecal incontinence using behavioral techniques, only two recent ones are given here. They convey the alternate strategies one might use to correct this somatic disorder.

Engel, Nikoomanesh, and Schuster [1974] used a combination of verbal reinforcement and biofeedback to eliminate incontinence in six patients ranging in age from six to fifty-four who had suffered from the disorder for three to eight years. In each case a balloon was inserted in the patient's rectum, which, when inflated, signaled the patient to begin sphincter control. The patient's attempts to establish "normal" control were then visually fed

back to him via polygraph tracings, and he was praised (positive reinforcement) for more normal responding. If he did poorly in trying to establish normal sphincter control, this was also indicated to him, both visually and verbally. All six patients completed their training in four sessions or less, with four of the six (67 percent) maintaining continent behavior for substantial periods of follow-up.

In a somewhat different way, Wagner and Paul [1970] reduced incontinent behavior in a large group of mental patients. The patients were given positive reinforcers such as candy and cigarettes, meals, and uninterrupted sleep if they were successful in not soiling their beds during the day or night. They were also encouraged and praised for using the toilet at appropriate times. After thirty-one weeks of treatment all of the patients had improved. Fourteen of the nineteen patients (74 percent) showed no incidence of daytime soiling at all, with the remaining five showing only a minimal amount of such behavior. Nighttime results were equally encouraging. Follow-up thirteen months later indicated continuing continence in nearly all of the patients.

Enuresis

There are many reports available that indicate the successful use of behavioral techniques in treating nocturnal enuresis, with success rates close to 90 percent in some cases [Lovibond 1964]. Reported here are two somewhat different strategies for correcting enuresis.

A study by Sloop and Kennedy [1973] illustrates the traditional behavioral approach to enuretic behavior, that is, urinating in bed causes an electrical buzzer to sound, which awakens the child who is then taken to the toilet. In treating a group of institutionalized retardates, Sloop and Kennedy noted a significant improvement in enuretic behavior following eleven weeks of treatment. Fifty-two percent of the youngsters receiving the treatment achieved dryness for fourteen successive nights during this period compared to a control group (who were taken to the bathroom twice nightly noncontingently whether they urinated in bed or not) in which only one child (5 percent) showed improvement. Here, learning to control urination is an avoidance response—i.e., to avoid the unpleasant consequences of being awakened abruptly during the night and taken to the toilet.

Kimmel and Kimmel [1970] and Paschalis, Kimmel, and Kimmel [1973], using a different approach, have attempted to reinforce bladder control positively rather than focus on enuretic behavior as such. In effect, they teach the enuretic child to "hold it in" for longer and longer periods (the program is individualized) in order to obtain social reinforcement (parental praise) and tangible rewards in the form of candy, cookies, and soda pop or tokens which may be exchanged for gifts. In both studies they noted dramatic success in altering both daytime and nighttime urinating behavior of children being treated, and in a relatively short time.

In addition, the successful effect of their approach has lasted for up to ninety days. They suggest that continuation of an intensive behavioral program can turn some preliminary failures into successes, that failures appear to be mainly the result of insufficient care and attention to detail by parents in administrating the program.

Insomnia

Geer and Katkin [1966] report a case in which systematic desensitization was used to treat a patient suffering from insomnia. The patient, a twenty-nine-year-old female student, had been having prolonged periods of sleeplessness (five or six nights consecutively) for a year before seeking treatment. She said that the insomnia had noticeably interfered with her school performance as well as many other aspects of her daily life and that she was increasingly irritable because of her insomia.

Treatment was carried out during a total of fourteen sessions which included an initial intake session, four sessions for training the patient in relaxation procedures, and nine therapy sessions in which she was progressively trained to relax while visualizing a single stimulus situation, such as lying in bed at home trying to fall asleep.

There was no change in her behavior for the first six treatment sessions. Then, between her sixth and seventh therapy sessions, she reported sleeping more, and by the ninth session she reported sleeping well each night. At follow-ups of 1 1/2 weeks, 1 1/2 months, and eight months she reported continuing good sleep as well as an improved disposition as a result of less fatigue.

Promises and Problems

The application of behavioral techniques to the treatment of somatic disorders is relatively new and is just beginning to be explored. Of the 656 articles appearing in the four major behavioral journals *(Behavior Research and Therapy, Behavior Therapy, Journal of Applied Behavioral Analysis,* and the *Journal of Behavior Therapy and Experimental Psychiatry)* during the period 1970–72, only twelve (2 percent) described the treatment of somatic, as opposed to mental, disorders. Of all the somatic disorders known to man, only a handful—as is illustrated in the literature review in this module—have so far been treated successfully with behavioral techniques. Not surprisingly, the area has yet to achieve firm scientific underpinning or adequate clinical trials. The fifty-eight therapeutically oriented studies, which represent the bulk of the published literature in this area, are reported on in detail above. Of these, only fifteen (26 percent) fall under the heading of basic research, and they are studies dealing exclusively with the cardiovascular system (heart and blood pressure). The remaining forty-three studies are more aptly described as clinical applications, which, for the most part, involve case studies of only one or a few individuals per report.

The results of these studies suggest that behavioral techniques hold promise for the treatment of somatic disorders. However, a number of problems exist which should be considered before one decides whether this promise is real or rather, as Blanchard and Young [1973] have said, it is "as yet . . . a promise unfulfilled."

Some critics may suggest that the initial success enjoyed in this area results from selecting patients who manifest something other than *real* or organic problems. Note that several of the studies discussed in this module involve, patients having a *psychogenic* or *functional* disorder [Gray, England,

& Mahoney 1965] or a "hysteric-type" personality [Gardner 1967]. Defenders of behavioral techniques offer two answers to such criticism. First, behavioral methods have been applied successfully to organically based problems. In fact, the bulk of the studies reported here do indicate an organic etiology for the disorder in question, e.g., cardiac damage [Weiss & Engel 1971], spasms associated with cerebral palsy [Sachs & Mayhall 1971], and chronic pain resulting from a herniated disc or spinal fracture [Fordyce et al. 1968]. Second, and more important, most clinicians who use behavioral methods to treat somatic disorders regard the issue of etiology as irrelevant. For example, Fordyce and coworkers [1968, p. 189], in describing the behavioral treatment for chronic pain, note: "The thesis . . . is not that pain is originally produced by operant conditioning (i.e., that pain originates from its consequences in the environment) but that much of the behavior occurring subsequent to presentation of a presumed noxious stimulus may be accounted for and modified by principles of learning, whatever the original cause of pain" (p. 189).

While the application of behavioral techniques may not be limited to disorders of psychogenic origin, the data suggest that one must nonetheless take into consideration the minimal constitutional requirements necessary for successful learning or relearning, especially with respect to changes in the autonomic nervous system. Weiss and Engel [1971] have noted that a heart that is too diseased to beat more regularly is incapable of benefiting from behavioral treatment no matter how motivated the patient is to perform as directed. Similarly, Davis and coworkers [1973] found that children with "severe" asthma failed to respond positively to combined relaxation and biofeedback procedures. They concluded that it is "possible that the degree of illness of the severe S's eliminated any chances for improved respiratory functioning on their part" (p. 126). Finally, Engel and colleagues [1974] had one patient end biofeedback training for incontinence after only one session because she found the procedure too painful. They noted that she was the only patient out of seven who complained of pain and the only one who exhibited an anal fissure.

Still another factor is the patient's level of motivation, which can be a determining factor in whether or not behavioral treatment is effective in modifying somatic disorders. While one might imagine that the possibility of becoming healthy or of prolonging one's life would be sufficient reinforcement for all patients to avail themselves of treatment, this is not the case. As Weiss and Engel [1971] noted with cardiac patients, competing reinforcement contingencies can affect the course and outcome of treatment. In their study two patients failed to participate fully in the biofeedback training program, one because of a drinking problem and the other because he "was afraid that if his PVCs improved, he might lose his disability benefits" (p. 318). He died shortly after being discharged from the hospital. It is sometimes both possible and desirable to provide other incentives for enlisting in a behavioral program and thus becoming healthier, especially where young children are being treated and the disorder is not life-threatening, e.g., money or tokens [Gardner 1968] and the opportunity to watch television [Creer 1970].

There is also the problem of determining just which techniques or reinforcement strategies are the most effective, whether various procedures are successful for all of the disorders being treated. For example, the existing evidence suggests that punishment (primarily in the form of electric shocks) may not be a desirable technique for modifying many somatic disorders. In one instance, punishment failed to achieve a complete reduction of symptoms [Ratliff & Stein 1968] and in another produced a dramatic increase in maladaptive behavior [Alexander et al. 1973]. In both reports the patients experienced an emotional reaction which caused them to resist or become less involved in the treatment. In other studies, however, punishment resulted in positive alterations in the somatic behavior [Lang & Malamed 1969; Sachs & Mayhall 1971]. Thus punishment as a treatment technique does appear to have some merit.

Most investigators have relied almost totally on simple applications of positive reinforcement, extinction, and avoidance conditioning. The reinforcement has been delivered continuously. There have been no attempts to use more complex, intermittent schedules of reinforcement in treating such patients. Other questions about the mechanics of operant and respondent conditioning with somatic disorders have been raised by Engel [1972], specifically for cardiac disorders. These include such issues as the need for feedback and feedback training, generalization of effects outside the treatment situation, and so on. Similarly, Miller [1974] has raised the issue of "placebo effects," that is, the possibility that almost any type of procedure which the patient believes will be effective will have beneficial effects. Some of the success of behavioral techniques may be attributed to these nonspecific placebo effects.

In at least one area of treatment—cardiovascular disorders—there has been some justifiable criticism of the "quality of the evidence." For example, Blanchard and Young [1973, 1974] point out that much of the work in the area of cardiac disorders and hypertension lacks sufficient methodological control to warrant definite conclusions about the efficacy of such techniques in treating this type of patient. They label several reports—for example, Engel and Melmon [1968]—as "unsystematic case studies," referring to the investigators' failure to provide a report of how the effects of treatment were measured and to their failure to provide adequate control groups or situations in which the patient serves as his own control. Blanchard and Young also believe that some studies in this area, while producing statistically significant results, do not bring all patients into the normal range of functioning, for example, in terms of blood pressure [Benson et al. 1971]. Such criticism might be leveled at other areas of treatment as well, but it is

encouraging that more and more studies of behavioral treatment of somatic disorders are including control (no-treatment) and/or comparison treatment groups and are contrasting the effects of treatment of both the subjective state of the patient ("my head doesn't hurt as much") and his physiological functioning.

Summary

Despite the problems mentioned in this module, the future of behavioral treatment of somatic disorders seems assured. Physicians, social scientists, and laymen alike are beginning to realize that any comprehensive understanding of physical illness and its treatment must include multiple, alternative theories and techniques, including the behavioral model. It seems clear that no individual can experience physical pain, suffering, and organic dysfunction without it drastically disrupting his relationship with his external environment. If someone cries out in pain, someone usually answers; this is positive reinforcement. If someone's back hurts for a prolonged period of time, he is generally excused from normal daily activities such as work, sex, and recreation; in certain individuals this constitutes a form of avoidance conditioning. On the other hand, anxiety and physical tension can result in physical illness, for example, headaches and asthma; the person is responding to an emotional antecedent or cause of the illness rather than to an organic one. In both instances the maladaptive behavior need no longer be regarded as "not real." Instead, it may optimistically be the subject of behavioral treatment.

BIBLIOGRAPHY

W. Stewart Agras, *Behavior Modification: Principles and Clinical Applications.* Little, Brown, 1972.

Stewart Agras and Carlton Marshall, "The Application of Negative Practice to Spasmodic Torticollis." *American Journal of Psychiatry,* 1965, 122:579–582.

Franz Alexander, "Emotional Factors in Essential Hypertension." *Psychosomatic Medicine,* 1939, 1:173–179.

A. B. Alexander, H. Chai, T. L. Creer, D. R. Miklich, C. M. Renne, and R. R. Cardoso, "The Elimination of Chronic Cough by Response Suppression Shaping." *Journal of Behavior Therapy and Experimental Psychiatry,* 1973, 4:75–80.

A. B. Alexander, D. R. Miklich, and H. Hershkoff, "The Immediate Effects of Systematic Relaxation Training on Peak Expiratory Flow Rates in Asthmatic Children." *Psychosomatic Medicine,* 1972, 34:388–394.

K. Eileen Allen and Florence R. Harris, "Elimination of a Child's Excessive Scratching by Training the Mother in Reinforcement Procedures." *Behavior Research and Therapy,* 1966, 4:79–84.

American Psychiatric Association, *Behavior Therapy in Psychiatry.* Task Force Report 5, 1973.

J. C. Ascough and C. N. Sipprelle, "Operant Verbal Conditioning of Autonomic Responses." *Behavior Research and Therapy,* 1968, 6:363–370.

Albert Bandura, *Principles of Behavior Modification.* Holt, Rinehart, and Winston, 1969.

H. Benson, D. Shapiro, B. Tursky, and G. E. Schwartz, "Decreased Systolic Blood Pressure through Operant Conditioning Techniques in Patients with Essential Hypertension." *Science,* 1971, 173:740–742.

A. J. Bernhardt, M. Hersen, and D. H. Barlow, "Measurement and Modification of Spasmodic Torticollis: An Experimental Analysis." *Behavior Therapy,* 1972, 3:294–297.

Edward B. Blanchard and Larry D. Young, "Self-Control of Cardiac Functioning: A Promise as Yet Unfulfilled." *Psychological Bulletin,* 1973, 79:145–163.

Edward B. Blanchard and Larry D. Young, "On Promises and Evidence: A Reply to Engel." *Psychological Bulletin,* 1974, 81:44–46.

E. R. Bleecker and B. T. Engel, "Learned Control of Ventricular Rate in Patients with Atrial Fibrillation." *Psychosomatic Medicine,* 1973, 35:161–175.

John Paul Brady, "Metronome-Conditioned Relaxation: A New Behavioral Procedure." *British Journal of Psychiatry,* 1973, 122:729–730.

John Paul Brady, Lester Luborsky, and Reuben E. Kron, "Blood Pressure Reduction in Patients with Essential Hypertension through Metronome-Conditioned Relaxation: A Preliminary Report." *Behavior Therapy,* 1974, 5:203–209.

D. Brierley, "The Treatment of Hysterical Spasmodic Torticollis by Behavior Therapy." *Behavior Research and Therapy,* 1967, 5:139–142.

T. Budzynski, J. Stoyva, and C. Adler, "Feedback-Induced Muscle Relaxation: Application to Tension Headaches." *Journal of Behavior Therapy and Experimental Psychiatry,* 1970, 1:205–211.

T. Budzynski, J. Stoyva, C. Adler, and D. Mullaney, "EMG Biofeedback and Tension Headache: A Controlled Outcome Study." *Psychosomatic Medicine,* 1973, 35:484–496.

A. J. Cooper, "A Case of Bronchial Asthma Treated by Behaviour Therapy." *Behavior Research and Therapy,* 1964, 1:351–356.

Thomas Creer, "The Use of Time-Out from Positive Reinforcement Procedure with Asthmatic Children." *Journal of Psychosomatic Research,* 1970, 14:117–120.

M. H. Davis, D. Saunders, T. Creer, and H. Chai, "Relaxation Training Facilitated by Biofeedback Apparatus as a Supplemental Treatment in Bronchial Asthma." *Journal of Psychosomatic Research,* 1973, 17:121–128.

Leo V. DiCara, "Learning in the Automatic Nervous System." *Scientific American,* 1970, 14:117–120.

S. Thomas Elder, Debra A. Leftwich, and Lynn A. Wilkerson, "The Role of Systolic- Versus Diastolic-Contingent Feedback in Blood Pressure Conditioning." *Psychological Record,* 1974, 24:171–176.

S. T. Elder, Z. R. Ruiz, H. L. Deabler, and R. L. Dillenkoffer, "Instrumental Conditioning of Diastolic Blood Pressure in Essential Hypertensive Patients." *Journal of Applied Behavior Analysis,* 1973, 6:377–382.

B. T. Engel, "Operant Conditioning of Cardiac Function: A Status Report." *Psychophysiology,* 1972, 9:161–177.

B. T. Engel and R. A. Chism, "Operant Conditioning of Heart Rate Speeding." *Psychophysiology,* 1967, 3:418–426.

B. T. Engel and S. P. Hansen, "Operant Conditioning of Heart Rate Slowing." *Psychophysiology,* 1966, 3:176–187.

B. T. Engel and L. Melmon, "Operant Conditioning of Heart Rate in Patients with Cardiac Arrhythmias." *Conditional Reflex,* 1968, 3:130.

B. T. Engel, P. Nikoomanesh, and M. M. Schuster, "Operant Conditioning of Rectosphincteric Responses in the Treatment of Fecal Incontinence." *New England Journal of Medicine,* 1974, 290:646–649.

W. E. Fordyce, R. S. Fowler, and B. DeLateur, "An Application of Behavior Modification Technique to a Problem of Chronic Pain." *Behavior Research and Therapy,* 1968, 6:105–107.

W. E. Fordyce, R. S. Fowler, J. F. Lehmann, and B. DeLateur, "Some Implications of Learning in Problems of Chronic Pain." *Journal of Chronic Diseases,* 1968, 21:179–190.

C. M. Franks, *Behavior Therapy: Appraisal and Status.* McGraw-Hill, 1969.

J. E. Gardner, "Behavior Therapy Treatment Approach to a Psychogenic Seizure Case." *Journal of Consulting Psychology,* 1967, 31:209–212.

J. E. Gardner, "A Blending of Behavior Therapy Techniques in an Approach to an Asthmatic Child." *Psychotherapy: Theory, Research, and Practice,* 1968, 5:46–49.

James H. Geer and Edward S. Katkin, "Treatment of Insomnia, Using a Variant of Systematic Desensitization: A Case Report." *Journal of Abnormal Psychology,* 1966, 71:161–164.

Burl B. Gray, Gene England, and Jack L. Mohoney, "Treatment of Benign Vocal Nodules by Reciprocal Inhibition." *Behavior Research and Therapy,* 1965, 3:187–193.

Allan G. Hedberg, "The Treatment of Chronic Diarrhea by Systematic Desensitization: A Case Report." *Journal of Behavior Therapy and Experimental Psychiatry,* 1973, 4:67–68.

Chase P. Kimball, "Conceptual Developments in Psychosomatic medicine: 1939–1969." *Annals of Internal Medicine,* 1970, 73:307–316.

H. D. Kimmel and Ellen Kimmel, "An Instrumental Conditioning Method for the Treatment of Enuresis." *Journal of Behavior Therapy and Experimental Psychiatry,* 1970, 1:121–123.

Leonard Krasner, "Behavior Therapy." *Annual Review of Psychology,* 1971, 22:483–532.

P. J. Lang and B. G. Malamed, "Avoidance Conditioning Therapy of an Infant with Chronic Ruminative Vomiting." *Journal of Abnormal Psychology,* 1969, 74:1–8.

Arnold A. Lazarus, *Behavior Therapy and Beyond.* McGraw-Hill, 1971.

H. I. Levene, B. T. Engel, and J. A. Pearson, "Differential Operant Conditioning of Heart Rate." *Psychosomatic Medicine,* 1968, 30:837–845.

O. I. Lovaas, *Behavioral Treatment of Autistic Children.* General Learning Press, 1972.

S. H. Lovibond, *Conditioning and Enuresis.* Pergamon Press, 1964.

E. R. Lutker, "Treatment of Migraine Headache by Conditioned Relaxation: A Case Study." *Behavior Therapy,* 1971, 2:592–593.

V. Meyer and E. S. Chesser, *Behavior Therapy in Clinical Psychiatry.* Science House, 1970.

Neal E. Miller, "Learning of Visceral and Glandular Responses." *Science,* 1969, 163:434–445.

N. E. Miller, "Biofeedback: Evaluation of a New Technio." *New England Journal of Medicine,* 1974, 290:684–685.

N. E. Miller and L. V. DiCara, "Instrumental Learning of Heart Rate Changes in Curarized Rats: Shaping and Specificity to Discriminative Stimulus." *Journal of Comparative and Physiological Psychology,* 1967, 63:12–19.

K. R. Mitchell and D. M. Mitchell, "Migraine: An Exploratory Treatment Application of Programmed Behaviour Therapy Techniques." *Journal of Psychosomatic Research,* 1971, 15:137–157.

N. Moore, "Behaviour Therapy in Bronchial Asthma: A Controlled Study." *Journal of Psychosomatic Research,* 1965, 9:257–276.

J. T. Neisworth and F. Moore, "Operant Treatment of Asthmatic Responding with the Parent as Therapist." *Behavior Therapy,* 1972, 3:95–99.

A. P. Paschalis, H. D. Kimmel, and Ellen Kimmel, "Further Study of Diurnal Instrumental Conditioning in the Treatment of Enuresis Nocturna." *Journal of Behavior Therapy and Experimental Psychiatry,* 1973, 3:253–256.

G. L. Paul and D. A. Bernstein, *Anxiety and Clinical Problems: Systematic Desensitization and Related Techniques.* General Learning Press, 1973.

L. A. Plumlee, "Operant Conditioning of Increases in Blood Pressure." *Psychophysiology,* 1969, 6:283–290.

R. G. Ratliff and N. H. Stein, "Treatment of Neurodermatitis by Behavior Therapy: A Case Study." *Behavior Research and Therapy,* 1968, 6:397–399.

David A. Sachs and Bill Mayhall, "Behavioral Control of Spasms, Using Aversive Conditioning with a Cerebral Palsied Adult." *Journal of Nervous and Mental Disease,* 1971, 152:362–363.

J. D. Sargent, E. E. Green, and E. D. Walters, "Preliminary Report on the Use of Autogenic Feedback Training in the Treatment of Migraine and Tension Headaches." *Psychosomatic Medicine,* 1973, 35:129–135.

Gary E. Schwartz, "Voluntary Control of Human Cardiovascular Integration and Differentiation through Feedback and Reward." *Science,* 1972, 175:90–93.

D. Shapiro, B. Tursky, E. Gershon, and M. Stern, "Effects of Feedback and Reinforcement on the Control of Human Systolic Blood Pressure." *Science,* 1969, 163:588–590.

D. Shapiro, B. Tursky, and G. E. Schwartz, "Differentiation of Heart Rate and Systolic Blood

Pressure in Man by Operant Conditioning." *Psychosomatic Medicine,* 1970a, 32:417–423.

D. Shapiro, B. Tursky, and G. E. Schwartz, "Control of Blood Pressure in Man by Operant Conditioning." *Circulation Research,* 1970b, supplement to vols. 26–27:I-27-I-41.

D. Shapiro, G. E. Schwartz, and B. Tursky, "Control of Diastolic Blood Pressure in Man by Feedback and Reinforcement." *Psychophysiology,* 1972, 9:296–304.

D. W. Shearn, "Operant Conditioning of Heart Rate." *Science,* 1962, 137:530–531.

E. Wayne Sloop and Wallace A. Kennedy, "Institutionalized Retarded Nocturnal Enuretics Treated by a Conditioning Technique." *American Journal of Mental Deficiency,* 1973, 77:717–721.

M. B. Sterman and L. Friar, "Suppression of Seizures in an Epileptic Following Sensorimotor EEG Feedback Training." *Electroencephalography and Clinical Neurophysiology,* 1972, 33:89–95.

M. B. Sterman, L. R. MacDonald, and R. K. Stone, "Biofeedback Training of the Sensorimotor EEG Rhythm in Man: Effects on Epilepsy." *Epilepsia,* in press.

B. R. Wagner and G. L. Paul, "Reduction of Incontinence in Chronic Mental Patients: A Pilot Project." *Journal of Behavior Therapy and Experimental Psychiatry,* 1970, 1:29–38.

D. Walton, "The Application of Learning Theory to the Treatment of a Case of Neurodermatitis." In Hans Eysenck, ed., *Behaviour Therapy and the Neuroses,* Pergamon Press, 1960.

T. Weiss and B. T. Engel, "Operant Conditioning of Heart Rate in Patients with Premature Ventricular Contractions." *Psychosomatic Medicine,* 1971, 33:301–322.

Ian E. Wickramaskera, "Temperature Feedback for the Control of Migraine." *Journal of Behavior Therapy and Experimental Psychiatry,* 1973, 4:343–345.

M. Wolf, J. Birnbrauer, T. Williams, and J. Lander, "A Note on Apparent Extinction of the Vomiting Behavior of a Retarded Child." In L. Ullmann and L, Krasner, eds., *Case Studies in Behavior Modification.* Holt, Rinehart, and Winston, 1965.

S. Yen and R. W. McIntire, "Operant Therapy for Constant Headache Complaints: A Simple Response-Cost Approach." *Psychological Record,* 1971, 28:267–270.

7

Behavioral Treatment of Autistic Children

O. IVAR LOVAAS
University of California, Los Angeles

IF you become a clinical psychologist, a special education teacher, a psychiatrist, a nurse, or some other mental health professional, then you will someday meet an extremely deviant child who may have been diagnosed as a childhood psychotic. There are some 620,000 psychotic children in America [cf. Treffert 1970] which makes it very likely that such a child will be brought to you and you will be asked to help.

Childhood psychosis is a broad diagnostic category that refers to children who have failed to a rather extreme extent in their behavioral development. Several subcategories are included in this label, and there are certain related developmental problems that are not always easy to distinguish from one another. Thus, if a child has been seen in more than one clinic, he is likely to have more than one diagnosis. He could have been given previous diagnoses such as childhood schizophrenic, autistic, brain-damaged, retarded, aphasic, etc. The exact guidelines for diagnosing the child into these various categories are not well known; however, since there is no direct relationship between diagnosis and recommended treatment anyway, and the relationship between etiology ("causes") and diagnosis is also not well understood, we do not have to concern ourselves a great deal about exactly what to call these children.

Although we are unable to offer exact guidelines on how to diagnose the various children, we can offer an accurate description of their various behaviors. As we single out and treat the various behaviors, we also recognize that other children, and sometimes normal children, may show the same kind of behavior. When we learn how to manage a particular behavior in a normal child, then that knowledge becomes applicable for the treatment of similar behavior in psychotic or retarded children and vice versa.

This module will describe certain research and treatment efforts with various behaviors of a group of children who psychologists would label as autistic. Autistic children comprise the group of psychotic children that is most "out of touch," "undeveloped," and "psychotic."

An autistic child often appears different from normal children during his first year of life, and certainly by the time he is 2 years old, he is dramatically different from normal children. He can be described as follows:

1) *Apparent sensory deficit.* One may move directly in front of the child, smile and talk to him, yet he will act as if no one is there. One may not feel that the child is avoiding or ignoring him, rather that the child simply does not seem to see or hear. The mother also reports that she did, in fact, incorrectly suspect the child to be blind or deaf. At one time or another she has taken him for a medical examination, but he was not diagnosed as blind or deaf. As one gets to know the child better, one becomes aware of the great variability in this obliviousness to stimulation. That is, though the child seems to give no visible reaction to a loud noise, such as a clapping of hands directly behind his ears, he may respond appropriately to the crinkle of a candy wrapper or excessively to a distant and barely audible siren. Similarly, though he does not notice the comings or goings of people around him, or other major changes in his visual field (turning off the lights may have no effect on his behavior), he will sometimes spot a small piece of candy on a table some 20 feet away from him. Obviously he is not blind or deaf in the way we usually use these terms.

2) *Severe affect isolation.* Another characteristic that one frequently notices is that attempts to love and cuddle and show affection to these children meet with essential disinterest on the child's part. Again, the parents relate how their children seem not to know or care whether they are alone or in their company. The children are indifferent to being liked by their siblings. Already as small babies they do not cup or mold when they are held, and do not respond with anticipation to being picked up. They do not laugh or cry appropriately, if at all.

3) *Self-stimulation.* Another strikingly different kind of behavior of these children centers on very repetitive stereotyped acts, such as rocking their bodies when in a sitting position, twirling around, flapping their arms at the wrists, or humming a set of three or four notes over and over again. The parents often report that their child may spend entire days gazing at his cupped hands, staring at lights, spinning objects, etc.

4) *Tantrums and self-mutilatory behavior.* Although the child may not engage in self-mutilation when one first meets him, the parents may report that the child sometimes bites himself so severely as to bleed; or that he beats his head against walls or sharp pieces of furniture so large lumps rise and his skin turns black and blue. He may beat his face with his fists. Some of the children bear scars from their self-mutilation; for example, one can observe skin discolorations that remain from biting wounds on the inside of their wrists. One is likely to trigger self-mutilatory behavior in such a child if one imposes some restriction on their movement, such as holding them still. Often they will engage in self-destructive behavior if one attempts to impose even minimal standards for appropriate behavior, such as requesting the child to sit at his desk or table. Sometimes their aggression will be directed outward, against their parents or teachers in the most primitive form of biting, scratching, kicking, and other tantrum behavior. Some of these children absolutely tyranize their parents, never sleeping through the night, tearing curtains off the window, spilling flour in the kitchen, etc., and the parents are at a complete loss as to how to cope with this situation.

5) *Echolalic and psychotic speech.* Most of these children are mute; that is, they do not talk; however, the speech of those that do talk may be echos of other people's attempt to talk to them. For example, if one addresses a child with the question, "What is your name?" the child is likely to answer (preserving, perhaps, the exact intonation of the one who spoke to him) "What is your name?" At other times the echolalia is not immediate but delayed in that the child will repeat statements he had heard that morning or on the preceding day, or he may repeat TV commercials or other such announcements.

6) *Behavioral deficiencies.* Although the presence of the behaviors sketched above are rather striking, it is equally striking to take note of many behaviors that the child does *not* have. That is, such a child has little if any self-help skills but needs to be fed and dressed. He may, in many ways, at the age of 5 or 10, show the social or intellectual repertoire of a 6-month-old baby. Very strikingly he is mute, and very likely has the same deficiency in receptive speech as he has in expressive speech.

Problems in Etiology

Why did the child become this way? What has caused this problem? Nobody really knows. But there have been three major hypotheses to account for the development of the disorder. These are based on psychoanalytic theory, developmental theory, and physiological theory. We will discuss these theoretical orientations very briefly here, with the primary purpose of suggesting reference material appropriate to each for those who want to familiarize themselves with the various theories in more detail.

Psychodynamic theories. The specifics of various psychodynamic theories on the etiology of autism may vary, but generally they can be summarized as follows. When the child was an infant, he developed in an environment that was singularly cold and destructive. Both Kanner [1943] and Bettelheim [1967] implicate the parents in the development of autism. According to Bettelheim, the child believes that his parents wish to destroy him and he, therefore, withdraws into his inner autistic world as a defense against his parents who frighten him. Kanner suggests that the typical parents of autistic children are cold, detached, unaffectionate, and emotionally insulated. The child then fails to form a meaningful warm relationship with them and therefore never moves on to relate himself to ("cathect") the external world. The essential aspect, but admittedly very simplified version, of psychodynamic treatment approaches to autism consists of attempts by therapists or teachers to create a loving, accepting and warm adult-child relationship—which the parents had supposedly failed to provide—in the hope that once the child accepts the adult he will then move out toward the world, lose the various "symptoms" (the behavioral deviations) of autism, and his acquisition of new behaviors would naturally follow from the change in the emotional relationship he had to that world.

Large comprehensive formulations, such as the psychodynamic attempt to understand autism, have not been adequately evaluated and perhaps they never will be. In any case, on the purely empirical level, the outcome studies on psychoanalytic attempts to treat these children have failed to produce significant results. Kanner and Eisenberg [1955], Brown [1960], and Rutter [1966] all report data that suggest that autistic children treated with psychodynamic frameworks did not do significantly better than children who received no treatment. A loving, understanding environment (to replace the supposedly cold parents) does not seem to help these children. Similarly more laboratory-like experimental studies, which were designed to test specific hypotheses derived from psychodynamic formulations, have failed to find data which support the

social and parental etiology. For example, studies have failed to identify the parents as cold and detached or any other emotional type.

Developmental theories. There is considerable speculation that infantile autism arises on the basis of a developmental perceptual disorder. Goldfarb [1961]; Schopler [1965]; and Rutter [1971] have all commented on this point. The term developmental disorder describes conditions in which there is an abnormal delay in the development of some normal function, so that what is abnormal at one age would be normal at a younger age. Basically the theory is based on a developmental model of receptor preferences. It holds that there is a normal transition from preference and dependence on the near receptors (e.g., tactile, kinesthetic, and gustatory) in early life, to a dominance of the far receptors (e.g., visual and auditory) in later years. It is speculated that autistic children fail to develop beyond the near receptors' stage, and therefore they fail to comprehend the social, linguistic, and intellectual environments that are mediated primarily by the distance receptors.

There are several directions in treatment and education which are based on such models of faulty reception. Schopler and Reichler [1971] have designed their teaching programs based on the child's "availability via his various receptor systems." The great emphasis on perceptual motor-training in education, as exemplified in the work of people like Kephart [1960] and Frostig and Home [1964] is also consistent with this theoretical orientation. It is too early to decide whether intervention based on this model has been successful, since no systematic data have been put forth to evaluate it. But it is important to note that experimental laboratory work designed to test the notion of distorted receptor hierarchies in autistic children [Schopler 1966; Lovaas, Schreibman, Koegel, & Rehm 1971; Lovaas & Schreibman 1971] failed to support the notion of a distorted receptor orientation along the lines which we have outlined here.

Arousal theories. Since it appears that the level of physiological arousal is an important determinant of how much an organism will be affected by environmental stimulation, a number of theories of abnormal arousal levels have surfaced in an attempt to account for autistic behavior. One theory suggests that autistic children suffer from a chronically high level of arousal [Hutt et al. 1965]; a second theory suggests that autistic children suffer from a chronically low level of arousal [Rimland 1964]; and a third theory suggests that there are alternating periods of high and low levels of arousal [Ornitz & Ritvo 1968]. Although these theories may become supported in empirical work in the future and provide suggestions for how to treat and educate these children, they have not as yet been adequately evaluated; nor have there been any systematic treatment-educational formulations that are clearly derived from these arousal hypotheses. Furthermore, as suggested by the comprehensive line of speculation, the relationship between arousal mechanisms and autistic behavior appears as yet to be rather unclear.

Perhaps it sounds discouraging that these three formulations, encompassing as they are, have failed to isolate the cause of autism. Let us warn, however, that to become involved in discovering "the cause of autism," noble as that sounds, may not be altogether wise at this point for the following reasons:

1] We are far from certain that there exists an underlying solitary entity or "disease" that we can call autism. Instead it may be that we can observe autistic-like behaviors owing to a large variety of reasons. We do not have one "cause," but many causes. "Autism," therefore, may be a diagnostic mislabel referring to a phenomenon that does not exist.
2] Once the child comes for treatment at the age of 2 or 3, and usually much later than that, so many things have already happened to him (diet, disease, concussions, experiences) and so much information about him has been lost, that to look for the "cause" of autism is to look for the famous "needle in the haystack." There are so many methodological problems associated with the question of early cause that the answers need too many qualifications to be useful.
3] The initial cause may not be the current cause. That is, a child may engage in autistic behaviors when he is an infant because of a certain set of circumstances that are very different from those that cause him, later in his life, to maintain his autistic behaviors. Initial cause and current causes are not necessarily synonymous.
4] Finally, it is not necessary to know the initial cause of autism in order to help these children. It may be necessary for prevention, but not for treatment. A colleague of mine, Professor Israel Goldiamond, has an apt analogy: one can put out forest fires without knowing why they started.

In conclusion, then, we do not know the cause of autism; we are not even certain that it is helpful to talk about "autism." Autistic children show many problem behaviors such as self-destruction and self-stimulation; and there are all kinds of behaviors they do not have, such as not talking and not playing. So it is at this point we will start to help them—treating or remediating at a behavioral level.

Managing Self-destructive Behavior

With which behaviors do you start? To some extent, the child will tell you what you have to do first. You definitely have to do something about his self-destructive behaviors right away. He may be tearing, with his teeth, large amounts of tissue from his shoulders and arms, chewing off parts of his fingers, hitting his head so violently against the wall that he detaches his retina, and so on. Many of these children, although only 8 or 9 years old, have spent most of their lives in restraints, being tied down both by their feet and arms, to prevent them from incurring too much damage to themselves. Tying a child down, of course, is no solution.

Let us tell you what we did with the self-destructive behavior of the first autistic child we saw. Her name was Beth, she was 10 years old, and she had been severely autistic since her first year of life. That is, she did not want to be loved, neither did she seem to love anybody, and she did not know how to play. She had often acted as if blind or deaf (she spent her life "in a shell," "turned inward"); and she could not speak, but rather would just echo back the speech of others. She was seriously self-destructive, beating her head against the sharp corners of the furniture, banging it against the walls of the room with loud booms, tearing her skin open with her teeth or nails, bleeding, opening wounds, and so on. Her self-destruction had begun when she was about 3 years old for reasons no one knew. One day she put her hair in the wall heater, burning it off. Beth was the only patient we saw at the time (she being the first one). We were four adults. We had her with us most of the day and got to know her quite well. It could hardly be said that she was being neglected. We explored some programs designed to teach her how to talk, to dress and comb her hair, to play, and so on, and we made some progress in these areas. But it seemed pointless, since we would take her home to her parents in the afternoon with her head and face still bleeding.

So this is what we then did. First we *measured* the strength of her self-destruction. We did this by simply counting the number of self-destructive acts (bites, head bangs) for a certain time during the day when Beth was with a particular person in a particular room. To record her self-destruction was critical because we wanted a *baseline* against which to evaluate the effect of any treatment. We then asked several professional people how to handle her self-destruction. The predominant philosophy at the time [1963] was to treat the self-destruction as a symptom or expression of an underlying problem, such as guilt, poor concept of herself, and the like. We were advised to express our concern and love for her when she was self-destructive, to reassure her that we cared for her. Her parents were similarly advised.

It is now very important to note that we were in a position to actually measure how such therapy affected her. It is surprising, as well as instructive, to note that despite its widespread use nobody had tested the effectiveness of this treatment before. Perhaps it was felt that it obviously would work (if you persist, how can anyone turn down your love, particularly a "sick" child who needs it so much); and then, perhaps, it was felt that human behavior could not be subjected to such an objective assessment. In any case, we introduced the treatment ("Beth, I love you," and other sympathetic comments) on certain days, removed it, reintroduced it, and so on, in what has been called a "within-subject," or "single-subject" design, or ABA design (where A is baseline, and B represents the treatment).

To our surprise, she was worse on the days we treated her [Lovaas, Freitag, Gold, & Kassorla 1965]. That is important to know. The clearest example of how damaging such love can be is seen in the case of Greg, another self-destructive child, whom we treated in the same way. His data are presented in figure 1, as cumulative curves. This means that if he did not hit himself, the line is flat (i.e., horizontal); and each time he injured himself, it is recorded on a pen that makes one small step upward for each response. The steeper the curve, the more hits. Notice that we have, in sessions 1 and 2, baseline data that tell us that his self-destructive behavior is very low; the curves are almost flat. In session 3, we started our treatment with him, expressing our concern and affection for him when he hit himself. Note also that each time we treated him in this manner the pen on the graph gave a signal by an upward-moving stroke or hatchmark. Session 3 shows a marked increase in the rate of self-destruction when we treated him like that. In session 4, we removed the treatment and the curve flattens out; he gets better. In session 5 we reintroduced the treatment, and he now hits himself some 200 times in the short period of 10 minutes. When we again remove the treatment (sessions 6 and 7) we recover his baseline. This, then, is an ABABA design. Incidentally, it would have been quite possible for us to have killed Greg through this treatment. All we needed to do was to thin out the reinforcement schedule a bit (i.e., follow self-destructive acts by sympathetic comments less than 100 percent of the time) and to have given love contingent on more vicious blows, closer to the eyes or other vulnerable spots.

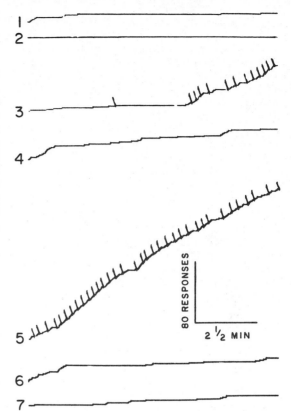

Figure 1. A child's self-destructive behavior (self-inflicted hurts, like head bangs, bites, etc.) recorded as cumulative response curves over daily 10-minute sessions (1 through 7). The child was treated in sessions 3 and 5, where the upward moving hatchmarks mark the delivery of sympathetic comments, play, etc., contingent on self-destruction.

Notice this about our approach so far: We have *measured* the behavior with which we are concerned, and have systematically *manipulated* the treatment in order to assess its effects. By that we mean that we, as investigators, introduced, removed, and reintroduced the treatment in such a manner that we reduced the effect of *confounding* variables. Confounding variables are those events that operate concurrently with the treatment variables and which could have contributed to the observed behavior change.

For example, the first time we introduced our treatment (session 3) he got worse; but this could have been caused by something else that, by chance, happened to him on that same day. For example, his favorite nurse left the ward. To reduce the effect of such confounding variables (the nurse leaving) we *reintroduced* the treatment (session 5). It is less likely that the same confounding variables (the nurse leaving) would, by chance, be present on the second (and future) presentation(s) of the treatment variable. Each time you *replicate the independent (treatment) variable*, you become increasingly confident about your inferences —namely that it is A which causes B. In any case, we became increasingly confident that attending to the self-destructive behavior did not help that behavior but may, in fact, have worsened it.

Let us stop for a moment to make a minor observation. The fact that we *measured* behavior and *systematically manipulated* the treatment for that behavior, controlling for confounding variables, is called a controlled-experimental or laboratory-experimental method. This method (as contrasted with free-observational, naturalistic, or correlational approaches) is a defining feature of that school of clinical psychology called *behavior modification* (or applied behavior analysis). For any scientist, the belief is very strong that the *method* with which he attempts to obtain answers about behavior is critical, and that, given the appropriate research method, answers will be forthcoming.

Now let us return to Beth to complete the story about how we discovered a treatment that actually helped her overcome her self-destruction. When we knew that our attention to her self-destruction made her worse, we had become very familiar with her. Since she spent so much time with us she became like "one of the family." There was a healthy matter-of-factness that came to characterize our relationship and which afforded us the opportunity to observe Beth without too many interfering preconceptions. For example, we had ceased to treat Beth as a patient. She had become, in a sense, like one of us. To drop one's preconceptions of the person one studies (and particularly to ignore labels such as "autistic," "psychotic," or "disturbed") is extremely important. The circumstances or conditions under which one makes one's observations are at least as important as having a good research design. Few people have written about that; yet without the right conditions for observation, a free "frame of reference," one will not see anything. One needs to adopt a naive attitude about nature, assuming only that behavior is determined.

In any case, one day while I was talking to Beth's teacher about her language program, Beth hit her head against the wall right behind me. This made me turn around and, without thinking, slap her quite hard on

her rear. She turned around, visibly surprised, but delayed hitting herself for about 30 seconds. She then went back to the wall to hit herself once more, but by that time we had the upper hand. The second time she hit her head she was smacked even harder on the rear. She did not hit herself on the head the rest of that day. Later we "sharpened" up this treatment (using painful but harmless electric shock), replicated its effects on other kids, and published on it [Lovaas & Simmons 1969]. Others [Bachman 1972] have replicated these findings. The point, of course, is that we would never have spanked Beth if we had viewed her as a patient; no one hits a "sick" child.

Let us return to the self-destructive behavior once more. We now knew how to make it worse, and how to make it better. Was anything left over? Yes, we had a hunch by now that we should try extinction procedures. On the basis of certain principles of learning, such as those involved in "operant conditioning" or reinforcement theory, we began to expect that the self-destructive behavior was operant, particularly since it increased in strength when certain *consequences* were provided. It seemed that when we expressed our concern it served as a positive reinforcer for the self-destruction, *increasing* its strength. If it were operant behavior then it should also *decrease* in strength, if one made sure that there were no extrinsic consequences such as social attention contingent on the behavior. Wolf, Risley and Mees [1964] had already published a finding where they had successfully used extinction to reduce tantrums and self-destruction in an autistic child that suggested it might work.

This is what happened. When the children were left free to injure themselves without parents or nursing staff intervening, the self-destructive behavior decreased in a very gradual but lawful manner. Data on one such child which we ran on extinction, is presented in figure 2. Again, we have recorded the behavior on cumulative curves, and, as you can see, the initial rate is *very* high. During the first session, which lasted for about 90 minutes (the child was merely left alone to hit himself, nobody intervened), he hit himself more than 2,700 times. Note this, however: that when he had been on extinction for half an hour into the first session, his rate was falling slightly and we had the first inkling that the treatment might work. You can determine the falling rate by laying a ruler along the curves to measure their steepness, and the various curves (the pen resets itself once it hits the top of the graph) very slowly fall off. There would have been no way to know this had we not taken data; one cannot determine the falling rate by merely looking at the child. It is important to know immediately whether the treatment will work because the child is in bad shape indeed, bleeding profusely, and so forth. If we did not have some confidence that the treatment would work we would have quit; and if we had quit and given in, say by the end of the second session, we would probably have reinforced a high rate of self-destruction.

There is something else in these curves that you may appreciate: they are regular, smooth, lawful. It gives you the feeling that you are dealing with a phenomenon you can understand. We say that we *understand* self-destructive behavior because we can *control* it. As used here, terms like understanding and knowledge are nearly synonymous with the term control. We infer from these figures that the self-destructive behavior is controlled by a set of *external* events; self-destruction does not appear to be an "expression" of some internal psychotic state or some shattered, guilty, worthless self.

The children also told us that they were very tough indeed by subjecting themselves to such self-inflicted pain in order to gain sympathy from people around them. And we began to see how miserably the world treats its sick children when they have to hurt themselves to make their needs known.

Surprisingly, perhaps, and certainly disappointingly, the reduction in self-destructive behavior did *not* bring with it a simultaneous change in other classes of behavior. The children who stopped mutilating themselves did not simultaneously become normal. Change in one response did not produce large changes in other responses; we speak of this as limited *response generalization*. We therefore had to develop other programs to help the child become appreciably better. These programs were devised to teach the child to play, to talk and read, to dress himself, and so on. Let us use our language program as an example of how one may want to build new behaviors.

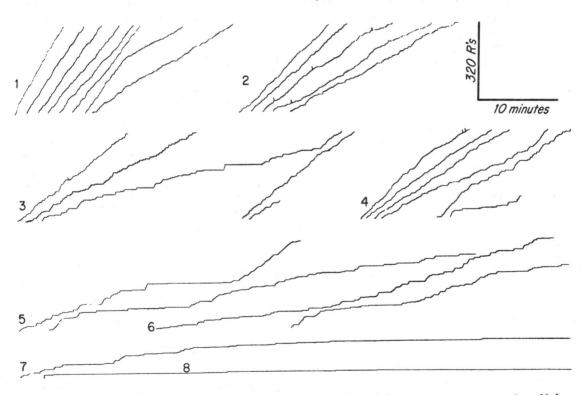

Figure 2. Extinction of a child's self-destructive behavior over 8 daily, 90-minute sessions. The self-destructive behavior was recorded as cumulative response curves. Session 7 shows a high of some 2,700 hits, gradually falling over subsequent sessions to zero rate in session 8.

SOURCE: This figure first appeared in "Manipulation of Self-Destruction in Three Retarded Children," by O. Ivar Lovaas. *Journal of Applied Behavior Analysis*, 1969, 2, 143–157. Reprinted with permission.

Building Language

It is surprising how little is known in psychology of a *practical* nature—how little we know of ways to help man. Language is a good example. For centuries people have written extensive essays on how children learn to talk, and yet no one has actually worked with children and showed what one should do to help them to talk. If, therefore, one wants to teach a child language, one pretty much has to develop one's own procedures. Some investigators will even argue that one can not teach language in the first place, the language is so complicated that it can not be taught. Language is considered to be determined by certain innate, neurochemical mechanisms. It is best to ignore such statements if one wants to help. So let us look at our language program because it illustrates how one may build or engineer a behavioral repertoire.

When one sets about building verbal behavior, or any other meaningful behavior, there are two jobs which one has to accomplish. First, one has to build a *behavioral topography*. We have to place certain verbal responses in each child's repertoire; "mama," "baby," "I want to eat," and similar words and simple phrases. Then we have to place these behaviors in the appropriate environmental context to give it meaning. This parallels a child's psychological development which can be said to consist of the acquisition of *behaviors* and *stimulus functions* [Bijou & Baer 1961].

Building vocal behavior. Briefly, we built the verbal behavioral topography by training the children in verbal imitation. The program involved building various discriminations, and we define a discrimination as behavior that occurs in some situations and not in others. One can teach discrimination by reinforcing (rewarding) the child for emitting a behavior in one situation, and not reinforcing it if it occurs in other environments. When one does this, it seems as if a particular situation comes to "trigger" or "cue" the response. The verbal imitation training consisted of the following steps. In Step 1, the therapist increased the child's vocalizations by reinforcing him (usually with food) contingent on such behavior. We did this so as to get more vocal behavior with which to work. In Step 2, the child was trained in a temporal discrimination. His vocalizations were reinforced only if they were in response to the therapist's speech (e.g., if they occurred within 5 seconds of the therapist's vocalization). The therapist's vocalization became a stimulus (SD) for the child's vocalization. In Step 3, finer discriminations were reinforced. That is, the child was reinforced for making successively closer approximations to the therapist's speech until he could match the particular sound given by the therapist (e.g., emit "a" when the

therapist said "a"). In Step 4, the therapist replicated Step 3 with another sound very dissimilar to the first one (e.g., "m"), interspersed this sound with the previous one, only reinforced the child for correct reproductions and in this manner demanded increasingly fine discriminations and reproduction from the child. Starting with sounds that were quite different (such as "m" and "a") the child was taught to imitate an increasingly large range of more similar sounds, then words, and later sentences. Imitation, then, was defined as discrimination when the response resembled its stimulus.

The acquisition of such imitation is presented in figure 3. We present the data for Billy and Chuck, the first two children we treated. The sounds/words are presented in lower case letters on the day they were introduced and practiced, and in capital case letters on the day they were mastered. As can be seen, the curves are *positively accelerated*, each child learning at an increasing rate (more and more behavior per unit time) the longer he is in the program. He is "learning to learn," as it is said; it looks as if he is acquiring the discrimination we wanted to teach him.

Several features are noteworthy about this program in verbal-imitation training. One feature to bear in mind is that the new behaviors are acquired through *behavior-shaping*. In shaping procedures one sets up a *terminal behavior* (one's behavior goal) to be reached through a set of steps that are graded in difficulty from easy to difficult. An "easy" step is defined in terms of what the child can do at the outset of training; that is, behavior which he will emit at a certain rate *so that the shaper can reinforce it*. Note that if one were to start at too difficult a level, then the shaper would not be able to reinforce the child (the behavior occurred too infrequently) and the child would not learn anything (because learning is dependent on reinforcement). In order for the shaping procedures to work (for reinforcement to be given and behaviors to be acquired) the child has to be successful; there are no unsuccessful children. The rate of acquiring the new behaviors may vary across the children, but each child is learning.

Teaching stimulus functions (meanings). Once the child can imitate the speech of others he does not simultaneously know the meaning of the words he utters. His speech exists without meaning. A program for the establishment of meaningful speech involves establishing a *context* for speech, which we viewed as two basic discriminations. In the first discrimination the stimulus is nonverbal and the response is verbal, as in "expressive" speech (e.g., the child may be taught to label a food). In the second discrimination, the stimulus is verbal, but the response is nonverbal, as in language "comprehension" (e.g., the child learns to follow instructions, obey commands, etc.). Most language situa-

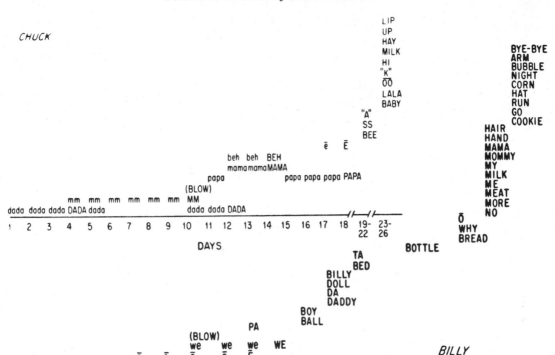

Figure 3. The first 26 days of imitation training for Billy and Chuck, who were both psychotic and mute before training. The abscissa denotes training days. The sounds and words are printed in lower case letters on the days they were introduced and trained, and in capital letters on the days they were mastered.

tions involve components of both discriminations, such that both the stimulus and response have both verbal and nonverbal components. The speech program, based on these two discriminations, begins with simple labeling of common objects and events and is made functional as soon as possible. For example, as soon as a child knows the label for a food, he is fed contingent on asking for food. The program gradually moves on to making the child increasingly proficient in language, including training in more abstract terms (such as pronouns, time, etc.); some grammar, such as the tenses; the use of language to please others, as in recall or storytelling, etc.

Figure 4 gives an example of how one of these "meaning-acquisitions" are acquired. The figure shows the acquisition of verbal labels of common everyday events (objects and behaviors) in two previously mute, psychotic children. Note the high degree of similarity between figure 4 and 3. The similarity is probably attributable to the same underlying process, discrimination learning.

We have produced a film [Lovaas 1969] that describes the language-training program in more detail. It also illustrates the kinds of children with whom we have worked. The film shows the shaping procedures, discrimination training, and so on, in considerable detail. The program is also presented in detail in a book [Lovaas 1973].

As with the work on self-destruction, the findings from the language program also have been replicated by other investigators, sometimes independently, which gives added support to the validity of these treatment procedures. In particular, our program has extensive overlap with that presented by Risley and Wolf [1967].

Throughout our treatment there is an emphasis on teaching behaviors that are both socially desirable and useful to the child. Thus, although the majority of the

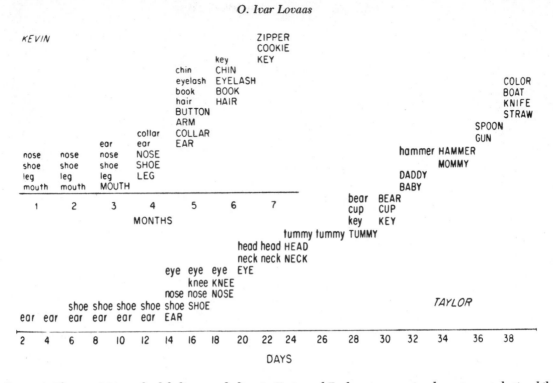

Figure 4. *The acquisition of a labeling vocabulary in Kevin and Taylor, two previously mute, psychotic children. The abscissa denotes training days. The sounds and words are printed in lower case letters on the days they were introduced and trained, and in capital letters on the days they were mastered.*

research has focused on attempts to build language, there have also been several attempts to facilitate social and self-help skills. Like others, we have [Lovaas et al. 1967] developed procedures for initially building non-verbal imitation which then were used to build social and self-help skills. This included methods for building those behaviors that make the child easier to live with—such as friendly greetings and expressions of affection, dressing himself, feeding himself, brushing his teeth, and so on. This method also was based on shaping procedures where the child is rewarded for making closer and closer approximations to increasingly complex adult behaviors. As the children learn to discriminate the similarity in their own and the model's behaviors, they gradually acquire imitative behavior as they did in the speech program.

We have given just the barest introduction to behavior-shaping procedures. Over the last 10 years there has been an enormous increase in the application of operant principles to the education of psychotic and retarded children, and it is beyond the scope of this module to review this large body of research. We might point out that many of the techniques that have

been developed to treat psychotic children also appear equally applicable to retarded children, and vice versa.

Generalization and Follow-up Results

We now have some data that provide an estimate of the changes one might expect in autistic children undergoing behavior therapy [Lovaas et al. 1973]. We examined three measures of the generality of treatment effects: [1] Stimulus generalization, the extent to which behavior changes that occurred in the treatment environment transfer to situations outside the treatment; [2] Response generalization, the extent to which changes in a limited set of behaviors effected changes in a larger range of behaviors; and [3] Generalization over time (or durability), how well the therapeutic effects maintained themselves over time.

Let us illustrate the kinds of treatment changes and follow-up data we have collected, by presenting certain data on the first children we treated. We recorded five behaviors in a free-play situation, which was different from the treatment environment, and in the presence of people who had not treated the child. This would give us an estimate of the extent to which our treatment produced stimulus generalization. Two of the behaviors were inappropriate behaviors —*self-stimulation* and *echolalia*, which we have described earlier and three of the behaviors were appropriate—*appropriate verbal*, which was speech related to an appropriate context, understandable, and grammatically correct; *social nonverbal*, which referred to appropriate nonverbal behavior that depended on cues given by another person for its initiation or completion, and *appropriate play* referred to the use of toys and objects in an appropriate age-related manner. The recordings were made before treatment started, at the end of 12–14 months of treatment and in a follow-up, some 1 to 4 years after treatment was terminated.

The children were divided into two groups, those who were discharged to a state hospital and those who remained with their parents.

The data are presented in figure 5. Percent occurrence of the various behaviors is plotted on the ordinate for before (B) and after (A) treatment, and shows the latest follow-up (F) measures. "I" refers to the average results for the four children who were institutionalized (discharged to a state hospital), and "P" refers to the six children who lived with their parents since their discharge from treatment. If one examines the change in the children's behavior between B and A, it is apparent that they improved with treatment. After 12 months of treatment there was a substantial reduction in inappropriate behavior and a corresponding increase in the appropriate ones. The follow-up data (F)

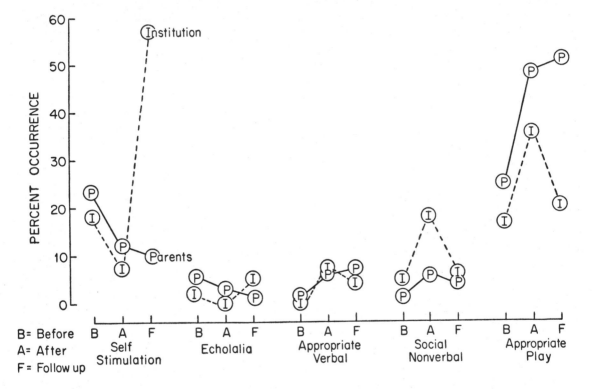

Figure 5. Multiple response follow-up measures. Percent occurrence of the various behaviors is plotted on the ordinate for Before (B) and After (A) treatment, and for the latest Follow-up (F) measures. "I" refers to the average results for the four children who were institutionalized and "P" refers to the average results for the nine children who were discharged to their parents' care. Percent occurrence of the behaviors is presented on the ordinate.

SOURCE: This figure first appeared in "Some Generalization and Follow-Up Measures on Autistic Children in Behavior Therapy," by O. Ivar Lovaas, *Journal of Applied Behavior Analysis*, 1973, 6, 131–166.

pose a warning: the children who were discharged to a state hospital lost what they had gained in treatment; they increased in their psychotic behavior (self-stimulation and echolalia) and lost what they gained of social nonverbal behavior, as well as appropriate verbal and appropriate play behaviors. The children who stayed with their parents, on the other hand, maintained their gains or improved further. For the children who regressed in the state hospital, a brief reinstatement of behavior therapy could temporarily reestablish the original therapeutic gains.

These findings clearly emphasize certain important points underlying the use of behavior modification with psychotic children. It is not enough to help the child acquire appropriate behaviors and to overcome the inappropriate ones; it is also important to provide maintaining conditions that insure that the improvements will last. To help insure generalization and maintenance of the treatment effects, we now teach the child's parents to become the child's primary therapists. The parents have to pass a "test" before we accept them as clients: they have to learn how to record behavior reliably, and they have to show us that (with our help) they can at least gain control over one of the child's behaviors. If they meet these criteria, then we train them as therapists.

Current Research on Perceptual Deviance

We still need to know a lot more in order to help effectively, and many important questions remain unanswered. Behavior therapy for severely psychotic children is still a very slow process. The treatment effects are reversible. Few children become normal. Let us conclude this discussion by reviewing some current research that hopefully will suggest improvements in the use of behavior modification with autistic children, starting out with research on perceptual variables.

Many researchers and clinicians have emphasized the extreme inconsistency with which autistic children respond to sensory input. At one time they appear to be blind and deaf, while at another time they show extremely fine visual and auditory acuity. In one situation they respond correctly to an instruction; at another time they appear to have learned nothing about how to respond. Such pecularities in the childrens' responding led us to conduct the following studies.

In the first study [Lovaas et al. 1971], we trained normal and autistic children to respond to a complex stimulus involving the simultaneous presentation of auditory, visual, and tactile cues. Thus, we turned on a loud tone and a bright light, and inflated a pressure cuff

on the child's leg. All this lasted for about 5 seconds, and if the child responded by depressing a bar at that time he would get reinforced. These stimuli were then removed, and if he responded in their absence he would not be reinforced. In this way he learned the discrimination, and we knew he was attending to this stimulus input because he responded on the bar when the stimulus was on but did not respond when the stimuli were removed. Once this discrimination was established, elements of the stimulus complex were presented separately to assess which aspects of the complex input had acquired control over the child's behavior. We found that the autistics had primarily come under the control of only *one* of the components, while the normal children we tested responded uniformly to all three components. For example, the autistic child would hit the bar when we presented the light, but he would remain completely indifferent when we presented him with the sound or the touch. It was as if he had learned about only one of the elements and nothing about the others. The normal children, on the other hand, learned about each component; the separate elements had each become functional stimuli. We also found that we could arrange conditions such that a component that had remained nonfunctional when presented in the complex, could be established as functional when trained separately. Thus the autistic children did not appear to show a deficit in any one particular sensory modality but rather, when presented with multiple sensory input, a very restricted range of that input gained control over their behaviors. It was as if they were functionally blind in those situations when they were responding to visual cues. Subsequently we replicated this finding in a two-stimulus situation (light and tone), and Koegel and Wilhelm [1973] showed the same to occur with multiple visual stimuli.

This finding, which we called overselective attention (or stimulus overselectivity) may have certain implications for understanding the difficulty autistic children experience in complex learning and social environments. First, let us illustrate the social problems. In one study [Schreibman & Lovaas 1973] autistic children were trained to discriminate between a boy and a girl figure (Ken and Barbi dolls). The results showed that for the autistic children, this discrimination would break down (return to chance level) when a specific clothing component (such as the shoes) were removed from the dolls. This pointed out that the autistic children learned to tell the two figures apart on the basis of a very trivial detail, and again indicated the problems caused by the extreme selectivity with which autistic children respond to their environment. If, for example, an autistic child recognizes his mother on the basis of her shoes, he will indeed have problems getting along when she removes them. The autistic children typically show these wide fluctuations and inconsistencies in their social behavior.

Such overselective attention may also have implications for understanding why autistic children fail to acquire an adequate range of affect. Rarely do autistic children show sadness, remorse, joy, or many of the emotions which help us relate to others. Many psychologists think that such feelings are acquired through classical conditioning. The problem for the autistic child is that in classical conditioning, he is presented with a contiguous or near-contiguous presentation of two stimuli (a CS and a US). If he overselects in this situation, he will respond to either one or the other of the two, but not both, and therefore fail to condition and acquire appropriate affect.

Their acquisition of meaningful behavior may be retarded for a similar reason. The establishment of meaningful behavior, such as meaningful speech, involves establishing a *context* for that behavior and thus requires response to multiple inputs. For example, in attempting to teach a child the meaning of the word "book," the most common teaching procedure involves *saying* "(This is a) book," while *showing* a book. If the child responds to the auditory input alone he may fail to perceive the visual referent, hence not associate the appropriate label. Koegel [1971] presented the first study that showed that "extra" stimuli (such as prompt cues) that one may use to guide learning of normal children, become a source of interference for the autistic child.

Let us review a study by Schreibman [1972] that shows the beginnings of a solution to this problem. This study will be described in some detail since it illustrates how, by identifying their specific weaknesses and strengths, we may be able to construct the kinds of teaching environments for psychotic children where they will be able to move toward normalcy by acquiring the behaviors that normal children do possess.

Schreibman wanted to teach the child to tell the difference between various geometric forms that were difficult to tell apart. In everyday life, the child is asked to make a great number of discriminations between stimuli that differ only to a minor degree, such as stimuli that differentiate between a man and a woman, a smile from a frown, between letters like "b" and "d," and so on. In one of Schreibman's discriminations the children were required to identify one of two (very similar) stick figures, as given in figure 6. These figures are identical except that one has his hand raised. The child was asked to "Point to the correct figure." One of

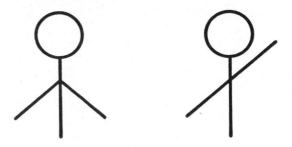

Figure 6. The stick-figure stimuli used for the discrimination tasks.

the figures was correct (S+); the other was incorrect (S−). For some of the children the figure with the raised hand was correct; for some children, the other was correct. The autistic children failed to learn this discrimination even though the teacher went through extensive and elaborate prompting procedures. In these prompting procedures the teacher initially prompted the correct response by pointing to the correct stimulus. The autistic children learned to discriminate between increasingly fine teacher-pointing cues, but did not "transfer" their response from the teacher's finger to the figures. It was as if they saw only the teacher's finger and not the figures to which she was pointing. Schreibman then changed her approach to teaching them by altering and exaggerating the relevant aspect of the stimuli. Figure 7 illustrates how Schreibman proceeded. The child was initially presented with two cards. One card was blank, and the other card had a diagonal line across its surface. Step 1 of figure 7 shows this discrimination. It is a relatively simple one to learn, and the autistic child learned it. Then, in gradual steps (as illustrated from steps 2 to 5 in the figure) the incorrect stimulus (S−) was gradually faded in. Then size and position cues were faded out (steps 6 through 10); and finally, when the child could discriminate between the position of the arms (the only relevant aspect of the discrimination), the other parts of the stimuli (head, legs, etc.) were slowly faded in, as shown in steps 11 to 15, figure 7.

The point of Schreibman's study is, of course, that the environment that helps the normal (average) child does not necessarily help but in fact may retard the deviant child. Instead of putting the blame on the child ("He is too disturbed to learn") we do better by analyzing and redesigning the learning environments to which the child is exposed. Schreibman changed a typical teaching procedure, and the autistic children learned. Failure in the current environment means failure in the "average" environment. We already have

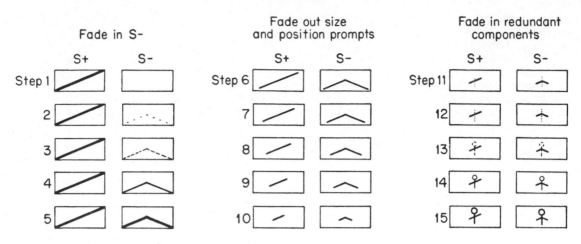

Figure 7. *The fading steps used to teach the child to identify the correct stick figure.*

an "average" environment because it is the least expensive environment to construct. It has been designed for the "average" child, who (by definition) represents the majority. As society's financial condition improves, it can spend money on research to help educate the deviate. With time we will be able to design the unusual environment that helps the unusual child learn.

Current Research on Motivation

Apparently we are beginning to get the kind of information about perceptual deviance among psychotic children that will allow us to design and test certain specific teaching procedures. Another research problem deals with motivation. Motivational variables affect both the acquisition of new learning as well as maintenance of that which is learned. In the kind of behavioristic system we have followed, the question of motivation becomes a question concerning the effectiveness of reinforcing stimuli. Can we understand the autistic child's problems by analyzing how reinforcing stimuli operate for him? Let us try.

It seems safe to assume that at birth most of what happens around the child is essentially neutral to him; most of the stimuli he encounters neither rewards nor punishes him. But as he gradually interacts with his environment, various stimuli acquire rewarding and punishing functions for him. For example, his mother's smile, though initially not affecting him, becomes a reward (or a punishment) as he has certain experiences with it; we say it *acquires* reinforcing functions. The child learns new behaviors to obtain (or avoid) that smile. Stimuli that have acquired reinforcing power are called *secondary* (conditioned) reinforcers.

Let us be more explicit about the interaction between secondary reinforcers and behavioral development. Although the child's behavior during the first few months of life seems regulated by primary (biological) reinforcers, such as food and pain, secondary reinforcers soon take over an essential controlling function. To illustrate, when the child is a baby, the mother may respond to his various behaviors by stroking him, cuddling him, or feeding him. We say that she administers primary (biological) reinforcing stimuli that serve to shape and maintain his various behaviors. Later in life, however, she is less likely to give him primary reinforcers but responds to him with what is technically called secondary reinforcing stimuli. That is, when he has behaved in a certain way she will smile at him, talk to him, or frown, and so forth.

Most stimuli generated by other people, such as closeness to others, affection, support of peers, correctness, and so forth, can serve as secondary reinforcers. We speculate that when a child emerges as a human being, he does so essentially because his behaviors are reinforced by stimuli from his social environment. For example, a child may visually fixate on his mother's face to the extent that her face has secondary reinforcing properties for him. If her face possessed no reinforcing function for him (he did not care one way or the other about her face) he probably would not look at her. Technically we call "looking" an operant behavior; that is, behavior that exists insofar as there in turn exist reinforcing stimuli to maintain it. To illustrate further, the child may seek others if closeness to other people is reinforcing for him. And he may explore his first sound or word production because he hears himself sound like his parents; that is, the matching of stimulus inputs has acquired reinforcing properties for him. Apparently an enormous variety of such emotional or intellectual behaviors is regulated by secondary reinforcers, that is, environmental consequences which have acquired their rewarding or punishing properties.

Given these assumptions, then, it seems to follow that an autistic child has failed to develop behaviorally because his natural environment is not sufficiently reinforcing for him. If his developmental failure was based on a deficiency in social and other acquired reinforcers, as Ferster [1961] claimed it was, then an intervention at this level would seem to strike at the very base of the problem. A treatment program centered on the establishment of a normal hierarchy of secondary reinforcers would give the child's everyday environment (his parents, teachers, peers, etc.) the tools with which to build and modify the myriad behaviors necessary for the child to function effectively within the environment. In a sense, the child's behavioral changes would "take care of themselves," provided he returned from treatment to a normal environment that possessed reinforcing functions for him.

When we first began to treat autistic children we explored this alternative of enriching and normalizing reinforcing stimuli for these children. We did succeed at establishing certain social stimuli as reinforcing for the autistic child, using either pain reduction [Lovaas, Schaeffer, & Simmons 1965] or food presentations [Lovaas et al. 1966]. For example, we delivered social stimuli (smiles, verbal approval, etc.) at the same time as the child was fed, hoping that he would associate the social stimuli with the pleasurable biological ones (as in a classical conditioning paradigm, where the social stimuli were the CS and the food the US). Or, we reasoned that parents did acquire reinforcing properties not just because they were associated with the delivery of pleasurable events, but also because they helped their children overcome frightening situations. Therefore we constructed a dangerous environment for the child and proceeded to rescue him from that danger. In brief, we delivered a painful but physically harmless electric shock through the floor, which was turned off as soon as the child sought us out. Ideally we would have liked to help him overcome a more "natural" fear than shock; but autistic children seem quite void of natural fears, so we could not help them in that respect. Although we produced some very durable reinforcers in these ways, they were too discriminated (situational) and the procedures too cumbersome to be of much practical significance. For example, the child showed great affection for us when in the "dangerous" room, but more and more became unaware of us on the outside.

When we finally designed our treatment environ-ment, we sidestepped the child's motivational deficiency by selecting powerful, largely primary reinforcers such as food and pain. For example, the children were only fed provided they talked or otherwise behaved appropriately. But there are certain serious problems inherent in the use of primary reinforcers. Primary reinforcers are "artificial" for the older children since such reinforcers exist only in specially constructed environments, such as our treatment environment. What happens with artificial reinforcers is that one observes limited *stimulus generalization,* the behaviors one builds with those reinforcers are limited largely to those environments where such reinforcers are available. Our use of primary reinforcers is the probable reason why the children showed behavior losses when they were institutionalized on discharge from us. The institutional environment like most environments, did not prescribe primary reinforcers for the children, hence the behaviors we had built were extinguished (the reinforcement being withheld). The child's parents, on the other hand, had been specifically taught by us how to use powerful reinforcers, and because the parents used the correct reinforcers their children did not lose the progress they had made. But these are only makeshift solutions. The ideal treatment would normalize the child's motivational structure so that his everyday environment could help him.

What can we do at this point? We can try harder to find efficient and practical ways of building secondary social reinforcers; that is, we can pursue the motivation problem as a problem in the acquisition of secondary reinforcers. Or, we can take quite another view of the motivational problem. Perhaps our analysis has placed too much emphasis on the social consequences of behavior. Maybe most of normal human behavior is *not* maintained by social or extrinsic reinforcement.

Let us illustrate an alternative viewpoint. We now know from animal research that organisms respond to obtain reinforcing stimuli unrelated to "social" reinforcers or primary reinforcers as we now know them (appetitive reinforcers, sex, pain reduction, etc.). Animals will respond just to obtain sensory input, such as changes in light intensity, sound productions, and so on. It seems as if organisms have a "need" for sensory stimulation and are controlled by such consequences. Similarly, psychotic children give evidence of the same "craving" for stimulation. They are never still but rather in continuous motion, rocking, spinning, twirling, jumping, etc. We have labeled this behavior self-stimulatory because it seemed to have no other function than providing the child with sensory input from his own behavior; the sensory feedback he gave himself seemed very important to him. Similar instances of self-stimulatory behavior can be observed in small babies, normal children, and adults when they have nothing else to do.

We therefore propose [Lovaas 1973] that there exist *two kinds of operants* depending on the kind of reinforcers that maintain the operant. We may talk about *external* or *social operants* when other people (society) control the reinforcer, and hence shape the behavior. And we may talk of *self-stimulatory operants* when the reinforcing stimulus for that response is controlled by the person himself, as in the case of sensory reinforcement.

The next question that faces us, then, concerns the extent to which common, everyday, normal human behavior is self-stimulatory. Obviously certain behaviors seem to qualify, such as games people play (like chess and athletics). But let us also propose that many instances of language or thought have the same self-stimulating function. One can think of several examples, such as daydreaming, mulling on the present, exclaiming and soothing oneself with words, attacking others in private verbal exchanges, and so on. It is virtually impossible to "pull a blank," one is always "thinking." Since there is scant evidence that one is actually solving any problems or achieving any social effects by these thoughts, it seems unlikely that the reinforcers which maintain them are extrinsic or social. Rather, language and thought may be prime examples of self-stimulatory behavior.

If we now return to formulate research questions about motivation we may propose that an essential problem in motivational research concerns the discovery of those conditions that change inappropriate self-stimulatory behavior (such as rocking) to socially appropriate forms of self-stimulation (such as language and thought).

Summary Comment

Behavior therapy with psychotic children is quite new; in fact, it is less than 10 years old. It has been shown to be of more benefit than other approaches to treating psychotic children. Its application is becoming increasingly widespread, and it appears to be the treatment of choice for the more undeveloped children in particular.

Despite the apparent success of behavior therapy with autism, it is important to remember that we avoid getting trapped within a particular conceptual framework, operant or otherwise. The most important feature to remember is that behavior therapy is a treatment based on research rather than one deduced from theory. Insofar as we are accountable and remain sensitive to the consequences of our interventions, we will have an immense and often unappreciated advantage over those who preceded us, because the research methodology enables us to contribute in a *cumulative* manner to psychological treatment.

BIBLIOGRAPHY

John A. Bachman, "Self-Injurious Behavior: A Behavioral Analysis." *Journal of Abnormal Psychology*, 1972, 80:211–224.

Bruno Bettelheim, *The Empty Fortress.* Free Press, 1967.

Sidney W. Bijou and Donald M. Baer, *Child Development, A Systematic and Empirical Theory, Vol. I.* Appleton-Century-Crofts, 1961.

Janet L. Brown, "Prognosis From Presenting Symptoms of Preschool Children With Atypical Development." *American Journal of Orthopsychiatry*, 1960, 33:382–390.

Charles B. Ferster, "Positive Reinforcement and Behavioral Deficits of Autistic Children." *Child Development*, 1961, 32:437–456.

Marion Frostig and D. Home, *The Frostig Program for the Development of Visual Perception.* Follett, 1964.

William Goldfarb, *Childhood Schizophrenia.* Harvard University Press, 1961.

S. J. Hutt, C. Hutt, D. Lee, and C. Ounsted, "A Behavioral and Electroencephalographic Study of Autistic Children." *Journal of Psychiatric Research*, 1965, 3:181–197.

Leo Kanner, "Autistic Disturbances of Affective Contact." *Nervous Child*, 1943, 2:217–250.

Leo Kanner and Leon Eisenberg, "Notes on the Follow-up Studies of Autistic Children." In P. Hoch and J. Zubin, eds., *Psychopathology of Childhood*, Greene & Stratton, 1955.

Newell C. Kephart, *The Slow Learner in the Classroom.* Charles E. Merrill Books, 1960.

Robert Koegel, *"Selective Attention to Prompt Stimuli by Autistic and Normal Children."* Unpublished doctoral dissertation, University of California, Los Angeles, 1971.

Robert Koegel and Hannelore Wilhelm, "Selective Responding to the Components of Multiple Visual Cues." *Journal of Experimental Child Psychology*, 1973, 15:442–453.

O. Ivar Lovaas, *Behavior Modification: Teaching Language to Psychotic Children*, instructional film, 45 min., 16 mm-sound. Appleton-Century-Crofts, 1969.

O. Ivar Lovaas, *Teaching Language to Non-linguistic Children*, 1973, in preparation.

O. Ivar Lovaas, Gilbert Freitag, Vivian J. Gold, and Irene C. Kassorla, "Experimental Studies in Childhood Schizophrenia: Analysis of Self-Destructive Behavior." *Journal of Experimental Child Psychology*, 1965, 2:67–84.

O. Ivar Lovaas, Gilbert Freitag, Melvyn I. Kinder, Bruce D. Rubenstein, Benson Schaeffer, and James Q. Simmons, "Establishment of Social Reinforcers in Two Schizophrenic Children on the Basis of Food." *Journal of Experimental Child Psychology*, 1966, 4:109–125.

O. Ivar Lovaas, Lorraine Freitas, Karen Nelson, and Carol Whalen, "The Establishment of Imitation and Its Use for the Development of Complex Behavior in Schizophrenic Children." *Behaviour Research and Therapy*, 1967, 5:171–181.

O. Ivar Lovaas, Robert Koegel, James Q. Simmons, and Judith Stevens, "Some Generalization and Follow-up Measures on Autistic Children in Behavior Therapy." *Journal of Applied Behavior Analysis*, 1973, 6:131–166.

O. Ivar Lovaas, Benson Schaeffer, and James Q. Simmons, "Experimental Studies in Childhood Schizophrenia: Building Social Behaviors in Autistic Children by Use of Electric Shock." *Journal of Experimental Research in Personality*, 1965, 1:99–109.

O. Ivar Lovaas, Laura Schreibman, Robert Koegel, and Richard Rehm, "Selective Responding by Autistic Children to Multiple Sensory Input." *Journal of Abnormal Psychology*, 1971, 77:211–212.

O. Ivar Lovaas and James Q. Simmons, "Manipulation of Self-destruction in Three Retarded Children." *Journal of Applied Behavior Analysis*, 1969, 2:143–157.

Edward M. Ornitz and Edward R. Ritvo, "Perceptual Inconstancy in Early Infantile Autism." *Archives of General Psychiatry*, 1968, 2:389–399.

Bernard Rimland, *Infantile Autism*. Appleton-Century-Crofts, 1964.

Todd Risley and Montrose M. Wolf, "Establishing Functional Speech in Echolalic Children." *Behaviour Research and Therapy*, 1967, 5:73–88.

Michael L. Rutter, "Prognosis: Psychotic Children in Adolescence and Early Adult Life." In John K. Wing, ed., *Early Childhood Autism*. Pergamon, 1966.

Michael L. Rutter, "The Description and Classification of Infantile Autism." In Don W. Churchill, Gerald D. Alpern, and Marion K. DeMyer, eds., *Infantile Autism*. Charles C. Thomas, 1971.

Laura Schreibman, "Within-stimulus versus Extra-stimulus Prompting Procedures in Discriminations with Autistic Children." Unpublished doctoral dissertation, University of California, Los Angeles, 1972.

Laura Schreibman and O. Ivar Lovaas, "Overselective Response to Social Stimuli by Autistic Children." *Journal of Abnormal Child Psychology*, 1973, in press.

Eric Schopler, "Early Infantile Autism and Receptor Processes." *Archives of General Psychiatry*, 1965, 13:327–335.

Eric Schopler, "Visual versus Tactile Receptor Preference in Normal and Schizophrenic Children." *Journal of Abnormal Psychology*, 1966, 71:108–114.

Eric Schopler and Robert J. Reichler, "Psychobiological Referents for the Treatment of Autism." In Don W. Churchill, Gerald D. Alpern, and Marion K. DeMyer, eds., *Infantile Autism*. Charles C. Thomas, 1971.

D. A. Treffert, "Epidemiology of Infantile Autism." *Archives of General Psychiatry*, 1970, 22:431–438.

Montrose M. Wolf, Todd Risley, and Hayden L. Mees, "Application of Operant Conditioning Procedures to the Behavior Problems of an Autistic Child." *Behaviour Research and Therapy*, 1964, 1:305–312.

[*The research which is reported in this article was supported by USPHS Research Grant MH 11440 from the National Institute of Mental Health. Many persons have helped in this research, and I am particularly grateful for the help my students have given me, and for the confidence the parents showed us when they trusted us to treat their psychotic children.*]

8

Instrumental Autonomic Conditioning

EDWARD S. KATKIN
State University of New York at Buffalo

In order to read this page you have just engaged in a variety of voluntary activities. You have fixed your eyes on these words; you have used your arms to position the page at a reasonable reading distance; and you have adjusted your body to a comfortable reading position. No doubt also you may at will change any or all these adjustments. You are in control of your behavior. Some of your behavior, however, cannot be so easily controlled. Try if you will to reduce your blood pressure, or to set your heart to beat at 85 beats per minute; and while you are at it, tell your kidneys to decrease the rate at which they are forming urine! Those among you who pride yourselves on having complete self-control may feel somewhat humbler at recognizing that you do not in fact have any direct control of these major life functions of your body; for the blood vessels, smooth muscles, and glands of your body are controlled by a system of nerves that is virtually *autonomous.* For that reason this system is referred to as the *autonomic nervous system* (ANS). This autonomic division of your nervous system is responsible for maintaining your body in what Cannon in 1939 called homeostasis—a state of equilibrium in which circulation, digestion, growth, and metabolic processes carry on without attention or concern, except in those unfortunate circumstances when they break down as a result of disease.

Probably because of its relative independence of conscious control, and certainly because its effects are expressed exclusively on inner organs of the body and are not visible to observers, the ANS has been described traditionally by psychologists as secondary or "inferior" to the "somatic" nervous system (SNS), which controls voluntary actions of the skeletal-muscular system. The history of second-class citizenship for the ANS and for the study of emotions (which are presumed to depend on autonomic activity for their existence) has been well documented. Averill suggested that the Western intellectual tradition, stemming from the Greeks, has relegated the supposedly involuntary aspects of man's behavior—those autonomous functions associated with emotional expression—to an inferior position relative to the more voluntary, rational functions. Averill argued further that throughout scientific history such symbolic considerations have altered the way scientific concepts have been defined and studied. This is certainly how psychologists have dealt with the distinctions between the autonomic and somatic nervous systems. It has been usual for twentieth-century psychology to assume that the autonomic system is not capable of responding to training techniques as well or as much as the somatic system. Specifically, it has been argued that the ANS is subject only to the laws of learning subsumed under the rubric of "classical conditioning," while the SNS is subject both to classical conditioning and to conditioning of the "instrumental" or "operant" type. Before continuing with our discussion of the distinction between ANS and SNS conditioning, we shall distinguish between these two types of learning procedures, and then return to the importance of the distinction for an understanding of autonomic conditioning.

Classical and Instrumental Conditioning

Classical Conditioning

The term "classical conditioning" is applied to those forms of conditioning developed by Pavlov, the Russian physiologist who discovered the conditional reflex and developed most of the major techniques of conditioning employed during the past sixty years.

When a physician taps your patellar (knee) tendon properly with a hammer, your knee jerks. The relationship between the hammer tap and the knee jerk is literally unconditional; it always happens. It is a reflex. Pavlov defined this as the *unconditional reflex* (incorrectly translated from the Russian as *unconditioned reflex,* and often referred to as such); its two observable components are the *unconditional stimulus* or *UCS* (the hammer tap) and the *unconditional response* or *UCR* (the knee jerk). Another example of an unconditional reflex is the one with which Pavlov did his experimenting, the salivary reflex. If you place meat powder (a UCS) in the mouth of a hungry dog, he will salivate (a UCR). Now, Pavlov's great discovery was that if you strike a tuning fork

(or bell) just before you place the meat powder in the dog's mouth and repeat the sequence a few times, soon the dog will begin to salivate upon hearing the bell, even if the presentation of the meat powder is now omitted. It is important to understand the critical elements of this discovery. First, it must be understood that repeated presentations of a bell by itself will *not* cause that dog to salivate; in that sense the bell is said to be a *neutral* stimulus. Only if the bell is followed by the meat powder will the bell eventually elicit the salivation; the eliciting of a salivary response by the bell is conditional upon its being presented at about the same time (actually just before) as the meat powder. Therefore the bell is referred to as the *conditional stimulus* or *CS*; the salivation that follows the bell is called the *conditional response* or *CR*; and the sequence of presenting the bell and eliciting the salivation is called the *conditional reflex.* This reflex is conditional on the fact that there is an unconditional relationship between the meat powder and the salivation, and also on the fact that the bell is associated with the meat powder.

The general outline of classical, or Pavlovian, conditioning appears in figure 1. In classical conditioning the experimenter calls the shots; it is the experimenter who determines whether or not meat powder will be presented. The subject has no control over the "pure" classical conditioning situation, for the experimenter makes no alterations in procedures as a result of any action the subject takes.

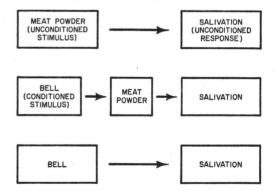

Figure 1. A classical conditioning procedure schematically diagrammed. In the top row an unconditional stimulus elicits an unconditional response; in the middle row the unconditional stimulus is preceded by a conditional stimulus; and in the bottom row the conditional stimulus becomes effective in eliciting what appears to be the same response elicited in the two prior situations, but which is now conditional on the presentation of the conditional stimulus.

Instrumental Conditioning

Suppose you place a rat in an empty box and provide it with no stimulation. You will observe that the rat may groom himself, walk around, or turn his head in many directions. These acts are all examples of what the learning psychologist, B. F. Skinner, has identified as an *operant* response, behavior that occurs spontaneously without being specifically evoked by a stimulus. Skinner contrasts operants with *respondents*. Respondents are elicited by specific stimuli (for example, a rat jumping when his feet receive an electric shock from the floor of his cage) and are similar to Pavlov's unconditional responses. In operant or instrumental conditioning, the emphasis is not on the respondent, but on the operant, and the goal is to train the animal (or person) to increase the frequency with which a certain operant is performed. In the most popular technique for instrumental conditioning a rat is placed in a cage (commonly called a Skinner box), which is empty except for a lever at one end of it. The rat normally will exhibit a variety of operants: walking, scratching, grooming, and perhaps pressing on the lever. If the experimenter were interested in training the rat to press the lever with great frequency relative to other operants he would have to try something other than the Pavlovian technique, for there is not a readily available stimulus which will *unconditionally* evoke lever-pressing behavior from a rat. But suppose the rat has been deprived of food and receives food every time he happens to press the lever. At the outset he may press the lever, say, once a minute; but soon the rat is pressing the lever at a rate considerably faster than once a minute. The food is called a reinforcer since it "strengthens" the behavior it follows, in the sense that the behavior occurs more frequently. In this situation the animal is reinforced —receives food—only when he presses the lever. Thus his behavior is instrumental in the receipt of food; the course of events is in the paws of the rat, not in the hands of the experimenter. Through this procedure the rat becomes conditioned to press the lever, and this is known as instrumental conditioning.

Instrumental Conditioning and the Somatic-Autonomic Distinction

As was mentioned earlier, psychologists have assumed traditionally that autonomic (ANS) responses could be acquired by a "simple" form of learning, classical conditioning, but were not subject to a more complex, superior form of learning, instrumental conditioning. The traditional belief in the "inferiority" of the ANS was based in part on scientific observation and in part on "common sense." For instance, the ANS has been traditionally defined by neuroanatomists as solely a motor system [Peele]. Therefore, it was believed to be incapable of receiving incoming stimuli, capable only of sending out impulses. This factor, Smith argued, rendered the ANS incapable of being responsive to external reinforcement. Furthermore, common sense indicated that in order for instrumental conditioning to take place a response (e.g., lever pressing) had to have some demonstrable effect on the external environment (e.g., the food-dispensing magazine of a Skinner box). Clearly, ANS responses such as changes in heart rate or blood pressure do not interact with the external environment, and therefore were seen to be entirely incapable of acting instrumentally. It seemed obvious to most investigators, as it must seem obvious to you now, that to demonstrate instrumental conditioning of, say, blood pressure level, you would have to train a subject to change his blood pressure level in order to receive reinforcement. As we noted at the beginning of this discussion, this kind of "voluntary" control seems quite beyond the capabilities of mere mortals.

These arguments were not based merely on conjecture. They were heavily influenced by the fact that many experimenters had tried to condition autonomic responses instrumentally—and had failed. The evidence was so uniformly discouraging that Skinner declared in his influential treatise on instrumental learning in 1938 that the ANS could not respond to instrumental training techniques. Other prominent learning psychologists shared this conclusion, so that for two decades psychologists influenced by their views essentially ignored the problem, assuming that the issue had been closed.

Yet the past decade has witnessed a dramatic shift in our knowledge and understanding of the abilities of the ANS to respond to instrumental training. In the following pages we shall describe the development of a scientific assault on the traditional belief in the distinction between somatic and autonomic learning. This attack was carried out by scientists with an egalitarian view of the nature of learning, a view that holds that all segments of the nervous system, skeletal as well as autonomic, are equal, and capable of equal learning, provided they have equal opportunity.

You may ask at this point why scientists should be so interested in finding evidence to support this new idea. Why does it matter whether autonomic functions do or do not respond to the same manipulations as skeletal functions? What is the importance of gaining instrumental control over them? In addition to the esoteric theoretical interest that some scientists have in the problem, there are also some clear practical reasons for the interest. If people can be trained to control their autonomic responses and to make them instrumental in responding to external rewards, great strides forward may be envisioned in the field of psychosomatic medicine. For instance, consider ulcer patients trained to inhibit acid secretions in the stomach, or cardiac patients trained to control voluntarily cardiac arrhythmias, or people who suffer from intense, unrealistic fears being trained to control the autonomic components of their fear. Furthermore, if it can be proved that autonomic functions are subject to instrumental reinforcement, we can begin to explore the possible ways such reinforcement actually takes place in natural life, with a view toward further explanation of the early development of psychosomatic symptoms, and the development of individual differences in visceral functions.

So you see, the issue has broad implications for some very real problems of behavior and all these reasons have further spurred attempts to break down the traditional distinction between autonomic and somatic learning. As we shall see, this radical assault upon traditional beliefs required endless patience, new techniques, and the ability to provide evidence sufficiently convincing to be entertained seriously. The eventual establishment of a new view based on solid evidence was a long and difficult task. We shall follow the historical course of the research that has been carried out on this problem.

Background

Twenty-three years after Skinner in 1938 concluded that instrumental conditioning of ANS functions was impossible, Razran in 1961 reported evidence that Lisina, in the Soviet Union, had instrumentally conditioned dilatation of the blood vessels (vasodilatation). Razran's report of Lisina's work stimulated considerable interest in the United States and may have been responsible, at least in part, for the resurgence of research endeavors during the past decade; however, when Lisina's work was published in English in 1965, and became available for more careful scrutiny by American investigators, it appeared that she did not claim to have conditioned vasodilatation directly. Rather, Lisina

concluded that her subjects gained voluntary control over their blood vessels by "using a number of special devices, mainly the relaxation of the skeletal musculature and changing of the depth of respiration" [p. 456]. She suggested further that the changes observed in vascular activity may not have been conditional responses but rather unconditional responses to muscular changes and breathing changes that the subject exhibited. That is, Lisina suggested that her subjects may have learned a certain muscular response and/or breathing response which in itself acted as a UCS, thereby eliciting unconditional changes in vascular activity.

Lisina's results demonstrate the difficulty of defining clearly the effect of instrumental conditioning procedures on ANS function. In Skinner's earlier discussion (1938) of instrumental conditioning of autonomic behavior he attempted to analyze this problem in depth. Skinner emphasized that human beings can and do exert voluntary control over their autonomic functions. For instance, think of the child who has learned to cry "real tears" or the boy who has learned not to cry in public. But is this voluntary control exercised directly or is it the indirect result of voluntary control of skeletal activity? Is it possible that the apparent direct control of autonomic function is really only a by-product of direct control over somatic functions? The following discussion, adapted from Skinner, suggests that instrumental ANS conditioning may sometimes be nothing more than an epiphenomenon associated with skeletal conditioning and/or previous classical conditioning. The following four cases describe ways in which such apparent, but not true, instrumental conditioning may occur.

1. *An autonomic response may be a UCR to an external source of stimulation.* For instance, an individual may stick himself with a pin thereby causing his blood pressure to change. If an experimenter delivered reinforcement upon detecting a change in blood pressure, the subject might resort to sticking himself with a pin to obtain reinforcement. Admittedly this pin-sticking strategy seems rather unlikely either in nature or in laboratories, but there is a variety of less obvious sources of external stimuli (e.g., light, visual patterns) to which a subject might learn to expose himself.

2. *An autonomic response may be a UCR to an internal source of stimulation.* That is, a subject may engage in rapid muscular activity thereby eliciting unconditional blood pressure changes. If an experimenter delivered reinforcement upon detecting such a blood pressure change, the subject might show an

increase in muscular activity resulting in apparent conditioning of blood pressure. Indeed this case is identical to the sequence of events described by Lisina in her study of vasodilatation.

3. *An autonomic response may be a CR to an external source of stimulation.* That is, an individual may read an exciting book or look at an arousing picture to which autonomic responses have been classically conditioned previously. Although it is unlikely that an individual in a laboratory would be able to subject himself voluntarily to this type of external stimulation, the following variation of this case suggests that there are other forms of stimulation which are more susceptible to self-presentation in a laboratory.

4. *An autonomic response may be a CR to an internal source of stimulation.* In this case an individual may engage in subvocal activity (thinking) and this activity may elicit a previously conditioned (classical) ANS response pattern. For instance, a subject might have a sexually arousing thought, thereby eliciting a previously conditioned autonomic response. If an experimenter delivered reinforcement upon detecting the autonomic response, the subject might show an increase in the frequency of occurrence of sexually stimulating thoughts, resulting once again in apparent instrumental ANS conditioning.

To illustrate the confounding effect of previously conditioned autonomic responses Skinner referred to work by Hudgins in 1933 in which subjects said the word "contract" at the same time that a bright light was flashed on their eye. The bright light, of course, caused their pupils to constrict unconditionally. Subsequently the mere vocalization of the word "contract" became sufficient to elicit classically conditioned pupillary constriction. This is an example of case 3 above because the spoken word constituted an external stimulus. Had the subject merely *thought* the word "contract" the results would conform to the paradigm of case 4. Thus, the subject may be reinforced, as we have seen, not only for skeletal-muscular activity but for verbal or cognitive activity, and this activity may serve either as a conditional or as an unconditional stimulus for ANS responses.

In order for investigators interested in the possibilities of conditioning the ANS by instrumental techniques to provide us with convincing evidence they should be able to deal with the problems raised by these four alternative explanatory mechanisms. Ideally, animal studies might use curare to eliminate skeletal-muscular activities; for that matter such controls are not out of the question in human research [Birk, Crider, Shapiro, & Tursky; Smith,

Brown, Toman, & Goodman]. Furthermore, such experiments should be designed to reduce the possibility of self-stimulation eliciting previously conditioned autonomic responses. In the following discussion we shall review first the studies on human subjects during the past decade and then we will turn to the research on infrahuman subjects. In each case, the evidence offered by the various investigators will be evaluated against the possibility of alternative explanations. We shall examine the extent to which scientifically obtained data can be seen to be definitive, or at least convincing, and we shall examine also the extent to which scientifically obtained data may be seen to be ambiguous and subject to alternative interpretations. We will review experiments that have been conducted on a variety of basic autonomic response systems: the electrodermal response system, the peripheral vascular system, the cardiac regulatory system, and visceral regulatory mechanisms.

Instrumental Conditioning of Electrodermal Responses

Some Definitions

If a pair of electrodes were placed on your skin and a voltage impressed upon them, the surface of your skin would offer considerable resistance to the flow of current between the electrodes. This resistance, or apparent resistance to be more technically accurate, can be measured on a galvanometer and quantified. The measurement of such skin resistance is referred to as *electrodermal* measurement. The impetus for the interest in electrodermal activity was stimulated originally by Féré in 1888, who discovered that levels of skin resistance seem to change reflexively to applied stimulation, and by Richter in 1927 who demonstrated that an intact autonomic nervous system (specifically the sympathetic division) was necessary for the elicitation of reflex electrodermal responding.

Figure 2 shows a typical polygraph recording of basal skin resistance and a specific electrodermal response to a stimulus. As may be noted in figure 2 basal skin resistance can be read on a polygraph in electrical units of resistance called ohms; the presentation of a stimulus to a subject elicits a discrete drop in the resistance level followed shortly by a return to the predeflection level of resistance. This discrete drop is sometimes referred to as a galvanic skin response (GSR). In more recent years, as technology has become more sophisticated and measure-

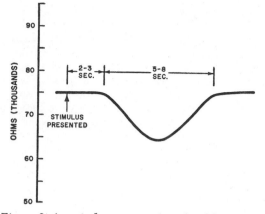

Figure 2. A typical representation of a GSR.

ment more precise, it was discovered that subjects often emitted GSRs in the absence of any specific stimulation to elicit them. These unelicited GSRs, which may be considered operants in Skinner's terms, are often very small in magnitude but sometimes can be as large as the specific elicited GSRs.

On the assumption that both elicited GSRs (respondents) and unelicited GSRs (operants) may be indexes of emotional behavior (due to their link with the autonomic nervous system), both of these responses have been the subjects of extensive investigation by psychologists, and a large amount of this investigation has concerned their conditionability. Some investigators have been interested in conditionability of autonomic responses solely because of the implications of such conditioning for the study of emotional behavior and psychotherapy. Other investigators have been concerned with the investigation of classical conditioning in and of itself and have chosen the galvanic skin response as a convenient measure of choice with which to pursue theoretical interests. In the following discussion we will review first the empirical literature on *instrumental* modification of unelicited GSRs using reward to increase their frequency of occurrence and punishment to decrease their frequency of occurrence. Then we will look at the literature on the instrumental modification of the elicited GSR in which subjects are trained to respond instrumentally with a specific GSR to a cue in order to avoid some negative consequences.

Rewarding the Unelicited GSR

The earliest of the recent attempts to condition an autonomic response by instrumental techniques was published in 1960 by Kimmel and Hill who at-

tempted to modify the frequency of emission of unelicited GSRs by rewarding or punishing their subjects with pleasant or unpleasant odors. Working on the assumption that GSR responses were related to emotional state, Kimmel and Hill tried to increase the frequency of GSRs by presenting subjects with pleasant smells only when the subjects emitted a spontaneous or unelicited GSR. It was expected under these circumstances that the rate of GSR responding would increase. Conversely, the investigators attempted to decrease the rate of emission of GSRs for some subjects by presenting them with unpleasant odors and predicting that unpleasant reinforcement would result in a decrease in GSR response rate. The results of Kimmel and Hill's experiment were essentially negative. No differences were obtained between their experimental and control groups during the conditioning period and no overall differences were obtained in the subsequent "extinction" period in which no rewards were presented regardless of GSR rate of response. These early negative findings were consistent with the then prevalent assumptions of psychology that instrumental modification of autonomic functions was not feasible. However, the experiment was flawed in a variety of ways, the most obvious of which was that the experimenters found it difficult to control carefully the presentation of odors. Ironically, then, instead of deterring further experimentation this early report by Kimmel and Hill instead stimulated considerably more effort in the area, directed toward the elimination of the flaws.

The next three attempts to modify the frequency of unelicited GSRs [Fowler & Kimmel 1962, Kimmel & Kimmel 1963, Mandler, Preven, & Kuhlman 1962] used flashing lights instead of odors as reinforcers, since lights can be easily controlled by experimenters. Fowler and Kimmel employed the following procedure: they allowed their subjects to rest for approximately two minutes during which time they recorded all the unelicited GSRs given by the subjects. After this two-minute period, they flashed a light each time a subject emitted a GSR that was equal to or greater than the average magnitude of all responses emitted during the two-minute rest period. A "control" group of subjects was also employed, and it also received flashing lights; however, the control group received the flashing lights at random intervals not contingent upon the emission of GSRs. Fowler and Kimmel reported a difference between the "contingent" and "noncontingent" groups beyond what statistical tests suggested would be expected by chance. There are some difficulties in interpreting the significance of these differences, however. It turns out that neither the contingent nor the noncontingent group of subjects showed a higher rate of GSR emission during the conditioning period than during the rest period. In fact, both groups showed a somewhat lower rate. At no time in the course of training did the experimental (contingent) group emit more than 80 per cent of their rate of responding obtained in the initial two-minute rest period. Although there was a higher number of responses for the experimental group than the control group, both groups showed a general pattern of decline from the initial rest period.

To deal with this interpretive problem, Kimmel and Kimmel replicated the Fowler and Kimmel study with several modifications, the most important being an increase in the length of the initial rest period. This is an important experimental modification, for it is apparent that when subjects first arrive at a laboratory their operant rate of GSR emission is extremely high and there is a strong general tendency for it to decline for ten to fifteen minutes. To begin an experimental procedure after only two minutes, as Fowler and Kimmel did, is to cause the experiment to intervene in the natural process of adaptation. By increasing the initial rest period and allowing the subjects time to reach a minimal rate of GSR activity, the effects of the experimental manipulation can be more clearly understood. The Kimmels' experiment also used an experimental group that received reinforcement contingent on the emission of *any* response and a control group that received an equal number of reinforcers only at times when no response was observed.

The results of the Kimmels' study were far more dramatic than those of the earlier Fowler and Kimmel experiment which they set out to replicate. In this second experiment the experimental group showed clear increases up to 120 per cent of the initial resting level and the noncontingent control group declined in rate of emission to below 80 per cent of initial level. This pattern of acquisition, which was clearer than that obtained in the original Fowler and Kimmel study, may be attributed to either or both of the following factors. First, the longer initial rest period used by the Kimmels overcame the difficulty of the general decline in response frequency during the early stages of conditioning. Second, in the Kimmels' study every response detectable was reinforced instead of the Fowler and Kimmel technique of reinforcing only responses equal to or greater than the average magnitude of all responses during rest.

Yet the results of both of the studies from Kimmel's laboratory may be subjected to interpretation on other grounds. Neither the Fowler and Kimmel nor the Kimmel and Kimmel studies included direct controls for skeletal-muscular mediation. Although no evidence of gross body movement was observed in the GSR records obtained by Kimmel and associates, muscle potential, or electromyogram (EMG), recordings were not taken to confirm this. The authors themselves recognized that their "conclusion that autonomically mediated responses can be conditioned instrumentally can be challenged on the basis of an almost infinite number of possible somatic mediators" [Kimmel & Kimmel 1963, p. 213].

In yet another early study on unelicited GSRs, Mandler et al. (1962) reinforced GSRs equal to or greater than 500 ohms resistance and found no effects of contingent reinforcement on learning. Mandler et al. also presented evidence which suggested that the general effect of reinforcement was to increase the general activation level of their subjects. This increase in activation, they suggested, might easily have resulted in increased skeletal-muscular activity which might in turn have caused any increase in GSR frequency which was observed. Mandler and his colleagues concluded that instrumental conditioning of autonomically mediated responses remained to be demonstrated.

Although these reports were not entirely positive and in the case of Mandler et al. were downright negative, the general impact on the field was to stimulate thinking and activity. After the publication of these studies in the early 1960's, three further reports from the Harvard Medical School appeared [Birk et al. 1966, Crider, Shapiro, & Tursky 1966, Shapiro, Crider, & Tursky 1964]. In the Shapiro et al. and Crider et al. studies subjects were told that they should think emotional thoughts and that they would hear a tone which was worth five cents each time the experimenter's machinery detected such thoughts. In the Shapiro et al. study respiration was simultaneously monitored as a way of determining whether or not subjects were moving, and in the Crider et al. study an ingenious device was utilized to detect even the slightest body movement in the subjects. Although both experiments indicated some differences between an experimental and a control group of subjects, which might have been indicative of an instrumental conditioning phenomenon, both studies are clearly susceptible to alternative explanations under the case 4 argument presented earlier. That is, the GSR might have been a conditioned response to internal stimuli, for it is quite obvious that the subjects were instructed to produce subvocal operants (translated, think emotional thoughts) which may have been conditional stimuli for ANS responses.

In the Birk et al. study a single subject was run under conditions of partial curarization. Curare, a drug that must be used with extreme care, interferes with the chemical transmitters that are necessary for nerve impulses to be delivered to skeletal muscles, but does not interfere with autonomic nerve activity. Here we have the only known attempt in this area to control skeletal muscular artifact by curarization of a human subject. Figure 3 shows the acquisition curve for this subject during curarization and during a similar period in which the same subject was not curarized. It may be observed that the curare session yielded *lower* frequencies of response throughout, although both curves showed an acquisition like trend. Unfortunately, the authors did not obtain a control "noncontingent reinforcement" session from this subject with which to compare the two conditioning sessions. Thus, the safest conclusion that can be drawn from this demonstration is simply that the administration of curare resulted in reduced muscle activity (obviously) and reduced frequency of GSR responding as a consequence.

Rice attempted to control for muscle movements without the use of paralyzing drugs. In his experiment he used the EMG to record small amplitude muscle potential changes in the forearm muscle group which mediates flexion of the fingers from which the GSRs were then recorded. By using this technique any small muscle movement in the arm which might have caused an unconditional GSR was recorded and Rice could subsequently disregard any GSRs that were associated with muscle activity. Furthermore, Rice divided his subjects so that half

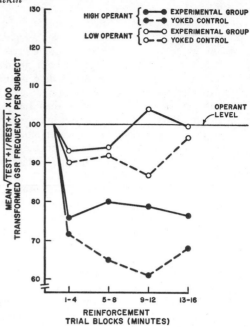

Figure 4. *Mean transformed GSR frequency for subjects in the contingent and noncontingent groups, irrespective of EMG, divided by operant level, during reinforcement [Rice].*

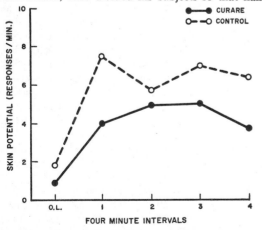

Figure 3. *Number of skin potential responses per minute over a 16-minute period and an operant period for a single subject under normal and curarized conditions [Birk et al.].*

received reinforcement for any GSR they emitted and half received reinforcement only for GSRs emitted *in the absence of the EMG responses.* Using this technique Rice could compare the conditioning results for subjects who might be showing unconditional responses to muscle activity as compared to subjects who were reinforced only for showing GSRs entirely independent of muscle activity. The reinforcement used was a light presented in an otherwise dark room. Rice also used noncontingent control groups as a comparison and, in addition, he divided his subjects as a function of their initial level of responding. That is, subjects who showed a high level of operant responding in the initial rest period were compared with those subjects who showed a low level of operant responding in the initial rest period.

Rice's findings are complex and must be considered in detail. Figure 4 presents his data for those subjects who were reinforced irrespective of muscle action. Consistent with previous reports there were differential rates of adaptation for the contingent and noncontingent groups, with the contingent group demonstrating a greater resistance to habituation regardless of their initial operant level. Figure 5 presents data obtained from those subjects who re-

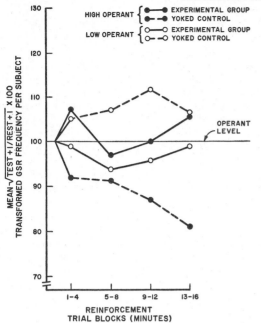

Figure 5. Mean transformed GSR frequency for subjects in the contingent and noncontingent groups, reinforced only in the absence of EMG, divided by operant level, during reinforcement [Rice].

ceived reinforcement only when no muscle action (as recorded on the EMG) was associated with the response. These data yielded no notable effect. The results of figure 5 indicate that the only subjects for whom the trend was in the expected direction (i.e., showed evidence of conditioning) were those subjects in the low operant *non*contingent group. In other words, the data in figure 5 indicate that the best conditioning curve was obtained from some of the control subjects, for whom there was no conditioning situation! These results indicate that the differences between experimental and control groups seen in figure 4 may really reflect differences in muscle activity, for the significant differences between experimental and control groups seemed to fade away when only those responses independent of muscle action were analyzed. However, Rice observed that the subjects represented in figure 5 received fewer reinforcements than those represented in figure 4, because they received no reinforcement for GSRs that were associated with muscle changes. Therefore, Rice ran eighteen additional pairs of subjects for longer time periods, reinforcing only those responses that were independent of muscle action and delivering to these subjects the same number of reinforcements given to the initial groups repre-

sented in figure 4. Under these conditions even the differential habituation trends seen in figure 4 disappeared and Rice concluded "the evidence is somewhat equivocal as to whether operant GSR conditioning is possible when only those GSRs given in the absence of preceding muscle tension changes are reinforced" [p. 912].

Rice's study was not the only one concerned with the problem of somatic or skeletal mediation in GSR conditioning. Van Twyver and Kimmel also attempted to increase the rate of unelicited GSR activity while simultaneously investigating the possibility of somatic mediation. Van Twyver and Kimmel controlled carefully for respiration rate, respiration irregularity, and muscle potentials. At the conclusion of their experiment, they evaluated the EMG records and the respiration records and concluded that there were no differences between groups for any of these possible mediators. Furthermore, all GSRs that were accompanied by muscle activity or breathing irregularity were discarded in a subsequent analysis. The data obtained by Van Twyver and Kimmel were clear—the contingent reinforcement group showed a smooth acquisition curve and the noncontingent group showed a clear adaptation curve. Acquisition was clear and more gradual than in the Kimmel and Kimmel experiment recorded previously in which muscular mediation was not controlled. Thus, the Van Twyver and Kimmel study reported clear evidence for instrumental modification of GSR frequency independent of skeletal-muscular or cognitive mediation.

To recapitulate, then, these studies on the reward of unelicited GSRs yielded conflicting results. Some investigators were unable to demonstrate any positive findings at all while other investigators implicated the skeletal-muscular system as a mediator, or causal link, in the apparent conditioning of GSRs. Finally, after a number of attempts in his laboratory Kimmel was able to offer apparently definitive results indicating that, in fact, the rate of occurrence of unelicited GSRs could be increased by rewarding subjects with a light flash upon the emission of a GSR; but this report by Van Twyver and Kimmel did not stand unchallenged. Two subsequent reports [Stern 1967, Stern, Boles, & Diones 1966] raised questions about the adequacy of all previous attempts to reward the unelicited GSR.

Stern and his associates reported that they had consistently obtained negative results when attempting to demonstrate operant conditioning of spontaneous GSRs in a manner similar to Kimmel's. Stern and his colleagues discussed this difficulty in some detail and proposed some alternative explanatory mechanisms for the positive findings reported by other investigators, explanations that incorporate some of the arguments presented at the beginning of this paper concerning skeletal-muscular and cognitive mediation. As you will recall, it is common in the instrumental conditioning paradigm to utilize a control group in which subjects receive reinforcement only at times when they are not giving GSRs. Stern became interested in the cognitive evaluations that subjects might place upon the reinforcement they received, and he was particularly interested in whether the subjects in the control condition would evaluate the meaning of reinforcement in a different manner than the subjects in the experimental condition. To investigate this question, subjects in Stern's experiments were presented with questionnaires and asked to respond to certain specific queries concerning the meaning for them of the reinforcement stimuli. In this manner, Stern obtained empirical evidence that suggested that in the control group subjects reinforced for *not* responding tended to develop the cognitive belief that they were being reinforced for being "relaxed" or "drowsy"; the experimental subjects, on the other hand, who were reinforced only when they *were* responding tended to develop the belief that they were being reinforced for doing things such as "muscular reaction," "slight movements," or "thinking about exciting things." Stern suggested that these different kinds of beliefs led to different courses of action on the part of the subjects, and that the different courses of action resulted in unconditional ANS responses that were then incorrectly considered to be conditional responses. In other words, Stern and his associates are suggesting that the control subjects, who believe they are being reinforced for being relaxed or drowsy, then act relaxed or drowsy, thereby inhibiting muscle activity. The experimental subjects, on the other hand, who are reinforced only when they are responding, tend to believe that they are being reinforced for slight movements, muscular actions, or cognitive activity and, therefore, tend to move their bodies more and/or think more "exciting thoughts."

Stern's comments provide a basis for reinterpreting data obtained from experiments in which the control subjects were given equal numbers of reinforcements only at times when they were not responding. However, Stern's comments are not the only critical points raised about the early research. A controversy has also arisen about the experimental technique in which control subjects receive reinforcement at exactly the same time as the experimental subjects. This technique is called the "yoked-control." The term "yoking" developed from the literal yoking of subjects, usually animal subjects. Specifically, in a yoked experiment the reinforcing apparatus is designed to be triggered only by a correct response from a subject in the experimental group, yet the delivery of reinforcement occurs simultaneously for subjects in the control group. Consequently, a subject in a control group receives exactly the same number of reinforcements as the subject in the experimental group, and he receives them at exactly the same time; but whereas the experimental subject receives the reinforcement only after a correct response (i.e., GSR), the control subject may or may not have emitted a correct response just before receiving reinforcement. Thus, for the control subject, the reinforcing pattern tends to be random (sometimes, by chance, reinforcement accompanies a response, but more often than not it does not). It is also common practice for psychologists to use yoked control designs which are not "truly" yoked. That is, an experimental subject may be run by himself and a record kept of exactly the times at which he gave reinforceable responses. A control subject then is subsequently run, matched identically to the experimental subject for number and time of reinforcements.

Now let us return to the controversy that has arisen about the use of yoked-control techniques. In 1964 Church published an influential article which stated that the yoked control design establishes an inherent bias in favor of experimental groups and that the yoked control design therefore was entirely inadequate to interpret the results of instrumental conditioning studies. In a critical argument concerning the relevance of Church's discussion to autonomic conditioning, Katkin and Murray in 1968 argued that otherwise satisfactory reports of instrumental modification of ANS responses (such as the one offered by Van Twyver and Kimmel) had to be interpreted cautiously and perhaps rejected because they had employed yoked control designs. Katkin and Murray were quickly disputed by Crider, Schwartz, and Shnidman who pointed out that there was an error in Church's original formulation of the difficulties with the yoked control design. Consequently, Crider et al. have suggested that Katkin and Murray's conclusion (that research on instrumental conditioning of autonomic functions which employs the yoked control design should be rejected) was premature. It is not possible to go into lengthy discussion of the technical considerations entailed in the analysis of experimental designs; however, Black [1967a] has had perhaps the last word on the topic in his suggestion that discretion in the face of confusion is the better part of valor. Black has stated that it is theoretically impossible to determine whether yoked designs are appropriate in any given experiment. "In general, if yoked designs are inappropriate under at least one of a given set of possible assumptions about how conditioning takes place, and if one does not know which set of assumptions is correct, then he cannot employ yoked designs" [p. 8].

Support for Black's general warning may be inferred from data that came from Kimmel's laboratory approximately one year after the successful Van Twyver and Kimmel experiment. Kimmel and Sternthal [1967] became aware of Church's argument which suggested that the yoked-control design was inadequate and so they attempted to replicate some earlier findings in Kimmel's laboratory [Kimmel & Baxter, 1964] which had employed a yoked-control design. In brief, Kimmel and Sternthal reported that "the results of this study tend to support Church's contention that the yoked-control design may lead to spurious or exaggerated evidence of avoidance conditioning" [p. 145]. Kimmel and Sternthal reported that in their replication study, which did not use a yoked-control design, differences favoring an experimental group over the yoked-control group tended to shrink. The results of the Kimmel and Sternthal paper presented some difficulty for advocates of the position that autonomic functions could be modified by instrumental techniques. How could this failure to replicate previous findings be interpreted? Perhaps the best interpretation was that Black's admonition was well taken—the biasing effects of the yoked-control design are intricate and difficult to predict. When in doubt it should be avoided. If, on the other hand, Crider et al.'s argument in favor of the yoked-control design is accepted, then we must still explain why Kimmel and Sternthal were unable to replicate early experimental findings. So you see, whether or not we dismiss some of the early positive findings because of inappropriate experimental design, we are faced with the fact that up to this point the existing evidence for instrumental modification of autonomic functions in human subjects was at best weak.

Perhaps an examination of other experimental techniques to modify autonomic function will yield more conclusive and convincing evidence. We turn next to a discussion of the use of punishment to *decrease* the frequency of unelicited GSRs as compared to the previous discussion of the use of reward to *increase* the frequency of unelicited GSRs.

Punishing the Unelicited GSR

There have been fewer attempts to decrease the frequency of electrodermal responses than there

have been to increase the frequency, and in this section we will review two seminal papers in this area—one by Johnson and Schwartz and one by Senter and Hummel. In the earlier of these two studies, Senter and Hummel used an electric shock as a punishing stimulus and delivered the shock to a subject's forefinger only when the subject emitted an unelicited GSR. Senter and Hummel's assumption was that this punishing shock would be instrumental in reducing the rate at which subjects emitted spontaneous GSRs.

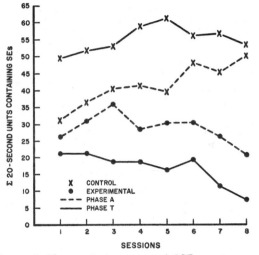

Figure 6. Changes in frequency of GSR spontaneous emissions (SEs) during phase A and phase T [Senter & Hummel].

The best way to understand the meaning and results of Senter and Hummel's experiment is to examine closely figure 6. All of the subjects in the Senter and Hummel study were allowed an initial period of rest in which no shocks were delivered to their fingers and in which the rate of spontaneous emissions was counted. This initial resting period is referred to in figure 6 as phase A. On the vertical axis of the figure we see that the unit of measurement was the sum of time units, in this case 20-second time units, which contained spontaneous emissions. On the horizontal axis of the graph we see that there were eight sessions altogether. In other words, for each of the eight sessions the time units were broken down into 20-second units and the number of such 20-second units in which at least one spontaneous emission was noted was plotted on the graph. After the initial resting period (phase A) subjects were trained for 15 minutes. Training meant that each time a subject emitted a GSR during that 15-minute period he received an electric shock. It was expected then that subjects in the experimental group who received a shock every time they gave a GSR would show fewer GSRs after training than before training. The graph shows that for the period *after* training—phase T—subjects in the experimental group did indeed show fewer GSRs than they did in phase A. This is seen by inspection of the lower two lines of figure 6. The lowest line represents experimental subjects after training and the line above it represents the same experimental subjects before training. It may also be noted in figure 6 that for the control subjects who received random shocks unrelated to their GSR activity there was actually some evident increase in the total number of time units containing responses in phase T as compared to phase A. This finding is to be expected on the assumption that random shocks, as delivered to the control group, cause a general increase in autonomic activity. On the other hand, the decrease in autonomic activity during phase T for subjects in the experimental group, on the surface, seems to be explicable only in terms of a conditioned or learned avoidance response. That is, the subjects have been conditioned *not* to respond in order to avoid receiving electric shocks. Unfortunately, Senter and Hummel recorded neither muscle potentials nor respiration activity and hence it is impossible to determine adequately whether their results indicate instrumental conditioning of autonomic functions or just instrumental conditioning of the inhibition of muscular activity resulting in *unconditional* autonomic changes.

In a second study that used punishment Johnson and Schwartz avoided the unpleasantness of shocking their subjects and used instead a loud noise as a punishing stimulus. Subjects in their experimental group received the loud noise only when they emitted a GSR; subjects in their control groups received a loud noise an equal number of times, but it was not contingent on GSR activity. Johnson and Schwartz took precautions to try to satisfy any potential criticisms of their results. They used EMG recordings in an attempt to control for artifactual muscle activity and they interviewed each of their subjects in depth to determine the extent to which cognitive activity, or thinking, might have influenced their results. In brief, Johnson and Schwartz discovered that the delivery of a contingent loud noise after the emission of a GSR resulted in suppression of GSR activity. The control subjects, on the other hand, showed no similar suppression of their activity. The Johnson and Schwartz results are quite persuasive for a number of reasons. First, the magnitude of the differences between experimental and control groups was quite large—much larger than usually reported in such

experiments. Second, the use of muscle potential recording resulted in data that were reasonably free of possible skeletal artifact. And finally, the results of the extensive interviewing of the subjects indicated that subjects in both the experimental and control groups had approximately the same ideas about the experiment and were trying out approximately the same mental strategies to avoid receiving loud noises. Thus, Johnson and Schwartz were able to conclude that alternative explanations such as those presented earlier in cases 2 and 4 could be dismissed.

To summarize, the bulk of studies which tried to *increase* the frequency of GSR responding by the use of reward have provided us with conflicting results and only hints of success. Although most of these studies reported positive findings, close inspection of them indicated that the findings were not definitive and in most cases could be explained by any of a variety of alternative explanations, most of which were discussed thirty years earlier by Skinner. The smaller number of studies which attempted to *reduce* the frequency of unelicited GSRs also showed conflicting results. While Johnson and Schwartz's paper seems to be an adequate demonstration of the phenomenon, Senter and Hummel's paper was somewhat less clear.

Not all of the research on electrodermal activity has addressed itself to the control of *unelicited* (operant) GSRs. There have been a few studies that have attempted to elicit a specific GSR (respondent) to a stimulus and then to make that elicited GSR instrumental in achieving some goal. We shall now discuss these studies.

Avoidance Conditioning of the Elicited GSR

Avoidance conditioning involves a different experimental paradigm than the one we have been discussing. Avoidance conditioning is similar to classical conditioning in that the subject is presented first with a neutral stimulus and then with a reinforcing stimulus a few seconds later. The difference between classical conditioning and instrumental avoidance conditioning is that in the instrumental avoidance conditioning situation the second stimulus, or UCS, does not necessarily *always* follow the first one (CS). In the instrumental situation the second stimulus occurs *only* if the subject fails to respond to the neutral stimulus. A concrete example may help to explain the avoidance conditioning paradigm. A rat is placed in a Skinner box and is presented with a flash of light. This light is a neutral stimulus that in and of itself evokes no particular unconditional response (except perhaps pupillary constriction). Now a few seconds after the light is flashed the floor of the Skinner box may be electrically charged causing the rat to experience pain. In the instrumental avoidance conditioning situation the rat may avoid receiving the electric shock if, and only if, he responds with an appropriate response (for instance, lever pressing) to the light flash. In other words, if the rat is presented with a light flash and then presses the lever he will not receive the electric shock. It is as if he has been conditioned to press the lever to the neutral light flash. The differences between this paradigm and classical conditioning, once again, are the following. First in classical conditioning the electric shock would be presented to the rat on each and every trial irrespective of his behavior; in the instrumental avoidance conditioning paradigm the rat can avoid the punishment by making an appropriate instrumental response. Second the response conditioned (lever pressing) has no unconditional relationship to the UCS employed (shock).

Now, with respect to avoidance conditioning of the GSR, the experimental expectation would be that subjects presented with paired lights and shocks or paired tones and shocks or any other neutral stimuli with shocks would learn to avoid those shocks by giving an appropriate autonomic response to the neutral stimulus. The first of such studies was reported by Kimmel and Baxter in 1964. In this experiment subjects were presented with a neutral tone followed four seconds later by a painful electric shock. Kimmel and Baxter set up the experiment so that the shock would *not* be presented if subjects gave a large GSR to the neutral tone. Now it is very likely that upon the first presentation of a tone all subjects will show some GSR response. But it is also well known in research on autonomic responses that if you simply present the same tone to a subject repeatedly he will soon show a complete adaptation to it and will stop responding. Thus, Kimmel and Baxter first presented all subjects with the neutral tone repeatedly until they stopped responding to it. Afterwards they began presenting systematically a painful electric shock approximately four seconds after the tone was presented. If the autonomic response could become instrumental in avoiding the shock, we would expect that an experimental group of subjects who could avoid shocks only when they gave GSRs to the tones would soon begin to show increased GSR responses to the presentation of the tone. A control group of subjects who received electric shocks only randomly and not necessarily when a GSR was elicited would not be expected to show

an increase in GSR responding. In this particular experiment Kimmel and Baxter used a control group that was yoked to the experimental group in the manner described in our earlier discussion.

Kimmel and Baxter obtained positive results. That is, in this experiment the experimental group showed evidence of learning to aviod the shock by giving a GSR to the tone, i.e., their GSRs to tones systematically increased over time, whereas the control group showed no increase in GSR over trials. However, there were difficulties in definitive interpretation not only because of the use of the yoked-control design but because the study included no simultaneous measure of muscle activity, and the responses very conceivably could have been artifacts of learned skeletal-muscular activity. Kimmel himself recognized these problems, especially the methodological one raised by the use of the yoked-control design. Therefore, as we mentioned in the last section, Kimmel and Sternthal attempted to replicate the positive findings which Kimmel and Baxter had obtained by using both muscle potential measurement and sophisticated methodological techniques for overcoming the possible biases of the yoked-control design. In this replication and in another by Kimmel, Sternthal, and Strub no significant results were obtained. This failure to replicate led Kimmel and Sternthal to conclude (as we saw earlier) that the results "tend to support Church's contention that the yoked-control design may lead to spurious or exaggerated evidence of avoidance conditioning" [p. 45]. Thus, it may be seen that the research on avoidance conditioning of autonomic responding led to similar conclusions as did the earlier research on conditioning of unelicited GSRs.

The results discussed up to this point indicate only tentative evidence for successful instrumental conditioning of autonomic responses. And yet each additional study, while failing to be definitive, continued to be provocative. So far we have discussed only research conducted on human electrodermal reflections of autonomic behavior. It could be argued that of the variety of functions mediated by the autonomic nervous system, electrodermal activity is among the least likely to be subject to control. After all, it seems somewhat less central and important to the adaptive functioning of the organism than cardiac functions or peripheral vascular functions and somewhat more remote from our consciousness. In the sections to follow we shall investigate the history of the development of research on instrumental modification of these other autonomic functions, and shall move finally to a consideration of research conducted on infrahuman animals in which there exists greater experimental freedom to manipulate the biological state of the subject.

Instrumental Control of Peripheral Vascular Responses

The flow of blood through the periphery of your body is controlled largely by the ANS. This flow is evident to even the most unsophisticated observers of neuroanatomy at times of embarrassment, when the blood rushes to your face and you blush, and at times of distress or fear when the blood drains from your face and you turn pale. As you are well aware, you have very little voluntary control over either the blushing or the paling of your skin, just as you have very little control directly over the course of blood rushing through your veins and capillaries. But whether or not you can control it, peripheral blood flow is an integral part of your emotional life and according to some current Soviet theoreticians [Sokolov 1960, 1963] peripheral blood flow serves an important purpose in mediating perceptual behavior and in discrimination between threatening and nonthreatening stimuli. Because of the variety of theoretical interests in vascular activity, Lisina's report of apparently successful conditioning of vasodilatation has been cited frequently and has provided a major impetus for the present interest in the entire area of instrumental ANS conditioning. As mentioned earlier, it was Razran's early report of Lisina's work which stimulated a reawakening of interest in this area. Yet, as also mentioned earlier, a close examination of Lisina's paper indicated that even she provided no clear evidence of such conditioning.

Although Lisina's early work was an important stimulus for future research in instrumental conditioning of autonomic functions, the work that followed was not often directed toward the conditioning of peripheral vascular activity. In fact, the sum total of American human research on this issue has come from only one laboratory at Kansas State University [Snyder & Noble 1965, 1966, 1968]. It is somewhat ironic that there has been so little general interest in the instrumental modification of peripheral vascular function because Snyder and Noble's reports are clearly among the most successful and most productive of all the studies on human subjects.

The research reported in the three papers by Snyder and Noble proceeded along the following lines. Subjects were connected to a polygraph in such a way that spontaneous changes in the constriction of peripheral blood vessels could be observed easily.

After an initial rest period in which the experimenters were able to determine the operant frequency of spontaneous vasoconstrictions, reinforcement conditions were begun. During the reinforcement period a subject was presented with a light flash if and only if he showed a spontaneous vasoconstriction that was equal to or larger than a predetermined criterion. A yoked-control group was employed but Snyder and Noble were careful also to employ a second control group which received no reinforcements at all at any time. Thus, they were able to compare the results of their experimental group not only with the possibly contaminated yoked-control group but with a non-reinforced control group as well. Furthermore, Snyder and Noble recorded respiration patterns and muscular movements in order to clearly eliminate these possible skeletal-muscular mediators from the analysis of their results. The results of Snyder and Noble's work indicated that the experimental groups, which received a light flash reinforcement for spontaneous vasoconstrictions, showed definite increases in the frequency of vasoconstrictions. The control group that received no reinforcement showed no change from the operant level, and a yoked-control group, which received reinforcement only when not responding, showed a modest decrease in the frequency of responding. These results, which are depicted more clearly in figure 7, are quite impressive and subject to much less interpretive debate than the results of the studies discussed previously. Therefore,

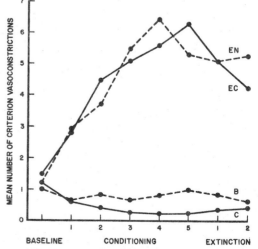

Figure 7. Mean number of conditioned vasoconstrictions for subjects in two experimental groups (EC and EN), a yoked control group (C), and a group that received no reinforcement at all (B) [Snyder & Noble 1968].

it must be concluded that Snyder and Noble's work provides relatively strong evidence for the possible instrumental modification of peripheral vascular responses.

On the basis of this small amount of work, we must conclude tentatively that a greater degree of success has been achieved in the conditioning of vascular activity than in the conditioning of electrodermal activity. If this trend is borne out by future research, some explanatory mechanisms will have to be postulated for it. It would be instructive at this point to look at the results of research on other aspects of the cardiovascular system such as the instrumental modification of heart rate itself. As we mentioned before, although we have no direct control over our peripheral blood vessels, we are sometimes more aware of their functioning than we are of electrodermal function. When we blush we feel and we recognize the change in blood vessel activity in our faces; we do not feel and/or usually recognize the change in our skin resistance during the same emotional experience (although we might notice some increased sweat activity in the palms). Along this dimension of recognizability we can probably all conclude that our heart is more well known to us than other internal organs that are mediated by the ANS. During periods of excitement or stress or athletic acitvity we become aware of our heart beating and pounding within our chest. The accuracy of such perception of our heart rate activity is still a question for research, but at least we can probably all agree on an intuitive basis that we have some awareness of our heart's activity, although we do not seem to have direct control over its beat. In the following section we will review the wide variety of investigations which have been carried out on the instrumental modification of heart rate activity in both human and animal subjects.

Instrumental Control of Cardiac Rate

Human Subjects

As in the research on electrodermal activity the early attempts to instrumentally modify cardiac activity were characterized by inconclusive results and a fair degree of controversy. The first report of instrumental modification of human heart rate was published in 1962 by Shearn, who presented subjects with a modified avoidance conditioning paradigm in which the "correct response" did not enable the subject to avoid a subsequent shock but did enable him

to delay its occurrence. Although Shearn presented the results of his experiment in a very positive light and optimistically concluded that he had evidence for instrumental modification of cardiac activity, he himself cautioned that his results were subject to a variety of alternative explanations. For instance, Shearn reported significant differences in the respiratory patterns between subjects in his experimental group and subjects in his yoked-control groups, and he suggested that these differences in respiratory patterns might have resulted in unconditional cardiac changes. Second, Shearn pointed out that although he had obtained some evidence to show that the heart rate response was capable of instrumentally delaying the occurrence of a shock the significance of these findings was unclear.

After the appearance of Shearn's initial work, Harwood in 1962 reported two attempts to condition cardiac deceleration instrumentally. According to Harwood both of these attempts were complete failures and the main thrust of his paper was to forewarn future investigators of the complexity of attempting such work under "normal" conditions. Harwood suggested, among other things, that a serious assault on the problem should employ multiresponse measurement to enable evaluation of cardiac activity independent of respiratory or skeletal mediation. Harwood suggested further that any definitive research on this problem should probably employ infrahuman subjects who could be treated with drugs such as curare to eliminate skeletal mediation problems. (Harwood's suggestion had already been taken up by investigators at Yale University whose work will be discussed in the following section.)

But the issue had been joined and the gloomy and negative report by Harwood did not stand unchallenged. Engel and his associates [Engel & Chism 1967, Engel & Hansen 1966] criticized Harwood's report on the grounds that he had not been able to deliver reinforcement appropriately because of unsophisticated electronic apparatus. Engel's point was that heart rate activity is much more difficult to treat in the conditioning situation than other autonomic responses because of its rapid response rate. For instance, if an average subject in a laboratory has a heart rate of approximately 80 beats per minute, then each heartbeat occurs less than one second after another and each beat must be dealt with individually and reinforced appropriately on a beat-to-beat basis. Let us look at a concrete example to make this point clear. To make the numbers easy to deal with, imagine that a subject has an average heart rate of

60 heartbeats per minute. This means that on the polygraph we record a heartbeat once every second. If the purpose of the experiment is to increase the rate at which the subject's heart is beating, then the experimenter must wait until a given heartbeat occurs less than one second after a previous heartbeat. As you can see, if any given heartbeat occurs less than one second after the previous heartbeat, then the rate per minute between those two beats is somewhat faster than 60 beats per minute. Conversely, if the object of the experiment were to reinforce subjects for a slower heart rate, the experimenter would have to wait until a heartbeat occurred *more* than one second after a previous heartbeat for, in that case, the rate for that beat would be slower than 60 beats per minute. Reinforcement should occur immediately after *each* heartbeat exhibiting the criterion latency. But it should be obvious that with heartbeats that occur more than once a second, on an average, it is virtually impossible for any unaided human experimenter to discern the appropriate heart rate and apply reinforcement after a specific beat in the small interval of time before the next beat.

Engel and his associates suggested that proper experimentation on cardiac activity necesarily required sophisticated electronic apparatus such as provided by digital computer equipment, which would allow delivery of reinforcement on a beat-to-beat basis. Employing such sophisticated electronic apparatus, Engel and Hansen (1966) reported that they had successfully slowed the human heart rate instrumentally, and Engel and Chism (1967), using the same apparatus, later reported successful heart rate speeding in human subjects. The fact that Engel and his associates could demonstrate speeding of the heart rate in one experiment and slowing of the heart rate in another experiment was seen to be extremely important because the ability to condition the heart both to increase and to decrease would lend some credibility to the fact that the conditioning procedure was highly effective, for if the results were simply artifactual one would expect the artifact to be unidirectional. That is, if putting the subjects in the experimental situation and doing *anything* to them caused them to become excited and excitement caused their heart rate to increase, then we would not know if the increase was a function of the experimental conditions in general or the conditioning procedures specifically. However, by demonstrating that the heart rate could be either increased or decreased in an essentially identical situation credibility is added to the "conditioning" interpretation.

Yet, despite this powerful bidirectional demonstration the results reported by Engel and his associates

did not stand up under intensive scrutiny. In both of these studies Engel and his co-investigators interviewed their subjects to see if there were any systematic differences in the evaluation of the experimental situation between experimental and control subjects. As you may remember from our earlier discussion of electrodermal conditioning, Stern and his associates showed that interviewing the subjects revealed that experimental subjects held clearly different evaluations of the experiment than control subjects. In a detailed analysis of the interview material published by Engel and his associates, Murray and Katkin demonstrated that subjects' reports of their voluntary actions were highly correlated with the obtained heart rate changes in both studies, irrespective of the reinforcement used. Murray and Katkin provided statistical analyses which supported the notion that neither the Engel and Hansen paper nor the Engel and Chism paper demonstrated successful instrumental conditioning of the heart rate.

Augmented feedback. As we mentioned at the beginning of our discussion of cardiac conditioning, a critical difference between cardiac functions and electrodermal functions concerns the degree to which the human subject is aware of them. In the first report on instrumental cardiac conditioning, Shearn amplified the sounds of his subjects' heart rates and played them over a loudspeaker during the course of the experiment. In so doing, he augmented the ability of the subjects to perceive the sound of their own hearts beating. Although the later studies by Harwood and by Engel and his associates did not augment feedback from the heart in this manner, a number of studies have appeared that utilized augmented sensory feedback in the course of attempting to demonstrate instrumental control of cardiac function.

In the first of these studies in 1965 Hnatiow and Lang presented their subjects with an ingenious visual display of their heart rate activity in an experiment which they referred to as "driving your own heart." Hnatiow and Lang's description of heart rate control as a "driving" problem undoubtedly was stimulated by the nature of the apparatus they used. Subjects were presented with a visual display of a pointer whose movements were synchronized with their own heartbeats. The pointer moved left and right as the subject's heart slowed down or speeded up, and the pointer was placed on a background of white paper with a red stripe down the center. This striped paper moved continuously on a drum and the subjects were told that their job was to keep the pointer on the central red stripe and not let it deviate off to the white fields on the sides. This task is reminiscent of automobile skill tasks found in penny arcades and amusement parks. As long as the subject kept the pointer on the red stripe he knew that he was a success. As soon as the pointer moved to the white part of the field, he got immediate feedback that he was a failure. The reinforcement then is defined in this experiment as the feedback to the subject of success or failure in controlling the pointer. Since the position of the pointer, of course, was determined only by the subject's heart rate the degree to which he was a success depended exclusively on the degree to which he could voluntarily keep his heart beating within the narrow limits of the red line. In this experiment, then, subjects were being reinforced not for slowing or speeding their heart rate, but for narrowing the variability of its rate. Hnatiow and Lang's results indicated clearly that subjects in the experimental group were able to reduce the variability of their heart rates while subjects in the control group were not. The control group was presented with the same task, but their heartbeats did not control the pointer.

While Hnatiow and Lang's experiment addressed itself to the *variability* of the heart, two subsequent experiments by Brener and Hothersall in 1966 and in 1967 were addressed to the instrumental control of heart *rate,* using augmented sensory feedback to facilitate the conditioning. Brener and Hothersall obtained apparently successful results in their first experiment, showing that under conditions of augmented feedback subjects could be trained to either increase or decrease their heart rates. However, Brener and Hothersall felt that their initial results may have been an artifact of learned changes in respiration which could have affected the heart. Thus they replicated their experiment in 1967 using controls for respiration rate. Once again they demonstrated that the positive results obtained in their first experiment were replicable and that they were independent of changes in respiratory behavior; however, Brener and Hothersall reported that "the possibility that the observed cardiac control was mediated by learned changes in muscle tension remains a problem worthy of empirical investigation" [1967, p. 6]. Again we are faced with the problem that apparently successful results may be explained in terms of the case 2 argument presented at the beginning of this paper. Neither the Hnatiow and Lang paper nor the two Brener and Hothersall papers investigated the possibility of skeletal-muscular mediation of the obtained heart rate changes. Nevertheless, Brener and Hothersall concluded that their results were consistent with the results of Hnatiow and Lang and that taken together all these findings suggest that the extent to which subjects can gain voluntary control over their behavior may be a function of the amount of feedback about that behavior that they received. Since they did not directly investigate the relationship between the cardiac changes and skeletal-muscular activity, it seems possible to conclude that the augmented sensory feedback which they utilized served *merely to facilitate the learning of skeletal-muscular responses which in turn elicited unconditional autonomic responses.*

These arguments all lead us to the inevitable conclusion that it is probably impossible to find any research on human subjects that can definitively solve the basic question at issue. Let us remind ourselves of the question: can autonomic functions be modified by instrumental conditioning techniques and *can this modfiication be demonstrated to be free of potential skeletal-muscular mediation?* Perhaps the only definitive answer will have to come, as Harwood suggested, from experimentation on curarized animals.

Animal Subjects

Shortly after the publication of the studies on humans described above, a series of experiments on instrumental conditioning of autonomic functions in curarized animals was reported from Neal Miller's laboratory first at Yale University and later at Rockefeller University. The first experiments to be reported from his laboratory concentrated on conditioning of the cardiac rate. But later in the research program, interest was shifted to vascular activity and internal glandular activity. We shall review these reports in a roughly chronological manner.

One of the first studies from Miller's laboratory was undertaken by Trowill because he felt that "none of the studies yielding positive results has conclusively ruled out the possibility that Ss learned skeletal responses which had an unlearned tendency to elicit the visceral responses recorded" [p. 7]. To rule out conclusively the possibility of skeletal-muscular mediation Trowill used animals who were curarized deeply. Curare drugs (as mentioned earlier) interfere with the chemical transmitters that are necessary for nerve impulses to be delivered to skeletal muscles, but do not interfere with transmitters that innervate autonomic functions. Therefore, a curarized animal is incapable of showing skeletal responses, but his autonomic functions continue unimpeded. Because he is incapable of showing skeletal responses, however, he is incapable of eating or drinking; thus the positive reinforcement procedures usually used in reinforcement research (food and water to hungry or thirsty subjects) are impossible in curare experiments. For this reason, Trowill introduced another variation in the usual instrumental autonomic conditioning procedure. As a reinforcement, Trowill employed electrical stimulation of the "pleasure center" in the brain, specifically the medial forebrain bundle in the lateral hypothalamus. It has been well demonstrated in the past two decades (e.g., Olds & Milner in 1954) that electrical stimulation of this portion of the brain has powerful rewarding effects on animals. Therefore, it is likely that the reinforcement of instrumental behavior with electrical stimulation of the pleasure centers in the brain is an excellent and highly efficient reinforcement to use.

Trowill's procedure was straightforward. The curarized rats were observed during a rest period in order to determine their average heart rate. Their heart rate signal was fed into an electronic computer which kept a continuous record of the beat-to-beat heart rate. The computer was programmed so that animals would receive electrical stimulation of the brain only if their heart rate deviated to some predetermined level above average. Similarly, another group of subjects received electrical stimulation of the brain only if their heart rate deviated to some predetermined level below average. In this manner, half the subjects were being reinforced for heart rate *increases* and half the subjects were being reinforced for heart rate *decreases*.

Trowill's results indicated that 15 of the 19 rats rewarded for fast heart rates increased their rates and that 15 of the 17 rats rewarded for slow heart rates decreased their rates. Statistical tests showed that both these changes were unlikely to be due to chance. However, the amount of change reported for both groups of subjects was small—approximately 5 per cent up or down from their baseline. Miller and DiCara felt that the magnitude of change obtained by Trowill was so small as to be "not completely convincing" [1967, p. 12]. Therefore, they endeavored "to see (a) whether larger changes in the heart rates of curarized rats can be achieved by 'shaping' their responses, i.e., progressively shifting rats to a more difficult criterion after they have learned to meet an easier one, and (b) whether a visceral discrimination can be learned so that the response will be more likely to occur in the stimulus situation in which it is rewarded than in the one in which it is not" [1967, p. 12]. To accomplish these aims, Miller and DiCara replicated Trowill's experiment with some modifications. The major modification consisted of the use of increasingly stringent requirements for reinforcing the animal. That is, the electronic apparatus was

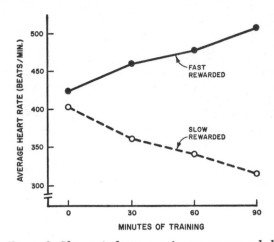

Figure 8. Change in heart rate for groups rewarded for fast or for slow rates. Each point represents average of beats per minute during five minutes [Miller & DiCara 1967].

programmed so that at first an animal received reinforcement if its heart rate changed 2 per cent above or below its initial baseline. If an animal successfully increased (or decreased) its heart rate by 2 per cent, its new level was then considered baseline and he was required to change again by 2 per cent to receive reinforcement. Each successive time the animal met the criterion for reinforcement, the criterion was shifted another 2 per cent. If an animal failed to meet a new criterion, the criterion was then shifted down to the prior one and the procedure was tried again. Figure 8 presents the results of Miller and DiCara's experiment on 12 rats trained to increase and 11 rats trained to decrease their heart rates over a 90-minute training period. These dramatic findings are clear; both groups showed changes of approximately 100 beats per minute!

During Miller and DiCara's experiment the rats received reinforcement for heart rate changes only during times when a complex pattern of tone and light was presented to them. If their heart rate changed during times when this pattern of tone and light was not presented they received no reinforcement. Usually in instrumental conditioning situations subjects learn to discriminate between the so-called "time-in" period, in this instance the period when the complex pattern of tone and light was presented, and the "time-out" period when this pattern was not present. However in Miller and DiCara's experiment the rats tended to increase or decrease their rates both during time-in and time-out periods. This lack of discrimination is very different from traditional findings on the instrumental conditioning of skeletal responses. To determine if the heart rate response was capable of being more discriminating Miller and DiCara subjected some of their animals to an additional period of training at approximately the same reinforcement criterion obtained at the end of the initial training period. After 45 minutes of additional training, Miller and DiCara discovered that the rats indeed showed discriminative heart rate learning such that their heart rates were increasing or decreasing significantly more during the "time-in" than the "time-out" period. Thus, Miller and DiCara were able not only to modify heart rate instrumentally but were also able to train the curarized animals to respond discriminatively to external stimuli without any apparent skeletal mediation.

Miller and DiCara's demonstration seems to be considerably more convincing than the previous studies on human subjects. Yet, even this carefully controlled demonstration did not stand unchallenged by other investigators. In 1966 Black presented evidence that suggested that dogs who are sufficiently curarized as to be incapable of making muscular movements still show evidence of *muscle action potentials* when an EMG is recorded. Thus Black concluded that although skeletal-muscular activity may be interrupted by curare the activity of the cerebral motor cortex has not been interrupted, and there may be conditioned motor cortex responses which mediate instrumental conditioning of the heart rate. In 1967 [b] Black presented this argument in more detail, and it may be understood more clearly by observation of figures 9, 10, and 11. In figure 9 we see a schematic representation of a situation in which an autonomic change (the heart rate) is operantly reinforced directly. In this diagram you see that an incoming stimulus activates some area of the brain which in turn activates the heart directly. The skele-

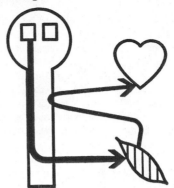

Figure 10. Schematic representation of situation in which instrumental conditioning results in innervation of skeletal musculature which in turn activates autonomically innervated organ [Black 1967b].

tal muscle which is included in the diagram is not at all affected in this situation. In figure 10 the incoming stimulus triggers a different area of the brain—presumably an area of motor cortex which in turn sends signals to a skeletal muscle whose activation then affects the heart. This situation was discussed originally in our case 2 argument and is also the situation to which Miller and DiCara as well as Trowill addressed themselves in the use of curare drugs. Curare intervenes in the chain between the cortex and the muscle therefore making it impossible for the muscle to be activated. Successful instrumental autonomic conditioning in curarized animals such as Miller and DiCara demonstrated could not occur if this model were correct. Figure 11 represents yet another possible situation postulated by Black [1967b] as a possible alternative. Here the incoming stimulus triggers an area of the brain which simultaneously

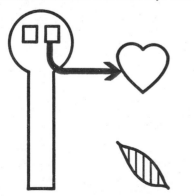

Figure 9. Schematic representation of situation in which instrumental conditioning affects the autonomically innervated organ directly [Black 1967b].

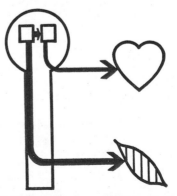

Figure 11. Schematic representation of situation in which instrumental conditioning results in motor impulses being sent simultaneously to skeletal musculature and to centers which innervate organs via ANS [Black 1967b].

sends signals to a skeletal muscle and to another area of the brain which innervates an autonomic structure, in this case the heart. In this situation it is obvious that the use of curare drugs would intervene only in the skeletal chain and would not prevent the motor cortex from sending impulses to the heart. Thus Black suggests that a slim possibility remains that motor cortex activity, prevented from activating the muscles by curare, may nevertheless influence the heart.

Unless and until alternative arguments such as Black's could be eliminated by appropriate experimental design the question of whether or not instrumental modification of autonomic functions was successful could not be resolved. The demonstration that instrumental ANS conditioning was in fact a genuine phenomenon hinged on the argument presented by Miller and Banuazizi in 1968, who pointed out that the autonomic nervous system (and especially the sympathetic division of that system) tends to act uniformly. Therefore, activation of the ANS by impulses from the motor cortex (as in figure 11) should result in generalized activation of *all* the structures influenced by the ANS. If it could be demonstrated that reinforcement of heart rate change resulted only in heart rate change and no other autonomic change, and that reinforcement of a different visceral response resulted solely in the conditioning of that response, then one would be able to conclude that the responses in question were modified only by the reinforcement technique and were not unconditional artifactual responses of motor cortex activity.

Miller and Banuazizi attempted such a demonstration by comparing the effects of rewarding either heart rate change or spontaneous intestinal contractions on the rate of response of both the heart rate and the intestines. As a first step, deeply curarized rats were reinforced for intestinal relaxation, resulting in a decrease in the rate of spontaneous contractions of the intestine. Subsequently, the same rats were reinforced for increases in intestinal contraction, resulting in a clear increase in their rate of contractions. Having thus demonstrated that intestinal contractions were subject to the same effects of reinforcement as the heart rate had been in earlier experiments, Miller and Banuazizi proceeded to reinforce one group of rats only for heart rate changes, and another group of rats only for intestinal changes; however, they monitored response levels of *both* systems for *all* subjects irrespective of which system was being reinforced. Miller and Banuazizi found "that intestinal contraction increased when it was rewarded, decreased when relaxation was rewarded and remained virtually unchanged when either in-

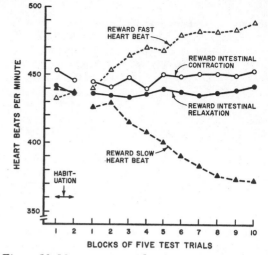

Figure 12. Measurement of heart rate during periods when heart rate is rewarded for increase and decrease; and during periods when intestinal activity is rewarded. Note that heart rate is affected only when heart rate is rewarded [Miller & Banuazizi].

creased or decreased heart rate was rewarded. Similarly, heart rate increased when a fast rate was rewarded, decreased when a slow rate was rewarded, and remained virtually unchanged when either intestinal contraction or relaxation was rewarded" [p. 5]. These results are summarized more clearly in figures 12 and 13. Miller and Banuazizi concluded that if

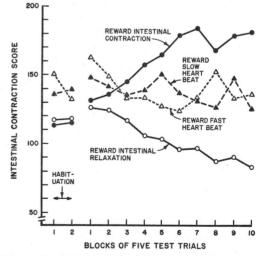

Figure 13. Measurement of intestinal contractions during periods when intestine was rewarded for constricting and relaxing; and during periods when heart rate was rewarded. Note that intestinal activity changed only when intestinal activity was rewarded [Miller & Banuazizi]

the findings of their experiment had been a result of artifactual phenomena such as impulses sent out from the motor cortex then these impulses should have affected both response systems simultaneously. Obviously, this was not the case. Heart rate and intestinal activity had been conditioned independently.

At this point in the history of the problem it appeared that Miller and his colleagues had presented truly convincing evidence for instrumental conditioning of ANS responses independent of any possible alternative explanations. However, their experiments differed in one crucial manner from all others reviewed. In each case the reinforcement used was electrical stimulation of the hypothalamic area of the brain. This raised a new and important question. Simply put, could such dramatic results be obtained using any reinforcement other than direct stimulation of the brain? DiCara and Miller [1968a] attempted to answer this question by training curarized rats to increase or decrease their heart rates in order to escape or to avoid electric shock, or both. In this experiment the reinforcement was the avoidance of pain, a paradigm essentially similar to the avoidance paradigm used with human subjects by Kimmel and Baxter [1964] and Kimmel and Sternthal [1967]. Following essentially the same procedures used in the earlier studies conducted in Miller's laboratory, DiCara and Miller obtained evidence that heart rate changes can be effectively reinforced by escape or avoidance of electric shock. Thus, they concluded that the instrumental learning of a visceral response could be accomplished by other procedures than the direct electrical stimulation of the brain as a reward.

Taken together with the earlier results from Miller's laboratory these findings by DiCara and Miller leave little room for the alternative interpretation that instrumentally modified heart rate activity observed in their laboratory was an artifact of impulses from the motor cortex. Miller and his associates appear to have come as close as possible to providing foolproof evidence for the phenomenon of instrumental conditioning of the heart rate. In a continuing series of experiments, Miller and his colleagues extended their research to other organs innervated by the ANS.

Extension of Infrahuman Research to Other Visceral Organs

Kidney Functions

Having concluded that the heart rate was capable of being modified by instrumental techniques, Miller and DiCara in 1968 proceeded to test the possibilities of their new techniques on the modification of the rate of urine formation by the kidney. To conduct this experiment, a catheter had to be permanently inserted in curarized rats and electronic devices had to be developed to measure the rate of urine formation. Having solved these technical problems, Miller and DiCara proceeded to reinforce their rats with electrical stimulation of the brain when their rate of urine formation decreased. An initial experiment indicated results equally as dramatic as their earlier results on cardiac conditioning; a group of seven rats that were rewarded for decreased amounts of urine formation showed significantly slower rates of such formation, while another group of seven rats rewarded for increasing the rate of urine formation showed similar increases in their rate of formation.

In order to analyze more closely exactly what aspect of kidney functioning was being modified, a variety of additional measures were taken from the rats. Miller and DiCara discovered that the rats who were rewarded for increasing their rate of urine formation showed an increased rate of renal blood flow, whereas those rats who were rewarded for decreased urine formation showed a decreased rate of renal blood flow. Furthermore, Miller and DiCara discovered that these changes in renal blood flow were independent of any changes in general blood pressure or heart rate. Thus, they concluded that the instrumental conditioning technique exercised a highly specific effect on vascular changes in the renal arteries.

Peripheral Vasomotor Responses

Having demonstrated that urine formation could be modified as a function of instrumental modification of internal vasomotor changes in the kidney, DiCara and Miller [1968c] turned their attention to the instrumental conditioning of peripheral vasomotor responses, an area that had been investigated earlier in human subjects by Lisina in the Soviet Union and by Snyder and Noble in the United States. As you may remember the experiments reported by Snyder and Noble were among the most successful experiments carried out on human subjects. In DiCara and Miller's attempts to condition peripheral vasomotor activity in the rat they began by measuring the amount of blood in the tail of a curarized rat and rewarding changes in the peripheral blood flow in the tail with electrical stimulation of the brain. DiCara and Miller successfully demonstrated that rats could learn either to constrict or dilate blood vessels of the tail in order to gain hypothalamic stimulation.

DiCara and Miller attempted next to test the limits

of the specificity of this peripheral vasomotor learning. In their earlier experiment on conditioning of urine formation, they discovered that the renal blood flow changes seemed to occur independently of cardiovascular changes in the rest of the organism. In this experiment DiCara and Miller attempted to find out if they could condition specific peripheral vasomotor changes. In order to do this, they placed measuring devices on both ears of curarized rats and connected them to a reinforcing apparatus so that the rats received electrical stimulation in the hypothalamus only when blood flow in both ears showed relative imbalance. Six rats who were rewarded for vasodilatation of the left ear showed vasodilatation of that ear, while six other rats rewarded for vasodilatation of the right ear showed dilatation of that ear. Thus, DiCara and Miller produced the remarkable findings that with proper reinforcement a rat can be trained to increase the rate of blood flow to one ear relative to the other. In addition to the curiosity value inherent in this research there is an important theoretical point; these results cannot be explained readily as artifacts of either general changes in heart rate or blood pressure, nor can they be explained very easily as artifacts of mediated responses of any sort since such mediation would be expected to affect both sides of the body equally.

Blood Pressure Independent of Heart Rate

Finally, DiCara and Miller [1968b] attempted to influence the blood pressure levels of curarized rats. In this experiment rather than using electrical stimulation of the brain, DiCara and Miller reverted to an avoidance conditioning paradigm. Seven rats were trained to increase their blood pressure in order to avoid or escape from a mild electric shock and seven other rats were trained to decrease their blood pressure in order to avoid or escape similar shock. The results of this experiment indicated that rats readily learned either to increase or to decrease their blood pressure in order to avoid or escape a mild electric shock. Furthermore, the results of the experiment indicated that the increases and decreases in blood pressure were entirely unrelated to changes in the heart rate. Thus, DiCara and Miller provided even further evidence for the specificity of autonomic learning in an instrumental conditioning situation.

Summary, Discussion, and Some Unanswered Questions

This essay has reviewed a number of studies on instrumental conditioning of autonomic functions in human and animal subjects. In general, the results of research on humans have been relatively inconclusive while the research reported on curarized animals has been much more definitive. The few clearly positive reports of instrumental conditioning in human subjects were subject to reinterpretation on the basis of a variety of alternative explanations including skeletal or cognitive mediation. The more recent studies on curarized animals, on the other hand, have provided quite convincing evidence that a variety of autonomic functions can be conditioned instrumentally.

It is important to note that the most definitive experiments to date have been conducted on curarized animals. In a report in 1969, Miller described attempts in his laboratory to obtain similar results from noncurarized animals. Although he reported that he was able to obtain some positive evidence for instrumental modification of autonomic functions in noncurarized animals, Miller also pointed out that the effects were not as large and were obtained less consistently. Although we cannot be sure of the reasons why curare seems to facilitate the conditioning of such autonomic functions, Miller has postulated that one possibility may be that free skeletal activity results in unconditional autonomic responses which get confounded with the spontaneous autonomic responses the experimenter is attempting to condition. Thus, in the noncurarized condition the experimenter may be reinforcing both genuine autonomic spontaneous responses and unconditional autonomic responses to skeletal activity. In this case it becomes more difficult for the subject to discriminate the nature of the response for which he is being rewarded. Miller suggested, therefore, that the most effective modification of autonomic functions would be expected to occur under curarized conditions in which the "noise" of skeletally mediated responses is eliminated. In this case, future research with human subjects seems necessarily limited and the potential for employing these new found techniques for the treatment of psychosomatic symptoms may be impaired.

There are at least two possible ways to deal with this problem. One strategy suggested by Miller would be to try to approximate a curarized state through such techniques as hypnosis, in which the human subject can be hypnotically entranced and instructed to inhibit skeletal-muscular activity, thereby simulating a curarized state. Another approach to the problem has been suggested by Katkin and Murray. These authors have suggested that although we have conclusive demonstrations of "pure" instrumental conditioning of ANS functions in animals, it may not be necessary to obtain a "pure" state of instrumental conditioning in humans. Katkin and Murray, drawing upon suggestions by Black [1966], have drawn a distinction between *conditioning* and *controlling* the autonomic nervous system. For those researchers whose primary goal is to gain control over ANS function and for whom theoretical problems concerning possible mediators are less important, it may be unnecessary to demonstrate the pure phenomenon of instrumental conditioning. In fact, Katkin and Murray have suggested that it is probably fruitless to pursue further any attempts at providing such demonstrations in humans because they would require unconscious subjects (to eliminate cognitive mediation) and complete curarization (to eliminate somatic mediation). Instead, the desired control of autonomic activity might be more efficiently produced in human subjects by proper reinforcement of both the somatic and cognitive mediators. That is, for those who want to control autonomic activity for clinical or therapeutic reasons an alternative procedure would be first to determine accurately the relationship between certain voluntary skeletal actions and their associated autonomic response patterns, and then to reinforce the voluntary responses. Similarly, Katkin and Murray have postulated that relationships between cognitive activity and autonomic responses can be determined, and subjects may then be reinforced for certain specified thoughts.

Regardless of which course of action is pursued it is clear that the theoretical work has been largely done. The groundwork has been laid for an exciting future in which our innermost functions may be subject to modification by appropriate applications of external reward. Between now and 1984 you may well discover that you can voluntarily reduce your blood pressure, set your heart to beat at any rate you desire, and tell your kidneys just how fast to produce urine for your maximum convenience. The future, as Professor Irwin Corey has boldly proclaimed, lies ahead!

BIBLIOGRAPHY

J. R. Averill, "Emotion and Visceral Activity: A Case Study in Psychophysiological Symbolism." Paper, Society for Psychophysiological Research, Monterey, October 1969.

L. Birk, A. Crider, D. Shapiro, and B. Tursky, "Operant Electrodermal Conditioning under Partial Curarization." *Journal of Comparative and Physiological Psychology*, 1966, 62:165–166.

A. H. Black, "The Operant Conditioning of Heart Rate in Curarized Dogs: Some Problems of Interpretation."

Paper, the Psychonomic Society, St. Louis, October 1966.

A. H. Black, "A Comment on Yoked Control Designs." Technical Report No. 11, McMaster University, September 1967. (*a*).

A. H. Black, "Operant Conditioning of Heart Rate under Curare." Technical Report No. 12, McMaster University, October 1967. (*b*)

J. Brener and D. Hothersall, "Heart Rate Control under Conditions of Augmented Sensory Feedback." *Psychophysiology*, 1966, 3:23–28.

J. Brener and D. Hothersall, "Paced Respiration and Heart Rate Control." *Psychophysiology*, 1967, 4:1–6.

W. B. Cannon, *The Wisdom of the Body.* Norton, 1939.

R. M. Church, "Systematic Effect of Random Error in the Yoked Control Design." *Psychological Bulletin*, 1964, 62:122–131.

A. Crider, G. Schwartz, and S. Shnidman, "On the Criteria for Instrumental Autonomic Conditioning: A Reply to Katkin and Murray." *Psychological Bulletin*, 1969, 71:455–461.

A. Crider, D. Shapiro, and B. Tursky, "Reinforcement of Spontaneous Electrodermal Activity." *Journal of Comparative and Physiological Psychology*, 1966, 61:20–27.

L. V. DiCara and N. E. Miller, "Changes in Heart Rate Instrumentally Learned by Curarized Rats as Avoidance Responses." *Journal of Comparative and Physiological Psychology*, 1968, 65:8–12. (*a*)

L. V. DiCara and N. E. Miller, "Instrumental Learning of Systolic Blood Pressure Responses by Curarized Rats: Dissociation of Cardiac and Vascular Changes." *Psychosomatic Medicine*, 1968, 30:489–494. (*b*)

L. V. DiCara and N. E. Miller, "Instrumental Learning of Vasomotor Responses by Rats: Learning to Respond Differentially in the Two Ears." *Science*, 1968. 159:1485–1486. (*c*)

B. T. Engel and R. A. Chism, "Operant Conditioning of Heart Rate Speeding." *Psychophysiology*, 1967, 3: 418–426.

B. T. Engel and S. P. Hansen, "Operant Conditioning of Heart Rate Slowing." *Psychophysiology*, 1966, 3:176–187.

C. Féré, "Note sur les modifications de la résistance électrique sous l'influence des excitations sensorielles et des émotions." *Comptes Rendus Société de Biologie*, 1888, 5:217–219.

R. L. Fowler and H. D. Kimmel, "Operant Conditioning of the GSR." *Journal of Experimental Psychology*, 1962, 63:563–567.

C. W. Harwood, "Operant Heart Rate Conditioning." *Psychological Record*, 1962, 12:279–284.

M. Hnatiow and P. J. Lang, "Learned Stabilization of Cardiac Rate." *Psychophysiology*, 1965, 1:330–336.

C. V. Hudgins, "Conditioning and the Voluntary Control of the Pupillary Light Reflex." *Journal of General Psychology*, 1933, 8:3–51.

H. J. Johnson and G. E. Schwartz, "Suppression of GSR Activity through Operant Reinforcement." *Journal of Experimental Psychology*, 1967, 75:307–312.

E. S. Katkin and E. N. Murray, "Instrumental Conditioning of Autonomically Mediated Behavior: Theoretical and Methodological Issues." *Psychological Bulletin*, 1968, 70:52–68.

E. Kimmel and H. D. Kimmel, "A Replication of Operant Conditioning of the GSR." *Journal of Experimental Psychology*, 1963, 65:212–213.

H. D. Kimmel and R. Baxter, "Avoidance Conditioning of the GSR." *Journal of Experimental Psychology*, 1964, 68:482–485.

H. D. Kimmel and F. A. Hill, "Operant Conditioning of the GSR." *Psychological Reports*, 1960, 7:555–562.

H. D. Kimmel and H. S. Sternthal, "Replication of GSR Avoidance Conditioning with Concomitant EMG Measurement and Subjects Matched in Responsivity and Conditionability." *Journal of Experimental Psychology*, 1967, 74:144–146.

H. D. Kimmel, H. S. Sternthal, and H. Strub, "Two Replications of Avoidance Conditioning of the GSR." *Journal of Experimental Psychology*, 1966, 72:151–152.

M. I. Lisina, "The Role of Orientation in the Transformation of Involuntary Reactions into Voluntary Ones." In L. G. Voronin, A. N. Leontiev, A. R. Luria, E. N. Sokolov, and O. S. Vinogradova, eds., *Orienting Reflex and Exploratory Behavior*. American Institute of Biological Sciences, 1965.

G. Mandler, D. W. Preven, and C. K. Kuhlman, "Effects of Operant Reinforcement on the GSR." *Journal of the Experimental Analysis of Behavior*, 1962, 5:317–321.

N. E. Miller, "Learning of Visceral and Glandular Responses." *Science*, 1969, 163:434–445.

N. E. Miller and A. Banuazizi, "Instrumental Learning by Curarized Rats of a Specific Visceral Response, Intestinal or Cardiac." *Journal of Comparative and Physiological Psychology*, 1968, 65:1–7.

N. E. Miller and L. V. DiCara, "Instrumental Learning of Heart Rate Changes in Curarized Rats: Shaping, and Specificity to Discriminative Stimulus." *Journal of Comparative and Physiological Psychology*, 1967, 63: 12–19.

N. E. Miller and L. V. DiCara, "Instrumental Learning of Urine Formation by Rats: Changes in Renal Blood Flow." *American Journal of Physiology*, 1968, 215: 677–683.

E. N. Murray and E. S. Katkin, "Comment on Two Recent Reports of Operant Heart Rate Conditioning." *Psychophysiology*, 1968, 5:192–195.

J. Olds and P. Milner, "Positive Reinforcement Produced by Electrical Stimulation of Septal Area and Other Regions of Rat Brain." *Journal of Comparative and Physiological Psychology*, 1954, 47:419–427.

T. L. Peele, *The Neuroanatomic Basis for Clinical Neurology*, 2nd ed. McGraw-Hill, 1961.

G. Razran, "The Observable Unconscious and the Inferable Conscious in Current Soviet Psychophysiology: Interoceptive Conditioning, Semantic Conditioning, and the Orienting Reflex." *Psychological Review*, 1961, 68:81–147.

D. G. Rice, "Operant Conditioning and Associated Electromyogram Responses." *Journal of Experimental Psychology*, 1966, 71:908–912.

C. P. Richter, "A Study of the Electric Skin Resistance and Psychogalvanic Reflex in a Case of Unilateral Sweating." *Brain*, 1927, 50:216–235.

R. J. Senter and W. F. Hummel, Jr., "Suppression of an Autonomic Response through Operant Conditioning." *Psychological Record*, 1965, 15:1–5.

D. Shapiro, A. B. Crider, and B. Tursky, "Differentiation of an Autonomic Response through Operant Reinforcement." *Psychonomic Science*, 1964, 1:147–148.

D. W. Shearn, "Operant Conditioning of Heart Rate." *Science*, 1962, 137:530–531.

B. F. Skinner, *The Behavior of Organisms: An Experimental Analysis*. Appleton-Century, 1938.

K. Smith, "Conditioning as an Artifact." *Psychological Review*, 1954, 61:217–225.

S. M. Smith, H. O. Brown, J. E. P. Toman and L. S. Goodman, "The Lack of Cerebral Effects of *d*-Tubocurarine." *Anesthesiology*, 1947, 8:1–14.

C. Snyder and M. Noble, "Operant Conditioning of Vasoconstriction." Paper, Midwestern Psychological Association, Chicago, April 1965.

C. Snyder and M. Noble, "Operant Conditioning of Vasoconstriction." Paper, Psychonomic Society, St. Louis, October 1966.

C. Snyder and M. Noble, "Operant Conditioning of Vasoconstriction." *Journal of Experimental Psychology*, 1968, 77:263–268.

E. N. Sokolov, "Neuronal Models and the Orienting Reflex." In M. A. B. Brazier, ed., *The Central Nervous System and Behavior*. Josiah Macy Foundation, 1960.

E. N. Sokolov, "Higher Nervous Functions: The Orienting Reflex." *Annual Review of Physiology*, 1963, 25: 545–580.

E. N. Sokolov, J. Boles, and J. Dionis, "Operant Conditioning of Spontaneous GSRs: Two Unsuccessful Attempts." Technical Report No. 13, Office of Naval Research, Indiana University, 1966.

R. M. Stern, "Operant Conditioning of Spontaneous GSRs: Negative Results." *Journal of Experimental Psychology*, 1967, 75:128–130.

J. A. Trowill, "Instrumental Conditioning of the Heart Rate in the Curarized Rat." *Journal of Comparative and Physiological Psychology*, 1967, 63:7–11.

H. B. Van Twyver and H. D. Kimmel, "Operant Conditioning of the GSR with Concomitant Measurement of Two Somatic Variables." *Journal of Experimental Psychology*, 1966, 72:841–846.

9

Behavioral Training: A Skill-Acquisition Approach To Clinical Problems

RICHARD M. MCFALL
University of Wisconsin

The purpose of this module is to introduce the reader to a behaviorally oriented psychotherapy approach called *Behavioral Training*.[1] In contrast to most other therapy approaches, Behavioral Training is not a well-defined, specific set of intervention techniques; instead, it is a general conceptual orientation toward treatment. Within the Behavioral Training approach as much attention is devoted to the fundamental issues of how clients' problems are defined, how treatment objectives are formulated, and how intervention efforts are assessed as is de-

---

1. *Behavioral Training* is only one of several names that have been used by different authors writing on this general topic. It was chosen for use here because it seemed to be the simplest, most accurately descriptive, and most generic of the alternative labels. Not coincidentally, it also happens to be the label that the present author has used most consistently in reporting his own research. Apologies are extended to the authors who find their work relabeled here in the interest of an orderly presentation.

voted to the technical, "nuts-and-bolts" issue of how behavioral changes are produced. Because of its comprehensive conceptual focus, Behavioral Training is not another therapy technique for practitioners to add to their list of procedures; it represents an incompatible, competitive alternative to most other approaches.

In order to communicate fully the theoretical and practical implications of the Behavioral Training approach, this presentation will begin by examining the manner in which Behavioral Training deals with the most fundamental treatment issues. This will include an examination of the purpose of psychotherapy, the nature of behavioral disorders, and the development and evaluation of specific behavior-change procedures. In the process Behavioral Training occasionally will be contrasted with other therapeutic approaches to highlight important distinctions — that is, to show what it *is not*, as well as what it *is*. After this therapeutic approach has been placed in its proper conceptual context, there will be a review of the experimental and clinical literature on Behavioral Training, describing the variety of clinical problems to which it has been applied, outlining the various specific treatment programs that have been developed within this framework, and summarizing the empirical evidence for and against this general approach. Finally, future prospects of Behavioral Training will be explored.

What Is Psychotherapy?

One summer, while visiting a large midwestern mental hospital for chronically disturbed patients, I heard about an innovative-sounding psychotherapy program called *landscape therapy* being used at the facility. I asked to see the program in operation. From the name, I expected to see lush greenhouses tended by patients whose enthusiasm for life was being rekindled through their newfound relationship to growing things. Instead, I was led to the hospital lawn where I saw four husky attendants stationed at the corners of an area approximately fifty feet square. Inside the area ten or fifteen regressed patients wandered about aimlessly, each pushing a lawnmower. When the patients' collective meanderings had grazed most of the staked-off area, the "therapist" herded them to an adjacent patch of

uncut lawn. Then an "advanced" patient stepped in to polish off any spots that they had missed.

My skepticism about this "therapy" must have shown because my hospital guide rather defensively began extolling the virtues of fresh air, sunshine, and exercise. As he saw it, the treatment's main flaw was that it was highly seasonal. I did not suggest it, but I wondered why they had not considered solving that problem by simply making a wholesale purchase of snowshovels.

As this experience illustrates, the term *psychotherapy* means different things to different people. It seems as though almost any human activity imaginable might be considered by someone to be a form of psychotherapy. The ambiguity and confusion surrounding the term make it difficult to compare and evaluate various therapy methods. Obviously, all therapies are not created equal, but on what basis can the various claims and counterclaims be judged in order to determine which methods are legitimate and which are not? On the basis of what criteria is it possible to conclude that landscape therapy, for example, is implausible, exploitive, or invalid as a therapeutic procedure? Obviously, such criteria exist, for we do make evaluative judgments regarding the validity of various therapy procedures; the real issue is whether such criteria can be stated explicitly in objective terms or whether we must be satisfied with subjective judgments based on personal tastes and prejudices.

Despite differences in language, goals, and methods, all forms of psychotherapy have at least one thing in common: all psychotherapy represents a commercial problem-solving enterprise in which certain individuals (clients), who are experiencing certain problems in living, purchase the services of other individuals (therapists), whose training and experience purportedly qualify them as experts at helping others solve their life problems.[2]

By viewing psychotherapy as a problem-solving

---

2. There are two apparent exceptions to this formulation, but on closer inspection both still fit it. First, when the client does not actually pay for the service, he, nevertheless, is the purchaser — albeit, with someone else's funds — as long as he contracts for the service. Second, when the designated "client" is coerced into therapy by "significant others," then the *real* client is actually these significant others. They are the ones who have a problem and want something done about it; the so-called "client's" behavior is a problem to them, and they want the behavior changed.

enterprise in this way, all specific forms of treatment can be evaluated on at least three common criteria. First, the *effectiveness* of particular treatment methods can be evaluated by assessing the extent to which they fulfill their implied promise to do something to resolve the client's specific life problems. Second, the *efficiency* of treatment methods can be evaluated by assessing their relative costs — in time, money, personal discomfort, and negative side effects. Third, the *ethical* status of different treatments can be appraised, at least in part, by examining whether or not they are honest about whose problems they are designed to resolve. It is dishonest and unethical for a therapy to be presented as if it were designed to help the designated client when, in fact, it is aimed at producing changes in the client that would be of primary benefit to others. My objections to landscape therapy, for example, were based largely on ethical grounds. It seemed obvious that the hospital administration was deriving more benefits from the "therapy" — in the form of cheap labor — than were the patients.

While all psychotherapies are similar in that they are problem-solving procedures, they tend to differ considerably in the specifics of how they go about the problem-solving task. They may differ in their conceptualization of the client's problem; they may perceive and define the objective of treatment differently; they may employ dissimilar intervention methods to effect desired changes; and they may disagree about the best way to assess the effects of their problem-solving efforts.

Actually, these four areas of difference correspond to the four steps involved in *any* problem-solving process. The steps are sequential, interdependent, and logically related: the first, the way a problem is defined, influences the second, how its goal solution will be perceived; the problem definition and goal specification, in turn, will determine the third, what intervention methods are selected and implemented; and all of these factors will dictate the fourth, how the success of the intervention efforts will be assessed. If any one of these steps is slighted or poorly conceived, the problem-solving effort will be less effective than it might have been.

Unfortunately, many treatment approaches have tended to stress the importance of their techniques without making explicit how such techniques are logically related to the other aspects of the problem-solving process. If the underlying conceptions of various treatment approaches were exposed and subjected to critical scrutiny, perhaps it would be possible to decide that certain approaches are more promising than others, simply on logical grounds.

Defining the Problem

Sign versus Sample

When a client enters therapy the therapist's first task is to cast the client's self-reported problem into a conceptual framework that will prove fruitful for subsequent problem solving. From the outset the therapist generally has one of two different preconceptions about the client's reported problem. He will perceive it either as a *sign* or as a *sample* of the problem that actually needs treatment. When the reported problem is perceived as a sign, the therapist discounts the validity of the client's overt problem statements and seeks instead to discover the "real" underlying problem, of which the overt problem is only an indirect and often symbolic expression. When the reported problem is perceived as a sample, the therapist accepts the client's report as an essentially valid description of the very problem situations and behaviors in need of treatment.

Traditional therapy approaches with a dynamic conception of personality generally take the sign view, whereas behaviorally oriented therapies take the sample view. Thus if a client entered therapy complaining about an overwhelming fear of snakes, the traditional therapist would typically interpret the fear of snakes as being symbolic of a hidden problem, such as an unconscious sexual conflict, while the behaviorally oriented therapist would conclude that the client's problem is that he has an overwhelming fear reaction to snakes.

The relative merits of the sign and sample views have been discussed in detail elsewhere [Goldfried & Sprafkin 1974; Mischel 1968]. Generally, there are so many theoretical and methodological problems with the sign view that the sample view, by default, is the more tenable conceptual choice. Behavioral Training, like other behaviorally oriented approaches, takes the sample view of the client's reported problems.

Behavioral Excess versus Behavioral Deficit

Within the general view that a client's reported problem provides a sample of the actual problems requiring treatment, there are at least two possibilities. On the one hand, the client's problem could be perceived as representing an instance of a behavioral excess; alternatively, it could be perceived as reflecting a behavioral deficit. The first view emphasizes what it is that the client is doing wrong; the second view emphasizes what it is that the client is not doing right. The first sees the problem as one of commission, the second as one of omission. In some ways this distinction may seem relatively inconsequential, like the difference between saying that a glass is half full versus saying that it is half empty. In practice, however, it is a distinction with implications for the subsequent problem-solving steps of specifying treatment objectives, choosing intervention methods, and evaluating treatment outcome.

As an illustration, consider the case of an alcoholic client. On the surface this client's problem seems to fit logically into the behavioral-excess category, that is, the client drinks alcoholic beverages in excessive quantities. Viewed from this perspective, the logical treatment objective would be to reduce the client's drinking behavior; the logical choice of treatment would be a technique designed to decrease or eliminate the drinking behavior; and the logical criterion of treatment success would be a significant reduction in the client's rate of alcohol consumption.

It is possible, however, to construe the same behavioral problem as an instance of a behavioral deficit. From this alternative perspective the fact that the client drinks excessively is seen as secondary to the fact that when he engages in such maladaptive behavior, he is not engaging in some other behavior that is more desirable, adaptive, and potentially reinforcing. This view has different implications for the subsequent steps of problem solving. Treatment would begin with a situational analysis of the function served by the current drinking behavior; the treatment objective would be to replace the drinking behavior with a more positive adaptive behavior; the treatment method would be designed to teach the client more functional and effective ways of dealing with the life situations in which he currently resorts to the drinking response; and treatment success would

be measured by the extent to which the client replaces his former drinking behavior with the new, more adaptive behavior.

The prevailing view among many behaviorally oriented psychotherapists has been that almost all clinical problems represent instances of behavioral excess. Even problems such as social isolation, depression, sexual impotence, or irrational avoidance responses, which seem at first to be clear-cut examples of an absence of desirable responses, typically have been translated into problems of excess. The observable lack of desirable responses in such problems is explained as being caused by an *excess* of another response — anxiety — which somehow blocks the desired responses from being emitted. From this perspective the goal of therapy is to eliminate the excessive anxiety; it is assumed that a decrease in anxiety will lead more or less automatically to an increase in the desirable responses.

J. Wolpe's [1958, 1969] reciprocal-inhibition hypothesis, which served as the initial theoretical foundation for such treatment techniques as systematic desensitization and assertion training, provides a concrete example of how the behavioral-excess formulation is used to explain and treat problems involving apparent behavioral deficits. According to Wolpe, the rationale behind the therapeutic practice of pairing relaxation, assertive responses, or sexual responses with previously anxiety-evoking stimuli is that such responses are incompatible with anxiety, and thus they will serve to weaken the previous bond between the stimuli and anxiety. [For a review of this approach, see Paul & Bernstein 1973.]

According to the view being presented here, this rationale can be challenged on logical grounds as unnecessarily indirect, incomplete, and elliptical. To argue that clients should be trained to relax, to behave assertively, or to engage competently in sexual responses primarily in order to inhibit their anxiety seems analogous to arguing that the primary function of education is to drive out ignorance.

If the reciprocal-inhibition hypothesis were strictly interpreted, the so-called anxiety-inhibiting responses that clients are trained to emit could be treated as equivalent and interchangeable since they all are incompatible with anxiety. In practice the anxiety-inhibiting response selected for use in a particular case is almost always directly related to the specific problem behavior being "disinhibited." Thus snake phobics are given imaginal training in relaxed snake handling; withdrawn clients are taught assertive responses, and sexually inadequate clients are painstakingly taught sexual skills. Clearly, the so-called anxiety-inhibiting responses are not merely means to ends; they are ends in themselves.

Consistent with this view, M. R. Goldfried [1971] has suggested that the most positive and parsimonious explanation for the effectiveness of systematic desensitization is that it works precisely because it provides clients with systematic training in more adaptive alternative responses to previously fear-arousing stimuli. In other words, Goldfried is suggesting that the problems with which systematic desensitization has been employed successfully might be viewed most simply as response-deficit problems rather than as response-excess problems; moreover, the therapy technique itself might be construed more accurately as a Behavioral Training procedure, emphasizing the acquisition of new positive responses rather than as a disinhibition procedure, emphasizing the elimination of excessive anxiety.

With a little ingenuity one can construe almost any problem, alternatively, as involving either a deficit or an excess in behavior, although certain problems may seem to fit more naturally into one view than the other. It may not be readily apparent, for example, what the specific behavioral deficits might be in such clinical problems as stuttering, obesity, exhibitionism, or paranoia; nevertheless, it is possible to formulate such problems in terms of specific response deficits. The ultimate test of the relative merits of the excess versus deficit formulations is not their initial obviousness but their eventual therapeutic utility. Do they point to different treatment objectives, which imply different intervention strategies, that are associated with different treatment outcomes?

Maladaptive Behavior Viewed as a Performance Deficit

The response-deficit view, which is that of the Behavioral Training approach to treatment, seems especially compelling because it is logically consistent with an analysis of the circumstances under which persons enter therapy. Ordinarily, a client's behavior is labeled *maladaptive*, either by the client or by significant others in his life, only when that behavior is perceived to be deficient relative to certain implicit or explicit performance criteria. Thus when a behavior is labeled maladaptive, this invariably implies that in the judgment of the person using the label there is some alternative behavior that should be emitted instead because it would be judged as "better," more desirable, or more adaptive according to the criteria held by the labeler.

Clearly, this labeling process is inherently relativistic, value-laden, and judgmental. There are no absolute or universal standards for deciding that a particular behavior is maladaptive; at best, the use of the label always represents only a prediction by the labeler that if the client behaved in certain alternative ways, it would lead to more positive consequences. Whether or not the implied alternative behavior would, in fact, result in the predicted positive consequences is really an empirical question. In order to answer that question properly, however, we first must be clear about one additional matter. From whose perspective are we to evaluate the value of the actual consequences? It is to be hoped that the implied alternative behavior will be regarded as better only if its consequences are more reinforcing *for the client*.[3]

This analysis helps focus attention on the fact that a response deficit is implied anytime we define a behavior as maladaptive, or perceive an individual as being in need of treatment. It is this implied response deficit, growing out of a perceived discrepancy between the current behavior and some preferred behavioral alternative, that serves as the explicit

---

3. In footnote 2 it was pointed out that when a "client" is coerced into treatment by significant others who want the "client's" behavior changed because it causes them problems, then these others are the *real* clients. In the present context it should be clear that significant others may label a so-called "client's" behavior as maladaptive when they feel that certain alternative behaviors by the "client" would be more reinforcing *to them* but not necessarily to the "client." There may be circumstances under which a therapist will feel justified in helping the significant others effect such a change, but the therapist must not lose sight of who his *real* clients are in this case. To change one person in order to please another person, without the consent of the first person, is extremely difficult to defend ethically; perhaps that is why the issue of who the *real* client is often is kept obscure.

conceptual basis for the Behavioral Training approach to treatment. Although it may not always be apparent what the implied deficit is in every case, the logic of the above analysis indicates that the perception of a behavioral deficit underlies all clinical problems.

Identifying Performance Deficits

The performance criteria on which a client's current behavior is judged to be deficient often are obscure, even to the person making the judgment. Their existence and specific nature usually become more apparent, however, when the question of therapeutic objectives is explored. The performance criteria are revealed by the answers obtained to the following question: How would the client have to behave differently, or what different consequences would have to follow from the client's behavior in order for the client's problem to be considered "successfully treated"?[4] Thus identifying the specific performance deficits implicit in the judgment that a client has a problem is something that is discussed in connection with the second step of the problem-solving process — specifying treatment objectives.

Origins of Performance Deficits

One of the cornerstones of learning theory is the *law of effect* — the premise that the future probability of a particular response is determined by its previous consequences. That is, the most probable response in a particular stimulus situation will be the one that has been most highly reinforced in that situation in the past. It follows from this proposition that the term "maladaptive behavior" is something of a misnomer; the law of effect dictates that an individual's behavior in a given situation always will be the behavior that previously has proven most reinforcing (that is, most adaptive) for that individual

---

4. Answers to this question sometimes illustrate clearly the importance of distinguishing between the definition of a problem and the specification of that problem's solution. The answers sometimes show how different individuals can agree completely that a client's behavior is a problem but disagree completely regarding how that behavior must change in order for it to cease being a problem.

in that situation. In other words, a particular behavior can not be considered maladaptive when viewed solely within the context of the individual's learning history; it is maladaptive only when viewed from an independent, external perspective that takes into account positive reinforcement consequences that would be available to the individual if he were to behave differently, but which the individual has not experienced.

Consistent with this learning-theory conception, Behavioral Training is based on the fundamental assumption that each individual always does the best that he can, given his physical limitations and unique learning history, to respond as effectively as possible in every situation. To the extent that his "best effort" behavior is judged to be deficient, we can conclude, quite literally, that it is because he "does not know any better." That is, he has not learned those responses that would be considered skillful or competent in that situation. Furthermore, if he knew of a better, more functional way to behave, he would!

Ordinarily, it is virtually impossible to reconstruct through retrospective analyses a valid account of the learning history of a particular performance deficit. Thus it ordinarily is not possible to say why an individual has not acquired competent behavior in a particular situation. In the abstract, however, we can see that his skill deficit might have come about in several ways: lack of experience or opportunity to learn, faulty learning as a result of unrepresentative or faulty experiences, obsolescence of a previously adaptive response, learning disabilities resulting from biological dysfunctions, or traumatic events, such as injuries or diseases, that nullify prior learning or obstruct new learning. More than one of these factors might be involved in any particular skill deficit, and the factors can operate interactively. For example, the social skill deficits characteristic of schizophrenic behavior may develop through an interaction between a genetically transmitted biological dysfunction and the unusual social learning experiences, such as failure, frustration, rejection, and isolation, likely to be encountered by persons with this dysfunction.

Rather than searching out the specific origins of various skill deficits, the Behavioral Training approach focuses on the general fact that each individual's response repertoire has evolved through a process of natural selection; that is, the repertoire consists of tnose responses, out of all those that have been tried, that have proven most functional or reinforcing for the individual in the past. This focus has direct implications for therapy. Treatment procedures should be designed to help the individual acquire new response skills in precisely those areas where their response repertoire is deficient. To the extent that the new responses result in more positive consequences than the previous "best effort" responses, the process of natural selection will assure that the new responses will displace the old.

It should be noted that for treatment to be effective the new responses that clients are taught must be more reinforcing *to the individuals emitting them* or they will not successfully displace the previous maladaptive responses. This means that considerable attention must be given to the next step of the problem-solving process, specifying the treatment objective.

Specifying the Treatment Objective

Is it Necessary?

There is no such thing as a behavioral vacuum. If one behavior is eliminated, then the time and space it occupied will necessarily be filled by some other behavior. Unless we specify what new behavior should fill the void, the replacement may not be any more adaptive than the behavior that it replaced. In fact, the principle of natural selection suggests that since the new behavior is lower in the person's response hierarchy, it probably will be *less* adaptive. Thus behavior modification techniques that focus on eliminating maladaptive behaviors without showing equal concern for controlling what new behaviors will replace them risk the possibility of merely exchanging one maladaptive behavior for another.

Treatments that focus on eliminating maladaptive behavioral excesses are implicitly based on the assumption that adaptive functioning is the normal state of the organism and that this state will return spontaneously once the behavioral excesses have been eliminated. The use of aversion-therapy procedures to "stamp out" undesirable behavior, for

example, must assume that desirable behavior is latent somewhere in the client's response repertoire. Similarly, systematic desensitization, implosive therapy, and other techniques aimed at eliminating anxiety also must assume that desirable behaviors exist in the repertoire, waiting to appear once the inhibiting effects of anxiety are gone. Therapies based on this assumption state their therapeutic objectives in negative rather than positive behavioral terms; they focus on what the client should *stop doing wrong* rather than on what he should *start doing right*. To be complete, however, therapeutic objectives must be stated in both positive and negative behavioral terms; certain behaviors should increase, while others should decrease.

There is a simple way of testing whether specific statements of treatment objectives meet these criteria. It is called the "dead-man" test.[5] If a dead man could satisfy the criteria for the treatment objective, then the treatment's goal response is incomplete in that it does not adequately specify positive response criteria. Examples of treatment objectives that fail the dead-man test are "stop smoking," "be quiet," "stay out of jail," "stop behaving anxiously," or "stop complaining." A dead man could do any of these, so they all are inadequate statements, specifying only the absence of certain behaviors without specifying positive behavioral alternatives.

Why is it necessary to specify treatment objectives positively as well as negatively? First, most clients who seek therapy already know that their current behavior is deficient and that they could function more effectively if they behaved differently, but they do not know how to become more effective on their own. Therapies that stress what they are doing wrong are only minimally helpful; they leave the clients to their own resources to discover through trial and error how to function more effectively. Moreover, whereas the therapist is likely to consider therapy a success once it has eliminated the negative behavior, the clients may regard treatment as incomplete until it has taught them how to function more effectively.

Therapy approaches that assume, without sup-

---

5. The author can find no published reference for this test, which he heard described in a talk by Ogden Lindsley at the University of Wisconsin Medical School in the late 1960s.

porting evidence, that adaptive responses exist in the client's response repertoire are taking unnecessary risks. The client may or may not have such responses available to him. A therapist simply cannot tell whether or not such responses exist in the client's repertoire since it is not possible to measure unobservable behavior. Therefore, from the practical standpoint of minimizing error and maximizing treatment success, it would be best, in every case, to make the conservative assumption that the desired response is *not* in the client's repertoire. This assumption avoids the error of deciding that a latent response exists when it actually does not. While it might result in the opposite error — deciding that a latent response does not exist when it actually does — such an error should have fewer detrimental effects. That is, it probably would not be harmful, and might even prove therapeutic, to provide a client with training in responses that he already has in his repertoire.

In general, then, there are compelling logical and theoretical reasons why it is necessary to specify treatment objectives in explicit terms, indicating not only what current behaviors should be eliminated, but also what future behaviors should be developed.

Perhaps the only exception to this requirement would be in those rare circumstances where virtually any behavior would be an acceptable substitute. Even then, however, long-term considerations might make it necessary to determine which substitutes would be most functional or reinforcing since behavior changes will not be maintained unless the newly acquired responses are genuinely effective and positively reinforcing.

Objective: Competence

If therapy is a problem-solving enterprise and if clinical problems are performance deficits, it follows that the objective of treatment is to overcome such deficits by increasing performance competence. *Competence* can be defined as the learned ability, acquired through training or experience, to perform with sufficient skill to produce an effect that meets the needs of a life situation. This definition of treatment objectives focuses attention on the learned aspect of skills, on the situational specificity of performance criteria, and on Behavioral Training as

a preferred mode of treatment. Furthermore, its emphasis on learned situational skills places the locus of disordered behavior in an interpersonal, task-oriented context. Clients are seen as striving to achieve valued personal goals in specific situational tasks rather than as struggling to fight off psychological disease processes or handicapped by internal psychic conflicts. The most appropriate way to deal with disordered behavior, from this point of view, is to teach the individual specific response skills that will improve his ability to achieve his own objectives in specific situational tasks.

Defining Situation-Specific Competence

To say that increased competence is the goal of treatment is not of much practical value to therapists who must translate this abstract objective into specific behavioral referents in each individual case. What behaviors, for example, should be taught to an alcoholic, an impotent man, an obese woman, a delinquent boy? The current problems represented by such cases seem fairly clear; but what are the new behaviors that each of these individuals should acquire to overcome his or her current problem? Unfortunately, the definition and assessment of situational competence has not been the focus of much research among psychopathologists. Their research has concentrated on examining the ineffectual, incompetent performance of disturbed individuals without also studying how effective, competent individuals handle similar life situations. This lack of research on competence is serious indeed, since therapists cannot help clients acquire the performance skills that they need to function more effectively without knowing what specific behaviors comprise these skills.

Therapists have used several methods to define situation-specific competence. Perhaps the most common, although the least satisfactory, has been definition by *fiat*. Certain behaviors are identified as desirable merely because someone in a position of authority arbitrarily decides that they are. There are many examples of such arbitrary definitions: the mental hospital administrator who regards passive compliance as an indication of competency for discharge; the teacher who treats such classroom behaviors as sitting quietly in one's seat as an indication of academic competence; or the psychotherapist who insists that certain behaviors are "healthier" simply because some theorist has asserted that they are.

A better method of defining competence is by *consensus*. It is an improvement over the first method because it substitutes the opinions of several individuals for the opinion of one individual. In effect, it substitutes democracy for autocracy. Moreover, it involves more systematic and quantitative procedures; the judgments of several raters are obtained, scored, intercorrelated, and averaged. In the end, this method defines competence as whatever the majority says that it is. It should be noted that consensus does not assure validity; the opinions of several judges are not necessarily any more valid than the judgment of a single individual. Consensus may reflect little more than commonly held biases or pooled ignorance.

An even better approach to defining situational competence is the *known-groups* method. This is a purely empirical method in which the situational performance of two groups known to differ in some general skill is compared. Any specific behavior that significantly differentiates between these two groups is treated as an essential component or manifestation of the general skill on which the two groups were originally sorted. One problem with the known-groups method is that it commits the *error of the assumed essence*. This is the logical error of deciding that the group difference that served as the original basis for sorting the individuals reflects the *essential* difference between the groups and that all subsequently observed differences are necessarily related to this assumed essence. The method overlooks the possibility that the groups may differ in other important respects as well and that some unforeseen and unrelated third factor may account for some of the subsequently observed differences. The known-groups method also suffers from its tendency to treat performance samples as though they were indices of underlying personality traits. It assumes that "skillful" individuals will perform in a consistently skillful manner across all situations and that all aspects of their performance are relevant to their skillful*ness*. In fact, the so-called skillful persons seldom show the expected degree of cross-situational consistency [Mischel 1968]; moreover, certain

aspects of their performance may be superfluous, or even detrimental, to their overall success in some situations. In general, then, the primary value of the known-groups method is as a source of hypotheses to be examined more systematically in subsequent research.

The best way to define situation-specific competence is the *experimental* method. This method takes proposed definitions — hunches, personal opinions, opinions reflecting group consensus, hypotheses based on known-groups comparisons — and subjects them to an empirical test. The behavioral alternatives suggested as solutions for the client's life problems are compared, and the behavior that comes closest to achieving the client's goal in the problem situation is defined as the most competent. Of those discussed, this is the only method capable of separating the relevant from the irrelevant, the essential from the nonessential, and the effective from the ineffective. Unfortunately, it also is the most time-consuming, difficult, and neglected method.

There are few examples in the clinical literature of psychotherapists experimentally pretesting the effectiveness of the behavioral solutions that they prescribe for their clients' life problems. J. B. Rotter [1971], who has deplored this fact, has suggested that perhaps the prescription and administration of psychological treatments should be regulated in a manner not unlike the current regulation of drugs by the Food and Drug Administration. Perhaps psychotherapists should be required to specify each treatment's target problem and expected outcomes and be required to demonstrate not only that the treatment actually does everything it claims to do, but also that it does not have negative side effects that might outweigh its benefits. If therapists were required to prove the validity of the behavioral solutions they prescribe for their clients, it probably would mean not only that most psychotherapists would be put out of business, but also that far more effort would be devoted to the important, but neglected, business of experimentally defining situation-specific behavioral competence.

A major advantage of defining competence experimentally is that it tends to resolve the thorny question of who decides what new, adaptive behaviors the client should acquire. The ultimate responsibility for the answer to this question is delegated to the naturalistic environment and the reinforcement contingencies imposed on behavior by the "real world." That is, once the client's personal goals in his problem situation have been identified, then the empirical evidence will impartially determine which of the various behavioral alternatives being examined actually is best for achieving those goals. With the experimental method both the therapist and client are committed to taking an objective approach toward problem solving, and personal opinions and values play less of a role.

If the definition of competence depends on the particular situation, the particular person, and the particular objectives involved, does this mean that competence can never be defined the same way for any two persons or situations? Fortunately not. Within cultural and subcultural groups there often are similarities in backgrounds, goals, and problems that make it possible to develop conceptions of competence with general relevance for co-members of a group. Therefore, it is not always necessary to start from scratch with each new client; however, the validity of the culturally based definition must always be tested when being applied to a particular individual. In the final analysis the selection of the best behavioral solution to an individual's problem involves an experiment with only one subject; the ultimate definition of competence depends upon what works for the particular client.

Possible Objections?

To some the idea that psychotherapy should teach clients to behave in a situationally competent manner may sound unappealing or even objectionable. Perhaps the therapist seems like a tool of the establishment who teaches clients to behave in ways that merely perpetuate the status quo. Behavioral Training may sound to some like an approach that, for example, might encourage women who are oppressed by sexual biases to "adapt" (that is, capitulate) to their second-class status. Perhaps the treatment also sounds as though it would foster conformity, squelch spontaneity, or discourage originality. After all, if clients are taught to behave more effectively, is not that equivalent to "getting along," and does not that imply a decrease in individuality and personal freedom? Why should the individual be expected to change in response to the environment rather than the other way around, especially when the environment seems morally wrong?

All of these concerns are legitimate and deserve answers. Consider the last question first: Why *should* the therapist focus on changing the individual rather than on changing those unjust aspects of society that may be causing the client's problems? The answer is that Behavioral Training's mission is to help the individual acquire precisely those skills necessary for increased personal control over the environment. Thus the goal is to change the client, but to do so in ways that increase *the client's* ability to alter those aspects of society that are personally disturbing. Even if it were possible for the therapist to rearrange the environment to suit the client, this would only serve to increase the client's dependence on the therapist; on the other hand, teaching the client to exert control over life situations fosters independence. In other words, Behavioral Training actually can be seen as one way to increase personal freedom and individuality. It starts, as it must, by temporarily accepting as a "given" the constraints of the current environment; they must be dealt with in any problem-solving effort. For example, it treats sexual biases as part of the problem to be solved by women; with that reality as a constraint it assesses what response options each woman has available for achieving her personal goals. Of course, for some women one of the highest priority goals would be to eradicate sexual biases.

Does Behavioral Training result in rigid, conforming, uncreative behavior on the part of clients? This concern must be answered both yes and no. When clients are first learning and trying out new, alternative behaviors, they often may perform these in an uncertain, stilted, stereotyped manner. This unnaturalness is only natural; it would be expected with any newly acquired behaviors, such as when learning to drive a car or to speak a new language. It is reassuring to realize that many of the behaviors we emit so smoothly now were originally acquired through imitation and were performed awkwardly at first. With repeated practice and application new behaviors gradually become more natural, smoother, less self-conscious. They also become less stereotyped because the individual gradually begins to personalize them, performing them in a distinctive manner. Actually, this entire concern over the originality of a client's responses seems a bit inappropriate when viewed from a different perspective. It is a concern that would only occur to someone who is not in the client's shoes and therefore can afford the luxury of worrying about such fine points as the originality of responses. As a practical matter, the client who is faced with a seemingly insurmountable problem seldom worries about such fine points. The client typically welcomes any behavioral solutions; often he prefers solutions that have been thoroughly tested.

Goal Limitations

Suppose that a male client is seeking therapy in the hopes of learning to be as heterosexually successful as Steve McQueen is portrayed as being in movies. Suppose further that the therapist perceives this objective to be unrealistic, knowing of no behavior to teach the client that would enable him to achieve his goal. In this case the therapist is obligated to inform the client that the goal seems unattainable, within the limits of available knowledge, and to decline to enter into a therapy "contract" involving that particular goal. The therapist might then suggest alternative goals that are related to the client's initial goal, are more attainable, and hence, are more acceptable as a basis for a workable therapy contract. The client is left with three options: (1) he can choose to work toward an alternative goal suggested by the therapist; (2) he can propose a new goal alternative of his own; or (3) he can decide to go elsewhere to find a smarter therapist who knows how to help him fulfill his dream.

Suppose, instead, that the prospective client wants the therapist's advice on how to kill someone without getting caught for the crime. In this case the therapist may even have a vague idea of how the client might accomplish his goal, but he is unwilling to enter into a therapy contract with the client because the stated goal is personally repugnant and morally unacceptable. Again, the therapist is obliged to tell this to the client. The therapist might suggest that there are other behavioral solutions, short of murder, that the client had not considered and that perhaps one of these alternatives might even be a more effective solution, all things considered. The therapist could offer to enter into a therapy contract aimed at exploring and evaluating these alternatives. Again, the client has the three options of (1) accepting the therapist's proposed substitute goal, (2) suggesting a more acceptable substitute goal of his own, or (3) looking elsewhere for a more cooperative therapist.

The two hypothetical cases illustrate the limits of the Behavioral Training approach when it comes to specifying treatment objectives. In both, the ultimate decision about treatment objectives resided with the client. In the first case the therapist refused to offer treatment because the client's objective was acceptable but unattainable; in the second case the therapist refused to offer treatment because the client's goal was attainable but unacceptable. In other words, the goals of therapy are up to the client, with the only external limitations being the therapist's technical knowledge, on the one hand, the therapist's willingness to collaborate, based on personal moral and ethical considerations, on the other hand. This formulation resolves some of the ethical problems raised by other treatment approaches. Specifically, the therapist *never* imposes a solution on a client; the therapist either works toward the client's goals or not at all.

What if the client's problem is that he does not know what goals to choose? Then the immediate therapeutic goal would be to help the client define personal goals. This would be done empirically, first making a list of possible objectives that the client feels might be personally meaningful and then systematically exploring, sampling, and trying out these goals to determine which ones the client actually wants to pursue.

What if the client does not even know what his problem is, let alone his goal? Then the immediate therapeutic goal would be to help the client identify and define the problem in a way that is meaningful to him. It would involve a systematic behavioral analysis. If and when the problem were defined, then a new therapy contract involving other goals (for example, defining goals, learning new skills) might be arranged.

What if the therapist does not know of an effective behavior for solving a problem situation presented by the client but believes that a solution may exist? Then the therapist should be willing to explore alternative solutions in collaboration with the client, drawing on available outside resources and using the best methods possible to find the most valid solution. An incidental, but by no means trivial, aspect of this procedure is the involvement of the client in the search for a solution. In effect, the procedure teaches the client how to find solutions in general as well as teaching him a specific solution.

Finally, what if the therapist does not like the client's goals? For example, what if the therapist feels that it is sexist for a client to pursue the objectives personified by Steve McQueen in movies? Therapists will vary with regard to where they draw the line on goals that they can comfortably work toward. Some may agree to any goals short of serious crimes. Others may feel so strongly about certain religious, political, or economic matters that they draw the line on these. The therapist has the right, as a matter of conscience, according to the view being presented here, to refuse to collaborate on any goals that are personally unacceptable — but he does *not* have the right to try and impose his values or goals on the client.

Selecting Therapy Techniques

Psychotherapy techniques hold a special fascination for mental health professionals and laypersons alike. As part of this fascination, there often is a tendency to attribute far too much importance to the role of the techniques per se and to pay too little attention to how such techniques relate to the more general process of psychotherapy. In some instances interest in techniques for their own sake has created a situation in which techniques that have become divorced from their original purpose have continued to exist in the absence of any valid reason for being [Astin 1961]. The unfortunate effect of this has been to undermine the role of reason in selecting among techniques and to foster a climate in which choices are made largely on the basis of fad, fashion, and personal taste.

A personal experience stands as a vivid reminder of the irrationality of some therapists' choice of techniques. I was giving a research presentation on Behavioral Training to a group of practicing clinical psychologists. As most of these practitioners had a traditional orientation, I had "loaded" my presentation with data in the hope that I might influence as well as inform. At the conclusion a listener came up to pay his compliments, so I asked if he thought that the talk might influence how he would do therapy in the future. His reply was mystifying. He said that although he found the evidence compelling, he thought such behavioral techniques sounded too boring to administer. He thought he would continue with his old technique because he enjoyed it and felt it was more interesting.

One way to put psychotherapy techniques back into their proper perspective is to think of them simply as tools. All tools are instruments of change, designed to solve specific problems and accomplish specific goals. Thus their value can be assessed only in relation to their intended function. As an example, think of two tools: a hammer and a saw. It would be meaningless to talk about which of these is the *best* tool without specifying for what purpose; only when we know what the job is, can we pick the best tool for *that* job. The value of a particular tool, in other words, depends on two things: first, it depends on how appropriate the tool is for the particular job, and second, it depends on how well the tool actually does what it is supposed to do.

If therapy techniques are considered to be tools, then the therapist's choice of techniques should be a rational, pragmatic affair, based solely on an analysis of what needs to be done and the best way to do it. The therapist should ask, what is the nature of the client's current problem? How should things be different in order to consider the problem solved? What is the best tool for getting from where things are now to where they should be? The first two questions have been the focus of the module to this point. We shall now focus on the third question.

Most behaviorally oriented therapy techniques fit into one of four general models of therapy [cf. Bandura 1969, 1971] — response inhibition, response disinhibition, response facilitation, or response acquisition. Behavioral Training fits within the response-acquisition model; but to explain what the response acquisition involves, it would be helpful to present a brief description of the three contrasting models.

The Response-Inhibition Model

Advocates of the response-inhibition model, which includes such treatments as aversive conditioning [Rachman & Teasdale 1969] and covert sensitization [Cautela 1969], regard a number of clinical problems in terms of behavioral excesses. In treating these problems they specify the treatment goal in terms of the inhibition of these excesses and use the systematic presentation of aversive stimuli as the primary tool for eliminating the undesirable behaviors. For example, the smoker may be asked to imagine all sorts of physically unpleasant sensations in conjunction with smoking, or the alcoholic may be given a substance causing nausea immediately before being given a drink. Little attention is paid to what new behaviors will replace the old, since it is assumed that once the behavioral excess has been eradicated, appropriate behavior will appear spontaneously.

The Response-Disinhibition Model

Therapists using the response-disinhibition model, which is represented by Wolpe's [1958] systematic desensitization technique, perceive a particular clinical problem as resulting from the excess of one particular inappropriate behavior — conditioned anxiety — which, in turn, inhibits the occurrence of appropriate alternative behaviors. Typically, the technique is employed in instances in which the client complains that some object or activity causes him to be fearful. The model's treatment objective is to increase appropriate behaviors by removing the anxiety that is inhibiting them. The tool used for this in systematic desensitization is relaxation training, which is designed to obstruct the occurrence of anxiety through the systematic and repeated pairing of anxiety-incompatible relaxation responses with previously fear-evoking stimuli. In effect, the response-disinhibition model represents merely a special instance of the response-inhibition model, in which the response to be inhibited is an inhibition. Doing this presumably clears the way for appropriate behavior to surface spontaneously.

The Response-Facilitation Model

None of the prominent therapy techniques follow the response-facilitation model, probably because its underlying assumptions are too restrictive to apply to most clinical problems. The facilitation model explicitly excludes from consideration the acquisition of any new behaviors or any behaviors inhibited by negative social sanctions [cf. Bandura 1969].

A nonclinical example of behavioral influence that falls within this model would be the tendency for a person waiting on a crowded curb at a stop light to lunge forward when someone else moves, even though the light has not changed. Another example would be the tendency for a passerby to stop and look into a store window merely because others are doing so. As these examples illustrate, the absence of desirable behaviors in the facilitation model is not explained in terms of inhibitions or pathological factors but simply in terms of the absence of appropriate discriminative stimuli. The implication is that the way to elicit desired behavior is to arrange the necessary environmental cue conditions.

Summary and Critique of Three Conceptual Models

The response-inhibition approach to solving problems focuses on eliminating undesirable behaviors; response facilitation concentrates on eliciting desired behaviors; and response disinhibition involves a combination of the other two, stressing the elimination of undesirable behaviors in order to elicit desirable behaviors. Despite these differences, the three models are alike in one crucial respect. They all are based on the fundamental assumption that the desired *adaptive* behaviors exist in the client's response repertoire, even though such responses are not observable because they are not now being emitted in the stimulus situation of therapeutic interest. The models assume that the behaviors are latent, ready to emerge once appropriate steps are taken to free them (that is, by inhibiting the competing undesirable behaviors) or to coax them out (that is, by arranging for the necessary environmental cues). The dangers inherent in making this assumption were mentioned previously when the reasons why treatment objectives should be specified in positive as well as negative terms were discussed. It was suggested, at that point, that since it is impossible to determine what latent responses may exist in a person's repertoire, the most practical and error-free solution would be to assume in every case that the only responses a person has are those that can be observed. The full implication of taking this conservative view could perhaps not be wholly appreciated when it was first suggested. Now, however, it is apparent that acceptance of this view would logically preclude the use of the three models just presented and by default make the response-acquisition model, which does not assume the existence of any unobservable reservoire of latent responses, the only feasible treatment model.

Dismissing the first three models on purely logical grounds seems a drastic step. Is there not any reasonable way to infer that a particular response, or a *potential* for that response, exists in a person's repertoire even though the response is not currently emitted in the stimulus situation of interest? For example, can we not reasonably infer that a person is potentially able to engage in a response once he has observed others making it? Unfortunately, although there is abundant evidence that responses can be acquired through observation, it is equally evident that observation does not guarantee learning. The only basis for concluding that learning has taken place is an actual change in performance.

Perhaps we can infer that a person has a latent response if that response has been emitted in the past, even though it is no longer observable. But how are we to decide between the possibility, on the one hand, that the response exists in a latent form and the possibility, on the other hand, that the response may have been lost, forgotten, or modified? It appears that all we can safely infer from the historical evidence is that the response previously existed in the person's repertoire.

Perhaps we can infer that a person has a particular response in his repertoire when we see him either engage in that behavior in other stimulus situations or engage in very similar behavior in the stimulus situation of interest. The problem with this solution is that it ignores the evidence indicating that learned behavior is highly situation-specific [Mischel 1968]. Thus the absence of a *particular* response in a *particular* situation may mean it was never learned *in that situation* or that it was learned but subsequently lost or modified. We simply cannot tell which.

Another possibility is that we might be able to infer that a person has a response if we could demonstrate that he emitted it when we arranged special stimulus conditions or response consequences (for example, if his life depended on it or if he were paid enough money). One problem with this solution is that it does not involve an inference; rather, it involves an observation of performance. In addition, however, it involves an alteration of the conditions and incentives for performance so that it still does not demonstrate whether the person has the response available for use in the original stimulus situation. Again, the situational specificity of learned behavior prevents us from making the inference that the person has learned to make the response in the stimulus situation of interest.

There is still another possibility. Perhaps we can assume that a person has a response if he tells us he does or if he provides a verbal description of the response. This solution suffers from its failure to consider the evidence that the three response systems — verbal-cognitive, overt-motor, and autonomic — are often poorly correlated [Lang 1969]. It is part of folk wisdom that "Sayin' and doin' are two different things." If a person tells us that yes, he can, but we observe that he does not, which are we to believe?

Finally, what if a person tells us that he has the response in his repertoire, but he contends that he cannot emit it because he is too anxious? Like the preceding solution, this one relies on the validity of self-report that contradicts direct observation, and it is subject to error. It also raises another issue — namely, the assumed causal relationship between anxiety and performance. Contrary to popular belief, anxiety is not always detrimental to performance. Even when anxiety measures are correlated with a performance decrement, which causes which? Is the person unable to perform competently because he is inhibited by anxiety? Or does the person feel anxious because he is unable to perform competently? In the response-acquisition model, the fourth model of therapy, the client's sentence, "I can't because I'm anxious," is turned around to say, "I feel anxious because I can't." In other words, whereas the first three treatment models make the untestable and seemingly unwarranted assumption that the desired behavior is latent in the client's repertoire, the response-acquisition model assumes that a client who does not engage in the desired behavior does not know how!

What is meant by "know how"? One example was given to me by a father who told about the time his son accidentally broke a neighbor's window. The father instructed the boy to go next door and apologize, but the son only slinked around the house, despite the father's urgent and repeated prods. Finally, in desperation, the father said, "You *do* know *how* to apologize, don't you?" to which his son meekly replied, "No." Seeing his error, the father practiced with the son what he might say, and then the son, smiling and without hesitation, went next door and apologized!

"Know how" does not refer merely to intellectual knowledge; it refers to performance competence, which may or may not be related to a cognitive or intellectual understanding. In fact, it is not unusual for persons identified as competent — artists, cooks, athletes, scholars, leaders — to be unable to provide an intellectual explanation of *how* they do what they obviously "know how" to do very well. "Know how" is not like a trait; it refers to situation-specific learned skills, which may not show a high degree of consistency across situations or across time. As an example of this, consider the performance of a concert pianist. No pianist knows how to play all conceivable piano pieces. This will be true even though the pianist may know how to play certain specific pieces brilliantly, may have a thorough mastery of the subcomponent skills, such as fingering, that are essential to the performance of virtually every piece, and may be able to learn new pieces very quickly. It is also true that the pianist's performance on a particular piece will vary from time to time and from place to place as a function of such diverse factors as practice, fatigue, concentration, age and so on.

Another important aspect of "know how" is that it generally refers to an integrated and coordinated sequence of behaviors, not merely a single response; to be competent, the sequence must be performed successfully as a unit and accomplish the desired objective. Thus in the examples cited previously, going-next-door-to-apologize was one functional unit made up of a sequential chain of responses, and performing-a-piano-piece was a whole unit comprised of many parts. Often we conclude that a person does not know how to do something when actually he cannot perform only a particular aspect of the whole unit. The task of identifying the specific deficit sometimes is complicated by the tendency for persons to avoid engaging in the whole behavioral unit when they are uncertain about their ability to handle a small part of it. A teen-aged boy, for example, avoided social interactions with peers for nearly a whole summer because he felt awkward about explaining why he was staying away from the community swimming pool; he avoided the pool because he felt awkward about explaining his hesitancy to join the other boys in diving off the high board to impress the girls; and he avoided diving because he had never learned how to keep water from getting up his nose. Once the deficit was identified and corrected, the entire problem disappeared. An even more extreme example involved a woman who was about to marry a man she did not even like because, according to her, she did not know how to say no when he asked.

Response-Acquisition Model

It should be apparent from the preceding discussion that the response-acquisition model of treatment is quite different from the other three models. It defines behavioral problems in terms of performance deficits. Implicit in the judgment that a deficit exists is the judgment that the individual lacks certain alternative behaviors that would be "better." In other words, the definition of a problem in terms of a performance deficit invariably carries with it the implicit specification of how things should be, which amounts to the change objective. The change techniques in this model are essentially educational techniques, designed to teach clients new, more adaptive behaviors.

There are two main treatment approaches within the response-acquisition model — the *consequation* approach, which is represented by operant-conditioning procedures, and the *instigation* approach, which is represented by Behavioral Training procedures.

There are numerous differences between the consequation and instigation approaches, but only some of the important contrasts will be noted. The central difference is that consequation therapies attempt to modify responses indirectly by manipulating their consequences, whereas instigation therapies attempt to modify responses directly through training. In the consequation approach it is assumed that desired behavior will result naturally if behavior is allowed to vary freely in relation to the intervention, which focuses on systematically arranging for more appropriate response consequences. In the instigation approach it is assumed that if response consequences are allowed to vary freely while the responses themselves are altered in the direction of new, more effective behavior, then more positively reinforcing consequences will occur naturally, and these, in turn, will influence subsequent responses.

Although the distinctions between these two approaches are subtle, they have ramifications that seem to favor the instigation formulation. First, the instigation approach seems to be more efficient because it modifies responses directly, through the use of instructions and modeling, rather than indirectly, through "shaping" procedures, which require that the therapist "teach" by waiting for the desired response or an approximation of it to be emitted and then introducing a positive consequence. Second, the instigation approach tends to be more practical to implement. The consequation approach requires that the therapist can arrange for a high degree of environmental control over response-reinforcement contingencies, but this is feasible only in the most restricted or regimented of settings, such as prisons, mental hospitals, or school rooms. Third, the instigation approach is designed to initiate change. The consequation approach, in contrast, is designed to alter reinforcement contingencies *following* behavior; therefore, the main effect is not to initiate change but to maintain change once it has occurred.

Perhaps the most serious problem with the consequation approach involves the logical dilemma it poses for therapists regarding the specification of treatment goals. The approach assumes that deviant behavior is maintained by its reinforcing consequences and, therefore, that intervention efforts should be aimed at altering the naturalistic contingencies causing the deviance. But suppose that the therapist overthrows the constraints of the contingencies and gains control over the reinforcing stimuli. How then does the therapist decide what behaviors should be reinforced? A behavior's adaptiveness ordinarily would be defined in terms of its effectiveness; but once the therapist determines a

behavior's effects, there is no longer any independent and objective criterion for defining adaptive behavior. Adaptiveness becomes whatever the therapist wants it to be.

Of course, the arbitrariness of the therapist's power raises serious ethical questions such as, Who controls the controller? It also raises practical problems. By design the therapist's artificially imposed contingencies will conflict with the naturalistic contingencies that they have displaced. For example, hospitalized psychotic patients may be rewarded for performing routine acts of self-care or for socializing with other patients, activities which are taken for granted in the outside world. What effect will this have, therefore, on the likelihood that treatment effects will generalize to settings where the therapist does not control the reinforcers? The available evidence is not encouraging [Krasner & Krasner 1972]. And how likely is it that treatment effects will persist after the therapist's control over contingencies has been withdrawn? To make matters worse, there is recent evidence suggesting that artificially imposed reinforcement contingencies actually may have harmful effects; the use of external incentives, such as rewards or tokens, seems to decrease the responsiveness of subjects to the intrinsically reinforcing aspects of performance [Levine & Fasnacht 1974].

Reports of therapeutic success using consequation techniques (such as contingency contracting [Homme et al. 1969] and token economies [Kazdin & Bootzin 1972]) suggest that the approach may be effective despite its problems. On closer examination, however, such successes may be open to alternative interpretation. One such technique, for example, is contingency contracting in which client and therapist reach a formal contract about performance goals, with agreed-upon pay-offs to the client for successful performance. The beneficial effects, however, occur after the establishment of a formal performance contract but *precede* the actual payoffs dictated by the contract. Thus the treatment has a strong instigative component, with the delivery of agreed-upon contingencies serving primarily to strengthen and maintain changes prompted by the contract-writing process.

Another major consequation technique for which success has been claimed is the token economy in which individuals in a controlled environment (school, hospital, and so on) gain privileges, material goods, or money by earning tokens for performing specified acceptable behaviors.

Like contingency contracting, most token economy systems are complex interventions involving far more than the contingent dispensing of tokens. Those employed in elementary classrooms, for example, often include such instigative features as providing students with instructions, with coaching regarding "appropriate" behavior, and with modeling of such behavior so that students may learn from observing. The token systems also provide teachers and school administrators with extensive training in effective ways to handle the problems that they face (for example, how to control disruptive students). Whether one chooses to regard token economy systems as examples of the consequation or the instigation approach will depend largely on one's perspective on the problem being treated.

To illustrate, imagine a therapist who has been asked by a teacher to help change the behavior of a child whom the teacher perceives as "disruptive." The therapist's intervention consists of training the teacher to use a token reinforcement system in which disruptive behaviors are ignored (not reinforced) and appropriate behaviors (or failures of disruptive acts to occur) are reinforced by tokens. What is happening from the perspective of the consequation approach? The child is the designated patient because the child's "disruptive" behavior is seen as the target problem; the goal is to decrease the child's disruptive behavior and to increase appropriate behavior (both defined by the teacher); the technique employed involves modifying the teacher's behavior as a means of altering the reinforcement contingencies, which, in turn, would modify the child's behavior.

Consider the same intervention within the framework of the instigation approach. The teacher becomes the designated client because it is the teacher's inability to control the child, along with the teacher's distress about this, that has prompted the therapist's intervention. The objective is to increase the teacher's skill at interacting effectively with children (that is, to teach ways to get the disruptive child to conform with the teacher's standards for good behavior); and the technique used is to teach the teacher "token-dispensing behavior," which is just one of several possible strategies that might increase the teacher's control over the child's classroom behavior.

It is interesting that the instigation interpretation of token economies is most consistent with the general finding that successful token systems often have a more lasting, generalized and pervasive effect on the behavior of the staff carrying them out than on the behavior of the so-called patients for whom they were intended. The staff members, more than the patients, seem to be acquiring new performance strategies and interpersonal skills that they can use for solving similar problems in future situations.

One other positive implication of the instigation view, as demonstrated in the example, is an ethical one. The instigation approach helps clarify who the *real* client is at all times. It forces the therapist to consider as the client the person who identified the problem and who specified the change objectives. The criteria of who identified the problem and who specified the objectives help the therapist avoid the ethical trap of working to change the behavior of one person at the request of another person and claiming that the first person, who never asked for help, is the real client. In the example of the teacher and the disruptive child the teacher clearly is the client according to these criteria. Although the teacher may have the best interests of the child genuinely in mind when seeking help, it is important to recognize that the therapist is the teacher's agent: it is the teacher's definition of the problem that the therapist is responding to and the teacher's objectives that the therapist is working to achieve.

Specific interventions invariably can be interpreted from more than one perspective and often can be seen as fitting within more than one of the four treatment models. Thus when examining the results of therapy outcome studies, it is important to distinguish between the empirical fact that a technique is effective and the theoretical explanation given for the fact that the technique worked. Techniques are not the exclusive property of any particular conceptual model. Whereas the ultimate test of a technique's value is its effectiveness, the value of a conceptual explanation is assessed primarily on the basis of its relative capacity for encompassing existing data, for generating new hypotheses, and for stimulating procedural innovations. Thus reconstruing existing treatment procedures from the perspective of different conceptual frameworks is not merely an intellectual exercise; sometimes it can prove fruitful by suggesting ways that the treatments might be modified to make them even more effective or to make them applicable to problems previously considered irrelevant.

To illustrate this point, consider M. P. Feldman and M. J. MacCulloch's [1971] reported success using aversive conditioning procedures to treat volunteer male homosexuals. They found that their procedure (pairing of noxious stimuli with stimuli initially leading to sexual arousal) was not equally effective for all subjects. Their goal was to achieve a satisfactory heterosexual adjustment. Those patients who did achieve a satisfactory adjustment tended to be those who had a history of heterosexual interest and experience. Among these "secondary" homosexuals posttreatment interviews revealed that the treatment was successful primarily for those who, on their own initiative, actively engaged in imaginal rehearsal of heterosexual behaviors in between treatment sessions. This finding suggests that the aversive conditioning procedure per se may not have been primarily responsible for the outcome; it may have served instead to mediate the effects of other, unprogrammed therapeutic factors. Specifically, perhaps the aversion treatment forced patients to seek out and rehearse response alternatives that would make it possible for them to avoid receiving the experimentally imposed aversive stimuli. Patients with prior heterosexual experience would be more likely to have such alternatives available to them. This possible explanation suggests that a more complete treatment approach might be one that explicitly provides behavioral training in heterosexual skills, perhaps using aversive contingencies only temporarily, if at all, to enhance the incentive for change or to suppress any response tendencies that might interfere with the acquisition of the new skills.

Tools of Behavioral Training

Behavioral Training has been characterized as an educational therapy in which the purpose of treatment is to help clients overcome specific performance deficits by teaching them new adaptive responses. If therapy techniques are viewed as nothing but the tools used to achieve particular therapeutic objectives, then the principle tools of Behavioral

Training obviously would have to be teaching techniques. The possible range of such techniques would be as varied and extensive as the whole field of education itself. For the sake of convenience, however, teaching techniques can be organized into four general categories, with the specific techniques included in each category tending to represent variations on a common theme. The following is a summary of teaching techniques. It is intended to be illustrative, not exhaustive.

1. *Demonstration.* If a person is going to learn a new response, it is very important that this person know what the specific response to be learned *is* — that is, what it looks like or how it sounds. In the "show-and-tell" jargon of the elementary school classroom this category refers to the use of "showing" tools. Demonstration procedures can be extremely effective teaching tools because they have the capacity to convey an enormous amount of rich information about behavior, and they do it simply, quickly, and efficiently. There are certain behaviors, in fact, that are all but impossible to teach without using some form of demonstration. Modeling, which is a form of demonstration, is an indispensable tool for teaching gross motor skills (for example, how to drive a car), activities requiring dexterity (for example, how to use hand tools), subtle responses (for example, postural or vocal cues), or cognitive responses (for example, reasoning or logic). In fact, it is difficult to see how any of the remaining teaching tools could be employed with a person who had not had some direct observational experience with the response being taught.

Demonstrations can be live, recorded, or imaginary; they can occur *in situ* or in simulation; they can be presented auditorily, visually, or in combination; they can involve persons and animations of many types; they can be broken into units involving whole response sequences, into parts of sequences, or into small bits of behavior; they can be in slow motion, in stop-action, or in almost any time frame one chooses; and they can be presented alone or in combination with other teaching techniques. In other words, there are numerous different ways to demonstrate behavior. The particular form chosen usually depends upon the kind of behavior being demonstrated, who is being taught, who is doing the teaching, and so on.

2. *Instruction.* Within the instruction category are those tools representing the "tell" half of "show-and-tell." Just as there are some things that cannot be taught very easily without being shown, there are other things that are extremely difficult to convey without the use of verbal communication or other symbolic processes. For example, relationships, principles, rules, response sequences, directions, classifications, and other abstractions are taught most efficiently using language. Words are capable of focusing attention on the relevant and essential aspects of performance. They also can be manipulated to express hypotheses, convey information about unobservable events and feelings, and represent relational concepts. Telling can communicate more economically than showing, once words have acquired behavioral referents. The instruction may be verbal, written, or symbolic, live or recorded, individualized or impersonal, directive or reflective. In general, the possible variations on instructional techniques are too numerous to mention. "Coaching" is a term that describes one particular type of instruction that is used most often in Behavioral Training. This term emphasizes the importance of analyzing, directing, instructing, and prompting behavior in this kind of therapy.

3. *Practice.* It may be a bit extreme to say that practice makes perfect, but without practice the acquisition of new responses will not be complete and the retention of previously acquired responses will be difficult. Practice is the active part of the learning process. It tends to stabilize newly acquired responses. We learn best by doing. Experience, drill, recitation, rehearsal, homework, and exercise are some of the terms used to describe teaching tools fitting the practice category. The following dimensions illustrate just a few of the ways in which practice procedures may vary: massed versus distributed trials, focused versus broad response categories, overt versus covert rehearsal, *in situ* versus in simulation settings, and part versus whole response units.

4. *Knowledge of Results.* The teaching tools that provide knowledge of results function as the catalysts of the learning process. Imagine a person who has been shown what to do, has been told when, why, and how to do it and then has actually gone out and done it. As the final step in the learning process, this person needs to know what happened as a result of doing it. Some of the various ways of describing this aspect of learning are: consequences, reinforcements, results, products, effects, and outcomes. We can receive feedback about the effects of our behavior via all of our senses, with input coming from the most basic tissue level to the most abstract cognitive level. Knowledge of results involves both the informational and the incentive effects of performance. Therefore, negative information indicating that certain responses are incorrect or ineffective is potentially as valuable for improving performance as is positive information.

Investigators have devoted considerable research attention to studying various aspects and forms of this particular teaching tool. The following is only a partial list of different factors influencing how knowledge of results affects learning: real versus imagined consequences, frequent versus infrequent feedback, feedback following whole versus partial response units, direct versus vicarious experience of consequences, positive versus negative feedback, immediate versus delayed feedback, consequences with extrinsic versus intrinsic reinforcement value, the effects of programmed, individualized feedback, and the effects of audio- or videotaped playback of rehearsal responses.

Relationship between Therapy Techniques and Therapy Content

In principle, the selection of educational techniques is inextricably tied to the particular response content that the techniques are supposed to teach. Thus while all of the various techniques described have been employed at one time or another in a Behavioral Training program, their inclusion in any particular program has tended to be a function of the particular program and its purpose. In contrast to most other behavior therapy techniques, Behavioral Training does not involve only one set of well-defined therapeutic procedures; it involves as many different procedures as there are different problems and populations. This is because Behavioral Training calls for the use of tailor-made educational procedures to teach the specific skills needed to overcome the performance deficits associated with the specific life problems of particular persons.

Unfortunately, much of the research on Behavioral Training to date has been ill conceived. It has tended to put the cart before the horse by concentrating on evaluating the relative effectiveness of various training methods without first developing the response content of the training programs in a careful and empirical manner. Few studies have attempted to determine which responses actually represent competent, effective solutions to the particular life problems of particular clients. Such studies must be done, however, since we cannot reasonably begin to assess which methods are best for teaching until we have decided what we are going to use the methods to teach. In the end, of course, our teaching methods must be good since even the most carefully developed content will be of little value to clients if they fail to learn it because the teaching methods were inadequate. By the same token, however, if the content of the training program is not valid — that is, if the "competent" responses taught clients do not arm them with genuinely effective solutions to their life problems — then the program will fail no matter what training methods have been used.

Actually, a considerable amount is known already about *how* to teach response skills [see Lumsdaine 1961], but comparatively little is known about *what* the skillful responses are that should be taught. Basic methodological guidelines for analyzing situation-specific behavioral competence in a systematic and empirical manner have been set forth by M. R. Goldfried and T. J. D'Zurilla [1969] and by R. F. Mager and P. Pipe [1970]. Unfortunately, these guidelines have been ignored by most of the investigators interested in Behavioral Training. Perhaps because the behavioral assessment and definition of competence seems so time-consuming and tedious, most investigators simply have preferred to rely almost entirely on their clinical experience and intuition to decide what skill deficits plagued their clients and what response skills their clients needed to acquire.

It might help to illustrate what can happen when investigators fail to develop their training program's content empirically and rely on their intuition instead. A group of investigators was interested in developing an experimental Behavioral Training program to treat heterosexually anxious college-aged

men. Rather than developing their program empirically, by conducting systematic studies into the deficits of shy males and the performance characteristics of competent males, they wrote it "off the top of their heads." The program represented little more than their consensual guess as to what their clients needed to learn. In one phase of their program, the investigators devoted considerable attention to teaching the importance of maintaining eye contact when conversing with a woman. Apparently, they had decided that eye contact per se is a good thing and that the higher the absolute percentage of time the clients did it, the better. Of course, theirs was an overly simplistic analysis of the role of eye contact in social interactions. Other research on eye contact has shown that its value, or appropriateness, depends upon the particular situational context and what is happening in the interaction at the time. At the extreme, incessant staring is as ineffectual as never looking. What is most critical about eye-gaze behavior, though, is not really *how much* one person looks at the other person but *when*. At certain points in an interaction it is most functional and appropriate to look away; whereas at other points it is best to look toward the other person. This means that the investigators who taught their clients to engage in a high rate of undifferentiated eye contact may have decreased rather than increased their clients' competency. In fact, subsequent research has shown that eye contact is not even a variable that distinguishes between groups of shy and confident college males, and that it may not need to be included in the content of skill-training programs for shy males [Arkowitz et al. 1975].

Assessing Treatment Effects

The assessment of treatment effects in Behavioral Training is similar to the assessment of learning in other educational contexts. The purpose of assessment is to determine the extent to which the Behavioral Training program is doing what it is supposed to be doing. There are three levels of assessment. At the most basic level the concern is with evaluating changes within the ongoing training program itself. This involves measuring specific learning as it occurs and then using this information to make subsequent training decisions. It deals with the questions, Are the tools working, and are we progressing in the right direction?

At the next level assessment focuses on the client's performance relative to the specified training goals. This is referred to as *criterion-referenced* assessment. Rather than asking how well the client is performing in comparison to his past performance or how well the client is performing relative to how well other persons might perform, this assessment asks how the client's performance compares to the criterion level of performance that was set as the treatment goal. It asks, Are we there yet?

The third level of assessment focuses on evaluating the effectiveness of the newly acquired behaviors for resolving the original life problem. For example, if a depressed housewife were trained to behave more assertively on the assumption that increased assertion would lead to less depression, then an assessment of the training program's overall effectiveness could not stop merely with a demonstration that the client was behaving assertively in the problem situations; it also would have to show that the client's depression had decreased too.

Assessment involves taking performance samples of the very behavior being taught. It might involve self-report, behavioral or autonomic measures. The samples should be taken under conditions that are as representative as possible of the stimulus situations for which the newly acquired behaviors were intended. It is not sufficient to show that the depressed housewife, for example, can respond assertively on a paper-and-pencil survey. It is not sufficient to show positive changes in her behavioral samples collected in role-played situations in the training context. Nor is it wholly satisfactory to accept her verbal reports or diary accounts of increased assertions in relevant real-life situations. Ideally, performance samples should also be collected in the naturalistic environment in an unobtrusive manner. Of course, it is not always possible to gather such ideal performance samples, but one should strive to come as close as possible to the ideal.

It is important to determine whether or not the newly acquired responses are being emitted as planned in the real world because without such evidence therapists may draw erroneous conclusions about their treatment programs. Using the example of the depressed housewife again, if we were to look only for changes in her depressed behavior following assertion training and were to find no such change, we might conclude that the training was unsuccessful. It is possible, however, that the training program succeeded in increasing her assertive behavior but that it did not have the anticipated parallel effect of decreasing her depressed behavior. Armed with real-life measures of both behaviors, we could see that our original definition of the problem was faulty and, as a result, that the treatment failed to accomplish one-half of its objective even though the training did increase her assertion.

It should be apparent from this description of assessment in Behavioral Training that the clarity with which the target problem is defined, the specificity with which the treatment objective is identified, and the precision with which the treatment is administered all will influence the degree to which it is possible subsequently to assess whether therapy has succeeded [see Goldfried & Sprafkin 1974]. Moreover, well-designed assessment systems can have a corrective effect on the other three aspects of treatment. That is, the assessment data can sharpen our understanding of the problem, help us decide what treatment goals would be most appropriate, and enhance our ability to construct highly specific training programs. As stated at the beginning of this module, the four parts of the problem-solving process are interdependent and each is essential to the development of effective Behavioral Training programs.

Relationship between Behavioral Training and Psychopathology

As a clinical psychology graduate student, I spent part of one year working in the Blind Rehabilitation Program at the Hines Veterans Administration Hospital near Chicago. The program was designed to transform helpless, immobile, emotionally overwhelmed individuals into self-reliant, active, and independent persons — all in a period of eighteen weeks. Virtually every patient who entered the program showed some signs of serious psychological disturbance — depression, suspiciousness, suicidal fantasies, social withdrawal, passivity. The program's staff, comprised almost entirely of teachers, ignored the symptoms and attended to the practical matter of teaching specific skills that would enable the blind patients to function as effectively and independently as possible. Mobility trainers, for example, taught the patients to navigate independently with a cane, to feed themselves, to dress, and the like. Mobility training culminated with a tough final exam — a performance sample — requiring each patient to travel unaccompanied to downtown Chicago and to bring back a specific purchase. There also were teaching specialists in communication skills for the blind, such as typing, braille, and the use of tape recorders. Other teachers focused on helping each patient acquire appropriate marketable job skills. In essence, the performance requirements for living independently as a blind person had been carefully analyzed, and a program had been designed to teach all of the necessary skills to each patient in a programmatic, individualized manner. The program not only accomplished its goal, but it had an intriguing side effect. As the patients increased in competence, their psychological symptoms gradually disappeared.

A Behavioral Training program designed to deal with another target problem was developed by F. P. Robinson [1946]. In an effort to help failing college freshmen stay in school he conducted a systematic analysis of their common academic performance deficits. Relative to successful students, he found that the poor students did not know how to study effectively. He developed and validated a method of effective study (known as the SQ3R method, standing for Survey, Question, Read, Recite, Review) and successfully taught students to use it. Robinson also discovered that many of these students received low grades on term papers and that spelling errors were a major reason. He was able to identify and compile a relatively short list of frequently used words that accounted for the majority of the spelling errors. When poor students were taught to spell this finite list of words, their written papers tended to become indistinguishable from those of other students, and their grades improved. Robinson's program for teaching students academic skills, published in the

1940s, is in use today at colleges and universities across the country.

The two programs described are examples of systematic applications of Behavioral Training. The reader may wonder, however, about the relevance of the training programs employed in these two examples to the treatment of more severe psychological problems. What do cane technique and braille or study methods and spelling lists have to do with the profound life problems of the clients encountered in a clinic, correctional facility, or mental institution? In the first place, the blind veteran and potential college failure belong to high-risk populations. Unless they receive assistance in learning to deal with their immediate life problems, they will be more likely to need even greater help with more serious problems at some later point in their life. By providing Behavioral Training to the veteran, symptomatic behavior disappeared. By helping the college freshmen avoid academic failure, personal distress was decreased and life goals were kept alive.

The two examples are relevant to the treatment of clinical problems in another respect. In the case of the blind rehabilitation training, a known physical disorder accounted for most of the patients' problems. Although the blindness was never cured, the behavioral problems associated with it were successfully treated with a Behavioral Training approach. In the second case the specific origins of the students' problems were unknown, yet they too were responsive to treatment by Behavioral Training procedures. Thus the examples illustrate that the relevance and effectiveness of Behavioral Training programs do not necessarily depend upon the etiology of the particular problem being treated.

Finally, these examples are considered relevant analogies for the treatment of more extreme psychopathological behaviors because the Behavioral Training approach assumes that a common set of principles should be able to explain both adaptive and pathological behavior and that the learning principles underlying effective treatment should be relevant to both as well. It is on the basis of this assumed similarity that a fairly large proportion of the experimental studies on Behavioral Training to date have focused on treating relatively normal clients. The next section will survey a representative group of these analogue studies, and the section following that will present a sample of studies in which Behavioral Training has been used with more severely disturbed subjects.

Behavioral Training Programs for Psychological Handicaps

Assertion Training

The term *assertion* refers to all situationally appropriate expressions of personal rights and feelings and includes such behaviors as refusing unreasonable requests, expressing anger and indignation, expressing affection and appreciation, and showing compassion and tenderness. There are occasional situations in which most of us find it difficult to behave assertively. Some persons are unable to behave assertively in many situations, and to them this represents a psychological handicap with far-reaching significance. These persons tend to compromise themselves to such an extent that they experience a distressing loss of control over their own life circumstances. An extreme example of this is the woman, mentioned previously, who was about to marry a man she did not like because she was unable to decline his proposal.

Several investigators have developed training programs aimed at teaching nonassertive individuals to behave more assertively. My associates and I have contributed to this effort by developing an experimental training program focusing on one particular type of assertive behavior — namely, the refusal of unreasonable requests. In a programmatic series of experiments [McFall & Lillesand 1971; McFall & Marston 1970; McFall & Twentyman 1973] we have demonstrated that two twenty-minute sessions of assertion training are capable of producing a significant increase in the assertive-refusal behavior of previously nonassertive college students. The program is prerecorded and employs the training components of overt or covert response rehearsal, the presentation of tape-recorded assertive models, the use of instructional coaching, and the use of various forms of performance feedback, including corrective feedback and playback of recorded rehearsal responses. Treatment effects have been assessed in several ways, including self-reports, performance

samples of assertion in simulation tasks, and real-life samples of refusal behavior obtained via unobtrusive telephone calls in which an experimental assistant, posing as a fellow student, makes unreasonable requests. For a better idea of the actual treatment procedure, an excerpt from a transcript of the tape-recorded program is presented. This example represents only one of the ten assertion situations on which subjects received training, but essentially the same format was followed for all situations.

Narrator Presents Situation:	A person you don't know very well is going home for the weekend. This person has some books that are due at the library. The books are heavy; it's a twenty-five minute walk to the library from where you live, and you hadn't planned on going near the library that weekend. This person says, "Would you be willing to take these books back for me so they won't be overdue?"
	(Bell cues subject to respond. Subject responds covertly.)
Narrator:	Now, listen to two assertive responses to this situation.
Female Model:	I'd like to help, but that's quite a walk and I'm really busy. Sorry.
Male Model:	No. I'm not going to be anywhere near the library. You had better ask somebody else.
Narrator Presenting Coaching Material:	Notice that these responses were tactful but firm. They made it clear that the request was too much of an imposition. They didn't go into long excuses or apologies and made it clear that they would not do it. The other person would probably say something like, "Okay. Don't sweat it. I'll find somebody else to do it." Now, think back to your response and compare it with the assertive examples.
	(Ten-second pause)
Narrator:	Here's the situation again. This time, respond out loud. A person you don't know too well is going

home for the weekend. This person has some books that are due at the library. The books are heavy; it's a twenty-five minute walk to the library from where you live, and you hadn't planned on going near the library that weekend. This person says "Would you be willing to take these books back for me so they won't be overdue?"

(Bell rings.)

(Subject responds overtly. Subjects's response is recorded and played back.)

Our research evidence, coupled with evidence contributed by other investigators, supports the view that assertion training programs can be of benefit to individuals suffering from this particular type of psychological handicap.

Heterosexual Skills Training

A dominant area of concern among teenagers and college-aged adults centers on acquiring the interpersonal skills necessary for satisfying heterosexual relationships. Persons with problems in this area often are described as having "dating problems." This is a misleading descriptive label because the problem is not nearly as trivial as the word "dating" suggests. In our society heterosexual relations are extremely important throughout the lives of most adults; an inability to relate easily and effectively to the opposite sex (or to one's own sex too, for that matter) can be a psychological handicap with ominous implications, especially if it is treated lightly and if steps are not taken to overcome it.

Several investigators have made serious attempts to study so-called dating problems using systematic, empirical methods. Attention has focused on three main areas. First, the research has attempted to determine what factors may be related to dating problems. Using the known-groups approach, researchers compared low-frequency daters with high-frequency daters on a number of different measures. Second, the research has evaluated the effectiveness of various training programs supposedly designed to

teach heterosexually anxious males how to interact more satisfactorily and effectively with women. Third, some investigators have been concerned with the more fundamental question of defining interpersonal competence in situation-specific behavioral terms. Whereas most of the early research was oriented toward evolving effective treatments, much of the later work reflects a growing recognition that an accurate definition of the problem and a sound knowledge about interpersonal competence are prerequisites to developing the best possible treatment package. Nevertheless, results from some of the early, intuitively constructed training programs — despite their crudeness — were encouraging [Twentyman & McFall 1975].

Other Psychological Handicaps

Assertion and heterosexual skills account for most of the Behavioral Training research thus far in the general category labeled psychological handicaps. Research inroads also have been made into several other areas. A few of these deserve to be mentioned, if for no other reason than to indicate the potential range of problems for which the Behavioral Training approach might prove valuable in the future.

M. R. Goldfried and C. S. Trier [1974] developed and evaluated an experimental Behavioral Training program for use with college students suffering from the handicap of public-speaking anxiety. The program taught subjects relaxation responses and stressed that these were active coping skills that the subjects could employ to achieve increased self-control over their speech anxiety. The experimental results were especially interesting because subjects continued to improve even after therapy was terminated.

J. C. Wright [1972] reported generally positive results using a group-administered Behavioral Training program to treat college students who reported being anxious about participating in quiz-section discussions. Subjects who were given training in quiz-section behaviors received instructional coaching, participated in group discussion, observed models, rehearsed responding, received constructive feedback, and were given homework assignments. Experimental comparison groups received either systematic desensitization (a technique aimed solely at removing the students' anxiety) or no treatment; neither of these groups showed as much improvement on most of the measures as the Behavioral Training group.

Behavioral Training procedures also have been employed experimentally to treat a number of specific fear and avoidance behaviors. Typically, these experimental treatments have been reported under other labels (for example, contact desensitization, participant modeling), but they are appropriate to this discussion because of their use of response training methods, including the presentation of real-life stimuli in conjunction with the rehearsal of situation-specific coping responses, the use of live models, and a heavy emphasis on instructional coaching and response prompting. Some of the specific fears with which treatment reportedly has been successful are fear of snakes [Bandura, Blanchard, & Ritter 1969], fear of heights [Ritter 1969], and fear of water [Sherman 1972].

Behavioral Training for Serious Dysfunctions

Sexual Dysfunctions

Impotence, frigidity, and premature ejaculation are examples of sexual dysfunctions that typically represent more debilitating problems than those covered in the preceding section. Historically, such sexual problems have been interpreted as symbolic manifestations of very serious and difficult-to-treat psychodynamic conflicts. Of late, however, they have seemed much less formidable owing largely to the results of the widely publicized sex research of W. H. Masters and V. E. Johnson [1966, 1970]. The first phase of their research was devoted to analyzing the psychological and biological foundations of normal and deviant sexual functioning. The second phase, which grew out of the first, was devoted to developing effective treatment programs for specific dysfunctions. Because the treatments were empirically grounded, they stand as models to other investigators.

As presented by Masters and Johnson, the therapy program has the appearance of a response-disinhibition treatment because it ostensibly focuses on the elimination of performance-inhibiting factors, such as the fear of evaluation or the tendency to assume a "spectator" role. On closer inspection, however, the treatment obviously includes response-acquisition features too. It relies heavily on the use of Behavioral Training methods to overcome specific performance deficits. Couples are systematically taught precisely those performance skills that they need to achieve mutually satisfying sexual intimacy. After several sessions devoted to an analysis of the couple's problems and an introduction to the treatment's rationale, the couple is assigned homework exercises that concentrate on systematically developing each of the progressively more advanced stages of a full sexual interaction. Each of the assignments includes explicit rules of conduct. (For example, no touching of breasts or genitals is allowed in the first exercise, which focuses on pleasurable sensations with each person taking turns giving pleasure to the partner through touching.) Gradually, as each stage is assigned, practiced, and discussed afterward in the therapy sessions, the specific problems are overcome.

The work by Masters and Johnson is not the only example of the application of Behavioral Training to sexual dysfunctions; it simply is the most extensive and best known to date. Other investigators have experimented with additional training methods for specific problems. W. C. Lobitz and J. LoPiccolo [1972], for example, have used masturbation, erotic stimuli and fantasies, and role-played orgasm to enhance sexual responding. On balance, the available evidence suggests that such treatment methods can be effective with sexual dysfunctions.

Alcoholism

A common psychiatric conception of alcoholism is that it is an addictive disease in which the physical craving for alcohol is so great that a single drink is sufficient to cause a total loss of control and start a chain reaction leading to drunkenness. Understandably, treatment approaches based on this conception insist that total abstinence is the only solution and concentrate on helping alcoholics avoid temptation. Unfortunately, such treatments have not been too successful. Moreover, studies have challenged the validity of the disease conception itself [see Marlatt, Demming, & Reid 1973].

An alternative conception of alcoholism is that it is a learned behavioral problem in which the consumption of alcohol is an instrumental response associated with specific stimulus events. Investigators interested in this conception have studied possible stimulus determinants of drinking behavior, have studied the characteristics of the drinking response itself, and have experimented with various treatment strategies for dealing with alcoholism as learned behavior.

Some interesting results have emerged from these studies. For example, comparisons between the drinking patterns of social drinkers and alcoholics revealed that in addition to ordering more drinks, alcoholics tend to prefer more straight as opposed to mixed drinks, to take larger sips, and to drink faster [Sobell, Schaefer, & Mills 1972]. Such findings suggested that perhaps alcoholics could be helped by training them to drink as social drinkers do. M. B. Sobell and L. C. Sobell [1973a, 1973b] subsequently incorporated training in social-drinking behaviors as one part of a comprehensive, seventeen-session therapy program for alcoholics in a state hospital. The major emphasis of their program (ten sessions) was on analyzing the stimulus conditions for each patient that elicit heavy drinking, generating effective alternative responses to each situation, anticipating the potential favorable consequences of the alternative actions, and practicing these new behaviors in simulation exercises. The program's effectiveness was evaluated by comparing it to the hospital's regular treatment program. The experimental and control treatment groups were divided into two subgroups. For some patients the express treatment goal was one of total abstinence; for others it was to become controlled social drinkers. A one-year follow-up revealed that the outcome for the experimental treatment condition was superior to that for the control treatment on virtually every measure (daily drinking, emotional adjustment, vocational adjustment, arrests, and so on). It also showed that experimental subjects with a social-drinking orientation were at least as successful as subjects with an abstinence orientation. Of these two groups, 70 percent and 68 percent, respectively, were either abstinent or drinking in a controlled manner after one year, whereas the comparable rates for the subjects in the associated control groups were only 35 percent and 38 percent respectively. In general, these results are encouraging and suggest that Behavioral Training may be an effective treatment approach with alcoholics. Additional research is needed, however, to replicate these findings and to isolate the treatment components contributing to the outcome.

G. A. Marlatt [1974] has taken a slightly different tack in his efforts to develop a Behavioral Training program for alcoholics. After achieving disappointing long-term results with various aversion treatment paradigms (for example, avoidance, escape, punishment), he examined his subjects' descriptions of the circumstances under which they resumed drinking. He found that two classes of situations accounted for approximately 60 percent of the relapses. The central feature of the first class was the subjects' apparent inability to deal with anger and frustration (for example, resulting from an argument with a spouse). The second class was characterized by the subjects' inability to cope with social pressures to drink (for example, the boss offers to buy a drink). Based on his relapse data and other experimental evidence indicating that alcoholics need to perceive themselves as being in control of their environment, Marlatt has begun to develop an experimental training program aimed at increasing alcoholics' control over their lives by teaching them skillful ways to cope with common problematic situations.

Delinquency

Another category of dysfunctional behavior for which Behavioral Training seems to be a promising treatment approach is delinquency. The rationale is straightforward. It is assumed that many delinquents simply are deficient in critical social skills and that they engage in self-defeating, socially unacceptable behavior because they literally do not know any better. This implies that if the delinquents were taught more effective behavioral solutions to the problems that they face, they would engage in less delinquent behavior.

The results of an experimental treatment study by I. G. Sarason and V. J. Ganzer [1969] provided partial support for this view. Social skill training was given to one group of institutionalized male adolescent delinquents, while subjects in comparison groups received either a group-discussion treatment or no treatment. The training program employed instructional coaching, modeling, response rehearsal, and, in some cases, videotaped playback of rehearsal responses. The training content was designed to teach effective responses to situations presumed to be related to delinquency. These involved interpersonal conflicts with parents, peers, and authorities. The experimental results seemed to favor the skill-training program. The subjects in this program tended to be released sooner from the institution and to stay out longer following release than subjects receiving no special treatment. Those in group-discussion treatment also did better than those in the no-treatment control group. However, since these subjects also focused on finding effective behavioral solutions to problem situations (without guided practice), the results of this treatment are difficult to interpret.

A common shortcoming in many of the studies reviewed thus far has been the failure to determine empirically what the specific skill deficits are that are associated with the specific problems and populations being treated. As a result of this oversight, it is possible that the training programs would succeed in teaching new skills — but that the new skills would not be directly relevant to the target problem.

B. J. Freedman [1974] has conducted one of the few systematic assessment studies of skill deficits. She performed a behavioral analysis of situation-specific performance competence among male adolescent delinquents, following the methodological guidelines suggested by Goldfried and D'Zurilla [1969]. First she extracted from the literature and from interviews problem situations in which adolescents might get into trouble with peers, parents, teachers, police, and others. Responses to these situations were elicited from a cross section of persons — delinquents, nondelinquents, counselors, and so on. The responses were rated for competence by another sample of persons, and a scoring manual reflecting these ratings was developed. Finally, performance samples to these situations were obtained from three groups of adolescents: institutionalized delinquents, nondelinquents matched for age and socioeconomic class, and "superstar" peers (high school leaders) matched for age. Performance samples were obtained by asking subjects to role play in response to each of the problem situations. Each subject's competence in each situation was scored on an 8-point scale, using the criteria in the previously developed scoring manual. An example of one item and its scoring criteria follows:

> You're visiting your aunt in another part of town, and you don't know any of the guys your age there. You're walking along her street, and some guy is walking toward you. He is about your size. As he is about to pass you, he deliberately bumps into you, and you nearly lose your balance. What do you say or do now?
>
> 8 — *S* ignores the boy, says nothing, or walks on (he *may* give the boy a dirty look), OR gives an assertive, calm response, or tries to get to know the other boy.
>
> 6 — Polite but conciliatory or apologetic response. *Example:* Excuse me; Sorry about that.
>
> 4 — Response is unassertive, wishy-washy, overly wordy, or otherwise ineffective, but not likely to provoke a fight.
>
> 2 — Response is insulting, antagonistic, or provocative. *Example:* Watch where *you're* going. What'd you do that for?
>
> 0 — *S* pushes or fights the other boy, in any way. (It does not matter what else he says or does. Fighting takes precedence, unless he says that he would try to avoid a fight, but if the other boy swung first, he'd hit back. That receives 2.) [Freedman 1974.]

When compared to the two nondelinquent groups, delinquents were found to earn significantly lower competence scores on forty-one out of forty-four of the problem situations. If we assume that the scoring criteria in the manual actually reflected the relative real-life effectiveness of various behavioral solutions to the selected problem situations, then these results support the hypothesis that delinquents tend to be deficient in social skills. In addition, the Freedman study provides an empirically derived and validated set of delinquency-related problem situations and associated competent responses that could be used as the content of a skill-training program for delinquents.

Depression

M. E. P. Seligman [1973, 1975] has defined depression as a learned belief in one's own helplessness. He came to this conception of depression as the result of laboratory experiments, many involving animals as subjects, showing that subjects confronted with circumstances over which they cannot exert control will develop behavior similar to the clinical symptoms of depression. The depressed person, in Seligman's view, has learned that he is helpless to control his environment; therefore, his depression will be alleviated only when he learns that he is an effective person. This suggests that the best therapy for depression would be one, such as Behavioral Training, that is aimed at increasing the person's repertoire of effective responses. At least in the laboratory the only technique that has succeeded in "curing" learned helplessness has been directive therapy — forcing the subject to see that his responses can have an effect.

P. M. Lewinsohn and his associates [Lewinsohn, Weinstein, & Shaw 1969] have offered a similar explanation for depression. They have hypothesized that depression occurs because depressed persons are deficient, relative to nondepressed persons, in social skills. They define social skill in terms of the social consequences of behavior: that is, a skillful response is one that elicits reinforcing consequences from the environment and is not punished or extinguished. Like Seligman, they believe that the best therapeutic approach with depression is to increase patients' social skills by teaching them responses that enable them to control their own environment.

J. M. Libet and P. M. Lewinsohn [1973] conducted an experimental test of the hypothesized relationship between social skill and depression. Depressed and nondepressed subjects were observed interacting in various structured interpersonal tasks for two hours, twice each week, for eight weeks. Skill was measured in terms of five categories of coded behavior: total rate of behavior, efficiency of emitted behavior (rate of emitted behavior relative to the rate of responses elicited from others in return), interpersonal range (number of persons toward whom behavior is emitted and from whom responses are elicited), relative frequency of positive reactions emitted, and response latency. Significant performance differences between groups were found on four of the five skill measures (on all but efficiency), thus lending general support to the experimental hypothesis. Depressed persons apparently are less able than nondepressed persons to maximize the positive consequences and minimize the punishing or extinguishing consequences that they elicit from their

social environment. The implication of this study is that depressed persons might benefit from skill-training therapy aimed at increasing their ability to elicit environmental reinforcement.

There is another aspect of depression that may be susceptible to a Behavioral Training approach. Some depressed persons are not actually ineffectual; they only treat themselves as though they were. They disparage their own abilities, deny responsibility for their own successes, and find fault with virtually everything that they do. These persons seem to suffer from a lack of reinforcement primarily as a result of their own doing. They set unrealistically high performance standards for themselves, and, then when they fail to satisfy these standards, they self-administer punishment in the form of derogatory self-statements. Perhaps depressed persons fitting this description would benefit from training that focused less on their ability to elicit environmental reinforcers and more on their ability to provide reinforcement to themselves. To some extent, this might involve teaching them to set more realistic standards for self-praise. However, it also might require teaching them to make different, more positive self-statements [see Meichenbaum 1974].

To date, formal Behavioral Training programs for the various dysfunctional behaviors associated with depression have not been systematically developed and evaluated. The conceptual rationale for doing so is available, however, so it will be only a matter of time before it is done. Meanwhile, evidence for the therapeutic value of treating depression with such procedures must come from clinical reports of its successful use [for example, Lazarus 1974].

Schizophrenia

The dysfunctional behaviors included under the label of schizophrenia represent some of the most difficult of all problems to treat. Nevertheless, there is growing evidence that they, too, may respond favorably to Behavioral Training.

It has been recognized for some time that schizophrenic patients tend to be deficient in social skills [Phillips 1953]. Attempts to treat these skill deficits directly, however, generally have been regarded as offering little more than a superficial palliative. This contention is based on the argument that schizophrenia probably is caused by biological factors, as suggested by the research on heredity; therefore, skill training represents a superficial treatment because it can deal only with the symptoms and not the cause. This argument, of course, misses the point. A treatment can alleviate or ameliorate a problem without "curing" its original cause. A simple example of this was the blind rehabilitation program described earlier. The skill training did not restore patients' vision, but it certainly alleviated the incapacity caused by blindness. Viewed from this perspective, treating schizophrenics with Behavioral Training would be no different, in principle, from using tranquilizing medications. Both treatments are aimed at increasing patients' capacity to function, and neither allows any conclusions to be drawn about what caused the performance deficits. If a patient's behavior improves on certain medications, we cannot conclude from this that the absence of these medications was the original cause of the problem. Similarly, if a patient's functioning improves as a result of skill training, we cannot conclude from this that the patient's problem was caused by a lack of skills. From a practical standpoint, the cause and the treatment of a problem often can be considered quite separately, and any treatment that works can be accepted as valid and valuable without special regard for the problem's cause.

There is another aspect of Behavioral Training that makes it an especially suitable treatment for schizophrenics. A. P. Goldstein [1973] has pointed out that hospitalized schizophrenics tend to be from the lower class and to be relatively nonverbal, nonintrospective, and action-oriented. He reasoned that the emphasis of Behavioral Training procedures on active problem solving might be far more appropriate for such persons than the emphasis of traditional "talk" therapies on achieving "insight." Consistent with this view, Goldstein and his associates [Gutride, Goldstein, & Hunter 1973] conducted an experiment in which they used skill-training procedures with psychiatric inpatients to enhance their performance on several dependent measures. Compared with patients receiving psychotherapy, the skill-training subjects generally seemed to improve more, although the results were not consistent across all measures.

Other investigators have reported positive experimental results using training procedures to modify other behaviors in schizophrenic subjects. D. Meichenbaum and R. Cameron [1973], for example, taught hospitalized schizophrenics to use self-instruction as a means of exercising self-control over their attentional processes. In addition, these subjects were taught to monitor their own behavior, to assess its effects on others, and to read the interpersonal cues emitted by others. The combined effect of this training was to improve subjects' performance, relative to that of control subjects, on several experimental measures of attention. In another study [Hersen et al. 1973] a training program consisting of videotaped models and focused instructions to increase the situation-specific assertive behaviors of nonassertive psychiatric patients was successfully used.

At the University of Wisconsin a series of experimental studies has developed and evaluated specific skill-training programs for psychiatric populations. In the first study K.W. Clark [1974] compared the relative effectiveness of three separate group-administered treatments — skill training, dynamically oriented role playing, and dydactic therapy — for increasing self-assertion, heterosexual skills, and job-interview performance among Vietnam era veterans on a psychiatric ward. Two of the three categories of behavior selected for training (assertion and heterosexual skills) were chosen primarily because they had been used previously in laboratory training studies and thus provided a direct link to past research. Of course, there also was good reason to believe that training in these behaviors would help the young veterans succeed in their posthospital adjustment. The third category (job-interview behavior) was selected because of the importance of successful job placement as a predictor of posthospital adjustment. The situations used in training were developed empirically in a preliminary study, as were the experimental measures (self-report and behavioral) and the situation-specific responses taught the subjects. Each group of three subjects received treatment in four sessions over a two-week period. Subject groups were seen by one of three different therapists, thus permitting an analysis of therapist effects. Training methods consisted of overt role rehearsal, role reversal, modeling, therapist coaching, and group feedback and discussion. The experimental results indicated that the training condition generally was more effective than either the dynamic role playing or the dydactic conditions. Treatment differences were evident on all three target behaviors. In addition, there were therapist effects on subjects' self-reports of improvement but not on behavioral measures. A one-year follow-up also revealed a nonsignificant tendency for more subjects in the training condition to be employed and to have remained out of the hospital than subjects in the other two conditions. In light of the brevity of treatment, the positive results suggest that a carefully constructed, more extensive training program might be of considerable therapeutic value.

The second of the experiments [Goldsmith & McFall 1975] represented the most systematic attempt yet to apply Goldfried and D'Zurilla's [1969] methodological guidelines to the task of developing and evaluating an interpersonal skill-training program for psychiatric inpatients. The research was conducted in two phases. The first was a program-development phase. This involved (1) empirically identifying patient-relevant problem situations (obtained from interviews with psychiatric patients rather than being selected in advance by the experimenter, as was done by Clark), (2) eliciting and analyzing effective responses to each of these situations, (3) deriving a set of principles governing situation-specific competence, and (4) developing explicit scoring criteria for such competence and incorporating them into a scoring manual.

The second phase of the study was devoted to an experimental evaluation of the training program developed in the preceding phase. Subjects were male psychiatric inpatients, half of whom were diagnosed as schizophrenic. They were assigned to one of three conditions: skill training, pseudotherapy, or assessment-only control. Each of the subjects in the first two groups received a total of three hours of individual treatment that focused on improving their performance in such interpersonal tasks as initiating and terminating conversations, dealing with rejection, and behaving in a more assertive and self-disclosing manner. Subjects in the training condition received overt rehearsal, tape-recorded models, therapist coaching, recorded playback of rehearsal responses, and corrective feedback. Subjects in the pseudotherapy condition

received equivalent exposure to all training situations, but they concentrated on gaining "insight" into their problems rather than on exploring specific ways to behave more effectively. Treatment effects were assessed on self-report, behavioral role playing, real-life similation, and follow-up measures. Results on most of these measures showed that skill training was superior to the other two treatments and that it was as effective with the schizophrenic patients as with the nonpsychotic patients. Once again, it is encouraging to find that only three hours of training can produce positive effects in patients with such serious behavioral problems.

Evaluation and Conclusion

Beware of psychologists bearing panaceas — the present author included! Thus far the rationale and supporting evidence for Behavioral Training has been presented, with the emphasis always being on what is positive about the approach. No conceptual framework, no technique, however, can apply to *all* problems or do *all* things equally well. What are the *limitations* of Behavioral Training?

The answer to this question is not a simple one. If the general treatment concept of teaching individuals to function more effectively through the use of training procedures is under consideration, then the limitations are few. There is virtually no aspect of human behavior that automatically can be considered beyond the realm of Behavioral Training. The limits of the general concept can only be determined empirically, by pushing the use of the approach until those areas where it no longer seems to work are discovered. At a specific level, however, there are many limitations. If a particular Behavioral Training program is being evaluated, its relevance and effectiveness are highly restricted. A particular training program is constrained by the particular behavioral problem, subject population, stimulus environment, treatment objective, training methods, and outcome measures for which it was designed and validated.

Generalization

Many of the treatment studies surveyed in this module have failed to show evidence of generalization of training. The training effects usually were evident only in those very specific performance areas where training was given. Subjects taught to make assertive refusal responses in specific situations, for example, generalized what they had learned only to the extent that they could make refusal responses in novel situations. Refusal training did not seem to help them behave more assertively in other ways, such as in situations where they needed to make a request of someone else. This limitation is not difficult to understand if it is kept in mind that the treatment is basically an educational procedure. Education is very content-specific. A student who learns one foreign language, for example, is not expected to be able suddenly to speak all foreign languages. This implies that if we want to see an improvement in a particular area of a patient's performance, we must include that specific performance area in our training program. In other words, we must develop as many different specifically focused skill-training programs as there are types of behavioral problems requiring treatment. To do this properly, we map out the important areas of human functioning that frequently cause problems for individuals and cause them to seek psychological help. Then, for each of these common problem areas we need to develop specific training programs. In essence, this would be equivalent to developing a course curriculum for a school of life skills. We would have a library of specific skill-training programs from which each person could select the ones most appropriate to his or her particular needs.

Transfer

Research evidence also suggests that Behavioral Training effects sometimes do not transfer readily from the treatment setting to the real world. This is another potential limitation of the treatment approach. To the extent that it is a limitation at all, it is a fatal limitation; new skills that patients can use only in the presence of their therapist have little practical value. Actually, the evidence regarding transfer of training is difficult to interpret because so few investigators have even attempted to assess whether transfer takes place. This remains an open issue and requires the development of better methods for measuring training effects on behavior in the naturalistic environment.

The best way to insure transfer is to build procedures into the training program specifically for the purpose of promoting transfer. In other words, transfer is not something that should be left to chance. Bearing in mind that Behavioral Training is an educational procedure, we should not expect transfer to occur unless we have programmed for it. Drawing upon the educational methods used in other areas, we should make use of such training techniques as homework assignments, progressively realistic simulation exercises, and the equivalent of "on-the-job" training. The skill-training programs that have demonstrated real-life effects to date [for example, Masters & Johnson 1970] have programmed for transfer by using such methods.

Future prospects

Although education has a long history, its relevance to the treatment of clinical problems has not been recognized, at least not in this century, until very recently. Thus Behavioral Training is a treatment approach that is only in its infancy. We seem to have discovered something that has been right under our noses all along. The fact that we are discovering the obvious is something that became painfully clear to me several years ago during a social conversation with an insurance executive. He asked about my work. I told him about my research on assertion training. He listened politely as I described the experimental training procedures that I had been developing so painstakingly in my controlled laboratory research. When I finished, he told me about his job. He was associated with his company's job-training program for newly hired insurance adjustors. As he described his company's training programs, I realized that I had been empirically rediscovering the techniques that his company had been using for years. In certain respects their techniques were more sophisticated and had been tested more comprehensively than mine.

The special contribution of Behavioral Training to the treatment of human problems, therefore, is not technological since the technology is not new. The primary contribution is its demystification of psychotherapy through its recognition that existing training techniques are relevant to the process of solving behavioral problems. The emphasis of future research in Behavioral Training should be on developing a better understanding of human problems and on the search for realistic, effective behavioral solutions to such problems.

BIBLIOGRAPHY

H. Arkowitz, E. Lichtenstein, K. McGovern, and P. Hines, the "Behavioral Assessment of Social Competence in Males." *Behavior Therapy*, 1975, 6:3–13.

A. W. Astin, "The Functional Autonomy of Psychotherapy." *American Psychologist*, 1961, 16:75–78.

A. Bandura, *Principles of Behavior Modification*. Holt, Rinehart and Winston, 1969.

A. Bandura, *Social Learning Theory*. General Learning Press, 1971.

A. Bandura, E. B. Blanchard, and B. Ritter, "Relative Efficacy of Desensitization and Modeling Approaches for Inducing Behavioral, Affective, and Attitudinal Changes." *Journal of Personality and Social Psychology*, 1969, 13:173–199.

J. R. Cautela, "Behavior Therapy and Self-control." In C. M. Franks, ed., *Behavior Therapy: Appraisal and Status*. McGraw-Hill, 1969.

K. W. Clark, "Evaluation of a Social Skills Training Program with Psychiatric Inpatients: Training Vietnam Era Veterans in Assertion, Heterosexual, and Job Interview Skills." Unpublished doctoral dissertation. University of Wisconsin at Madison, 1974.

M. P. Feldman and M. J. MacCulloch, *Homosexual Behaviour: Theory and Assessment*. Pergamon Press, 1971.

B. J. Freedman, "An Analysis of Social-Behavioral Skill Deficits in Delinquent and Nondelinquent Adolescent Boys." Unpublished doctoral dissertation. University of Wisconsin at Madison, 1974.

M. R. Goldfried, "Systematic Desensitization as Training in Self-control." *Journal of Consulting and Clinical Psychology*, 1971, 37:228–234.

M. R. Goldfried and T. J. D'Zurilla, "A Behavior-analytic Model for Assessing Competence." In C. D. Spielberger, ed., *Current Topics in Clinical and Community Psychology*. Academic Press, 1969.

M. R. Goldfried and J. N. Sprafkin, *Behavioral Personality Assessment*. General Learning Press, 1974.

M. R. Goldfried and C. S. Trier, "Effectiveness of Relaxation as an Active Coping Skill." *Journal of Abnormal Psychology*, 1974, 83:348–355.

J. B. Goldsmith and R. M. McFall, "Development and Evaluation of an Interpersonal Skill-training Program for Psychiatric Inpatients." *Journal of Abnormal Psychology*, 1975, 84:51–58.

A. P. Goldstein, *Structured Learning Therapy*. Academic Press, 1973.

M. E. Gutride, A. P. Goldstein, and G. F. Hunter, "The Use of Modeling and Role Playing to Increase Social Interaction among Asocial Psychiatric Patients." *Journal of Consulting and Clinical Psychology*, 1973, 40:408–415.

M. Hersen, R. M. Eisler, P. M. Miller, M. B. Johnson, and S. G. Pinkston, "Effects of Practice, Instructions, and Modeling on Components of Assertive Behavior." *Behaviour Research and Therapy*, 1973, 11:443–451.

L. Homme, A. Csanyi, M. Gonzales, and J. Rechs, *How to Use Contingency Contracting in the Classroom*. Research Press, 1969.

A. E. Kazdin and R. R. Bootzin, "The Token Economy: An Evaluative Review." *Journal of Applied Behavior Analysis*, 1972, 5:343–372.

L. Krasner and M. Krasner, "Token Economies and Other Planned Environments." In C. E. Thoresen, ed., *Behavior Modification in Education: I*. National Society for the Study of Education, 1972.

P. J. Lang, "The Mechanics of Desensitization and the Laboratory Study of Human Fear." In C. M. Franks, ed., *Behavior Therapy: Appraisal and Status*. McGraw-Hill, 1969.

A. A. Lazarus, "Multimodal Behavioral Treatment of Depression." *Behavior Therapy*, 1974, 5:549–554.

F. M. Levine and G. Fasnacht, "Token Rewards May Lead to Token Learning." *American Psychologist*, 1974, 29:816–820.

P. M. Lewinsohn, M. S. Weinstein, and D. A. Shaw, "Depression: A Clinical Research Approach." In R. D. Rubin and C. M. Franks, eds., *Advances in Behavior Therapy*. Academic Press, 1969.

J. M. Libet and P. M. Lewinsohn, "Concept of Social Skill with Special Reference to the Behavior of Depressed Persons." *Journal of Consulting and Clinical Psychology*, 1973, 40:304–312.

W. C. Lobitz and J. LoPiccolo, "New Methods in the Behavioral Treatment of Sexual Dysfunction." *Journal of Behavior Therapy and Experimental Psychiatry*, 1972, 3:265–271.

A. A. Lumsdaine, *Student Response in Programmed Instruction*. National Academy of Sciences, National Research Council, 1961.

R. M. McFall and D. B. Lillesand, "Behavior Rehearsal with Modeling and Coaching in Assertion Training. *Journal of Abnormal Psychology,* 1971, 77:313–323.

R. M. McFall and A. R. Marston, "An Experimental Investigation of Behavior Rehearsal in Assertive Training." *Journal of Abnormal Psychology,* 1970, 76:295–303.

R. M. McFall and C. T. Twentyman, "Four Experiments on the Relative Contributions of Rehearsal, Modeling, and Coaching to Assertion Training." *Journal of Abnormal Psychology,* 1973, 81:199–218.

R. F. Mager and P. Pipe, *Analyzing Performance Problems.* Fearon, 1970.

G. A. Marlatt, "Outcome Research in Alcoholism: Analysis of Data in Relation to Determinants of Drinking." Paper presented at Iowa Symposium on Clinical Problems, Iowa City, April 11, 1974.

G. A. Marlatt, B. Demming, and J. B. Reid, "Loss of Control Drinking in Alcoholics: An Experimental Analogue." *Journal of Abnormal Psychology,* 1973, 81:233–241.

W. H. Masters and V. E. Johnson, *Human Sexual Response.* Little, Brown, 1966.

W. H. Masters and V. E. Johnson, *Human Sexual Inadequacy.* Little, Brown, 1970.

D. Meichenbaum, *Cognitive Behavior Modification.* General Learning Press, 1974.

D. Meichenbaum and R. Cameron, "Training Schizophrenics to Talk to Themselves: A Means of Developing Attentional Controls." *Behavior Therapy,* 1973, 4:515–534.

W. Mischel, *Personality and Assessment.* Wiley, 1968.

G. L. Paul and D. A. Bernstein, *Anxiety and Clinical Problems: Systematic Desensitization and Related Techniques.* General Learning Press, 1973.

L. Phillips, "Case History Data and Prognosis in Schizophrenia." *Journal of Nervous and Mental Disease,* 1953, 117:515–525.

S. Rachman and J. D. Teasdale, "Aversion Therapy: An Appraisal." In C. M. Franks, ed., *Behavior Therapy: Appraisal and Status.* McGraw-Hill, 1969.

B. Ritter, "The Use of Contact Desensitization, Demonstration-plus-Participation, and Demonstration Alone in the Treatment of Acrophobia." *Behaviour Research and Therapy,* 1969, 7:157–164.

F. P. Robinson, *Effective Study.* Harper & Row, 1946.

J. B. Rotter, "On the Evaluation of Methods of Intervening in Other People's Lives." *The Clinical Psychologist,* 1971, 24:1–2.

I. G. Sarason and V. J. Ganzer, "Social Influence Techniques in Clinical and Community Psychology." In C. D. Spielberger, ed., *Current topics in Clinical and Community Psychology,* Vol. 1. Academic Press, 1969.

M. E. P. Seligman, "Fall into Helplessness." *Psychology Today,* 1973, 7:43–48.

M. E. P. Seligman, *Learned Helplessness and Depression in Animals and Humans.* General Learning Press, 1976.

A. R. Sherman, "Real-life Exposure as a Primary Therapeutic Factor in the Desensitization Treatment of Fear." *Journal of Abnormal Psychology,* 1972, 79:19–28.

M. B. Sobell, H. H. Schaefer, and K. C. Mills, "Differences in Baseline Drinking Behavior between Alcoholics and Normal Drinkers." *Behaviour Research and Therapy,* 1972, 10:257–267.

M. B. Sobell and L. C. Sobell, "Individualized Behavior Therapy for Alcoholics." *Behavior Therapy,* 1973a, 4:49–72.

M. B. Sobell and L. C. Sobell, "Alcoholics Treated by Individualized Behavior Therapy: One-year Treatment Outcome." *Behaviour Research and Therapy,* 1973b, 11:599–618.

C. T Twentyman and R. M. McFall, "Behavioral Training of Social Skills in Shy Males." *Journal of Consulting and Clinical Psychology,* 1975, 43:384–395.

J. Wolpe, *Psychotherapy by Reciprocal Inhibition.* Stanford University Press, 1958.

J. Wolpe, *The Practice of Psychotherapy.* Pergamon Press, 1969.

J. C. Wright, "The Relative Efficacy of Systematic Desensitization and Behavioral Training in the Modification of Universtiy Quiz-section Participation Difficulties." Unpublished doctoral dissertation. University of Wisconsin at Madison, 1972.

10

Attribution Processes in the Development and Treatment of Emotional Disorders

STUART VALINS
State University of New York at Stony Brook

RICHARD E. NISBETT
University of Michigan

An increasing number of experimental studies of attribution processes are relevant to the problems encountered by psychotherapists (see Nisbett and Valins 1971 for a review of these studies). In this paper we attempt to describe systematically how attribution processes may help explain the development of some emotional disorders and how attribution processes may be incorporated into treatment procedures. We hope that this undertaking will help to create a common language with which the problems of clinical practice and the experimental analysis of attribution processes may speak to one another.

Attribution Processes and Emotional Disorders

Attribution is a process whereby the individual "explains" his world. In doing so he often uses social consensus as a criterion for validating his explanations. Indeed, when objective evidence is not available, it is the opinion of relevant others that largely determines the confidence he has in his explanations of the world. Social comparison theory [Festinger 1954] and research on affiliation [Schachter 1959] have provided the major impetus for investigations of the conditions under which we actively seek out the opinions of other people. This research, however, has identified circumstances in which individuals seem to avoid obtaining the opinions of others. To the degree that our preliminary evaluations indicate that our attitudes or behavior are bad or shameful, we may not want to check the validity of our evaluations by discussing them with other people [Sarnoff & Zimbardo 1961]. Likewise, to the degree that other people are dissimilar or do not share our experiences, we may not want to use them as a source of information against which to check our evaluations [Schachter 1959]. It is thus apparent that effective social comparison often *cannot* take place, even though the individual might desire it or benefit from it. Effective social comparison is impossible when there are no individuals available who could provide adequate information and unlikely when the comparison process is personally painful. Social comparison is also unlikely when the person does not realize that there is a social comparison question to be asked, as when he thinks he already has correct explanations for his experiences.

In this section we argue that the failure or inability to use social consensus to check shameful evaluations can lead to self-ascriptions of mental abnormality and personal inadequacy that can be profoundly debilitating. We also argue that under conditions in which no one else shares the individual's experiences he is apt to distrust other people, and left alone he may develop incorrect and seemingly bizarre interpretations of his experiences. In the absence of social consensus, unusual feelings or events may be explained by delusional systems—a symptom characteristic of the paranoid schizophrenic.

Attributions of Abnormality

There exist in the popular culture ready explanations for feelings or behaviors that the individual believes to be inappropriate or wrong. The concepts of modern psychology, in particular those of Freud, have had a profound impact on the naive psychology of the common man. George Miller [1969] has referred to man's changed conception of himself as the major effect of the psychological enterprise on society. One consequence of this new conception is that we have all become amateur psychologists and are quite ready to infer unconscious or hidden motives to account for all sorts of behavior. In most cases attributions of this nature are relatively harmless and have few important implications, even if they are correct. They are evident in cocktail party banter and function more as jokes or to highlight the wit of the observer than to explain the motives of the actor. These attributions take the form of "You spilled that drink because you dislike me and want to stain my carpet," or "She dresses like that because she's afraid of growing old," or "He's a flirt because he's very insecure about his masculinity."

In other contexts these attributions have more serious effects. If one evaluates his own behavior as inadequate or explains it by referring to hidden motives that are shameful or pathological, profound personal upset can occur. Unfortunately, pathological interpretations of behavior now abound in the popular culture. Educated people use the concepts of repression, projection, and defensiveness with as much facility as they use terms such as emphysema and gastritis. The characters in soap operas are likely to be motivated by devious and unconscious forces. The media continually present us with "expert" opinion on the underlying unconscious and often unsavory reasons for our behavior. Magazine articles feature self-administered tests that allow us to evaluate our success or failure in such roles as parent, spouse, or lover. Medical columns in the newspaper saddle us with psychic responsibility even for our physical aches and pains. (The individual who avoids reading popular psychodynamics is likely nevertheless to encounter it in the physician's office. A young married woman of our acquaintance complained of abdominal pain at bedtime and was informed that it had its origin in "sexual fears." A more old-fashioned physician subsequently diagnosed the ailment as a tomato allergy, with symptom onset roughly six hours after consumption of tomatoes. The young woman dropped tomatoes from her diet, and her sexual fears diminished greatly.) Although much of this information may be shrugged off or taken with a grain of salt, most of us are frequently faced with "scientific evidence" of our inadequacy or psychological abnormality. It is thus not surprising that there are individuals who are continually monitoring their behavior and who interpret behaviors that are common and normal as being "abnormal."

Consider as an example of such a person a case study described by John Neale [personal communication 1970]. The client, a twenty-five-year-old black, unmarried male, came for therapy because he thought he was homosexual. Deeply upset by this prospect, he found himself frequently in states of severe anxiety and depression. His attribution of homosexuality was based on several observations. Sexual intercourse was unsatisfactory, he often found himself looking at the crotch area of other men, and he believed that his penis was abnormally small. This latter belief appeared to be the major source of his difficulties. As he put it, "black people are supposed to be hung like horses and I'm not." Therapy was initiated by explaining the laws of optics—to wit, viewed from above objects in the same plane as the line of vision appear shorter. The client was advised to view himself in a mirror and this procedure helped convince him that his penis, though not of superhuman proportions, was of "normal" size. The therapist also explained that the client's glances toward the crotch area of other men were a natural consequence of his belief that his own penis was small. The client was thus persuaded that this behavior was an indication of self-evaluation and not homosexuality. It was "normal" for him to be curious about the size of other men's penises. Finally his unsatisfactory sexual experiences were explained as not being a result of inadequate heterosexual interest but a "normal" consequence of anxiety about possible inadequate performance. Neale reports that these discussions subsequently relieved the symptoms with which the client entered therapy. The client no longer considered himself homosexual and his anxiety and depression substantially diminished.

Neale's therapy, which may be called "attribution therapy" (after Ross, Rodin, & Zimbardo's 1969 suggestion) or (as Davison 1969 has labeled a similar technique) "assessment therapy" evidently consisted of providing "normal" explanations for the behavior the patient presumed to be "abnormal." Such explanations did not support a homosexual attribution and as a result reduced the client's fears. Note, however, that to correct the patient's attributions a psychotherapist may not have been required. A therapist was necessary mainly because the client was too ashamed of his possible homosexuality to check his beliefs with other people. His fears about homosexuality led to incorrect interpretations of behavior. These interpretations might very well have been corrected had he spoken to friends and been influenced by their interpretations. Many beliefs, however, are simply too undesirable to discuss, and in such cases we often do not check their validity through social consensus. Under these circumstances normal behaviors can be used incorrectly to generate a diagnosis of abnormality.

Attributions of Inadequacy

Attributions damaging to mental health are not limited to erroneous interpretations of one's own behavior but also include interpretations of the behavior of others toward oneself. *Time* magazine [1969] reported an important development in military psychiatry practiced in Vietnam. Army psychiatrists observed that the men in long-established combat units were in the habit of greeting new arrivals with strong suspicion and hostility. The new man, ignorant of battle and the unwritten rules of his new unit, seems stupid and unsocialized to his seasoned but uncharitable companions. The pattern, which the psychiatrists labeled the f.n.g. (for "f——g new guy") syndrome, produces a considerable number of psychiatric casualties among the new men. In a program that might be called "preventive attribution therapy," field commanders are now urged to prepare the new man for his cold reception. When the new man joins his unit he is equipped with the attribution "they hate the f.n.g." instead of the far more distressing attribution "they hate me."

The Vietnam psychiatrists recommend a similar preventive technique when rotating unit commanders. Often a departing commander relaxes discipline and lets his hair down with his men, aware that the taut control that psychological distance helps to maintain will soon be unnecessary. The new commander, intent on establishing authority, looks like a martinet by comparison and is sometimes engulfed by the rejection and anger he encounters. Army psychiatrists now urge the departing commander to tighten discipline and control before he leaves. This serves to prevent anger against the new commander and the subsequent damaging self-evaluations.

These techniques have obvious applications to civilian life. There are many life situations that regularly produce severe stress, and there are probably regularities in the damaging attributions that individuals employ to account for their tension and unhappiness in these situations. The new job is probably one of these situations. Damaging self-attributions are likely when the individual observes himself worrying excessively about the prospect of job change, or when he makes the job change and finds himself making errors, or when he incurs criticism from his new colleagues, or when he observes himself upset and tense in his new job.

Clearly to the extent that the problems associated with situations like the job change are universal, self-attributions of inadequacy are not merely damaging but erroneous. These errors are not likely to be discovered, however, because a given individual experiences such situations too seldom to perceive the situational nature of the stress and apparent inadequacy. Reassuring social comparison agents are often not available, even if the individual were motivated to seek them out. And, unfortunately, the explanations offered by the cultural milieu are as likely to reinforce as to counteract self-attributions of inadequacy. The individual who is inclined to label his stress-produced anxiety as "neurotic" readily finds support for that interpretation in the new naive psychology.

Attributions to Account for Unusual Sensory Phenomena: Schizophrenic Delusional Systems

Certainly some interpretations of one's behavior and the behavior of others toward oneself can be quite damaging. The interpretation can generate additional unhappiness and an unflattering self-concept and, as we shall emphasize later, can exacerbate through worry and anxiety the very symptoms the interpretation seeks to explain. The unflattering self-attributions in our examples, however, are not themselves evidence of pathological belief systems. They are not neurotic or "crazy" interpretations and no one would take them as evidence of a thought disorder. They are simply attributions that are wrong or damaging or both. Other explanatory systems, however, usually are taken as evidence of deranged thinking. These are the delusional systems characteristic of the schizophrenic. We shall argue in this section, following Brendan Maher [1970], that it is fruitful to treat such delusional systems as explanatory devices, which like the other attributions we have discussed are not pathological in their own right but merely the results of the patient's attempts to understand certain phenomena.

Let us begin by discussing Davison's [1966] treatment of a schizophrenic by "cognitive restructuring." The client, a forty-four-year-old married male, sought treatment because of twitches over his eye, heart, and solar plexus. He was particularly worried about "pressure points" over his right eye. These pressure points were interpreted as being caused by a "spirit" that was helping him to make decisions. The "messages," however, had begun to impart conflicting information, which troubled the client. When he was admitted to the hospital, "his speech was described as tangential, with loose associations, its content concerned with grandiose schemes and persecutions by others, but centering around information from his pressure points. There was no evidence of hallucinations" [p. 177]. The diagnosis was paranoid schizophrenia.

Therapy consisted of systematically teaching the client that his pressure points were situationally induced and an indication of extreme tension and upset. The client was shown that a tense situation (a game of blackjack with the therapist) produced these pressure points and that muscle relaxation exercises reduced them. Given a "normal" explanation for these pressure points, the client began to refer to them as "sensations" and gradually stopped referring to them as spirit-induced. Furthermore, realizing that his previous spirit explanation was an indication of crazy or abnormal behavior, the client was now considerably relieved to have a "normal" explanation for his pressure points.

Davison's therapy, like Neale's, can best be described as attribution therapy. Just as Neale provided his client with a "normal" explanation for his "homosexual" behavior, Davison provided his client with a "normal" explanation for his "spirit-induced" sensations. Both clients were greatly relieved to realize that they were less deviant than they had supposed. The cases were different, however, in that Neale's client was merely holding a false belief whereas Davison's client had developed a delusional system. Davison's client held a belief with which anyone else would have disagreed and which even the client realized was "crazy." Why did he develop this delusional system? The answer is at the core of the problem we are faced with in understanding and treating the schizophrenic. Brendan Maher has begun to outline an answer that is quite speculative but worthy of close attention.

Maher points out that schizophrenic delusions have usually been regarded as evidence that the patient has an underlying thinking disorder. This view rests on the assumption that the same sensory data are available to the patient as to others. The patient is assumed to be incapable of making reasonable inferences from these data. Maher opposes to this view the possibility that the schizophrenic's inference processes are intact, but that the data available to him really are very different from those available to others. Citing evidence from, among others, Payne [1962] and Venables [1964], Maher argues that an impairment in the patient's sensory input channels may distort the available information. These impairments are probably of biochemical origin, and might conceivably result from a malfunction of the central nervous system arousal mechanisms, perhaps an overactivity of the reticular formation. Such an impairment of arousal mechanisms might reasonably be expected to produce a good many of the other bizarre experiences and behaviors of schizophrenics, including the phenomenon of "word salad" (perhaps from overactive associative links between words and phrases that ordinarily have low associative values), hallucinations, and a variety of somatic sensations.

If it is correct that schizophrenic experiences are "real," then delusional beliefs may appropriately be seen simply as the patient's attempts to explain his unusual experiences. Since other people apparently do not share his experiences, the schizophrenic must reject their opinions when evaluating his experiences. Indeed, by virtue of the fact that others do not share his experiences, the schizophrenic is pushed toward delusions of self-reference. His experiences are considered unique because others are in a conspiratorial fashion producing them, or, because of his special qualities, he has been "chosen." Maher thus argues that there is no reason to assume that the cognitive activity by which patients arrive at their delusions (explanations) is distinguishable in any way from that employed by nonpatients, or for that matter by scientists. The intelligence of the particular patient determines the structural coherence and internal consistency of the explanation. The cultural experiences of the patient determine the content—political, religious, or scientific—of the explanation. In brief, "a delusion is an hypothesis designed to explain unusual perceptual phenomena and developed through the operation of normal cognitive processes" [p. 4].

There is an intriguing similarity between Maher's analysis of schizophrenia and Schachter's analysis of emotion. Schachter [1964] has proposed that the individual in a state of autonomic arousal has a need to explain the arousal. If the explanation is consistent with emotion, the individual will feel emotional. Maher proposes that the schizophrenic has unusual, arousal-producing experiences he needs to explain. If the explanation he hits upon is unusual enough, the individual is called "crazy" and his explanation a "delusion." The implied cure for these delusions is similar to the technique used by Schachter and his colleagues to forestall an emotion, which is to provide a nonemotional explanation for the arousal. Maher proposes that schizophrenic delusions may be similarly circumvented by acknowledging the reality of the patient's experiences and by providing the patient with a "normal," that is, biological, explanation of them. The patient might be told, in effect, that just as some people have weak hearts or inefficient gall bladders, he has an overactive reticular formation. Such an explanation might effectively undermine the delusional system, which the patient himself often knows to be crazy but which he perhaps finds more acceptable than the traditional demand of the therapist that the patient deny the reality of his experiences.

Maher's proposal (which has been anticipated by Davison and Neale) seems to us to be of great importance. It is also thoroughly consistent with recent attribution research indicating that the explanation accepted by an individual for his experiences is of paramount importance for subsequent cognitive, emotional, and motivational processes. Nevertheless, we would like to distinguish between two features of Maher's argument. The reluctant reader can agree

that delusions may profitably be viewed as incorrect explanations for the schizophrenic's experiences without however acceding to Maher's belief that these experiences arise from atypical or unusual biological phenomena. It is possible to hold the traditional view that the arousal mechanisms and sensory apparatus of the schizophrenic are intact but still agree that the *context* in which he receives and evaluates stimuli may be radically different. Just as a subject in a sensory deprivation experiment is apt to develop minor delusions, the isolated, distrustful individual who persistently ignores consensus information would be apt to develop bizarre explanations for his "normal" experiences.

Therapeutic Undermining of Dispositional Self-Diagnoses

Diverse as these examples are, it seems to us that they have several elements in common. Neale's "homosexual," the Vietnam soldier, and Davison's schizophrenic resemble one another in the following ways. (1) Each of the individuals had developed a dispositional explanation to account for some behavioral effect. Neale's client attributed various effects to a homosexual disposition, the Vietnam soldier to personal inadequacy, and Davison's client to an ability to communicate with spirits. (2) Each went about making his dispositional interpretation in perfectly logical ways, but because of a lack of social consensus for the observed effect or an inability or unwillingness to seek social comparison agents each arrived at an erroneous belief that there was a relatively unique, personal cause for the observed effects. (3) Each suffered in one or more of the following ways for his erroneous causal attribution: from depression and anxiety caused by an unfavorable view of the self; from a consequent exacerbation of the very symptoms that gave rise to the attribution; from an increasing distance and sense of difference from his fellow men.

The treatment for each of the three types of client may also be described in terms of common elements: (1) In each case the individual's underlying dispositional assumption was challenged (or in the military case prevented). The result was to render the symptom more "normal," which is to say, more nearly a result of situational forces than of personal dispositions. Neale's client did not have a homosexual disposition but a common worry and a natural response to it. The Vietnam soldiers were told to expect a set of reactions that would be common to anyone in their situation. Davison's schizophrenic was assured of a reality base for his "pressure points" but was offered an explanation that served to relate the symptoms to specific situational determinants and to a form of stress reaction that was not unique. (2) In each case the new interpretation resulted in symptom improvement, presumably because the interpretation did not support the anxiety and depression generated by the old attribution and did not have the effects either of furthering a sense of differentness and apartness or of prompting behaviors that would serve to exacerbate the symptoms.

We should say that the tone of this analysis is very much out of step with prevailing clinical practice, which is to make inferences about the patient's personality and dispositions and to share them with the patient in the hope that he will change the disabling dispositions. Whether the dispositional interpretations of the therapist are generally correct or not, we wish to point out that a given patient can sometimes be helped most by attacking the dispositional interpretations he has already made for himself and supplying less damaging situational attributions. The dispositional interpretations generated by the client, it should be noted, will often (and probably increasingly) be misapplications of psychodynamic principles developed since the beginning of the twentieth century.

Attribution Processes, Drugs, and the Treatment Situation

There is reason to be concerned about a patient's attributions even when faulty attributions are not the source of his emotional disorder. All aspects of the treatment situation—including drugs, the conversations between therapist and patient, and the new behaviors the patient is encouraged to attempt—together with the shifting elements of the patient's life situation, are fair game for the patient's attribution processes. Change or lack of change, improvement or worsening, are effects whose causes the patient is likely to try to infer. Knowledge of the attributions patients are likely to make should be helpful to the clinician who wishes to maximize his treatment effects.

Just as a distinction between dispositional and situational causes of behavior was useful earlier, a distinction between stimulus and circumstance causes will be useful here. Nisbett and Valins [1971] have developed a distinction between causal factors seen as *intrinsic to a given stimulus* and those seen as *extrinsic or circumstantial*. In contrast to the dispositional-situational distinction that is concerned with the causal role of the person versus the causal role of the environment, the stimulus-circumstance distinction is concerned with the allocation of cause to various aspects of the environment. A *stimulus attribution* occurs when an individual attributes his reaction (e.g., visceral arousal, subjective fear, avoidance behavior) in the presence of a particular salient stimulus to the stimulus itself (for example, electric shock). A *circumstance attribution* occurs when an individual attributes his reaction to some aspect of the situation other than the particular salient stimulus (e.g., to a drug taken before the electric shock is given). There is a relationship between the two types of distinction. Logically, stimulus and circumstance are subcategories of situational causes, as distinct from dispositional causes. However, dispositional inferences can be coordinated to either type of situational cause. Thus an individual may infer that he has low or high *tolerance for shock* or that he has low or high *susceptibility to a drug* that influences the effects of electric shock.

The remainder of this paper is concerned with the consequences of stimulus attributions and circumstance attributions. In the next section we deal with situations in which it may be beneficial for an individual to attribute his behavior more to extrinsic circumstances than to an intrinsic reaction to the salient stimulus. We believe this to be generally so when (a) attribution to the stimulus is likely to result in maladaptive behavior (extreme fear, phobic or inappropriate avoidance) and (b) attribution to the stimulus is likely to result in a damaging dispositional inference (e.g., neuroticism, inadequacy). Then we deal with situations in which it may be beneficial for an individual to attribute his behavior more to an intrinsic reaction to the salient stimulus than to extrinsic circumstances. We believe this to be generally so when (a) attribution to the stimulus is likely to result in adaptive behavior (e.g., effective coping behavior) and (b) attribution to the stimulus is likely to result in a self-enhancing dispositional inference (e.g., belief that he is capable, healthy, etc.).

Almost all the research we discuss has dealt exclusively with drugs as the alternate (circumstance) attribution. Although drugs are often an important part of the treatment regimen and at times constitute the entire treatment, we believe that our discussion is also relevant to treatment situations where drugs are not used.

266

Therapeutic Effects of Attributing Undesirable Symptoms to an Extrinsic Cause

The distinction between extrinsic and intrinsic causes of behavior is grounded in Schachter's [1964] theory of emotion. We have thoroughly discussed Schachter's theory elsewhere [Nisbett & Valins 1971], but it will be helpful briefly to review the central experiment of the theory. Schachter and Singer [1962] gave subjects epinephrine (adrenalin), a drug that produces marked bodily sensations of autonomic arousal. Subjects were then placed in situations designed to elicit either euphoria or anger. When the arousal symptoms were attributed to the situation (what we would call the salient stimulus), the subjects reacted differently than when the arousal symptoms were attributed to the true source of the sensations—the drug (what we would call the circumstance). When arousal sensations were attributed to the situation, the subjects "caught" the salient emotion present in the situation. They became more angry or euphoric than subjects who attributed the source of their sensations to the drug. Subjects who attributed their arousal to the drug actually tended to be less emotional than subjects who had received no external boost to their arousal at all.

While Schachter and Singer were the first to demonstrate this phenomenon in the laboratory, experiences in the dentist's office suggest that it may occur in many real-life situations. Dentists often inject local anesthetics such as procaine in a solution that includes a vasoconstrictor. The purpose of the vasoconstrictor is to retard the absorption of the anesthetic to maintain its effectiveness. The vasoconstrictor typically used is epinephrine—the same drug Schachter and Singer used to produce the visceral groundwork of emotion! Consider how a bright and well-informed individual, Bertrand Russell, reacts in such a situation.

> On one occasion my dentist injected a considerable amount of adrenalin into my blood, in the course of administering a local anaesthetic. I turned pale and trembled, and my heart beat violently; the bodily symptoms of fear were present, as the books said they should be, but it was quite obvious to me that I was not actually feeling fear. I should have had the same bodily symptoms in the presence of a tyrant about to condemn me to death, but there would have been something extra which was absent when I was in the dentist's chair. What was different was the cognitive part: I did not feel fear because I knew there was nothing to be afraid of. In normal life, the adrenal glands are stimulated by the perception of an object which is frightful or enraging; thus there is already a

cognitive element present. The fear or rage attaches itself to the object which has stimulated the glands, and the full emotion arises. But when adrenalin is artificially administered, this cognitive element is absent, and the emotion in its entirety fails to arise [1927, p. 226].

It seems clear from the Schachter and Singer experiment that if dental patients are not informed about the side effects of the anesthetic (the circumstance), as Bertrand Russell was, they will often find a cause in the situation. We might expect that an uninformed patient would readily find an adequate stimulus explanation for his arousal while the dentist is hovering over him. A clear implication of the laboratory research is that dental patients should be informed of the symptoms that these drugs might produce. Certainly enough fear is experienced in the dental situation without compounding it by allowing patients to misattribute their drug-produced symptoms to fear. Although we are aware of the limitations of informal observation, we should report that we are familiar with at least one dentist who knows of attribution processes and who has found that his patients are "easier to handle" when they are correctly informed of the side effects of anesthetics.

From the standpoint of our concern with psychotherapy, it is intriguing to consider more fully what our dentist may be doing for the emotional processes of his patients. It is likely that the chief source of a given dental patient's arousal symptoms is not the drug but the state of fear he is in. If fear is the true cause of the side effects, or at least one cause, then our dentist may be engaged in a form of attribution therapy with potentially broad applications. It may be that he gives his patients a "drug-attribution" for symptoms actually produced by fear. His patients may be less fearful as a result of this reattribution. The research of Nisbett and Schachter [1966] indicates that such a reattribution is entirely possible. Under conditions in which subjects could be convinced that the arousal symptoms produced by electric shock—palpitations, tremor, and so on—were caused by a capsule they had taken (the circumstance), considerably more intense shocks were tolerated than when subjects attributed their symptoms to the true cause, the shocks themselves (the stimulus).

Ross, Rodin, and Zimbardo [1969] have replicated Nisbett and Schachter's finding in a setting with strong implications for the therapeutic situation. By a clever juxtaposition of stimuli they persuaded their subjects to attribute arousal symptoms accompanying fear of anticipated electric shock to a loud noise piped in over a headset. Subjects were then allowed the opportunity to work on either of two insoluble puzzles while listening to the noise. They were led to believe that the solution of one of the puzzles would allow them to escape the electric shock, while the solution of the other puzzle would bring them a monetary reward. The extent to which subjects spent time working on the shock puzzle, as opposed to the reward puzzle, could thus be used as a behavioral indicator of fear of shock. Subjects who were encouraged to attribute their arousal symptoms to the noise (the circumstance) quickly abandoned work on the shock puzzle and spent more time working on the reward puzzle than did subjects who were left to attribute their symptoms to fear of the shock alone (the salient stimulus).

Ross et al. argued that a version of this reattribution technique might successfully be employed as therapy for phobic patients. For example, an acrophobic might be told that his symptoms are "a common physiological consequence of the optical effects of viewing converging vertical lines" [p. 288]. Such a re-attribution of arousal symptoms might counter the emotional response to height. Similarly, the individual with a great fear of flying might be told that autonomic arousal is produced by other factors associated with flying—the anticipation of a trip, entrance into a confined space filled with people, the marked acceleration of takeoff, and so on. When arousal symptoms occur, an airplane phobic with this information would have a ready explanation in circumstantial, nonfearful terms.

A variant of this reattribution device was employed, with therapeutic results, by Storms and Nisbett [1970]. Some of their subjects, all of whom were insomniacs, were given placebos described as drugs capable of producing alertness, heart-rate increase, and high temperature—the arousal symptoms accompanying insomnia. It was reasoned that subjects taking the pills would be able to attribute their arousal to the "drug" (the circumstance) instead of to the emotional thoughts accompanying and intensifying their state of insomnia. Such a nonemotional symptom attribution would be expected to result in lowered emotionality and quicker sleep onset. Such subjects did in fact report getting to sleep about 12 minutes sooner on the nights they took the placebo "pep pills" than they had on nights without the pills.

The exact cognitive process that made it possible for insomniac subjects to get to sleep more quickly was unclear to Storms and Nisbett. The investigators had made the initial assumption that insomnia is produced in part by emotionality at bedtime—the rehearsal of angry, fearful, or exciting memories or anticipations. They reasoned that if they offered their subjects an alternative explanation of the arousal produced by their emotions, the emotions would diminish and sleep would ensue correspondingly quickly. However, comments volunteered by the subjects suggested to Storms and Nisbett that a rather different process might have occurred. Several of the subjects made it clear, in informal conversation, that they were worried about the fact that they were insomniacs—about their inability to control such a basic function as sleep and about the state of insomnia as evidence of more general pathology. There is good reason to believe that the experimental manipulation would have had an effect on a worrisome dispositional inference of this sort. Subjects were told, in effect, that on certain nights their insomnia would be caused by a drug. On those nights, therefore, subjects did not have to view their symptoms as evidence of inadequacy or pathology. They may have worried less about their condition and may have got to sleep more quickly for this reason. The drug attribution, then, may not have resulted in a general reduction in emotionality, but only in a reduction in the degree of worry about being an insomniac. To the extent that such worries interfere with sleep, such a change could have produced the experimental results.

Although it was not possible to be certain as to just what kind of process occurred in their experiment, Storms and Nisbett speculated that:

> It is quite likely that there are pathologies involving a vicious cycle of the following type: (1) occurrence of symptoms, (2) worry about symptoms, (3) consequent exacerbation of symptoms. For example, males with problems of impotence probably respond with alarm to signs of detumescence in the sexual situation. Alarm, of course, would increase the likelihood of continued loss of erection. If it were possible to change the meaning which detumescence has for the individual, alarm and consequent impotence might be prevented. Such an individual might be given a "drug," for example, and told that it might occasionally produce momentary detumescence, or he might be assured that occasional detumescence in the sexual situation was characteristic of most normal males. A cycle of symptoms, worry about symptoms, and intensified symptoms might be expected to occur with a number of other behaviors as well, including perhaps stuttering, extreme shyness, and excessive awkwardness in athletic situations. With each condition, an externalization of the symptoms or a reinterpretation of the symptoms in nonpathological terms might help to break the cycle [p. 326].

We would argue, therefore, that it may often be

beneficial for patients to attribute their reactions to "extrinsic" or circumstantial causes. We suggest that it may be valuable for the individual to attribute his reactions to extrinsic sources when stimulus attribution would lead to maladaptive behavior, when the reactions are regarded as undesirable or as evidence of pathology, or when his worries about his reactions and efforts to change them are likely to result only in further exacerbation.

Yet in the next section, we argue that it is sometimes beneficial to encourage the patient to attribute his behavior or symptoms to the salient stimulus and to discourage attribution to an extrinsic agent. In general, the circumstances where this is true are the reverse of the circumstances where attribution to an external agent is desirable. Attribution to the stimulus is likely to be beneficial when the symptoms are desirable or indicative of psychological health or when there is in fact something that the individual can do through his own efforts to produce the desired behavior or symptoms. In addition, we argue that when the clinician includes external agents such as drugs in his treatment regimen, it may be unwise to encourage the patient to attribute too much causal effectiveness to them. This is especially true when the clinician cannot be sure that the external agent will in fact produce the desired improvement or when it appears likely that the patient's faith in the external agent may leave him uncertain of his ability to maintain the improvement when the agent is withdrawn. As we shall see, these recommendations directly contradict much current clinical theory and practice.

Therapeutic Effects of Attributing Desirable Symptoms to an Intrinsic Cause

Most clinicians are well aware of the "placebo effect." They assume that the effectiveness of a drug is the additive result of its pharmacological effect and the psychological effect of the "suggestion" that the patient will improve. The practitioner is typically not unwilling to capitalize on the possibility of a placebo effect. Thus, when he is treating an individual with drugs or some other procedure, he often describes the treatment's effectiveness in a strong and exaggerated fashion ("This drug is a very effective tranquilizer. Relax, you need not worry any longer"). Although the literature dealing with the placebo effect certainly implies that this procedure is correct, we speculate on its possible negative consequences. In the present terminology, such a procedure is an attempt to get the patient strongly to attribute desirable effects to an extrinsic agent. However, describing

a drug as very strong may lead an individual (*a*) to rely solely on the drug's curative powers and thereby apply himself less to other aspects of the treatment procedure; (*b*) to infer extreme illness if the drug does not work in the expected manner; and (*c*) to become psychologically dependent on the drug and to infer negative consequences when he is taken off the drug.

Exclusive Reliance on Drugs. Let us first consider the possibility that an individual may rely exclusively on the curative power of a drug. Interest has recently been expressed in the use of drugs to facilitate the effectiveness of systematic desensitization therapy. The therapy is based upon the notion that "If a response antagonistic to anxiety can be made to occur in the presence of anxiety-evoking stimuli so that it is accompanied by a complete or partial suppression of the anxiety responses, the bond between these stimuli and the anxiety responses will be weakened" [Wolpe 1958, p. 71]. The client is usually trained to relax his musculature and is then asked to imagine various anxiety scenes while he is relaxed. This therapeutic procedure obviously requires the client to expend much effort. He must maintain his state of relaxation and he must try to imagine vividly the anxiety scenes.

Davison and Valins [1968] have discussed the possibility that such efforts are necessary features of desensitization and have expressed doubts about the efficacy of drugs to relax clients. Without going into their entire argument, we would point out one consequence of using a drug to relax during the desensitization procedure. Individuals so treated may become passive and contribute less to the treatment procedure. They may, for example, try less hard to imagine the required scenes. Since according to the theory a vividly imagined scene must be paired with the relaxation response, the failure to do so should adversely affect treatment. Perhaps as a consequence, there has been some confusion in the literature as to whether a muscle-relaxing drug (methohexital sodium) is effective during desensitization. Among those who have found it to be effective, Brady [1967] reports that he tells clients that the drug will help them to relax but that they must work along with it to achieve the desired results. Brady's observations suggest that it may be unwise to "oversell" the effectiveness of drugs. It may be better to tell the client that the drug is not so powerful as to cure completely by itself. Instead, the patient should believe that he must actively engage himself in the therapeutic process. We suggest that the drug or circumstance attribution be weakened so that the client can be encouraged to contribute to the therapeutic situation.

The Negative Placebo Effect. Let us now consider a situation in which the placebo effect might literally backfire. What might happen if an individual takes a drug described as strong and effective, but the drug does not change his behavior? The present line of reasoning leads us to expect that he might get worse. If he knows that his functioning has remained at the predrug level, but also "knows" that he is under the influence of a strong medication, he might be expected to reach the logical conclusion that his functioning has in reality deteriorated. He would thus infer a worsening of his state from the failure of a presumably strong medication. Some evidence relevant to this expectation has been accumulated in the context of experiments designed to evaluate the effectiveness of various tranquilizers.

Rickels and his colleagues [Rickels, Baumm, Raab, Taylor, & Moore 1965, Rickels & Downing 1967, Rickels, Lipman, & Raab 1966] have performed a series of evaluations of tranquilizers, always including control conditions where subjects were given placebos but told that they had been given tranquilizers. The present line of reasoning leads to the expectation that subjects in the control conditions would get worse. They might be expected to say to themselves, in effect, "I still feel about the same as I did before taking the tranquilizers, so I must be getting more anxious." The data reported by Rickels and his colleagues, while not presented in a form that makes it possible to determine the extent of worsening, do indicate that at best placebo patients do not improve as a group and that certain categories of patients get decidedly worse. The characteristics of the patients least likely to improve are quite interesting from the standpoint of attribution theory. Patients in the placebo condition did not improve if they had had previous experience with tranquilizers, if their anxiety state was a long-standing one, or if their anxiety state was severe. Each of these circumstances would provide the patient with clearer information about the effects of anxiety and tranquilizers and would increase the probability that he would make the attribution that the pill is not working.

The hypothesis that an unfulfilled expectation of improved psychological state results in a worsened condition has been directly tested by Storms and Nisbett [1970]. In this experiment (of which one condition was described above), self-reported insomniacs were asked to take a drug before bedtime, which, they were told, would serve to reduce alertness, heart rate, and body temperature. These symptoms are, of course, the symptoms of an effective

sleeping pill, but the "drug" was actually a placebo. The investigators reasoned that if insomniacs believed themselves under the influence of an arousal-reducing drug, they would regard anything less than a noticeable reduction in arousal as evidence that their emotional thoughts and insomniac state were unusually intense. This in turn should result in a worsening of the insomnia. Subjects given the "sleeping pills" did in fact report taking about fifteen minutes longer to get to sleep than on nights without the pills. The experiment thus provides confirmation of the proposition suggested by Rickels' work: "placebo effects" may backfire when subjects can infer a deterioration of their state from the absence of a promised improvement.

The phenomenon of "suggestion" therefore cannot necessarily be counted upon when patients are given a placebo. In some circumstances, the clinician can expect "suggestion" to work against him. What can we expect when patients are given not placebos, but genuine psychoactive drugs? A clear answer is not currently available. Three investigations have been made of the effects of "overselling" versus "underselling" psychoactive drugs (Uhlenhuth, Canter, Neustadt, & Payson 1959, Uhlenhuth, Rickels, Fisher, Park, Lipman, & Mock 1966, Kast 1961]. The results of these investigations are rather confused and contradictory, indicating that overselling sometimes, with some populations, lessens the effectiveness of psychoactive drugs and sometimes enhances their effectiveness. However, without exception the studies allowed a confounding of overselling with the relative warmth of the therapist and underselling with relative coldness of the therapist.

The most suggestive evidence on the question to date comes from a study by Valins, Adelson, Goldstein and Weiner [1971]. They found some evidence for the negative placebo effect in an experimental situation in which a psychoactive drug was first administered but then withdrawn. Their S's participated in two experimental sessions. During the first session all S's were given nitrous oxide (N_2O), a gas that many modern dentists use to relax their patients. At customary dosages people typically feel quite relaxed, a bit lightheaded, and in general mildly intoxicated. The study was described as an investigation of the psychological effects of N_2O. After experiencing N_2O for ten minutes, subjects completed various questionnaires and were then scheduled for a second session several days later. During this session, all the S's were administered pure oxygen. However, half the S's were told that the same dosage of N_2O was being administered while the remaining S's were told that a considerably weaker and imperceptible dosage was given. All S's were also led to expect that a test of their tolerance for electric shock would be given after the experience with the gas. It was hypothesized that S's who thought they were getting the strong dose of N_2O, and thus expected to be relaxed, would explain their failure to be relaxed by reference to the shocks they thought they would be getting. As expected, these S's said they were more frightened of the forthcoming shocks than did S's who thought that they were receiving a very weak dose (p = .05). This study is further evidence that negative placebo effects can occur if a drug is oversold or if an individual is not told that the drug might not work. In this instance, we again advise that the drug or circumstance attribution be weakened in advance. If a drug is described in somewhat less than enthusiastic terms and if it then does not work, the individual does not then have to search among the disturbing stimuli in his life situation to find an explanation for his failure to improve.

Maintenance of Drug-Produced Improvement. Finally, let us consider the problem of transferring a drug-produced behavior change to the nondrug state. Current use of psychoactive drugs follows this general pattern. The patient takes the drug, knows what he is taking, expects a particular effect, usually experiences the effect, and at some point sees himself being withdrawn from his "crutch" in order to test whether he can function without the drug in a manner similar to his improved behavior while under its influence. This is particularly likely to be the modus operandi in the outpatient treatment of "neurotics," individuals who are unduly upset about certain aspects of daily life. That this procedure leads to only very poor generalization from drugged to undrugged conditions has been cited numerous times as a major problem in the therapeutic use of psychoactive drugs.

Neal Miller's [1966] systematic work with rats constitutes some of the most clear-cut evidence of the failure of drug-induced behavior change to generalize to the nondrug state. In one experiment in Miller's paradigm, rats were shocked for pressing a food lever until the lever-pressing response was completely suppressed. Then the shock was turned off and animals were allowed access to the lever for several trials. During these trials without shock, some animals were given the tranquilizer amobarbital sodium while some were given only placebos. As expected, the tranquilized animals were more likely to press the lever than the animals given placebos. The following day, all animals were given placebos and again allowed access to the lever without shock.

Animals previously given placebos were somewhat more likely to press the lever than they had been the previous day, the extinction process having advanced somewhat further. Animals previously given tranquilizer, however, were less likely to press the lever than on the preceding day and actually somewhat less likely to press the lever than animals previously given placebos. The experiment is especially discouraging from the standpoint of drug therapy carry-over effects, because, as Miller points out, "the drug had allowed the animals to resume pressing the bar, a response which not only gave them an opportunity to discover that the shock was no longer present, but also to secure rewarding pellets of food which might have been expected to countercondition the fear" [p. 7].

Fortunately, when the subjects are people instead of rats, it is possible to encourage them to attribute improved functioning to a new-found reaction to the stimulus. Taking note of the transfer problem, Davison and Valins [1969] have suggested that maintaining drug-produced changes in behavior might be facilitated by allowing individuals to think that part of their behavior change is due to themselves rather than being solely the result of the drug. The Davison and Valins experiment, reviewed in Nisbett and Valins [1971], found that subjects who attributed increased shock tolerance to themselves (because they had previously received only a "placebo") subsequently continued to tolerate more shock than subjects who attributed increased shock tolerance to a "drug." Davison and Valins speculated that when a patient can attribute his behavior change to himself:

> the patient would now have to accept the responsibility for his changed behavior and because of this might make three inferences: (*a*) "The world can't be that frightening after all" (he will reevaluate the stimulus situation); (*b*) "I have succeeded and am competent" (he will feel happy and proud of himself); (*c*) "I will subsequently be able to behave differently when in stressful situations" (his expectations and aspirations for improved behavior will be higher). These kinds of inferences would seem to facilitate the maintenance of the behavior change once we have actually terminated the drug. Such subjects should maintain their improved behavior to a greater degree than those who have a drug-attribution for their behavior change [p. 26].

The implications of the Davison and Valins experiment seem clear. The maintenance of a drug-produced behavior change is likely to be greater if the individual can attribute part of the change to his new reactions to stimuli. Such an attribution will be facilitated if the drug is described as being *not* very strong. If the drug or circumstance attribution is relatively weak, the patient's view of the salient stimulus is more likely to change and his improved behavior more likely to carry over into the nondrug situation.

In summary, we have good reason to suspect that it may not always be wise to trust to the "placebo effect" in the drug-taking or general treatment situation. Describing a drug as very strong can have negative consequences. If the drug is effective an individual may not apply himself to relevant aspects of the treatment procedure, and, furthermore, whatever change is produced may disappear when the drug is withdrawn. If the drug is not effective, the individual may infer extreme illness and this belief can further exacerbate his condition. We would like to emphasize that, while we have spoken almost exclusively of drugs as the extrinsic, circumstance attribution, it is possible to think of all aspects of the treatment situation as potential circumstance attributions. The individual should benefit to the extent that he can attribute change to new-found reactions to the stimuli that constitute his life situation. He should fail to benefit to the extent that he believes that behavior change is due merely to the circumstances of his treatment regimen. When the patient behaves in healthier ways, the therapist should stress the causal role of the patient's new attitudes in prompting the behavior.

A Note on Deception

There may be those who feel that the deception described in some of the present research is unwise or even unethical. It should be made clear, however, that none of the principles underlying our recommendations for clinical practice rest upon any necessity to deceive the patient. While we have used deception in our therapy-relevant research, we have done so not because we believe that deception is usually necessary or desirable but because deception techniques are economical ways of answering research questions. In the therapeutic situation it is usually sufficient merely to withhold information that could be harmful and to emphasize those aspects of the truth, as the clinician sees it, most likely to help. For example, our recommendations for the use of psychoactive drugs do not intrinsically involve deception. Practitioners could simply tell their patients little or nothing about the strength of the drug they are being given, rather than state that the drug is very weak. Similarly, no deception is necessary either in persuading the patient that he must work

along with the drug or, upon withdrawal, that his efforts have been responsible in part for his improvement.

Deception is even less necessary for attribution therapies that do not involve drugs. On the contrary, most of our recommendations involve giving the patient explanations for his symptoms that are closer to the truth as the scientist and therapist see it than those that the patient himself has employed. It is unlikely that Neale was telling his patient a benign lie: it is very implausible that his patient was the homosexual he supposed himself to be. And as evidence mounts that schizophrenia is a biological phenomenon and that psychosis-like phenomena can be produced by drugs, it becomes more and more likely that an acceptance of schizophrenic experiences as "real" is scientifically correct, as Davison [1966] and Maher [1970] suggest. Even the proposal that arousal symptoms be reattributed to extrinsic causes does not necessarily involve deception. For example, it is plausible that insomnia is produced in part by an inconvenient diurnal rhythm or by a high resting level of autonomic activity. If so, insomniac patients might be told this, and the resulting nonemotional attribution might be effective in helping them to sleep. To the extent that nonpathological, nonemotional factors work to produce the patient's symptoms, it is scientifically valid as well as therapeutically helpful to emphasize them.

Summary and Conclusions

We have suggested that an understanding of attribution processes may help to account for the development of some emotional disorders and help to modify various treatment procedures. People usually need other people to help them evaluate their behavior, yet social comparison is often not obtained when the individual considers his behavior to be "bad" or shameful or when he distrusts other people. Under such circumstances people may develop dispositional explanations for their behavior when situational explanations may be more appropriate. Dispositional explanations of homosexuality, inadequacy, and the ability to contact spirits were discussed, and we suggested that therapy should sometimes consist of a systematic attack on the dispositional explanations individuals make and that less damaging situational attributions should be supplied.

We also suggested that it might often be valuable for an individual to attribute his reactions to an extrinsic source (for example a drug) when a stimulus attribution would likely lead to maladaptive behavior, when the individual regards the reactions as undesirable, or when he cannot improve and may possibly exacerbate his untoward reactions by his worries about them and efforts to conquer them. We also suggested that it might be beneficial for an individual to attribute his reactions to intrinsic sources (for example, a new-found attitude toward the stimulus) when such a stimulus attribution would be likely to lead to adaptive behavior, or when the reactions are indicative of psychological health.

Much of our discussion centered on research in which drugs or placebos were given. This research suggests that it may be unwise to try to capitalize on the "placebo effect" in the drug-taking situation. Describing a drug as very strong can have negative consequences. If the drug is effective, the individual may not apply himself to other relevant aspects of the treatment procedure and any change that is produced might disappear when the drug is withdrawn. If the drug is not effective, the individual may infer extreme illness and this belief can further exacerbate his condition.

BIBLIOGRAPHY

John P. Brady, "Comments on Methohexitone-Aided Systematic Desensitization." *Behavior Research and Therapy,* 1967, 5:259–260.

Gerald C. Davison, "Differential Relaxation and Cognitive Restructuring in Therapy with a 'Paranoid Schizophrenic' or 'Paranoid State.'" *Proceedings of the American Psychological Association,* 1966, 177–178.

Gerald C. Davison, "Appraisal of Behavior Modification Techniques with Adults in Institutional Settings." In Cyril M. Franks, ed., *Behavior Therapy: Appraisal and Status,* McGraw-Hill, 1969.

Gerald C. Davison and Stuart Valins, "Drug-Produced and Self-Produced Muscular Relaxation: Letting Go and the Issue of Attribution." *Behavior Research and Therapy,* 1968, 6:401–402.

Gerald C. Davison and Stuart Valins, "Maintenance of Self-Attributed and Drug-Attributed Behavior Change." *Journal of Personality and Social Psychology,* 1969, 11: 25–33.

Leon Festinger, "A Theory of Social Comparison Processes." *Human Relations,* 1954, 7:117–140.

Edward E. Jones and Richard E. Nisbett, "The Actor and the Observer: Divergent Perceptions of the Causes of Behavior." General Learning Press, 1971. Also in E. E. Jones, D. E. Kanouse, H. H. Kelley, R. E. Nisbett, S. Valins, and B. Weiner, *Attribution: Perceiving the Causes of Behavior.* General Learning Press, 1971.

Eric C. Kast, "Alpha-Ethyltryptamine Acetate in the Treatment of Depression: A Study of the Methodology of Drug Evaluation." *Journal of Neuropsychiatry,* 1961, 2, suppl. 1:114–118.

Brendan Maher, "Delusional Thinking and Cognitive Disorder." Paper presented at annual meeting of the American Psychological Association, 1970.

George Miller, "Psychology as a Means of Promoting Human Welfare." *American Psychologist,* 1969, 24: 1063–1075.

Neal Miller, "Some Animal Experiments Pertinent to the Problem of Combining Psychotherapy with Drug Therapy." *Comprehensive Psychiatry,* 1966, 7:1–12.

Richard E. Nisbett and Stanley Schachter, "Cognitive Manipulation of Pain." *Journal of Experimental Social Psychology,* 1966, 2:227–236.

Richard E. Nisbett and Stuart Valins, "Perceiving the Causes of One's Own Behavior." General Learning Press, 1971. Also in E. E. Jones, D. E. Kanouse, H. H. Kelley, R. E. Nisbett, S. Valins, and B. Weiner, *Attribution: Perceiving the Causes of Behavior,* General Learning Press, 1971.

R. W. Payne, "An Object Classification Test as a Measure of Over-Inclusive Thinking in Schizophrenic Patients." *British Journal of Social and Clinical Psychology,* 1962, 1:213–221.

K. Rickels, C. Baumm, E. Raab, W. Taylor, and E. Moore, "A Psychopharmacological Evaluation of Chlordiazepoxide, LA-1 and Placebo, Carried out with Anxious, Neurotic Medical Clinical Patients." *Medical Times,* 1965, 93:238–242.

K. Rickels and R. Downing, "Drug- and Placebo-Treated Neurotic Outpatients." *Archives of General Psychiatry,* 1967, 16:369–372.

K. Rickels, R. Lipman, and E. Raab, "Previous Medication, Duration of Illness and Placebo Response." *Journal of Nervous and Mental Disease,* 1966, 142:548–554.

Lee D. Ross, Judith Rodin, and Philip G. Zimbardo, "Toward an Attribution Therapy: The Reduction of Fear through Induced Cognitive-Emotional Misattribution." *Journal of Personality and Social Psychology,* 1969, 12:279–288.

Bertrand Russell, *An Outline of Philosophy.* George Allen and Unwin, London, 1927.

Irving Sarnoff and Philip Zimbardo, "Anxiety, Fear, and Social Affiliation." *Journal of Abnormal and Social Psychology,* 1961, 62:356–363.

Stanley Schachter, *The Psychology of Affiliation.* Stanford University Press, 1959.

Stanley Schachter, "The Interaction of Cognitive and Physiological Determinants of Emotional State." In L. Berkowitz, ed., *Advances in Experimental Social Psychology,* Academic Press, 1964.

Stanley Schachter and Jerome E. Singer, "Cognitive, Social and Physiological Determinants of Emotional State." *Psychological Review,* 1962, 69:379–399.

Michael D. Storms and Richard E. Nisbett, "Insomnia and the Attribution Process." *Journal of Personality and Social Psychology,* 1970, 16:319–328.

Time Magazine, October 10, 1969, p. 60.

E. H. Uhlenhuth, A. Canter, J. O. Neustadt, and H. E. Payson, "The Symptomatic Relief of Anxiety with Meprobamate, Phenobarbital and Placebo." *American Journal of Psychiatry,* 1959, 115:905–910.

E. H. Uhlenhuth, Karl Rickels, Seymour Fisher, Lee C. Park, Ronald S. Lipman, and John Mock, "Drugs, Doctor's Attitude and Clinical Setting in the Symptomatic Response to Pharmacotherapy." *Psychopharmalogia,* 1966, 9:392–418.

Stuart Valins, Richard Adelson, Joel Goldstein, Michael Weiner, "The Negative Placebo Effect–Consequences of Overselling a Treatment." Paper presented at the International Association for Dental Research, 1971.

P. H. Venables, "Input Dysfunction in Schizophrenia." In B. A. Maher, ed., *Progress in Experimental Personality Research,* Academic Press, 1964.

Joseph Wolpe, *Psychotherapy by Reciprocal Inhibition.* Stanford University Press, 1958.

[This paper grew out of a workshop on attribution theory held at UCLA in August 1969, supported by Grant GS-2613 from the National Science Foundation. The paper was written while Richard Nisbett was supported by a Morse Faculty Fellowship from Yale University and a National Science Foundation postdoctoral fellowship. The writing of the paper and some of the research reviewed was facilitated by NSF Grant 2587 to Nisbett and by NIMH Grant 14557 to Valins.]

11

Cognitive Behavior Modification

DONALD MEICHENBAUM

University of Waterloo
Waterloo, Ontario, Canada

WARNING: Reading this module may be dangerous to your mental fictions.

Picture the following scene. Two individuals, both of whom possess essentially the same speaking skills, are asked on separate occasions to present a public speech. The two individuals differ in their levels of speech anxiety: one has high speech-anxiety while the other has low speech-anxiety. During each speaker's presentation, some members of the audience walk out of the room. This exodus elicits quite different self-statements or appraisals from the high versus the low speech-anxiety individuals. The high speech-anxiety individual is likely to say to himself: "I must be boring. How much longer do I have to speak? I knew I never could give a speech," and so forth. These self-statements engender anxiety and become self-fulfilling prophecies. On the other hand, the low speech-anxiety individual is more likely to view the audience's departure as a sign of rudeness or to attribute their leaving to external considerations. He is likely to say something like: "They must have a class to catch. Too bad they have to leave; they will miss a good talk."

A similar pattern of differential thinking styles is evident for high and low test-anxiety individuals. Consider an exam situation in which some students hand in their exams early. For the high test-anxiety individual this event elicits worrying type self-statements, namely, "I can't get this problem. I'll never finish. How can that guy be done?", resulting in increased anxiety and further task-irrelevant and self-defeating thoughts. In comparison, the low test-anxiety student readily dismisses the other students' performance by saying to himself: "Those guys who handed in their papers early must know nothing. I hope they score this exam on a curve."

In short, the high test-anxiety individual tends to be self-oriented and to personalize the situations and challenges with which he is confronted. There is considerable evidence that the high test-anxiety individual is strongly self-deprecating and ruminative in evaluative situations [Sarason 1972]. Whereas the low test-anxiety-person plunges into a task when he thinks he is being evaluated, the high test-anxiety individual plunges inward.

Note that the same stimulus event (in the first case people walking out in the middle of a speech, in the second students handing in their examinations early) elicits different perceptions, attributions, and self-statements in high- and low-anxiety individuals. One can find similar examples of negative self-statements contributing to maladaptive behaviors in a number of situations and among a variety of different populations. For example, consider individuals who experience anxiety about participating in classroom discussion, individuals who feel anxious in dating situations, and so on. Most recently, a similar pattern of negative self-statements was observed among college students who performed poorly on creativity tests [Meichenbaum, 1973a]. When such "noncreative" subjects were asked to describe the thoughts and feelings they experienced while taking a battery of creativity tests, they reported task-irrelevant, self-critical thoughts (e.g., "I'm not very original or creative. I'm better at organizing tasks than at being creative.") *or* thoughts which disparaged the value of the creativity tests (e.g., "Is this what psychologists mean by creativity, telling all the unusual uses of a brick? What a waste."); *or* if they did produce a creative response, they devalued their own performance by thinking, "Anyone could have pro-

duced such an answer." Such cognitive activity is obviously counterproductive and interferes with the creative process.

The concern of this essay is to present some of the evidence that exists for the importance of cognitive variables, such as self-statements, as determinants of behavior patterns, and to illustrate the range of therapeutic procedures that have been used to modify both the maladaptive self-statements and the maladaptive behaviors of high-anxiety individuals and other types of clinical patients. We will examine some of the ways in which clinicians of very different theoretical and philosophical persuasions try to modify what clients say to themselves, their belief systems, and their behaviors.

Before we move to a description of the therapeutic strategems, it may be helpful to examine some of the recent literature on the role of cognitive variables in stress and emotional reactions.

Cognitive Variables in Stress Reactions

Men are disturbed not by things, but by the views they take of them.

Epictetus, 1st century A.D.

The evidence for the important role of cognitive variables in stress and emotional reactions comes from several sources. A primary contributor to our understanding of this phenomenon has been Richard Lazarus, whose analysis of stress reactions starts with the assumption that a human being is an *evaluating* organism who searches the environment for cues about what is needed or desired and evaluates the relevance and significance of each input. Lazarus has chosen the term *appraisal* to describe the cognitive process of apprehending and interpreting that mediates between the environmental situation and the emotional reaction:

Three formal kinds of appraisal processes may be distinguished: primary appraisal, secondary appraisal, and reappraisal. Primary appraisal refers to the judgment that a situation is relevant or irrelevant, or that it will have either a beneficial or harmful outcome. Secondary appraisal is a judgment about the forms of coping available for mastering anticipated harm, or for facilitating potential benefits. Reappraisal involves changed evaluations based on new cues, feedback from one's response or the effects of the response, or further reflection about the evidence on which the original appraisals were based [Lazarus & Averill 1972, p. 242].

In short, since cognitive processes mediate between a situation and the emotional response, every emotion must be understood in terms of a particular kind of *appraisal.* One research strategy that has been used to assess the role of cognitive factors in stress reactions attempts to influence directly the subject's appraisal system. For example, the subject may be provided with an interpretive framework before or during the stressful experience or the environmental circumstances may be manipulated so as to influence the subject's sense of self-control and competence. The exact nature of the experimental manipulation depends in part upon the theoretical orientation of the investigator, with each investigator focusing on some particular aspect of the cognitive process.

For some researchers the subject's sense of control over the threatening situation seems most critical. Presumably, an individual will appraise a potentially aversive situation as less threatening if he perceives himself as having some measure of control over the aversive stimulus. Thus, a number of investigators [Bandler et al. 1968; Corah & Boffa 1970; Glass & Singer 1972; Hokanson et al. 1971; Staub, Tursky, & Schwartz 1971] have provided subjects with the opportunity to self-administer or to escape from an aversive event. In each case the *perception* of control appeared to reduce the negative effects of stress, whereas unpredictability and lack of control led to a sense of ''learned helplessness'' [Seligman, Maier, & Solomon 1969; Thornton & Jacobs 1971].

Perhaps a study that illustrates this line of research is the one by David C. Glass and Jerome E. Singer [1972] on the effect of noise on tasks requiring persistence and attention to details (e.g., puzzles and proofreading). The subjects were exposed to tape recordings of loud, randomly occurring noise, which included a combination of people speaking foreign languages and office equipment in operation; the net effect was a jumbled roar that served as an aversive stimulus. Half the subjects were provided with a button that enabled them to terminate the noise. These subjects were instructed in the use of the button but

were encouraged to use it only if the noise became too much for them to bear. These subjects were thus provided with what Lefcourt [1973] calls the best modern analog of control — the off switch. As the authors had predicted, subjects with access to the off switch attempted almost five times as many insoluble puzzles and made significantly fewer omissions in proofreading than did their counterparts who were given no such control option [Glass, Singer & Friedman 1969]. These differences were obtained despite the fact that subjects who had potential control did not actually exercise it. The mere knowledge that one can exert control mitigates the debilitating effects of aversive stimuli. The question for the clinician is, how can patients be trained to generate their own off-switches, to develop a set that they are in control, in other words, to modify what they say to themselves?

Another aspect of the appraisal system that has been manipulated is the cognitive labeling process. The research by Stanley Schachter and his colleagues has demonstrated that the specific emotion experienced by an individual depends not only upon his state of physiological arousal but also on the way he *interprets* or *labels* this state [Nisbett & Schachter 1966; Schachter & Singer 1962; Schachter & Wheeler 1962]. They also found that this labeling process in turn is influenced by what the individual believes is the origin of the arousal. Velten [1968] has provided evidence to support the notion that what the subject says to himself influences his mood state. Velten had subjects read self-reference statements. Some of these statements reflected elation (''This is great — I really do feel good — I am elated about things'') whereas others were depressive in quality (''I have too many bad things in my life''), and still others were neutral (''Utah is the beehive state''). Using verbal report as well as various indirect indicators (e.g., writing speed, reaction time) as measures of mood state, Velten found that mood varied as a function of the type of statements read. A subsequent study by Rimm and Litvak [1969] similarly supported the finding that one's self-verbalizations significantly affect emotional arousal.

Perhaps the clearest demonstration of the direct manipulation of subjects' cognitive processes are the studies by Richard Lazarus and his colleagues, who found that under certain conditions information about the nature of the stimulus may affect its assessment and in turn its impact on people. Lazarus and his associates found that the same, potentially disturbing movie produces very different degrees of emotional disturbance depending upon how it is interpreted (i.e., on the kind of appraisal the person makes of it). They found that one can "short-circuit" or reduce the subject's stress reaction by providing suggestive information. The potential stress-inducing effects of two films were reduced by accompanying suggestions that, in one case, the surgical operation that was part of a primitive initiation ceremony did not produce harm [Lazarus & Alfert 1964; Speisman et al. 1964] and in the other, that the injury suffered by someone in the film was enacted rather than real [Lazarus et al. 1965]. On the other hand, the stress reaction was increased by information that emphasized the harm inflicted by the observed operation [Speisman et al. 1964].

In *summary*, the research on the role of cognitive variables in stress reactions indicates that how one responds to stress in large part is influenced by how he appraises the stressor, to what he attributes the arousal he feels, and how he assesses his ability to cope. The research has also indicated that under laboratory conditions the subject's cognitive set can be directly influenced.

Clinical Examples of the Role of Cognitive Activities in Stress Reactions

Researchers with broad therapeutic concerns have attempted to identify and categorize general types of faulty thinking patterns in clinical patients. An examination of these thinking patterns illustrates the role played by the client's perceptions, attributions, and self-statements. The following brief list, taken mainly from the work of psychiatrist Aaron Beck, illustrates some characteristics of the faulty or disordered thinking of patients that influence their maladaptive behaviors [1970a].

Dichotomous reasoning refers to the tendency to divide everything into opposites or to think solely in terms of extremes. The patient has a proclivity to see things in absolutes, either black or white, good or bad, right or wrong. This is often exemplified by remarks such as, "I must do my job perfectly," or "Everyone is against me."

Overgeneralization refers to a tendency to make far-reaching conclusions on the basis of little data. Often a patient makes an unjustified generalization on the basis of a single incident. Illustrative of this is the patient who thinks "I'll never succeed at anything!" when he has a single, isolated failure. As Arnold Lazarus [1971] has pointed out, the dichotomous reasoner usually tends also to overgeneralize — for example, "My girlfriend Betty let me down again; I'll never trust another woman as long as I live."

Magnification refers to the tendency to view things as being much more important, fearful, or catastrophic than they objectively are. The patient exaggerates the meaning or significance of a particular event. Beck gives as an example a person with a fear of dying who interprets every unpleasant sensation or pain in his body as a sign of some fatal disease. Ellis [1962] terms this kind of reaction "catastrophizing".

Arbitrary inference refers to the process of drawing conclusions when evidence is lacking or is actually contrary to the conclusions. The depressed patient may observe a frown on the face of someone and think, "That person is disgusted with me," or the person who notes that no one greets him upon arrival at a party may think, "What's the use of my coming — no one wants to talk to me. I'm just worthless." The patient tends to take certain features out of context and emphasize them to the exclusion of others.

It is interesting to think back to our speech-anxious and test-anxious individuals in light of these faulty thinking patterns, and to consider the ways in which their thinking may be faulty. One can gain a further appreciation of such styles of thinking by noting in television commercials the number of instances in which the advertiser is trying to sell his product by employing or capitalizing on an audience propensity to have negative self-statements. What the advertiser does is associate the absence of his product with the presence of negative self-statements, and the use of his product with the occurrence of positive consequences. For example: "What will others think if I don't use [the product]?" "The kids are upsetting me; I'm going to pieces; I'd better use [the product]." "If I use [the product], I will be like so and so, who has all these wonderful traits. Then I will be worthwhile." Obviously the way to cope and the way to enhance one's self-worth is to use the product. Consider the impact of such repetitive bombardment of neurotic thinking styles upon our culture.

This brief survey of both laboratory studies of emotional reactions to stress and the clinical literature on patients' faulty thinking styles indicates the important influence of cognitive variables on behavior. In particular, the laboratory research on stress has indicated that the direct manipulation of the subject's sense of control, his self-attributions, and his emotional appraisals is not only feasible but a strategy of great potential value. However, the full practical and clinical value of these laboratory studies has not been fully assessed. In each of the laboratory studies described the subject's cognitive set and appraisal system were modified only within the context of a brief laboratory experiment. The question arises whether such cognitively directed procedures can be employed to alter meaningfully both the client's thinking style and his maladaptive behavior. That is, can one use the general strategy of directly modifying the subject's cognitions to accomplish long-range change and to alter significantly the stress reactions and coping behaviors of clinical populations?

Semantic Therapies

Reason does not function automatically; the exercise of man's rational faculty is volitional.

Ayn Rand, 20th century A.D.

Semantic or cognitive therapy is a generic term that refers to a variety of therapeutic approaches whose major mode of action is modifying the faulty pattern of the patient's thinking and the premises, assumptions, and attitudes underlying these cognitions. The focus of therapy is on the ideational content involved in the symptom, namely, the irrational inferences and premises. Thus, the semantic or cognitive therapist attempts to familiarize himself with his patient's thought content, style of thinking, feelings, and behaviors, in order to understand their interrelationships.

For the semantic therapist, mental illness is fundamentally a disorder of thinking by which the patient consistently distorts reality in an idiosyncratic

manner. These thought processes adversely affect the patient's view of the world and lead to unpleasant emotions and behavioral difficulties. The cognitive therapist helps the patient to identify specific misconceptions, distortions, and maladaptive attributions, and to test their validity and reasonableness. Such popular aphorisms as, "As you think so shall you feel," and, "If you are not feeling well you are probably not thinking right," capture the spirit of this approach. Like many areas in psychology, the use of semantic therapies to alleviate maladaptive behavior has a long past but only a short history. As Albert Ellis has emphasized, several Greek and Roman philosophers (including Epictetus), as well as ancient Buddhist thinkers, perceived the close connection between reason, emotion, and behavior and offered advice for changing behavior by altering thinking patterns (see Ellis [1962] for a discussion of this past). In this century a number of therapists, including Coue [1922], Korzybski [1933], Johnson [1946], Kelly [1955], Phillips [1957], Frank [1961], Ellis [1962], Blumenthal [1969], Beck [1970a], and Lazarus [1971], have emphasized the role of cognitive factors in mental illness and have focused on altering the client's maladaptive self-verbalizations. Typical of this view is Shaffer, who defined therapy as a "learning process through which a person acquires an ability to speak to himself in appropriate ways so as to control his own conduct" [1947, p. 463].

The short history of semantic therapies derives from the fact that only within the last several years has there been a systematic attempt to evaluate the efficacy of such semantic therapies. The semantic therapy that has received most attention is Albert Ellis' rational-emotive therapy (RET). The basic premise of rational-emotive therapy is that much, if not all, emotional suffering is due to the irrational ways people construe the world and to the assumptions they make. The construing and assumptions lead to self-defeating internal dialogue or self-statements that exert an adverse effect on behavior. Thus, the task for the RET therapist is threefold. He must first determine precipitating external events that upset his patient. Then he must determine the specific thought patterns and underlying beliefs that constitute the internal response to these events and give rise to negative emotions. Third, he must assist the client in altering these beliefs and thought patterns. The following quote from Ellis captures the thrust of his therapeutic approach:

> Cognitively, RET teaches clients the A–B–C's of personality formation and disturbance-creation. Thus, it shows people that their emotional *C*onsequences (at point C) do *not* directly stem from the *A*ctivating events (at point A) in their lives, but from their *B*elief Systems (at point B) *about* these Activating events. Their Belief systems, when they feel disturbed, consist of, first, a set of empirically-based, rational Beliefs (rB's). For example, when they fail at a job or are rejected by a love partner (at point A) they rationally convince themselves, "How unfortunate it is for me to fail! I would much rather succeed or be accepted." If they stick rigorously to these rational Beliefs, they feel appropriately sorry, regretful, frustrated, or irritated (at point C); but they do *not* feel emotionally upset or destroyed. To make themselves feel inappropriately or neurotically, they add the nonempirically-based, irrational Beliefs (iB's): "How *awful* it is for me to fail! I *must* succeed. I am a thoroughly *worthless person* for failing or for being rejected!" *Then* they feel anxious, depressed, or worthless.
>
> In RET, the therapist or teacher shows people how to vigorously challenge, question, and *D*ispute (at point D) their irrational Beliefs. Thus, they are shown how to ask themselves: "*Why* is it awful that I failed? Who says I *must* succeed? Where is the evidence that I am a *worthless person* if I fail or get rejected?" If people persistently and forcefully Dispute their insane ideas, they acquire a new cognitive *E*ffect (at point E), namely, the Beliefs that: (1) "It is not awful but only very inconvenient if I fail"; (2) "I don't *have* to succeed, though there are several good reasons why I'd *like* to"; (3) "I am never a *worthless person* for failing or being rejected. I am merely a person who has done poorly, for the present, in these areas, but who probably can do better later. And if I never succeed or get accepted, I can *still* enjoy myself in *some* ways and refrain from downing myself" [Ellis 1972, p. 19].

It should be stressed that an individual, before treatment, is unlikely to "tell himself" various things consciously or deliberately when he is confronted with real-life situations. Rather, because of the habitual nature of one's expectations or beliefs, it is likely that such thinking processes become automatic and seemingly involuntary, like most over-learned sets. Moreover, the patient's faulty cognitions may take a pictorial form instead of or in addition to the verbal form [Beck 1970a]. For example, a woman with a fear of walking alone found that her spells of anxiety followed images of her having a heart attack and being left helpless. A college student discovered that her anxiety at leaving the dormitory was triggered by visual fantasies of being attacked. Such idiosyncratic cognitions (whether pictorial or verbal) are usually very rapid and often contain an elaborate idea compressed in a few seconds or less. Beck points out that these cognitions are experienced as though they were automatic and involuntary, and that they usually possess the quality of appearing plausible.

The semantic therapist attempts to make his client aware of negative self-statements and images, and of the anxiety-engendering, self-defeating, and self-fulfilling prophecy aspects of such thinking. The first goal of therapy is to have the patient entertain the possibility that his maladaptive behaviors and emotional upset are contributed to by what he says to himself. The therapist, after initially listening to the patient's complaints, may give the patient the assignment of listening to himself over the course of the week and conducting a situational analysis of the times at which he experiences such negative self-statements. Through careful questioning by the therapist, the patient begins to accept a cognitive conceptualization of his problem, one that is shared by the therapist. When the patient returns with examples of his negative self-statements, the therapist may ask, with some tact and skill, "Are you telling me that these kinds of thoughts are part of your problem? How do they cause you to become upset?" At this point the patient begins to provide evidence that negative self-statements are contributing to his problem. Over the course of future sessions the patient and therapist examine whether incompatible thoughts and behaviors can be used instead of the negative self-statements. The patient, in collaboration with the therapist, is likely to generate assignments not only to monitor and test his self-statements rationally but also to act differently, to engage in new interpersonal interactions. The focus of the semantic therapy at first is on the patient's ideation so that patient and therapist may have a common conceptualization of the problem, but often therapy moves quickly into a phase of behavioral rehearsal and the expression of more assertive behavior. Once the patient entertains the possibility that his maladaptive state results from what he tells himself, then a whole set of therapeutic assignments make sense and are enthusiastically engaged in. From a therapeutic point of view whether the patient did or did not actually talk to himself is less important than that he now entertain this conceptualization. (Jerome Frank, in a delightful and important book called *Persuasion and Healing* [1961], has discussed the importance of a common patient-therapist conceptual framework for the achievement of behavior change.)

Evidence for the therapeutic efficacy of semantic therapies has been offered by several investigators, including Meichenbaum, Gilmore, and Fedoravicius [1971], Trexler and Karst [1972], Goldfried, Decenteceo, and Weinberg [in press]. Meichenbaum and his associates found, for example, that both individual and group forms of RET therapy were effective in the treatment of speech-anxiety, especially for those individual clients who experienced interpersonal anxiety across a variety of settings, including that of giving a formal speech.

In *summary*, the first objective of the semantic therapist, whether an advocate of RET or some other cognitive approach, is to make the patient aware of his own thinking style and to convey to the patient a sense that he can control such thinking. Second, the therapist attempts to teach the patient, by means of rational analysis, information giving, or other procedures, a set of self-statements that are incompatible with his previous negative self-statements and a more adaptive style of behavior. Often included in the treatment package are such things as behavioral and imagined rehearsal via hierarchically arranged stressful situations, modeling, therapist praise and attention, and self-observation. Semantic therapists differ in how directive they are in achieving these goals and in how much they utilize behavioral techniques.

Finally, it is important to understand that the cognitive change that the semantic therapist helps his client to achieve is not merely a purely intellectual insight. Rather, throughout therapy the semantic therapist refers to cognitive processes that are closely tied to motivational, emotional, and behavioral variables. The cognitive therapist is sensitive to the client's feelings, and semantic therapy does indeed focus on these emotions. But it is assumed that an important element of each emotion is a cognitive component and that the modification of this component provides the avenue for behavior change.

Behavior Therapies

As we have seen, the semantic or cognitive therapist listens for the pattern of the client's thinking processes in order to discern the underlying premises, beliefs, and idiosyncratic distortions that give rise to maladaptive self-statements and maladaptive behavior. By a process of cognitive restructuring the patient is helped to reformulate his experiences more realistically, with consequent behavior change.

The behavior therapist, in contrast, approaches the task of modifying the client's cognitions or self-statements with a different set. Two general treatment strategies seem to characterize the behavior therapy approach. The first strategy, which we will examine in some detail, views the client's cognitions explicitly as behaviors to be modified in their own right. The client's covert behaviors, private events, and higher mental processes, such as ideas, self-statements, and images, are viewed as behaviors and thus are subject to the same "laws of learning" as are overt or nonprivate behaviors. Thus, the behavior modification techniques that have been used to modify overt behaviors, such as operant and aversive conditioning, modeling, and rehearsal, may be applied to covert processes. In fact, Homme [1965] has offered the concept of "coverants" (covert operants) to describe covert behaviors within a learning framework. The second strategy of behavior therapists is to focus treatment *not* on the client's maladaptive cognitions but on his maladaptive overt behaviors and to teach him a set of adaptive behaviors that are incompatible with those maladaptive overt behaviors. It is assumed that as the client learns new behavioral skills and receives reinforcement for these from significant others in his environment, his thinking style in turn will change. The latter treatment approach is illustrated by the aphorism "It is easier to act your way into a new way of thinking than it is to think your way into a new way of behaving."

Two major sources of impetus for viewing cognitions within a learning framework are the writings of John Dollard and Neal Miller [1950] and B. F. Skinner [1953]. Dollard and Miller set out to translate Freudian psychoanalytic procedures into learning theory terms. In doing so, they indicated that the client's higher mental processes, such as the labels he uses in a situation, can be viewed as "cue-producing responses" that may facilitate or inhibit subsequent responses. The labels the client employs, or the things he says to himself, are viewed as responses that in turn may be stimuli for succeeding responses. Within such a mediational view of behavior, modification of the label the client attaches to a situation can be effective in altering the individual's emotional reaction (e.g., in reducing anxiety). The labels a person assigns to his own or others' behavior are learned, and learning techniques can be explicitly employed to teach the use of new, more adaptive labels. Dollard and Miller suggest that an important consequence of changing labels and reducing anxiety is an increase in the client's problem-solving capacities. The client's newly learned "cue-producing response" leads to significant behavior change.

Skinner's operant conditioning model of self-control contends that one controls his own behavior in precisely the same way that he would control the behavior of anyone else, through manipulation of the variables of which the behavior is a function. Skinner, for example, speaks of manipulating one's own behavior, thoughts, and images just as one might do with another person, or as the environment does through its reward and punishment contingencies. To decrease an undesirable behavior in himself, one makes the undesirable response less probable by altering the rewards and punishments on which it depends. For example, a behavior therapist with an operant orientation asks, what is the immediate effect of a disruptive thought or image (e.g., a depressing or anxiety-arousing idea)? Frequently, the immediate effect is that the person labels himself depressed or anxious and hence feels he is incapable of continuing work. The net effect is that the act of thinking such thoughts often leads to escape from an unpleasant situation, and thus reinforced, the act is maintained. The operant behavior therapist suggests that one can significantly and directly influence the client's thinking processes by systematically manipulating their consequences.

Illustrative of an operant and self-management treatment approach to changing covert behaviors is a recent case reported by Michael Mahoney [1971]. The goal of behavior therapy was to increase positive self-thoughts and to decrease self-deprecatory obsessions on the part of a 22-year-old male who experienced "pervasive and uncontrollable thoughts about being brain damaged, persecuted, and odd." In the first treatment phase a self-punishment (snapping a heavy rubber band worn around the wrist) was used immediately after each negative thought. The self-punishment procedure eliminated the obsessional thoughts. Eight weeks after treatment was begun, a "priming" technique was implemented. Four index cards were attached to the client's cigarette package. The client was asked to cite some positive things about himself. Positive comments were written on three of the four cards, for example, "I'm proud of being in good physical shape"; the fourth card was blank. Before taking a cigarette he read (subvocally) the top card attached to the cigarette package, placed it on the bottom, and then reinforced himself with a cigarette. When the top card was blank, the client had to generate a new positive self-thought. The procedure greatly increased the client's frequency of positive self-thoughts in a period of seven weeks. Mahoney reported: "The client stated that spontaneous positive self-thoughts were occasionally self-reinforced with cigarettes, but that most of them constituted their own reward because of their pleasantness." Gains in self-confidence and general behavioral adjustment followed treatment.

The case reported by Mahoney is included here because it is typical of a number of case studies and experimental investigations that apply "learning principles" to the modification of covert behaviors. Note the variety of techniques: self-monitoring of negative thoughts; the self-administration of a punisher; the pairing of the production of positive thoughts with the administration of an external reinforcer; and the eventual pairing of positive ideas with self-reinforcement. Although one must be cautious in reaching conclusions based on a single case study, due to the many possible contaminating factors and the number of rival hypotheses that might also explain the behavior change, the Mahoney study does illustrate the clinical potential of applying a learning theory framework to the modification of covert behaviors.

Indeed, the Mahoney approach is only one of many methods that behavior therapists have used to alter the strength or frequency of covert behaviors. The following section briefly reviews some of these treatment approaches.

Behavior Therapy Treatment Approaches

Pairing of Covert Behaviors with External Consequences.

The behavior therapist pairs the client's expression of a maladaptive thought or image with the onset of an aversive event, and pairs the expression of a positive coping cognition with the onset of an external reinforcing event or with the termination or avoidance of an aversive event. In most cases the externally administered consequence is electric shock administered by either the therapist or the patient. An example of this approach is the anxiety-relief conditioning technique introduced by Joseph Wolpe and Arnold Lazarus. They describe the treatment paradigm as follows: "If an unpleasant stimulus is endured for several seconds and is then made to cease almost immediately after a specified signal, that signal will become conditioned to the changes that follow cessation of the uncomfortable stimulus" [1966, p. 149]. Typically, the word "calm" or "relax" is the signal that is paired with the cessation of aversive stimulation (usually electric shock). Theoretically, the self-instruction "calm" takes on counterconditioning, anxiety-relief qualities that generalize across situations. The notion is that the client will be able to reduce his anxiety level in virtually any situation by instructing himself to be "calm" and thus evoking the conditioned "relief"

response. The anxiety-relief qualities of the self-instruction are enhanced by the conditioning process. A number of investigators have presented data that demonstrate the therapeutic value of such anxiety-relief techniques in alleviating phobic and obsessive behaviors [Solyom & Miller 1967; Thorpe et al. 1964].

An example of this approach is a recent study by Meichenbaum and Cameron [1973] who demonstrated that an elaborate anxiety-relief conditioning procedure can be successfully employed in treating snake-phobic adults [1973a]. The anxiety-relief conditioning procedure was arranged as follows: the therapist said the cue word "snake"; the client then verbalized the self-statements, thoughts, and descriptive images he experienced when confronted by a snake ("It's ugly"; "It's slimy"; "I won't look at it"; etc.). Following expression of these self-statements, electric shock was administered by the therapist to the client, thus punishing the anxiety-inducing, avoidant self-statements. The instrumental response used by the client to terminate shock (and in later sessions, to avoid onset of shock) was a set of positive coping self-instructions (e.g., "Relax"; "I can touch it"; "One step at a time."). The anxiety-relief conditioning treatment was successful in reducing the client's persistent avoidant behaviors.

In the anxiety-relief conditioning procedure the behavior therapist is treating the client's maladaptive ideations as behaviors, subjecting them to specific stimulus consequences. In a similar fashion, the Mahoney case study, described above, illustrates how the client can pair positive cognitions with the self-administration of external reinforcement, such as cigarettes, food, or money.

Pairing of Covert Behaviors with Other Covert Behaviors.

In the same way that one can make the onset and cessation of external stimuli contingent upon the production of the client's cognition, one can have the client make an aversive or reinforcing *covert* event, such as an image, contingent upon the production of a cognition. Joseph Cautela [1973] and his associates have demonstrated this in covert sensitization and covert reinforcement procedures. In the covert sensitization procedure the client is asked to image the maladaptive behavior (i.e., the behavior the client wants to control, for example, smoking, overeating, or drinking alcohol) and then the client is asked to imagine in detail a noxious or aversive scene, such as becoming sick and vomiting. For example, a client who wishes to stop smoking is instructed to imagine the following:

> As soon as you start reaching for the cigarette, you get a nauseous feeling in your stomach, like you are about to vomit. You touch the package and bitter spit comes into your mouth. When you take the cigarette out of the pack, some pieces of food come into your throat. Now you feel sick and have stomach cramps. As you are about to put the cigarette in your mouth, you puke all over the cigarettes, all over your hand. The cigarette in your hand is very soggy and full of green vomit. Snots are coming from your nose. Your clothes are full of puke [etc.] [p. 23].

The conditioning process of contiguously pairing the two images of smoking and vomiting results in a significant reduction of the maladaptive behavior. One can apply the same covert conditioning paradigm to the strengthening of desirable behaviors by covert reinforcement. The client now images a desirable behavior, which is to be strengthened by contiguous association with a rewarding scene. For example, a shy male client may be asked to pair the image of himself calling a girl for a date with a pleasant rewarding scene, such as swimming on a hot day in refreshing water and feeling wonderful. In addition to the covert sensitization and covert positive reinforcement procedures, Cautela has suggested the use of covert negative reinforcement and covert extinction as modification techniques.

Another interesting case was reported by Davison [1968], who trained a male college student to eliminate sexual fantasies of a sadistic nature by pairing these fantasies with images of a nauseating nature. Normal sexual fantasies were encouraged and strengthened by having the patient masturbate while looking at *Playboy* sexy pictures, while the sadistic fantasies were eliminated by their association with the obnoxious images.

The therapeutic potential of having patients contiguously associate two ideas or images is also illustrated by a procedure called emotive imagery [Lazarus & Abramovitz 1962]. The procedure, used mainly with children to alleviate phobic responses, pairs a pleasant affective state — which is instilled by means of an engrossing fantasy image — with a gradual introduction of anxiety-eliciting stimuli into fantasy. Thus, an attempt is made to change the meaning or anxiety-eliciting qualities of a given set of stimuli by pairing them with set of incompatible thoughts and feelings.

Staats [1972], in reviewing language behavior therapy studies, found a number of studies that illustrate that one can indeed change the "meaning" of a given stimulus word or image by consistently pairing it with a positive set of words. Two illustrations of the language conditioning procedure are the studies by Early [1968] on social isolation of children in school and by Hekmat and Vanian [1971] on snake phobics. The problem of social isolation was solved by changing the attitudes (emotional responses) of the isolates' classmates toward the names of the isolates; positive emotional words were paired with each isolate's name. Similarly, with snake phobics, pairing the image of a snake with positive emotional words for over a hundred trials, a significant reduction in snake avoidance and a more positive attitude toward snakes was achieved. Indeed, a number of other treatment techniques have been developed to foster behavior change by having the client juxtapose covert events (i.e., thoughts and images).

Pairing of Covert Behaviors with an Overt Behavior.

The basic treatment strategy is to pair the experience of a covert event such as a thought or image with a behavioral act of the client. The behavior or response usually chosen is bodily relaxation, which is incompatible with the experience of anxiety. The best known behavior therapy procedure, systematic desensitization, pairs the client's anxiety-inducing cognition with the experience of relaxation. In counterconditioning terminology, the ability of a given stimulus to evoke anxiety is permanently weakened, says Joseph Wolpe, if "a response antagonistic to anxiety can be made to occur in the presence of anxiety-evoking stimuli so that it is accompanied by complete or partial suppression of the anxiety responses" [1958, p. 71]. The incompatible response is relaxation, which is achieved by means of progressive training exercises. While the client is relaxed, he is asked to image in turn scenes ranked earlier in order of increasing anxiety. It is by this counterconditioning or pairing process of imaging an anxiety-eliciting scene and relaxing that behavior change is supposed to occur. Although there is a great deal of controversy over the mechanisms by which desensitization operates (e.g., see Goldfried [1971]; Locke [1971]; Paul & Bernstein [1973]; Weitzman [1967]), the technique does illustrate the therapeutic procedure of modifying behavior by directly influencing the client's cognitions. Interestingly, in vivo or live desensitization, especially when supplemented by modeling, has been found to be even more effective in alleviating phobic behaviors.

A number of variants of the desensitization treatment procedure have been offered. One of the more interesting is a procedure called dynamic behavior therapy [Feather & Rhoads 1972]. Instead of having the client image real life scenes while relaxed, the client is asked to image the fantasy that often underlies the phobic or anxiety condition. The therapist elicits the client's fantasies by asking him what is the worst thing that could happen if he were confronted by the phobic situation. For example, a speech-anxious subject might offer a fantasy of getting so angry with himself and the audience that he loses control and hurts someone. It is to this fantasy that the client is then desensitized. Feather and Rhoads argue that in many instances the client is phobic to his own ideation and that much of the client's behavior is a learned avoidance of experiencing such thoughts. The distinction between reality and fantasy, and the control of fantasy are achieved by having the client image the fantasies while relaxed. The author of this essay treated a radio broadcaster for microphone phobia by such a procedure. It turned out that the client was phobic not to some specific external stimulus event but to the fantasy that he would blurt out on the air that he was a homosexual.

Following the same principle of pairing covert events and overt behaviors, one can pair the expression of a self-instruction such as "relax" with the instrumental response of relaxing. A number of years ago, Dorothy Yates [1946] described an association set technique that essentially involved giving the client the set that he could relax by thinking of a soothing word, such as "calm," or a pleasant image.

Clients were encouraged to rehearse concentrating on the key word or image while relaxed, and to fasten upon the word or image in disturbing situations to counteract stress. She reported that a wide variety of patients improved after being taught this procedure. Similarly, Cautela [1966] taught patients to say to themselves, "I am calm and relaxed," while giving themselves a relaxation session, especially in anticipating a stressful situation. The clients reported "in a while that the mere words calmed them down." Kahn, Baker, and Weiss [1968] successfully used a similar procedure in the treatment of insomnia.

Jerome Singer [1972], in an excellent review article on imagery techniques, reports a rather old but fascinating study of the therapeutic potential of manipulating cognitive processes. Chappell and Stevenson [1936] trained a group of peptic ulcer patients to control body processes by having them image a pleasant experience each time they became anxious. Compared to an untreated control group of peptic ulcer patients, the cognitive training group showed a marked reduction in symptomatology and ulceration, and even after a three-year followup only two of twenty-eight experimental subjects had serious symptom recurrences. Since all patients had been ill with ulcer symptoms for a minimum of two years before treatment, the effectiveness of the "positive imagery" technique is impressive.

This brief review of the behavior therapy literature illustrates the therapeutic potential of directly modifying the client's cognitive processes. We have seen that behavior change can be achieved by contiguously associating the client's covert events with external stimuli, with other covert events, and with overt behaviors. Central to each of the behavior therapy procedures is an active self-monitoring process on the part of the client. In the early phases of therapy the client is taught how to conduct a situational analysis of his presenting problem, noting both the internal and external cues that trigger the maladaptive thoughts and behaviors, and the consequences or secondary gains that the client realizes from the maladaptive behavior. Then, the client and therapist together consider the incompatible adaptive thoughts and behaviors that the client can now emit. In order to accomplish such a situational analysis the client is often given the assignment of self-monitoring his urges, thoughts, images, and behaviors (e.g., by counting, graphing, keeping a diary, etc.). There is evidence that making explicit records of one's behavior is in itself a substantial intervention procedure that often results in behavior change. After this initial phase of treatment, the behavior therapist may then decide, with the client, whether treatment intervention should focus on modifying the client's thinking patterns, learning new behavioral skills, or manipulating the consequences of the problem behavior. Thus, the behavior therapist has many options and a varied clinical armamentarium upon which to draw. Often the behavior therapist uses a variety of clinical procedures in combination.

Finally, as one looks at the complex treatment options available to the therapist, it should become more and more obvious that it is impossible to proceed therapeutically along a single dimension, cognitive or behavioral. The distinction between "cognitive therapy" and "behavior therapy" is becoming more fuzzy all the time and indeed may be indistinguishable. "There may be highly specific interventions which have a behavioral or cognitive focus, but these are always embedded in a multidimensional context or have multiple consequences" [Bergin 1970, p. 208]. Even in a behavior therapy procedure such as operant conditioning, the subject's personal valuations of the experimenter's reinforcement influence the effectiveness of the treatment procedures (for example, see work by de Charms [1968]; Deci [1971]; and Steiner [1970]). A combination of procedures seems to represent best the true nature of the cognitive behavior modification process.

Some Criticisms of Behavior Therapies

Since the systematic experimental investigation of behavior therapy procedures is in its infancy, definitive conclusions regarding their efficacy cannot yet be drawn. Strong claims by both proponents and opponents are premature. One promising sign, however, is the commitment of behavior therapists to subject their procedures to experimental assessment. In the field of psychotherapy such an attitude has been all too infrequent. Almost all forms of psychotherapy have been introduced by charismatic figures (e.g., Freud, Jung, Adler, Ellis, Perls, Wolpe),

after which a "school" appears, with the accompanying fanfare, initial favorable results, sometimes accreditation procedures, etc. Objective assessment is not usually part of the entourage. Semantic and behavior therapies are not untouched by such criticisms. Perhaps by combining the rigor of the laboratory with clinical sensitivity the adequacy of behavior therapy treatment procedures can be determined. As Paul and Bernstein have indicated, the goal of treatment research is to find out "What treatment, by whom, is most effective for this individual with that specific problem under which set of circumstances?" [1973, p. 25].

A second criticism that has been leveled at behavior therapies is that, in fact, a learning theory approach is inadequate to explain the complex treatment techniques that behavior therapists employ. This criticism arises from a logical analysis of the definitions of stimuli, responses, and reinforcement as applied to covert events and from a recognition that there are a variety of learning theories, not merely the concepts underlying operant and classical conditioning (see, for example, Breger & McGaugh [1965]). A second source for this criticism comes from clinical observations of clients' reactions to specific treatment procedures, such as desensitization. Weitzman [1967], for example, reports that clients' images in the desensitization procedures do not function in the start-stop fashion often described by behavior therapists; rather, therapeutic change derives from a far more complex cognitive fantasy process. The same criticism may apply to other imagery procedures, such as Cautela's covert sensitization and covert reinforcement. What is going on when we ask a shy college student to imagine calling a girl for a date and then to imagine himself swimming? Can such cognitions be viewed simply within a stimulus-response model?

Perhaps the most telling criticism of a learning theory explanation of behavior therapy procedures comes from empirical investigations that have explicitly attempted to assess the underlying bases of the therapy procedures. For example, a number of investigators have assessed the importance of contingency of electric shock in aversive conditioning. If the efficacy of the treatment procedure is based on the learning principles claimed, then the sequence of the client's behavior or cognition and shock onset and cessation would be important to treatment outcome. However, if backward aversive conditioning or inverted anxiety-relief conditioning proves just as effective as straightforward conditioning, then some alternative explanation for behavior change may be required. Indeed, Carlin and Armstrong [1968] have reported that smokers treated in a noncontingent shock group showed significantly greater reduction in smoking than smokers treated according to a traditional aversive conditioning paradigm. McConaghy and Barr [1973] found that homosexuals who received inverted conditioning (i.e., for whom shock cessation was paired with onset of a "male" slide) improved as much as homosexuals who received straight aversive conditioning. Meichenbaum and Cameron [1973a] found that phobics exposed to an inverted anxiety-relief conditioning paradigm — in which shock onset was contingent upon coping self-statements and shock cessation was contingent upon anxiety-engendering, fear-avoidant self-statements — responded as well as did clients who received simple conditioning [1973a].

The validity of a learning theory explanation has been called into question with other behavior therapy procedures as well — for example, the mechanisms underlying such techniques as flooding or implosion therapy and stopping maladaptive thoughts [Marks 1973]. In flooding, phobic clients are asked to image intensely extreme phobic scenes; for example, a snake-phobic client may be asked to image being attacked and consumed by hundreds of snakes. Marks et al. [1971] report that asking such clients instead to image any intense emotional scene that is not related to the phobic scene, such as being attacked in a zoo by an escaped tiger, is as effective in reducing the phobic response. In the thought-stopping procedure the obsessive patient is trained to instruct himself to "stop" or to administer an electric shock while having obsessive thoughts. Marks [1973] reports that therapy which teaches the obsessive client to use the thought-stopping procedure with nonobsessive or neutral thoughts is just as effective as therapy that teaches thought stoppage with obsessive thoughts.

If learning theory concepts are open to question as explanations for behavior therapy procedures, then what other alternatives are available? One set of explanations, including social learning theory, dissonance theory, attribution theory, self-perception theory, and others, have as a common element their emphasis on the client's appraisal of the therapeutic process and on his perceptions of his ability to cope. Another source of explanations is client's descriptions of what is occurring in behavior therapy. For example, the phobic clients in the Meichenbaum and Cameron study [1973a], who received an inverted or backward anxiety-relief conditioning procedure that included exposure to an electric shock, reported that the treatment helped them to develop a general skill for coping with stress. Similarly, the clients in the Marks studies [Marks 1973; Marks et al. 1971] seemed to view the behavior therapy procedures as forms of self-regulation or coping training, which they could employ in other stressful situations. Perhaps, then, behavior therapies may be construed as techniques for teaching basic self-control skills by which the client can become his own therapist. This view is consistent with a recent analysis of the behavior therapy literature by Murray and Jacobson [1971]. They suggest that what the client learns in behavior therapy is a complex set of cognitive and behavioral skills that includes (1) changes in nonadaptive beliefs, which occur by means of a succession of nonconfirming experiences in the therapeutic interaction; (2) changes in one's self-concept and in the belief he has about others, which occurs by means of information learning; and (3) the development of new problem-solving skills and new interpersonal behavior skills. Skills-oriented therapy is another set of procedures that have been employed to modify what the client says to himself. This type of approach is outlined in the following section.

Skills-Oriented Therapy

The basic treatment strategy in skills-oriented therapy is to teach the client cognitive, behavioral, and interpersonal skills and then to provide opportunities for application of training either within the therapy setting or in real-life situations. The therapist attempts to teach the client a set of coping responses that he can apply in a variety of settings. The focus of therapy is to have the client become a better problem-solver so that when he is confronted by stress-inducing situations in the future he will be able to handle them adequately without need for professional help. In some sense, the client is trained to become his own therapist. The entire technology of behavior and semantic therapies, including modeling, cognitive-behavioral-imaginal rehearsal, rational analysis, informational learning, and other techniques, is directed to teaching the client new skills.

One can think of learning such skills in the same fashion as one learns motor skills, such as driving a car. Initially, the driver actively goes through a conscious mental checklist, sometimes aloud, which includes control or shifting of attention away from anxiety-engendering thoughts, verbal and imaginal rehearsal, cognitive self-guidance, and sometimes appropriate self-reinforcement, especially when driving a stick-shift car. Only with repetition and growing proficiency do the driver's cognitions become short-circuited and the cognitive and behavioral sequence become automatic and unconscious.

If this analogy has any merit, then a training procedure that makes the various steps explicit should facilitate the development of self-control and result in behavior change. Meichenbaum and his colleagues [Meichenbaum 1973b; Meichenbaum & Cameron 1974] have demonstrated that a cognitive self-guidance treatment program is helpful in teaching both attentional controls and general self-control to such varied populations as hyperactive impulsive school children, institutionalized adult schizophrenics, high test-anxiety college students, and low-creativity adults.

The cognitive self-guidance treatment consists of having the therapist model thinking patterns aloud and the client overtly and subsequently covertly rehearse the modeled self-statements. The logic of this procedure is the following: if the therapist can perform a task that the client cannot perform, then he should introspectively determine the thoughts, strategies, rules, etc., that he (the therapist) is employing to do the task. These cognitions can be translated into explicit self-statements to be modeled for and then rehearsed by the client. The therapist attempts to teach private speech or thinking styles by means of small steps and successive approximations. Operationally, the treatment proceeds as follows: first, the therapist performs a task while thinking aloud as the client observes (modeling phase); then

the client is asked to perform the same task while the therapist instructs the client aloud; then the client is asked to perform the task again while instructing himself aloud; then the client performs the task while whispering; and finally the client performs the task while instructing himself covertly. The verbalizations and images that the therapist models and the client rehearses include: (1) questions about the nature of the task; (2) answers to these questions in the form of cognitive rehearsal and planning; (3) guidance of performance by self-instruction; and (4) coping self-statements to deal with frustrations, uncertainty, and anxiety; and (5) self-reinforcement. In this way, the client is trained to develop a new cognitive approach or learning set in which he can size up the demands of a task, cognitively rehearse and "psych himself up," guide his performance by self-instructions, and finally, appropriately reinforce himself.

Interestingly, this training sequence parallels the developmental process, described by Soviet psychologists Vygotsky and Luria, by which the child's private speech comes to exert a regulatory and socializing influence on his behavior. Initially, it is the speech of others that exerts control over the growing child's behavior; then this speech is repeated by the child, initially aloud and subsequently covertly (to use Vygotsky's terms, the speech "becomes internalized" and "goes underground"). Although there is some controversy about whether self-control does evolve by such stages, the hypothetical sequence does lend itself to a most productive treatment program.

Although one might initially conjecture otherwise, teaching such explicit thinking styles appears to increase the client's creativity in approaching problems. This has been demonstrated in a program of research conducted by D'Zurilla and Goldfried [1971], which indicated that explicitly teaching clients problem-solving skills results not only in a reduction in the presenting problem but in creative application of these newly learned cognitive skills to other life problems. The training included helping the client to adopt a problem-solving set suited to his maladaptive behaviors and developing skills in specifying his problems, generating alternatives, and generating and verifying decisions. The clinical importance of such a problem-solving, skills-oriented treatment approach is indicated by the growing body

Table 1. *Examples of self-instructional statements used in creativity training*

Set-inducing Self-statements

(a) **What to do**
Be creative, be unique.
Break away from the obvious, the commonplace.
Think of something no one else will think of.
Just be free-wheeling.
If you push yourself you can be creative.
Quantity helps breed quality.

(b) **What not to do**
Get rid of internal blocks.
Defer judgments.
Don't worry about what others think.
Not a matter of right or wrong.
Don't give the first answer you think of.
No negative self-statements.

Self-statements arising from a mental-abilities conceptualization

---

(a) Problem analysis — what you say to yourself before you start a problem
Size up problem; what is it you have to do?
You have to put elements together differently.
Use different analogies.
Do the task as if you were Osborn brainstorming or Gordon of Synectics training.
Elaborate on ideas.
Make the strange familiar or the familiar strange.

(b) Task execution — what you say to yourself while doing a task
You're in a rut — okay try something new.
How can you use this frustration to be more creative?
Take a rest now; who knows when the ideas will visit again.
Go slow — no hurry — no need to press.
Good — you're getting it.
This is fun.
That was a pretty neat answer; wait till you tell the others!

Self-statements arising from a psychoanalytic conceptualization

---

Release controls; let your mind wander
Free-associate; let ideas flow
Relax — just let it happen
Let your ideas play
Ideas will be a surprise
Refer to your experience; just view it differently
Let your ego regress
Feel like a bystander through whom ideas are just flowing
Let one answer lead to another
Almost dreamlike, the ideas have a life of their own

---

of literature that demonstrates that clinical populations are characterized by poor problem-solving capacities [McGuire & Sifneos 1970; Platt & Spivack 1972; Shure & Spivack 1972].

An even more direct demonstration that teaching thinking styles may release an individual's creativity is the recent study in which Meichenbaum [1973a] attempted to enhance creativity by explicitly modifying what college students say to themselves. Each of three major conceptualizations of creativity represented in the literature was translated into a set of self-statements that could be modeled by a therapist and then practiced by clients on meaningful self-selected tasks. Table 1 illustrates the variety of self-statements used in training. The self-instructional training groups showed enhanced creativity relative to appropriate control groups. Moreover, the cognitive self-instructional training engendered a generalized set to handle life situations in a more creative fashion. The clients reported that they had spontaneously applied the creativity training to a variety of personal and academic problems.

The literature on psychotherapy is replete with examples of skills-oriented treatment procedures. A recently developed procedure, which will serve to illustrate such therapy, is called stress inoculation training [Meichenbaum 1973b]. The training was designed to accomplish three goals. The first was to educate the client about the nature of stress or fear reactions; the second, to have the client rehearse various coping behaviors; and finally, to give the client an opportunity to practice his new coping skills in a stressful situation.

The educational phase defined the client's anxiety in terms of Schachter's model of emotion [Schachter & Singer 1962]; that is, the therapist reflected that the client's fear or anxiety reaction seemed to involve two major elements, heightened arousal (e.g., increased heart rate, sweaty palms, body tension) and a set of anxiety-engendering thoughts and images. The therapist then suggested that treatment would be directed helping the client to control his physiological arousal by learning how to physically relax and learn how to replace his self-statements with more productive ones. Table 2 illustrates the self-statements the client rehearsed. This package of self-statements, like those for creativity training, was generated in full collaboration with the client. In

Table 2. *Examples of coping self-statements rehearsed in stress inoculation training*

Preparing for a Stressor

What is it you have to do?
You can develop a plan to deal with it.
Just think about what you can do about it. That's better than getting anxious.
No negative self-statements; just think rationally.
Don't worry; worry won't help anything.
Maybe what you think is anxiety is eagerness to confront it.

Confronting and Handling a Stressor

Just "psych" yourself up — you can meet this challenge.
One step at a time; you can handle the situation.
Don't think about fear; just think about what you have to do. Stay relevant.
This anxiety is what the doctor said you would feel. It's a reminder to use your coping exercises.
This tenseness can be an ally, a cue to cope.
Relax; you're in control. Take a slow deep breath. Ah, good.

Coping with the Feeling of Being Overwhelmed

When fear comes, just pause.
Keep the focus on the present; what is it you have to do?
Label your fear from 0 to 10 and watch it change.
You should expect your fear to rise.
Don't try to eliminate fear totally; just keep it manageable.
You can convince yourself to do it. You can reason your fear away.
It will be over shortly.
It's not the worst thing that can happen.
Just think about something else.
Do something that will prevent you from thinking about fear.
Describe what is around you. That way you won't think about worrying.

Reinforcing Self-statements

It worked; you did it.
Wait until you tell your therapist about this.
It wasn't as bad as you expected.
You made more out of the fear than it was worth.
Your damn ideas — that's the problem. When you control them, you control your fear.
It's getting better each time you use the procedures.
You can be pleased with the progress you're making.
You did it!

---

fact, the client helped generate a broad list and then was given an opportunity to "try on" various self-statements, picking for rehearsal those that worked best for him. Once he had mastered such coping skills, the client (e.g., a phobic) was given an opportunity to apply the coping mechanisms in a stress-inducing situation that involved a stressor unrelated to the presenting problem (e.g., receiving unpredictable electric shocks).

The stress inoculation training procedure is a complex, multifaceted treatment package. It attempts (1) to modify the client's appraisal of the fearful situation and of his ability to cope; (2) to teach the client specific skills, and (3) to provide him with an opportunity for application of training. The skills-training treatment approach was designed to translate the client's sense of "learned helplessness" into a feeling of "learned resourcefulness" so that he could cope with any stress-inducing situation.

Given the increasing demand upon individuals to deal with stress, the possibility of using stress inoculation training for prophylactic purposes is most exciting. The notion of arming the client with a defense he can use against anxiety is in some respects analogous to immunization against attitude change or medical inoculation against disease. The underlying principle in all these situations is that a person's resistance is enhanced by exposure to a stimulus that is strong enough to arouse the defenses but not so powerful as to overcome them. An examination of the way this principle is applied by social psychologists and physicians may suggest methods for refining and improving stress inoculation. For instance, it may prove helpful to expose the client to a variety of stressors (e.g., cold pressor test, stress-inducing films, fear-inducing imagery, deprivation conditions, fatigue, etc.). Presumably, the more varied and extensive the training, the greater the likelihood the client will develop a general learning set, a general way of talking to himself in order to cope. Films demonstrating cognitive coping can also be used to facilitate learning. There seems to be much promise in the possibility of explicitly teaching even nonclinical populations to cope by such diverse techniques as altering attributions and self-labels, imagery rehearsal, shifting attention, distractions, self-instructions, and relaxation, or to do what Janis [1958] calls the "work of worrying."

Comparisons between skills-training procedures and standard behavior therapies have indicated that greater therapeutic benefit, broader application of behavior change, and longer persistence of behavior improvement results from skills-training treatment programs. As already indicated, one problem with behavior therapy procedures has been the absence of generalization from treatment to other situations. For example, phobic clients desensitized to one phobic object often fail to generalize to another phobic object. Disruptive school children who are exposed to an operant conditioning program may shape up in the treatment class but often do not show improvement in other, nontreatment classrooms. Lang [1968] has indicated that the frequent lack of transfer effects in part results from failure to shape cognitive sets and attitudes in addition to overt behaviors. The skills-training programs are designed explicitly to change the client's cognitive set, and the results indicate that

doing so significantly increases generalization of treatment effects. The client's cognitive set and self-statements are indeed subject to modification by means of semantic and behavior therapies.

By now, the reader should be talking to himself in a task-relevant fashion about the clinical potentials of modifying what clients say to themselves. As Farber has stated, "The one thing psychologists can count on is that their subjects or clients will talk, if only to themselves; and not infrequently, whether relevant or irrelevant, the things people say to themselves determine the rest of the things they do" [1963, p. 336]. Cognitive behavior modification is designed to influence the nature of the client's internal dialogue.

BIBLIOGRAPHY

Richard J. Bandler, Jr., George R. Madaras, and Daryl J. Bem, "Self Observation as a Source of Pain Perception." *Journal of Personality and Social Psychology,* 1968, 9:205–209.

Aaron Beck, "Cognitive Therapy: Nature and Relation to Behavior Therapy." *Behavior Therapy,* 1970a, 1:184–200.

Aaron Beck, "Role of Fantasies in Psychotherapy and Psychopathology." *Journal of Nervous and Mental Disease,* 1970b, 150:3–17.

Allen Bergin, "Cognitive Therapy and Behavior Therapy: Foci for a Multidimensional Approach to Treatment." *Behavior Therapy,* 1970, 1:205–212.

Allan Blumenthal, "The Base of Objectivist Psychotherapy." *The Objectivist,* June 1969, 3–11.

Louis Breger and James L. McGaugh, "Critique and Reformulation of 'Learning Theory' Approaches to Psychotherapy and Neurosis." *Psychological Bulletin,* 1965, 63:338–358.

Albert S. Carlin and Hubert E. Armstrong, Jr., "Aversive Conditioning: Learning or Dissonance Reduction?" *Journal of Consulting and Clinical Psychology,* 1968, 32:674–678.

Joseph Cautela, "A Behavior Therapy Approach to Pervasive Anxiety." *"Behaviour Research and Therapy,* 1966, 4:99–111.

Joseph Cautela, "Covert Processes and Behavior Modification." *Journal of Nervous and Mental Disease,* 1973, 157:27–35.

M. Chappell and T. Stevenson, "Group Psychological Training in Some Organic Conditions." *Mental Hygiene,* 1936, 20:588–597.

Norman L. Corah and Joseph Boffa, "Perceived Control, Self-observation and Response to Aversive Stimulation." *Journal of Personality and Social Psychology,* 1970, 16:1–14.

Emil Coue, *The Practice of Autosuggestion.* Doubleday, 1922.

Gerald Davison, "Elimination of Sadistic Fantasy by a Client-controlled Counterconditioning Technique: A Case Study." *Journal of Abnormal Psychology,* 1968, 73:84–90.

Richard de Charms, *Personal Causation: The Internal Affective Determinants of Behavior.* Academic Press, 1968.

Edward Deci, "The Effects of Externally Mediated Rewards on Intrinsic Motivation." *Journal of Personality and Social Psychology,* 1971, 18:105–115.

John Dollard and Neal E. Miller, *Personality and Psychotherapy.* McGraw-Hill, 1950.

Thomas D'Zurilla and Marvin Goldfried, "Problem Solving and Behavior Modification." *Journal of Abnormal Psychology,* 1971, 78:107–126.

C. Joan Early, "Attitude Learning in Children." *Journal of Educational Psychology,* 1968, 59:176–180.

Albert Ellis, *Reason and Emotion in Psychotherapy.* Lyle Stuart Press, 1961.

Albert Ellis, "Emotional Education in the Classroom: The Living School." *Journal of Clinical Child Psychology,* 1971, 1, 19–22.

I. E. Farber, "The Things People Say to Themselves." *American Psychologist,* 1963, 18:185–197.

Ben W. Feather and John M.. Rhoads, "Psychodynamic Behavior Therapy: I. Theory and Rationale." *Archives of General Psychiatry,* 1972, 26:496–502.

Jerome Frank, *Persuasion and Healing.* Johns Hopkins Press, 1961.

David C. Glass and Jerome E. Singer, *Stress and Adaptation: Experimental Studies of Behavioral Effects of Exposure to Aversive Events.* Academic Press, 1972.

David C. Glass, Jerome E. Singer, and Lucy N. Friedman, "Psychic Cost of Adaptation to an Environmental Stressor." *Journal of Personality and Social Psychology,* 1969, 12:200–210.

Marvin Goldfried, "Systematic Desensitization as Training in Self-control." *Journal of Consulting and Clinical Psychology,* 1971, 37:228–234.

Marvin Goldfried, Edwin Decenteceo, and Leslie Weinberg, "Systematic Rational Restructuring as a Self-control Technique." *Behavior Therapy,* in press.

Hamid Hekmat and Daniel Vanian, "Behavior Modification through Covert Semantic Desensitization." *Journal of Consulting and Clinical Psychology,* 1971, 36:248–251.

Jack E. Hokanson, Douglas E. DeGood, Marvin S. Forrest, and Thomas M. Brittain, "Availability of Avoidance Behaviors in Modulating Vascular Stress Responses." *Journal of Personality and Social Psychology,* 1971, 19:60–68.

Lloyd Homme, "Perspectives in Psychology: Control of Coverants, the Operants of the Mind." *Psychological Record,* 1965, 15:501–511.

Irving Janis, *Psychological Stress.* Wiley, 1958.

Wendell Johnson, *People in Quandaries.* Harper, 1946.

Michael Kahn, Bruce L. Baker, and Jay M. Weiss, "Treatment of Insomnia by Relaxation Training." *Journal of Abnormal Psychology,* 1968, 73:556–558.

George Kelly, *The Psychology of Personal Constructs* (2 vols.). Norton, 1955.

Alfred Korzybski, *Science and Sanity.* Lancaster Press, 1933.

Peter Lang, "Fear Reduction and Fear Behavior: Problems in Treating a Construct." In J. M. Schlein, ed., *Research in Psychotherapy,* Vol. III. American Psychological Association, 1968.

Arnold Lazarus, *Behavior Therapy and Beyond.* McGraw-Hill, 1972.

Arnold Lazarus and Arnold Abramovitz, "The Use of 'Emotive Imagery' in the Treatment of Children's Phobias." *Journal of Mental Science,* 1962, 108:191–195.

Richard Lazarus and Elizabeth Alfert, "Short-circuiting of Threat by Experimentally Altering Cognitive Appraisal." *Journal of Abnormal and Social Psychology,* 1964, 69:195–205.

Richard Lazarus and James Averill, "Emotion and Cognition: With Special Reference to Anxiety." In Charles Speilberger, ed., *Anxiety: Current Trends in Theory and Research,* Vol. II. Academic Press, 1972.

Richard Lazarus, Edward M. Opton, Jr., Markellos S. Nomikos, and Neil O. Rankin, "The Principle of Short-circuiting of Threat: Further Evidence." *Journal of Personality,* 1965, 33:622–635.

Herbert Lefcourt, "The Function of the Illusions of Control and Freedom." *American Psychologist,* 1973, 28:417–425.

Edwin Locke, "Is 'Behavior Therapy' Behavioristic? (An Analysis of Wolpe's Psychotherapeutic Methods)." *Psychological Bulletin,* 1971, 76:318–327.

Michael Mahoney, "The Self-Management of Covert Behaviors: A Case Study." *Behavior Therapy,* 1971, 2:575–579.

Isaac Marks, "New Approaches to the Treatment of Obsessive Compulsive Disorders." *Journal of Nervous and Mental Disease,* 1973, 156:420–426.

Isaac Marks, John Boulougouris, and Pedro Marset, "Flooding Versus Desensitization in the Treatment of Phobic Patients." *British Journal of Psychiatry,* 1971, 119:353–375.

N. McConaghy and R. F. Barr, "Classical, Avoidance and Backward Conditioning Treatments of Homosexuality." *British Journal of Psychiatry,* 1973, 122:151–162.

Michael McGuire and Peter Sifneos, "Problem Solving in Psychotherapy." *Psychiatric Quarterly,* 1970, 44:667–673.

Donald Meichenbaum, "Enhancing Creativity by Modifying What Subjects Say to Themselves." Unpublished manuscript, University of Waterloo, 1973a.

Donald Meichenbaum, "Cognitive Factors in Behavior Modification: Modifying What Clients Say to Themselves" In Cyril Franks and Terence Wilson, eds., *Annual Review of Behavior Therapy: Theory and Practice.* Bruner/Mazel, 1973b.

Donald Meichenbaum, "A Self-Instructional Approach to Stress Management: A Proposal for Stress Inoculation Training." In Charles Speilberger and Irwin Sarason, eds., *Stress and Anxiety in Modern Life*. Winston and Sons, in press.

Donald Meichenbaum and Roy Cameron, "An Examination of Cognitive and Contingency Variables in Anxiety Relief Procedures." Unpublished manuscript, University of Waterloo, 1973a.

Donald Meichenbaum and Roy Cameron, "Training Schizophrenics to Talk to Themselves: A Means of Developing Attentional Controls." *Behavior Therapy*, 1973b, 4:515–534.

Donald Meichenbaum and Roy Cameron, "The Clinical Potential of Modifying What Clients Say to Themselves." In Carl Thoresen and Michael Mahoney, eds., *Self-Control, Power to the Person*, Brooks-Cole, 1974.

Donald Meichenbaum, Barney Gilmore, and Al Fedoravicius, "Group Insight Versus Group Desensitization in Treating Speech Anxiety." *Journal of Consulting and Clinical Psychology*, 1971, 36:410–421.

Donald Meichenbaum and Joseph Goodman, "Training Impulsive Children to Talk to Themselves: A Means of Developing Self-control." *Journal of Abnormal Psychology*, 1971, 77:115–126.

Edward Murray and Leonard Jacobson, "The Nature of Learning in Traditional Psychotherapy." In Allen Bergin and Sol Garfield, eds., *Handbook of Psychotherapy and Behavior Change*. Wiley, 1971.

Richard Nisbett and Stanley Schachter, "Cognitive Manipulation of Pain." *Journal of Experimental Social Psychology*, 1966, 2:227–236.

Gordon L. Paul and Douglas A. Bernstein, *Anxiety and Clinical Problems: Systematic Desensitization and Related Techniques*. General Learning Press, 1973.

E. Phillips, *Psychotherapy: A Modern Theory and Practice*. Prentice-Hall, 1957.

Jerome Platt and George Spivack, "Problem Solving Thinking of Psychiatric Patients." *Journal of Consulting and Clinical Psychology*, 1972, 39:148–151.

David C. Rimm and Stuart B. Litvak, "Self-Verbalization and Emotional Arousal," *Journal of Abnormal Psychology*, 1969, 74:181–187.

Irwin Sarason, "Experimental Approaches to Test Anxiety: Attention and the Uses of Information." In Charles Speilberger, ed., *Anxiety: Current Trends in Theory and Research,* Vol. II. Academic Press, 1972.

Stanley Schachter and Jerome E. Singer, "Cognitive, Social and Physiological Determinants of Emotional State." *Psychological Review*, 1962, 69:379–399.

Stanley Schachter and Ladd Wheeler, "Epinephrine, Chloropromazine and Amusement." 1962, 65:121–128.

Martin Seligman, S. Maier, Richard Solomon, "Unpredictable and Uncontrollable Events." In F. Robert Brush, ed., *Aversive Conditioning and Learning*. Academic Press, 1969.

Laurance F. Shaffer, "The Problem of Psychotherapy." *American Psychologist*, 1947, 2:459–467.

Myrna Shure and George Spivack, "Means-Ends Thinking, Adjustment and Social Class among Elementary School–aged children." *Journal of Consulting and Clinical Psychology*, 1972, 38:348–353.

Jerome L. Singer, "Imagery and Daydream Techniques in Psychotherapy: Some Practical and Theoretical Implications." In Charles Speilberger, ed., *Current Topics in Clinical Community Psychology*. Academic Press, 1972.

B. F. Skinner, *Science and Human Behavior*. Macmillan, 1953.

L. Solyom and S. B. Miller, "Reciprocal Inhibition by Aversion Relief in the Treatment of Phobias." *Behaviour Research and Therapy*, 1967, 5:313–324.

Joseph C. Speisman, Richard S. Lazarus, Arnold Mordkoff, and Les Davison, "Experimental Reduction of Stress Based on Ego Defense Theory." *Journal of Abnormal Psychology*, 1964, 68:367–380.

Arthur Staats, "Language Behavior Therapy: A Derivative of Social Behaviorism." *Behavior Therapy*, 1972, 3:165–192.

Ervin Staub, Bernard Tursky, and Gary E. Schwartz, "Self-control and Predictability: Their Effects on Reactions to Aversive Stimulation." *Journal of Personality and Social Psychology*, 1971, 18:157–162.

Ivan Steiner, "Perceived Freedom." In Leonard Berkowitz, ed., *Advances in Experimental Social Psychology*. Academic Press, 1970.

Jerry W. Thornton and Paul D. Jacobs, "Learned Helplessness in Human Subjects." *Journal of Educational Psychology*, 1971, 87:367–372.

J. G. Thorpe, E. Schmidt, P. T. Brown, and D. Castell, "Aversion Relief Therapy: A New Method for General Application." *Behaviour Research and Therapy*, 1964, 2:71–82.

Larry D. Trexler and Thomas O. Karst, "Rational-Emotive Therapy, Placebo, and No Treatment Effects on Public Speaking Anxiety." *Journal of Abnormal Psychology,* 1972, 79:60–67.

Emmett Velten, Jr., "A Laboratory Task for Induction of Mood States." *Behaviour Research and Therapy,* 1968, 6:473–482.

Bernard Weitzman, "Behavior Therapy and Psychotherapy." *Psychological Review,* 1967, 74:300–317.

Joseph Wolpe, *Psychotherapy by Reciprocal Inhibition.* Stanford University Press, 1958.

Joseph Wolpe and Arnold Lazarus, *Behavior Therapy Techniques.* Oxford: Pergamon Press, 1966.

Dorothy Yates, "Relaxation in Psychotherapy." *Journal of General Psychology,* 1946, 34:213–238.

12

Behavioral Personality Assessment

MARVIN R. GOLDFRIED
State University of New York at Stony Brook

JOYCE N. SPRAFKIN
State University of New York at Stony Brook

M AN has always been interested in personality—in the differences between himself and his neighbor and generally in why people behave as they do. The development of the science of personality assessment largely grew out of the practical needs of society. For example, World War I provided the impetus to devise, among other things, an efficient means of identifying severely disturbed men for disqualification from the Armed Services; hence, the development of Woodworth's Personal Data Sheet, the first self-report inventory. Similarly, World War II created the need for a reliable method of selecting men to serve as agents behind enemy lines; hence the development of one of the earliest situational tests, a test that involved performing tasks required of agents, such as building a bridge to transport equipment across a stream.

As one might expect in the development of any science, the actual measurement procedures involved in the study of personality have changed over the years. The different titles of one of the professional journals devoted to personality assessment serve as a useful barometer of the trends in the field. In 1936, when the Rorschach inkblot test was seen as *the* prime method used by clinical psychologists for understanding personality, the *Rorschach Research Exchange* was introduced. As other projective techniques gained in popularity, the scope of personality assessment expanded, as reflected in 1947 by the new title *Rorschach Research Exchange and Journal of Projective Techniques*. It soon became apparent that the Rorschach per se was playing an even less essential role in personality assessment, and that its use was being supplemented by still other projective tests. Thus in 1950 the title of the journal was again changed to read *Journal of Projective Techniques*. Subsequent changes in the field reflected greater recognition of nonprojective assessment procedures, such as the MMPI and other paper-and-pencil tests. The journal editors reflected this shift in orientation by changing the title in 1963 to *Journal of Projective Techniques and Personality Assessment*. With the accumulation of disappointing results in the use of projective techniques, these procedures began to wane in popularity, and in 1971 the journal became simply *Journal of Personality Assessment*. Rather than speculating what the next change will be, the authors would like to express the hope that *Journal of Behavioral Personality Assessment* will be the title in the future.

As a function of the growing interest in behavior therapy techniques, clinical psychologists have begun to take a new look at the whole area of personality assessment. For reasons that will become more apparent later in this module, the behavior therapist requires assessment procedures if he is systematically to develop and monitor intervention programs. Rather than using the currently available personality measurement techniques as is, however, a new orientation to assessment is required. The purpose of this module is to review the current status of this relatively new field, behavioral personality assessment; to raise certain issues that should be dealt with; and to outline potential future directions.

Basic Assumptions Underlying Behavioral Assessment

In behavioral personality assessment as in any area of study, new orientations are seldom completely independent of their predecessors. Many of the assessment techniques to be discussed here bear a similarity to long-standing methods of personality measurement (such as self-report inventories, interviews, and role-playing). Rather, the point of divergence between the traditional and behavioral approaches is found in the assumptions underlying the construction and interpretation of these assessment methods [Goldfried and Kent 1972]. A delineation of the contrasting assumptions

should provide the reader with the general principles of behavioral personality assessment.

The Definition of "Personality"

Although a number of different theoretical approaches are involved in traditional personality assessment, they all share a common conception of human functioning—one that views an individual's overt behavior pattern as a manifestation of some underlying and presumably more basic characteristic. Thus, constructs such as "drive," "trait," and "motive" have been proposed as the unit of analysis for assessment. Such a conception of personality naturally leads one to the conclusion that the best way to predict human behavior would be to concentrate on the assessment of those inferred characteristics of which the overt behavior is likely to be a function. By way of contrast, a more behavioral approach to personality assessment focuses on "what a person *does* in situations rather than on inferences about what attributes he *has* more globally" [Mischel 1968, p. 10]. In a detailed critique of traditional approaches to personality assessment, Mischel [1968] has provided convincing arguments that challenge the assumption that individuals possess generalized traits or behavioral stabilities that manifest themselves independent of situational variations. As he and several others have shown [Endler & Hunt 1966, 1969; Moos 1969], any failure to assess the situation as well as the individual's behavior is doomed to limit severely one's attempt to understand and predict human behavior. Unfortunately, a review of the history of personality assessment reveals that the neglect of situational variables has been the rule rather than the exception. As Rotter [1955] has observed: "In the half century or more that psychologists have been interested in predicting the behavior of human beings in complex social situations, they have persistently avoided the incontrovertible importance of the specific situation on behavior" [p. 247].

Although traditional personality theorists have tended to minimize the importance of situational variables in understanding human behavior, they nonetheless *have* acknowledged the fact that an individual's behavior will, at times, vary according to the situation. To deny behavioral inconsistencies would be to blatantly ignore a most common observation. This apparent contradiction to the assumption concerning consistency is integrated into the traditional approach as follows: Consistency of functioning is assumed to exist only in the underlying personality, not necessarily in the overt behavior. For example, an individual with what has classically been termed an "obsessive-compulsive" personality tends to be extremely neat and orderly in his style of living. Nevertheless, one may observe some inconsistencies in orderliness—such as a dresser drawer that is in a state of disarray. Psychodynamic theorists have typically incorporated such exceptions into their theoretical framework by offering an explanation that provides consistency to seemingly inconsistent behaviors. In the case of the obsessive-compulsive, then, instances of untidiness offer evidence for the contention that one of the factors underlying the obsessive-compulsive personality is the *desire* to be untidy. When the individual has been successful in defending against this impulse, an observer would label him "neat," and when unsuccessful, "untidy." Behaviorally oriented personality theorists would prefer a more parsimonious explanation of such inconsistencies, namely that an individual's behavior is in part a function of his ability to discriminate among varying situational contingencies. As suggested by Mischel [1969]: "What people do in any situation may be altered radically even by seemingly minor variations in prior experiences or slight modifications in stimulus attributes or in the specific characteristics of the evoking situation" [p. 1016]. Thus, it is possible that the otherwise orderly individual may neglect the appearance of his dresser drawers as a function of the fact that negative consequences may never have accrued to him because of their untidy appearance.

Although behaviorally oriented psychologists have not completely eliminated the concept of personality, they have tended to view it in a radically different light. An individual's behavior is not seen as being a function of his personality, but rather the reverse. In other words, "personality may be construed as an intervening variable that is defined according to the likelihood of an individual manifesting certain behavioral tendencies in the variety of situations that comprise his day-to-day living" [Goldfried & Kent 1972, p. 412]. The term "personality" is no more than an abstraction devised by psychologists to facilitate communication.

Selection of Test Items

Both the traditional and behavioral conceptions of personality functioning have important implications for the selection of test items in the development of personality assessment procedures. In the case of traditional views of personality, in which consistencies are believed to exist regardless of variations in the situation, relatively little importance has been attributed to the assessment of functioning within any particular situational context. In fact, the goal of projective methods has been to make the test items as ambiguous

as possible. It is thought that if the stimuli (for example, inkblots, pictures, incomplete sentences) are too directly associated with any salient situation, the test-taker would become too defensive to reveal his "real" self. In contrast, if one takes a behavioral view toward personality functioning, where the essential unit of investigation consists not of an underlying construct but rather the individual's response to particular situations, the situational aspect of the test items included in any assessment procedure becomes all important.

Depending upon what aspect of personality functioning one is interested, in measuring (assertive behavior, anxiety in heterosexual situations, and so on), it is crucial for the behavioral assessor to include an adequate sample of relevant situations within the test itself. Such an approach to test construction has typically been referred to as content validity, in the sense that included in the test itself is the content of those situations about which one is interested in making some prediction. The importance of establishing content validity for a test has been discussed at great length by experts in test construction, but primarily in the context of predicting an individual's achievements or learned proficiencies. For example, if one wishes to devise a test for secretarial competence, the typical procedure would involve sampling those tasks that a secretary must perform (shorthand, typing, filing, and so on), and then include miniature instances of such tasks within the measuring instrument. In the case of psychodynamic personality tests, on the other hand, content validity considerations have typically been deemed relatively unimportant [Anastasi 1968]. This goes directly back to the traditional conceptualization of personality as something above and beyond a learned ability to react in certain ways to given situations.

Interpretations of Test Responses

The final point of divergence between the assumptions underlying the traditional and behavioral approaches to personality assessment involves the interpretation of test responses. In this regard, the important consideration is whether or not the individual's response to a given test item constitutes a "sign" or a "sample." When viewed as a sign, the individual's response presumably is an indirect manifestation of some other characteristic; for example, an individual's emphasis on color in his response to an inkblot test presumably indicates emotionality. The sample interpretation makes no such inference, but instead construes the person's test responses as being indicative of the way he would react in similar nontest situations. The reader should be able to surmise by now that the traditional assessors employ a sign interpretation whereas behavioral assessors prefer the sample approach.

Methods of Behavioral Assessment

Above and beyond the basic assumptions underlying behavioral assessment, there exists the question of how to sample an individual's interactions with his environment. A variety of different approaches have been taken, including direct observation in real-life and contrived settings, self-report, role-playing, and physiological measurements. Each of these procedures has its assets and liabilities as a measure of behavioral functioning, as will be seen in the descriptions and evaluations that follow.

Direct Behavioral Observation

Behavioral observation procedures had been in existence long before their use by behavior therapists. In 1951, for example, Barker and Wright reported observing a seven-year-old boy during all of his waking hours. Several observers literally followed the boy around during the course of the day, each taking turns in recording the behavior as it occurred. The results of these efforts were included in a book, aptly called *One Boy's Day*.

Unfortunately, there are a number of limitations to such recordings of the "stream of behavior" as it occurs in naturalistic settings. A basic problem is that one obtains a large quantity of data that may have little or no bearing on the original purpose of the observation. One solution to this problem is the development of coding procedures that categorize behaviors in advance of the actual observation, thereby simplifying the assessment task itself by focusing only on those events that are specifically of interest. Unlike the continuous, all-day observation by Barker and Wright, such behavioral codes are utilized to obtain samples of the behavior of interest by coding the occurrence or nonoccurrence of particular behaviors for brief periods during the day. Behavioral codes for use with direct observational procedures have been developed for a variety of different settings, including schools, home situations, hospitals, and other relatively contained environments.

One of the first attempts to utilize a behavioral code within a classroom setting has been reported by O'Leary and Becker [1967], who used it to evaluate the effects of a token reinforcement program (that is, a training program in which specified behaviors are re-

warded, typically by tokens that can later be "cashed in") on the disruptive behavior of children in an "adjustment class." The program entailed explaining the token program to the children and specifying the behaviors that would be reinforced. The amount of reinforcement a child received was based on the teacher's ratings of the frequency of these specific behaviors. The objective outcome data consisted of behavioral observations that were recorded from the back of the classroom by college students who had been trained in the use of the code and in the art of being unobtrusive (saying nothing, showing minimal facial expressions and so on). Two observers simultaneously collected data during specified time periods that typically lasted slightly longer than 1½ hours. A few of the specific behaviors included in the code are pushing, making disruptive noise, and answering without raising one's hand. The average interobserver reliability ranged from 70 to 100 percent agreement during baseline period, and 80 to 96 percent agreement during the treatment phase. The results of the program were most favorable, as evidenced by the dramatic decrements in observed disruptive behavior.

The development of such a behavioral code to assess the outcome of treatment programs represents an advancement in methodological sophistication. However, to assess either the antecedent or the consequent events maintaining any given behavior, a method of coding the interactions between an individual and his environment is required. Such a code was developed by Patterson [1971], who focused on the interaction between predelinquent boys and their parents. Observations of family interactions are typically carried out in the home setting, and each behavior is coded under one of approximately thirty categories. The primary unit of observation consists of the interaction between the "subject" (the predelinquent boy, within this particular coding system) and one or more family members. Of necessity, there are certain arbitrary rules indicating at what point a sequence begins and where it ends. An example of the way in which complex streams of behavior may be coded can be seen in the following illustration taken from Patterson, Ray, Shaw, and Cobb [1969]. The subject in this case is "Kevin," and the interaction that follows involves him, his mother and father, and sister Frieda:

> Kevin goes up to father's chair and stands alongside it. Father puts his arms around Kevin's shoulders. Kevin says to mother as Frieda looks at Kevin, "Can I go out and play after supper?" Mother does not reply. Kevin raises his voice and repeats the question. Mother says, "You don't have to yell; I can hear you." Father says, "How many times have I told you not to yell at your mother?" Kevin scratches a bruise on his arm while mother tells Frieda to

get started on the dishes, which Frieda does. Kevin continues to rub and scratch his arm while mother and daughter are working at the kitchen sink. [p. 21]

The above sequence, which occurs within a relatively brief (30-second) period of time, can be coded into five separate sequences, as follows:

1. Kevin engages in "normative" behavior (i.e., appropriate behavior not falling under any specific category) and father shows positive physical contact.
2. Kevin talks and his mother ignores him.
3. Kevin yells and both mother and father show their disapproval.
4. Kevin is involved in self-stimulation, and Frieda engages in other activities and shows no response.
5. Kevin engages in self-stimulation while mother and Frieda are involved in other activities and show no response.

In order to facilitate the actual coding procedure, each family member is assigned a standard number code and each behavioral category is abbreviated. In the example cited above, Kevin, the deviant child, is considered 1; 2 signifies the father; 3 the mother; and 4 the sister. Thus the actual recording would be done as follows:

1. 1NO 2PP
2. 1TA 3IG
   4AT
3. 1YE 2/3DI
4. 1SS 4NR
5. 1SS 3/4NR

Inasmuch as there are limitations to the length of time an observer can reliably code ongoing behavior, a time-sampling procedure is typically utilized, in which two 5-minute observational periods are carried out for each family member at any given time. With practice and training, the agreement between independent observers is high (85 percent is typical).

Patterson and his coworkers have used this behavioral observation procedure to monitor various intervention procedures for predelinquent boys. The behavior modification program was implemented by the boys' parents, who were provided with techniques for modifying their child's deviant behavior. Trained observers were sent to the home, where they collected assessment data during baseline, intervention, and termination periods. Patterson's report [1971] of the results of several treatment programs supports both the effectiveness of the intervention method as well as the utility of the assessment procedures. Thus, for the average family involved in the treatment program, the deviant behavior showed a reduction of 59 percent

from baseline. In a study comparing the efficacy of the behavioral approach with a placebo treatment involving group meetings to discuss child management problems, the behavioral treatment resulted in a 61 percent decrease from baseline for problem behaviors, whereas the placebo group showed a 37 percent increase.

One may legitimately raise the question of why Patterson chose to include the particular behavioral categories in his coding system. There were undoubtedly certain general limitations that influenced the selection of both the number and type of categories—it would be unmanageable for observers to keep in mind too many categories, and the code would be potentially unreliable if categories requiring excessive inferences by observers were included. However, such considerations typically function to *exclude* various classes of behaviors, and provide little direction to the behaviors on which to focus. Included among the deviant child behaviors in the code are such categories as "tease," "yell," "whine," "hit," and "cry." Clearly, one might observe other "deviant" behaviors among children, such as the stereotypic, mechanical, and self-destructive behaviors of autistic children. However, Patterson's behavioral code was designed for intervention programs with predelinquent boys, and consequently was structured to include only those deviant behaviors likely to occur in such a population. The numerous revisions involved in the construction of Patterson's code reflect the difficult nature of selecting and categorizing relevant behaviors. This is not a problem specific to Patterson's system, or even to observational procedures in general, but rather is a basic issue involved in any attempt to develop a behavioral method for assessing human functioning. We shall return to this most important issue later on in this module.

Influenced by Patterson's work with predelinquent boys, Lewinsohn and Shaffer [1971] have integrated home observation procedures in the treatment of depressed adults. The time-sampled observations are typically obtained during mealtime, when all the family members are present. The coding system involves recording family interactions, in which an individual's behavior is classified as either an "action" or a "reaction." Although the distinction may at times be difficult to make, an action refers to a behavior more or less independent of another individual's behavior, whereas a reaction is a response to what another person has said or done. Actions include criticism, complaint, information request, and statement of personal problem. The reaction, or consequences of any particular behavior, may either be positive (that is, interest, approval, laughter) or negative (that is, ignoring, disagreement, criticism, physical punishment). The recording of such interactions provides information about "who is doing what to whom."

The Lewinsohn and Shaffer coding system is still in its development phase, and seems to have considerable potential for the assessment and treatment of depression. One possible limitation is that it focuses only on the individual's verbal behavior. Whether or not the exclusion of nonverbal behavior categories is, in fact, a limitation to the code awaits further research on the system.

Another variation of behavioral observation in naturalistic settings is currently being developed by Paul and his associates for use in hospital settings [Paul et al. in press]. The coding system is being constructed for use with chronic mental patients, and consists of a time-sample behavioral checklist on which the patients' behaviors are recorded and coded by trained observers for 2-second intervals during each of the patient's waking hours. Numerous classes of behavior have been included in the checklist, each of which reflects the bizarre behavior likely to be observed in this setting (such as grimacing or frowning without apparent stimulus, repetitive and stereotypic movements, destroying property). At present, the only information regarding the empirical status of this system consists of interrater reliability, which comes close to being perfect!

Some researchers have used behavioral observation techniques within hospital settings, but primarily as a means for determining exactly which aspects of the physical environment are associated with various forms of patient behavior. Thus, Ittelson, Rivlin, and Proshansky [1970] have described the development of "behavioral maps," which are based on frequency counts of particular classes of behavior (e.g., solitary and social behaviors) within different locations in the ward, and how such behaviors are additionally influenced by time of day, the presence of visitors, and other environmental variations. The potential utility of behavioral maps is intriguing, particularly as they may be applied within the context of environmental design.

All of the observational procedures described thus far are utilized within real-life situations—in the classroom, the home, and the hospital ward. One of the salient advantages of this approach is that, more than any other procedure, it represents a direct assessment of criterion behaviors. One potential limitation of observations in naturalistic settings, however, is that there is no means of controlling the situations preceding or following the behaviors of interest. Another limitation is that in order to obtain an accurate behavioral assessment, an adequate sample of interactions is necessary to insure the occurrence of any relevant controlling environmental events.

Toward the goal of making certain that particular events occur during the observational period, observation procedures in which the situations are controlled or contrived by the behavioral assessor have been developed. This approach to behavioral assessment has the additional advantage of greater standardization, which facilitates comparison of individuals being observed.

Observation in contrived situations might be implemented in a number of different ways. For example, Paul [1966] developed a behavior checklist for the assessment of anxiety in public-speaking situations. The checklist includes twenty behaviors presumably indicative of anxiety (e.g., extraneous hand movements, voice tremor, absence of eye contact, pacing, and so on), and the recording involves tallying the occurrence of these indicators during a speech-giving situation. An anxiety score is obtained by totaling the frequency of occurrence of each behavior. Although these behavioral indicators might appear relatively easy to observe, a fair amount of training is required before observers achieve acceptable levels of reliability. Research utilizing this checklist has demonstrated its usefulness in that it reflects decrements in anxiety following various treatment procedures. However, all the behavioral signs are not of equal utility. Although some of the indicators decrease as a function of anxiety reduction, some do not change, and others actually increase. The elimination of such nondiscriminating behaviors can only improve the utility of the checklist.

Farina, Arenberg, and Guskin [1957] have developed the Minimal Social Behavior Scale, which is a behavior rating scale to be used in a standardized interview with chronic psychotics. The scale specifies a series of behaviors to be carried out by the interviewer (such as dropping a pencil or asking various questions) and provides a recording format to score the adequacy of the patient's responses. Inasmuch as the interviewer records the occurrence of obvious behaviors, the interrater reliability is close to perfect. The scale has been demonstrated to be sensitive to behavior changes due to drugs, and to discriminate between levels of functioning.

Still another example of the use of a contrived situation to obtain observational data is the Behavioral Avoidance Test (BAT), which provides an assessment of an individual's degree of fearfulness to specific objects or situations. The test requires that the individual be placed a certain distance from the feared object, such as a snake, and asked to approach it and perhaps to touch it. The final distance between him and the feared object and the length of time it took to reach that point comprise the behavioral measures of fearfulness. The major use of this test has been to provide an objective dependent measure for outcome studies dealing with phobic individuals. There is virtually no limit to the types of phobias amenable to assessment by means of a BAT. Indeed, the types of objects that have been utilized in constructing BATs are as varied as the plagues that befell the ancient Egyptians—spiders, rats, cockroaches, dogs, are only a few. In addition to feared objects, the BAT may also include frequently occurring phobic situations, such as those involving enclosed places, wide-open spaces, and heights.

Another application of behavioral observation in controlled situations focuses on parent-child interactions. Unbeknownst to the child, parent, or both, the situation is constructed so that it has a high likelihood of stimulating certain behavior patterns. If, for example, one wished to observe the extent to which a particular child could independently carry out his school work, one might construct the following situation: Both mother and child are brought into the clinic or laboratory setting, where the child is provided with a rationale for having to complete his homework before engaging in some other activity. Both the child and mother are placed in a room, typically one with a one-way vision screen that shields the observer, and the child is instructed to do his homework. Similarly, the mother is given something else to work on, such as a written questionnaire. The frequency with which the child requests assistance from his mother may then be determined, by either a time-sampling or continuous-observation procedure. The parent's behavior may also be observed and coded; in this example, any behaviors that precede and follow the child's independent and dependent work activity would be of interest. By coding the interactions between the mother and her child, data useful for a functional analysis of the behavior would be provided.

Problems in the Development and Utilization of Direct Observation Procedures. First, there is the problem of reactivity, which involves behavior change as a function of the observation method. If someone were to tell you that for the next twenty-four hours he was going to follow you around and record the number of times you smiled at people with whom you interacted, such knowledge would undoubtedly make you more aware of this aspect of your behavior, and possibly influence it in some way. Relatively little actual research has been carried out on this particular issue,

although there are some findings that suggest that carrying a wireless radio transmitter has relatively little effect on behavior after the first few days [Moos 1968; Purcell & Brady 1966].

The extent to which a person's behavior changes as a function of being observed probably depends on his knowledge of the specific behaviors being observed and coded, and of the value attached to such behaviors. To tell an individual that his behavior is being observed would probably make him self-conscious, but it would provide little information as to *what* behaviors to be self-conscious about. Hence, little behavior change would be expected. When behavioral codes are used in the context of intervention programs, individuals may be aware of the fact that they are being observed during the baseline period, but may not as yet be informed about the specific code being employed. The introduction of the therapeutic intervention, specifying the target behaviors that are being modified—directly or by virtue of what is being differentially reinforced —may very well also provide individuals with clues to what specific aspects of their behavior are being recorded. If this is in fact true, then any changes between baseline and treatment may also be due to the fact that the individual is now aware of the behavioral code being employed. One way to partial out the potential effect of reactivity from the effects of treatment would be to inform individuals at the very outset of the baseline period of just what aspects of their behavior are being recorded. Although this does not rule out all possibilities that the observational procedures are causing some changes in behavior, it does allow one to determine the extent to which the actual therapeutic program contributes to any changes above and beyond those that may be a function of reactivity.

Although there is no sure-fire way to completely eliminate potential reactivity due to observation —unless the observations are carried out without the individual's awareness (which raises serious ethical questions)—behavioral assessors generally agree that the observers should try to be as unobtrusive as possible. In addition, a period of acclimation is required before collecting interpretable data; that is, the early phases of observation should be used primarily to enable the subjects to get accustomed to the presence of the observers.

Another potential source of error lies within the observer himself—in his *expectations* about what he observes. There exists a body of literature suggesting that an experimenter's hypothesis can greatly influence the kind of results he actually obtains [Rosenthal 1966]. To what extent does the observer's expectation about what he is supposed to see influence what he does see, or at least what he says he sees?

Kent, O'Leary, Diament, and Dietz [in press] have presented some evidence to indicate that this may not be a very significant issue when one utilizes a relatively specific behavioral code. Using the O'Leary coding system described above, these authors experimentally manipulated observers' expectations of therapeutic change. One group of observers was told that the treatment procedure would result in a decrease in disruptive behavior, while the other group was told that no change in disruptive behavior was anticipated. Groups of observers viewed the same videotapes of baseline and treatment sessions. The tapes, in fact, showed no change in rate of disruptive behavior from baseline to treatment. From the point of view of those using observational procedures, the results of this study were favorable—there was no significant difference between the behavioral recordings obtained under these two conditions. An additional interesting finding was that when the observers were asked the question, "What actually happened to the level of disruptive behavior from the baseline to the treatment condition?" a bias *did* emerge. Nine out of ten of the observers in the "decrease" condition reported seeing a decrease, whereas seven of the ten observers in the "no change" condition reported seeing no change. Thus, impressionistic as opposed to behaviorally anchored data appears to be more susceptible to any bias resulting from differential expectations.

A subsequent study by O'Leary, Kent, and Kanowitz [1973], however, provided evidence that when observers are aware of the experimental hypothesis *and* are exposed to the experimenter's reaction to the data recorded, biases in recording may occur. Observers were told that two categories of disruptive behavior would be the targets of a token reinforcement program and that two additional categories would remain untreated. In fact, no change in level of disruptive behavior from baseline to treatment conditions occurred in any of the four categories. When observers recorded data that tended in the direction of "predicted" change, the experimenter provided positive comments (for example, "Those tokens are really reducing the level of vocalization"). When no change from baseline levels was recorded, the experimenter provided negative reactions (such as, "We really ought to be picking up some decreases in the rate of playing by now"). Systematic feedback of this sort resulted in observation biases in the two categories of behavior supposedly treated with a token program. It is clear from this study that recordings made by observers may be influenced by the combination of predictions of experimental results and feedback from the experimenter.

Another potential methodological difficulty involved in behavioral observation consists of the extent to which independent observers can *reliably* code the same behaviors during an assessment session; that is, agree in a substantial proportion of cases as to whether or not a behavioral unit took place and as to how it should be categorized. Utilizing the procedures described above, most investigators report relatively high levels of interobserver reliability. Although no pun is intended, there may be more here than meets the eye. Results of research addressing this question have revealed that interobserver agreement is influenced by the observer's knowledge that reliability is assessed. Reid [1970] trained observers in the use of a behavioral observation code until they reached a criterion of 70 percent agreement. The observers were then provided with videotape recordings from which to code behavior, and led to believe that their observations were the only ones made. In comparison to a median correlation coefficient of .76 when the observers knew their accuracy was being checked, the interobserver agreement dramatically dropped to .51 when they felt that they had reached a sufficiently high level of agreement and were no longer to be monitored. More interesting yet is the Romanczyk, Kent, Diament, and O'Leary [1973] finding that not only was reliability higher when observers knew they were being monitored, but it increased even more when they knew specifically against whose recording theirs would be evaluated. In other words, there apparently was a shift in their observational criteria to match those held by the person who checked their reliability.

A difficulty related to this shift in criteria is what has been referred to by O'Leary and Kent [1973] as the "drift" problem. This is typically noted in situations in which teams of observers work together for a period of time and have occasion to compute their reliability estimates and discuss any discrepancies that may exist in their use of the behavioral code. Following such periodic discussions, one finds an increase in interobserver reliability. This is not in itself necessarily bad. However, it does become an issue when *other* teams of observers are doing the same thing and arriving at different interpretations of just how to use the code. Although the statistical estimates of reliability within teams of observers may be high, it is actually possible to reach a point where different teams are, in effect, using different behavioral codes. Although every attempt is made to operationalize the code in clear-cut behavioral terms, a certain degree of ambiguity nonetheless does exist. For example, the category "Playing" involves any behavior in which the child may be using his hands to play with some object, so that it interferes with the learning process—if a child toys with his pencil while doing arithmetic problems, the observer must decide whether this behavior is actually interfering with the child's on-task behavior. Different teams may arrive at relatively unique sets of additional criteria to be used in making such decisions.

Problems of a different kind are also involved in assessing interobserver reliability. Embarrassingly, there is the potential for "cheating" in the computation of reliability coefficients. Thus, O'Leary and Kent (1973) discovered a tendency for reliabilities to be higher when observers computed these estimates unsupervised. Two kinds of cheating (not necessarily intentional) were discovered—one involved observers changing recorded frequencies to match those of their partners; and the other, the making of mathematical errors in the consistent direction of increasing reliability.

Lest the reader conclude that behavioral observation procedures are riddled with too many methodological problems to be of any utility, what follows are recommendations on how to overcome these difficulties. As a means of dealing with the reactivity issue, every attempt should be made to have the observers be as unobtrusive as possible. Most important, observers should be trained to be totally unresponsive to those they observe. Further, on the assumption that subjects are likely to acclimate to the presence of an observer after a period of time, provision should be made for longer baseline periods before actually utilizing the data observed. As a means of dealing with the expectation problems—to eliminate the possibility that observers might be shaped to report observations that conform to the experimenter's hypothesis—precise behavioral categories should be used and observational data should not be inspected while a study is in progress. To deal with the interobserver reliability problem, observers should be extensively trained to apply the code accurately: they should be monitored regularly and their reliability checked covertly; members of observer teams should be periodically reassigned to minimize "drift"; and groups of observers should be rotated between experimental conditions to eliminate a confound of observer and treatment.

In designing a coding system with which one wishes to obtain acceptable levels of interobserver reliability, the behavioral assessor must ask himself if he is simply requiring too much of his observers. In this regard, a number of questions become relevant, such as: Can the observer reasonably keep in mind the number of different categories involved? Can each category be defined behaviorally? Are the distinctions among categories easy to make? Is sufficient opportunity provided for observers to code and record the behaviors they have observed? Have the observers all reached a common level of training that enables them to deal adequately with any ambiguities that may exist within the coding system? Is the total period of observation brief enough so as to prevent the observers from becoming fatigued or bored? Interobserver reliability will increase as each of these questions is answered in the affirmative.

Methodological problems also plague behavioral observations in contrived situations. As it is with observations in everyday settings, such as homes and classrooms, reactivity is a problem in the laboratory setting. However, here the nature of the problem relates less to the mere presence of observers and more to the demand characteristics of the situation. In a number of ingenious studies, Orne [1962] has demonstrated that a subject's behavior in any given situation can be influenced simply by the knowledge that he is in an experiment. For example, he showed that subjects in a laboratory setting are willing to add up columns of figures on paper, to tear up this paper, and then to repeat the procedure. As incredible as it seems, subjects continue to persist at this boring and nonsensical task, simply because they are "in an experiment." The characteristics of the experimental situation implicitly "demand" that the subject comply with the experimenter's instructions—even if compliance involves engaging in behavior very much out of character.

In the case of behavioral avoidance tests, there exists clear evidence that the subject's perception of the task can cause him to either approach or avoid the feared object. A study by Miller and Bernstein (1972) aptly illustrates this phenomenon. They divided twenty-eight claustrophobics into two conditions (low and high demand instructions) and put them individually into a small dark room. In the low demand group, subjects were informed that they could stop the process at any point, whereas those in the high demand group were encouraged to stay in the chamber the full ten minutes, even though they might experience anxiety during the process. After completing this procedure, the conditions were reversed so that the initially high demand group was given low demand instructions, and vice versa. Two interesting findings were revealed. First, the demand instructions had no effect on the anxiety experienced by subjects, as measured by subjective reports and various physiological indices. The second finding was that the demand instructions had a very powerful effect on the subject's actual behavior, in that they responded "phobically" in the low demand conditions and "fearlessly" with the high demand instructions. Thus, the high demand instructions resulted in subjects remaining in the chamber for a significantly longer time.

Bernstein [1973] has pursued the issue of situational demand characteristics in behavioral avoidance tests in other studies. In one of these, phobic subjects, who were screened on the basis of their scores on an independently administered Fear Survey Schedule, participated in a behavioral avoidance test in one of two contexts—the clinic or the laboratory. When the avoidance test was carried out in the clinic context, there was a fairly good relationship between the individual's report on the Fear Survey Schedule and his actual behavior in the avoidance test. However, the initial verbal reports of subjects who participated in the avoidance test in the laboratory setting were completely unrelated to their behavior when confronted with the phobic object. Specifically, there was far more approach behavior than the Fear Survey Schedule scores would have predicted.

The influence of demand characteristics on fear behavior should not be construed as something that necessarily invalidates the behavioral avoidance test. One should minimize the potential bias by making certain that the task presented to the subject parallels the real-life situation as closely as possible. Clearly, if you told a snake-phobic individual that you would give him a million dollars if he picked up the harmless garter snake in the cage in front of him, his approaching the snake would probably reflect more his desire for the money than his lack of fear. However, it is unlikely that he would encounter such circumstances in his day-to-day life. His fear of snakes is liable to occur in a more naturalistic context, such as a camping trip during which he sees a green object slither across his path. What one needs, then, is a behavioral avoidance test whose conditions more closely appoximate those found in real-life settings. If nothing else, the avoidance test contrived by the behavioral assessor should have demand characteristics as comparable as possible to those in the environment that actually creates the problem for the individual.

One final point regarding behavioral observations. For a number of reasons, it may not always be feasible or practical to observe behavior directly—whether in naturalistic or contrived settings. Inasmuch as behavior can be expected to vary as a function of the situation, one may want behavior samples obtained in a wide variety of situations and over long periods of time. As a

means of circumventing the practical limitations of direct observations, behavioral assessors have made use of observations by people who have frequent contact with the subject in a naturalistic setting. Thus, a number of behavior checklists have been developed, such as those for use by psychiatric nurses [Honigfeld, Gillis, & Klett 1966], classmates [Wiggins & Winder 1961], and teachers [Ross, Lacey, & Parton 1965].

Self-Report Measures

An obvious source of information about overt behavior that occurs in restricted or private settings is the self-report by the individual being assessed. In contrast to the way in which self-reporting was handled in the past, behavioral assessors have restructured their procedures so that the subject is asked to provide information on specific aspects of his behavior and not on his more general personality characteristics.

Paper-and-pencil procedures and problems. A self-report measure for the assessment of assertiveness—referred to as the Conflict Resolution Inventory—has been devised by McFall and Lillesand [1971]. The inventory, which focuses on the individual's ability to refuse unreasonable requests, is comprised of thirty-five items, each describing a situation in which the individual is asked to do something that is somewhat unreasonable (for example, "You are in the thick of studying for exams when a person whom you know only slightly comes into your room and says, 'I'm tired of studying. Mind if I come in and take a break for a while?'"). For each situation, the subject is asked to indicate the likelihood that he would refuse the request, and how comfortable he would feel about refusing or acquiescing. The original item-pool used in the construction of the measure was obtained from written descriptions by undergraduate students of situations in which they had difficulty saying no to unreasonable requests. The Conflict Resolution Inventory has been a useful measure in a number of clinical outcome studies [McFall & Lillesand 1971; McFall & Twentyman 1973], in which subjects' refusal scores were found to increase as a function of assertive training.

A paper-and-pencil measure used for the assessment of academic behavior is the Survey of Study Habits and Attitudes (SSHA) [Brown & Holtzman 1966]. The measure provides two separate scores: Study Habits, reflecting behavioral tendencies associated with effective academic work (such as handing in assignments on time and dealing with distractions while trying to study, and so on) and Study Attitudes, reflecting opinions and beliefs about academic matters. The validity of the SSHA is indicated by its correlation of .36 with grade-point average. A recent study by Goldfried and D'Zurilla [1973] has demonstrated, however, that the SSHA is an even better predicter than previous research would suggest. They point out that grades are dependent on many more factors than effective study habits and positive attitudes about academic work, and they suggest that the external validity criteria should be more behavioral in nature. Thus, they administered the SSHA to a group of entering freshmen, and correlated the scores with roommate and suitemate effectiveness ratings that were obtained at the end of the first semester. The peer ratings involved effectiveness in a number of academic and nonacademic areas (for example, study habits, handling difficult course material, relationships with roommate, relationships with opposite sex, and so on). The correlation of SSHA scores with ratings of academic effectiveness were higher than those reported earlier, which used grades as the external criteria—.51 compared to .36. The Study Attitude score of the SSHA—which theoretically should be less directly related to ratings of effectiveness—showed an average correlation of .31. Neither of the two scores was at all related to any of the peer ratings of effectiveness within interpersonal situations, indicating that the measure does, indeed, predict situation-specific effectiveness.

Whatever promise may exist for self-reports of overt behavior and behavioral observation procedures, they will always be limited by the fact that they focus only on observable behavior and provide little data regarding thoughts and feelings. An assessor's interpretation of overt behavior can often be significantly influenced by knowledge of relevant covert variables. A classic story, involving a boy playing with a worm, will serve to illustrate this point. During the course of play, he takes out a knife and cuts the worm in half. This is being observed by an onlooker, who disapprovingly interprets the child's behavior as an act of aggression of the worst kind. What the observer could not see, however, was what the boy—who happened to have few friends—thought as he cut the worm in half: "There! Now you will have someone to play with." While behavioral observation can provide us with most important information, it does not tell the whole story.

Some years ago, Kelly [1958] suggested the following for those interested in personality assessment: "If you don't know what is going on in a person's mind, ask him; he may tell you." On the assumption that covert behaviors (such as, thoughts and feelings) are among the variables of interest to the behavioral assessor, there can be little doubt that verbal self-report proce-

dures occupy an important place in the behavioral assessment of personality.

One of the self-report measures of emotional arousal frequently used by behavior therapists in their research is the Fear Survey Schedule (FSS) developed by Geer [1965]. The FSS is a questionnaire consisting of a list of fifty-one possibly fear-provoking objects or situations (such as snakes, being alone, looking foolish) about which the subject indicates his degree of fear (ranging from "none" to "terror"). A factor analysis by Bernstein and Allen [1969] has indicated that the individual items may be sorted into six separate categories—live organisms, social interaction, negative social evaluation, personal illness or death, water, and illness or death of others. Research on the relationship between FSS scores and overt fearful behavior has yielded mixed results. There are reports that FSS scores can predict performance on behavioral avoidance tests, especially for females. However, as we have already noted, the influence of the demand characteristics associated with behavioral avoidance tests often operates to undermine the predictive ability of the FSS. There is yet another reason why these two measures may be unrelated; namely, they are measuring different aspects of fearfulness. On the FSS, individuals are asked to indicate just how afraid they would feel in certain situations. On the behavioral avoidance test, however, they are asked not how they feel about the situation, but instead to approach the object as much as they are able. Although there is clearly some relationship between subjective fearfulness and behavior, people often engage in activities despite their anxiety (for example, going for a job interview) and actively avoid others for reasons unrelated to fear (for example, taking out the garbage).

Although the FSS has the clear advantage of being quite easy to administer and score, there are limitations associated with its use. The subject is asked to indicate the degree of his fear of situations or objects described in very general terms (such as being criticized). Furthermore, the many ways in which fear can manifest itself—such as increased heart rate or sweaty palms—are not taken into account. Consequently the FSS does not provide the specific information required for clinical use. As a measuring procedure for research purposes, it is recommended only as an initial screening device, to be followed by other measures of fearfulness.

A paper-and-pencil measure of anxiety that takes into account the situation as well as the nature of the response has been devised by Endler, Hunt, and Rosenstein [1962] and aptly called the S-R Inventory of Anxiousness. At the top of each page of the inventory there is a one-sentence description of a potentially anxiety arousing situation; for example, one item is, "You are just about to take an important final examination." Under the description of each situation there is a list of fourteen possible reactions, each of which reflects some aspect of the construct "anxiety." Thus, these response modes include "heart beats faster," "get an uneasy feeling," "emotions disrupt action," "perspire," and other similar reactions. Each response mode is rated on a 5-point scale by the subject, who indicates the extent to which he would react if actually in such a situation. Using the same format, Endler and Hunt (1968) have also constructed the S-R Inventory of Hostility.

In addition to their practical utility in predicting fearfulness and hostility, both of these instruments have been employed to study the relative importance of individual differences, situations, and modes of response in accounting for behavioral variations. The relative importance of these variables is judged by utilizing a statistical computation of the "proportion of variance" for each variable. The magnitude of the variance figure obtained for each variable reflects how potent the variable is in accounting for differences in inventory responses. If individual differences accounted for most of the variance, it would be useful to treat anxiety and hostility as "traits" that people manifest to various degrees and that could be used to make predictions about behavior in most situations. However, the research indicates that individual differences are relatively unimportant—the mode of response and the specific situation were ranked higher. For one group of individuals filling out the inventory, the situation described contributed more than eleven times the variance than did individual differences. The implication of this research is that predictions about anxiety and hostility must be based on a specification of the situation and on the particular response mode of interest.

In addition to using written self-report measures to obtain predictions of how an individual would react —or generalizations of how he typically reacts—to specific situations, self-report procedures have been devised that determine a person's emotional state while actually in a given situation. For example, Spielberger, Gorsuch, and Lushene [1970] require the individual to indicate on a 4-point scale the extent to which a number of descriptive statements apply to him at that particular moment, such as "I feel calm," "I am tense," or "I am jittery." This measure of anxiety is very similar to the adjective checklists developed by several researchers, in which subjects are asked to indicate the degree to which a number of different adjectives describe their current emotional state. For example, Zuckerman and Lubin's [1965] Multiple Affect Adjective Checklist has such a format and measures states of depression,

hostility, and anxiety. Research involving these assessment procedures has typically yielded favorable results, indicating that reported emotional states increase and decrease with appropriate experimental manipulations (for example, stress-producing films, relaxation instruction).

Although these measures of emotional states have the advantage of not requiring the individual to make predictions or generalizations about his reactions to various situations, they nevertheless share one serious methodological flaw with all self-report measures—that of response bias. The most commonly discussed bias is "social desirability." In order to present themselves in a favorable light, individuals can give the socially acceptable rather than the truthful response. On an anxiety questionnaire, for example, individuals may be embarrassed to indicate how anxious they really are, for fear of appearing "neurotic." Suffice it to say that self-reports of emotional states have the potential of being influenced not only by how the subject may actually feel at any given time, but also by his willingness to *report* how he feels.

Husek and Alexander [1963] have addressed themselves to this very issue and developed a measure of state anxiety that is less susceptible to response bias. The format has been derived from the semantic differential, in which different words are rated on 7-point bipolar adjectival scales. The words and rating scales comprising Husek and Alexander's Anxiety Differential include "TODAY: Straight . . . Twisted; SCREW: Nice. . .Awful; HANDS: Wet . . . Dry." In contrast to adjective checklist measures, the socially desirable way of responding to this questionnaire is not immediately apparent. Thus, in addition to finding that scores on the Anxiety Differential vary as a function of manipulations designed to increase or decrease anxiety level, the authors have demonstrated that their assessment procedure has a low susceptibility to faking.

Response bias is not the only methodological problem that must be dealt with by self-report measure constructers and users. In addition, one is confronted with the finding that scores on these measures have little or no correspondence with physiological indicators of anxiety. As one might be tempted to ask about the discrepancy between self-reported fear and fear manifested in a behavioral avoidance test: Will the real measure of anxiety please stand up? In fact, there *is* no real measure of anxiety; rather, there are various response systems within any individual (covert, physiological, and behavioral), each of which may react to differing degrees when an individual is placed in an aversive situation. This most intriguing issue will be discussed in greater detail later on in this module, when we deal with physiological assessment.

Lest we create the impression that behavioral assessors are preoccupied only with the assessment of negative emotional states, we might mention some of the work that has been done on the measurement of an individual's pleasurable feelings about situations, experiences, and objects.

Influenced by the Fear Survey Schedule, Cautela and Kastenbaum [1967] have developed a Reinforcement Survey Schedule to assess those experiences from which an individual is likely to derive pleasure. This paper-and-pencil measure consists of a number of objects (such as food) and activities (such as gardening), for which the subject is asked to give his personal preference on a scale from "not at all" to "very much." Although the survey undoubtedly has a number of potential uses, its utility has been limited by its method of construction. The items within the survey were apparently generated on an a priori basis, reflecting what the authors believed would be reinforcing to various individuals. Had Cautela and Kastenbaum used an empirical approach in the construction of their measure, they undoubtedly would have discovered a number of items not included in the present survey—among which might have been such situations as pleasing a loved one, walking barefoot through the grass, or having one's back scratched.

A recently developed measure described by Mac-Phillamy and Lewinsohn [1972] appears to have overcome the item selection problem inherent in the Reinforcement Survey Schedule. MacPhillamy and Lewinsohn asked college undergraduates to generate "events, experiences, or activities which you find pleasant, rewarding, or fun." After eliminating redundant items, the 320 remaining ones were sorted into social and nonsocial categories and the measure was labeled the Pleasant Events Schedule. The subject taking the Pleasant Events Schedule is asked to respond to two questions about each item: How often has this event occurred within the past month? How enjoyable or pleasant was this event? If the individual has not experienced the event recently, he is asked to indicate how enjoyable it would have been if it had occurred, thus providing a preference rating for events possibly unobtainable. Although research on the construction and validation of the Pleasant Events Schedule is still in progress, this measure seems to have potential. For example, consistent with the behavioral view that depression results from the relative absence of reinforcing events in a person's life, significantly negative correlations have been found between the scores on the schedule and feelings of depression [Lewinsohn & Libet 1972].

Interview procedures and problems. Thus far, we have discussed ways in which paper-and-pencil measures may be used in the assessment of covert and overt behaviors. In addition to paper-and-pencil measures, interview procedures have been used to obtain self-reports. As with other behavioral assessment procedures, the interview is used merely as a vehicle for sampling the individual's responses to various situations. In some respects, the interview provides a more flexible assessment procedure than do the paper-and-pencil measures, as the interviewer may ask questions about reactions to a variety of situations and engage in follow-up questioning if more detailed information is required.

In using the interview as a behavioral assessment procedure, it is essential that the respondent be as specific as possible in providing reports of his reactions in various situations. It is the responsibility of the interviewer to ask questions that elicit public referents instead of abstract terms. People differ in their interpretations of vague states such as "anxiousness." In order for the behavioral assessor to obtain useful information, he should ask specific questions, such as: How do you know you are anxious? How would a person observing you know that you are anxious? What was happening in the environment the last time you felt anxious? The reader is referred to Peterson [1968] and Storrow [1967] for behaviorally oriented interview guides.

Even in reporting their overt behavior in given situations, individuals have difficulty in providing specific accounts. Thus, in an attempt to enable individuals to provide accurate self-reports of behavior, behavioral assessors have frequently required clients to monitor and keep records of what they do on a daily basis. Although this enables individuals to be more specific in the self-reports, it frequently does something else as well; it changes the frequency or magnitude of the behavior being monitored. This is the issue of reactivity we discussed earlier, in conjunction with the potential effects of being observed by others. So it is that, although it was originally proposed as an assessment procedure, self-monitoring is now gaining considerable popularity as a means of changing behavior. Why and when behavior may change as a function of self-observation is a most interesting but as yet unanswered question. In all probability, the reactive effects of self-monitoring depend upon the specific behavior in question, and behavior that is under voluntary control (such as studying) is more likely to change as a function of self-monitoring than more involuntary reactions (such as anxiety). In addition, the direction of change will vary as a function of whether the individual perceives the behavior as having positive or negative consequences. For example, time spent studying would be expected to increase, but the number of cigarettes smoked would be expected to decrease as a function of self-monitoring.

Some behavior therapists apparently feel somewhat uneasy about their use of self-report measures within the context of therapy outcome research. Perhaps this is because the term "behavior" highlights their orientation, or perhaps it is because they are concerned about some of the methodological issues involved in the use of such procedures. Whatever the motivation, there is one excellent reason why self-report measures should be included in clinical outcome research. In the clinical practice of behavior therapy, the primary assessment procedure typically used consists of the client's self-report. Except in relatively clear-cut cases, where direct behavioral observation is feasible, the behavior therapist usually accepts the client's statement that he has a problem and is willing to terminate when the client reports the problem no longer exists. Thus, the use of self-report measures in outcome research provides the behavioral assessor with ecological validity, allowing him to readily generalize his findings to actual clinical situations.

Role-Playing

An early report on the use of role-playing for assessment is provided by Rotter and Wickens [1948]. Although their work predated the current behavioral orientation to assessment and therapy, their rationale for proposing role-playing was most consistent with the assumptions outlined earlier in this paper. Thus, they argued that role-playing situations were more similar to criterion situations than were traditional personality tests, and therefore might provide a valuable method of obtaining behavior samples. Subjects were required to enact their responses to different situations, and their behaviors in these situations were rated according to the degree to which "social aggressiveness" was reflected in each response. Although Rotter and Wickens made no attempt to determine the actual validity of the role-playing assessment, they did demonstrate that by providing judges with a list of behaviors indicative of "social aggressiveness," one could obtain a fairly high level of interrater reliability.

A later study by Stanton and Litwak [1955] involved the use of role-playing to assess interpersonal competence. Using both foster parents and students as subjects, the role-playing was carried out in three situations—meeting a troubled friend, criticizing an old employee, and handling an interfering parent. Rat-

ers were provided with a list of twenty behaviors antithetical to what was defined as "autonomy" under interpersonal stress (for example, being curt, impolite, belittling, or defensive). Stanton and Litwak found that interrater reliability was good (the average correlation was .90), and that the assessment procedures were highly valid. For example, the autonomy scores obtained from role-playing correlated highly with comparable ratings by people who knew the subjects well. In the case of foster parents, the correlation with caseworkers' ratings was .82; for students, the correlation with friends' ratings was .93. As an interesting side note, Stanton and Litwak also found that when they used informants who were less familiar with the subject, the findings were not as favorable. They also found that the half hour of role-playing had better predictive efficiency than twelve hours of intensive interviewing. Thus, a correlation of .82 was found between the role-playing scores of foster parents and caseworkers' judgment of the foster parents' ability to care for their child, whereas the results of the interviewing yielded a correlation of only .55. These findings are indeed impressive, especially in light of the fact that the scenes used in the role-playing were not representative of situations involving competence in handling children.

Some workers have made an attempt to standardize and semiautomate the role-playing procedure. For example, Rehm and Marston [1968] developed a procedure for assessing heterosexual anxiety in males, which involves presenting ten social situations orally on tape. Each situation is first described by a male, after which there is a comment by a female. In one situation the narrator described the scene by stating, "As you are leaving the cafeteria, a girl taps you on the back and says . . ." at which point a female voice states "I think you left this book." Subjects are asked to imagine themselves in this situation and respond as they would in real life. In Rehm and Marston's research with the measure, subjects' verbal responses to each situation were tape-recorded and subsequently rated by female undergraduates for anxiety, adequacy of response, and likability. The interrater reliabilities of .47, .69, and .65 for each of the three variables would seem to indicate that more detailed training is needed in order to achieve greater consistency of ratings. In addition to the rating procedure, subjects' responses were evaluated for the number of words used per response, the delay between the female's comment and the subject's response, and various verbal signs of anxiety, such as stuttering, failure to respond, and repetition of words. Evidence for the validity of the assessment procedure is provided by the significantly different scores obtained between normal subjects and subjects enrolled in a therapy program for social anxiety, as well as by the fact that the role-playing performance of individuals undergoing therapy improved significantly more than did that of those in control conditions.

The semiautomated innovation in role-playing assessment influenced McFall and his coworkers. In an additional study by McFall and Marston [1970], a behavioral role-playing test was devised to assess assertive behavior. McFall and Marston selected their situations to be representative of a variety of instances in which one might be required to assert oneself. Included among such interpersonal situations were those in which friends may interrupt while you are trying to study, your laundry has been lost by the cleaners, a waiter brings you a steak that has not been cooked according to your request, and your boss asks you to work late at a time when it is inconvenient for you to do so. These situations are presented on tape in much the same way as in the procedure devised by Rehm and Marston. For example, the narrator describes a situation in which the subject is standing in a long line outside a movie theater, hoping that he will be able to get a ticket. Just then, two people walk up to their friend standing in front of the subject, and one of the newcomers says: "Hey, the line's a mile long. How 'bout if we cut in here with you?" The person in line responds "Sure, come on. A couple more won't make any difference." At this point, the subject is asked to respond as he would if he were really in this situation, and his response is recorded on tape. The behavioral role-playing test was administered by McFall and Marston before and after treatment, which consisted of assertive-training therapy sessions. Improvement was determined by five independent judges, who listened to pre- and post-responses to each of the sixteen situations and made some judgment as to which of the two ways of reacting in the situation was more assertive. The consensus of such judgments was used as the index of each individual's improvement. Although McFall and Marston did not report about the reliability of the scoring, the results of their study indicated that assertive behavior on the role-playing test increased as a function of therapy and that this increase was greater than that obtained from individuals assigned to control groups.

In a later use of behavioral role-playing, McFall and Lillesand [1971] had subjects' responses rated on a five-point scale of assertiveness. Interrater reliability was reported to be in the .90's. McFall and Lillesand similarly used the role-playing measure to determine change resulting from assertive training, and obtained favorable results. The correlation of the role-playing scores with those from a paper-and-pencil measure of assertiveness, the Conflict Resolution Inventory, was also calculated. Unlike the low correlations typically found between behavior and self-report, the obtained correlations were moderate (in the .60's). However, as most of the items on the role-playing test were identical to those on the Conflict Resolution Inventory, a significant proportion of the obtained relationship can be attributed to the subject's desire to appear consistent.

McFall and Lillesand experimented with a slightly different version of role-playing. Instead of merely presenting a person with a situation and asking for his initial response, a greater attempt was made to parallel what might actually happen in real life. Thus, they extended the interaction so that even if the subject initially refused the unreasonable request, the antagonist continued to press him further. The antagonist pleaded and insisted until the subject either gave in or a total of five "pushes" had occurred. The score on the extended interaction test consisted of the number of requests made by the antagonist, which varied from one to five. The findings with the use of this variation indicated that it, too, was sensitive to the behavior change resulting from the assertive-training procedures.

Methodological problems with role-playing procedures. In devising role-playing procedures for the assessment of various types of behavior—whether it involves interpersonal competence, social anxiety, assertiveness, or anything else—there are several factors to take into consideration. To begin with, it is essential that the behavior of the individual with whom the subject must interact (that is, the stooge) be standardized in such a way that he presents a consistent impact. McFall and his coworkers have addressed themselves to this issue by tape-recording the stimulus situation and preprogramming the stooge's responses on the extended interaction role-playing. Another issue to consider is the way in which subjects' responses are rated. There are some data to indicate that a "halo effect" may occur when the rater evaluates the subsequent interactions of an individual whom he has already rated. Rotter and Wickens [1948] found, for example, that when a subject's role-played responses to two different situations were rated by the same judges, the average correlation between the rating of the subject's behavior in the two situations was .78. When the rating was carried out by different judges, the average correlations dropped to .55. Clearly, the judge's ratings of an individual's reaction to one situation are influenced by his observation of that individual in another situation, resulting in the subject's behavior appearing more consistent than it really was. Inasmuch as the role-playing method involves the observation and recording of an individual's behavior, many of the issues discussed earlier under behavior observation are relevant here. These involve such matters as the specificity of the behavioral criteria involved in the code, the potential influence of the observer's expectations, the tendency for interrater reliability to drop as a function of being unmonitored, and "drift" as a result of surreptitious changes in standards for scoring.

An even more basic question about the use of role-playing for behavioral assessment remains to be asked: How do you know when the subject is really "in role"? The appeal of role-playing as an assessment device is based on the assumption that the testing situation provides a very close parallel to the individual's real-life behavior. What we know little about as yet, however, are those variables that are likely to facilitate an individual's assuming the role that he would in similar, real-life situations. Although there are clear advantages to using tape-recordings, the question remains whether this is as effective a procedure as one that involves more realistic simulations. Another related question is whether or not it is realistic to expect individuals who are unaccustomed to playacting suddenly to feel comfortable and behave naturally with the assessment procedure. Therapists involved in the use of role-playing within the context of psychodrama have written extensively about this problem and have recommended a number of techniques with which an individual may "warm up" prior to actual role-playing. There may also exist individual differences in this regard—some people, regardless of the situation or the amount of warm-up they are given, might be too self-conscious to role-play.

These are but some of the more important methodological issues related to the use of role-playing as an assessment procedure, none of which has been the object of experimental study. In light of the fact that role-playing seems to be a potentially useful assessment technique, systematic study of the procedural and individual difference factors that may increase its predictive efficiency is clearly needed.

Physiological Measurement

Considering the methodological problems associated with the use of the behavioral assessment techniques discussed thus far, the need for a more "direct" way of measuring behavior—that is, a method that can circumvent the response-bias problems of self-report, the observer-expectation and response-coding difficulties of behavioral observation, and the acting demands of role-playing—seems obvious. Upon initial reflection, the direct measurement of physiological responses would appear to be the panacea for behavioral assessment. After all, one cannot fake involuntary responses, external observers are not needed, and the individual is not asked to behave in any particular way. Accordingly, workers in the field have created a technology to measure physiological responses—anxiety and sexual arousal in particular—in order to provide a direct route to internal states. However, as will be shown in this section, the route is not as direct as it was hoped.

Physiological assessment of anxiety. As we noted earlier, the construct of anxiety has three modes of expression: self-report, behavioral, and physiological. The assessment of anxiety by physiological means assumes first that autonomic arousal is indicative of anxiety, and second, that such physiological responses can be distinguished from other kinds of autonomic arousal (for example, anger and pain). The first assumption has ample empirical support from studies that have exposed individuals to an anxiety-provoking situation and simultaneously monitored physiological responses. The general finding is that blood pressure, heart rate, galvanic skin response, and adrenal gland secretions typically increase. The second assumption concerning response specificity is not as clearly documented, but is nonetheless generally accepted. One of the conclusions reached in a review of the area by Martin was, "In spite of some inconsistencies among the studies there does appear to be evidence for distinguishable response patterns that can be tentatively associated with the constructs of fear (anxiety) and anger" [1961, p. 236]. However, since specific patterns have not been established for other subjective states, the situation in which the individual is reacting should be specified so as to rule out other possible sources of influence.

The specific response systems monitored in the physiological assessment of anxiety vary across different studies. Circulatory activity has proved to be a good index of arousal. The electrocardiograph (EKG), which monitors the electrical activity of the heart, is widely used to measure heart rate. The sphygmomanometer is a device used to measure blood pressure, its drawback being that it can only provide intermittent measurement. A strain gauge placed around a finger is used to measure finger pulse volume. The galvanic skin response (GSR) is measured by passing a small electric current between two electrodes attached to the skin surface. The increase in sweat gland activity that accompanies anxiety causes a decrease in skin resistance, which in turn results in greater electrical flow and hence an increase in GSR. Muscle tension can be measured by using surface electrodes to monitor muscle activity. Finally, hormonal secretions can be assessed through the use of blood tests. For a more detailed description of those psychophysiological methods themselves, the reader is referred to Brown [1967].

The remainder of this section will be devoted to a discussion of the methodological considerations associated with the physiological assessment of anxiety. While many of them—such as low correlations with other anxiety measures, reactivity, and fakability —overlap with those discussed for the other behavioral assessment techniques, others are unique to physiological measurement (for example, response specificity).

The first general consideration in utilizing physiological measures of anxiety is that such measures yield very low correlations with self-report and behavioral measures. The research bearing on this issue indicates that measures of trait or general anxiety are totally unrelated to physiological measures. For example, Katkin [1965] found no correlation between GSR indices and scores on the Taylor Manifest Anxiety Scale, a questionnaire that assesses the general tendency to be anxious. However, the evidence for state or situational anxiety is far more promising. Several studies [e.g., Pillard et al. 1966; Mordkoff 1965] have demonstrated moderate correlations between self-report and physiological measures of anxiety when both measures reflect responses to an induced anxiety situation involving stressful films. These findings suggest that physiological responses are like overt and cognitive responses in that their magnitude varies as a function of the situation.

Not only do physiological measures bear at best only a moderate relationship to self-report and behavioral measures, but low or even insignificant correlations are obtained *between* the various autonomic measures. For any level of stress that is less than extreme, the responses of any one physiological system cannot be predicted from the reactions of any other system. For example, heart rate cannot be predicted accurately from GSR or blood pressure. However, the lack of intercorrelations between response systems may in part be attributable to individual differences in response-patterning. Lacey, Bateman, and Van Lehn [1952] reached this conclusion after they exposed subjects to various stresses, monitoring physiological responses throughout, and found that different subjects had different patterns of autonomic responses that were reproducible over time and were consistent across the various stress situations. Thus, one individual might react to stress with a markedly increased heart rate but only minor changes in GSR, whereas the reverse might be true for another individual. Further, each

pattern would be fairly consistent for each individual across different anxiety-provoking situations. This response specificity makes any consistency of response systems across individuals unobtainable. The methodological problem presented by this finding is that the physiological assessor would have no way of knowing whether the single response (or even the sample of responses) monitored included the individual's most reactive system. Failure to tap this particular system would be likely to lead to incorrect conclusions about the person's reactivity. Only by sampling *all* the physiological responses could this potential problem be overcome—an obviously overwhelming task and in most cases, one that represents inefficient use of assessment time and energy.

It should be interesting to note that the finding of response specificity is consistent with the findings of Endler and Hunt [1966] concerning the relative importance of the situation, response mode, and individual differences in determining the responses on the S-R Inventory of Anxiousness. Subjects differed significantly from each other in the response mode most reactive to anxiety, and the degree of the specific anxiety reaction by any given individual was also significantly influenced by the particular situation presented.

The implications of response specificity are sufficiently critical to warrant further investigation. First, this finding suggests a "trait" in physiological responding, in that individuals respond in "typical" patterns across stressful situations. Although one would still need to know whether or not a particular situation would be stressful for an individual, this knowledge of a unique response pattern affords greater predictive power than is the case for the traditionally hypothesized, cross-situational traits. Further, there are implications for an explanation of the development of psychosomatic disorders. Sternbach [1966] speculates, for example, that the most reactive response system is most susceptible to tissue damage due to stress.

Although it might seem that physiological measurement is immune to response biases, faking in particular, recent research evidence indicates that physiological assessment shares this problem with all of the other assessment methods. It is becoming more apparent that a subject can increase or decrease autonomic arousal "at will" by altering breathing rate, skeletal muscle tension, or even by thinking of emotionally-toned scenes—all of which directly influence the physiological data obtained. The ability of individuals to change various autonomic responses has been highlighted recently by the development of biofeedback methods that help people to gain control of "involuntary" systems. Bergman and Johnson [1971] and Stern and Kaplan [1967] have shown that individuals can significantly change heart rate and GSR, respectively, even without external feedback. Also, the favorable reports of biofeedback studies have led Lang, one of its earliest investigators, to say the following about the lie detector, which monitors the autonomic nervous system: ". . .if visceral responses can be shaped in the same way as any other behavior, the lie detector is no sure route to emotional truth" [1971, p.83]. However, the degree to which this assessment method is susceptible to faking is probably far less than with the behavioral methods discussed earlier.

Physiological measurement possibly shares the limitation of reactivity with the other assessment methods. Although this has not been the subject of systematic investigation, it would seem that an individual "hooked up" with numerous electrodes and strain gauges would react somewhat differently to stimuli in this contrived, confining situation than he would otherwise. As yet, there are no "unobtrusive methods" of physiological reactions.

Physiological assessment of sexual arousal. The physiological measurement of sexual arousal has received most of its impetus from the pioneering studies of Masters and Johnson [1966]. Using a variety of physiological measures during actual sexual encounters, they have demonstrated discrete physiological changes that accompany the four stages of sexual responding (excitement, plateau, orgasmic, and resolution). Among the nongenital reactions that correlate with sexual arousal are increased heart rate, higher blood pressure, more rapid respiratory rate, and increased muscle tension. The genital changes in the female include lubrication, lengthening and distension of the vagina, increased blood flow, and a change in the color of the vaginal walls. The male changes include penile erection, tensing of the scrotum, and sometimes color changes in the glans. Some of these nongenital and genital changes during sexual intercourse have been investigated by other researchers in less directly sexual situations. Researchers have become interested in assessing the degree to which these physiological changes occur when individuals are exposed to erotic films and pictures. The primary reason why research subsequent to Masters and Johnson has dealt more with films and pictures than with direct sexual encounters is undoubtedly its relative ease of implementation.

The research evidence for nongenital changes in response to erotic pictures and films is disappointing. Sexually arousing stimuli do not consistently produce increases in heart and respiratory rates across experiments. Increases in blood pressure and GSR have been more consistently found, with blood pressure showing graded reactions to more arousing stimuli. However, these general arousal measures do not discriminate between positive, sexual affect and negative, nonsexual affect. For example, Romano [1969] found no significant differences in GSR or blood pressure between individuals viewing erotic and atrocity films, and Bernick, Kling, and Borowitz [1971] found no differences in heart rate between individuals viewing a heterosexual stag film, a homosexual stag film, neutral slides, and an Alfred Hitchcock suspense film. This absence of affect response specificity is the major problem presented by the use of nongenital measures of sexual arousal.

Direct genital measures of arousal have provided more promising results. The penile plethysmograph, worn on the penis, provides a direct measure of penile erection and is the most sensitive measure to date. By differential erectile responses to various slides, Freund [1963] was able to discriminate successfully between homosexuals and heterosexuals, a finding that has been replicated many times [e.g., Zuckerman 1971]. The penile plethysmograph has been most often used in the treatment of homosexuals, transvestites, and fetishists. One widely used therapeutic technique for sexual deviations is aversion conditioning, in which the goal is to cause the individual to develop an aversion to the deviant sexual object. The two procedures used are classical conditioning, in which the deviant object is paired with an unpleasant stimulus (electric shock or nausea-producing drug), and avoidance conditioning, in which the patient can avoid the unpleasant stimulus only by avoiding the deviant sex object. Invariably the penile plethysmograph is used as a measure of the therapeutic progress—successful treatments being indicated by decreasing erections to the previously arousing deviant stimulus [Yates 1970].

The penile plethysmograph has recently been used in biofeedback studies in which males learn to control penile tumescence. Providing feedback regarding the level of physiological arousal has been shown to be effective in teaching males both to suppress [Rosen 1972] and to increase [Price 1973] tumescence.

The measurement of female sexual arousal has received less empirical investigation. This may be due in part to the fact that the female genitalia are less accessible than those of the male. However, Cohen and Shapiro [1970] reported the development of a "thermal flowmeter," which, when inserted within a diaphragm and placed in the vagina, measures blood flow. Preliminary reports seem to indicate that the procedure is sensitive to sexual arousal. The two major potential uses for such a device are in the investigation of stimuli arousing to females and in the assessment of sexual arousal for sexual dysfunction problems.

It should be apparent that physiological assessments of both the sexual and anxiety responses are closely related to the treatment process. The penile plethysmograph for the assessment and treatment of inappropriate sexual object problems was mentioned above as one current use of this measure. Further, the biofeedback research concerning the successful training of erective control has clear implications for the treatment of impotence. The thermal flowmeter offers a parallel potential for the treatment of orgasmic dysfunction in females. One observation often made is that a woman cannot readily discern her own bodily cues of arousal; the implication is that training in "tuning in" to these cues of arousal would enhance the level of arousal. Thus, for both males and females, the physiological assessment measures of sexual arousal have the potential of playing a major role in biofeedback training to overcome sexual dysfunctions. Similarly, the correlates of anxiety, such as increased heart rate, blood pressure, GSR, and muscle tension, have been controlled to varying degrees with biofeedback techniques [Barber, et al. 1971], offering the potential of effective therapeutic procedures for the self-control of anxiety.

Assessment for Behavior Change

Thus far, we have discussed some of the basic assumptions underlying behavioral assessment and reviewed the particular procedures for actually carrying out behavioral assessment. We would now like to turn our attention to the question of utility, particularly as it pertains to the behavior change process.

Although the relationship between assessment and psychotherapy should be a close one, this has not been the case within a traditional orientation. One would think that an initial assessment would serve the purpose not only of determining what aspect of an individual's problematic behavior needs to be changed, but also of selecting the specific therapeutic approach to utilize in bringing about such change. Goldfried and Pomeranz [1968] have discussed this issue at length and offer possible reasons for traditionally oriented psychologists' separation of assessment and therapy. With regard to the initial assessment of problems in need of change, Goldfried and Pomeranz suggest:

> . . .regardless of the problems or symptoms which may have brought a client to treatment, the goal of insight therapy remains constant—self-understanding and the search for meaning. . . . More often than not, the theoretical orientation of the therapist determines what issues are

crucial for self-understanding. Thus, the psychoanalytically oriented therapist would argue that the dynamics which must be dealt with in therapy are relatively universal; little in the way of any initial assessment is needed to delineate them. Nondirective therapists [Rogers, 1951] have gone even further by claiming that prior knowledge of conflict areas or focal problems is not only inappropriate but often detrimental to the effective progression of therapy [p. 78].

Four Basic Variables in Problem-Behavior Assessment

Unlike the insight-oriented therapist, the behavior therapist tailor-makes the therapy goals to suit each client's problems. The specific goals chosen depend on the problematic behaviors, the factors maintaining them, and the relative seriousness of each problematic behavior. Accordingly, the behavior therapist requires assessment techniques that enable him to specify this information. There are three classes of variables that are critical in the determination of the factors accounting for the problematic behaviors—situational antecedents, organismic variables, and consequences of responses. In addition, one variable class, that of response dimensions, is instrumental in assessing the seriousness of the problem behaviors. These four variables are considered to be the foundation on which a clinical behavioral assessment is constructed.

Stimulus antecedents. The stimulus antecedents of the problematic behavior may be categorized either as elicitors or as discriminative stimuli. An elicitor is a stimulus that, through classical conditioning, comes to evoke an emotional response automatically. For example, a child who is always beaten with a belt might respond quite emotionally upon merely seeing a belt; the prior association of pain and belts accounts for the child's emotional behavior. A discriminative stimulus is one that provides for the occurrence of a specific behavior, due to a prior learning experience in which certain consequences followed that behavior when performed in the presence of that stimulus. For example, a child might learn that every time there are visitors and he behaves, he is rewarded by his parents, positive consequences for certain behavior in the presence of guests causes the presence of guests to become a discriminative stimulus to be good. It is not always easy, however, to determine whether a stimulus is an elicitor or a discriminative stimulus. If a child cries every night when he's put to bed in the dark, it may be due to a conditioned fear response to the dark or to prior learning experiences in which crying at bedtime was reinforced by permission to stay up longer.

Organismic variables. Information relevant to accounting for the development and maintenance of the problematic behavior can also be provided by an assessment of organismic variables. Organismic variables are those that function within the individual; they include self-statements or thoughts, standards for self-evaluation, and feelings, as well as physiological, genetic, neurological, and biochemical variables. Self-statements such as "I am a worthless person" may, in part, account for a person's depressive reactions. The degree of concurrence between a person's view of himself and his objective accomplishments provides additional data about his standards for self-evaluation, which, in turn, influence overt behavior; very high standards may cause an individual to be persistent and to work extremely hard.

In any consideration of organismic variables, one should also include those aspects of physiological functioning that may influence a person's behavior. For example, research on infants has shown that even at birth, wide differences in general activity level exist among individuals. Unfortunately, much of our knowledge regarding the importance of constitutional and other biological factors of human behavior is limited, which leaves us more with a general appreciation of the importance of such factors than with any specific indications of how they may be used in understanding human behavior.

Consequences. Problematic behaviors are often maintained by their consequences. Very simply, behaviors resulting in positive consequences are increased in frequency or maintained over time, and those leading to aversive consequences decrease in frequency or are eliminated. Although there is a temptation to make this distinction on a subjective basis —positive consequences consist of those things we like and aversive consequences of those things we find distasteful or repugnant—these concepts are typically defined in a functional sense. Thus, a consequence is described as positive if it has been successful in maintaining the continuity of the immediately preceding response, and as aversive if it can suppress (at least temporarily) the behavior it follows. Admittedly, there is a fair amount of overlap between subjective evaluations of what is positive and aversive and what would be so evaluated on an empirical basis. For most of us, praise, money, and other "good things" in life function as positive reinforcers, and scorn, poverty and other forms of misery are indeed functionally aversive. Nonetheless, exceptions *do* exist, as in the case of the reinforcing properties of parental attention, however negative it may appear to the external observer, or in that of the so-called masochist, who not only thrives on pain but actively seeks it out.

Apart from these relatively few exceptions—where seemingly noxious events function as positive reinforcers—there exist more frequent instances in which stable behavior patterns result in unpleasant consequences. This condition has classically been referred to as the "neurotic paradox," in which the individual continues to engage in various behaviors despite the fact they are psychologically and at times physically harmful. The alcoholic drinks himself out of a job, the drug addict steals in order to support his habit, and the more common "neurotic" continues to get involved in interpersonal relationships that are doomed to make him unhappy. In all of these and other deviant behavior patterns that result in aversive consequences, a more detailed analysis reveals that such problems *can* be understood in terms of reinforcement contingencies, provided one takes into account the delay between the behavior and its consequence. In the case of such maladaptive behavior patterns, one typically finds that the immediate consequences are positively reinforcing (for example, positive feelings associated with being high on alcohol and drugs), whereas the more temporally delayed ones are aversive in nature. Thus it is the immediate consequences that function to maintain the particular behavior pattern, and the ultimate consequences have little direct impact on the response pattern.

Response dimension. The clinician can gain a perspective on the seriousness of the problematic behavior from an assessment of response dimensions—duration, frequency, pervasiveness, and magnitude. The duration of the behavior indicates the extent to which the response may be overlearned or of more recent origin. Frequency and pervasiveness are overlapping dimensions in the sense that the former refers to how often the behavior pattern occurs in the individual's life situation, while the latter indicates the extent to which the behavior occurs in a variety of situational contexts. A response may also be assessed for its magnitude. In the case of phobia, for example, the magnitude of the fear may be indicated by the extent to which the individual actively avoids approaching the feared object. In the case of each of these dimensions, an individual's response pattern is typically observed in the context of the specific situation in which it occurs. An assessment of the SORC variables facilitates the selection of the problematic behaviors to be modified and the variables to be manipulated. A second potential use of assessment procedures is in the selection of the appropriate therapeutic procedure. As observed by Goldfried and Pomeranz [1968], the therapeutic technique utilized by most traditionally oriented therapists is determined more by the therapeutic procedures associated with the particular school than by the client's problem.

The behavior therapist—more than any other—is confronted with the dilemma of having to select from an array of potentially effective therapeutic procedures. In part, the selection of the appropriate behavior therapy depends upon one's functional analysis of the problematic behavior. For example, one would hardly want to desensitize an individual experiencing anxiety in social situations if this anxiety was primarily due to a lack of social skills. There are instances, however, when even after a functional analysis of the presenting problem, some uncertainty exists as to the relevant therapeutic procedure. With certain types of anxiety reactions, one may have to choose between a variety of behavior therapies, such as systematic desensitization—a technique in which the individual learns to imagine (or is actually exposed to) a series of situations that are increasingly threatening while maintaining a relaxed, nonanxious state; implosive therapy—in which the individual is deliberately made progressively more anxious by being asked to imagine fearful scenes until the anxiety is extinguished or "implodes"; or modeling techniques—in which the individual observes fearless behavior. Comparative research on the relative effectiveness of these behavior therapy procedures is just beginning, and only after such data are available can we begin to make more sophisticated decisions regarding the selection of the most appropriate procedures.

Classification of Deviant Behavior

In conducting a functional analysis of problematic behaviors in order to decide how to best bring about behavior change, one may make use of a classificatory system suggested by Bandura [1968]. In contrast to past attempts to classify behavior pathology based on etiology, prognosis, or some combination thereof, Bandura's scheme categorizes behavior according to those variables—situational antecedents, organismic response, and consequences—that need to be modified to bring about a change in behavior. The approach is as follows:

I. *Difficulties in the stimulus control of behavior*

A. *Defective stimulus control.* This category refers primarily to instrumental behaviors, for which the antecedent stimuli function as a discriminative cue for the reinforcement or nonreinforcement of certain acts. Behavior classified under this category is presumably not inherently deviant but rather inappropriate to the specific situational context in which it occurs. In other words, the difficulty lies primarily in the individual's inability to respond in

accordance with the discriminative stimuli dictating the functionally appropriate response. For example, a person who laughs and tells jokes at funerals would be considered to be behaving inappropriately. However, that same behavior at a cocktail party would be quite acceptable.

B. *Inappropriate stimulus control.* Included in this category are various intense and presumably maladaptive emotional reactions that are elicited by previously innocuous cues. The assumption is that the emotional reactions elicited by such stimuli have been learned by a conditioning process, either direct or vicarious. Typical deviant behaviors for which inappropriate stimulus control may be said to be operating include various forms of anxiety and fear responses, that have not been elicited by anything intrinsic in the stimulus situation.

II. *Aversive Self-Reinforcing Systems*

Bandura has proposed this category to account for those cognitive processes that mediate between an event and an individual's reaction to it. In deciding whether to positively reinforce their own behavior, individuals vary with regard to the standards by which they evaluate their performance. The relationship between these covert standards and overt behavior may be understood in these terms:

> Many people who think themselves maladjusted and seek the help of psychotherapists have relatively competent behavior repertoires under adequate control and are not encumbered by debilitating, externally stimulated inhibitory or avoidant repertoires. Despite their social competence and favorable reinforcement conditions, these people nevertheless experience a great deal of self-generated feelings of misery and self-imposed deprivations. These feelings often stem from excessively high standards of self-reinforcement, standards often supported by unfavorable comparisons with historical or contemporary models noted for their extraordinary achievements. This process characteristically gives rise to depressive reactions, feelings of worthlessness and lack of purpose, and a lessened disposition to perform because of the unfavorable ratio of work to self-reinforcement. [Bandura 1968, p. 328]

III. *Deficient Behavioral Repertoires*

In line with the conceptualization of personality outlined in the beginning of this module, deviant behaviors included in this category involve the absence of skills needed to cope effectively with various types of situations. On the basis of their early social learning experience, certain individuals may never have learned the appropriate things to say or do in various types of situations, including those of a social, vocational or academic nature. In the typical clinical case manifesting a behavioral deficit, the picture is frequently complicated by factors that are likely to be associated with such a deficit. For example, the individual who shows a deficit in interpersonal relations in that he never learned how to behave in a social setting has probably had minimal (if any) social reinforcement from other individuals. As a result, he may have developed various negative attitudes toward himself, may harbor intense resentment toward others, and may react with feelings of anxiety when placed in a social situation. Nonetheless, such an individual's problems should be placed within this category, as these other maladaptive reactions are the result, rather than the cause, of the behavioral deficiency.

IV. *Aversive Behavioral Repertoires*

In contrast to individuals manifesting deficient behavioral repertoires, those included in this category are capable of responding to various life situations but do so in a way that alienates others. Here the term "aversive" refers to the effect on others and not to the subjective reaction experienced by the person. Thus, the overly aggressive or antisocial individual would be placed within this category.

V. *Difficulties with Incentive Systems (Reinforcers)*

The problematic behaviors included under this general category consist of those that are maintained by the presence or absence of reinforcing consequences, either as a function of a characteristic of the individual or due to some aspect of the environment in which the person may be functioning.

A. *Defective incentive systems in individuals.* A defective incentive system may be said to exist for an individual when those social stimuli that typically achieve secondary reinforcing characteristics within a particular environment are not functioning. An extreme example of this would be autistic children, who respond minimally, if at all, to the social reinforcement offered by parents and other individuals. Another example would be antisocial individuals, for whom praise and approval have little effect on controlling behavior.

B. *Inappropriate incentive system in individuals.* Here, too, the problem of reinforcement rests within the individual. Rather than being absent, however, the reinforcers are physically harmful, culturally disapproved of, or both. Drug addiction, alcoholism, and various forms of deviant sexual behavior would all be included within this category.

C. *Absence of incentives in environment.* In contrast to the above two subcategories, problem behaviors here are primarily a function of the individual's environment. There are a number of possible reasons why a person's environment may deliver relatively few reinforcers—the death of a loved one or a shift in physical location or social status resulting in a situation in which certain behaviors no longer "pay off" as they did previously. Reactions to instances in which reinforcers are no longer forthcoming include feelings of depression, boredom, loneliness, and apathy.

D. *Inappropriate incentives in environment.* Although this particular category was not suggested by Bandura, it would seem to be useful in understanding certain forms of maladaptive behavior. What is involved here is a basic inconsistency inherent in the particular environment, in that the social milieu reinforces certain behaviors and at the same time labels them as maladaptive. This phenomenon is most clearly seen in psychiatric hospital settings, where the patients are reinforced for functioning in a passive and dependent manner, and at the same time are judged to be "mentally ill" for not being capable of functioning on an independent, adultlike level. In addition to the unwitting double standard found in particular environmental settings, the inconsistency may also exist as a function of the complexity of a particular social setting. Thus, although a teacher may label the class clown's behavior as problematic, such behavior may be maintained by the positive reaction of others in that particular environment—the other children.

In the application of Bandura's social learning taxonomy to any maladaptive behavior, it becomes apparent that the several categories are not mutually exclusive. This should not be viewed as a serious criticism of the classificatory scheme, but rather as a reflection of the multitude of determinants involved in understanding and modifying human behavior.

Inseparability of Assessment and Therapy

In conducting a behavioral assessment for the purpose of carrying out a therapeutic intervention, one frequently reaches a point at which the two clinical procedures become indistinguishable in a practical sense. The only difference, in fact, may be the "set" of the clinician.

In our discussion of the use of assessment for behavior therapy, we made the point that one of the tasks involves specifying those variables that maintain the particular problem, as they are the ones that should be manipulated to bring about behavior change. The question here is how does one know which variables are, in fact, the important ones to manipulate? In clinical practice, the behavior therapist will use clinical experience and research data to arrive at a hypothesis about the important variables; however, this assessment clearly entails a guess albeit an educated one. In order for him to know for sure that he was correct in his initial assessment, the therapist must engage in therapeutic manipulations to determine whether the hypothetically functional variable is actually the one maintaining the problem.

This very close interplay between assessment and therapy is nicely illustrated in a case report by Wahler, Winkel, Peterson, and Morrison [1965]. They observed the interactions between a mother and her problem child in a playroom located behind a one-way mirror. The child's problem was that he tended to be too demanding, as indicated by frequent verbal commands such as, "Now we'll play this," and "You go over there, and I'll stay here." A record was also kept of the mother's responses. After observing the mother and child interacting behind the one-way mirror, it was hypothesized that the mother's compliance with the child's demands was the crucial factor maintaining his deviant behavior. The mother was then instructed how to respond more appropriately to her child (that is, to ignore the deviant behavior and to reinforce cooperative statements), and a light signal was used as a cue for her to reinforce appropriate behaviors. This procedure resulted in a dramatic reversal in the child's behavior.

The above example can serve as an illustration of either sophisticated assessment, where variables are manipulated to determine whether they are functionally effective, or therapy, where variables are manipulated to bring about a change in certain maladaptive behaviors. Thus, it may be concluded that not only does behavioral assessment provide the foundation for the implementation of behavior therapy, but the two processes may at times be indistinguishable.

Future Directions in Behavioral Assessment

Where do we go from here? Perhaps one of the most important future directions for behavioral assessment is the development of standardized procedures for the measurement of human functioning. Although a number of investigators have been working on this task, it is still only in its beginning stages.

Goldfried and D'Zurilla [1969] have outlined certain general guidelines that may be followed in the development of behavioral measures. Their *behavioral-analytic* model stresses not only the importance of the individual and his reactions to specific situations, but also the way in which a person's behavior is likely to be evaluated within the context of his environment. The behavioral-analytic approach to test construction involves (a) situational analysis, (b) response enumeration, (c) response evaluation, and (d) development of the format of the measurement instrument. Each of these steps is designed to produce a close parallel between the assessment procedure and the criterion behaviors of interest.

In the situational analysis, the objective is to obtain a sample of those situations with which an individual must cope in the real-life setting. Rather than relying on "armchair speculation" in enumerating potential situations, the sampling is carried out empirically. There are a number of different ways in which the situational analysis may be implemented, including interviews with individuals who are familiar with a particular environment, direct observations of what actually occurs in the particular setting, and the self-observation and recording of those individuals who frequently cope with such situations. Once a wide array of situations has been accumulated by any or all of the above means, those situations that occur least frequently, and hence affect a small number of individuals, are eliminated.

In response enumeration, the objective is to sample a variety of potential responses to each of the circumstances described in the situational analysis. The response enumeration may be carried out via direct observation in naturalistic or contrived situations, by means of role-playing, or through self-reports of how individuals have responded under such circumstances. The major goals of response enumeration are threefold.

First, situations that are likely to elicit only a very narrow range of responses are eliminated. Situations in which most people either respond adequately (or ineffectively) tend not to be useful in discriminating among individuals. Second, this step provides the test constructor with information about the specificity of the situation presented. Even though an attempt may have been made to obtain highly concrete instances during the situational analysis, a certain amount of vagueness or ambiguity is likely to remain, producing a difficulty in describing responses to a situation as presented. This would be the case when the actual response in a particular circumstance would depend on as-yet unspecified aspects of the situation. Thus, an individual may not know how he would react to a description of a hypothetical classmate asking him for lecture notes unless it is clear how well he knows the other person. The final purpose of the response enumeration is to delineate a list of potential responses that may then be evaluated.

As with the previous steps, the response evaluation involves an empirical rather than an a priori determination. Rather than determining which responses are socially appropriate himself, the test constructor elicits these evaluations from persons who typically label such behavior in the real-life setting. This may involve peers, teachers, employers, or therapists, depending on the situations and behaviors of interest.

The first three steps noted above comprise what may be considered a behaviorally oriented criterion analysis, whereby the effectiveness of any particular class of behavior is determined. In addition, it provides one with the items to be included in the measure, as well as the criteria which may be employed for scoring. In the fourth phase, development of the measurement format, a decision is made regarding the method of sampling the situation-response interactions. Depending upon the particular class of responses being assessed as well as realistic limitations imposed by the measurement setting, any one of the procedures described earlier in this paper (that is, direct observation, self-report, role-playing, or physiological procedures) may be employed.

In addition to the need for a number of behavioral assessment procedures focusing on specific aspects of behavior, a more comprehensive assessment device should be developed for use prior to the application of any of the more specifically focused measures. The need here is primarily within a clinical context, in which it would not be feasible to administer each of the many behavioral measures. Thus, perhaps by means of a comprehensive questionnaire or interview procedure, a general overview of potential areas for further assessment may be obtained which can then be evaluated further by the relevant and more detailed assessment procedure available.

Some Unanswered Questions

We have been optimistic in our discussion of the behavioral assessment of personality, not so much because we believe that we now have the techniques available for describing and understanding human functioning, but rather because of the exciting potential that the field holds. Before this hope can be turned into a reality, however, there are certain basic questions that need to be answered. Since we do not as yet know the answers to these questions we will simply raise them and hope that some readers may be intrigued enough to attempt to provide the answers.

On what specific aspects of human functioning should behavioral assessment focus?

At various points in this module, we have referred to techniques for assessing "behaviors of interest." On what basis should we decide that certain aspects of functioning are "of interest" and that others are not? In the most general sense, behavioral assessors have been directing their attention to situational antecedents, organismic variables, responses, and consequences. However, these are very general classes of variables, each containing a number of potential subcategories. What should determine our interest in the specific variables? To date, targets for assessment have been selected largely on the availability of therapeutic procedures for changing such behaviors. Thus, behavioral assessors have dealt with the assessment of assertive behavior because of the utility such measures have in evaluating the effectiveness of assertive training procedures. Although the relevance of assessment procedures to therapeutic intervention is clearly a legitimate reason for the development of a behavioral measure, this approach clearly limits the scope of assessment to only those aspects of behavior that we know how to change. In contrast to psychologists of other orientations, who have more specific theories of personality to direct them in their assessment endeavors, there exists as yet no behavioral theory of personality per se that can help us in this regard.

What is the best method of behavioral assessment to employ?

In our discussion of the methods used in behavioral assessment to date, we have described them as if they were all equally valid. But are they? Does one achieve comparable findings if one uses direct behavioral observation and role-playing procedures? Perhaps some approaches are more valid than others. Perhaps there are interactions with particular aspects of behavior, so that certain methods are more valid for given target behaviors than for others.

Is the relationship between behavioral assessment and behavior therapy as close as it might be?

Apart from further information about the various problem behaviors, we need more information about individual differences between clients—these may be involved in the effective use of each of the several behavior therapy techniques. A client's level of motivation or expectation for improvement might potentially influence the choice of a therapeutic procedure. Also, there are probably prerequisites for the effective use of certain procedures. For example, the effective use of systematic desensitization requires that the client be able to imagine stimuli, and for role-playing he must be willing and able to "act".

What is the best way to validate a behavioral test?

One of the basic assumptions underlying behavioral assessment is that the measurement procedure provides a sample of actual criterion behaviors, rather than an index or "sign" of underlying traits. For this reason, the question that needs to be raised is whether or not the traditional methods of test validation apply to behavioral assessment. One of the typical methods for establishing the validity of a traditional personality test is to determine the extent to which that test correlates with an empirically defined criterion. If, however, the behavioral assessment procedure involves a direct sampling of the criterion itself, would not such a procedure have more to say about the measure's reliability than it would about its validity?

What is a behavioral test, anyway?

We asked ourselves this question as we set out to write this module. In the most general sense, a behavioral test is defined in terms of the assumptions we outlined in the beginning. However, what does it mean when one "takes into account the situation" in which an individual is to respond? The S-R Inventory of Anxiousness should qualify, in that it specifies the particular situation in question. How about paper-and-pencil measures of social anxiety [Watson and Friend, 1969] or test anxiety [Alpert and Haber, 1960]? They do not take into account a specific situation, but rather a class of situations—involving various social interactions and various types of test-taking activities. Do we disqualify such measures from inclusion in our list because of the assumption that a person's response is being assessed cross-situationally, albeit within a given class of situations? In many ways, such measures seem no less situation-specific than the S-R Inventory of Anxiousness items, such as "You are about to go to a party" or "You are taking an important exam."

Are there cross-situational consistencies in behavior?

Although we have emphasized the importance of the specific situation in behavioral assessment, an individual's behavior may sometimes be quite consistent from situation to situation. This is the case, in fact, when one looks at the extremes on any particular measure. For example, if an individual is very anxious, as determined by a given paper-and-pencil measure of generalized anxiety, one is really saying that this person is likely to react with anxiety in a wide variety of situations. Conversely, there exist placid individuals who typically remain calm regardless of the situation confronting them. But what about most of us, who fall somewhere between these two extremes? Undoubtedly, there are classes of situations in which one may find behavior to be consistent. Toward the goal of discovering those areas of behavioral consistency, it will probably be best to classify situations not according to their physical similarity or even their implicit demand characteristics, but more on a functional basis, as determined by some aspect of response similarity. This is clearly no easy task, but it nonetheless remains an essential one if we are ever to develop adequate behavioral procedures for assessing personality.

BIBLIOGRAPHY

Richard Alpert and Ralph N. Haber, "Anxiety in Academic Achievement Situations." *Journal of Abnormal and Social Psychology*, 1960, 61:207–215.

Anne Anastasi, *Psychological Testing*. 3d. ed. Macmillan, 1968.

Albert Bandura, "A Social Learning Interpretation of Psychological Dysfunctions." In Perry London and David Rosenhan, eds., *Foundations of Abnormal Psychology*. Holt, Rinehart, & Winston, 1968.

Theodore Barber, Leo DiCara, Joe Kamiya, Neal Miller, David Shapiro, and Johann Stoyva, eds., *Biofeedback and Self-Control—1970*. Aldine-Atherton, 1971.

Roger G. Barker and Herbert F. Wright, *One Boy's Day*. Harper & Row, 1951.

Joel S. Bergman and Harold J. Johnson, "The Effects of Instructional Set and Autonomic Perception on Cardiac Control." *Psychophysiology*, 1971, 8:180–190.

Niles Bernick, Arthur Kling, and Gene Borowitz, "Physiological Differentiation, Sexual Arousal, and Anxiety." *Psychosomatic Medicine*. 1971, 33:341–352.

Douglas Bernstein, "Behavioral Fear Assessment: Anxiety or Artifact?" In H. Adams and P. Unikel, eds., *Issues and Trends in Behavior Therapy*. Charles C. Thomas, 1973.

Douglas A. Bernstein and George J. Allen, "Fear Survey Schedule (II): Normative Data and Factor Analyses Based Upon a Large College Sample." *Behaviour Research and Therapy*, Oxford, 1969, 7:403–407.

Clinton C. Brown, ed. *Methods in Psychophysiology*. Williams & Wilkins, 1967.

William Brown and Wayne Holtzman, *Survey of study habits and attitudes. Form C*. The Psychological Corporation, 1966.

Joseph R. Cautela and Robert A. Kastenbaum, "A Reinforcement Survey Schedule For Use in Therapy, Training, and Research." *Psychological Reports*, 1967, 20:1115–1130.

Harvey D. Cohen and Arthur Shapiro, "A Method for Measuring Sexual Arousal in the Female." Paper presented at Society for Psychophysiological Research, New Orleans, October 1970.

Norman S. Endler and J. McVicker Hunt, "Sources of Behavioral Variance as Measured by the S-R Inventory of Anxiousness." *Psychological Bulletin*, 1966, 65:336–346.

Norman S. Endler and J. McV. Hunt, "S-R Inventories of Hostility and Comparisons of the Proportions of Variance From Persons, Responses, and Situations for Hostility and Anxiousness." *Journal of Personality and Social Psychology*, 1968, 9:309–315.

Norman S. Endler and J. McV. Hunt, "Generalizability of Contributions From Sources of Variance in the S-R Inventories of Anxiousness." *Journal of Personality*, 1969, 37:1–24.

Norman S. Endler, J. McV. Hunt, and Alvin J. Rosenstein, "An S-R Inventory of Anxiousness." *Psychological Monographs*, 1962, 76:1–33.

Amerigo Farina, David Arenberg, and Samuel Guskin, "A Scale for Measuring Minimal Social Behavior." *Journal of Consulting Psychology*, 1957, 21:265–268.

K. Freund, "A Laboratory Method for Diagnosing Predominance of Homo- and Hetero-Erotic Interest in the Male." *Behaviour Research and Therapy*, 1963, 1:85–93.

James H. Geer, "The Development of a Scale to Measure Fear." *Behaviour Research and Therapy*, Oxford, 1965, 3:45–53.

Marvin R Goldfried and Thomas J. D'Zurilla, "A Behavioral-Analytic Model for Assessing Competence." In C. D. Spielberger, ed., *Current Topics in Clinical and Community Psychology*, Academic Press, 1969.

Marvin R. Goldfried and Thomas J. D'Zurilla, "Prediction of Academic Competence by Means of the Survey of Study Habits and Attitudes." *Journal of Educational Psychology*, 1973, 64:116–122.

Marvin R. Goldfried and Ronald N. Kent, "Traditional vs. Behavioral Assessment: A Comparison of Methodological and Theoretical Assumptions." *Psychological Bulletin*, 1972, 77:409–420.

Marvin R. Goldfried and David M. Pomeranz, "Role of Assessment in Behavior Modification." *Psychological Reports*, 1968, 23:75–87.

Gilbert Honigfeld, Roderic D. Gillis, and James C. Klett, "A Treatment-Sensitive Ward Behavior Scale." *Psychological Reports*, 1966, 19:180–182.

Ted Husek and Sheldon Alexander. "The Effectiveness of the Anxiety Differential in Examination Stress Situations." *Educational and Psychological Measurement*, 1963, 23:309–318.

William H. Ittleson, Leanne G. Rivlin, and Harold M. Proshansky, "The Use of Behavioral Maps in Environmental Psychology." In Proshansky et al., eds., *Environmental Psychology*, Holt, Rinehart & Winston, 1970.

Edward S. Katkin, "The Relationship Between Manifest Anxiety and Two Indices of Autonomic Response to Stress." *Journal of Personality and Social Psychology*, 1965, 2:324–333.

George A. Kelly, "The Theory and Technique of Assessment." In Paul R. Farnsworth and Quinn McNeniar, eds., *Annual Review of Psychology*, Vol. 9, 1958.

Ronald N. Kent, Daniel K. O'Leary, Charles Diament, and Allen Dietz, "Expectation Biases in Observational Evaluation of Therapeutic Change." *Journal of Consulting and Clinical Psychology*, in press.

John I. Lacey, Dorothy E. Bateman, and Ruth Van Lehn, "Autonomic Response Specificity: An Experimental Study." *Psychosomatic Medicine*, 1952, 14:256–260.

Peter Lang, "Autonomic Control or Learning to Play the Internal Organs." In Theodore Barber, Leo DiCara, Joe Kamiya, Neal Miller, David Shapiro, and Johann Stoyva, eds. *Biofeedback and Self-control—1970*, Aldine-Atherton, 1971.

Peter Lewinsohn and Julian Libet, "Pleasant Events, Activity Schedules, and Depressions." *Journal of Abnormal Psychology*, 1972, 79:291–295.

Peter M. Lewinsohn and Martin Shaffer, "Use of Home Observations as an Integral Part of the Treatment of Depression: Preliminary Report and Case Studies." *Journal of Consulting and Clinical Psychology*, 1971, 37:87–94.

Douglas J. MacPhillamy and Peter M. Lewinsohn, "Measuring Reinforcing Events." *Proceedings of the 80th Annual Convention*, American Psychological Association, 1972.

Barclay Martin, "The Assessment of Anxiety by Physiological Behavioral Measures." *Psychological Bulletin*, 1961, 58:234–255.

William H. Masters and Virginia E. Johnson, *Human Sexual Response*. Little, Brown, 1966.

Richard M. McFall and Diane V. Lillesand, "Behavior Rehearsal With Modeling and Coaching in Assertive Training." *Journal of Abnormal Psychology*, 1971, 77:313–323.

Richard M. McFall and Albert Marston, "An Experimental Investigation of Behavior Rehearsal in Assertive Training." *Journal of Abnormal Psychology*, 1970, 76:295–303.

Richard M. McFall and Craig T. Twentyman, "Four Experiments on the Relative Contributions of Rehearsal, Modeling, and Coaching on Assertive Training." *Journal of Abnormal Psychology*, 1973, 81:199–218.

Barbara Miller and Douglas Bernstein, "Instructional Demand in a Behavioral Avoidance Test for Claustrophobic Fears." *Journal of Abnormal Psychology*, 1972, 80:206–210.

Walter Mischel. *Personality and Assessment.* Wiley, 1968.

Walter Mischel, "Continuity and Change in Personality." *American Psychologist*, 1969, 24:1012–1018.

Rudolf H. Moos, "Behavioral Effects of Being Observed: Reactions to a Wireless Radio Transmitter." *Journal of Consulting and Clinical Psychology*, 1968, 32:383–388.

Rudolf H. Moos. "Sources of Variance in Responses to Questionnaires and in Behavior." *Journal of Abnormal Psychology*, 1969, 74:405–412.

Arnold M. Mordkoff, "The Relationship Between Psychological and Physiological Responses to Stress." *Psychosomatic Medicine*, 1965, 26:135–150.

K. Daniel O'Leary and Wesley C. Becker. "Behavior Modification of an Adjustment Class: A Token Reinforcement Program." *Exceptional Children*, 1967, 33:637–642.

K. Daniel O'Leary and Ronald N. Kent, "Behavior Modification for Social Action: Research Tactics and Problems." In L. Hamerlynck et al., eds., *Critical Issues in Research and Practice*, Research Press, 1973.

K. Daniel O'Leary, Ronald N. Kent, and Jay Kanowitz, "Shaping Data Collection Congruent with Experimental Hypotheses." Unpublished manuscript, SUNY at Stony Brook, 1973.

Martin T. Orne, "On the Social Psychology of the Psychological Experiment: With Particular Reference to Demand Characteristics and Their Implication." *American Psychologist*, 1962, 17:776–783.

Gerald R. Patterson, "Intervention in the Homes of Predelinquent Boys: Steps Toward Stage Two." Paper prepared for the workshop "Delinquent Behavior: Some Psychological Research and Applications," at the Annual Convention of the American Psychological Association, 1971.

Gerald R. Patterson, Roberta S. Ray, D. A. Shaw, and Joseph Cobb, "Manual for Coding of Family Interactions," 1969. Available from ASIS/NAPS % Microfiche Publications, 305 E. 46 St., New York, N.Y. 10017. Document #01234.

Gordon L. Paul, *Insight vs. Desensitization in Psychotherapy.* Stanford University Press. 1966.

Gordon L. Paul, Lester L. Tobias, and Beverly L. Holly, "Maintenance Psychotropic Drugs in the Presence of Active Treatment Programs: A "Triple-Blind" Withdrawal Study With Long-Term Mental Patients." *Archives of General Psychiatry*, in press.

Donald R. Peterson, *The Clinical Study of Social Behavior.* Appleton-Century-Crofts, 1968.

Richard C. Pillard, James Carpenter, Kim W. Atkinson, and Seymour Fisher, "Palmer Sweat Prints and Self Ratings as Measures of Film Induced Anxiety." *Perceptual and Motor Skills*, 1966, 23:771–777.

Kenneth Price, "Feedback Effects on Penile Tumescence." Paper presented at Eastern Psychological Association Convention. May, 1973.

Kenneth Purcell and Kirk Brady, "Adaptation to the Invasion of Privacy: Monitoring Behavior With a Miniature Radio Transmitter." *Merrill-Palmer Quarterly of Behavior and Development*, 1966, 12:242–254.

Lynn P. Rehm and Albert R. Marston. "Reduction of Social Anxiety Through Modification of Self-Reinforcement." *Journal of Consulting and Clinical Psychology*, 1968, 32:565–574.

John B. Reid, "Reliability Assessment of Observation Data: A Possible Methodological Problem." *Child Development*, 1970, 41: 1143–1150.

Carl R. Rogers, *Client-Centered Therapy*. Houghton, Mifflin, 1951.

Raymond G. Romanczyk, Ronald N. Kent, Charles Diament, and K. Daniel O'Leary. "Measuring the Reliability of Observational Data: A Reactive Process." *Journal of Applied Behavior Analysis*, 1973, 6:175–184.

K. Romano, "Psychophysiological Responses to a Sexual and an Unpleasant Motion Picture." B.S. thesis. University of Manitoba, Canada, 1969.

Ray Rosen, "The Use of Contingent Feedback in the Suppression of an Elicited Autonomic Response: Penile Tumescence." Ph.D. dissertation. SUNY at Stony Brook, 1972.

Robert Rosenthal, *Experimenter Effects in Behavioral Research*. Appleton, 1966.

Alan O. Ross, Harvey H. Lacey, and David A. Parton, "The Development of a Behavior Checklist For Boys." *Child Development*, 1965, 36:1013–1027.

Julian B. Rotter, "The Role of the Psychological Situation in Determining the Direction of Human Behavior." In M. R. Jones, ed., *Nebraska Symposium on Motivation*, University of Nebraska Press, 1955.

Julian B. Rotter and Delos D. Wickens, "The Consistency and Generality of Ratings of 'Social Aggressiveness' Made From Observations of Role Playing Situations." *Journal of Consulting Psychology*, 1948, 12:234–239.

Charles D. Spielberger, Richard L. Gorsuch, Robert E. Lushene, *The State-Trait Anxiety Inventory (STAI) Test Manual For Form X*. Consulting Psychologists Press, 1970.

Howard R. Stanton and Eugene Litwak, "Toward the Development of a Short Form Test of Interpersonal Competence." *American Sociological Review*, 1955, 20:668–674.

Robert M. Stern and Burt E. Kaplan, "Galvanic Skin Response: Voluntary Control and Externalization." *Journal of Psychosomatic Research*, 1967, 10:349–353.

Richard A. Sternbach, *Principles of Psychophysiology*. Academic Press, 1966.

H. A. Storrow, *Introduction to Scientific Psychiatry*. Appleton-Century-Crofts, 1967.

Robert G. Wahler, Gary H. Winkel, Robert F. Peterson, and Delmont C. Morrison, "Mothers as Behavior Therapists For Their Own Children." *Behavior Research and Therapy*, Oxford, 1965, 3:113–124.

David Watson and Ronald Friend, "Measurement of Social-Evaluative Anxiety." *Journal of Consulting and Clinical Psychology*, 1969, 33:448–457.

Jerry S. Wiggins and C. L. Winder, *"The Peer Nomination Inventory: An Empirically Derived Sociometric Measure of Adjustment in Preadolescent Boys."* *Psychological Reports*, 1961, 9:643–677.

Aubrey Yates, *Behavior Therapy*. John Wiley & Sons, 1970.

Marvin Zuckerman, "Physiological Measures of Sexual Arousal in the Human." *Psychological Bulletin*, 1971, 75:297–329.

Marvin Zuckerman and Bernard Lubin, *Manual for the Multiple Affect Adjective Checklist*. Educational and Industrial Testing Service. 1965.

[Work on this paper was facilitated by research grant MH–24327 from the National Institute of Mental Health.]